Human-Computer Interaction in the New Millennium

Human-Computer Interaction in the New Millennium

John M. Carroll, Editor

ACM Press
New York, New York

 ADDISON–WESLEY

Boston • San Francisco • New York • Toronto • Montreal
London • Munich • Paris • Madrid
Capetown • Sydney • Tokyo • Singapore • Mexico City

Many of the designations used by manufacturers and sellers to distinguish their products are claimed as trademarks. Where those designations appear in this book, and we were aware of a trademark claim, the designations have been printed in initial capital letters or in all capitals.

The authors and publisher have taken care in the preparation of this book, but make no expressed or implied warranty of any kind and assume no responsibility for errors or omissions. No liability is assumed for incidental or consequential damages in connection with or arising out of the use of the information or programs contained herein.

This book is published as part of ACM Press Books—a collaboration between the Association for Computing Machinery (ACM) and Addison-Wesley. ACM is the oldest and largest educational and scientific society in the information technology field. Through its high-quality publications and services, ACM is a major force in advancing the skills and knowledge of IT professionals throughout the world. For further information about ACM, contact:

ACM Member Services
1515 Broadway, 17th Floor
New York, NY 10036-5701
Phone: (212) 626-0500
Fax: (212) 944-1318
E-mail: ACMHELP@ACM.org

ACM European Service Center
108 Cowley Road
Oxford OX4IJF
United Kingdom
Phone: +44-1865-382338
Fax: +44-1865-381338
E-mail: acm.europe@acm.org
URL: http://www.acm.org

The publisher offers discounts on this book when ordered in quantity for special sales. For more information, please contact:

Pearson Education Corporate Sales Division
One Lake Street
Upper Saddle River, NJ 07458
(800) 382-3419
corpsales@pearsontechgroup.com

Visit AW on the Web: www.awl.com/cseng/

Library of Congress Cataloging-in-Publication Data

Human-computer interaction in the new millennium / John M. Carroll, editor.
    p. cm.
  Includes bibliographical references and index.
  ISBN 0-201-70447-1
  1. Human-computer interaction. I. Carroll, John M. (John Millar), 1950–
QA76.9.H85 H857 2001
004'.01'9—dc21   2001035288

ISBN 0-201-70447-1
Text printed on recycled paper
1 2 3 4 5 6 7 8 9 10—CRW—0504030201
First printing, July 2001

Contents

PART IV GROUPWARE AND COOPERATIVE ACTIVITY   277

PART VII HCI AND SOCIETY   603

CHAPTER 27 Learner-Centered Design: Reflections and New Directions   605

Chris Quintana, Andrew Carra, Joseph Krajcik, and Elliot Soloway

Preface

Human-Computer Interaction (HCI) has been a focal area for innovative multidisciplinary computing research and development for the past 25 years. At the dawn of a new millennium, we should ask where the HCI project is going; what critical technical challenges and opportunities will define HCI research and development work beyond the year 2001; what approaches will sustain and enhance the vitality and effectiveness of HCI in this new era; and how HCI will be different from and similar to what it is today. These questions can be addressed both in the broad view and with respect to specific subdomains within HCI.

In spring 1998, Jonathan Grudin, editor of *ACM Transactions on Computer-Human Interaction,* and Tom Moran, editor of *Human-Computer Interaction,* suggested a coordinated special issue project celebrating "Human-Computer Interaction in the New Millennium." Because I serve on both editorial boards—and probably because I was unable to attend this meeting—I was asked to coordinate the project.

In late spring, an initial call for papers was circulated for the *Transactions*. About 50 research groups expressed initial interest, and in the end, 30 papers were submitted for the January 1999 deadline. Thirteen associate editors of the *Transactions,* Joelle Coutaz, Paul Dourish, Wayne Gray, Jim Hollan, Scott Hudson, Hiroshi Ishii, Robert Jacob, Sirkka Jarvenpaa, Allan MacLean, Brad Myers, Bonnie Nardi, Randy Pausch, and I, helped to manage the review process. The result was a double special issue of the *Transactions* in March and June 2000. The ten papers from that double special issue are included in this book, with some revision to make them briefer and more accessible to a larger audience.

In February 1999, the Human-Computer Interaction Consortium held a workshop on research visions and directions for the new millennium. A special issue of the *Human-Computer Interactions* was organized from the papers presented at this workshop. It was edited by Wendy Kellogg, Clayton Lewis, and Peter Polson. The five papers from that special issue are also included here. *Human-Computer Interactions* has a tradition of presenting rather lengthy and comprehensive papers. I thank this group of authors in particular for heroic revision efforts. In some cases, excellent papers were cut to less than half their original length, with their excellence preserved!

I think both journal special issue projects were highly successful. But journal projects are always limited by what papers are submitted. To help balance content,

I solicited 14 papers in addition to the 15 special issue papers from the two journals. Frankly, however, even 29 papers cannot begin to cover the scope of human-computer interaction. I thank this group of authors for writing to my half-baked specifications with such creativity and good nature.

Many experts from throughout the human-computer interaction community served as referees. The energy and insight that can be marshaled for projects like this is awesome. I tried to collate all the names: Gregory Abowd, Phil Agre, Erik Altmann, Izak Benbasat, Steve Benford, Gary Bishop, Susanne Bodker, Alan Borning, Amy Bruckman, Michael Byrne, Tom Carey, Chris Dede, Matthias Denecke, Andrew Dillon, Stephanie Doane, Paul Dourish, Keith Edwards, Thomas Erickson, Carolanne Fisher, Ken Fishkin, Edward Fox, George Furnas, Craig Ganoe, Bill Gaver, Nancy Green, Saul Greenburg, Christine Halverson, Beverly Harrison, Rex Hartson, Bill Hefley, Austin Henderson, Ken Hinckley, Andrew Howes, Scott Hudson, Hiroshi Ishii, Robin Jeffries, Bonnie John, Simon Kaplan, John Karat, David Kasik, Irvin Katz, Wendy Kellogg, David Kirsh, Brian Kleiner, Joseph Konstan, Clayton Lewis, Edwin Li, Kee Yong Lim, Scott MacKenzie, Gloria Mark, Jon May, David Millen, Michael Muller, Brad Myers, Beth Mynatt, William Newman, Jakob Nielsen, Dan Olsen, Gary Olson, Judith Olson, Sharon Oviatt, Leysia Palen, Jeff Pierce, Peter Polson, Blaine Price, Naren Ramakrishnan, David Redmiles, Paul Resnick, John Richards, Frank Ritter, Jeremy Roschelle, Mary Beth Rosson, Angela Sasse, Michael Schoelles, Doug Schuler, Abigail Sellen, Chris Shaw, Ben Shneiderman, Simon Buckingham Shum, Philip J. Smith, Lucy Suchman, Niels Taatgen, Desney Tan, Loren Terveen, John Thomas, Elaine G. Toms, Brygg Ullmer, Robert Virzi, Alex Waibel, Dieter Wallach, Wayne Ward, Colin Ware, Greg Welch, Alan Wexelblatt, Steve Whittaker, Terry Winograd, Richard Young.

I hope the efforts of all those who were involved in trying to take stock of where we are and to ponder where we are going will benefit them and the whole HCI community as we take our first steps into the future.

John M. Carroll
Department of Computer Science
Center for Human-Computer Interaction
Virginia Tech

Introduction: Human-Computer Interaction, the Past and the Present

John M. Carroll

The Emergence of Usability

Human-Computer Interaction (HCI) is the study and the practice of usability. It is about understanding and creating software and other technology that people will want to use, will be able to use, and will find effective when used. The concept of usability, and the methods and tools to encourage it, achieve it, and measure it are now touchstones in the culture of computing.

Through the past two decades, HCI emerged as a focal area of both computer science research and development and of applied social and behavioral science. Some of the reasons for its success are straightforwardly technical: HCI evoked many difficult problems and elegant solutions in the recent history of computing—for example, in work on direct manipulation interfaces, user interface management systems, task-oriented help and instruction, and computer-supported collaborative work. Other reasons are broadly cultural: The province of HCI is the view the nonspecialist public has of computer and information technology and the impact that technology has on their lives in the sense that it is the visible part of computer science and technology. The most recent reasons are commercial: As the underlying technologies of computing become commodities, inscribed on generic chips, the noncommodity value of computer products and services resides in applications and user interfaces—that is, in HCI.

The beginning of HCI is sometimes traced to the March 1982 (U.S.) National Bureau of Standards conference, "Human Factors in Computer Systems," though related conferences and workshops were conducted throughout the world at about that time. It is surely true that after the Bureau of Standards conference, HCI experienced meteoric growth. However, four—largely independent—threads of technical development from the 1960s and 1970s provided the foundation that allowed this interdisciplinary program to gel so rapidly in the early 1980s.

These four threads were prototyping and iterative development from software engineering; software psychology and human factors of computing systems; user interface software from computer graphics; and models, theories, and frameworks from cognitive science. It is interesting to remember these four roots of HCI, since the concerns that evoked them and that brought them together are still underlying forces in HCI today.

Prototyping and Iterative Development

In the 1960s, advances in computer hardware enabled new applications requiring software systems of far greater scale and complexity than before. But these greater possibilities exacerbated problems of software development: cost overruns, late delivery, and ineffective and unreliable systems that were difficult to maintain. This was termed the "software crisis." It led to the emergence of software engineering as a professional discipline.

The software crisis was never resolved per se. Rather, it helped to establish design and development methods as a central topic in computing. Early approaches emphasized structured decomposition and representation of requirements and specifications, and a disciplined workflow of stages and hand-offs called the "waterfall." Indeed, this was part of a broad movement toward more formal design methods during the 1960s (Jones 1970).

However, empirical studies of the design process and practical experience in system development raised questions about the new design methods. A prominent case was Brooks's (1975/1995) analysis of the development of the IBM 360 Operating System, one of the largest and most scrupulously planned software design projects of its era. Brooks, the project manager, observed that critical requirements often emerge during system development and cannot be anticipated. He concluded that software designers should always "plan to throw one away."

This was a striking lesson and one that continues to inspire studies of design. Design is now seen as opportunistic, concrete, and necessarily iterative. Designers typically work toward partial solutions for subsets of requirements, using prototypes to evoke further requirements and, indeed, to reformulate the goals and constraints of the problem. By providing techniques to quickly construct, evaluate, and change partial solutions, prototyping has become a fulcrum for system development.

Software Psychology and Human Factors

The software crisis intensified interest in programming as a human activity. It heightened the need for more programmers, for better-trained programmers, for more productive programmers. The development of time sharing and interactive computing allowed new styles of programming and made the dynamics of individual programmer activity more salient. Programming became recognized as an area of psychology involving problem solving and symbol manipulation (Weinberg 1971).

Through the 1970s, a behavioral approach to understanding software design, programming, and the use of interactive systems developed rapidly. This work addressed a wide assortment of questions about what people experience and how they perform when they interact with computers. It studied how system response time affects productivity; how people specify and refine queries; how syntactic constructions in programming languages are more or less difficult; and how aids like mnemonic variable names, in-line program comments, and flowcharts support programming. By the end of that decade, a software psychology research community had formed (Shneiderman 1980).

This work inspired many industrial human factors groups to expand the scope of their responsibilities toward support for programming groups and the usability of software. During the latter 1970s, several extensive compilations of research-based guidelines appeared, and most computer manufacturers (there were no exclusively-software companies at that time) established usability laboratories, whose scope of responsibility steadily expanded.

New User Interface Software

Before the 1960s, the notion of "user interface" was completely unarticulated. The focus of computing was literally on computations, not on intelligibly presenting the results of computations. This is why the early visions of personal, desktop access to massive information stores (Bush 1945), graphical and gestural user interfaces (Sutherland 1963), and synchronous collaboration through direct pointing and shared windows (Engelbart and English 1968) are historically so significant.

Through the 1970s, advances in workstation computers and bit-mapped displays allowed these early visions to be consolidated. A prominent example is work at the Xerox Palo Alto Research Center on the Alto computer and the Smalltalk-72 environment. It is striking that the essential concepts of desktop computing that guided the next 20 years of research and development emerged during this early period.

Models, Theories, and Frameworks

During the latter 1970s, cognitive science had coalesced as a multidisciplinary project encompassing linguistics, anthropology, philosophy, psychology, and computer science. One principle of cognitive science was that an effective multidisciplinary science should be capable of supporting application to real problems and to benefit from it. Many domains were investigated, including mechanics, radiology, and algebra. HCI became one the original cognitive science domains.

The initial vision of HCI as applied science was to bring cognitive science methods and theories to bear on software development. Most ambitiously, it was hoped that cognitive science theory could provide substantive guidance at very early stages of the software development process. This guidance would come from general principles of perception and motor activity, problem-solving and language, communication and group behavior, and so on. It would also include developing a domain theory, or theories, of HCI.

A prominent early example was the Goals, Operators, Methods, and Selection (GOMS) rules model for analyzing routine human-computer interactions (Card, Moran, and Newell 1983). This was an advance on prior human factors modeling, which did not address the cognitive structures underlying manifest behavior. But it was also an advance on the cognitive psychology of the time: It explicitly integrated many components of skilled performance to produce predictions about real tasks. The GOMS model is important because it set a standard for scientific and theoretical rigor and innovation that became a defining characteristic of HCI.

The foundations of HCI remain an active focus of research. The first group of papers in this volume shows how these foundations are continuing to expand the disciplinary scope and relevance of HCI models, theories, and frameworks to practitioners.

User-Centered System Development

These four starting points converged in the early 1980s through organizational initiatives including ACM's Special Interest Group in Computer-Human Interaction (SIGCHI) and IFIP's Task Group on Human-Computer Interaction (later, Technical Committee 13). Initially, HCI had two foci, methods and software, and a major theme was the integration of the two in a framework called user-centered system development.

The methods focus was on techniques to achieve better usability. This entailed explicating the concept of usability with respect to learning, skilled performance, and subjective experiences, like satisfaction and fun. It involved the development and empirical validation of models and theories. It involved laboratory studies of people learning and using systems, and of techniques for evaluating systems. And it involved working within development organizations to understand how to involve usability professionals earlier and more effectively in software development. The methods focus became known as usability engineering.

The software focus of HCI was concerned with inventing and refining graphical user interface concepts and techniques to make systems more powerful, more useful, and more usable. An important consequent objective was to make new user interface concepts and techniques easier for developers to employ. This entailed the development of toolkits and software frameworks. The software focus became known as user interface software and tools.

The method and software foci often cross-leverage one another. For example, new user interface metaphors are developed from theory and from user studies, refined and implemented in prototype systems, evaluated in further user studies, and then incorporated into toolkits. Through the past two decades, these original focus areas have continued to expand and diversify, though their synergistic relationship remains a cornerstone of HCI. Other focal areas have developed, such as groupware/cooperative activity and media/information.

Usability Engineering Methods and Concepts

The early focus of usability engineering was evaluation: gauging the success of implemented software and systems with respect to measurable criteria. It was patterned on the laboratory-oriented human factors paradigm in telecommunications. However, the ascendance of prototyping and iterative development in software and the ambition of engaging cognitive science as a foundation for human-computer interaction pushed the focus of evaluation work upstream in the system development process.

Prototyping and iterative development place a high premium on formative, rather than summative, evaluation (Scriven 1967)—that is, on evaluation that is carried out within the development process and that can guide redesign, rather than merely gauge attributes of a design result. Formative evaluation methods are often qualitative; a typical method involves having people "think aloud" as they perform a task. Theory-based models and tools took an even more ambitious position, seeking to enable analytic evaluations of designs before they were implemented even as prototypes. Usability engineering has remained a core concern of the ACM SIGCHI community, and its CHI Conference, but subcommunities have also developed for usability methods (the Usability Professional's Association) and for theory-based models (the Conference on User Modeling).

The objective of providing guidance earlier in the system development process entrained fundamental changes in usability engineering. An example is the recognition that the earliest point for impact is requirements analysis. The sociologists and anthropologists who had come to HCI through its connection to cognitive science showed through field studies of work practices that people do their work and use their tools in surprisingly creative ways (Suchman 1987). But their work practices are often not easy to anticipate without direct study or direct user participation in the development process. A subcommunity addressing these themes has formed around the Participatory Design Conference and the ACM Conference on Computer-Supported Cooperative Work (CSCW).

A second example is the growing focus on design methods: Usability can be designed as well as evaluated, but a design-time usability process entails coordination with graphical and interaction designers that is still just beginning. This design thread has led to another subcommunity formed around the ACM Symposium on Designing Interactive Systems (DIS), a conference series started in 1995.

Complementary to moving usability work further upstream in design and development is a focus in usability engineering on cost-benefit tradeoffs in methods (Bias and Mayhew 1994). The most evident manifestation of this theme has been widespread effort at developing "low-cost" inspection and walkthrough methods. But cost-benefit is a complex issue. Different methods have different goals, producing different types of benefits. Some continuing questions for usability engineering are how methods can leverage foundations in science and theory; how methods can be evaluated; and how different types of methods, like laboratory studies, field studies, walkthroughs, and analytic models, can be integrated with one another and with other methods and processes of system development.

The second group of papers in this volume shows how usability engineering is developing. It is addressing an ever-greater variety of types of systems and usability phenomena, such as worker adaptation. It is developing new approaches, such as the integration of user interface management systems with cognitive models. But it is also focusing on better consolidation and utilization of results and concepts in hand.

User Interface Software and Tools

User interface software and tools is concerned with user interface concepts and metaphors, display and interaction techniques, and software development methods. This is surely the most visibly successful area of HCI. The user interfaces that more or less everyone encounters more or less every day—the mouse and bitmap display, the desktop metaphor and window management, display widgets like scroll-bars, menus, and dialog boxes—emerge from this research and development work. This area is a distinct professional subcommunity within HCI, with its own ACM conference, User Interface Software and Tools, since 1987.

A continuing research thread in this area is architectures for user interface software. An early objective was separation of the user interface and application functionality into distinct layers. This approach modularized the user interface in user interface management systems, encouraging iterative redesign (for example, Tanner and Buxton 1985). However, layering entrained limitations on the granularity of user interface interactions. It also proved to be an obstacle to incremental development methods, because it presupposed top-down decomposition with respect to what was user interface and what was application functionality. Current approaches favor developing user interfaces and functionality in the same language, either in new languages invented for this purpose, like Visual Basic, or through extensions to standard languages for implementing functionality, such as libraries and toolkits for C++ or Java.

A key goal in this area has always been to ease the development of interactive systems. Through time, this goal has become more challenging because the skills of application developers have become more diverse. For example, this motivated a family of prototyping tools based on the premise that user interface software could be directly created "by demonstration."

The third group of papers summarizes the progress to date in user interface software and tools and identifies some of the key challenges for the future. The key questions for user interface software and tools are what models and techniques will be most appropriate for creating interfaces with controls and displays quite different from those of the graphical user interface paradigm of the past 20 years. For example, what are suitable architectures and tools for interfaces with voice, gesture, or position-sensing controls and immersive or wearable displays?

Groupware and Cooperative Activity

The early vision that interactive computing would enable human collaboration was already borne out in the 1970s by ARPA Net e-mail and Usenet newsgroups. Before HCI even existed, there had been considerable research on teleconferencing and other networked collaboration (Hiltz and Turoff 1978/1993). In the 1980s, possibilities for computer-supported cooperative work (CSCW), as well as the scope human-oriented issues considered, became more diverse. E-mail became a universal communication tool. Videoconferencing, electronic meeting rooms, and workflow support systems became common. Several very visible experiments with media spaces and shared virtual environments were carried out. Through the 1990s, networked collaboration became richer and more accessible—for example, through the World Wide Web.

CSCW, as a subcommunity in HCI, formed around the ACM CSCW Conference series starting in 1986. At first, the focus was on collaborative systems (groupware) and human-computer interactions with collaborative systems. But the more significant impact of CSCW, one that goes beyond the conference, is the recognition that all systems are used in a social context. In this sense, CSCW has become more a view of HCI than a subcommunity with it. CSCW has served as a conduit for the expansion of the science foundation of HCI to incorporate activity theory, ethnomethodology, and conversation analysis, among others.

Studies of work practices and of technology in the workplace have radically altered the scope of HCI concerns. Subtle features in the organization of work are often critical but easily missed in standard requirements processes. Some of the powerful features may be idiosyncratic to a particular type of work context, such as air traffic control rooms, or even to individual workplaces and groups. Even when technology appropriately addresses workplace needs, adopting new technology ineluctably disrupts work, at least temporarily. The effects of technology are not uniform across an organization; some workers benefit, but others may lose. And technology can be a double-edged sword: Making someone's work easier reduces the skill required to perform the work. In a given organizational context, it may reduce status, pay, and even job security.

Much of the focus of CSCW continues to be on new groupware systems. In the past decade, this thrust of CSCW has emphasized Internet systems. For example, there are many current reworkings of the classic multi-user domain (MUD) paradigm but bundling suites of communication tools, such as chats, multi-user whiteboards, videoconferencing, and shared applications, with graphical Web-clients.

Recently, work on groupware systems and cooperative activity has converged around the concept of "community." Examples of communities are varied, including dispersed groups of collaborating scientists, people subscribed to given newsgroups or other online services, and towns or neighborhoods with local networking infrastructures. On the one hand, this work investigates how a variety of interactions can be coherently supported to foster the qualities of community in participants. On the other hand, it investigates the social and psychosocial consequences of participation in such communities.

The fourth group of papers in this volume examines the history, current approaches, and challenges of groupware and cooperative activity.

Media and Information

In the early 1980s, possibilities for media other than formatted text were quite limited. Toward the end of the 1980s, this had changed dramatically: Hypertext was everywhere. In 1987, Apple began including HyperCard with all of its personal computers. At the same time, standard image formats were making it easier to create and share graphics and visualizations. Relatively good quality synthetic speech became available on personal computers. In the 1990s, these trends accelerated: The World Wide Web made hypertext a standard information design, Web-pages and single-click e-mail attachments made sharing images as easy as sharing text, and surprisingly good speech recognition became available on personal computers.

Where CSCW was initially a subcommunity of HCI that ended up providing a new perspective on what HCI is about, multimedia and hypermedia were initially a small collection of enhancements to user interface presentations but have continued to develop and diversify to produce half a dozen new subareas of HCI. Each of these areas is redefining the scope of HCI. Some examples are digital libraries, visualization and virtual environments, spoken-language interfaces, and agent-based and recommender systems.

The World Wide Web is a vast collection of information, but it is not a library. Finding things in the Web may be hit or miss, but it has helped to focus research and development interest on the human aspects of building and accessing large hypertext databases. Digital libraries were originally conceived of as an integration of database systems, multimedia, and information retrieval. However, the rapid growth of interest in digital libraries and the consequent need to make them accessible to a wider range of people has transformed digital libraries into a subarea of HCI as well.

Graphics and visualization techniques were central to the development of the contemporary user interface paradigm. However, continuing advances in hardware speed and other underlying technologies now allow large-scale graphical animations. Users do not merely display and inspect static visualizations; they can view animated sequences of visualizations and navigate through visualized spaces. In a limiting case, users are surrounded by wall-sized displays, viewed through depth-enhancing goggles, perceptually immersed in their data.

Twenty years ago, sound in the user interface meant warning beeps. Sound got attention in circumstances where flashing text boxes sometimes did not. During the 1980s, HCI incorporated a wider range of nonspeech sounds into the user interface (sometimes called "earcons") and made progress enhancing the quality of synthetic speech and applying it in telephone-based information systems. More recently, advances in speech recognition and natural language processing, and in underlying hardware and software technologies, have allowed remarkable progress in speech input, particularly in dictation applications.

Artificial intelligence has always played a role in HCI. Intelligent help and tutoring systems have been heavily researched through the past two decades. One of the obstacles to widely deploying such techniques in user interfaces is the amount of knowledge engineering required. This is one reason that intelligent tutoring systems tend to be developed for relatively closed domains of knowledge, like elementary mathematics. More recent approaches are exploring self-organizing agents and recommendation systems that aggregate the decisions and actions of many people to provide information resources.

The hypertext conference has continued, but the digital library community now has its own ACM conference series. There is also an ACM conference on multimedia. The fifth group of papers in this volume presents a diverse view of ongoing work in this area. It seems this "subarea" of HCI is already too rich and too diverse to cohere. In the new millennium, media and information will surely become several distinct areas. For example, the sixth group of papers addresses the integration of computation with real environments, a focus that has become distinctive only recently and promises to be become far more important in the future.

The last group, "HCI and Society," includes discussions of challenges and possibilities for education, community-building, and the development of social capital more generally, as facilitated, or at least modulated, by information technology. In the new millennium these considerations may yet become mainstream as foundations for HCI and as criteria for usability engineering methods.

Toward the New Millennium

At the inception of HCI, the notion that computer systems and software should be designed and developed with explicit consideration of the needs, abilities, and preferences of their ultimate users was not a dominant view. Most writings about computing from the mid-1970s are stunningly dismissive of usability and rather patronizing of users. After only a decade, the computer industry and the discipline of computer science were transformed. The case had been made for a user-centered system development process, a process in which usability was a primary goal. People began to distinguish sharply between technology-driven exploratory development, which is now often accompanied by explicit disclaimers about usability, and real system development, in which empirically verified usability is the final arbiter.

With the advent of the 1990s, HCI research had become relatively well integrated in computer science. A 1988 Association for Computing Machinery (ACM) task force enumerated HCI as one of nine core areas of the computer science discipline (Denning et al. 1989). A joint curriculum task force of the ACM and the IEEE (Institute of Electrical and Electronic Engineers) recommended the inclusion of HCI as a common requirement in computer science programs (Tucker and Turner 1991). And HCI was included as one of ten major sections of the first Handbook of Computer

Science and Engineering (Tucker 1997). In the 1990s, computer science students and the corporations that hire them demanded HCI courses in university curricula. Several major computer science departments have designated HCI as a research focus, and several comprehensive undergraduate texts have appeared.

In the computing industry, HCI practitioners have become well integrated in system development. HCI specialists have moved into a great variety of roles beyond human factors assurance. They have been routinely included in customer/user interactions to understand the need for new products, product planning and specification; in the development and evaluation of prototypes and systems; in the design of documentation and training; and in installation and user support. There has been an obvious trend for HCI specialists to be promoted into project management.

HCI remains an emerging area in computer science. Its four roots from the 1960s and 1970s—software engineering, software human factors, computer graphics, and cognitive science—have grown and intertwined. New influences and strands have been incorporated—broader social science, networking, media, information management, and artificial intelligence. HCI has become the focus for a new view of what computing is about. The future promises to be far more exciting than the quite exciting recent past. HCI only existed for the final quarter-century of the second millennium—time enough to irrevocably shake up the discipline of computer science and the trajectory of computing technology, but not a lot of time. HCI in the new millennium gives us much to look forward to.

Acknowledgment

This is a much revised and broadened descendant of a survey paper that appeared in *Annual Review of Psychology,* Volume 48, Palo Alto, CA: Annual Reviews, 1997, pages 501–522. That earlier version develops some of the points here in more detail and with more complete citations. I am grateful to Andrew Dillon, Brad Myers, Sharon Oviatt, Ben Shneiderman, Alistair Sutcliffe, Terry Winograd, and an anonymous reviewer for guidance, discussion, and comments on this essay.

References

Bias, R.G., and Mayhew, D.J., Eds. (1994). *Cost-justifying usability.* Boston: Academic Press.

Brooks, F.P. 1975. (1995). *The mythical man-month: Essays on software engineering.* (1995 Anniversary Edition). Reading, MA: Addison-Wesley.

 Bush, V. (1945). As we may think. *Atlantic Monthly,* 176, 1, 105–108.

Card, S.K., Moran, T.P., and Newell, A. (1983). *The psychology of human-computer interaction.* Hillsdale, NJ: Erlbaum.

Denning, P.J., Comer, D.E., Gries, D., Mulder, M.C., Tucker, A.B., Turner, A.J., and Young, P.R. (1989). Computing as a discipline. *Communications of the ACM, 32,* 9–23.

Engelbart, D.C., and English, W.K. (1968). A research center for augmenting human intellect. *AFIPS Proceedings of the Fall Joint Computer Conference, 33,* 395–410.

Hiltz, S.R., and Turoff, M. (1978). *The Network Nation: Human communication via computer.* Reading, MA: Addison-Wesley. (Revised edition, 1993 by MIT Press, Cambridge, MA.)

Jones, J.C. (1970). *Design methods: Seeds of human futures.* New York: John Wiley & Sons.

Kay, A., and Goldberg, A. (1977). Personal dynamic media. *IEEE Computer, 10,* 3, 31–41.

Scriven, M. (1967). The methodology of evaluation. In R. Tyler, R. Gagne, and M. Scriven (Eds.), *Perspectives of Curriculum Evaluation,* 39–83. Chicago: Rand McNally.

Shneiderman, B. (1980). *Software psychology: Human factors in computer and information systems.* Cambridge, MA: Winthrop.

Suchman, L.A. (1987). *Plans and situated actions: The problem of human-machine communication.* New York: Cambridge University Press.

Sutherland, I. (1963). Sketchpad, a man-machine graphical communications system. *Proceedings of Spring Joint Computer Conference,* 329–346. New York: Spartan Books.

Tanner, P.P., and Buxton, W.A.S. (1985). Some issues in future user interface management system (UIMS) development. In G.E. Pfaff (Ed.), *User interface management systems: Proceedings of the workshop on user interface management systems,* held in Seehiem, FRG, November 1–3, 1983, 67–79. New York: Springer Verlag.

Tucker, A.B. (Ed.) (1997). *The handbook of computer science and engineering.* Boca Raton, FL: CRC Press.

Tucker, A.B., and Turner, A.J. (1991). A summary of the ACM/IEEE-CS Joint Curriculum Task Force Report: Computing Curricula 1991. *Communications of the ACM, 34,* 68–84.

Van Dam, A. (1966). Computer driven displays and their use in man/machine interaction, In F.L. Alt and M. Rubinoff (Eds.), *Advances in Computers, 7,* 239-290. New York: Academic Press.

Weinberg, G.M. (1971). *The psychology of computer programming.* New York: Van Nostrand Reinhold.

PART I

Models, Theories, and Frameworks

On the Effective Use and Reuse of HCI Knowledge

Alistair Sutcliffe

1.1   Introduction

Studies of industrial practice suggest that the systematic, methodical practice of HCI is not widespread (Dillon et al. 1993), although usability engineering is making headway in industry (Muller and Czerwinski 1999). Although guidelines and principles have emerged, HCI has exerted only a minor influence on the current generation of object-oriented development methods (see UML: Rational Corporation, 1999; OOA: Coad and Yourdon 1991). While HCI has created structured methods from both academic research (Lim and Long 1994) and industrial authors (Redmond-Pyle and Moore 1995), these have largely been ignored by software engineers. The conception of HCI proposed by Long and Dowell (1989) drew the distinction between (1) craft practice with no generalization of knowledge; (2) scientific disciplines that generate new knowledge; and (3) engineering disciplines that systematically apply scientific knowledge in design practice. They argued for an engineering approach to HCI that complemented and integrated with software engineering, a quest that has proved elusive.

A fundamental mission of HCI is bringing psychology and other sciences such as sociology to bear upon design. If HCI fails to employ knowledge about the very people it is designing for, then it is left with technology and creative inspiration. The quest to effectively utilize knowledge from cognitive science has been a Holy Grail for many HCI researchers. Several generations of cognitive models have been produced, from early beginnings in the Model Human Processor (Card et al. 1983) to a range of cognitive architectures (Duke et al. 1998; Kitajima and Polson 1997). The

©2000 ACM. Reprinted with permission from *ACM Transactions on Computer-Human Interaction*, Vol. 7, No. 2, June 2000.

dilemma of cognitive models has been to try and accommodate the detail necessary for theoretically sound and accurate modeling while delivering useful predictions to designers. While the GOMS family of models has successfully survived in a niche of detailed prediction of error-free operation times (John and Kieras 1995), the influence of other cognitive models on the design process has been less successful. In spite of slow progress, HCI must be encouraged to continue this quest in the new millennium. Failure to do so would leave us with little more than craft-level experience.

Carroll's task-artifact theory (Carroll et al. 1991; Carroll and Rosson 1992) proposed an alternative means of applying psychological knowledge to design via artifacts that embody theoretically sound principles. The development of HCI knowledge proceeds through cycles of principles design, evaluation, extraction of generalizable knowledge (that is, claims analysis), and redesign. The task-artifact cycle provides a means for reusing HCI knowledge; however, the knowledge in claims is anchored in a specific artifact and scenario of use that limit its scope of future reuse. Reuse in HCI has attracted little attention in comparison to software engineering (see Gamma et al. 1995). Some preliminary ideas were proposed at a CHI workshop (Bayle et al. 1997), but reuse has yet to take root in user interface design even though its practice in user interface toolkits—such as MS-Windows—is widespread. It is the prospects for reuse-led development in HCI that I wish to examine. Also, in contrast to software engineering, where reuse is essentially a pragmatic exercise, I will argue that reusable interactive artifacts should embody sound theory. Two questions motivate this chapter: first, how can HCI knowledge be delivered from theory in a tractable form for designers? By HCI knowledge I mean the insights and predictions that are generated from theoretical analysis about why a design should be usable and which design properties should be selected to ensure usability. The second question is, how can such knowledge be delivered in a form that is reusable in many different applications?

The chapter investigates the prospects for reusable user interfaces as well as knowledge reuse in UI design. In Section 1.2, the prospects for HCI theory will be reviewed, along with theory that has influenced the design process. Section 1.3 introduces claims as grounded examples of theory-based advice linked to HCI artifacts. Section 1.4 discusses how claims may be generalized for reuse and gives a case study example of creating claims in one application, generalizing and contextualizing them for reuse via generic task models, and then applying them in a new application. The chapter concludes in Section 1.5 with discussion of the synergy between claims and theory and the future of intermediate forms of representing HCI knowledge as an effective means of communicating with designers.

1.2   Theories and Cognitive Models

Some may argue that HCI doesn't need theory. I disagree. Any discipline that fails to make a principled explanation to justify its practice is building on sand. HCI's problem is that its theories are shared with and, in many cases, borrowed from cognitive science. Cognitive science theories are complex, "big science" endeavors that can only be carried forward by communities of researchers, notably ACT-R (Anderson and Lebiere 1998) and SOAR (Newell 1990). Both of these theories have been applied to HCI problems, but the range of phenomena that they can account for is narrow. For instance, ACT-R/PM (process motor extension) can recognize characters on a computer screen and predict subjects' attention, reading latencies, and memory for simple character displays (Anderson and Lebiere 1998). This, however, is a long way from predicting similar user behavior in a complex multimedia system. The EPIC model (Kieras and Meyer 1997) provides an architecture of perceptual and cognitive processors with rules that predict the user's attention, recognition, and understanding of user interface features. While EPIC can accurately predict user performance and behavior with simple user interfaces (searching menu displays), it suffers from an increasing burden of configuration as the complexity of the external artifact is increased.

Cognitive theories, implemented as computational cognitive models, have a problem of scale. The relatively simple image illustrated in Figure 1.1 would have to be represented in a large number of propositions, and this involves judgment by the designers about which propositions, and how many, the interface contains. The design question is, which components will the user attend to and comprehend from this multimodal presentation? Propositions have to encode the objects, captions, commands, speech segments, and timing, and this changes for each frame in an animated sequence.

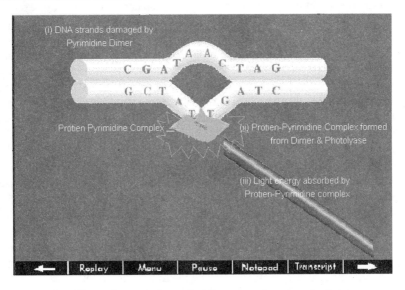

" . . . Next, the protein pyrimidine complex absorbs light
from the visible range . . ."

FIGURE 1.1 Screen image from a multimedia application with the speech track below the image

Multimedia and virtual reality are increasing this complexity with thousands of image components that may have important effects on interaction. Designers need to know whether a component in a complex image will be recognized, comprehended, and afford useful interaction to a user.

Theoretically, EPIC and ACT-R/PM might be able to answer questions about user behavior with multimedia applications, but they depend on preprocessing of complex multisensory input. The cognitive architecture has to be supplied with a list of objects attributed with perceptual properties to represent a computer display. The motivation to invest preprocessing effort will depend on the perceived payback in answering industrial scale design questions. More effort may be expended in modeling the user than is justified by the benefits gained in predicting the affordances that should be designed.

So what are the prospects for predictive cognitive theories in HCI? Barnard (Barnard 1991; Barnard and May 1999) has argued for families of theoretical models that address different aspects of users' cognition and interactive system designs with a means of exchanging knowledge between different theories and models. Modelers from cognitive, AI, and software engineering backgrounds can contribute solutions to design problems from different perspectives using design rationale to summarize design issues and modeling recommendations (Bellotti et al. 1995). This study, however, did not show how knowledge could be exchanged between models from separate academic traditions, even though some progress has been made on linking cognitive and software engineering models (Harrison and Barnard 1993). Unfortunately, design rationale has little to offer in organizing the semantics of knowledge exchange, so more rigorous definitions of HCI issues and arguments are required to create a common language for designers and researchers. Barnard and May (1999) provide a partial answer in Transition Path Diagrams (TPDs), which are derived from running a computational cognitive theory (Barnard's Interacting Cognitive Subsystems augmented with task/domain knowledge to create a Cognitive Task Model: CTM). TPDs represent snapshots of the user's mental model during interaction with a specific design that are created by a CTM analysis. However, understanding the design recommendations from TPDs still requires understanding the CTM analysis in some depth.

Another direction is to develop bridging models based on Norman's model of action (Norman 1986), perhaps the first bridging model in HCI. We have extended Norman's model to indicate the design features that should be combined with users' knowledge and abilities to achieve successful interaction in graphical user interfaces (Sutcliffe et al. 2000) and virtual reality (Kaur et al. 1999; Sutcliffe and Kaur 2000). Models of the user and machine are made explicit with a specification of the contributions each should, ideally, make for successful interaction at each stage in the process. Rules generate advice by defining the combination of user knowledge, abilities, and machine affordances, typically with the following format:

When at interaction stage <physically manipulate> object
If user ability <motor precision limitations> and device characteristics <minimal size, shape of target object>
Then interaction will proceed

Else usability errors <inability to manipulate/manipulation precision> are probable.

In this manner the model advises on a set of "generic design properties (GPDs)," essentially abstract requirements, for interaction in a context, but these abstractions are still intangible for designers. Mapping generic design properties to concrete guidelines is the next step (Kaur et al. 1999), providing a model that can be walked through to diagnose potential usability problems with an existing user interface (see Figure 1.2).

Kaur's theory has three interacting submodels for task action, exploration, and reactive behavior. Rules link components of user knowledge for each interaction stage to the necessary contributions from the design (GDPs). GDPs in turn are linked to specific guidelines and examples.

This extends cognitive walkthroughs (Wharton et al. 1994) with a richer set of evaluation techniques and allows guideline style knowledge to be recruited in appropriate contexts of interaction. But there are limitations in this approach. Cognitive phenomena are implicit in the requirements for interaction. Furthermore, the model has no explanation of user behavior with a complex interface. It may predict that a virtual reality environment should provide salient objects with affordances appropriate for the task, but this is a long way from informing designers how virtual objects should appear and

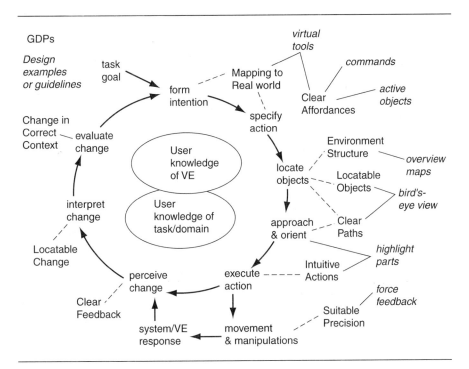

FIGURE 1.2   Abbreviated version of Kaur's model of VR interaction based on Norman's (1986) model of action

react—for example, a virtual scalpel in a medical surgery VE. Interaction models need to be linked to cognitive models of the user (for example, EPIC: Kieras and Meyer 1997) and the task to predict how users may react to several objects in a VE that have different saliences and affordances for interaction in a particular task/domain context.

A basic problem is how theory-based knowledge can be conveyed to designers who are not experts in cognitive science. Relevant results from psychology may be presented as principles or constraints and then related to cut down views of theory. For instance, channel contention in multimodal communication (trying to attend to more than one video at once in multimedia) could be explained by reference to Barnard's (1991) ICS architecture, as illustrated in Figure 1.3. Once the basic concepts of the theory have been explained, it can be used to explain usability issues for different classes of design problems.

In conclusion, cognitive models will be an essential component for progressing theory that underlies HCI, but they have considerable restrictions on their applicability to HCI design problems. These restrictions become severe for complex multimodal and multi-user interfaces. Furthermore, their complexity presents a barrier for delivering HCI knowledge as predictions for usable designs in a manner that is tractable for designers. Bridging models may be a means of transferring more theoretically principled knowledge in a digestible manner for designers, but the nature of knowledge transfer

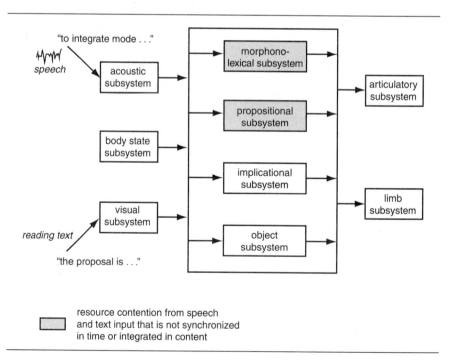

FIGURE 1.3 Bridging model that combines a design problem with a theory-based usability explanation, in this case motivated by the ICS cognitive model (Barnard 1991)

between theory and practice is not clear. Furthermore, examples are frequently necessary to make the application of design advice tangible and advice has to be represented in a digestible manner for designers. Prototypes and examples are a powerful means of anchoring usability arguments, a theme taken up in the next section.

1.3   Claims, Products, and Artifacts

If cognitive models cannot keep pace with the requirements of designers, then an alternative is to deliver usability via examples of good practice and/or reusable artifacts. This direction has been followed by Carroll and coworkers over a number of years (Carroll and Rosson 1992). Design improvement arises by usability evaluation and extracting claims that represent more generally applicable HCI knowledge. Claims are psychologically motivated design rationales that express the upsides and downsides (advantages and disadvantages) of a design as a usability issue, thereby encouraging designers to reason about tradeoff rather than accepting a single guideline or principle. Claims provide situated advice because they come bundled with scenarios of use and an artifact that illustrates application of the claim. Claims and the task-artifact theory follow in the empiricist tradition of HCI (Landauer 1995) that sees usability develop through incremental improvement of artifacts by evaluation and redesign.

The validity of claims rests with their grounding in theory or on the evolution of an artifact with usability demonstrated via evaluation. Theoretically-based knowledge may be recruited to design, which is also informed by task analysis (see Figure 1.4). Hence the artifact should embody not only features that enhance usability from a theoretical viewpoint but also the results of a thorough user-centered analysis

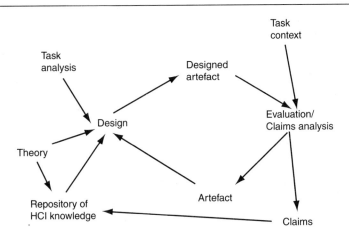

FIGURE 1.4   Task-artifact cycle (after Carroll and Rosson 1992)

of requirements. The weakness of claims is their very situatedness in a specific context provided by the artifact and usage scenario. This limits the scope of future applicability of any one claim to similar artifacts.

Artifacts are usually complex and consequently pose a problem in attributing the contribution that different claims and features make toward the usability of the whole product. To illustrate the point, the Goalposter claim (Carroll et al. 1992; see Figure 1.5) describes functionality to support learning. However, the usability of the artifact depends not only on effective functionality but also on a well-designed visual user interface and dialogue.

A schema of claims-related knowledge (see Figure 1.6) helps to make the assumptions and dependencies in the claim explicit. The theory slot points the designers toward the designer's motivation for the claim in more basic cognitive theory or HCI principles based on psychology. Downsides and some design issues point toward subclaims or design guidelines. Dependencies indicate architecture components or steps in the development process. The extended schema offers designers advice that links theory with psychological design rationale, scenario, and examples. Furthermore, claims can be partitioned by a walkthrough method (Sutcliffe and Carroll 1999) that questions the usability contributions made by different user interface components.

The act of classifying and relating claims exposes different levels of granularity of claims and the artifacts they belong to. Furthermore, decomposing the contributions of claims may lead to the design of new artifacts with associated claims. For example, the contribution of different components of the Goalposter artifact can be factored and expressed as new "child" claims. The telegraphic display claim evolved from its original motivating example into a more general and widely applicable claim for progress tracking user interfaces in any system with hierarchical, deterministic tasks. However, the usability of this claim still rested on several design issues. For instance, linear representations (see Ahlberg and Shneiderman 1994) rather than trees might be more suitable for temporal or sequential information, while lower-level design issues (such as choice of color) can be resolved with guidelines. To enable effective reuse, claims need to be classified and organized in a library. A framework is needed to organize claims into families so designers can locate the appropriate claims for their current application problem.

An initial view of such a framework is illustrated in Figure 1.7. The motivation for the framework is to classify claims with a context for reuse that designers will recognize. One set of families classifies claims that relate to general user interface components according to architecture (such as PAC: Nigay and Coutaz 1995). A second group of families associate claims with generalized models of application functionality, using a classification of generic tasks and domains (Sutcliffe and Maiden 1998). Claims for general user interaction families provide advice on information presentation, low-level interaction, exception handling, and dialogue controller functions. The user interaction family could be populated by claims associated with specifications for agents or interactors (Duke and Harrison 1995) for design of features such as undo (Dix and Mancini 1997), window managers, cascading style sheets, and so forth. The presentation family may contain visualization design advice for complex

Claim ID:	Color-Coded Telegraphic Display
Author:	Singley, M. K.; Carroll, J. M.
Artifact:	MoleHill tutor—Goalposter tool
Description:	The presentation of individual goals in the window is telegraphic, several words at most. However, the learner can expand any of the telegraphic goals (through a menu selection) to display a fuller explanation of whether it is worthwhile to pursue the goal. Thus, the system provides both shorthand feedback on correctness and access to further help.
Upside:	Provides persistent feedback on the correctness of actions as well as access to further information.
Downside:	Learners must learn the display's feature-language and controls.
Scenario:	The learner is trying to create an UpperCaseTextPane; the system infers that the learner is "searching for relevant classes and methods" and posts this phase in the GoalPoster; the learner selects the posted goal to display an expansion of why the goal should be pursued and how it can be advanced; the learner resumes work navigating to the Window class and causing this subgoal to be posted in the GoalPoster.
Effect:	Improved learning by provision of appropriate feedback.
Dependencies:	Tracking user's progress in learning tasks, known goal structure.
Issues:	What sorts of feedback displays are effective and under what circumstances? Is hue coding effective for indicating the three-way distinction between achieved subgoals, apparently correct subgoals, and apparently incorrect subgoals?
Theory:	Feedback in discovery-based learning (Lewis and Anderson 1985).

FIGURE 1.5   The telegraphic feedback claim based on the Goalposter artifact in the MoleHill Smalltalk tutor

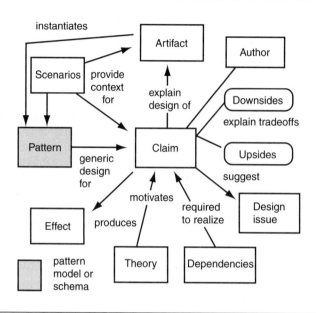

FIGURE 1.6   Claims description schema from Sutcliffe and Carroll (1998)

information structures such as Cam cones (Card et al. 1991) or multimedia scripts to represent generic explanations—for example, multimedia explanation of procedures (Sutcliffe and Dimitrova 1999). In the task layer, three families are proposed: claims that advise on supporting generic tasks, transaction processing in domains such as inventory control, and cognitive activities such as learning and decision making. The Goalposter and many of Carroll's claims belong in the third family. Artifacts in the task support layer should be novel designs with demonstrated usability and functionality to support the user's working practice and to empower users to achieve their goals in new ways. Organizing such a framework of claim families depends on a library of generic models for different tasks and applications. Partial libraries of such models do exist in software engineering (see Sutcliffe and Maiden 1998), but these need to be augmented with a more user-centric task analysis before classes of usable artifacts and claims can be proposed. The framework illustrated in Figure 1.7 is a speculation based on some experience. No doubt it will need refining. The main point is that such a framework is necessary.

Representing knowledge in a federation of claims (Carroll 2000) may help designers by providing a rich network of knowledge to draw upon. Although claims can deliver design advice as a theoretically motivated explanation, they do so within a specific context of an artifact and scenario that appears to restrict their scope for reuse. The following section explores the problem of how claims can be constructed to make their design advice more generally reusable.

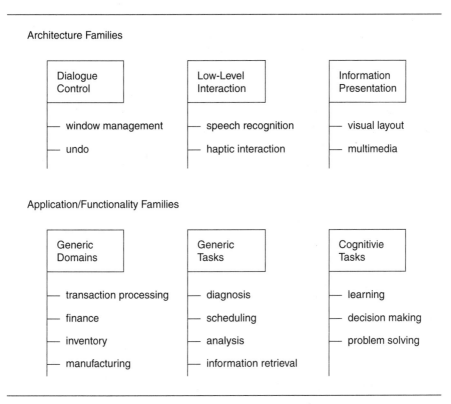

FIGURE 1.7   Framework for claims reuse, showing claims organized into hierarchically structured families that share the same high-level design motivation

1.4   Generalizing Claims and Reusing HCI Knowledge

Reuse of claims and their associated artifacts entails solving two problems: creating a generic version of claims and artifacts and then matching appropriate claims with a new application context. We have made some progress on the generalization problem (Sutcliffe and Carroll 1999) by developing a method that analyzes specific claims into child claims that address different issues following the taxonomy described in Figure 1.7. Briefly, the walkthrough method splits the functional aspect of specific claims into more general components that address user interface dialogue and interaction issues from task-related functionality. A variant of Norman's (1986) model of interaction (see Figure 1.8) is "walked through" by the HCI specialist with question prompts at each stage that indicate the type of new claim that may be discovered at each stage. Some claims may be high-level conceptions—for instance, of learning strategy—while others pertain to smaller-scale features of user interfaces.

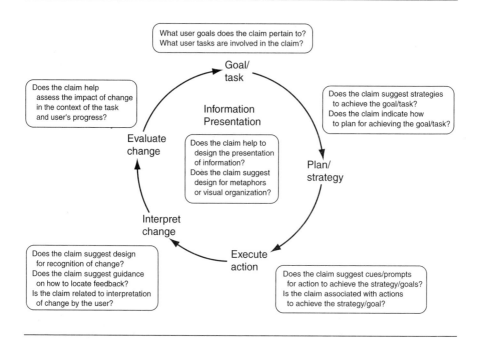

FIGURE 1.8 The claims factoring walkthrough method, composed of questions attached to stages in the process model of interaction (after Norman 1986). Norman's stages to recognize and evaluate change have been merged, as they tend to implicate the same artifact components.

Factoring claims suggests extensions or generalizations of the original claim, new artifacts, descriptions, upsides, downsides, scenarios, and so forth. The questions illustrated in Figure 1.8 are used to step through the task described in the originating claims scenario. Each task initiates an interaction cycle that should achieve its goal. Goal-related questions, however, may suggest subgoals in the task structure. The original goal may, for instance, be underspecified, or a different means of supporting the task may become apparent. Questions within each cycle focus more directly on the user interface components rather than task support functionality. The contribution that the claim and the artifact make in supporting interaction are assessed using the model to structure questions. Hence if the artifact is primarily intended to support formation and monitoring of users' goals, it has a task-goal contribution, whereas a display feature is more likely to support interpretation and evaluation of change. This process results in claims that pertain to tasks, transactions, or what we have termed metadomains (for example, learning) (Sutcliffe and Carroll 1998), which have been separated from claims for general user interface features (for example, undo facilities) that can be applied in a wide variety of interactive systems. The next step is to make the claim and its scenario more generic by substituting references to domain specific objects and actions with general types.

Once claims have been generalized and placed in a library, claims that are pertinent to a new design problem must be retrieved by designers. The retrieval problem is addressed by a multiple strategy approach. First, retrieval of appropriate components is a familiar problem in software engineering, where faceted classification schemes have been the favored approach. Faceted classification can be combined with indexing of general domain models that enable retrieval by browsing a library of generic models or via more sophisticated searching based on theories of analogy. For instance, factored claims are associated with diagnostic tasks or loans transaction processing applications (Sutcliffe and Carroll 1998). The Domain Theory models (Sutcliffe and Maiden 1998) are supported by software search tools that use structure matching (Gentner 1983) between a specific model of the new application and generic models in the Domain Theory library. This process partially escapes from the lexical trap by employing the schema of the domain model to constrain the search space and asking the user to mark up the application model with the schema types. For more details see Sutcliffe and Maiden (1998). However, the Domain Theory library only contains a restricted set of conceptual models describing information systems and real time problems, so it cannot help with all areas of the claims framework shown in Figure 1.7. Fortunately the extended claims schema provides other access paths. Searches could be made on the dependencies, artifact, and usage scenarios. In the latter we are investigating use of Latent Semantic Indexing (Landauer and Dumais 1997) to match an input scenario of use to scenarios associated with claims. Because LSI works by structural comparison of documents, we can escape the dependency on controlled vocabularies and indexes.

One example of classification for reuse with domain models is claims related to monitoring applications, derived from our previous research into safety critical user interface design (Sutcliffe et al. 1998). These describe how displays may be designed to improve the reliability of human monitoring and interpreting events. For instance, claim 1 (see www.acm.org/pubs/citations/journals/tochi/2000-7-2/p197-sutcliffe for details) in Figure 1.9 relates to tradeoffs in displaying a model of the sensed world for monitoring; claim 2 describes tradeoffs in filtering detected events; and in claim 3, automatic highlighting of rare events has the upside of making events more noticeable but the downside of decreasing user awareness by detecting too many false alarms. Claims are attached to either the whole model (as in 5) or specific components, depending on their intended usability effect on the associated artifact. The artifact for these claims is a shipboard emergency management system (see Sutcliffe and Carroll 1998).

The claims originally developed for a shipboard emergency management system were reused in the safety critical user design of a scientific instrument application (Sutcliffe 1998); see Figures 1.10 and 1.11.

Note the effect of generalizing the claims by substitution of specific references in the claim and scenario (Figure 1.11). Substitution is guided by the Domain Theory schema that contains types (such as agents, objects, events, structures) and by the

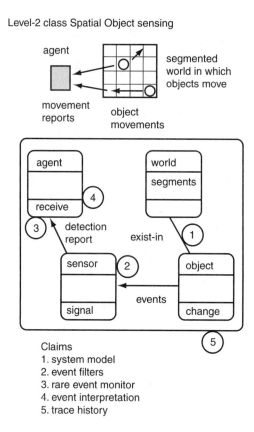

FIGURE 1.9 Object Sensing Model illustrated as an informal diagram and an object-oriented analysis model

models with which the claim is being associated—for example, object sensing OSMs (Object System Models) are associated with agent control OSMs and specify control subsystems, effector agents, and so on. In practice the generic and specific scenarios are separate texts, but both are used to promote understanding of the abstraction.

These domains apparently have little in common. However, at a deeper level of abstraction, the problems are related. Most safety critical applications involve the problem of monitoring a controlled system for events that may indicate dangerous states. Software engineering problems of event detectability are implicit in monitoring, while the HCI issues concern transmission of warnings to the user, situating warnings in context, and avoiding false alarms.

A context for claims reuse may also be provided by generic tasks acting as an indexing mechanism. Design advice expressed in claims format can be attached to

Original Claim

Claim ID: Rare event monitor 1

Author: A. G. Sutcliffe

Artifact: Shipboard emergency monitoring system

Description: The autopilot [control subsystem] is moni-
                   tored to ensure that course corrections [out-
                   put events] are being signaled to the rudder
                   [effector agent] and electronic circuits
                   [subsystem behavior] are working normally.
                   If abnormalities are detected, the user is
                   warned that the autopilot [control subsystem]
                   has failed.

Upside: Automatic detection of dangerous events
                   relieves the user of constant monitoring;
                   automatic detection and warning gives the
                   user time to analyze the problem.

Downside: Issuing too many warnings may lead the user
                   to ignore critical events; automated monitor-
                   ing may lead to user overconfidence in the
                   automated system and decrease their situation
                   awareness.

Scenario: No autopilot course corrections [control sys-
                   tem commands] are detected in a five-minute
                   period [time, frequency parameters], and the
                   circuit monitor detects no activity in the
                   rudder controls [effector agent], the system
                   gives an audio warning of autopilot failure
                   [control subsystem] to the user and visually
                   signals the location of the problem on a dia-
                   gram of the ship's controls.

{dependencies, etc. omitted because of space constraints}

FIGURE 1.10   Safety critical application: the original claim

Reused Claim

Claim ID: Rare event monitor 2

Target artifact: User interface for a chemical analysis
                   instrument control system

Description [of the new claim]:

                   Infrequent, dangerous events are detected
                   by the system, and a warning is issued to
                   the user; in this case, operational fail-
                   ures in a laser gas chromatograph control
                   system.

Upside: Automatic detection of dangerous events
                   relieves the user of constant monitoring;
                   automatic detection and warning gives the
                   user time to analyze the problem.

Downside: Issuing too many warnings may lead the
                   users to ignore critical events; automated
                   monitoring may lead to user overconfidence
                   in the automated system and decrease their
                   situation awareness.

Scenario: No events are detected in the laser emis-
                   sion controller or power supply, so the
                   system gives an audio warning to the user
                   and visually signals the location of the
                   problem on a diagram of the instrument.

FIGURE 1.11   Safety critical application: the reused claim

generalized task models (such as TKS: Johnson 1992), or to reach the software engineering community, claims can be associated with interaction diagrams following
use case notations. A generic model of information searching is illustrated in Figure
1.12 with associated claims based on research into information-seeking tasks (Sutcliffe and Ennis 1998) and information visualization (Sutcliffe and Patel 1996).

The first three claims describe tradeoffs for design features that help query formulation by either providing libraries of preformed query libraries, conceptual maps of
the database, or an active thesaurus that suggests alternative query terms (see
http://www.acm.org/pubs/citations/journals/tochi/2000-7-2/p197-sutcliffe for details).
The first claim, preformed queries (Figure 1.13), was derived from research on the
INTUITIVE information retrieval system (Sutcliffe et al. 1995).

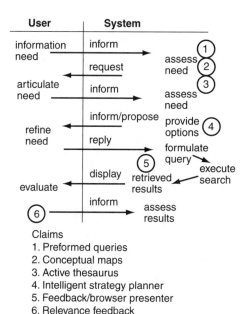

Claims
1. Preformed queries
2. Conceptual maps
3. Active thesaurus
4. Intelligent strategy planner
5. Feedback/browser presenter
6. Relevance feedback

FIGURE 1.12   Interaction diagram (use case) for the information-searching generic task. Claims are attached to either the whole task or specific components, depending on the original task/artifact context.

This claim was reused in the Multimedia Broker system, a Web-based broking application that also required information-searching facilities (see Sutcliffe and Carroll 1998). The prototype embodying this claim is illustrated in Figure 1.14. In this case not only the claim but also its associated software artifact could have been reused. The basic functionality of the reusable query class and its components—that is, a library of queries, a selection mechanism for the user, and a means of submitting the query to a database—could be transferred to the Broker. The new requirements, however, also specified tailorable queries. In INTUITIVE, the user interface manifestation (see Figure 1.13) of preformed queries were icons that enabled hypertext-like query by pointing. The user interface for preformed queries is different in the Broker system, since the query buttons were redesigned as mini-menus allowing limited customization of the query. In addition the user could enter a limited set of keywords to customize the query. This mitigated one of the claim's downsides (inflexible queries), but the claim now appears in a different user interface context and has new functionality in the keyword additions. This illustrates how reuse and evolution of claims often proceed in tandem because this reuse produced a new claim (customizable queries). Four other claims (conceptual maps, thesaurus, browser/presenter, and relevance feedback) all transferred to the Broker with little modification of the UI components.

Claim ID: Preformed query claim

Author: A. G. Sutcliffe

Artifact: Preformed query library (INTUITIVE class) and
                 UI menu selector

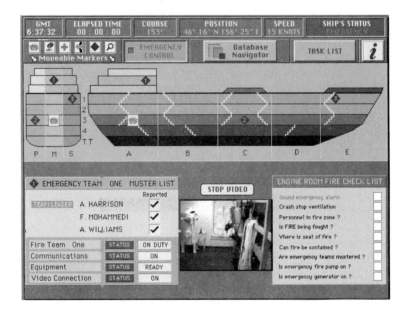

INTUITIVE shipboard emergency management system, showing
the checkbox artifact (bottom right) and preformed queries
as diamond icons leading to the answer box (bottom left).

Description: A preformed query is attached to an icon or
                  placed in a menu.

Upside: Provides rapid access to information; saves
                  users effort in articulating queries.

Downside: Finding queries in a large library can be
                  difficult; queries inflexible, cannot be
                  adapted.

Usage Scenario: The user interface presents a menu of queries
                  that can be reused. The user selects a query
                  that matches the need by selecting an icon or
                  a menu option, and the system retrieves the
                  information for presentation.

Effect: The user can retrieve information by reusing
                 familiar queries.

Dependencies: Information needs and queries must be
                 known; future information needs must be
                 predictable.

Issues: Query format, customizability of values and
                 constraint clauses, addressing queries to
                 different databases.

Scope: Information-seeking tasks with predictable
                 needs.

FIGURE 1.13   Preformed query claim and the original artifact it was derived from in
the INTUITIVE information retrieval system

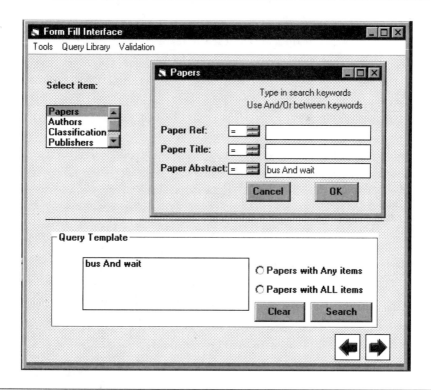

FIGURE 1.14   Multimedia Broker implementation of the generic preformed query
claim to support the user's information retrieval task

Specific claims may be reused and applied to the design of a new artifact. Alternatively, the original needs to be generalized and the user interface feature redesigned for reuse. This frequently implies considerable reengineering. As a partial solution we have related claims to design patterns (Sutcliffe and Dimitrova 1999), which have enjoyed considerable success in the object-oriented design community (Gamma et al. 1995). This creates a package of reusable knowledge composed of a generalized specification (a pattern), psychological design rationale (the claim), a designed artifact that embodies the claim and pattern, along with a scenario of use that situates the claim and artifact in a real world context. One example of a pattern is in multimedia explanations where patterns describe generic models of content linked to an explanation goal—for example, how to explain causal arguments (see Figure 1.15). Media application rules are then applied to this amodal content pattern to derive a media representation pattern. Claims provide arguments to justify patterns and explain design tradeoffs.

Claim ID: Multimedia-causal explanation

Artifact: Etiology of Cancer (SilverPlatter)

Pattern: Media representation script for causal
                   explanations (see below).

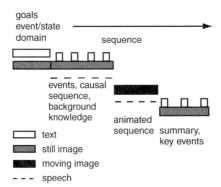

Description: The presentation starts with the goal and
                   then describes the causal sequence of events
                   with a summary. A combination of media is
                   used to reinforce different aspects of con-
                   tent with diagrams showing abstract views
                   linked to realistic images.

Upside: The media combination of abstract and realistic
                   images provides causal concepts linked to a
                   realistic context to reinforce the explanation.

Downside:	The presentation may be too simple for experts; insufficient links to background knowledge may frustrate users; too much detail may overwhelm novices.
Scenario:	The presentation shows how DNA is repaired by a photoactivated enzyme. A beam of light strikes the enzyme, causing the repair reaction to start.
Effect:	Learning is improved by media combination that reinforces the message.
Dependencies:	Conceptual diagram, image media, speech explanation.
Issues:	What level of detail is necessary for learners with different levels of knowledge and abilities? How far should the explanation trace backward into background knowledge?
Theory:	Causal knowledge structures, depth of encoding, memorability of static versus dynamic media (Gardiner and Christie 1987), linking viewpoints (Rogers and Schaife 1998).

FIGURE 1.15   Multimedia pattern for causal explanation and its associated claim

Multimedia patterns also demonstrate how cognitive models can contribute to the creation of reusable HCI knowledge—first in generating patterns and second as an explanation justifying claims. The ICS model (see Figure 1.3) was used to walk through the content patterns and check that application of media selection rules had not created a usability problem by overloading the user's cognitive resources. Some examples are obvious from simple inspection of the ICS architecture—for example, that use of text and speech concurrently will compete for the linguistic processing resource. Likewise, attending to video and still image will contend for image processing. In this way the cognitive model can act as a justification and explanation for claims associated with this pattern.

This vision of future reuse has several hurdles to cross before even its feasibility can be accepted. First, specific tasks come in different flavors, just as diagnosing a fault in a television set is very different from medical diagnosis. Presumably, subclasses of generic task models may be produced, but they will have an impact on the retrieval problem as the task/claims library scales up, since the designer has to find an appropriate generic model that matches the current application. A second problem is the applicability of specific claims, artifacts, and scenarios as solutions to the generic problem. Unfortunately, reusing claims creates a clash in levels of abstraction. Artifacts and scenarios are specific, whereas patterns are more generic, and whole claims are somewhere in between. This raises the problem of the applicability of a claim that was validated by usability evaluation of a specific artifact to a more general scope for reuse expressed in a pattern. The immediate response is to generalize claims, scenarios, and artifacts. Claims express general and theoretically motivated design knowledge, contextualized for reuse by association with abstract models and patterns. The link between claims and specific artifacts and scenarios helps to explain abstract ideas with grounded examples.

Inevitably there is a tradeoff between generality and specificity. Generic artifacts have a wider potential target for future reuse by virtue of their abstraction but pay the penalty of delivering less detailed advice to the designer. The converse is true for specific artifacts. These issues are being debated and have not as yet been solved in the software reuse community. In the future, HCI is also going to have to resolve the key issues of the appropriate chunk size and level of abstraction for effective reuse. Defining the levels of abstraction, scope, and applicability of HCI knowledge is another challenge that awaits resolution in the new millennium.

1.5   Conclusions

I have argued that HCI will need to adopt a new perspective on delivering theoretical insights into design advice in the new millennium and that design by reuse will become a dominant development paradigm. Two problems have to be solved. First, the complexity of theory has to be hidden from the designer while providing advice that is comprehensible yet faithful to predictions of theoretical models. Second, advice has to be generalized so it can be reused in a wide range of contexts. One might argue that guidelines (Gardiner and Christie 1987), generally applicable advice from cognitive models (Kitajima and Polson 1997), or design methodologies (Lim and Long 1994) address this point. These approaches, however, have met with limited success. The same is true for structured and formal methods in software engineering. In contrast, reusable design knowledge as patterns is having an increasingly important impact. In HCI we need to heed this lesson, and claims may provide the representation we seek.

However, reuse of claims (and patterns in software engineering) alone may not be enough. Design is a complex process that requires tradeoffs, so I have argued that knowledge needs to be reused by active reasoning using claims and cut-down versions of theories to promote better understanding of usability issues. Others have also proposed integration of informal notations, particularly design rationale, with more formal cognitive (Bellotti et al. 1996) and computational theories (Johnson 1996). Claims are partially motivated by design rationale, but their advantage may lie in the combination of the specific with the general. Design advice is expressed as tradeoffs associated with a theoretically motivated principle. In this chapter I have argued that the effectiveness of claims reuse might be extended, associating them with a design context of generic tasks and domain models. This might provide the best of both worlds: generalized, theoretically motivated claims, associated with specific scenarios and artifacts as well as general patterns. The disadvantage is increased complexity. Usability studies of design rationale have shown that users experience problems in assimilating advice even in a simple notation (MacLean and McKerlie 1995; Sutcliffe and Ryan 1997). The answer may lie in gradually unfolding design advice in increasing layers of complexity, following the minimal manual principle (Carroll 1999).

However, the fundamental problem of how to effectively transfer knowledge from theory into design still must be resolved. Claims may form one conduit for such a transfer, possibly in combination with patterns, that express more generalized specifications and models. However, patterns and reuse raise significant and difficult questions that require a new theory of abstraction in user interfaces to provide answers about the granularity and contents of UI patterns and their relationship to specific scenarios and artifacts. Without such a theory, pattern libraries will be developed in an ad hoc manner, leading to incompatibility and hindering development by reuse.

Patterns and claims may enable theoretically sound knowledge to be incorporated into designs to improve quality and help the evolution of usable designs. However, the means of communication between theory and design practice is probably the most significant challenge for the new millennium. Some hints were suggested in this chapter, such as creating question-like templates for design issues or building cut-down cognitive theories as digestible chunks of knowledge that can be applied to design. Reuse and incorporating sound theory from cognitive science can help to deliver usability. In the future, however, the utility of artifacts may be better shaped by sources of knowledge other than branches of psychology. However, reuse on its own is not the answer. Some innovation might arise from novel recombination of reusable components, assuming that the interoperability of HCI components could be solved.

Acknowledgments

Many of the ideas for claims analysis and reuse have been developed in collaboration with Jack Carroll and are published in recent papers. It is a pleasure to acknowledge the stimulus of that work. The development of claim families and other ideas contained in this chapter are the author's own responsibility.

References

Ahlberg, C., and Shneiderman, B. (1994). Visual information seeking: Tight coupling of dynamic query filters with starfield displays. *Proceedings CHI'94 Boston,* 313–317. New York: ACM.

Anderson, J.R., and Lebiere, C. (1998). *The atomic components of thought.* Mahwah, NJ: Lawrence Erlbaum Associates.

Barnard, P. (1991). Bridging between basic theories and the artifacts of human computer interaction. In J.M. Carroll (Ed.), *Designing interaction: Psychology at the human computer interface.* New York: Cambridge University Press.

Barnard, P., and May, J. (1999). Representing cognitive activity in complex tasks. *Human-Computer Interaction,* 14, 1–2, 93–158.

Bayle, E., Bellamy, R., and Casaday, G. (1997). Putting it all together. *SIGCHI Bulletin,* 30, 1, 17–23.

Bellotti, V., Blandford, A., Duke, D., MacLean, A., May, J., and Nigay, L. (1996). Interpersonal access control in computer-mediated communications: A systematic analysis of the design space. *Human-Computer Interaction,* 11, 4, 357–432.

Bellotti, V., Buckingham-Shum, S., MacLean, A., and Hammond, N. (1995). Multidisciplinary modelling in HCI design: Theory and in practice. In I.R. Katz, R. Mack, L. Marks, M.B. Rosson, and J. Nielsen (Eds.), *Proceedings CHI'95: Human Factors in Computing Systems, Denver CO 7–11 May 1995,* 146–153. New York: ACM.

Card, S.K., Moran, T.P., and Newell, A. (1983). *The psychology of human computer interaction.* Hillsdale, NJ: Lawrence Erlbaum Associates.

Card, S.K., Robertson, G., and Mackinlay, J.D. (1991). The Information Visualizer: An information workspace. *CHI'91 Proceedings: ACM Conference on Human Factors in Computing Systems, New Orleans,* 181–188. New York: ACM.

Carroll, J.M. (2000). *Making use: Scenario-based design of human-computer interactions.* Cambridge, MA: MIT Press.

Carroll, J.M. (Ed.) (1999). *Minimalism: Beyond the Nurnberg Funnel.* Cambridge, MA: MIT Press.

Carroll, J.M., Kellogg, W.A., and Rosson, M.B. (1991). The task-artifact cycle. In J.M. Carroll (Ed.), *Designing interaction: Psychology at the human-computer interface,* 74–102. New York: Cambridge University Press.

Carroll, J.M., and Rosson, M.B. (1992). Getting around the task-artifact framework: How to make claims and design by scenario. *ACM Transactions on Information Systems,* 10, 2, 181–212.

Carroll, J.M., Singley, M.K., and Rosson, M.B. (1992). Integrating theory development with design evaluation. *Behaviour and Information Technology,* 11, 247–255.

Coad, P., and Yourdon, E. (1991). *Object oriented analysis.* Englewood Cliffs, NJ: Yourdon Press.

Dillon, A., Sweeney, M.T., and Maguire, M.C. (1993). A survey of usability engineering within the European IT Industry: Current practice and needs. In A. Alty, D. Diaper, and S. Guest (Eds.), *People and Computers VIII; Proceedings: HCI'93,* 81–94. New York: Cambridge University Press.

Dix, A., and Mancini, R. (1997). Specifying history and backtracking mechanism. In P. Palanque and F. Paterno (Eds.), *Formal methods in human computer interaction, 1–23.*

Duke, D.J., and Harrison, M.D. (1995). From formal models to formal methods. In N. Taylor and J. Coutaz (Eds.), *Software Engineering and Human Computer Interaction: ICSE workshop on SE-HCI: joint research issues, 159–173.* Berlin: Springer Verlag.

Duke, D.J., Barnard, P.J., Duce, D.A., and May, J. (1998). Syndetic modelling. *Human-Computer Interaction, 13, 4, 337–393.*

Gamma, E., Helm, R., Johnson, R., and Vlissides, J. (1995). *Design patterns: Elements of reusable object-oriented software.* Reading, MA: Addison-Wesley.

Gardiner, M., and Christie, B. (1987). *Applying cognitive psychology to user interface design.* Chichester: Wiley.

Gentner, D. (1983). Structure-mapping: A theoretical framework for analogy. *Cognitive Science, 7, 155–170.*

Harrison, M.D., and Barnard, P. (1993). On defining the requirements for interaction. In S. Fickas and A.C.W. Finklestein (Eds.), *Proceedings: 1st International Symposium on Requirements Engineering, RE'93, San Diego CA, 50–55.* Los Alamitos: IEEE Computer Society.

John, B.E., and Kieras, R.E. (1995). The GOMS family of user interface analysis techniques: Comparison and contrast. *ACM Transactions on Computer-Human Interaction, 3, 320–351.*

Johnson, P. (1992). *Human computer interaction.* London: McGraw-Hill.

Johnson, C.W. (1996). Documenting the design of safety critical user interfaces. *Interacting with Computers, 8, 3, 221–239.*

Kaur, K., Maiden, N.A.M., and Sutcliffe, A.G. (1999). Interacting with virtual environments: An evaluation of a model of interaction. *Interacting with Computers, 11, 4, 403–426.*

Kieras, D.E., and Meyer, D.E. (1997). An overview of the EPIC architecture for cognition and performance with application to human computer interaction. *Human-Computer Interaction, 12, 4, 391–438.*

Kitajima, M., and Polson, P.G. (1997). A comprehension based model of exploration. *Human-Computer Interaction, 12, 4, 345–390.*

Landauer, T.K. (1995). *The trouble with computers: Usefulness, usability and productivity.* Cambridge, MA: MIT Press.

Landauer, T.K., and Dumais, S.T. (1997). A solution to Plato's problem: The latent semantic analysis theory of acquisition, induction and representation of knowledge. *Psychological Review, 104, 211–240.*

Lewis, M.L., and Anderson, J.R. (1985). Discrimination of operator schemata in problem-solving: Learning from examples. *Cognitive Psychology, 17, 26–65.*

Lim, K.Y., and Long, J.L. (1994). *The MUSE method for usability engineering.* New York: Cambridge University Press.

Long, J.L., and Dowell, J. (1989). Conceptions for the discipline of HCI: Craft, applied science, and engineering. In A.G. Sutcliffe and L.A. Macaulay (Eds.), *People and Computers V; Proceedings Fifth Conference of the BCS HCI SIG.* New York: Cambridge University Press.

MacLean, A., and McKerlie, D. (1995). *Design space analysis and user-representations* (Technical Report EPC-1995–102). Cambridge: Xerox Research Centre Europe.

Muller, M.J., and Czerwinski, M. (1999). Organizing usability work to fit the full product range. *Communications of the ACM, 42,* 5, 87–90.

Newell, A. (1990). *Unified theories of cognition.* Cambridge, MA: Harvard University Press.

Nigay, L., and Coutaz, J. (1995). A generic platform for addressing the multimodal challenge. *Proceedings of CHI'95, Human Factors in Computing Systems,* 98–105. New York: ACM.

Norman, D.A. (1986). Cognitive engineering. In D.A. Norman and S.W. Draper (Eds.), *User-centred system design: New perspectives on human-computer interaction.* Hillsdale, NJ: Lawrence Erlbaum Associates.

Rational Corporation (1999). *UML: Unified Modeling Language Method.* Available online at <http://www.rational.com> Accessed 1999.

Redmond-Pyle, D., and Moore, A. (1995). *Graphical user interface design and evaluation.* London: Prentice Hall.

Rogers, Y., and Scaife, M. (1998). How can interactive multimedia facilitate learning. In J. Lee (Ed.), *Intelligence and multimodality in multimedia interfaces: Research and applications.* Menlo Park, CA: AAAI Press.

Sutcliffe, A.G. (1998). Scenario-based requirements analysis. *Requirements Engineering Journal, 3,* 1, 48–65.

Sutcliffe, A.G., Bennett, I., Doubleday, A., and Ryan, M. (1995). Designing query support for multiple databases. In K. Nordby, P.H. Helmersen, D.J. Gilmore, and S.A. Arnesen, (Eds.), *Proceedings INTERACT-95: 5th International Conference on Human-Computer Interaction, Lillehammer, Norway 27–29 June 1995,* 207–212. London: Chapman & Hall.

Sutcliffe, A.G., and Carroll, J.M. (1998). Generalizing claims and reuse of HCI knowledge. In H. Johnson, L. Nigay and C. Roast, (Eds.), *People and Computers XIII; Proceedings: BCS-HCI Conference, Sheffield 1–4 September 1998,* 159–176. Berlin: Springer-Verlag.

Sutcliffe, A.G., and Carroll, J.M. (1999). Designing claims for reuse in interactive systems design. *International Journal of Human-Computer Studies, 50,* 3, 213–241.

Sutcliffe, A.G., and Dimitrova, M.T. (1999). Claims, patterns and multimedia. In A. Sasse and C. Johnson, (Eds.), *Proceedings of INTERACT-99: Human Computer Interaction,* 329–335. Amsterdam: IFIP/IOS Press.

Sutcliffe, A.G., and Ennis, M. (1998). *Towards a cognitive theory of information retrieval, IWC Special issue: Information retrieval and human computer interaction*, Vol. 10, 321–351.

Sutcliffe, A.G., and Kaur, K. (2000). Evaluating the usability of virtual reality user interfaces. *Behaviour and Information Technology,* 19, 6, 415–426.

Sutcliffe, A.G., and Maiden, N.A.M. (1998). The Domain Theory for requirements engineering. *IEEE Transactions on Software Engineering,* 24, 3, 174–196.

Sutcliffe, A.G., Maiden, N.A.M., Minocha, S., and Manuel, D. (1998). Supporting scenario-based requirements engineering. *IEEE Transactions on Software Engineering,* 24, 12, 1072–1088.

Sutcliffe, A.G., and Patel, U. (1996). 3D or not 3D: Is it nobler in the mind? In M.A. Sasse, R.J. Cunningham, and R.L. Winder (Eds.), *People and Computers XI. Proceedings: HCI-96, London August 1996,* 79–94. London: Springer-Verlag.

Sutcliffe, A.G., and Ryan, M. (1997). Assessing the usability and efficiency of design rationale. In S. Howard, J. Hammond, and G. Lindgaard (Eds.), *Proceedings of Human Computer Interaction INTERACT-97.* 148–155. London: Chapman & Hall.

Sutcliffe, A.G., Ryan, M., Springett, M.V., and Doubleday, A. (2000). Model mismatch analysis: Towards a deeper explanation of users' usability problems. *Behaviour and Information Technology,* 19, 1, 43–55.

Wharton, C., Reiman, J., Lewis, C., and Polson, P. (1994). The cognitive walkthrough method: A practitioners guide. In J. Nielsen and R.L. Mack (Eds.), *Usability inspection methods,* 105–140. New York: Wiley.

2

Macrotheory for Systems of Interactors

Philip Barnard
Jon May
David Duke
David Duce

2.1   Theory Development in a Boundless Domain

In less than a quarter of a century information technologies and their users have diversified into an extraordinary range of sociotechnical ecosystems. Few would disagree with the proposition that the study of HCI is now effectively a boundless domain. At the outset, many shared the vision of Card et al. (1983) that step by step task analysis could be combined with theories of the human information-processing mechanism and human knowledge representation to yield engineering methods to support design decision-making. As applications and interfaces diversified, the limitations of assumptions about a prototypical user's cognitive mechanism became all too readily apparent. It was, of course, recognized from the outset that the development of theory lagged developments in interface design and had other limitations (Newell and Card 1985). They were of restricted scope, applying mostly to local features of interface design. It also proved hard to re-use them in novel contexts or to scale up theoretical exercises from laboratory examples to real design settings.

We could now abandon serious attempts to maintain theory development within HCI. There is an obvious problem with this strategy. In the absence of a good body of formal theory, practitioners will undoubtedly invent their own informal, or folk, theories to help them represent and think about the problems and issues that are important to them in their context. The practice of HCI could become like that of psychoanalysis, with one school of thought communicating among themselves about a given set of issues in very different terms from those adhering to another school of thought. We would end up with a range of theories dealing with different facets of individual user performance, of the behavior of groups, and of larger organizations. Our theories would be unlikely to "fit together" in a coherent way to resolve the conceptual jigsaw puzzles that exist in real design spaces (Bellotti et al. 1996; Blandford and Duke 1997).

In this chapter, our immediate aim is to stimulate further debate on alternative routes to theory development and its integration. Our discipline will not be best served in the new millennium either by abandoning theory or by the unconstrained development of more and more unconnected local theories at different levels and in different domains. After all, HCI theories are not simply concerned with humans or computers but with their *interactions,* and these interactions are often situated in the context of teams, networked computers, and larger organizations. Our body of theory should directly address the problem of linking the different ways of modeling the properties and behaviors of these different entities. We argue here that greater integration within a boundless domain such as HCI is a tractable proposition for research in the new millennium. Integration can be facilitated through the development of generic representations of "systems of interactors."

2.2   Systems of Interactors, Macrotheory, Microtheory, and Layered Explanation

The general idea that the behavior of systems can be analyzed with a focus on different entities or at different levels of abstraction has been approached in many different ways in theoretical and applied contexts. Newell (1990), for example, describes a system level as "a collection of components that are linked together in some arrangement and that interact, thus producing behavior at that system level." In a system with multiple levels, the components at one level are realized by systems at the next level down and so on for each successive level (p. 117). Marr (1982) also stratified theories along a dimension of abstraction. He described a computational level of theory, which specifies the essential logic of what needs to be computed for a task to be carried out, and distinguished it from algorithmic and hardware levels of theory. The algorithmic level specifies the implementation of the computational theory, whereas the hardware level refers to the realization of the algorithm in some physical system. From the more practical perspective of systems engineering, Chapanis (1996) uses hierarchical diagrams to illustrate how humans, hardware, and software are grouped together in subsubsystems that are embedded in subsystems that make up a complete system, be it a team or wider organization.

We draw upon components of all these ideas in a generalized form and summarize here arguments developed at greater length elsewhere (Barnard et al. 2000). Much HCI theory has been "X-centric": user-centered, system-centered, team-centered, and so on. Rather than taking users, computers, or teams as specific points of departure for theory development, we start by defining all of these entities as "interactors." The use of this term originates in computer science (Duke and Harrison 1993). This term has a number of advantages. First, by being generically—as opposed to specifically—X-centric, it enables us to refer to things that interact without carrying the implicit semantic overheads that come with terms such as computers, users, or teams. Second, an interactor is something that is composed of other interactors and as such is a relative rather than absolute construct. Third, an interactor is something whose behavior can, in principle, be mathematically described in terms of the properties of the lower-order interactors of which it is composed. Finally, any interactor is an entity that behaves over time.

To model the behavior of an interactor over time, we need to understand how its behavior is constrained. The behavior of any interactor will be determined in part by constraints originating in its own constituents and in part by the behavior of the other interactors with which it engages as a part of some superordinate system. This implies that a complete theory of the behavior of a system requires two distinct components: a body of microtheory and a body of macrotheory. Figure 2.1 illustrates a hypothetical system of basic interactors—[B]'s. These are the basic units that interact, and their behavior is constrained by their constituent [C]'s and by the superordinate organization of the system they make up [SUPER].

In the case of human computer interaction, a system of basic interactors might minimally be composed of a user, a computer, and other things used in the task context, such as a printed document. The behavior of the user (a [B]) will be constrained by the properties of components ([C]'s) within their mental architecture (for example, perceptual mechanisms, decision mechanisms, and mechanisms for the control of action), as well as by human biomechanics. Likewise, the behavior of the computer system (a different [B]) will be constrained by its components (I/O devices, processor properties, operating system, and application characteristics). The "behavior" of the document (a third [B]) would also be constrained by factors like the flexibility of its physical components and how they were bound together. For this system of interactors, at least three types of microtheory are required: a model of the psychological system, a model of the computational system, and a model of a physical system. However, as components of a

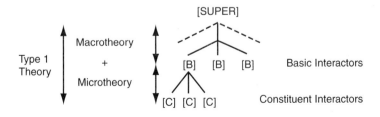

FIGURE 2.1   Type 1 theory composed of macrotheory and microtheory applied to any system of interactors

system these three are not independent; the behavior of each depends on the others. The relevant macrotheory for this system of interactors would specify how their conjoint behavior is constrained. Only the combination of micro- and macrotheory would provide a complete theory of this particular system of interactors. A coherent theory made up of an interrelated body of micro- and macrotheory will, for the purposes of a later contrast, be referred to as a "Type 1" theory.

For those interested in modeling the operation of a psychological system or of a computing system, the workings of their components require more detailed specification. At the apex of Figure 2.2 is a system composed of a user, a computer, and some other interactor, which might again be documentation. The topmost level is labeled a behavioral, or "syndetic," system. The term *syndetic* (Duke et al. 1998) is derived from the Greek term *syndesis* meaning "to bind together." We use the term syndetic to refer to the specific case of behavioral systems that are composed of interactors of fundamentally different types. To the sides of the apex are shown a psychological system of interactors and a computing system of interactors, and to the side of these are shown their respective refinements into neurological and electronic systems. This diagram can readily be extended "upward" to include the syndetic system as a basic interactor in a larger system of interactors, such as a team.

Systems are distinguished in terms of the focus of scientific attention. Each system in Figure 2.2 consists of entities that behave. In the neurological system, the things that behave are neurons. In the psychological system, the things that behave are processes that construct or change mental representations. In a behavioral or syn-

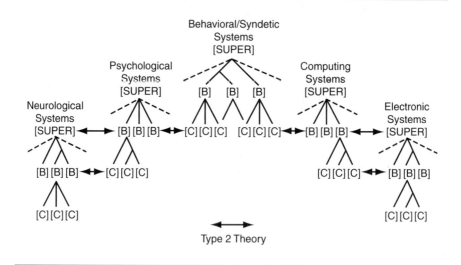

FIGURE 2.2 Systems of interactors at different levels of explanation organized by Type 1 and Type 2 theories

detic system, the things that behave are humans in interaction with technological arti-facts. Unlike a strict hierarchical decomposition of successive systems, Figure 2.2 overlaps hierarchies at different levels. This enables us to highlight two characteris-tics. First, when we focus our attention on the behavior of a system, we adopt a frame of reference appropriate to the entities that make it up. We must consider both the organi-zation of the superordinating system and the subordinate constituents of the entities. A complete Type 1 theory is composed of macrotheory and microtheory. Newell's (1990) main arguments were applied to the unification of theories *within* a cognitive layer. We take this form of argument and generalize it to *any* system level. Second, when we adopt a frame of reference for model building or theory development, we do so in terms of the scientific semantics of a particular class of theory. When we move the focus of scientific attention from one level of system to another, we use theories with different form and content, as identified by Marr (1982) and others. This is shown in Figure 2.2 by introducing the notion of a Type 2 theory, which is the map-ping from the macrotheory of one level of explanation into the microtheory of another and vice versa.

A Type 2 theory specifies the transformations that occur in the semantics of theo-ries when we move from one layer of systems analysis to another. Figure 2.2 suggests that these transformations have two components: a mapping from the superordinate composition of one system into the basic units of the higher system and a mapping from the basic units of the lower system into the constituents of the higher system. When we move up a level we discard the microtheory of the lower level, and when moving down, we add microtheory to support more detailed explanation or imple-mentation. This is marked in Figure 2.2 by the offsets to the right and left of the cen-tral behavioral or syndetic system. In moving to either a human or computer system, a basic unit of the behavioral or syndetic system becomes the superordinate entity of our new theoretical domain. Its constituent interactors become the basic interactors of our new theory, and we need a new microtheory to add in the new constituent structures, which were not specifically represented in the theoretical analysis of the behavioral or syndetic system.

The transformations that occur are not just those of adding or discarding detail. In the regions where macrotheory at one level overlaps with microtheory at a higher level, the two representations differ. One form of transformation is selection. A par-ticular theoretical project may be concerned with abstracting or refining only those components that are relevant to a specific modeling objective. A second is recombi-nation. The syndetic system incorporates basic interactors of different types and must draw on microtheories of each. In the years since Newell and Card's (1985) discus-sion of the problems faced by theory development in HCI, there can be little doubt that significant advances have been made in the development of unified cognitive architectures and placing modeling on firm computational foundations. SOAR (Newell 1990), ACT-R (Anderson 1993), and EPIC (see Meyer and Kieras 1997) have all achieved significant application successes in this domain. Progress has been rather more modest on other topics, such as modeling human understanding and use of dynamic graphical interfaces, multimodal perception, and emotion. Much the same observation could be made in relation to our ability to model the behavior of software systems before they are built or of team behavior before the teams are formed. In all these areas, our existing microtheories require considerable development, and forms of macrotheory need to be specified into which they too can be more readily integrated. Only then might we expect mature Type 1 theories of psychological and computational systems to emerge.

The gulfs also remain wide between different levels of analysis. We are not very good at establishing coherent theoretical connections of Type 2. Someone whose primary interest lies in the overall design of a human-computer work system is unlikely to be interested in the fine grain details of the limitations on human spatial working memory or in the limitations of graphics algorithms used to render a particular image. All of this can make it extremely difficult to deliver an interdisciplinary synthesis at one level that is based on principled reasoning grounded in other levels (Bellotti et al. 1996; Blandford and Duke 1997).

Within the overlapped hierarchy of Figure 2.2 macrotheory provides the connective tissue that binds together those microtheories of the entities that make up the system of interactors. It also provides the key level of abstraction that should enable us to carry over relevant knowledge, in a systematic way, from the science base of one level of system analysis to the next level up. Our current theory base may well be getting better at modeling and predicting the behavior of humans and computers in specific task contexts. However, it will remain of limited utility until and unless we develop true macrotheories that can meet the challenge of providing the connective tissue for both Type 1 and Type 2 theory.

As a boundless domain, HCI needs Type 1 microtheories of interactors and macrotheories of their interaction. It needs such theories at different levels of abstraction that extend from the fundamentals of the behavior of users and computers all the way up to the coordination of people and technologies in large-scale organizations (Malone and Crowston 1994). If HCI as a whole is to maintain some overall unity and coherence, it will also have to nurture Type 2 theories. They are needed to support effective communication between those whose focus of attention is at different levels. Their development is vital to enable knowledge in all the relevant disciplines to be brought to bear systematically on the solution of design problems involving the use of computers by individual users, by groups, and in organizations.

2.3   Macrotheory and Interaction

Our conjecture is that macrotheories at all levels can be represented within a general modeling framework. The objective is to capture the interdependencies between interactors. The key claim is that the behavior of any system of interactors will be a function (Fn) of four distinct classes of constraint.

System behavior = Fn (*Configuration* of interactors;
The interactors' individual *Capabilities*;
The *Requirements* that must be met to use those
capabilities; and
The regime of *Dynamic Control and
Coordination* of the interactors)

This four-component framework was first introduced as a basis for developing an explicitly formulated body of macrotheory concerning the behavior of the human mental architecture (Barnard 1987). Here we represent that framework in a form that can be generalized to all systems of interactors.

The *Configuration* defines the identity of the basic interactors that make up a system of concern and specifies their potential for engagement with each other. Their engagement might have physical or informational properties. For example, a system of three interactors might be configured so that they can all communicate with each other directly, or the channels might be more constrained with Interactor 1 being able to communicate with Interactor 3 only indirectly via Interactor 2.

The *Capability* of an interactor is defined as the transformations in information states, or of physical states, that it can accomplish. As basic interactors within a cognitive architecture, mental processes can be defined as having the generic capability to change the form or content of a mental representation. The generic capability of an interactor composed of a human and a technological device might be that of document preparation, with a repertoire of more specific capabilities for the human and the software.

The *Requirements* that must be met for an interactor to realize a specific capability are essentially the states that they need to function, be they physical or information states. An automobile needs enough fuel for its journey, while a mental process used in language understanding may require a clear incoming phonological representation in a language it has learned.

Systems behave over time, and the fourth component of the framework, the regime of *Dynamic Control and Coordination,* is intended to summarize properties of system activity on a temporal dimension. If we take a time slice of activity within a system, there will be some dynamic properties that characterize the overall state of the interaction. So, for example, a system may be in a state where the pattern of information or physical exchange among interactors is stable over time. Alternatively, a system may be engaging in two or more patterns of information exchange repeatedly over some period, perhaps with a dominant and a subsidiary activity oscillating rapidly or with more prolonged phases of each pattern being interleaved.

The ways in which activities are synchronized and controlled are also included in this fourth class of constraint on system operation. In some systems, wider control may be an emergent property of synchronous exchanges between interactors. In other systems, some interactors have the explicit capability to direct or control the activities of others. At a macrotheoretic level, we still need to capture any states of activity where the effective *locus of control* lies within a set of interactors and how the pattern of control changes over time.

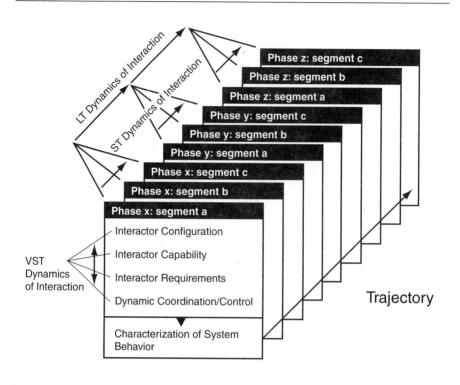

FIGURE 2.3 An outline characterization of a behavior trajectory subject to four "generic" classes of constraint (Modified for the current perspective from Barnard, Wilson, and MacLean 1987).

The behavior of any system of interactors evolves over time, and that behavior can usefully be thought of as a trajectory through a set of possible states. Figure 2.3 depicts a trajectory of continuous interaction divided into segments. These each approximate a state of activity among the interactors. One segment captures the properties of system behavior in the very short-term (VST). A phase of activity is a sequence of related short-term (ST) transitions among related segments. A transition from one phase to another would typically be associated with longer-term (LT) changes in the properties of systems. A number of distinct phases may contribute to a trajectory.

Thinking about a system's behavior as a trajectory governed by systematically structured sets of constraints is quite different from the more usual forms of step-by-step task analysis conducted in HCI and traditional human factors research. As with simulations of artificial life, the way in which system behavior evolves over time is an interaction of constraints. Each segment or phase of interaction has a point of departure and an outcome. The outcome of one phase is the point of departure for the next, and each will be defined in terms of the attributes of configurations, capabilities, requirements, and dynamic control and coordination that apply at that point.

2.4   Capturing Significant Variation in Interaction Trajectories

The problem of theory development for an area as boundless as HCI can be stated as two requirements. One requirement is to develop Type 1 theories of system behavior, composed of a unified body of macrotheory and microtheory. The other requirement is to develop Type 2 theories that map from one level of analysis to another. Type 2 theories also have two components, a mapping from the superordinate organization of one system to the basic units of another, and a mapping from basic units at one level into the constituents of another. Up to this point, the arguments have necessarily been general. In this section, we provide concrete illustrations of what we mean by a behavior trajectory for a system of interactors before going on to discuss how the wider schema can actually be specified and delivered in practice.

When interactions go wrong, traditional forms of analysis try to eliminate specific causes of error by redesigning the system, redesigning the task, and retraining users, or by changing the allocation of function between users and technologies. An analysis based around systems of interactors and the trajectories of their conjoint behavior can help us to think about what is going on in new ways. Couched in these terms, errors represent detours in an interaction trajectory (Blandford et al. 1995). Once a computer user makes an error, he or she typically must take a number of additional steps to recover.

A well known example of this is the unselected window scenario. A computer user who is interleaving activities conducted in different windows may start typing only to find that the products appear in a window she is not looking at, or that one window changes from being inactive to active. Trajectories for this situation are shown in Figure 2.4. It is assumed that the microtheory for the trajectory of a user's mental activity can be captured in a cognitive model. This model constrains the sequence of mental events that causes outcomes in segments of mental activity. These are represented by the linear sequence of cognitive events CE 1 . . . CE n linked to the cognitive model. Exactly the same description applies to the model of the devices—in this case computers and device events. These are represented in the lower part of the figure by the sequence DE 1 . . . DE n+. Alternative trajectories for the interaction are shown in the center as a series of phases (Px, Py, Pz), one of which is decomposed further into segments (PzSa, PzSb) according to the schema introduced in Figure 2.3. Each of these represents not a user state or a device state but a state of interaction, or engagement, between the interactors within the system.

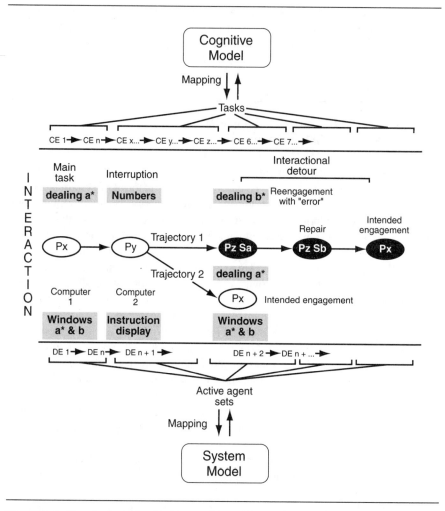

FIGURE 2.4 Two trajectories for interactions with a "selected" and "unselected window" (Modified from Barnard and Harrison 1992)

The trajectory shows a case where a user is conducting a main task on one computer—in this case share dealing—and is periodically interrupted by requirements to deal with a separate task on a different computer (in this case a numbers task). The share dealing task has two windows and requires frequent movement from one to another. The figure shows a phase of interaction (Px) on the main task followed by an interruption (Py). When returning to the dealing task, interaction may be reengaged with the active window on trajectory 2, or it may be reengaged with an inactive window (PzSa), requiring a segment of trajectory for repair (PzSb). The trajectory description is not a combination "user does this, system does that." It is a representation of a state of engagement between the two. In many other types of interaction—for example, human conversation—it is clear that people do not just stop one activity and start another. There tend to be transitions that are explicitly marked as distinct phases of interaction. We reasoned that the situation with unselected windows could be improved by redesigning the interaction trajectories to introduce two kinds of transitional phases. These are illustrated in Figure 2.5.

One transitional phase (TPs) is labeled "Possible Disengagement" and the other "Transitional Resumption" (Barnard and Harrison 1992). We designed a system that responded to potential disengagement by taking the initiative. After a period of zero input, the computer changed a property of the currently active window. The window border gradually started to "fizz," and pixels in the border went off and on. If at any point in the gentle increase in this attribute, the user did anything with the mouse or keyboard, the window border returned immediately to its passive state. If the user continued to do nothing, the border reached the maximum extent of its "fizzing" capability (steady state disengagement). At any point when the user reengages with this system (transitional resumption), the properties of the active window attract the user's attention. As soon as the user carries out an action, the border returns to its more passive indication that it is in an active state. Work with an experimental system demonstrated that it led to substantially fewer unselected window errors than occurred with systems that did not mark the transitions in this way (Lee 1992).

What is interesting about Lee's experimental results is that the new design changed the overall pattern of behavior across the whole interaction trajectory. Although there was a small reduction in the occurrence of unselected window errors

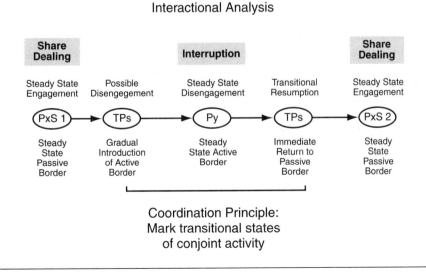

FIGURE 2.5   A trajectory designed to include overt marking of transitional phases

when the user returned to the main task following an interruption, the greatest reduction occurred during continuous segments of engagement on the main task. During such phases conditions virtually never arose where the user was inactive for long enough for the border to become fizzy; this was designed to happen only when the subsidiary task was interleaved. Users presumably developed a generic schema for interaction that led to an evaluation of border state on each move among windows, whatever the exact context. The general pattern is best understood by reference to more abstract macrotheoretic principles concerning interaction in the higher-order system. The dynamic control and coordination of the interaction depends on a number of interrelated attributes that can be represented in the four-component framework. These link a principle to mark transitional phases in a trajectory with system and user capabilities as well as their coordination.

- A property of system capability—dynamic and passive attributes on window border
- A property of user capability—the schema for monitoring window state
- A property of dynamic control and coordination—where the system acts as the locus of control in one phase and the user in others

A change to any of these properties may change the likelihood of detours occurring. Indeed, the same reduction in errors does not occur when active window fizzes all the time and is not sensitive to the transitional phases (Lee 1992).

This form of analysis does not represent or distinguish concrete properties of good or bad trajectories. It is necessary to understand the range of trajectories that may be possible and their relationship to the design context. Complex trajectories may be bad where the requirements include a concern for efficiency and speed. Just as there can be no absolute gold standard for the complexity of trajectory properties, so it is unlikely that there will be any simple recipes for deciding when it is appropriate to add functionality to a system. Successive periods of technology development have often led researchers to ask direct empirical questions about the consequences of adding functionality. Adding video channels to communication links may deliver benefits only in specific circumstances (Veinott et al. 1997). The addition to an interface of faces that show emotion, or agents with a humanlike persona, can have subtle influences on properties of an interaction, perhaps affecting user satisfaction more than traditional measures of the efficiency of task performance (Walker et al. 1994; van Mulken et al. 1998). As with the unselected window problem, empirical variation in these kinds of settings is unlikely to yield up all of its secrets to step-by-step forms of task analysis. We suggest that modeling the abstract properties of trajectories will be a productive basis for understanding the significant variation evident in the results from user testing in HCI.

2.5   Realizing Coherent Type 1 Theories of Interaction

The unselected window scenario introduced the general idea of an interaction trajectory, but it did so in informal terms. It was not a formally specified model or theory of interaction. To achieve a Type 1 theory of the behavior for a syndetic system of interactors involving both people and computers, we need well-formed microtheories of both the user interactor and the system interactor and a macrotheory of their interaction. It would be helpful to represent all these in a common modeling language. Within computer science, it has been acknowledged that the behavior of computational systems needs to be modeled at an abstract level. When designing a concurrent system, it is, for example, important to establish that it cannot enter deadlock. To model computational systems, the formal methods community has sought to evolve a body of mathematics and a family of methods that enables them to represent abstract properties of systems. When a computer scientist does produce a formal model of the behavior of a system before it is refined and built, it fulfills the role of macrotheory for computational systems. In fact, the four-component framework maps directly onto the schema for applying the mathematics of control theory. This schema includes a generalized construct of an array of data (requirements) on which functions (capability) operate to update the array according to selection restrictions (coordination and control). Configurations can then be an emergent property of what functions can operate on what data types within the array at what time. Likewise, the operation of an appropriately specified mental architecture can also be represented in the same four-component form, with a configuration of mental processes, each with particular capability, having requirements for information and governed by specific principles of coordination and control (Barnard et al. 1987; Barnard and May 1995, 1999).

We should be able to use the mathematics being developed within computer science to model abstract properties of the behavior of the mental architecture and to bind it to an equally abstract model of the behavior of a computer system. In principle, any model of mental architecture is amenable to this process, and indeed, formal descriptions have been developed based on a number of architectures including SOAR (Newell 1990) or EPIC (Meyer and Kieras 1997). In practice, however, the utility of such an approach is moderated by two key constraints.

- To allow reasoning about the behavior of the "mental interactor," the requirements on the deployment of resources and the regime for dynamic control and coordination need to be made explicit. This task is rather more difficult for operational styles of model—for example, the class of model originating from AI-style simulations.

- The type of mathematics used affects the ease with which the capabilities and configuration of an interactor can be described, the methods by which theories at one level can be composed to give a theory at the next level up, and the kinds of questions that can be asked of the resulting model.

The concepts of theory development and application described in this paper are not based on speculation. They are grounded in practical experience obtained in constructing models of software systems and from long-term work on developing a framework for understanding human information processing, the Interacting Cognitive Subsystems (ICS) architecture (see Barnard 1987; Barnard et al. 1987; Barnard and May 1995, 1999). ICS has several properties that make it well suited to serve as the architecture component of a Type 1 theory of interaction. It consists of a set of nine independent subsystems that process and exchange mental representations subject to a set of principles. As the subsystems share the same generic structure, the resources and capabilities of the architecture can be modeled conveniently using standard mathematical tools from computing—for example, function spaces in a state-based description or parallel composition in a process-oriented account. Similarly, the language of predicate logic, or the operators of a process algebra, provide convenient tools for expressing the requirements that govern when components of the ICS architecture can engage and thereby mediate information flow and interaction with interactors in the environment. Further details of ICS and its representation as a mathematical model can be found in Duke et al. 1998.

To develop a coherent Type 1 model of the system that results from combining user and device interactors, some macrotheory needs to be added to capture constraints on the exchange of information and action between the two components. Such a representation is called a syndetic model. In the Type 2 transition (Figure 2.2), macrotheory from psychology and macrotheory from computer science are both rerepresented to form microtheory at the level above in the overlapped hierarchy of abstraction. Axioms or properties of the syndetic model thus further constrain the space of possible trajectories of the combined system, from those that represent arbitrary interaction between user and device interactors to those that reflect the coordination and control inherent in the combined system. For example, when building a model of a user interacting with a window, we may need to indicate that the position of a "mouse" interactor is constrained by the output of the user's motor control. Representations perceived via the user's visual system are similarly constrained to reflect the actual layering of windows within the display context.

Our first attempt at this form of theoretical integration is fully reported in the journal *HCI* (Duke et al. 1998). Working within a large-scale European project on the integration of theory within design processes (AMODEUS 1995), we focused on a number of concrete design scenarios for advanced systems. One of these was a Multimodal Air Travel Information System (MATIS) capable of integrating typed, voice, and gestural inputs. The user could say, "Flights from [here] to [there]" and click on reference to the relevant cities by pointing at the appropriate referent with a mouse (Nigay and Coutaz 1995). The second scenario was a specific form of gestural language. This was designed to be used with the sort of data glove interfaces where the hand movements can be used to issue commands to the computer and where an image of the glove is concurrently rendered on the user's display (Bordegoni and Hemmje 1993). With well-defined configurations for information flow, ICS provides some generic rules for how the cognitive mechanism handles multimodal integration (see Barnard and May 1995). Since the properties of the two computing systems were known and specifiable, the constraints on key components of the two computing systems were modeled using modal action logic. The equivalent properties of the ICS architecture were also modeled using modal action logic but adding deontic extensions to capture aspects of the indeterminacy of mental processing.

As with simulation methods, the process forced us to be more precise in our specification of human information processing theory than we had been in our earlier attempts to model cognitive activity. The result of this modeling was two sets of axioms. One set of axioms represents assumptions about the constraints governing computer system behavior, and the other set represents assumptions about how the user's mental mechanism would function in the same setting. The axioms illustrate two aspects of the Type 2 transition. They discarded detail from more detailed psychological or system models. They were also selective in that they represented only those parts of the lower-level models that were necessary to deal with specific applied issues. These axioms were microtheories of user and system components. The added value of a Type 2 theory is the addition of a new superordinate level of organization. This was represented by a third set of axioms that specified assumptions about conditions that must apply in the interaction itself. The combination of micro- and macrotheory represented a coherent Type 1 syndetic model grounded in specifications of cognitive and computing mechanisms.

Once expressed in mathematical form, the model can do work. Unlike a simulation, this class of specification does not run and make a prediction. Newell (1990) noted, "Theories don't make predictions, *theorists* do." In this case, conjectures can be postulated and tested. The abstract model of a syndetic system is used to answer questions formulated by designers and to evaluate claims about the behavior of systems of interactors. In the case of the airline system, we might want to know how the user will cope with this design and develop a set of conjectures about it. The model is used *to derive a formal proof* of that conjecture. Duke et al. (1998) provide examples of this process.

In the case of the multimodal airline information system, the proof indicated that mental activity would not be well coordinated with the system behavior and that deictic reference using speech and mouse with this particular system would be problematic. Although the functionality was available, the analysis suggested that the likelihood that it would be used was low. As with the detours of the unselected window scenario, the analysis provided an insight into the properties of a behavior trajectory for a system composed of user and computer. It also provided an example of where additional functionality could be shown to be insensitive to wider properties of interaction.

As the underlying cognitive and system models provide the microtheory supporting the syndetic macrotheory, the reason why a particular difficulty occurs can be traced to somewhere in the Type 1 theory for that system of interactors. Alternative design solutions can then be driven by theoretical insight rather than by generate-and-test cycles of ad hoc change. Using mathematics, the consequences of theory can be explored in much the same way as they are in other physical sciences. What Duke et al. (1998) show is that axioms developed in one context can be reused to model generically related circumstances. Once in place, a body of psychological theory, such as ICS, can be combined with models of different computer systems. Although the specifications and proofs presented by Duke et al. cover several pages, they rely on inferences that could, in principle, be carried out using the current generation of theorem provers.

2.6   Extension to Higher Order Systems of Interactors

Part of our argument is that four generic classes of constraint need to be modeled at all levels of systems analysis. To support wider integration across the field of HCI, it needs to be shown that very similar forms of analysis might also hold for a characterization of behavior trajectories for groups and yet larger organizations.

An example of how principles of similar form and content may also apply to the behavior of groups originates in research on communication nets. Starting with Leavitt (1951), psychologists carried out research on tasks performed by collaborative groups working in configurations where they could only communicate along the kinds of constrained paths shown in Figure 2.6. The only interactors in this setting that have the capability to change representations or physical states are the people. They communicate by passing written messages through slots in reconfigurable walls. The paper, writing implements, and walls are, of course, subordinate interactors in this setting, and they too have definable capabilities (paper affords writing, slots afford message passing). In this setting the basic interactor is Human agent + paper + pencil, and it has the capability to construct task-relevant messages and pass them through one or more slots.

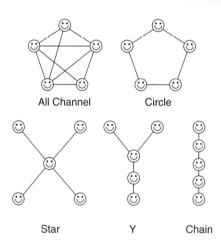

FIGURE 2.6   Centralized and decentralized communication networks

Leavitt found that of the circle, star, and Y configurations, the circle configuration gave rise to most errors, took the most time, and involved the greatest number of messages exchanged. While least efficient according to conventional criteria, people actually liked being in this configuration more than the other ones. An essential requirement for the group level interactor is to bring information together, and the centralized networks have, by their very structure, a locus of control through which all information is channeled.

The point to take from this example is not the specification of a particular trajectory or its properties. What is more important are the findings demonstrating that the relationships are not constant. With more complex tasks, Shaw (1954) found that decentralized networks gave rise to better performance. The requirements of bringing information together, and the issues that must be resolved in doing so, exceed the capabilities of the single individual acting as the locus of control. They have to interleave information and control transactions and keep track of everything that is going on. In contrast, activity in decentralized networks supports concurrent activity on different parts of the problem, ultimately resulting in fewer exchanges and less time.

Clearly, in order to model this example—including the alternative outcomes of participant satisfaction—the attributes and principles of a four-component analysis would need to be captured with more precision and completeness. Our reasoning about why different trajectories are followed from a particular point of departure to outcome is nonetheless framed by *interrelationships* that hold between properties of configurations, capabilities, requirements, and the dynamic control and coordination of the system itself. No amount of task description, knowledge analysis, or considerations of the limits on human cognition would provide such an analysis without referencing some other factors not normally considered to be within their scope.

In the case of yet higher order systems of interactors, the very terminology of the four component framework should have a strong sense of familiarity. Military strategists tend to think in terms of how the basic units of their forces are configured, what their capabilities are, what requirements must be met for them to use that capability, and, of course, how command and control is to be exercised. There might indeed be interesting similarities between the behavior of such systems and those of more traditional topics in HCI. For obvious reasons, our final concrete scenario is historic rather than drawn from our current research.

On August 2, 216 B.C. at Cannae, a Carthaginian army commanded by Hannibal slaughtered over 60,000 Roman soldiers, while losing only 6,000 of their own, a much smaller force. The three main phases representing the behavior trajectory for this highly concurrent system of interactors are shown in Figure 2.7.[1]

The progress of the battle can be succinctly summarized. In the opening phase of the battle, Hannibal advanced his infantry toward the Romans, and the Romans advanced to meet them. At the end of this phase Hannibal executed a preconceived tactical withdrawal. In the second phase the Roman army, believing that they were already in sight of victory, was drawn into Hannibal's trap as he maneuvered his infantry around the

---

[1]Details of the battle from Dupuy and Dupuy (1993).

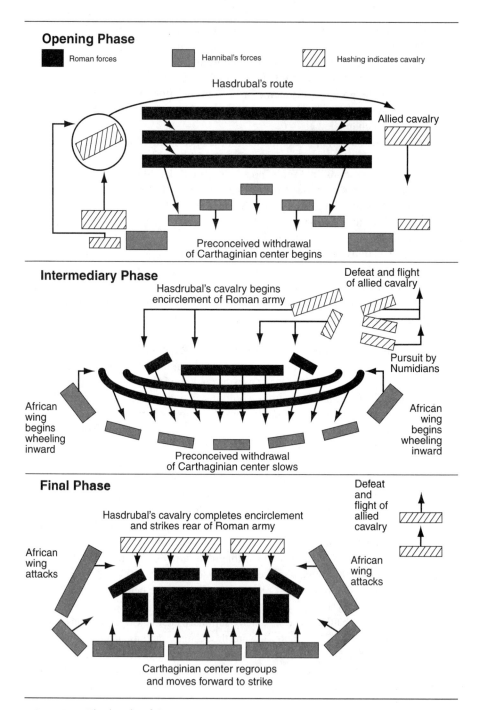

FIGURE 2.7 The battle of Cannae

flanks of the advancing Romans. At the end of the second phase of the battle, Hanni-bal's cavalry, who had engaged the Roman cavalry to the rear during the first phase, now disengaged and completed the encirclement of the Roman army. In the third phase of the battle, the Romans became a herd of panic stricken individuals, their force struc-ture losing all coherence and unity at the point when they realized that they had been enveloped. Hannibal's numerically inferior force quite literally cut them to pieces.

Given that their infantry outnumbered the Carthaginians by more than two to one, the Romans should have won. Hannibal had negated the Roman's numerical superiority in two ways. First, once encircled, a significant portion of the Roman units was trapped behind the line of engagement. They could not be configured to interact physically with the Carthaginians. Second, being only human, the Romans panicked, and the individual units lost the ability to fight as constituents within a higher-level force structure. The loss of coordination and control within basic units of organization translates upward into a degradation in the capability of interactors at the higher level of systems analysis.

The analysis of the unselected windows scenario and the modeling of interactions with the multimodal air travel information system involved both reasoning about dynamic control and coordination of simple user and system exchanges. When mapped upward to the concerns of designers of the higher-order system, the conclu-sions may need to be captured, not in the detailed model but in a Type 2 mapping. As in the case of Cannae, if coordination and control is degraded in a lower-order sys-tem, then it impacts the capability of the higher-order system. One sort of window improves capability of the combined system relative to the existing variant. It simpli-fies behavior trajectories by reducing the likelihood of detours. An envisaged design for multimodal integration of speech and mouse action in airline inquiries is unlikely to be used. Only when it could be argued that an envisaged design would facilitate behavior trajectories for the higher-order system might further investment in that aspect of software development be justified.

If those operating at different levels of systems analysis and on different topics were able to relate their own contributions to some common vehicle of expression, such as talking about generic constraints on interaction, then communication should be enhanced. Individual researchers might even gain substantial benefit from advances made by those working on quite different systems of interactors. Those working on modeling computational systems, cognitive systems, social systems, or military systems might improve their own tools and models on the basis of greater interdisciplinary coordination and reciprocated insight.

2.7   Conclusion

We have argued that the future course of theory in HCI might not be best served by the unconstrained development of more and more local theories and models specifically tailored only to the meet needs of different levels of analysis or different software applications. Because of the different systems of scientific semantics adopted, such an approach makes it hard to realize connections—either within or between levels of systems analysis.

We have offered some arguments for developing macrotheories. These provide connective tissue to bind together different concerns within a level of explanation. We also argued that macrotheories were needed to support a different kind of theory. The second form of theory provides the connective tissue between the systems of scientific semantics adopted at adjacent levels of analysis. A specific framework was proposed for the consistent organization of macrotheory across levels of analysis. This assumed that the behavior of any system was determined by four classes of constraint.

Hannibal's plan for the battle of Cannae provided military theorists with an oft-cited model of tactical perfection. Some two thousand years later, General Schwarzkopf remarked that he reused Hannibal's model for the battle of Cannae when he directed operation Desert Storm. An abstract model that is reusable over a couple of millennia, and from the technologies of swords and shields to those of tanks and missiles, is a significant achievement. As HCI moves into the next millennium, the development of new forms of theory, or a viable mathematics for modeling systems at different levels of analysis, still poses a whole range of exciting and important challenges. Before reliable and enduring models are achieved, research may well go up numerous blind alleys. Nonetheless, we believe the case for the development of models and theories is just as strong, if not stronger, as it was when Newell (1990) and Card et al. (1983) laid out their earlier visions for how theories might be integrated and applied to the practice of HCI.

Acknowledgment

This paper is based on the plenary address given at HCI '98, Sheffield by the first author. Some of the ideas were also developed in collaborations with others on the ESPRIT AMODEUS-2 project and with the UK Defence Evaluation and Research Agency. Both are gratefully acknowledged.

References

Amodeus (1995). *Assaying means of design expression for users and systems. AMODEUS-2 Project Final Report,* D13, Barnard, P.J., Bernsen, N.O., Coutaz, J., Darzentas, J., Faconti, G., Hammond, N.H., Harrison, M.D., Jørgensen, A.H, Löwgren, J., May, J., Young, R.M. CEC Brussels. http://www.mrc-cbu.cam.ac.uk/amodeus/abstracts/d/d13.html

Anderson, J.R. (1993). *Rules of the mind.* Hillsdale, NJ: Erlbaum.

Barnard, P.J. (1987). Cognitive resources and the learning of dialogues. In J.M. Carroll (Ed.), *Interfacing Thought,* 112–128. Cambridge, MA: MIT Press.

Barnard, P.J., and Harrison, M.D. (1992). Towards a framework for modeling human computer interactions. In J. Gornostaev (Ed.), *Proceedings of the East-West International Conference on Human Computer Interaction, EWCHI'92,* 189–196. Moscow: ICSTI.

Barnard, P., and May, J. (1995). Interactions with advanced graphical interfaces and the deployment of latent human knowledge. In F. Paternó (Ed.), *Eurographics Workshop on Design, Specification and Verification of Interactive Systems,* 15–49. Berlin: Springer-Verlag.

Barnard, P., and May, J. (1999). Representing cognitive activity in complex tasks. *Human-Computer Interaction,* 14, 93–158.

Barnard, P., May, J., Duke, D., and Duce, D. (2000). Systems, interactions and Macrotheory. *ACM Transactions on Computer-Human Interaction,* 7, 222–262.

Barnard, P.J., Wilson, M., and MacLean, A. (1987). Approximate modeling of cognitive activity with an expert system: A strategy for the development of an interactive design tool. *Proceedings of CHI+GI'87,* 2–26. New York: ACM.

Bellotti, V., Blandford, A., Duke, D., Maclean, A., May, J., and Nigay, L. (1996). Interpersonal access control in computer-mediated communications: A systematic analysis of the design space. *Human Computer Interaction,* 6, 357–432.

Blandford, A., and Duke, D. (1997). Integrating user and computer system concerns in the design of interactive systems. *International Journal of Human-Computer Studies,* 46, 653–679.

Blandford, A., Harrison, M., and Barnard, P. (1995). Using interaction framework to guide the design of interactive systems. *International Journal of Human-Computer Studies,* 43, 101–130.

Bordegoni, M., and Hemmje, M. (1993). A dynamic gesture language and graphical feedback for interaction in a 3d user interface. *Computer Graphics Forum,* 12, 3, 1–11.

Card, S.K., Moran T.P., and Newell, A. (1983). *The psychology of human computer interaction.* Hillsdale, NJ: Lawrence Erlbaum.

Chapanis, A. (1996). *Human factors in systems engineering.* New York: John Wiley.

Duke, D.J., Barnard, P.J., Duce, D.A. and May, J. (1998). Syndetic modelling. *Human Computer Interaction,* 13, 337–393.

Duke, D., and Harrison, M. (1993). Abstract interaction objects. *Computer Graphics Forum,* 12, 3, C-25–C-36.

DuPuy, R.E. and DuPuy, T.N. (1993). *The Collins encyclopedia of military history: From 3500 B.C. to the present.* Glasgow: HarperColins.

Leavitt, H. J. (1951). Some effects of certain communication patterns on group performance. *Journal of Abnormal and Social Psychology,* 46, 38–50.

Lee, W-O. (1992). The effects of skill development and feedback on action slips. To appear in A. Monk, D. Diaper, and M.D. Harrison (Eds.), *People and Computers VIII.* Cambridge: Cambridge University Press.

Malone, T.W., and Crowston, K. (1994). The interdisciplinary study of coordination. ACM Computing Surveys, 26, 87–119.

Marr, D. (1982). Vision, New York: W.H Freeman and Company

Meyer, D., and Kieras, D. (1997). A computational theory of executive cognitive processes and multiple-task performance: Part 1. *Psychological Review,* 104, 3–65.

Newell, A. (1990). *Unified theories of cognition.* Cambridge, MA: Harvard University Press.

Newell, S., and Card. S.K. (1985). The prospects for science in human computer interaction. *Human Computer Interaction,* 1, 209–242.

Nigay, L., and Coutaz, J. (1995). A generic platform for addressing the multimodal challenge. *Proceedings of the CHI'95 Conference on Human Factors in Computing Systems,* 98–105. Reading, MA: Addison Wesley.

Shaw, M.E. (1954). Some effects of problem complexity upon problem solving efficiency in different communication nets. *Journal of Experimental Psychology,* 48, 211–217.

van Mulken, S., André, E., and Müller, J. (1998). The persona effect: How substantial is it? In H. Johnson, L. Nigay, and C. Roast (Eds.), *People and Computers XIII,* 53–66. Berlin: SpringerVerlag.

Veinott, E.S., Olson, J.S., Olson, G.M., and Fu, X. (1997). Video matters! When communication ability is stressed, video helps. *Proceedings of ACM CHI'97 Conference on Human Factors in Computing Systems,* 2, 315–316.

Walker, J.H., Sproull, L., and Subramani, R. (1994). Using a human face in an interface in proceedings of CHI'94, 85–91. New York: ACM.

Design in the MoRAS

George W. Furnas

3.1 Introduction: ++HCI and the MoRAS

The field of Human Computer Interaction is on a trajectory of triply expanding scope. Each component of the name is taking on increased span. In a trend well anticipated by Grudin (1990), the scope of concern is advancing beyond the individual human user to the work group, the organization, markets, and society. Similarly, in more personal spheres, concern has moved to design for better impact on nuclear and extended family, neighborhoods, and communities. Meanwhile, the scope of the computer has expanded as well. No longer just boxes on our desktops, they have become communication intense, information rich, and increasingly ubiquitous and embedded, expanding into a broader, more seamless web of information technology and systems. Finally, what began as a human interaction with a computer now includes individuals interacting with others via computational and communication media, families confronting unvetted content on the World Wide Web, and organizations participating in electronic markets. We are not interacting *with* the technology so much as interacting with information, tasks, and other people *via* the technology, carrying on activities made possible by those technologies. In a sense, then, the successor to HCI as we have known it—let us call it ++HCI—is made up of ++H, ++C, and ++I.[1]

---

[1]The "++" operator in the Bell Labs family of languages (C, C++, AWK, etc.) indicates the successor function. In prefix form it means that the value of the variable should be incremented *before* being interpreted in the current context. Thus, by analogy, "++HCI" is meant to refer to "the successor of HCI."

©2000 Lawrence Erlbaum Associates, Inc. Adapted with permission from "Future Design Mindful of the MoRAS," *Human-Computer Interaction*, Vol. 15, No. 2/3, September 2000.

We need to be more explicitly mindful of the larger scope we care about—a broader sense of human spheres of interest, a broader conception of computation and information technology, and a broader view of interactivities. Attempts to be mindful of this larger scope are already manifest in the interdisciplinary habit of leading HCI research. Once the barely heeded task of programmers, it has become the work of computer scientists, psychologists, sociologists, information scientists, anthropologists, information economists, and organizational theorists, among others.

This chapter presents a framework for the interdisciplinary effort to design information technology in larger spheres of human concern. The framework views the world relevant to ++HCI design as being composed of a whole set of systems, ranging from the human mind to work groups, communities, markets, and society. The dominant considerations that shape the structure and dynamics of this set of systems arise by noting that they individually respond to their environments and adapt to remain viable over time. Further, they are coupled with one another in a kind of multiscale mosaic, influencing each other in a variety of ways. Information is at the essence of coupling, and as such, information technology is altering the coupling structure of this system of systems, with each responding and adapting in turn. This conception is similar in spirit to that of Rasmussen et al. (1994), whose HCI design methodology considers multiple dynamic systems and the role of effective couplings between them. It is also similar to the approach of Harris and Henderson (1999), who emphasize the adaptive character of organizations in adopting computer technology and how intentional design can be more supportive of these adaptive organizational processes. Here, though, an even larger set of coupled, adaptive systems is taken as relevant in design, a scope closer to that of Miller's (1978) grand monograph on *Living Systems*. Construing the world relevant to ++HCI as a coupled Mosaic of Responsive Adaptive Systems (MoRAS) should help us articulate and understand the proper context for the design of information technology in ways that will bring greater value to these human systems. In short, to do better ++HCI, we must be more mindful of the MoRAS.

3.2   The MoRAS

A sketch of the various systems of the MoRAS and how they are connected provides a framework for delineating current and future roles for information technology. These in turn help identify opportunities for ++HCI efforts and the influences those efforts must consider.[2]

A dominant aspect of the MoRAS is its successive layers of social aggregation—for example, a person within a work organization or a neighborhood within a community

---

[2]Furnas (2000) discusses some of the dynamics and theoretical issues related to how the pieces work together. In the space here we emphasize the structure.

(Figure 3.1). This nested system of systems is much like that presented in detail in Miller (1978). All these different layers of the MoRAS contain roles, or potential roles, for IT. At the level of markets, efficiency can be added with cyberauctions that increase information flow and reduce transaction costs. At the level of neighborhoods, local community networks can potentially provide new cohesion and build trust. Even at the low level of individual internal biological systems, information technology can provide smart pacemakers that can help hearts beat regularly according to demand. All these places for IT provide opportunities for more human centered ++HCI design efforts. Thus, while the various systems have typically been studied by different academic disciplines, from economists to sociologists to psychologists and biologists, bringing them back together yields the increasingly interdisciplinary nature of ++HCI efforts.

The dynamics and processes at the different levels of the MoRAS often exhibit interesting similarities. To be viable, each of the systems in Figure 3.1 must respond

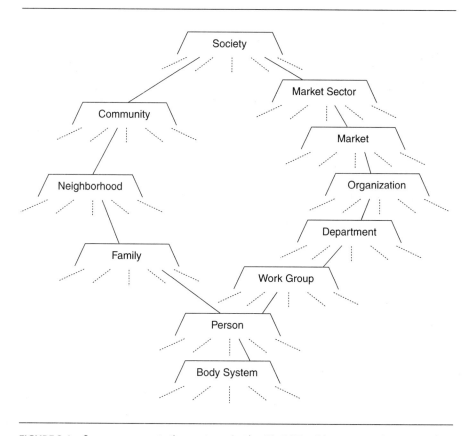

FIGURE 3.1   Some representative systems in the MoRAS, with system-subsystem relationships shown. Note that society can be subdivided independently into the market and community hierarchies, with people participating in both.

and adapt to external events in ways that are in some sense approximately appropriate to their environments. For example, each must be able to "sense" its external environment, "remember" the past and bring it to bear usefully on the present, make reasonable "decisions," and implement those decisions in a coordinated fashion in its environment. Analyzed in this way, libraries in society are analogous to memory systems in individual humans. Also, the coordination of a corporation is in many ways similar to coordination of the human body. As will be shown later, these similarities can not only inspire cross-disciplinary dialog leading to deeper understanding but they can provide ideas for concrete design by using solutions found in analogous systems.

The nesting relationships in the MoRAS do not form a strict hierarchy, or tree, as Figure 3.1 illustrates. There are multiple paths of aggregation—for example, those focusing on the personal and work sides of our lives. Each path will have different IT opportunities and different impacts on other systems. It is important to note the multiple paths so that major opportunities and influences are not overlooked. It is also important to recognize the multiple constraints and roles that components must sometimes balance and to consider the ways IT might help balance those constraints. For example, most of us are familiar with the difficulties arising from the fact that a Person is both in a Family and a Work Group, each making conflicting demands. Resolving those conflicts requires information, evaluation, decision making, planning, and coordination—all properly the domain of "generalized" information technology.

Many of the systems in Figure 3.1 include specialized subsystems playing differing roles (Figure 3.2). For example, there are departments in firms that do marketing and others that do finance, and together with other groups they serve the various needs of the comprising organization. Likewise, at a higher level, there are market sectors that manufacture goods and others that provide telecommunications services, serving the aggregate needs of society. At a lower level, there are biological subcomponents of the individual human that take care of movement (muscles) or respiration (lungs) in service of the needs of the individual.

This specialization is another aspect of the structure of the MoRAS useful for noting where information technology is most critical and thus where our ++HCI understanding and intentional design efforts are most important. To do so it is useful to distinguish between those subtypes that have a primary focus on (generalized) IT and those that focus on other fundamental concerns. The former would include Libraries, the Media, and Government in society; the R&D, Executive, and IT support groups in firms; the Central Nervous System of the human body (IT "wetware"). These subsystems focus on "cognitive" sorts of activities like information aggregation, evaluation, integration, storage, retrieval, as well as exploration, decision making, and decision implementation. Such subsystems are clearly foci of IT technology application and hence of potential ++HCI concern.

The other sorts of subsystems are associated with the many other, noncognitive functions vital to the viability of the larger system. These would include muscles and digestive systems in the human body; purchasing, maintenance, and production units within firms; the roads and social welfare departments within a society. Here the

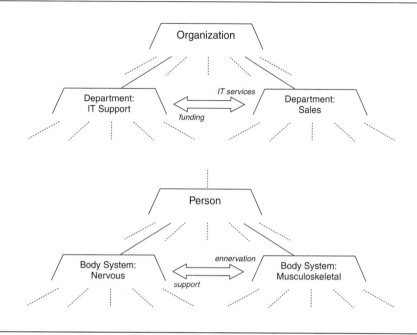

FIGURE 3.2   Sample specialization within subsystems and related nonhierarchical relationships in the MoRAS. It is not uncommon for some subsystems to specialize in IT functions.

generic noncognitive roles include physical resource accumulation, energy production, materials processing, and distribution.

While the IT and the related potential ++HCI concerns might be immediately obvious in the "cognitive" subsystems, these other systems also have significant information infrastructure, particularly for communication, coordination, and control. Indeed, the IT infrastructure in these non-IT components is what allows them, and hence the larger system, to derive benefit from the more centralized IT/cognitive subsystems. A brain is useless without a body with sensory and motor nerves; an executive group is blind and powerless without links that couple it to the rest of the firm. Thus ++HCI work is needed in centralized IT subsystems, in support of IT infrastructure in other subsystems, and, as appropriate, coupling these usefully to one another and/or to the center.

The links coupling generalized IT to other subsystems, shown in Figure 3.2, are among many other important horizontal relationships in the MoRAS—for example, trust between individuals in a work group, reciprocity between members of a community, competition between firms in a market, and supply-chain relationships between market subsectors. These horizontal links also often have information components and can be supported by IT and ++HCI design efforts.

So far we have focused on human systems, with technology mentioned in piece-meal, auxiliary roles. If the technology is serving well, however, it is perhaps more proper to think of it in a more integrated way. Thus, many of the human systems we have discussed so far have associated with them a corresponding layer of technology, together forming a larger sociotechnical system that is essentially the original system extended by artifacts and technology. One might, for example, redraw each of the systems of Figure 3.1 with a surrounding technology envelope, drawn suggestively to embrace it and perhaps the levels below. Thus, a person extended by a well-designed computer system forms a human/computer system, the standard focus of HCI. Work groups are extended by technology aggregates to create group + technology systems (for example, the airline cockpit of Hutchins 1995). Society is augmented by its transportation and telecommunications technology systems. Like the human subsystems of Figure 3.2, some artifacts are primarily aiding cognitive activities and others are for more general purposes. For examples at the individual level, a book is cognitive while a can opener is not. At the societal level, telecommunications networks are "cognitive" while power grids are not. The efforts of ++HCI presumably play two roles: enhancing the value of the cognitive artifacts directly and adding cognitive elements to noncognitive ones. (In these efforts, it should be remembered that cognitive artifacts of concern for ++HCI can also be intangible, like an individual's idea, a hypertext protocol, or a society's language.)

Laying out all the systems, their connections, their technological extensions, and the respective loci of IT concentrations creates a cognitive artifact to better enable mindful ++HCI consideration of the role of information technology throughout the sphere of human concerns. Diagrams like those in Figures 3.1 and 3.2 can be used to look for design opportunities. For a simple example, looking at Figure 3.1, viewers familiar with the past two decades of traditional HCI will note the uneven attention the individual MoRAS components have received. There has been considerable effort at the individual level (particularly on the work side) and at the level of the work group (in the CSCW subcommunity). There is, however, little at the family level or community level. These are opportunities for both future research and future enterprise. Focus on supporting human activity at the geographic community level is a new research area (see Carroll and Rosson 1998; Cohill and Kavanaugh 1999; Schuler 1996, 1998). Similarly there is an opportunity to find new ways to help families coordinate, maintain awareness, and communicate. There may also be opportunities for more work at the market level (for example, supporting reputation and trust in the new e-commerce and e-auction efforts; see Friedman and Resnick 1999; Tadelis 1999; Kollock 1999) and market sector levels.

Such diagrams can also suggest design opportunities if one asks questions about *pairs* of components. For example, "Are there benefits to be gained by new real-time links between systems x and y?" Links between consumers and manufacturers can allow mass customization and inventory control. Links from individual factory line workers to executive groups can improve quality control. Links between communities and their individual members might support the monitoring of health and safety. Another question, "Are there benefits possible by accumulating history about system w

for use by z?" could inspire new areas of data collection. Better accumulation of health history of individual humans could be more effectively used by the Centers for Disease Control. The gathering of the minority lending histories of banks could support choices of prospective minority borrowers. The question, "What are the needs of p with respect to q?" could help us ask what an elder person needs from a community and what a community needs from its elders. Questions of the form, "Can certain things computed about r be useful to s?" might lead to focus on how market indices are useful to individual investors, or how correlations in individual consumption are useful to marketers. Note that these pairwise questions can be asked about not just the vertical relationships, shown in Figure 3.1, but also horizontal links (to structural "siblings," as in Figure 3.2, or variously remote "cousins") and diagonal links (to structural "aunts" or "nieces").

3.3   Illustrating the Consequences

This section illustrates several ways in which the MoRAS framework can provide value to ++HCI. Ignoring the MoRAS can result in a kind of blindness leading to naïve predictions of the future, sometimes with considerable cost. The examples here consider how digital displays were supposed to make paper quickly obsolete and video links were going to supplant travel. Explicitly considering the MoRAS not only gives deeper insight; it yields at least two direct design benefits. Taking the case of information access, we show how the mosaic of systems forms both a broader canvas of design opportunities and a source of concrete design inspiration as solutions worked out in one place can be reused in another. Finally, looking at dynamics in the larger picture of the MoRAS can even allow us to understand and address new sorts of problems. Here we bring MoRAS insight into a growing schism between needs and wants—an underexamined but arguably large and serious problem that is both in the technical domain and the motivated concern of the ++HCI community.

3.3.1   Blindness from Ignoring the MoRAS

The rise of the information age has brought with it various predictions of the transformation of work life by computer technology, predictions that have been remarkably slow in materializing. One particularly long-standing forecast was of the imminent demise of paper and the rise of the "paperless office." Certainly by the 1960s, it was commonly predicted that electronic representations of information would soon make paper obsolete (Bush 1945; Licklider 1965; see Landauer 1995, p. 354). This misprediction had significant economic consequences. At least one major paper company (Meade) made huge investment decisions (buying the electronic information service, Lexis/Nexis) to hedge its bets, a decision later reversed as the paper industry thrived and the data service proved more complex than anticipated.

The error resulted from a broadly held but simplistic understanding of the role of paper in the mosaic of human systems. By the simplistic model, the primary purpose of paper was to record and present information. Since computers could also record and present information and were in many ways more versatile, "clearly" paper was imminently obsolete.

There was, however, much more going on with paper than was first evident—a fact that is actually a strong testimonial to the multiple systems operating in the MoRAS. The adaptation processes of each of the systems amount to a kind of generalized design process. Like the processes of human intentional design we usually consider, these other processes help create regularities and structure in the world in service of the viability of the systems involved. Any system that has remained viable for an extended period of time has had to adapt to the changing challenges and opportunities of its environment, in effect "designing" itself in real time as it goes along.

Effective design processes, from generalized ones like biological evolution to human intentional design, are often opportunistic, exploiting the affordances of the situation. For example, paper has many features, including physical security, indelibility, portability, uniqueness, high resolution, stability, longevity, physical examinability, and ease of annotation. All these have been explored then exploited by adaptation (generalized design) in various parts of the MoRAS. Individuals quickly learn to capitalize on the portability of paper to get the comfort of curling up in bed with a paperback book. Taking additional advantage of the ease of annotation, individuals get the convenience of jotting a phone number on a small scrap of paper that can be tucked into a pocket, or the ease of marking revisions on paper drafts. Organizations took advantage of the uniqueness of an individual piece of paper, settling into routines that used individual pieces of paper as process tokens, where group tasks were coordinated by who had what copy of which form when. They also relied on informal annotations on shared documentation to accumulate local workgroup knowledge. Societal institutional processes similarly adapted to capitalize on the special opportunities of paper. Thus, postal systems developed the clever little paper technology of the postage stamp. The courts came to rely on ink signatures on paper documents. In general, the viability of many systems came to depend to greater and lesser degrees on these opportunistic designs.

Furthermore, in a second tier of effects, aspects of practice in these other systems coevolved to support the primary adaptations: government printing offices to produce stamps, a design culture for legal forms including the knowledge to put blank signature lines at the bottom of pages, and so on. The result was amplified efficiency of the original generalized designs on the one hand and embedded investment and inertia on the other.

Amidst all this, a few engineers' intentional design of new electronic ways of presenting characters visually was taking care of only one aspect of the paper medium. It both ignored paper's primary role in many of the systems and showed little regard for the second tier effects. The expectation that this simple electronic innovation would quickly supplant paper was fundamentally a naïveté about the MoRAS. If paper becomes obsolete it will only be when most of its roles throughout the various systems have been otherwise accounted for. It is likely this will happen only as the respective systems work out alternative "designs." At best, in ++HCI, we can hope to identify these systems and their uses of paper and augment their own respective adaptive processes with our more mindful intentional design efforts.

The misprediction about the imminent demise of paper was not unique. A similar misprediction was made about the "imminent demise" of travel. The claim was that telecommunication technology, in particular video substitution for face-to-face meetings, would render airline travel unnecessary. Much more goes on in the process of face-to-face meetings than the talking heads of televideo could capture (Olson and Olson 2000). Face-to-face meetings also allow the ability to see other listeners' reactions to the speaker, to spawn off easy side conversations and follow up fluidly. It allows people to have usefully ambiguous casual encounters and to see the environment within which others work and how that environment shapes their attitudes and actions. It gives participants the chance to see others in their more spontaneous, natural modes. And, quite nontrivially, it gives them power to have direct physical influence—to help or to harm—and the consequent ability to send important social signals by those choices. (It means much more for trust if you refrain from helping or harming when you could actually do so.) Individual behaviors, business routines, social behaviors, and cultural practices all have developed around these less obvious aspects of physical presence. Simply providing video links showing talking heads does not take care of these needs of other systems nor respect the designs those systems have worked out.

With regard to these mispredictions, the claim is not just that things are not as simple as they first appear. The MoRAS framework explains the nature of that lack of simplicity and the reason why it is not readily apparent. First, things are complicated because there are many identifiable systems involved, each with adaptive mechanisms "designing" to meet its respective needs. Second, visibility to human designers' conscious thought has never been a prerequisite for the development of all this other structure in the MoRAS. Our intentional processes represent only one of the many "designing" components involved. The MoRAS framework can remind us of the larger array of often invisible, generalized design processes that interact with our intentional ++HCI design efforts.

3.3.2   Design Opportunities from Considering the MoRAS

Taking the multiple systems of the MoRAS into consideration can enrich ++HCI design efforts in several important ways. The previous section illustrated how being mindful of the MoRAS allows us to be less naïve about the context of our design efforts, to see the many intertwined threads that constrain how interventions will play out. Thinking of the MoRAS can also guide design in at least two proactive ways. First, it helps point to the multiple places where concerted ++HCI efforts may make a larger difference. For example, in improving human information access, the MoRAS framework motivates a much broader sphere of design opportunities than the "one-shot query" focus that dominated Information Retrieval research for several decades. Many of the systems illustrated in Figure 3.1, from the workings of human memory to the societal institutions of libraries, are clearly involved in human information gathering activity. ++HCI efforts can have much more impact if they look at this larger suite of design opportunities. Second, examining various analogies between systems of the MoRAS can even suggest ideas for design solutions. For example, borrowing information access ideas worked out by evolutionary design processes in the memory systems of the human brain, we can get clever ideas for information technology in service of information access in other parts of the MoRAS.

3.3.2.1   Search Is More Than the One-Shot Query

From the 1960s through the mid-1990s, the dominant focus of Information Retrieval (IR) research was on improving search and comparison algorithms for query engines. In real life, however, much search and retrieval, even of the classical IR sort, actually involves large portions of the MoRAS. Trying to help human information gathering only by improving the query engine is tremendously myopic. Submitting a query is only a small part of the human information-gathering activity. The systems of Figures 3.1 and 3.2 can serve as a kind of checklist for thinking about the proper scope of the problem—helping us identify the many levels that are involved and for which it is often possible to design better IT supports.

Consider the various levels in turn, starting at the bottom of Figure 3.1. The human brain is involved before and after the computer search engine's query execution. Preceding the query there is both a nontrivial search through semantic and lexical memory for appropriate keywords and a problem space search through the set of possible Boolean query structures combining those words. After the query execution there is visual scanning of the return set. At the individual human level there are the ongoing search activities of which the query is a part (for example, Bates 1990; Belkin et al. 1982). At a still higher level of social aggregation, there is the organizational information gap and corresponding organizational memory processes that often define and scope the individual's search. At the market level there are abstracting and indexing services, and software companies designing search tools and information gathering environments. At the societal level there are whole cultural institutions, like libraries and archives, to facilitate the saving and subsequent finding and gathering of information.

The implication is that appropriate design of information technology in support of information gathering should be mindful of all these many components of the MoRAS. Those of us engaged in ++HCI efforts must be reminded that all these pieces are relevant parts of the picture, and we must have some clue about how the individual pieces work and how they work together. Information access is valuable throughout the MoRAS basically because it increases the viability of any system (a person, a work group, a firm, a society) by making information created in one context available to another remote in time or space. Information technology can help couple these contexts in new and better ways, with a general ++HCI strategy of strengthening couplings that make a web of processes work better.

At the level of an individual's brain, for example, the semantic and lexical memory search for query terms can be supported by aids that suggest related terms, or allow users to browse through thesaurus structures (Wallace et al. 1998), or by latent semantic indexing (Deerwester et al. 1988) or adaptive indexing (Furnas 1985). The search through the design space of Booleans appropriate for the query can be aided by structuring interaction—for example, with form filling for facetted-retrieval (Hearst 1995). The visual search through return sets can be improved by using various visual "pop-out" features (Treisman and Gormican 1988) to speed finding relevant parts of the return set information (such as highlighting keywords in the original texts, an early example of which is found in the Superbook system, Egan et al. 1989). These examples support human cognition by appropriately tightening the coupling between the user and the computer artifact to create a more coherent larger cognitive entity (cf. Hutchins 1995)—a general goal of traditional HCI.

At the next larger granularity, where the extended and adapting ongoing search activities dominate, there are also numerous design opportunities. Bates (1990), Pirolli and Card (1995), and Russell et al. (1993), for example, have all suggested specific information technology supports for the human adaptive processes of learning and abstraction, present in ongoing activities of berrypicking, foraging, and sensemaking.

At the level of the work group, there is a growing literature on cooperative information gathering (Oates et al. 1997; Karamuftuoglu 1998; Prasad et al. 1998). At the organizational level there has been more than a decade of increasing interest in organizational memory and its technological support (Walsh and Ungson 1991; Stein and Zwass 1995; Ackerman and Halverson 2000). At several social levels, there are collaborative filtering technologies (Resnick and Varian 1997) to better link people who know things to those who do not.

At the market level there are various businesses competing to provide search services for accessing particular content or general search engine software for use by others. At the societal level there are, for example, various digital library initiatives and international metadata standards and related protocols (such as Z39.50, XML, Dublin Core). All of these design efforts could use stronger ++HCI focus, paying attention to the human needs, not just the technological ones.

Considering improving human access to information from the MoRAS perspective thus yields a rich spectrum of explicit design opportunities. Many ++HCI concerns projected into the kind of structure diagrammed in Figures 3.1 and 3.2 should generate a similarly rich design space.

3.3.2.2 *Exploiting Analogies for Design*

A view of the MoRAS not only provides a map of systems that may be considered when addressing problems. Analogies within the MoRAS can also suggest solutions.

For example, consider the analogy between an old occurrence in biological evolution and a recent one in the marketplace of search engines. In nature, there was a presumed coevolution of the visual pop-out effect of red on a green background in many animal vision systems and the development of red-ripening berries by fruiting plants when their seeds were ready for dispersal (similar to the coevolution of bee vision and flower ornamentation). The value to the animal can be analyzed in terms of being able to front-load the payoff in extracting food value from the plant. (Being able to distinguish sweet from un-sweet berries by sight, the animals can get the valuable berries from the plant more quickly and shift to another plant without trying all the green unripe ones.) The animals, following foraging theory, can extract nourishment faster from these enhanced plants, prefer them, and hence visit and eat from those plants differentially. This increases the effectiveness of that plant's seed dispersal mechanism and hence the viability of that germ line. Thus, plants had to compete with one another to provide this "foraging enhancement service." Similar plants that did not adopt a comparable strategy were evolutionarily threatened.

In a similar effort, around the period 1997–1999, search engines on the Web were competing to front-load value in the information "fruits" they had to offer to those who came foraging. In part, this involved making new design efforts to present the results ordered by presumed relevance to the query. It also involved "painting the ripe berries red," so to speak, showing highlighted search terms in context, thereby better aiding human visual search for the potentially most valuable items. Information foraging theory (Pirolli and Card 1995, 1999) says that users can extract more information value at a higher rate from such sites and that users thus should prefer them in their information diet selection. Those sites get visited more often, a matter crucial to those sites' viability, and other sites that do not adopt comparable strategies can disappear from the marketplace. This analogy gives insight into changes in the search engines and how the market forces some of these design optimizations. It also can suggest how ++HCI designers might further this effort to front-load value in Web pages.

In the general area of information access there is also an interdisciplinary analogy between libraries and human memory, helpful both in understanding each structure better and for its useful design implications. The analogy presumably exists because the viability of sophisticated systems is significantly enhanced when they have mechanisms for bringing past experience to bear on the future in an organized way. Since the brain and current Western society have benefited from long adaptive processes, the analogy can be taken quite far.

According to the analogy, the biological evolution of our memories corresponds to the cultural evolution of the institution of libraries. The filling of an individual library corresponds to the filling of an individual's brain. There are collection development strategies in libraries for deciding what to acquire and what to get rid of. These correspond to human attentional and forgetting mechanisms. While there are culturally evolved general strategies for collection development, these are tailored locally by organizational learning processes to the circumstances of an individual library. So it is also with a human. The corporate library at the DuPont chemical company will tailor its acquisitions and holdings just as the chemists working there will tune what they attend to, encode, ignore, or forget. Information is important in making decisions, and quality, balanced information is important in making good decisions. This is true at the individual human level and at the societal level where, in the United States, decisions are made by democratic process. Thus, following Jefferson and Dewey, in the service of good democratic societal decision making, the collection development and access policies of public libraries place strong emphasis on freedom of information and avoiding certain biases—for example, making both sides of important political issues available for evaluation.

The extensive analogy is more than food for idle curiosity. It can be exploited for design if one probes a bit deeper. For example, a decade ago the eminent cognitive psychologist John Anderson did some seminal work on a "rational" analysis of human memory (Anderson and Milson 1989; Anderson 1990). A rational analysis tries to explain not *how* something works (in this case memory in terms of its basic mechanisms and processes) but *why* it does what it does. The analysis builds on the basic conjecture that design is approximately rational—that is, the observed structure and processes are optimized (within the constraints of available resources) to serve the needs of the organism. Such rational analysis is of specific use to ++HCI because it amounts to a kind of reverse engineering and task analysis for the design of the human brain—and as such is quite instructive for the design of other information systems similarly confronted.

Anderson's analysis of human memory took as central the idea that the main goal of memory was not just to save things but to estimate continually the probability that each thing was going to be needed at the next moment (the *need probability*) and make those items with the highest need probability most available.[3]

This need probability was analyzed further in terms of temporal components (recent or frequently used items were more likely to be needed next) and contextual components (co-occurrence structure of the world, reflected in the associative structure in memory, predicts what might be used after the current item). His analysis explained qualitatively, and often quantitatively, the character of much of the vast cognitive psychological literature on memory.

This rational analysis extends by direct analogy to instruct ++HCI and the design of interfaces to artificial information systems. First note that the typical library has a reference section for frequently used materials and a current periodicals section for recent journals. These represent the temporal components of the user population's need probabilities. Public libraries also often have thematic displays based on current topical content—for example, books on witches and goblins around Halloween. Similarly, in computer-based technology, information objects can be made more available by designers explicitly trying to estimate need probabilities. Web browsers are trying to make recently or frequently visited sites more available (via better history and bookmarking mechanisms, respectively). Site designers are paying more explicit attention to putting frequently used items or items of current topical interest up front. Microsoft is trying to put recency and frequency into its multi-tiered pull-down menu structure in Windows 2000. The Anderson analysis gives explicit insight into these design trends.

---

[3]Fittingly, Anderson's analysis was inspired in part by work in information science on the statistical patterns of book usage in libraries—the probabilities that a social aggregate of users would need the various holdings in this cultural memory institution.

Exploring these analogies between information systems in different parts of the MoRAS leads to deeper understanding of the phenomena, their processes, and their motivations. As a result, they can also suggest directions for design. Thus, in summary, considering the MoRAS can amplify ++HCI design efforts in two ways. First, by laying out the network of systems and processes that are relevant to design of human-centered, information-rich technologies, it can provide a much broader canvas for our work. Second, by exploiting the many rich analogies, it can bring the clever design accomplished in one sphere to bear in others.

3.3.3   New Problems Addressed—Needs and Wants

The final illustration of the relevance of the MoRAS framework to ++HCI concerns how a MoRAS perspective can illuminate new problems—in this case the roles of evolutionary design, technology, and the marketplace in creating a schism between human needs and human wants. The example is a MoRAS tale because it involves the interplay of several different responsive, adaptive systems: biological evolution of the human body and brain, the cultural evolution of science and technology, and the economic optimizations of the marketplace. It is of special interest to ++HCI because it represents a broad class of growing problems and fundamentally involves generalized information technologies and their alignment with human needs. It is treated at considerable length in Furnas (2000). Only a brief summary is given here.

As used here, *needs* are conditions that must be satisfied for a system to be healthy and viable. Want mechanisms, or simply *wants,* are designed technologies (in a very generalized sense of both of those terms) that recruit resources, focus attention, and organize behavior of the system in service of those needs. Thus, for example, we have a biological *need* for glucose, to produce energy. We also have, correspondingly, evolutionarily "designed" *want* mechanisms that organize behavior around obtaining glucose as needed. There are brain systems that monitor blood sugar, linked to a hunger system that increasingly gets our attention to seek sugars, starches, and fats. There are taste buds that detect sweet tastes, linked to pleasure mechanisms that fire when sweetness is detected in a state of hunger. There are so-called "operant learning" mechanisms that increase the frequency of behavior that preceded the pleasure.

Note that needs and associated want mechanisms occur in generalized form throughout the systems of the MoRAS. They occur at various levels of aggregation. For example, firms have sales and profit *needs,* and must create mechanisms (*want* mechanisms) to structure their attention and behavior (for example, employee incentive plans) in service of those needs. In addition, wants and needs can be noted in both direct material spheres (thwarting a predator or competitor) and derivatively in information spheres (getting information about predators or competitors)—a distinction closely related to specialization of subsystems at a given level in the MoRAS, sketched in Figure 3.2, where some have explicit cognitive/IT focus and others do not. General understanding of the concepts of needs and wants, and their IT implications, can therefore be highly leveraged, its utility multiplied by the many places it occurs in the MoRAS.

This pair of concepts, *needs* and *wants,* should be a particular focus for ++HCI. *Needs* are of interest because ++HCI is concerned with technology, not for its own sake but for its value in service of human needs. *Want* mechanisms are of particular interest because they have a dominant IT component. They detect and collect signals that correlate with future problems or opportunities. They then undertake decision and planning activities to structure and coordinate behavior in response. These are all information-rich activities that are designed to contribute to viability. Understanding and supporting them are thus natural fits for ++HCI.

The critical problem about needs and wants arises in our changing world from the fact that want mechanisms are only heuristic. In particular, their design relies for success on the structure of the world for which they were designed. Thus, we have, in addition to a glucose need, a biological need for vitamins to catalyze various biochemical reactions. We do not, however, have strong want mechanisms to organize our behavior in explicit pursuit of vitamins. Explicit mechanisms were not necessary because other want mechanisms served the purpose heuristically in our natural environment. The energy-seeking mechanisms were sufficient to get us eating fruits, grains, and meats. The vitamins, whose occurrence in the natural world was very highly correlated with those energy nutrients, came along for free. If, however, the correlational structure of the world is changed so that it is possible to get sugar, starch, and fat without the associated vitamins, the existing heuristic want mechanisms can be perfectly satisfied without the other nutritional needs being met.

At this point, a second part of the story comes in as increasingly efficient social institutions centered on advancing science and technology provide the tools for changing the correlational structure of the world. Indeed, such change is part of their purpose—to put roofs over heads where there were none and to bring health where disease was rampant. Advances also, however, make it quite technically possible to address needs and wants separately. Following our nutritional example, it has become possible to refine sugar, taking it out of its vitamin-rich natural package. To choose an example in the IT domain, it is now arguably possible with television to satisfy people's socio/informational wants without satisfying their corresponding needs (see Putnam 1995): People will stay at home watching *Friends* on TV, getting some of the satisfying feeling of actually having friends, when in fact they do not. None of those characters on TV will give them a ride to the airport, drop in when they are sick, or listen to their troubles.

The third piece of the story involves how market forces drive this technically possible dissociation in the direction of giving people what they want regardless of the satisfaction of their underlying needs. By definition, the organized expenditure of resources is mediated by want mechanisms, not directly by needs. People will work for sugar (or work to earn money to buy sugar) but not (without a strong educational campaign) for vitamins. This means that businesses can earn money only if they cater to their customers' want mechanisms and not to their customers' needs. (Indeed, businesses *need* to do so and must have corporate *want* mechanisms to ensure these corporate needs are met.)

The problem arises as these three threads, themselves products of different parts of the MoRAS, come together. The evolutionarily designed heuristic connection between needs and their associated want mechanisms creates a certain vulnerability if the structure of the world changes. The efforts of science and technology yield the power to change the structure of the world. The forces of the marketplace push this change in directions driven only by wants, not the more important underlying needs. The net effect of these is that there is a strong dynamic in the MoRAS at present to give individuals (or other systems in the MoRAS) more and more of what they *want* but not necessarily more (and likely less) of what they *need:* frosted cupcakes and potato chips, or sex and violence in movies.

Mechanisms for the realignment of needs and wants via various uses of information technology are discussed in Furnas (2000), based on examining how want mechanisms work and how they are modified in different parts of the MoRAS.

The alignment of wants and needs is a long-standing project of adaptive mechanisms, from biological evolution to implicit organizational design. The practice of ++HCI is one such adaptive mechanism: a growing cultural institution mobilizing human intelligence, observation, and intentional design to bring people, information, and technology together in better ways. Thus, on the face of it, needs/wants issues seem particularly important candidates for ++HCI focus. Want mechanisms are fundamentally generalized Information Technology, and such technology is the core of the ++HCI content domain. Moreover, the mechanisms are fundamentally in the service of human viability and value, the heart of the ++HCI mission.

3.4   The MoRAS and ++HCI Design

The basic claim of the MoRAS framework is that the proper context for the ++HCI enterprise is a large mosaic of systems. The introduction of IT alters these various systems and their couplings, and the systems respond and adapt in ways that co-design the result. As ++HCI designers, we must be mindful of the larger opportunities and impacts of our efforts and more aware of our virtual "partners" in the design process.

For example, to help find places to direct ++HCI efforts, a look at MoRAS diagrams (Figures 3.1 and 3.2) can suggest individual systems that seem underrepresented in efforts so far, or pairs of places in the MoRAS that might benefit from useful bridges built between them. Given a design focus, its MoRAS context can be understood by looking explicitly at where it fits in the structure of the MoRAS and then asking about the dominant processes operating in the corresponding components as well as their dependencies on other components and their needs and existing want mechanisms. From there one can consider how to extract value with new couplings across space, time, or situations. One can ask how basic IT roles—like collection, integration, reuse, synthesis, computation, planning, action, coordination, and feedback—might apply in new places in the MoRAS. In seeking solutions, one can ask if there are useful analogies elsewhere in the MoRAS that can provide design inspiration. Perhaps the adaptation mechanisms of other systems can be encouraged to support intended design efforts—for example, by the constructive engagement of their want mechanisms. Perhaps incidental aspects of the existing system (structure, artifacts, or behavior) are available for opportunistic use in the design. In evaluation, one can weigh the impact of a proposed design on other parts of the MoRAS, using diagrams like those of Figures 3.1 and 3.2 as a checklist. One can examine how the coupling between various components is being changed by the design, what incidental aspects of the world are being changed that may have been used opportunistically by other systems, or what adaptive processes in the MoRAS will respond to the intentional design efforts.[4] Only by such considerations will we maximize our effectiveness in trying to bring people, information, and technology together in more valuable ways.

3.5   Future Directions

Future work on the MoRAS framework would fall into three areas: research (basic and applied), education, and design. Basic research is needed to advance a unifying understanding of the structure and processes of the MoRAS, drawing both on classical cybernetic systems theory (Bertalanffy 1969; Buckley 1968; Bahg 1990), the theory of complex adaptive systems (Holland 1992, 1998), and the less traditional autopoietic theory (Maturana and Varela 1980; for relevance to HCI, see Winograd and Flores 1987). There is also basic research needed to understand more of how the systems of focus in the separate disciplines are situated within the MoRAS. What other systems rely on what properties of a given system of focus? Conversely, on what properties of other systems does that focal system rely? Is there a simple first-order model of a given system that could be exported to others for purposes of MoRAS considerations? Applied research is needed to identify the places of ++HCI leverage in the MoRAS. This includes not just options for placing information technology but also how to influence other "design" mechanisms in the MoRAS to respond and adapt appropriately.

Future work is also needed in education, since both researchers and designers will require a more multidisciplinary background. The general flavor of the education would be a kind of applied theory, integrating both fundamental understanding and design implications. A doctoral agenda would emphasize the theory and its integration, in support of a master's agenda that emphasizes its application. In either case there are three components. First, education in systems theory is needed to help to understand the overall structure of the MoRAS as a system of systems and to facilitate the understanding of individual component systems. Second, a general education about those component systems is needed—what outsiders really need to know about the domains,

---

[4]Some general design principles, explicit design questions, as well as a concrete design example are found in Furnas (2000).

structure, and primary adaptive and responsive features with respect to the MoRAS. Finally, there would be a heavy specialized focus on one or two specific systems of key interest to the student—the place where she will do most of her work, mindful of the web of the MoRAS. This educational mix gives more meaning to the student's component of special interest, provides triggers for seeking expertise in other disciplines, and supplies a minimal common ground for the ensuing interdisciplinary conversations.

The real design agenda is to carry on with the ++HCI mission, making information technology more valuable to humans in more ways throughout the MoRAS. Being mindful of the MoRAS highlights opportunities for design, as well as strategies and technologies to bring it to bear. It involves taking principles extracted by research about the MoRAS and its design systems and putting them into practice, gaining experience with this design approach, accumulating case studies and examples of tools, tactics and strategies, and developing design methodologies.

The goal of this paper has been to lay out the MoRAS in a preliminary framework to support the broader scope of design implicit in the ++HCI mission. While the scale of the MoRAS is daunting, this work represents the belief that ++HCI will benefit from participants in the converging disciplines foregoing some of their specialized focus for a valuable overview of other parts of the MoRAS and how they work together. Such an overview could provide sanity checks on our local views, give us a way to know whom to consult about other matters that arise, and create a shared framework for those conversations. Clearly, an extended formulation of any such framework can be achieved only by a prolonged, interdisciplinary community effort. This paper strives primarily to stimulate the interest that might engage such an effort.

Acknowledgments

I would like to thank colleagues here at SI for their inspiration, particularly Dan Atkins, the founding dean who brought our interdisciplinary team together, Michael Cohen for sharing early explorations in a course we co-taught, and the several dozen students in related graduate seminars. I would also like to thank Wendy Kellogg, Maria Slowiaczek, Jeff Mackie-Mason, Paul Resnick, and the several anonymous reviewers for their numerous helpful comments on drafts of this paper.

References

Ackerman, M.S. and Halverson, C.A. (2000). Reexamining organizational memory. *Communications of the ACM,* 43, 1, 58–64.

Anderson, J. (1990). *Adaptive character of thought.* Hillsdale, NJ: Lawrence Erlbaum.

Anderson, J., and Milson, R. (1989). Human memory: An adaptive perspective. *Psychological Review,* 96, 4, 703–719.

Bahg, C.-G. (1990). Major systems theories throughout the world. *Behavioral Science,* 35, 79–107.

Bates, M.J. (1990). The design of browsing and berrypicking techniques for the online search interface. *Online Review,* 13, 5, 407–424.

Belkin, N.J., Oddy, R.N., and Brooks, H.M. (1982). ASK for information retrieval: Part 1. Background and theory. *Journal of Documentation,* 38, 2, 145–164.

Bertalanffy, L. von. (1969). *General system theory: foundations, development, applications.* New York: G. Braziller.

Buckley, W.F. (1968). *Modern systems research for the behavioral scientist: A sourcebook.* Chicago: Aldine Publishing Company.

Bush, V. (1945). As we may think. *Atlantic Monthly,* 176, 7, 101–108.

Carroll, J.M., and Rosson, M.B. (1998). Network communities, community networks. *Tutorials/Proceedings of ACM CHI'98 Conference on Human Factors in Computing Systems* (Summary), 121–122. New York: ACM.

Cohill, A.M., and Kavanaugh, A.L. (Eds.) (1999). *Community networks: Lessons from Blacksburg, Virginia.* 2nd Edition. Boston: Artech House.

Deerwester, S., Dumais, S.T., Furnas, G.W., Landauer, T.K., and Harshman, R.A. (1988). Indexing by latent semantic analysis. *Journal of the American Society for Information Science,* 41, 6, 391–407.

Egan, D.E., Remde, J.R. Landauer, T.K., Lochbaum, C.C., and Gomez, L.M. (1989). Behavioral evaluation and analysis of a hypertext browser. *Proceedings of ACM Conference on Human Factors in Computing Systems (CHI'89),* 205–210.

Friedman, E., and Resnick, P. (1999). The social cost of cheap pseudonyms. Working paper available online at http://www.si.umich.edu/~presnick/papers/identifiers/. An earlier version of this working paper was presented at the 1998 Telecommunications Policy Research Conference.

Furnas, G.W. (1985). Experience with an adaptive indexing scheme. *Human Factors in Computing Systems CHI'85 Conference Proceedings,* 131–135.

Furnas, G.W. (2000). Future design mindful of the MoRAS. *Human Computer Interaction,* forthcoming.

Grudin, J. (1990). The computer reaches out: The historical continuity of interface design evolution and practice in user interface engineering. *Proceedings of ACM CHI'90 Conference on Human Factors in Computing Systems,* 261–268. New York: ACM.

Harris, J.A., and Henderson, A. (1999). Better mythology for system design. *Proceedings of ACM CHI'99 Conference on Human Factors in Computing Systems,* 88–95. New York: ACM.

Hearst, M. (1995). TileBars: Visualization of term distribution information in full text information access. *Proceedings of ACM Human Factors in Computing Systems (CHI'95),* 59–66. New York: ACM.

Holland, J.H. (1998). *Emergence: From chaos to order.* Reading, MA: Addison-Wesley.

Holland, J.H. (1992). Complex adaptive systems. *Daedalus,* Winter.

Hutchins, E. (1995). How a cockpit remembers its speeds. *Cognitive Science,* 19, 265–288.

Landauer, T.K. (1995). *The trouble with computers: Usefulness, usability, and productivity,* Cambridge, MA: MIT Press.

Licklider, J.C.R. (1965). *Libraries of the future.* Council on Library Resources, and Bolt Beranek and Newman Inc. Cambridge, MA: M.I.T. Press.

Karamuftuoglu, M. (1998). Collaborative information retrieval: Toward a social informatics view of IR interaction. *Journal of the American Society for Information Science,* 49, 12, 1070–1080.

Kollock, P. (1999). The production of trust in online markets. In E.J. Lawler, M. Macy, S. Thyne, and H. A. Walker (Eds.), *Advances in Group Processes* (Vol. 16). Greenwich, CT: JAI Press.

Maturana, H., and Varela, F. (1980). *Autopoiesis and cognition: The realization of the living.* In R.S. Cohen and M.W. Wartofsky (Eds.), *Boston Studies in the Philosophy of Science,* Vol. 42. Dordecht: D. Reidel Publishing Co.

Miller, J.G. (1978). *Living systems.* New York: McGraw-Hill.

Oates, T., Prasad, M.V.N., and Lesser, V.R. (1997). Cooperative information gathering: A distributed problem-solving approach. *IEEE Proceedings on Software Engineering,* 144, 1, 72–88.

Olson, G.M., and Olson, J.S, (2000). Distance matters. *Human Computer Interaction,* 2000.

Prasad, M.V.N., Lesser, V.R., and Lander, S.E. (1998). Learning organizational roles for negotiated search in a multiagent system. *International Journal of Human-Computer Studies,* 48, 1, 51–67.

Pirolli, P., and Card, S.K. (1995). Information foraging in information access environments. *Proceedings of the Conference on Human Factors in Computing Systems. CHI'95.* Part 1 (of 2), 51–58. Denver, CO; New York: ACM.

Pirolli, P., and Card, S.K. (1999). Information foraging. *Psychological Review,* 106, 4, 643–675.

Putnam, R. (1995). Bowling alone. *Journal of Democracy,* 6, 1, 65–78.

Rasmussen, J., Pejtersen, A., and Goodstein, L.P. (1994). *Cognitive systems engineering.* New York: Wiley.

Resnick, P., and Varian, H.R. (1997). Recommender systems. *Communications of the ACM,* 40, 3, 56–58.

Russell, D.M., Stefik, M.J., Pirolli, P., and Card, S.K. (1993). Cost structure of sensemaking. *Proceedings of the Conference on Human Factors in Computing*

Systems—INTERACT'93 and CHI'93, 269–276. Amsterdam, Neth.; New York: ACM.

Schuler, D. (1996). *New community networks: Wired for change.* New York: Addison.

Schuler, D. (1998). Designing across borders: The community design of community networks. *Workshops/Proceedings of ACM CSCW'98 Conference on Computer-Supported Cooperative Work,* 416. New York: ACM.

Stein, E.W., and Zwass, V. (1995). Actualizing organizational memory with information-systems. *Information Systems Research,* 6, 2, 85–117.

Tadelis, S. (1999). What's in a name? Reputation as a tradeable asset. *The American Economic Review,* 89, 3, 548–563.

Treisman, A., and Gormican, S. (1988). Feature analysis in early vision: Evidence from search asymmetries. *Psychological Review,* 95, 1, 15–48.

Wallace, R., Soloway, E., Krajcik, J., Bos, N., Hoffman, J., Hunter, H.E., Kiskis, D., Klann, E., Peters, G., Richardson, D., and Ronen, O. (1998). ARTEMIS: Learner-centered design of an information seeking environment for K-12 education. *Proceedings of ACM CHI'98 Conference on Human Factors in Computing Systems,* 195–202.

Walsh, J.P., and Ungson, G.R. (1991). Organizational memory. *Academic Management Review,* 16, 1, 57–91.

Winograd, T., and Flores, F. (1987). *Understanding computers and cognition.* Reading, MA: Addison-Wesley.

4

Distributed Cognition: Toward a New Foundation for Human-Computer Interaction Research

James Hollan
Edwin Hutchins
David Kirsh

4.1 Introduction

As computation becomes ubiquitous, and our environments are enriched with new possibilities for communication and interaction, the field of human-computer interaction confronts difficult challenges of supporting complex tasks, mediating networked interactions, and managing and exploiting the ever-increasing availability of digital information. Research to meet these challenges requires a theoretical foundation that is not only capable of addressing the complex issues involved in effective design of new communication and interaction technologies but also one that ensures a human-centered focus. In this paper we argue that the theory of distributed cognition (Hutchins 1995; Norman 1993; Saloman 1993) provides an effective theoretical foundation for understanding human-computer interaction and a fertile framework for designing and evaluating digital artifacts.

The theory of distributed cognition, like any cognitive theory, seeks to understand the organization of cognitive systems. Unlike traditional theories, however, it extends the reach of what is considered *cognitive* beyond the individual to encompass interactions between people and with resources and materials in the environment. It is important from the outset to understand that distributed cognition refers to a perspective on all of cognition, rather than a particular kind of cognition. It can be distinguished from other approaches by its commitment to two related theoretical principles.

The first of these principles concerns the boundaries of the unit of analysis for cognition. In every area of science, the choices made concerning the boundaries of the unit of analysis have important implications. In traditional views of cognition the boundaries are those of individuals. Sometimes the traditionally assumed boundaries are exactly right. For other phenomena, however, these boundaries either span too much or too little. Distributed cognition looks for cognitive processes, wherever they may occur, on the basis of the functional relationships of elements that participate together in the process. A process is not cognitive simply because it happens in a brain, nor is a process noncognitive simply because it happens in the interactions among many brains. For example, we have found it productive to consider small sociotechnical systems such as the bridge of a ship (Hutchins 1995) or an airline cockpit (E.L. Hutchins 1995; Hutchins and Klausen 1996; Hutchins and Palen 1997) as our unit of analysis. In distributed cognition, one expects to find a system that can dynamically configure itself to bring subsystems into coordination to accomplish various functions. A cognitive process is delimited by the functional relationships among the elements that participate in it, rather than by the spatial co-location of the elements.

The second principle that distinguishes distributed cognition concerns the range of mechanisms that may be assumed to participate in cognitive processes. Whereas traditional views look for cognitive events in the manipulation of symbols inside individual actors, distributed cognition looks for a broader class of cognitive events and does not expect all such events to be encompassed by the skin or skull of an individual. For example, an examination of memory processes in an airline cockpit shows that memory involves a rich interaction between internal processes, the manipulation of objects, and the traffic in representations among the pilots. A complete theory of individual memory by itself is insufficient to understand how this memory system works. Furthermore, the physical environment of thinking provides more than simply additional memory available to the same processes that operate on internal memories. The material world also provides opportunities to reorganize the distributed cognitive system to make use of a different set of internal and external processes.

When one applies these principles to the observation of human activity "in the wild," at least three interesting kinds of distribution of cognitive process become apparent.

1. Cognitive processes may be distributed across the members of a social group.

2. Cognitive processes may involve coordination between internal and external (material or environmental) structure.

3. Processes may be distributed through time in such a way that the products of earlier events can transform the nature of later events.

In order to understand human cognitive accomplishments and to design effective human-computer interactions, it is essential that we grasp the nature of these distributions of process. In the next section we elaborate a distributed cognition approach before describing in Section 4.3 how the theory of distributed cognition may provide a new foundation for HCI and in Section 4.4 how it can help the design of new digital work materials.

4.2   A Distributed Cognition Approach

4.2.1   Socially Distributed Cognition

The idea of socially distributed cognition, prefigured by Roberts (1964), is finding new popularity. Anthropologists and sociologists studying knowledge and memory, AI researchers building systems to do distributed problem solving, social psychologists studying small group problem solving and jury decision making, organizational scientists studying organizational learning, philosophers of science studying discovery processes, and economists and political scientists exploring the relations of individual and group rationality, all have taken stances that lead them to a consideration of the cognitive properties of societies of individuals. One idea that is emerging is that social organization is itself a form of cognitive architecture.

The argument is as follows. Cognitive processes involve trajectories of information transmission and transformation, so the patterns of these information trajectories, if stable, reflect some underlying cognitive architecture. Since social organization—plus the structure added by the context of activity—largely determines the way information flows through a group, social organization may itself be viewed as a form of cognitive architecture.

If this view is accepted, it has an odd consequence: We can use the concepts, constructs, and explanatory models of social groups to describe what is happening in a mind. Thus, for instance, Minsky (1985), in *The Society of Mind,* argues that ". . . each brain contains hundreds of different types of machines, interconnected in specific ways which predestine that brain to become a large, diverse society of partially specialized agencies." He then goes onto examine how coalitions of these agents coordinate their activities to achieve goals. The implication, of course, is that the cognition of an individual is also distributed.

Distributed cognition means more than that cognitive processes are socially distributed across the members of a group. It is a broader conception that includes phenomena that emerge in social interactions as well as interactions between people and structure in their environments.

4.2.2   Embodied Cognition

A second tenet of the distributed cognition approach is that cognition is embodied. It is not an incidental matter that we have bodies locking us causally into relations with our immediate environments. Causal coupling is an essential fact of cognition that evolution has designed us to exploit.

In recent years this idea has gained increasingly strong support (Brooks 1991; Clark 1997; Kirsh 1995, 1996; Lakoff 1987; Maturana and Varella 1987; Thelen 1995; Turvey et al. 1981; Varlea et al. 1991). Minds are not passive representational engines, whose primary function is to create internal models of the external world.

The relations between internal processes and external ones is far more complex, involving coordination at many different time scales between internal resources—memory, attention, executive function—and external resources—the objects, artifacts, and at-hand materials constantly surrounding us.

From the perspective of distributed cognition, the organization of mind—both in development and in operation—is an emergent property of interactions among internal and external resources. In this view, the human body and the material world take on central rather than peripheral roles. As Andy Clark (1997) put it, "To thus take the body and world seriously is to invite an emergentist perspective on many key phenomena—to see adaptive success as inhering as much in the complex interactions among body, world, and brain as in the inner processes bounded by the skin and skull."

For the design of work environments, this means that work materials are more than mere stimuli for a disembodied cognitive system. Work materials from time to time become elements of the cognitive system itself. Just as a blind person's cane or a cell biologist's microscope is a central part of the way they perceive the world, so well-designed work materials become integrated into the way people think, see, and control activities—part of the distributed system of cognitive control.

4.2.3 Culture and Cognition

A third tenet of the theory of distributed cognition is that the study of cognition is not separable from the study of culture because agents live in complex cultural environments. This means, on the one hand, that culture emerges out of the activity of human agents in their historical contexts, as mental, material, and social structures interact. And on the other hand, that culture in the form of a history of material artifacts and social practices, shapes cognitive processes, particularly cognitive processes that are distributed over agents, artifacts, and environments. Hutchins (1995) treats this at length in his book *Cognition in the Wild*.

Permitting the boundary of the unit of analysis to move out beyond the skin situates the individual as an element in a complex cultural environment (Cole 1996; Shore 1996; Strauss and Quinn 1998). In doing this, we find that cognition is no longer isolated from culture or separate from it. Where cognitive science traditionally views culture as a body of content on which the cognitive processes of individual persons operate, in the distributed cognition perspective, culture shapes the cognitive processes of systems that transcend the boundaries of individuals (Hutchins 1995).

At the heart of this linkage of cognition with culture lies the notion that the environment people are embedded in is, among other things, a reservoir of resources for learning, problem solving, and reasoning. Culture is a process that accumulates partial solutions to frequently encountered problems. Without this residue of previous activity, we would all have to find solutions from scratch. We could not build on the success of others. Accordingly, culture provides us with intellectual tools that enable us to accomplish things that we could not do without them. This is tremendously enabling, but it is not without cost. For culture may also blind us to other ways of thinking, leading us to believe that certain things are impossible when in fact they are possible when viewed differently.

Distributed cognition returns culture, context, and history to the picture of cognition. But these things cannot be added on to the existing model of cognitive processes without modifying the old model. That is, the new view of culturally embedded cognition requires that we remake our model of the individual mind.

4.2.4   Ethnography of Distributed Cognitive Systems

A major consequence of the tenets of embodiment, cultural immersion, and social distribution, is that we need a new kind of cognitive ethnography to properly investigate the functional properties of distributed cognitive systems. The ethnographic methods associated with cognitive anthropology in the 1960s and 1970s focused on meaning systems: especially, but not exclusively, the meanings of words (Agar 1986; Tyler 1969; Werner and Schoepfle 1987). Meanings were sought in the contents of individual minds (Hutchins 1980; Kronenfeld 1996; Wallace 1970). The ethnography of distributed cognitive systems retains an interest in individual minds but adds to that a focus on the material and social means of the construction of action and meaning. It situates meaning in negotiated social practices and attends to the meanings of silence and the absence of action in context as well as to words and actions (Hutchins and Palen 1997).

The theoretical emphasis on distributed cognitive processes is reflected in the methodological focus on events. Since the cognitive properties of systems that are larger than an individual play out in the activity of the people in them, a cognitive ethnography must be an event-centered ethnography. We are interested not only in what people know but in how they go about using what they know to do what they do. This is in contrast to earlier versions of cognitive ethnography that focused on the knowledge of individuals and largely ignored action.

Cognitive ethnography is not any single data collection or analysis technique. Rather it brings together many specific techniques, some of which have been developed and refined in other disciplines (for example, interviewing, surveys, participant observation, video and audio recording). Which specific technique is applied depends on the nature of the setting and the questions being investigated. Because of the prominence of events and activity in the theory, we give special attention to video and audio recording and the analysis of recordings of events (Goodwin and Goodwin 1995; Suchman 1985). In human-computer interaction settings we expect automated recording of histories of interaction (Hill and Hollan 1994) to become an increasingly important source of data.

The theory holds that cognitive activity is constructed from both internal and external resources and that the meanings of actions are grounded in the context of activity. This means that in order to understand situated human cognition, it is not enough to know how the mind processes information. It is also necessary to know how the information to be processed is arranged in the material and social world. This, in turn, means that there is no substitute for technical expertise in the domain

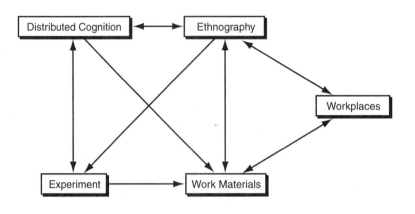

FIGURE 4.1   Integrated research activity map

under study. This is why participant observation is such an important component of cognitive ethnography.

The approach to human-computer interaction we propose here requires researchers to make a real commitment to a domain. If one is to talk to experts in a meaningful way about their interactions with structure in their task environments, one must know what that structure is and how it may be organized. One must also know the processes actors engage in and the resources they use to render their actions and experiences meaningful. This perspective provides new insights for the design of conceptually meaningful tools and work environments. It implies that their design should take into account the ways actors can achieve coordination with the dynamic behavior of active work materials.

4.3   An Integrated Framework for Research

The approach we propose for human-computer interaction research integrates distributed cognition with methods for design of digital work materials. It contains the elements shown in Figure 4.1. Although this entire integrated program has never before been assembled, our previous work has led us to this integrated program, and it promises to open up new opportunities for research in cognitive science and for designing new forms of human-computer interaction.

How then do the parts of this program fit together? The general idea is as follows. Distributed cognition theory identifies a set of core principles that widely apply, such as the following.

- People establish and coordinate different types of structure in their environment.
- It takes effort to maintain coordination.
- People offload cognitive effort to the environment whenever practical.
- There are improved dynamics of cognitive load-balancing available in social organization.

These principles serve to identify classes of phenomena that merit observation and documentation. Cognitive ethnography has methods for observing, documenting, and analyzing such phenomena, particularly information flow, cognitive properties of systems, social organizations, and cultural processes. Because cognitive ethnography is an observational field, the inferences we would like to draw are at times underconstrained by the available data. In these cases, the findings of cognitive ethnography may suggest "ethnographically natural" experiments to enrich our data.

The principles of distributed cognition are also at play in these experiments because the point of experimentation should be to make more precise the impact of changes in the naturally occurring parameters that theory tells us are important. As these three areas—principles, ethnography, and experiment—are elaborated, they mutually constrain each other and offer prescriptive information on the design of work materials. To be sure, the matter is more complicated. Work materials are themselves part of workplaces and themselves constitute important changes in the distributed cognition environment. So the introduction of a new work material is itself a form of ethnographic experiment, which allows us to test and revise the theory. But in general, we give pride of place to the principles of distributed cognition, for it is these that inform experiment, ethnographic observation, and design of work materials and workplaces.

Itis worth elaborating these relations. Consider how cognitive ethnography is used. Cognitive ethnography seeks to determine what things mean to the participants in an activity and to document the means by which the meanings are created. This is invariably revealing and often surprising. For example, in the world of aviation and ship navigation we have documented many cases of use of structure that were not anticipated by the designers of the tools involved. Experts often make opportunistic use of environmental structure to simplify tasks. A simple example is that pilots routinely display the test pattern on the weather radar as a reminder that a final fuel transfer is in progress. There is no method other than observation that can discover these sorts of facts of behavior and no other method that can teach us what really matters in a setting.

In order to make real world observations, it is necessary to establish rapport with the members of a community. While the skills required to do this are not normally part of a curriculum in cognitive science, they are as essential as the methods of experimental design. Cognitive ethnography feeds distributed cognition theory by providing the corpus of observed phenomena that the theory must explain. Most cognitive theories seek to explain experimental data. We believe there should be a single theory that covers cognition as it occurs in all settings. An experiment is, after all, just another socially organized context for cognitive performance. This means not only that we look at so-called *real world* settings but that we look differently at experiments, seeing them as settings in which people make use of a variety of material and social resources in order to produce socially acceptable behavior.

While the study of cognition in the wild can answer many kinds of questions about the nature of human cognition in real workplaces, the richness of real world settings places limits on the power of observational methods. This is where well-motivated experiments are required. Having observed phenomena in natural settings, we can set about designing more constrained experiments that address specific aspects of the behavior.

Design enters the story in several ways. First, ethnography offers clever ways of getting things done that can be incorporated into new designs. New uses can be found for old strategies, and techniques effective in one setting may be transferred to another. Experiments can refine the theory of distributed cognition that in turn can be applied to improve design. Finally, since the design process creates new tools for workplaces, there are new structures and interactions to study.

This loop from observation to theory to design and back to new ethnographic observations is an important cycle of activity in our framework. The design process, by virtue of posing design decisions, may also reveal novel aspects of behavior that should be attended to by cognitive ethnography or experimental studies. This forms yet another cycle of activity that can be used to refine each element in turn as the elements of the cycle interact with one another. The many loops and feedback circuits in the activity map reflect the multiple iterative processes involved in the successive refinement of theory, methods, and products.

Portions of the integrated approach have appeared in our previous work, but to date the entire activity has not been applied to a single problem domain. In the following sections we summarize our earlier work on a number of projects and show in each case the overlapping subsets of the elements of the activity that were conducted and the new opportunities that are presented by assembling the complete integrated research system.

4.3.1   Ship Navigation

In the 1980s, Hutchins did an extended cognitive ethnography of navigation aboard U.S. Navy ships (Hutchins 1995; Seifert and Hutchins 1992). The very notion of distributed cognition and the need for cognitive ethnography arose from the observation that the outcomes that mattered to the ship were not determined by the cognitive properties of any single navigator but instead were the product of the interactions of several navigators with each other and with a complex suite of tools. That work developed distributed cognition theory and extended the methods of cognitive ethnography. It examined the history of navigation practice in two very different cultural traditions to show how a single computational level of description could cover systems that had radically different representational assumptions and implementational means. It examined the details of tool use, showing how the cognitive processes required to manipulate a tool are not the same as the computations performed by manipulating the tool. It documented the social organization of work and showed how learning happened both in individuals and at the organizational level.

The integrated process we are proposing here could take that work much further. The observations of the practices of navigation suggest experiments. For example, when accomplished navigators talk about bearings expressed in numbers of degrees, they often report that in addition to thinking of the three-digit number, they *feel* a bearing as a direction in space relative to the position of their body. A navigator facing northeast may say that a bearing of 135 degrees true feels to be off to his right side. Some observed instances of navigators detecting errors appear to involve this sort of cross-modal representation. Since error detection is a key cognitive property of this system, it would be nice to know how this actually works. It is not possible to know from observation alone what role such representations might play in the navigation task. An experiment using expert subjects could shed light on this important process.

While Hutchins's work on ship navigation did not include any design activities, it could also be used as a basis for the design of electronic charting tools (an area of considerable interest to the Navy and the Coast Guard). An ethnography of the use of these new tools would be the beginning of the next phase of the cycle of research activity.

4.3.2   Airline Cockpit Automation

In the late 1980s, Hutchins moved his primary field location from the bridges of ships to the cockpits of commercial airliners. Since then he and his students have continued to refine the distributed cognition theory by applying it to cockpit (E.L. Hutchins 1995; Hutchins and Klausen 1996; Hutchins and Palen 1997) and air traffic control (Halverson 1995). This work included an extensive cognitive ethnography of airline pilots including observations in the jump seat of airliners in revenue flight, completion of training programs for state-of-the-art airliners, and work with airline training departments on the design of training programs. Based on a theoretical interpretation of the ethnographic findings, Hutchins designed a graphical interface to the autoflight functions of the Boeing 747–400 (Hutchins 1996). That interface uses direct manipulation technology, originally developed in the STEAMER project (Hollan et al. 1984), which is now nearly 20 years old. We now have the opportunity to apply the very latest technology to the problem of making the behavior of the autoflight system visible to the pilots.

4.3.3   Beyond Direct Manipulation

It is possible to create virtual social and material environments that have different properties than real environments. Hollan and Stornetta (1992) discuss how an unquestioned presupposition of the efficacy of imitating face-to-face communication restricts current human-computer interaction work on supporting informal communication. By paying close attention to how people actually exploit real environments, and describing those phenomena in appropriate theoretical terms, we can see how to go beyond the simple replication of felicitous features of the real world. An important research issue for the field of human-computer interaction is how to move beyond current direct manipulation interfaces.

One key focus of research based on distributed cognition is the nature of representations and the ways that people use representations to do work. Traditional information processing psychology focuses on symbols as tokens that refer to something other than themselves but pays little attention to strategies people may develop to exploit the physical properties of the representing tokens themselves. Our cognitive ethnographies show us that people often shift back and forth between attending to the properties of the representation and the properties of the thing represented, or intentionally blur the two. These strategies of shifting in and out of the symbolic stance support some very interesting cognitive processing. For example, Hazlehurst (1994) studied Swedish fishermen who coordinate their actions with other boats in a pair-trawl by interpreting and talking about what appears on a false-color sonar display. They talk about seeing *flecks* and *sprinkles* and also about seeing *fish*. And they mix the two kinds of talk, as in *that fleck is dense enough to set the net upon*.

Hutchins and Palen (1997) looked at how a meaningfully constructed space (the flight engineer's panel in a Boeing 727 airliner) and gesture and speech are all woven together in a brief cockpit episode in which the flight engineer explains to the captain and first officer that they have a fuel leak. He interacts with the panel both as if it is the fuel system it depicts and, at other times, as if it is just a representation of the fuel system (when he flicks a gauge with his finger to get the needle to move, for example). These shifts from attending to the representation to attending to the thing represented, whether in communication or in individual action, provide a range of cognitive outcomes that could not be achieved if representations were always only taken as representations of something else, and not as things in themselves.

Given the primary role of representation in interfaces to computational systems, there are likely to be many opportunities to exploit such shifts. That is, it might be possible to do one kind of cognitive work on the representations as things in themselves and another kind of cognitive work interacting with the representations as stand-ins for the things they represent. In direct manipulation interfaces, the objects on-screen are meant to be so closely coupled to the actual computational objects we are dealing with that we are supposed to feel as if we are manipulating the real objects themselves and not just their stand-ins. To achieve this feeling of immediacy (Hutchins et al. 1985), it is essential that meaningful interface actions have meaningful counterparts in the system. Thus, in dragging an icon of a file from one folder to another we are not to think we are just moving icons but rather moving the actual folders and all their contents.

There are limits, however, to how well a representation can resemble the thing it represents. For instance, many of the actions we perform on icons have no meaningful correlate when we consider their referent. This is especially true when we consider the way we can change the spatial relations between icons. For example, when we move an image of a hard drive to a more convenient position on the screen where could we be moving the real hard drive to? Distributed cognition theory makes this otherwise isolated observation an instance of an important class of events: those in which people manipulate the properties of a representation to encode information that does not pertain to and is not *about* the thing that the representation represents. Because we manipulate icons in *icon space,* it is possible to take advantage of the way they are displayed to help us further simplify our activity. We can opportunistically exploit structural possibilities of the interface. Files may be left near the trash can to remind us that we need to delete them. Files that are to be used for a single project can be bunched together or aliased so that they appear to be in two folders at once.

As users become more familiar with an environment, they situate themselves more profoundly. We believe that insights concerning the way agents become closely coupled with their environments have yet to be fully exploited in interface design. As we build richer, more all-encompassing computational environments, it becomes more important than ever to understand the ways human agents and their local environments are tightly coupled in the processing loops that result in intelligent action.

Discovering new models of active representations is fundamental to the future of human-computer interaction. Hollan et al. (1997) have proposed an informational physics model. Such models specify rules for how information presents and advertises itself and how it reacts to a changing environment. Changes can include the availability of alternative perceptual access routes, the presence of other informational entities, and the evolving nature of users' tasks, histories of interaction, and relationships with other information structuring entities.

The research framework we proposed here and our previous theoretical, ethnographic, and design efforts lead one to address questions such as the following.

1. How then can we design representations to facilitate their flexible use?

2. How can we make representations more active so that they help users see what is most relevant to deciding what to do next?

3. How can we shift the frame of interpretation so as to achieve a better conceptualization of what is going on and what ought to be done?

One way to address each of these questions is to specifically focus on creation of virtual social and material environments that go beyond mere imitation of the felicitous features of the real world to exploit the felicitous features of a computational world.

4.3.4 History-Enriched Digital Objects

Just as computation can be used to create potentially more flexible and effective active representations, it can also be used to allow representations to record their history of use and make that history available in ways that inform tasks and facilitate interaction. We think that automated gathering of activity histories provides rich opportunities for pursuing the event-centered ethnography we are proposing.

In interaction with objects in the world, history of use is sometimes available to us in ways that inform our interactions with them. For example, a well-worn section of a door handle suggests where to grasp it. A new paperback book opens to the place we last stopped reading. The most recently used pieces of paper occupy the tops of piles on our desk. The physics of the world is such that at times the histories of use are perceptually available to us in ways that support the tasks we are doing. While we can mimic these mechanisms in interface objects, of potentially greater value is exploiting computation to develop new history of interaction mechanisms that dynamically change to reflect the requirements of different tasks.

Studies of experts working in complex environments (E.L. Hutchins 1995) have shown that use-histories are sometimes incorporated in cognitively important processes. The side effects of use often provide resources for the construction of expert performance. Unfortunately, these supports for expert performance are sometimes actively but mistakenly designed out of "clean" and "simple" digital work environments. A striking example of this is the cockpit of the Airbus A-320 aircraft as discussed in Gras et al. (1991). By recognizing the functions of use-histories in simple media, we can exploit digital media to provide additional support in ways that are simply not possible with static media.

Digital objects can encode information about their history of use. By recording the interaction events associated with use of digital objects (such as reports, forms, source code, manual pages, e-mail, spreadsheets), it becomes possible to display graphical abstractions of the accrued histories as parts of the objects themselves. For example, we can depict on source code its copy history so that developers can see that a particular section of code was created based on a copy of other code and thus perhaps be led to correct a bug not only in code being debugged but also in the code from which it was derived.

In earlier efforts (Hill et al. 1992) we explored the use of attribute-mapped scroll bars as a mechanism to make the history of interaction with documents and source code available. Hollan and his colleagues modified various editors to maintain detailed interaction histories. Among other things, they recorded who edited or read various sections of documents or code as well as the length of time they took. Histories of those interactions were graphically made available in the scroll bar. These graphical depictions identified and highlighted sections that had been edited and who had edited them. Presenting this in the scroll bar made effective use of limited display real estate. To investigate any particular section, users need only click on that section of the scroll bar. Similarly, we and others (Eick et al. 1992) have explored representing histories of interaction on source code itself.

Records of the amount of time spent reading wire services, net news, manual pages, and e-mail messages can be shared to allow people to exploit the history of others' interactions. One can, for example, be directed to news stories that significant others have spent considerable time reading or to individuals who have recently viewed a manual page that you are currently accessing. There are, of course, complex privacy issues involved with recording and sharing this kind of data. Such data, in our view, should belong to users, and it should be their decision what is recorded and how it might be shared. Encryption should be used to prevent data from being obtained without the owner's permission.

The rich data resulting from recording histories of interaction and required to support active representations that conform to different use contexts is a crucially important area of research and potential resource upon which to base the design of future digital work environments. The integrated framework we propose here highlights the importance of ethnographic analysis of current use histories and encourages us to expand our exploration of digital artifacts that capture their use histories. But capturing such histories is only the first step in being able to effectively exploit them. The framework we are advocating suggests that we examine the activities of those systems at multiple scales.

4.3.5 PAD++: Zoomable Multiscale Interfaces

The observation that we move closer to items we wish to know more about, or that if we cannot get closer, we view them through magnifying optics, is so commonplace that it seems unworthy of mention. Yet, this simple and powerful idea can be exploited in computational media in ways that other media do not allow.

Pad++ (Bederson and Hollan 1994; Bederson et al. 1996) is an experimental software system to support exploration of dynamic multiscale interfaces. It is part of our research program to move beyond mimicking the mechanisms of earlier media to more effectively exploit computational mechanisms. It provides a general purpose substrate for creating and interacting with structured information based on a zoomable interface. Pad++ workspaces are large in extent and resolution, allowing objects to be placed at any location and at any size. Zooming and panning are supported as the fundamental interaction techniques.

Pad++ provides multiscale interface development facilities. These include portals to support multiple views, lenses to filter and furnish alternative views, search techniques to allow one to find information that matches selected characteristics and easily move to it, history markers and hypertext links to support navigation, layout and animation facilities, and other experimental multiscale interface techniques and tools.

While Pad++ provides a powerful substrate for creating multiscale work materials, here we mention only one example. PadPrints (Hightower et al. 1998) is a Pad++ application linked with Netscape that functions as a navigation aid for Web-based browsing. As a user follows links in the browser, a multiscale map of the history of traversals is maintained by PadPrints. The graphical views of pages can be used to select previously visited pages and are ideal candidates for visually representing the history of use information mentioned earlier. As a navigation aid, PadPrints exploits multiscale facilities for both representation and interaction. We have shown it to be more effective than traditional browsers (Hightower et al. 1998) in a variety of common information search tasks.

Information-intensive workplaces can be naturally viewed within a multiscale space. Dynamic multiscale spaces are particularly appropriate for hierarchical information because items that are deeper in the hierarchy can be made smaller yet because they are still in view they can easily be accessed by zooming. Similarly, the time structure of many information-based tasks is hierarchical in nature and fits well with multiscale representations.

Embedding Pad++ research within the distributed-cognition framework we propose here has important consequences. It helps us realize that some of what is powerful about multiscale representations comes from how individuals and groups adapt. As we discuss below, careful observation demonstrates that we constantly adapt to our environments at different spatio-temporal scales. Individually we adapt through interaction and creating scaffolding; collectively we adapt through culture and intelligent coordination. The very flexible multiscale representations that Pad++ makes possible allow us to explore representations that might better fit these differing spatio-temporal scales.

Distributed cognition encourages us to look at functional organizations that soften traditional boundaries between what is inside and what is outside. Because of the highly interactive nature of Pad++ interfaces, there is a rich interplay of cognitive processing, activity structure, and dynamic representational changes. How people manipulate the multiscale space and the multiscale objects within it is of particular interest. Distributed cognition encourages exploration of the tight coupling of interface components and cognition. Better understanding of this coupling may help in explaining why zoomable multiscale interfaces seem so compelling and assist in effective design of alternative multiscale representations. The integrated framework encourages us to augment experimental evaluation of Pad++ with ethnographic analyses, not only of usage patterns, but also of the general navigation activities people exploit in dealing with emergent structure in dynamic information displays.

4.3.6   Intelligent Use of Space

In observing people's behavior in Pad++, it is apparent that how they manipulate icons, objects, and emergent structure is not incidental to their cognition; it is part of their thinking process, part of the distributed process of achieving cognitive goals. They leave certain portals open to remind them of potentially useful information or to keep changes nicely visualized, they shift objects in size to emphasize their relative importance, and they move collections of things in and out of their primary workspace when they want to keep certain information around but have other concerns that are more pressing.

Studies of planning and activity have typically focused on the temporal ordering of action, but we think it is important to also explore questions about where agents lay down instruments, ingredients, work-in-progress, and the like. For in having a body, we are spatially located creatures: We must always be facing some direction, have only certain objects in view, be within reach of certain others. Whether we are aware of it or not, we are constantly organizing and reorganizing our workplace to enhance performance. Space is a resource that must be managed, much like time, memory, and energy. Accordingly we predicted that when space is used well it reduces the time and memory demands of our tasks and increases the reliability of execution and the number of jobs we can handle at once.

In Kirsh (1995) we classified the functions of space into three main categories: spatial arrangements that simplify choice, spatial arrangements that simplify perception, and spatial dynamics that simplify internal computation. The data for such a classification was drawn from videos of cooking, assembly, and packing, from everyday observations in supermarkets, workshops, and playrooms, and from experimental studies of subjects playing Tetris, the computer game. The studies, therefore, focused on interactive processes in the medium- and short-term: on how agents set up their workplace for particular tasks and how they continuously manage that workplace.

As with many such studies it is not easy to summarize our findings, though our main conjecture was strongly confirmed. In several environments we found subjects using space to simplify choice by creating arrangements that served as heuristic cues. For instance, we saw them covering things, such as garbage disposal units or hot handles, thereby hiding certain affordances or signaling a warning and so constraining what would be seen as feasible. At other times they would highlight affordances by putting items needing immediate attention near to them, or creating piles that had to be dealt with. We saw them lay down items for assembly in a way that was unambiguously encoding the order in which they were to be put together or handed off. That is, they were using space to encode ordering information and so were offloading memory. These are just a few of the techniques we saw them use to make their decision problems combinatorially less complex.

We also found subjects reorganizing their workspace to facilitate perception: to make it possible to notice properties or categories that were not noticed before, to make it easier to find relevant items, to make it easier for the visual system to track items. One subject explained how his father taught him to place the various pieces of his dismantled bicycle, many of which were small, on a sheet of newspaper. This made the small pieces easier to locate and less likely to be kicked about. In videos of cooking we found chefs distinguishing otherwise identical spoons by placing them beside key ingredients or on the lids of their respective saucepans, thereby using their positions to differentiate or mark them. We found jigsaw puzzlers grouping similar pieces together, thereby exploiting the capacity of the visual system to note finer differences between pieces when surrounded by similar pieces than when surrounded by different pieces.

Finally, we found a host of ways that embodied agents enlist the world to perform computation for them. Familiar examples of such offloading show up in analog computations. When the tallest spaghetti noodle is singled out from its neighbors by striking the bundle on a table, a sort computation is performed by using the material and spatial properties of the world. But more prosaically we have found in laboratory studies of the computer game Tetris that players physically manipulate forms to save themselves computational effort (Kirsh and Maglio 1995). They modify the environment to cue recall, to speed up identification, and to generate mental images faster than they could if unaided. In short, they make changes to the world to save themselves costly and potentially error-prone computations.

All the work we have just discussed points to one fact: People form a tightly coupled system with their environments. The environment is one's partner or cognitive ally in the struggle to control activity. Although most of us are unaware of it, we constantly create external scaffolding to simplify our cognitive tasks. Helpful workflow analyses must focus on how, when, and why this external scaffolding is created. We think an integrated research environment such as we propose is absolutely crucial to such analyses and as foundation for creating digital environments that make these cognitive alliances as powerful as possible.

4.4   Conclusions and Future Directions

Human-computer interaction as a field began at a time in which human information processing psychology was the dominant theory and still reflects that lineage. The human information processing approach explicitly took an early conception of the digital computer as the primary metaphorical resource for thinking about cognition. Just as it focused on identifying the characteristics of individual cognition, human-computer interaction, until very recently, has focused almost exclusively on single individuals interacting with applications derived from decompositions of work activities into individual tasks. This theoretical approach has dominated human-computer interaction for over twenty years, playing a significant role in developing a computing infrastructure built around the personal computer and based on the desktop interface metaphor.

For human-computer interaction to advance in the new millennium we need to better understand the emerging dynamic of interaction in which the focus task is no longer confined to the desktop but reaches into a complex networked world of information and computer-mediated interactions. A central image for us is that of future work environments in which people pursue their goals in collaboration with elements of the social and material world. We think that to accomplish this will require a new theoretical basis and an integrated framework for research.

Here we propose distributed cognition as a theoretical foundation for human-computer interaction research. Distributed cognition, developed over the past twelve years, is specifically tailored to understanding interactions among people and technology. The central hypothesis is that the cognitive and computational properties of systems can be accounted for in terms of the organization and propagation of constraints. This theoretical characterization attempts to free research from the particulars of specific cases but still capture important constituents of interactions among people and between people and material artifacts.

Taking a distributed cognition perspective radically alters the way we look at human-computer interaction. In the traditional view, something special happens at the boundary of the individual cognitive system. Traditional information processing psychology posits a gulf between inside and outside and then "bridges" this gulf with transduction processes that convert external events into internal symbolic representations. The implication of this for HCI is that the computer and its interface are "outside" of cognition and are only brought inside through symbolic transduction (see Card et al. 1983). Distributed cognition does not posit a gulf between "cognitive" processes and an "external" world, so it does not attempt to show how such a gulf could be bridged. Moving the boundary of the unit of cognitive analysis out allows us to see that other things are happening there. Cognitive processes extend across the traditional boundaries as various kinds of coordination are established and maintained between "internal" and "external" resources. Symbolic transduction is only one of myriad forms of coordination that may develop between a user and a feature of a computer system.

We propose an integrated framework for research that combines ethnographic observation and controlled experimentation as a basis for theoretically informed design of digital work materials and collaborative workplaces. The framework makes a deep commitment to the importance of observation of human activity "in the wild" and analysis of distributions of cognitive processes. In particular it suggests we focus on distributions of cognitive processes across members of social groups, coordination between internal and external structure, and how products of earlier events can transform the nature of later events.

This integrated approach strongly suggests that human-computer interaction research should begin in ethnographic studies of the phenomena of interest and with natural histories of the representations employed by practitioners. This in turn suggests that researchers must have a deeper understanding of the domains involved in order to, among other things, allow them to act as participant observers as well as to be theoretically and methodologically positioned to see existing functional organizations. The framework we propose holds that grounding in cognitive ethnography and integration of ethnographic methods with normal experimental analysis is fundamental to effective iterative evolution of interfaces. This framework also suggests that there are important opportunities available for designing and building systems that capture and exploit histories of usage. Such histories can not only be the basis for assisting users but also, with privacy concerns adequately addressed, provide researchers and developers with crucially important continuing data streams to assist future development.

As we mentioned earlier, the integrated research program described in this paper does not yet exist. We realize that it is quite ambitious in scope and in the skills demanded. The issues to be addressed are complex. Strategic advances will require considerable coordination of research activities on a scale not now associated with the field of human-computer interaction. In addition, graduate training programs will need to be expanded to incorporate training in a wider array of research skills. As a step in that direction, we have recently joined together to form a new research laboratory, Distributed Cognition and Human-Computer Interaction Laboratory, and are designing a graduate education and research training program for human-computer interaction based on the theory of distributed cognition. As part of that effort we are embarking on a research enterprise (Hollan et al. 1998) coordinated by the integrated framework we have described. We will need to await the results of these ventures to better understand the consequences of putting into practice what we propose. Still, we hope it is clear that without theories that view human-computer interaction within larger sociotechnical contexts and without a theoretically-based research framework that integrates ethnographic and experimental approaches, it is unlikely the field of human-computer interaction will do justice to designing the intellectual workplaces of the future and ensuring that they meet human needs.

Acknowledgments

This work was supported by grant #9873156 from the National Science Foundation. Additional support was provided by Intel, Sony, and Sun. The development of this paper has benefited from many discussions with members of our research group: Dan Bauer, Aaron Cicourel, Ian Fasel, Deborah Forster, David Fox, Mike Hayward, Jonathan Helfman, Ron Hightower, Barbara Holder, Sam Horodezky, Terry Jones, Todd Kaprielian, Tim Marks, Jonathan Nelson, Thomas Rebotier, Ron Stanonik, Scott Stornetta, and Peg Syverson.

References

Agar, M. (1986). *Speaking of ethnography.* Newbury Park: Sage Publications.

Bederson, B.B., and Hollan, J.D. (1994). Pad++: A zooming graphical interface for exploring alternate interface physics. *Proceedings of the ACM Symposium on User Interface Software and Technology,* 17–26.

Bederson, B.B., Hollan, J.D., Perlin, K., Meyer, J., Bacon, D., and Furnas, G. (1996). Pad++: A zoomable graphical sketchpad for exploring alternate interface physics. *Journal of Visual Languages and Computing,* 7, 3–31.

Brooks, R.A. (1991). Intelligence without reason. *Proceedings of the 12th International Joint Conference on Artificial Intelligence.* R. Myopoulos, John; Reiter, Ed., Morgan Kaufmann. 569–595.

Card, S.K., Moran, T.P., and Newell, A. (1983). *The psychology of human-computer interaction.* Hillsdale: Lawrence Erlbaum.

Clark, A. (1997). *Being there: Putting brain, body, and world together again.* Cambridge: MIT Press.

Cole, M. (1996). *Cultural psychology.* Cambridge, MA: Harvard University Press.

Eick, S.G., Steffen, J.L., and Sumner Jr., E.E. (1992). Seesoft—A tool for visualizing line oriented software statistics. *IEEE Transactions on Software Engineering,* 957–68.

Goodwin, C., and Goodwin, M.H. (1995). Formulating planes: Seeing as situated activity. In D. Middleton and Y. Engestro (Eds.), *Cognition and Communication at Work.* Cambridge University Press.

Gras, A., Moricot, C., Poirot-Delpech, S., and Scardigli, V. (1991). Le pilote, le controleur, et l'automate (reedition du rapport predefinition pirttem—cnrs et du rapport final sert—ministere des transports. ed.).

Halverson, C.A. (1995). Inside the cognitive workplace: Air traffic control automation. PhD thesis, Department of Cognitive Science. San Diego: University of California.

Hazlehurst, B. (1994) *Fishing for cognition.* PhD thesis, Department of Cognitive Science. San Diego: University of California.

Hightower, R.R., Ring, L.T., Helfman, J.I., Bederson, B.B., and Hollan, J.D. (1998). Graphical multiscale web histories: A study of padprints. *Proceedings of the Ninth ACM Conference on Hypertext.* Mapping and Visualizing Navigation. 58–65.

Hill, W.C., and Hollan, J.D. (1994). History-enriched digital objects: Prototypes and policy issues. *The Information Society,* 10, 139–145.

Hill, W.C., Hollan, J.D., Wroblewski, D., and McCandless, T. (1992). Edit wear and read wear. *Proceedings of ACM CHI'92 Conference on Human Factors in Computing Systems.* Text and Hypertext. 3–9.

Hollan, J., Hutchins, E., and Weitzman, L. (1984). STEAMER: An interactive inspectable simulation-based training system. *AI Magazine,* 5, 2, 15–27.

Hollan, J., and Stornetta, S. (1992). Beyond being there. *Proceedings of ACM CHI'92 Conference on Human Factors in Computing Systems.* Perspectives on the Design of Collaborative Systems. 119–125.

Hollan, J.D., Bederson, B.B., and Helfman, J. (1997). Information visualization. In M.G. Helenader, T.K. Landauer, and P. Prabhu, (Eds.), *The Handbook of Human Computer Interaction,* 33–48. Elsevier Science.

Hollan, J.D., Hutchins, E.L., and Kirsh, D. (1998). KDI: A distributed cognition approach to designing digital work materials for collaborative workplaces. http://www.nsf.gov/cgi-bin/showaward?award=9873156.

Hutchins, E. (1980). *Culture and inference.* Cambridge, MA: Harvard University Press.

Hutchins, E. (1995). *Cognition in the wild.* Cambridge: MIT Press.

Hutchins, E.L. (1995). How a cockpit remembers its speed. *Cognitive Science,* 19, 265–288.

Hutchins, E.L. (1996). The integrated mode management interface (final report for project ncc 92–578, nasa ames research center). Tech. rep., UCSD.

Hutchins, E.L., Hollan, J.D., and Norman, D.A. (1985). Direct manipulation interfaces. *Human-Computer Interaction,* 1, 4, 311–338.

Hutchins, E.L., and Klausen, T. (1996). Distributed cognition in an airline cockpit. In Y. Engeström and D. Middleton (Eds.), *Cognition and Communication at Work.* Cambridge University Press. 15–34.

Hutchins, E.L., and Palen, L. (1997). Constructing meaning from space, gesture, and speech. In L.B. Resneck, R. Saljo, C. Pontecorvo, and B. Burge (Eds.), *Tools, and Reasoning: Essays in Situated Cognition.* Springer-Verlag.

Kirsh, D. (1995). The intelligent use of space. *Artificial Intelligence(1–2),* 73, 31–68.

Kirsh, D. (1996). Adapting the environment instead of oneself. *Adaptive Behavior.*

Kirsh, D., and Maglio, P. (1995). On distinguishing epistemic from pragmatic actions. *Cognitive Science.*

Kronenfeld, D. (1996). *Plastic glasses and church fathers.* Oxford: Oxford University Press.

Lakoff, G. (1987). *Women, fire, and dangerous things. What categories reveal about the mind.* Chicago: University of Chicago Press.

Maturana, H., and Varella, F. (1987). *The tree of knowledge: The biological roots of human understanding.* New Science Library.

Minsky, M. (1985). *The society of mind.* New York: Simon and Schuster.

Norman, D.A. (1993). *Things that make us smart: Defending human attributes in the age of the machine.* Reading, MA: Addison-Wesley.

Roberts, J. (1964). The self-management of culture. In W. Goodenough (Ed.), *Explorations in Cultural Anthropology: Essays in Honor of George Peter Murdoc.* New York: McGraw-Hill.

Saloman, G., (Ed.). (1993). *Distributed cognitions: Psychological and educational considerations.* Learning in Doing: Social, Cognitive, and Computational Perspectives. Cambridge University Press.

Seifert, C.M., and Hutchins, E.L. (1992). Error as opportunity: Learning in a cooperative task. *Human Computer Interaction,* 7, 409–435.

Shore, B. (1996). *Culture in mind.* Oxford: Oxford University Press.

Strauss, C., and Quinn, N. (1998). *A cognitive theory of cultural meaning.* Cambridge: Cambridge University Press.

Suchman, L. (1985). *Plans and situated actions.* Cambridge: Cambridge University Press.

Thelen, E. (1995). Timescale dynamics and the development of an embodied cognition. In R. Port and T. van Gelder (Eds.), *Mind as Motion.* Cambridge, MA: MIT Press.

Turvey, M., Shaw, R., Reed, E., and Mace, W. (1981). Ecological laws of perceiving and acting. *Cognition* 9, 238–304.

Tyler, S. (1969). *Cognitive anthropology.* New York: Holt, Rinehart and Winston.

Varlea, F., Thompson, E., and Rosch, E. (1991). *The Embodied Mind.* Cambridge, MA: MIT Press.

Wallace, A. (1970). *Culture and cognition.* New York: Random House.

Werner, O., and Schoepfle, M. (1987). *Systematic fieldwork.* Sage Publications.

PART II

Usability Engineering
Methods and Concepts

5

The Strategic Use of Complex Computer Systems

Suresh K. Bhavnani
Bonnie E. John

5.1   Introduction

A dominant goal of the Human-Computer Interaction (HCI) field has been to design facile interfaces that reduce the time to learn computer applications. This approach was expected to enable users to quickly perform simple tasks with the implicit assumption that they would refine their skills through experience. However, several longitudinal and real world studies on the use of complex computer systems such as UNIX (Doane et al. 1990), word processors (Rosson 1983), spreadsheets (Nilsen et al. 1993), and computer-aided drafting (Bhavnani et al. 1996) have shown that despite experience, many users with basic command knowledge do not progress to an efficient use of applications. These studies suggest that knowledge of tasks, and knowledge of tools on their own are insufficient to make users more efficient.

In this paper we argue that, in addition to task and tool knowledge, users must also learn an intermediate layer of knowledge that lies between the layers of tasks and tools. This can be illustrated in even very simple tasks performed with simple tools. Consider the task of driving in a nail with a hammer. The task description (drive in a nail) together with the design of the hammer (designed to afford gripping), leads a user to grasp the handle, hold the nail in position, and hit it with repeated blows. While this method can achieve the goal, it often leads to bent or crooked nails, or fingers being accidentally hit with the hammer. In contrast, master craftsmen know that a quicker way to avoid these problems is (1) tap the nail to guarantee its proper angle of entry and to hold it in place, (2) remove the fingers holding the nail, and (3) drive in the nail with heavier blows. The knowledge of this efficient method is neither expressed in the task description nor expressed by the design of the handle. Instead, this knowledge lies between the layers of tasks and tools. This intermediate layer of knowledge has to be learned, and the cost of learning is amortized over subsequent use of the hammer to drive in nails.

This paper focuses on efficient strategies to use computer applications that lie in the intermediate layers of knowledge. We will show that these strategies are (1) efficient because they exploit specific capabilities provided by computers, (2) difficult to acquire from tool and task knowledge alone, and (3) general in nature and therefore have wide applicability.

Section 5.2 will introduce the preceeding three concepts in the context of *aggregation* strategies that exploit the iterative power of computer applications. Section 5.3 will provide empirical evidence that these strategies are not spontaneously acquired by experienced users but, if used, can reduce task time and errors. Section 5.4 will discuss possible explanations for why such strategies are not easily learned or used. Section 5.5 will expand the notion of strategies beyond those to perform iterative tasks and will briefly discuss our experience of using them to design training. In conclusion, we present some concepts that could lead to a general framework to systematically identify efficient strategies at different levels of generality. The goal is to help designers and trainers identify strategies that make users more efficient in the use of complex computer applications.

5.2   Strategies in the Intermediate Layers of Knowledge

Complex computer applications such as UNIX, CAD, word processors, and spreadsheets often provide more than one way to perform a given task. Consider the task of drawing three identical arched windows in a CAD system. As shown in Figure 5.1A, one way to perform this task is to draw all the arcs across the windows, followed by drawing all the vertical lines, followed by drawing all the horizontal lines. An alternate way to do the same task (as shown in Figure 5.1B) is to draw all the elements of the first shape (Detail), group these elements (Aggregate), and then make multiple copies of the aggregate to create the other shapes (Manipulate). Both these methods allow a user to complete the task. We call such *nonobligatory* and *goal-directed* methods *strategies*. The *Sequence-by-Operation* and *Detail-Aggregate-Manipulate* methods just described are prime examples of strategies that can be used in complex computer systems.

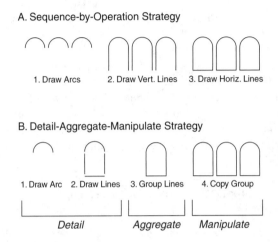

A. Sequence-by-Operation Strategy

1. Draw Arcs   2. Draw Vert. Lines   3. Draw Horiz. Lines

B. Detail-Aggregate-Manipulate Strategy

1. Draw Arc   2. Draw Lines   3. Group Lines   4. Copy Group

Detail   *Aggregate*   *Manipulate*

FIGURE 5.1   Two strategies to perform the task of drawing three windows in a CAD system

5.2.1   Strategies That Exploit the Iterative Power of Computers

The advantage of the *Sequence-by-Operation* strategy is that by drawing all arcs, followed by drawing all lines, the user reduces switching between tools. Although the Sequence-by-Operation strategy reduces tool switching, the user still has to perform the iterative task of creating each of the elements. In contrast, the advantage of the *Detail-Aggregate-Manipulate* strategy is that the user draws the elements of only one window, and the computer performs the iterative task of creating copies of the other windows when given their locations. However, a critical part of this strategy is that the user must make sure that all the elements in the original are complete and error-free *before* they are grouped and copied. This avoids having to make corresponding changes in each copy.

The Detail-Aggregate-Manipulate strategy exploits the iterative power of computers through the capability of aggregation provided by most computer applications. For example, most CAD systems, word processors, and spreadsheets allow users to aggregate groups of objects by dragging the cursor over a selection and then applying to this aggregate manipulations or modifications such as copy and delete. By grouping before applying operations, the user exploits the iterative power of the computer because the computer performs the iteration over all the elements in the group. This notion is captured in the basic strategy *Aggregate-Manipulate/Modify* of which the Detail-Aggregate-Manipulate is just one of several variations. We refer to all of these strategies as *aggregation strategies* (Bhavnani 1998). We will show in Section 5.3 that aggregation strategies are in fact much more efficient in terms of time and errors when compared to Sequence-by-Operation.

Figure 5.2 shows decompositions of the Sequence-by-Operation and Detail-Aggregate-Manipulate strategies for the draw three windows task. These decompositions reveal that the strategies exist in an intermediate layer of knowledge lying between the task description (at the top of the decomposition) and the commands to complete the task (at the bottom). The location of these strategies in the intermediate layers of knowledge profoundly affects their learnability and generalizeability.

5.2.2 Acquiring Strategies in the Intermediate Layers of Knowledge

Because strategies such as Detail-Aggregate-Manipulate reside in the intermediate layers of knowledge above commands, they are difficult to infer from command knowledge. For example, in the task to draw three windows, knowledge of how to use commands such as Draw Line and Group Elements in a CAD system is not sufficient to know that it is important to complete all the elements of the first window before grouping and copying. This has led to the general observation that good interface design on its own cannot lead to efficient use (Bhavnani and John 1997). Furthermore, when different strategies can accomplish the same task, the task itself also cannot express this strategic knowledge. This knowledge, therefore, has to be learned by various processes such as through trial and error or through explicit instruction. In

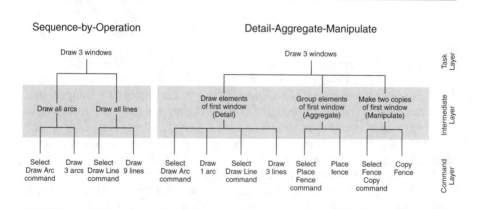

FIGURE 5.2 Decompositions of the task to draw three windows. The Sequence-by-Operation and Detail-Aggregate-Manipulate strategies lie in the intermediate layers of knowledge below the task, and above the commands.

fact, we will show in Section 5.3 that, despite mastery of basic commands, many users do not spontaneously acquire strategic knowledge to use commands efficiently.

There is a cost to learning strategies such as Detail-Aggregate-Manipulate. Users must learn to recognize opportunities to operate on groups of objects in order to exploit iteration and then know a sequence of actions to execute the strategy. As shown in Figure 5.2, the aggregation strategy requires a very different task decomposition compared to strategies that operate on single elements. However, this learning cost is amortized over the efficiency gains over many invocations of the strategy. This is similar to learning to use any new device efficiently whether it is a hammer or a computer application. Furthermore, we have empirical evidence to show that, when given appropriate instruction, users can easily learn to recognize and use strategies such as Detail-Aggregate-Manipulate (Bhavnani et al. 1999). After a few weeks of class instruction and practice, architectural graduate students learned to decompose complex architectural drawings by using aggregation strategies, in addition to learning commands. One important reason why these strategies were learned easily is that repeated elements are intrinsic to architectural designs (Flemming et al. 1997). Windows, doors, columns, and even entire facades are repeated or mirrored to create designs, and it is typical for an architect to exploit these repetitions while creating drawings. Aggregation strategies such as Detail-Aggregate-Manipulate, therefore, exploit how architects already think about objects in their designs. These results are not unique to teaching CAD strategies to architectural graduate students. Preliminary results from our ongoing research show that strategies can be taught in a short amount of time to a diverse population of freshmen students (Bhavnani et al. 2001).

5.2.3 Generality of Strategies in the Intermediate Layers of Knowledge

Because strategies such as Detail-Aggregate-Manipulate reside in the layers above the command layer, they are not dependent on specific implementations of commands in an application. For example, the step *Aggregate* in the Detail-Aggregate-Manipulate strategy can be executed by many different commands in different applications. Aggregation strategies, therefore, are generally applicable across computer applications. Figure 5.3 shows three aggregation strategies and how they generalize across computer applications. The first row shows how the Detail-Aggregate-Manipulate strategy can be used in CAD (as already discussed in Figure 5.1B, and in Bhavnani and John 1996) and in other applications. In a spreadsheet application it can be used to create a row of data, aggregate it into a range, and operate on the range using a formula. In a word processor the strategy could be used to copy paragraphs of text across files.

Next, the *Aggregate-ModifyAll-Modify Exception* strategy allows a user to exploit aggregation to handle exceptions. For example, if all except one of a group of elements need to share an attribute, it is better to modify all of them and then change the exception, instead of modifying each on its own. The Aggregate-ModifyAll-Modify

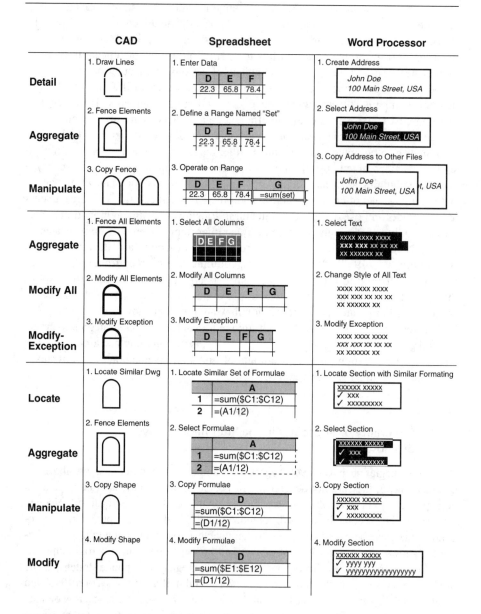

(© 1997 ACM, Inc., Included here by permission.)

FIGURE 5.3   Three strategies of aggregation and how they generalize across computer applications. Each cell shows an example of a task that can be performed using a strategy.

Exception strategy can also be used to modify the width of columns with an exception, as well as in a word processor to handle exceptions during the font modification of a paragraph.

Finally, the Locate-Aggregate-Manipulate-Modify strategy in CAD can be used to exploit similarity in a drawing by copying a figure that is already drawn and modifying it. In spreadsheets, this strategy could be used to copy and modify complex sets of formulae. The formulae shown contain absolute and relative referencing of cells that can be modified and reused in another location. In word processors, the strategy could be used to copy and modify a section containing complex formatting.

To summarize, this section described the existence of a set of aggregation strategies that reside in the intermediate layers of knowledge. We argued that these aggregation strategies are (1) efficient because they exploit the iterative power of computers, (2) difficult to acquire spontaneously from knowledge of commands or tasks, and (3) generalizeable across computer applications. The next section will analyze the first two points in more detail. First, we will describe a GOMS analysis of a real world task to precisely understand how aggregation strategies can affect performance. Second, we will provide empirical evidence from other studies to show that aggregation strategies are not spontaneously acquired by even experienced users.

5.3 Evidence for the Effects of Aggregation Strategies on Performance

To understand how strategies affect performance, we present a real world task performed by a CAD user during an ethnographic study (Bhavnani et al. 1996). One of the users from the study, "L1," had more than two years of experience in using a CAD system called MicroStation™ (version 4). His task was to edit a CAD drawing of ceiling panels that overlapped air-condition vents. The task of editing the panels overlapping these vents will be referred to as the *panel clean-up task*. This task is typical of drawing tasks performed by architects during the detail drawing stage of a building design. We observed nine other users who performed similar drawing tasks in our study.

5.3.1 The Panel Clean-up Task

As vents go vertically through ceiling panels, they both cannot occupy the same space. Therefore, as shown in Figure 5.4, L1 had the task of removing all the line segments (representing ceiling panels) that overlapped the rectangles (representing air-condition vents). The vents and panels were defined in two different drawing files that were simultaneously displayed on the screen to reveal their overlap. This

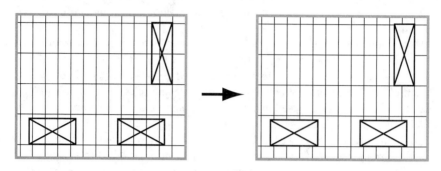

FIGURE 5.4   The panel clean-up task requires all ceiling panel lines that overlap
the air-condition vents to be modified. The drawings are schematic and not to scale.

enabled L1 to modify the panels without affecting the vents. The file had 21 such
vents, all of them similar to those shown in Figure 5.4. This meant that L1 had to
modify numerous lines that overlapped the vents.

5.3.2   How L1 Performed the Panel Clean-up Task

L1 zoomed in and panned a single window in order to view sets of vents to work on.
Figure 5.4 represents a typical example of such a window setup, with 3 of the 21
vents displayed. As shown in Figure 5.5, L1 first cut all the panel lines that overlapped the 3 vents by using the Delete Part of Element tool (which deletes a portion
of a given line between two specified points). He then cleaned up all the cut lines to
the edges of the vent using the Extend to Intersection tool (which extends or shortens
a line to the intersection point of any other line).

By sequencing all the cut operations across the vents, followed by all the cleanup
operations, L1 is effectively using the Sequence-by-Operation strategy described in
Section 5.2. This strategy reduces tool switches between the cutting and cleaning
operations but requires the user to perform the iterative task. Furthermore, the task
requires high precision, since L1 has to select each panel line in order to cut and
extend it to the edge of the vent.

Because of the highly repetitious and precise nature of the task, L1 committed
several errors of omission and commission. As shown in Figure 5.6, he did not notice
that two panel lines located very close to the boundary of the upper right-hand vent
overlapped the vent. He had to return to them after the rest of the lines had been cut
and extended. Second, he accidentally selected a panel line just above the lower
right-hand vent instead of the actual vent-line, thereby extending a panel-line to the
wrong place. This error went undetected, and the drawing was inaccurate after he

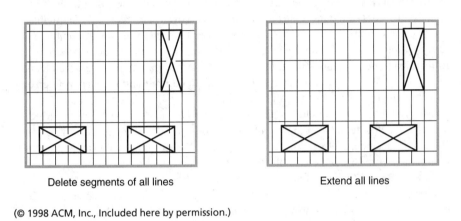

Delete segments of all lines   Extend all lines

FIGURE 5.5   The method used by L1 to perform the panel clean-up task.

completed the task. Finally, he committed five slips in the selection of panel lines, which had to be repeatedly reselected in order to get exactly the line he wanted. Despite these difficulties, L1 consistently used this time-consuming and error-prone strategy to clean up all 21 vents. In the process, he committed several more omission and commission errors and took approximately 30 minutes to complete the entire task.

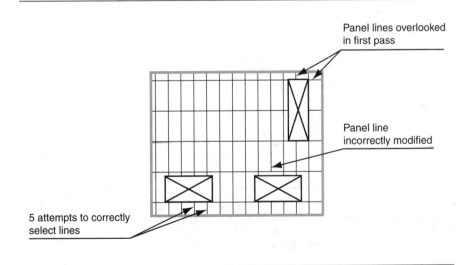

Figure 5.6   Errors in the panel clean-up task leading to inefficiencies and an inaccurate drawing. The figure shows the drawing after L1 completed the task.

To precisely understand the nature of these inefficiencies in terms of time and frequency of errors, the data was transcribed at the keystroke level and quantitatively analyzed. As shown in Figure 5.7, L1 took more than two minutes to complete the fairly simple task of deleting 11 very similar line segments (these numbers relate to the cleanup of 3 vents—the total task, as described earlier involved the cleanup of 21 vents). Furthermore, he spent 20 seconds to commit and recover from errors, which formed 16 percent of the total task time.

Many of these errors could have been avoided if L1 had used the Aggregate-Modify strategy to delegate to the computer the repetitive task of cutting and cleaning many lines. For instance, L1 could have used the Place Fence[1] command (an aggregation command) with a Snap mouse option (where the cursor jumps to the closest intersection) to accurately place a fence over the vent and then delete all the panel lines in one step. By using this procedure, all element segments within the fence, regardless of how visually close they were to the vent boundary, would have been selected. The errors related to precise line selection and of overlooking lines that had to be cut and

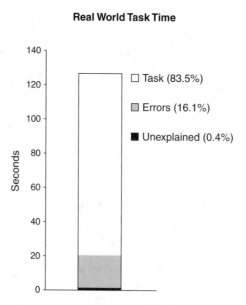

Real World Task Time

☐ Task (83.5%)

▨ Errors (16.1%)

■ Unexplained (0.4%)

FIGURE 5.7   Total time to complete the 3-vent clean-up task including the time to commit and recover from errors. Errors are all actions where a correct goal was incorrectly executed (slips). Unexplained behavior includes all behavior where it was not obvious what goal was being achieved.

---

[1]Ethnographic notes revealed that L1 had used the Fence command several times in other tasks to modify groups of objects. The missed opportunity to use the Aggregate-Modify strategy was therefore not due to the lack of knowledge of this command.

extended and could therefore have been avoided. Furthermore, because the iterative task of cleaning up each line would be delegated to the computer, it appears that the strategy could have reduced the time to perform the task.

5.3.3   Cognitive Analysis of the Panel Clean-up Task

To understand the differences between the Sequence-by-Operation and Aggregate-Modify strategies to perform the panel clean-up task, we first constructed hierarchical goal decompositions of each approach. Figure 5.8 shows a decomposition of the task as performed by L1 using the Sequence-by-Operation strategy. As shown, he used the Delete Part of Element command to cut each line across the three vents and the Extend to Intersection command to extend each of the cut lines to the boundary of the appropriate vent. The figure shows how L1's strategy choice resulted in many low-level mouse inputs. Figure 5.9 shows a task decomposition of how L1 could have performed the same task using multiple instances of the Aggregate-Modify strategy. When contrasted to the real-world task decomposition, there is a reduction in the number of low-level inputs due to the delegation of iteration to the computer.

To estimate the effect of this reduction in low-level inputs on performance, we developed GOMS (Card et al. 1983) models of both approaches. As shown in Figure 5.10, the model with the Aggregate-Modify strategy predicted a reduction in time of 71 percent. Furthermore, as shown in Figure 5.11, the frequencies of inputs were different between the two models. While there is an increase in the number of command selections (as the Fence and Delete operations have to be applied to three vents), there is a reduction in the number of precision inputs to select lines and intersections, as well as a reduction in the number of overall mouse clicks (command selections, accepts, tentative snaps). The large number of precision inputs may explain why L1 committed many errors, which added 20 seconds to the overall time.

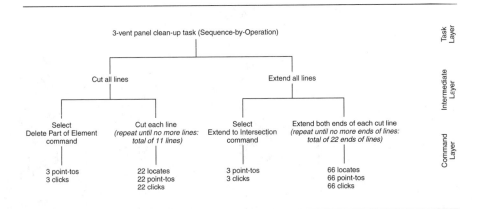

FIGURE 5.8   A GOMS decomposition of the 3-vent panel clean-up task using the Sequence-by-Operation strategy to clean up each vent.

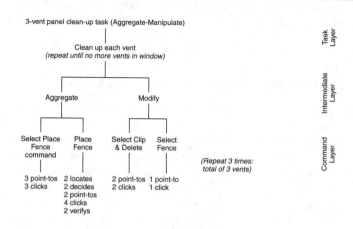

FIGURE 5.9 A GOMS decomposition of the 3-vent panel clean-up task using the Aggregate-Modify strategy to clean-up each vent.

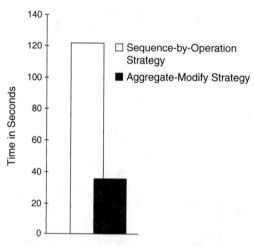

Figure 5.10 The Aggregate-Modify strategy used in the ideal model could reduce the time to do the panel clean-up task by 71 percent.

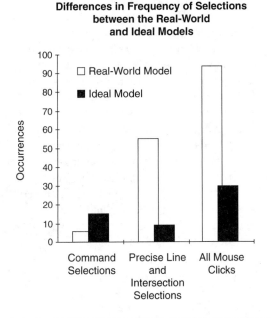

FIGURE 5.11   Change of input frequencies between the real-world data and ideal model for the 3-vent panel clean-up task.

The analysis of the panel clean-up task reveals many issues related to strategy use. First, despite experience and knowledge of the Fence command, L1 did not use an efficient strategy to perform a highly repetitive task requiring high precision. Second, despite making many errors, L1 was persistent in using his strategy over the course of the entire task. Third, the use of an aggregation strategy could have reduced time and errors, and could have led to a more accurate product.

5.3.4   Inefficient Use Reported in Other Studies

The preceding results are not unique to L1 performing the panel clean-up task. Our analysis of nine other experienced CAD users in the same office revealed a similar pattern of behavior (Bhavnani 1998). Users could have saved between 40 to 75 percent of their time to complete their tasks if they had used various forms of the aggregation strategies as shown in Figure 5.3. These results are also not unique to our study of CAD usage. Lang et al. (1991) report an experienced user who missed an opportunity to use the Detail-Aggregate-Manipulate strategy in a CAD task. When the task was redone after a brief discussion with an expert CAD user, it was completed in 67.5 percent less time. This study provides more evidence that although aggregation strategies need to be explicitly taught, they are easily learned through instruction and successfully executed.

The preceding results generalize even outside the domain of CAD. Nilsen et al. (1993) studied the development of 26 graduate business students learning how to use Lotus 1-2-3™ over a period of 16 months. Their results showed that even after 16 months of using the application in enrolled courses, the students did not use efficient strategies. For example, a task required five columns to be set to a particular width X and one to be set to a different width Y. The efficient method to perform this task involves two commands: one to set all the columns to width X and one to set the width of the exception to Y. Only 2 of the 14 students used this method. The other 12 students changed the width of each column individually. The authors make the observation that experience does not guarantee that users change their strategies to more efficient ones. It is important to note that the efficient strategy suggested by the authors is in fact the Aggregate-ModifyAll-ModifyException strategy described in Figure 5.3.

In a different study on spreadsheet use, Cragg and King (1993) have shown that 55 percent of users did not use the range option, an aggregation command to group and name many cells in Microsoft Excel. Once a range is created and named, it can be manipulated in other formulae merely by reference to the range name. This is in fact an instantiation of the Detail-Aggregate-Manipulate strategy in the use of a spreadsheet application, also shown in Figure 5.3.

This cognitive analysis of the panel clean-up task, together with the other empirical studies, suggest two basic points. First, despite experience, users do not easily acquire aggregation strategies to perform iterative tasks. The users tend to master the use of commands but do not appear to progress toward using them in an efficient way to complete complex tasks. Second, when used, aggregation strategies can in fact reduce time and errors and lead to a more accurate product.

While the GOMS analyses provide a rigorous account of the observed behavior, in addition to the improvements that could be achieved through the use of aggregation strategies, it cannot explain how the knowledge and behavior of the users got to be that way. The next section will explore possible explanations of why many users do not acquire and use efficient strategies.

5.4 Possible Explanations for Inefficient Computer Usage

Why don't experienced users learn and use efficient strategies, and why do these inefficient behaviors persist? This section will present possible explanations under two broad categories: (1) efficient strategies not known and (2) efficient strategies known but not used. These explanations will be derived from empirical studies done on computer applications where efficient strategies were not used, from both existing theories of knowledge acquisition, and from emerging theories of strategy choice and usage. Many of our explanations come directly from our experience studying CAD usage in detail. However, these results generalize to other complex computer applications. The goal of discussing these explanations is to identify approaches to improve the use of complex computer applications.

5.4.1 Efficient Strategies Not Known

The simplest explanation for the inefficient use of computer systems is that some users, despite many years of computer experience, had not yet acquired knowledge of efficient strategies. While it is well known that the acquisition of expertise is time-consuming, the following reasons explore why users of complex systems persist in not acquiring efficient strategies.

5.4.1.1 Efficient Strategies Have Not Been Made Explicit

One possible reason that efficient strategies are not known is that they are neither explicitly provided in instructional manuals nor explicitly taught in vendor-provided training. In a systematic search of libraries, publishers, and CAD vendors, we found that only 2 out of 26 books (randomly selected from the entire population of 49 books) went beyond the description of commands to perform simple tasks. One of the books (Crosley 1988) describes the importance of "thinking CAD." He states, "It's possible to use computer-aided drawing without really taking advantage of its capabilities. Even some experienced CAD users have simply transferred all their manual-drawing habits over to the computer" (p. 6). Later he adds, "The advantages of CAD are not free; they come at the expense of having to actually design the drawing" (p. 11). While this author stresses the importance of rethinking the drawing process, he does not present explicit strategies to "design the drawing," leaving the readers to discover and implement the strategies themselves.

5.4.1.2 Weak Causal Relationship between Method and Quality of Product

While the absence of strategic knowledge in books and manuals makes it difficult for users to obtain it directly, it cannot explain why CAD users do not discover the strategies while using their systems. An analysis of efficient manual drafting strategies provided some clues as to why strategy discovery in computer usage may be difficult. For instance, a well-known manual drafting strategy to prevent lines getting smudged and drawings getting dirty is to always "begin work at the upper left corner of the sheet of drafting paper and to finish at the lower right corner of the sheet" (Beakley et al. 1984, p. 47). In most cases, if such strategies are not followed, it is very hard to produce a quality drawing. A wrong strategy invariably leads to a visibly low-quality drawing. Because there is such a strong causal relationship between technique and quality, and because the flaws are publicly visible, drafters tend to be highly motivated to improve their technique.

This strong causal relationship between technique and drawing quality is absent in CAD. The drawing produced by Ll, when printed, is clean. Therefore, there is no visible indication that the drawing was produced by an inefficient strategy. As the flaws in the technique are not publicly visible, the users neither notice their inefficient techniques nor have motivation to change them. This phenomenon has also been observed in controlled studies. For example, Singley and Anderson (1989) note that "productions which produce clearly inappropriate actions contribute to poor initial performance on a transfer task but are quickly weeded out. Productions which produce actions which are merely nonoptimal, however, are more difficult to detect and persist for longer periods" (p. 137).[2]

5.4.1.3 Office Culture Not Conducive to Learning

The preceding explanations focus on an individual's interaction with a CAD system. However, real-world CAD usage typically occurs in a group environment where information is exchanged. This exchange can strongly affect the usage of a CAD system. For example, Gantt and Nardi (1992) recommend that CAD managers encourage "gurus" to develop expert knowledge and to act as disseminators of this information within an organization. Majchrzak et al. (1987) provide several recommendations: Managers should be well trained in the technology; CAD training should focus on presenting a general education in CAD concepts, thereby moving away from teaching only commands; and users should have biweekly meetings where they can discuss specific problems and keep abreast of changes.

However, as described in our ethnographic study of an architectural office (Bhavnani et al. 1996), such ideal conditions do not always occur in realistic office settings. The manager of the architectural section we observed was not trained in the use of CAD and did not use it to create drawings. Furthermore, training was perceived as a once-in-a-lifetime requirement, and the users were not encouraged to get follow-up training. As a result, the system had undergone many changes that were unknown to the users.

The lack of training was exacerbated by the absence of any regular discussions on system usage. Most discussions were confined to issues concerning design, and architects rarely discussed drawing strategies or looked over each other's shoulders during the drawing process. Additionally, there was an internal rule that prevented users from contacting the vendor phone support directly for help. The questions had to be routed through a system coordinator, who did not have a clear understanding of the problems faced by the architectural group and therefore was ineffectual in solving problems. These conditions severely inhibited the flow of CAD-related information within the group.

In cases when drawings are shared and modified within a group working on the same project, a poorly constructed CAD drawing can cause irritations and problems to other users. For example, a user might expect to move a shape by grabbing a side and, when that side moves away from the rest of the shape, realize the shape was

---

[2] Singley and Anderson are discussing a model of cognition where knowledge is encoded as if-then rules called *productions*.

constructed with single lines instead of as a polygon. In such cases, the drawing strategy becomes public and therefore presents opportunities for critical appraisal of inefficiencies. However, if all the users in a group share a flawed mental model of the CAD system, the inefficient strategy can remain undetected despite shared drawings. This was exactly the situation at the office where our data were collected. Therefore, the realities and complications in realistic office environments can make the dissemination of CAD-related information difficult and unreliable.

5.4.2   Efficient Strategies Known But Not Used

Another possible reason for the inefficient use of complex computer systems is that users know efficient strategies but choose not to use them. The following are some of the possible reasons and our evidence for and against those reasons.

5.4.2.1   *Efficiency Not Valued*

There is a possibility that users may know aggregation strategies but decide not to use them because they do not value the benefits they provide. That is, the users neither care for the savings in time nor for the accuracy that the strategies could produce.

This possibility is in fact *not* supported by our ethnographic data. Users explicitly stated the importance of saving time while performing drafting tasks. For example, in a discussion on advanced commands during the ethnographic study (Bhavnani et al. 1996), an architect explicitly stated, "Anything that saves time is of value to us." This observation is further substantiated by current research in the acquisition of strategic knowledge. For example, the adaptive strategy choice model (ASCM) developed by Siegler and Shipley (1995) predicts how children select strategies to solve problems in arithmetic. One of the predictions provided by ASCM, verified through empirical analysis, states that "when children can choose among alternative ways of executing a given strategy, they should increasingly choose the ones that are fastest and that yield the most accurate results" (Lemaire and Siegler 1995, p. 86). Although these predictions have to be verified with adults using computer applications, the aggregation strategies fit exactly into this category of strategy as they are predicted to be faster than the ones the users had and to produce more accurate results.

5.4.2.2   *Strategies Not Really Efficient*

It can be argued that the strategies we have identified as efficient require additional cognitive costs that are not taken into account in our GOMS models. If this were true, the strategies may not really be efficient, and users may therefore choose not to use them. While this argument may be potentially true for more complex tasks, we do not believe it to be true for the tasks we observed and modeled.

The tasks we observed and modeled were so simple that they did not involve time-consuming problem-solving or planning. For example, the panel cleanup task was simple and regular. There were many vents, all the vents had to be clear of ceiling panel lines, and the architect knew this at the start of the task. That was the only knowledge necessary to invoke the Aggregate-Modify strategy. There was nothing additional to figure out or plan. The user needed only to select a strategy and execute it. Such tasks are well modeled in the GOMS framework. In our models (Figure 5.8 and 5.9), the small amounts of perception and cognition needed to recognize the task situation are subsumed in the selection rules to pick the strategy and in the traversal of the goal hierarchy. Only perceptual operators (locate, verify), cognitive operators (decide), and motor operators (point-to, click) combine to give the time predictions because the theory and practice of GOMS does not assign time to selection rules or goal manipulation.[3] Therefore, we believe our models reflect any cognitive costs associated with using the strategies we identified, and they truly are efficient during the performance of simple tasks.

More generally, for users skilled in their task domain, the recognition of features like repetition, symmetry, and similarity are likely to be central to their task (for example, see Flemming et al. 1997 for a discussion of such domain knowledge known by architects). Therefore, users who are skilled in their domains need only learn the connection between these task concepts and the strategies that exploit them (see Section 5.4.1 for a discussion of learning costs) in order to invoke this knowledge in simple task situations.

However, there exist more complex tasks that may require problem solving and planning to recognize a structure and exploit it with efficient strategies. For example, given a cathedral with recursive symmetries, an architect, despite his or her domain experience, must first look for the recursive structure in the task, decompose it to the lowest level of symmetry, and then build up the drawing through the successive levels of symmetry using an aggregation strategy. This is what Crosley (1988) meant by "design the drawing" (p. 11). The more complex the structure in a drawing, the more mental effort is required to identify how best to decompose the drawing in order to

---

[3]It is true that adding each new strategy to a user's knowledge necessarily also adds at least one new selection rule to choose that strategy in the appropriate task situation. However, many cognitive modeling theories with good fit to empirical data assume no extra performance cost to having more selection rules that are not applicable to the task situation. For instance, GOMS (Card et al. 1983), Soar (Newell 1990), and ACT-R (Anderson and Lebiere 1998) all have this characteristic. Although some empirical evidence exists for the mere existence of different methods increasing decision time for skilled users (Olson and Olson 1990), it is small compared to the savings in execution time these strategies would provide.

It is also true that task decompositions using strategies often have slightly deeper goal-stacks than simpler strategies. For example, the Aggregate-Modify strategy for the 3-vent panel cleanup task (Figure 5.9) has a deeper goal stack than the Sequence-by-Operation strategy for the same task (Figure 5.8). Whether a deeper goal stack adds to performance time for skilled use is an open research question (John and Kieras 1996). Card et al. (1983) tried both approaches and found no additional predictive power from assigning time to goal decomposition and therefore left it out of the original GOMS formulation for simplicity's sake. On the other hand, Kieras (1997) included 100 msec per push or pop of a goal in GLEAN, and both Soar and ACT-R also include time on the order of 50–100 msec. Again, since the difference in depth is typically one or two levels at most, even this potential cost is small compared to the usually more substantial cost in keystrokes and mouse movements.

use an aggregation strategy. These are not the tasks we have modeled, and more research is required to understand how the aggregation strategies play out in such situations. (See Bhavnani et al. 1999 for how we taught students to decompose complex drawings and to use aggregation strategies.) Given the huge savings in execution time predicted by our GOMS models of simple tasks, it is likely that the more complex the drawing, the greater the cost of not using appropriate aggregation strategies. Therefore, we expect that the extra mental effort required to decompose complex tasks will be more than compensated by the overall savings in time that aggregation strategies provide.

For these reasons, we believe that in simple task situations similar to those we and others have observed (Doane et al. 1990; Rosson 1983; and Nilsen et al. 1993), the benefits of using aggregation strategies far outweigh the negligible performance costs. Therefore, if they had been known, they would have been used. In contrast, during the performance of more complex tasks, a tradeoff may arise between the cost of planning the task decomposition and the benefits of executing the appropriate aggregation strategies. Further research would be needed to understand such tradeoffs.

5.4.2.3 *Prior Knowledge Dominating Performance*

Several studies have shown how prior experience of manual tasks has a strong effect on performing computerized tasks. For example, many researchers have shown that the difficulties expert typists encounter when they first learn to use a text editor can be explained by their prior knowledge of using typewriters (Carroll and Thomas 1982; Douglas and Moran 1983; Halasz and Moran 1982; Lewis and Mack 1982; Mack et al. 1983; and Waern 1985). Marchionini (1989) found that many high school students, even after being trained to use online encyclopedias with sophisticated query searches, tended to use simple index-based searches similar to manual searches of printed encyclopedias. It may be the case that users know most efficient strategies but fail to use them because they are dominated by prior knowledge. The difficulty of breaking previously learned habits has been explored by cognitive theories such as ACT* (Singley and Anderson 1989).

The strong effects of prior knowledge may explain L1's interactions. Prior to using CAD, L1 had spent many years using manual drafting tools to create architectural drawings. The tools of manual drafting (such as the T-square, triangle, pencil, and eraser) are precision tools that assist users in creating accurate drawings. They are obviously not designed to assist users in iterative tasks. When using such tools, the user performs all the iteration. If 10 lines have to be drawn, then each line has to be individually drawn. Often, iterative drawing tasks require more than one tool such as the task of shortening 10 lines that requires each line to be erased and then redrawn accurately. For such tasks, it makes sense to use the Sequence-by-Operation strategy where all the 10 lines are erased, followed by redrawing all the 10 lines because it saves switching between the eraser and the pencil. This, of course, is exactly the strategy used by L1. Because L1 had spent many years using manual drafting tools, the well-learned Sequence-by-Operation strategy (efficient in manual drafting but inefficient in CAD) may in fact have blocked the use of the Aggregate-Modify strategy even though he knew it. It seems possible that if L1 had been cued to a better way, he might have switched to the better strategy.

5.4.3 Discussion of Possible Explanations of Inefficient Computer Usage

The preceding sections have presented several reasons that conspire against users employing strategic knowledge. Our evidence suggests that the more compelling reasons involve the difficulty of acquiring strategic knowledge or that this knowledge is insufficiently strong to routinely come into play in real-world tasks. Furthermore, users do seem to value the benefits provided by efficient strategies, and those benefits seem to be real.

While we do not deny that cognitive cost will be incurred in *learning* efficient strategies, we believe this cost does not extend in any meaningful way to skilled performance. There are situations where this may not hold—for example, when users are under the effects of fatigue, boredom, or low motivation. Neither present-day cognitive theory in HCI nor our data speak to this issue, and it should be investigated further. However, under the normal, goal-directed, skilled performance often studied in HCI, the aggregation strategies posited here are efficient at performance time and do add value to those task situations where time is important to users.

The cost of acquiring an efficient strategic level of knowledge is currently very high. It is so high, in fact, that it is not surprising that many studies of "regular" users report this lack of knowledge. There do exist subpopulations of users who enjoy experimenting with different methods in order to push the edge of their computer knowledge or other groups who experiment and compete with friends to find the fastest ways to perform tasks. Such users are motivated to invest the time necessary to acquire efficient strategies. However, as evidenced by the studies presented in this and other papers, such users are not universal.

Many approaches can be taken to alleviate this situation ranging from making strategic knowledge explicit through training, manuals, help systems, and tutorials, to making organizational changes to encourage exploration, feedback, and sharing of knowledge. However, we believe all these approaches depend on the central fact that the strategic knowledge must first be identified before it is disseminated. In the next section, we describe other general strategies that are important in the use of complex computer applications.

5.5   General Computer Strategies beyond Aggregation

The basic notion underlying all aggregation strategies is that an efficient way to deal with the iterative task of operating on many objects lies in the ability to aggregate the objects and to apply operations on that aggregate. As we discussed in Section 5.2, this ability shifts the task of iterating over each object from the user to the computer. Such strategies are possible because computers have the power to iterate over many objects in an aggregate. Aggregation strategies therefore exploit the power of iteration provided by computers. This insight motivated us to look for other powers provided by computer applications and to explore whether these powers could help identify other efficient strategies.

Our explorations led us to identify three other powers that were generally provided across computer applications: propagation, organization, and visualization.[4] As shown in Figure 5.12, each of these powers requires a set of strategies to exploit it. Propagation strategies exploit the power of computers to modify objects that are connected through explicit dependencies. These strategies allow users to propagate changes to large numbers of interconnected objects. Organization strategies exploit the power of computers to construct and maintain organizations of information. Such strategies allow for quick modifications of related data. Finally, visualization strategies exploit the power of computers to display information selectively without altering its content. Strategies of visualization can reduce visual overload and navigation time. Similar to the general aggregation strategies presented in Section 5.2, the following section will discuss how the seven strategies in the previous three categories are useful and meaningful in word processing, spreadsheet, and CAD tasks. These strategies also begin to extend our definition of efficiency from task time and errors to include other important variables such as modifiability of content, and visual overload.[5] All these strategies appear to be intuitively efficient but need to be rigorously tested through future research.

5.5.1   Propagation Strategies

The first two strategies in Figure 5.12 (Strategies 1 and 2) exploit the power of computers to propagate modifications to objects that are connected through explicit dependencies. Strategy 1 makes the dependencies between objects "known" to the computer so that (1) new objects inherit properties or receive information from another object, and (2) modifications can propagate through the dependencies. For

---

[4]We do not yet have a principle to generate these powers. We therefore do not claim this list is complete.

[5]Green (1989) has analyzed similar concepts such as *hidden/explicit dependencies* and *viscosity/fluidity* in the framework of "cognitive dimensions."

General Strategies	Word Processing Examples	Spreadsheet Examples	CAD Examples
Propagation			
1. Make dependencies known to the computer	Make paragraphs dependent on a format definition	Make formulas dependent on numbers in cells	Make window design dependent on a graphic definition
2. Exploit dependencies to generate variations	Modify style definitions to generate variations of the same document	Modify formula dependencies to generate different results for the same data set	Modify graphic definitions to generate variations of a building facade
Organization			
3. Make organizations known to the computer	Organize information using lists and tables	Organize yearly data in different sheets	Organize columns and walls on different layers
4. Generate new representations from existing ones	Generate table from tabbed words	Generate bar graph from table	Create 3-D model from 2-D floor plan
Visualization			
5. View relevant information, do not view irrelevant information	Magnify document to read fine print	View formulas, not results	Do not display patterned elements
6. View parts of spread-out information to fit simultaneously on the screen	Use different views of the same document to bring two tables together on the screen for comparison	Use different views of the same document to view column headings and data at the end of a long table	Use two views focused at the ends of a long building facade to make comparisons
7. Navigate in global view, manipulate in local view	Use outline view to view entire document and specify location of interest, use local view to make modification	Use outline view to view entire spreadsheet and specify location of interest, use local view to make modification	Use global view to view entire building and specify location of interest, use local view to make modifications

FIGURE 5.12   Seven general strategies beyond aggregation strategies and how they are useful in word processing, spreadsheet, and CAD tasks

example, word processor users can create paragraphs that need to share a common format to be dependent on a common definition. When the definition is modified, all the dependent paragraphs are automatically changed. Similarly, formulas in a spreadsheet can be linked to dependent data, or graphic elements in a CAD system can be linked to a common graphic definition of objects.

Strategy 2 exploits such dependencies to generate variations of the same information. For example, the strategy could be used to explore different looks of a document in a word processor, generate different results in a spreadsheet by altering a variable (such as an interest rate), or create several variations of window designs in a building facade while using a CAD system.

5.5.2 Organization Strategies

Strategies 3 and 4 exploit the power of computers to construct and maintain organizations of information. Strategy 3 reminds users to make the organization of information known to the computer to (1) enhance comprehension and (2) enable quick modifications. For example, a table constructed with tabs in a word processor is not "known" to the computer as a table, and therefore the tabular structure may not be maintained when the table contents are modified. On the other hand, a table that is known to the computer will be maintained under any modification of its contents. Similarly, data for different years in a spreadsheet can be organized in separate sheets for easy access, and different building elements such as columns and walls can be separated in different layers. Strategy 4 generates new representations from existing ones. For example, tabbed tables in word processors can be converted to tables and vice versa, data in a spreadsheet can be represented as charts, and 3-D graphic objects can be generated from 2-D representations and vice versa.

5.5.3 Visualization Strategies

The last three strategies in Figure 5.12 (Strategies 5–7) exploit the power of computers to view information selectively. Strategy 5 can be used to alter the amount of information displayed by viewing relevant information and not viewing irrelevant information. For example, when text is too fine to read while using a word processor, this strategy could be used to magnify the view instead of changing the font size. Similarly, in a CAD system, patterned elements can be undisplayed when not needed in order to make the relevant information more salient.

Strategy 6 addresses the limited screen space of most computer terminals. Often, users have tasks that require them to compare or manipulate objects that are difficult to view simultaneously in a single view. For example, a user might need to compare the contents of a table at the beginning of a long word processing document to the contents of a table in the middle of the same document. In such cases, instead of moving back and forth between the tables, it is more efficient to set up views that focus on each table to enable both to be viewed simultaneously on the screen. This strategy is clearly useful in large documents containing text, numbers, or graphic elements and therefore generally useful across applications using such objects.

Strategy 7 extends the notion of selective viewing to tasks involving a combination of navigation and manipulation. For example, a CAD user might need to make many precise changes to different parts of a large floor plan. A magnified view is needed to make the precision changes, while a global view is needed for navigation to the next task. One way is to zoom in to perform the precise modifications and then to zoom out of the same view to navigate to the next task. A more efficient method is to have one global view of the file for navigation and one local view to make the changes. The user then selects the location of interest in the global view, which automatically updates the local magnified view where the user can make the precise modifications. As shown in Figure 5.12, this strategy is useful when modifying a large word processing document as well as a large spreadsheet.

Currently we do not have a systematic way to identify powers of computers nor do we understand how to systematically identify efficient strategies from these powers. However, we are convinced that teaching such strategies would benefit users. To test this hypothesis, we taught one group of freshman students to use UNIX, Microsoft Word, and Microsoft Excel using commands and strategies, and compared them to another group of students who were taught only commands (Bhavnani 2000b; Bhavnani and John 2000; Bhavnani et al. 2001). Preliminary results from the experiment show that strategies could be taught effectively in the same amount of time as teaching just commands. Furthermore, the results also indicate that the students could transfer the strategies across applications. The analysis of strategies has therefore led to the reexamination of the content and delivery of computer literacy courses with promising results.

5.6   Summary and Future Research

To counteract the widespread inefficient use of computer applications, this paper identified and analyzed efficient strategies in the intermediate layers of knowledge. These strategies have three characteristics: (1) They are efficient because they exploit powers offered by computer applications such as iteration, propagation, organization, and visualization; (2) they need to be made explicit to users because the knowledge to use them is neither suggested by tools nor by task descriptions; and (3) they are generally useful across computer applications. The preceding characteristics inspired the design and testing of a strategic approach to training with promising results. These results suggest that the cost of learning and applying efficient strategies can be easily addressed by proper strategic instruction.

Based on our experience in teaching strategies, we believe that the identification of efficient strategies should be a key research goal. Therefore, we pose the question: Is there a framework that can systematically identify efficient strategies? There are several tantalizing clues that such a framework does exist. For example, we have observed that in addition to powers, computers also have limitations, such as in screen size, memory size, and processing speed. When task requirements exceed such resources, users may benefit by efficient strategies to circumvent the limitations (Bhavnani and John 1998). Therefore, powers, limitations, and their interactions could be the source of many strategies. A systematic identification of powers and limitations of computers could be an important step toward building the framework.

Another clue toward the framework is that efficient strategies in the intermediate layers could contain strategies at different levels of generality. For example, at one level, strategies could be relevant only to a particular application such as Microsoft Word. These strategies deal with eccentricities of the package but are generally useful for many tasks in that application. At another level, strategies could relate to an entire domain such as CAD but not outside. For example, strategies to precisely locate points using snap locks are generally useful across all CAD packages but not relevant to word processors. At yet another level of generality, strategies apply across domains, such as those on which we have focused in this paper. These levels could structure the search for efficient strategies.

Besides exploring a framework to identify efficient strategies, we are also exploring how strategies can guide the design of functionality. Designers could systematically check whether their designs provide the functionality to execute efficient strategies and test whether that functionality actually helps users become more efficient. Research on the systematic identification of strategies in the intermediate layers of knowledge can therefore not only lead to more effective ways of training but also to more principled methods to design functionality (Bhavnani 2000a). Both of these approaches should counteract the persistence of inefficient usage, which has plagued modern computers for many years.

Acknowledgments

The views and conclusions contained in this document are those of the authors and should not be interpreted as representing the official policies, either expressed or implied, of NSF or the U.S. government. The authors thank P. Polson, F. Reif, G. Vallabha, R. Young, and the reviewers for their contributions.

References

Anderson, J., and Lebiere, C. (1998). *The atomic components of thought.* Mahway, NJ: Lawrence Erlbaum Associates.

Beakley, G., Autore, D., and Patterson, T. (1984). *Architectural drawing and design.* New York: Macmillan Publishing Company.

Bhavnani, S. (1998). *How architects draw with computers: A cognitive analysis of real-world CAD interactions.* Unpublished Ph.D. dissertation. Carnegie Mellon University, Pittsburgh.

Bhavnani, S. (2000a). Designs conducive to the use of efficient strategies. *Proceedings of the DIS'00 Conference,* 338–345. New York: ACM.

Bhavnani, S. (2000b). Strategic approach to computer literacy. *Proceedings of the CHI'00 Conference on Human Factors in Computing Systems,* 161–162. New York: ACM.

Bhavnani, S., Flemming, U., Forsythe, D., Garrett, J., Shaw, D., and Tsai, A. (1996). CAD usage in an architectural office: From observations to active assistance. *Automation in Construction* 5, 243–255.

Bhavnani S., and John, B. (1996). Exploring the unrealized potential of computer-aided drafting, *Proceedings of the CHI'96 Conference on Human Factors in Computing Systems,* 332–339. New York: ACM.

Bhavnani, S., and John, B. (1997). From sufficient to efficient usage: An analysis of strategic knowledge. *Proceedings of the CHI'97 Conference on Human Factors in Computing Systems,* 91–98. New York: ACM.

Bhavnani, S., and John, B. (1998). Delegation and circumvention: Two faces of efficiency. *Proceedings of the CHI'98 Conference on Human Factors in Computing Systems,* 273–280. New York: ACM.

Bhavnani, S., Reif, F., and John, B. (2001). Beyond Command Knowledge: Identifying and Teaching Strategic Knowledge for Using Complex Computer Applications. *Proceedings of the CHI'01 Conference on Human Factors in Computing Systems.* 229–236. New York: ACM.

Bhavnani, S., and John, B. (2000). The strategic use of complex computer systems. *Human-Computer Interaction,* 15, 107–137.

Bhavnani, S., John, B., and Flemming, U. (1999). The strategic use of CAD: An empirically inspired, theory-based course. *Proceedings of the CHI'99 Conference on Human Factors in Computing Systems,* 42–49. New York: ACM.

Card, S., Moran, T., and Newell, A. (1983). The *Psychology of human-computer interaction.* Hillsdale, NJ: Lawrence Erlbaum Associates.

Carroll, J., and Thomas, J. (1982). Metaphor and the cognitive representations of computing systems. *IEEE Transactions on Systems, Man, and Cybernetics,* SMC-12, 107–116.

Cragg, P., and King, M. (1993). Spreadsheet modeling abuse: An opportunity for OR? *Journal of the Operational Research Society,* 44, 743–752.

Crosley, L. (1988). *The architect's guide to computer-aided design.* New York: John Wiley and Sons.

Doane, S., Pellegrino, J., and Klatzky, R. (1990). Expertise in a computer operating system: Conceptualization and performance. *Human-Computer Interaction,* 5, 267–304.

Douglas, S., and Moran, T. (1983). Learning text editor semantics by analogy. *Proceedings of the CHI'83 Conference on Human Factors in Computing Systems,* 207–211. New York: ACM.

Flemming, U., Bhavnani, S., and John, B. (1997). Mismatched metaphor: User vs. system model in computer-aided drafting. *Design Studies* 18, 349–368.

Gantt, M., and Nardi, B. (1992). Gardeners and gurus: Patterns of cooperation among CAD users. *Proceedings of the CHI'92 Conference on Human Factors in Computing Systems,* 107–117. New York: ACM.

Green, T. (1989). Cognitive dimensions of notations. *People and Computers V: Proceedings of the Fifth Conference of the British Computer Society Human-Computer Interaction Specialist Group,* 443–460. Cambridge: Cambridge University Press.

Halasz, F., and Moran, T. (1982). T.P. analogy considered harmful. *Proceedings of Human Factors in Computer Systems,* 383–386. Washington, DC: ACM.

John, B., and Kieras, D. (1996). The GOMS family of user interface analysis techniques: Comparison and contrast. *Transactions of Computer-Human Interaction,* 3, 4, 320–351.

Kieras, D. (1997). A guide to GOMS model usability evaluation using NGOMSL. In M. Helander, T. Landauer, and P. Prabhu (Eds.), *The Handbook of Human-Computer Interaction* (Second Edition), 733–766. Amsterdam: Elsevier Science B.V.

Lang, G., Eberts, R., Gabel, M., and Barash, M. (1991). Extracting and using procedural knowledge in a CAD task. *IEEE Transactions on Engineering Management, 38, 257–68.*

Lemaire P., and Siegler, R. (1995). Four aspects of strategic change: Contributions to children's learning of multiplication. *Journal of Experimental Psychology: General,* 124, 1, 83–97.

Lewis, C., and Mack, R. (1982). Learning to use a text processing system: Evidence from "thinking aloud" protocols. *Proceedings of Human Factors in Computer Systems Conference,* 387–392. Washington, DC: ACM.

Mack, R., Lewis, C., and Carroll, J. (1983). Learning to use word processors: Problems and prospects. *ACM Transactions on Office Information Systems,* 1, 245–271.

Marchionini, G. (1989). Information seeking in electronic encyclopedias, *Machine-Mediated Learning,* 3, 3, 21–26.

Majchrzak, A, Chang, T., Barfield, W., Eberts, R., and Salvendy, G. (1987). *Human Aspects of Computer-Aided Design.* London: Taylor Francis.

Newell, A. (1990). *Unified theories of cognition.* Cambridge: Harvard University Press.

Nilsen, E., Jong. H., Olson J., Biolsi, I., and Mutter, S. (1993). The growth of software skill: A longitudinal look at learning and performance. *Proceedings of INTERCHI'93,* 149–156. New York: ACM.

Olson, J., and Olson, G. (1990). The growth of cognitive modeling in human-computer interaction since GOMS. *Human-Computer Interaction,* 5, 221–265.

Rosson, M. (1983). Patterns of experience in text editing. *Proceedings of the CHI'93 Conference on Human Factors in Computing Systems,* 171–175. New York: ACM.

Siegler, R., and Shipley, C. (1995). Variation, selection, and cognitive change. In G. Halford and T. Simon (Eds.), *Developing cognitive competence: New Approaches to process modeling,* 31–76. Hillsdale, NJ: Erlbaum.

Singley, M., and Anderson, J. (1989). *The transfer of cognitive skill.* Cambridge, MA: Harvard University Press.

Waern, Y. (1985). Learning computerized tasks as related to prior task knowledge. *International Journal of Man-Machine Studies,* 22, 441–455.

6

User Interface Evaluation: How Cognitive Models Can Help

Frank E. Ritter
Gordon D. Baxter
Gary Jones
Richard M. Young

6.1 The Synergy between Cognitive Modeling and HCI

Cognitive models—simulations of human behavior—now perform tasks ranging in complexity from simple mental arithmetic to controlling simulations of complex real-time computer based systems, such as nuclear power plants. In the future these models will become even more powerful and useful.

We describe here an approach for allowing cognitive models[1] more direct access to the interfaces that users see. This is done by adapting ideas taken from user interface management systems (UIMSs) and extending them so that cognitive models can interact with any interface built within the UIMS. This will allow cognitive models to be utilized as an interface design and evaluation tool on a wider range of interactive systems as previously envisioned (Olsen et al. 1993). There are advantages of this approach for human-computer interaction (HCI) and for modeling.

6.1.1 The Advantages for HCI

HCI has used cognitive models successfully in three main ways (John 1998). The first way is to help examine the efficacy of different designs by using cognitive models to

---

[1]Unless otherwise specified, "model" refers to the model of the user, and "simulation" refers to the simulation of the task.

©2000 ACM. Adapted with permission from "Supporting Cognitive Models as Users," *ACM Transactions on Computer-Human Interaction,* Vol. 7, No. 2, June 2000.

predict task performance times (e.g., Sears 1993). The GOMS family of techniques (Card et al. 1983; John and Kieras 1996) particularly have been successfully deployed. These models can help create and choose better designs, sometimes saving millions of dollars (e.g., Gray et al. 1993). The next step is to provide these and more complex models in design tools to provide feedback for designers.

The second way is by using cognitive models to provide assistance, such as with an embedded assistant. In particular, models can be used to modify interaction to help users with their tasks. This technique has been employed in cognitive tutors (Anderson et al. 1995). Some of these model-based tutors can be regarded as an example of what are commonly described as embedded agents or embedded intelligent assistants. The next step is to make the development of such models a more routine process.

The third way is by using models to substitute for users. These models are useful for populating synthetic environments (Pew and Mavor 1998)—for example, to simulate fighter aircraft crews in a simulated war scenario (Jones et al. 1999). In the future they will also lead to models that can test interfaces by behaving like a user. Using models as users has been envisioned before (e.g., Byrne et al. 1994; Lohse 1997) but has not yet been widely applied. The next steps are to provide models with more realistic inputs and outputs mirroring human performance and to apply them more widely.

A real impediment to each of these uses has been the difficulty of connecting the cognitive models to their task environment (Ritter and Major 1995). Either the connection or the interface—or sometimes both—must be built. Further, this connection should mimic the limitations and capabilities of human performance.

6.1.2   The Advantages for Models

Providing models with access to interfaces facilitates further development of the models and will open up new applications and expand existing ones. The main advantage is that the models will gain access to a much wider range of tasks than can be simulated in modeling languages. Early modeling work examined static tasks, keeping track of the task state in the model's head, at least partly because it is difficult to develop a model of an interactive task without providing the model with a capability to interact with an external world (for a review of early models, see Ritter and Larkin 1994). If previous models (e.g., Bauer and John 1995; Howes and Young 1996; John et al. 1994) had been able to use the same interface as the corresponding subjects used, they would have been applied and tested on more tasks and would have been able to cover a wider range of behavior, skills, and knowledge.

Creating a model that is embodied (that is, with perception and motor actions) further constrains the model by restricting it to interact only through its hand and eye. Although the constraints imposed by physical interaction may be relatively small on simple puzzle tasks, they are much more significant on interactive tasks. The models described here incorporate knowledge related to interaction, such as where to look on the interface to find information. The models require a depth and range of knowledge about interaction, predicting that users do, too.

Keeping the task simulation distinct from the cognitive model has three advantages. First, it makes development easier because the model and the simulation can be tested and debugged independently. Second, it makes it less likely that the modeler will unintentionally incorporate assumptions about the task into the cognitive model or about cognition into the task simulation. Third, it makes it easier to use different cognitive models with the same task simulation or to apply the same cognitive model to different tasks. When a model performs a task in its own "mind," it is difficult to reuse the model or the task elsewhere. Where a model is developed that works with one interface, there may be other interfaces to which it can be applied as well.

Working with existing external simulations of tasks can make model development easier because it removes the need to create the task simulation using cognitive modeling languages, which is a difficult activity. There is less development required because only one interface has to be created and updated if the model (or others) suggest changes. There is also less question about whether the model and the subject had access to the same material. Several of the case studies use simulations that already existed, thus relieving the modeler from developing the task simulation.

Finally, this approach leads to theory accumulation. In the examples we describe later, the models are developed using a cognitive architecture (Newell 1990), also referred to as an integrated architecture (Pew and Mavor 1998) when interaction is included. Cognitive architectures are theories of the common modules and mechanisms that support human cognition. They are typically realized as a programming language specifically designed for modeling, such as Soar (Newell 1990) or ACT-R (Anderson and Lebiere 1998). Cognitive architectures offer a platform for developing cognitive models rapidly while still maintaining theoretical coherence between the models.

Although there are tools to develop user interfaces and there are tools that help develop cognitive models, there are none that support connecting cognitive models to a wide range of interfaces. In the rest of this chapter we develop an approach to allow cognitive models access to the same user interfaces as users. Section 6.2 describes the cognitive modeling process and introduces the concept of a cognitive model interface management system (CMIMS). Section 6.3 describes examples where models perform interactive tasks using the same type of simulated eye and hand implemented in different interface tools and modeling languages. These examples, when considered together with a review of related systems, suggest possible applications and indicate where further work is necessary. Section 6.4 assesses the implications of these projects and identifies ways in which integrated models could be exploited in the development of user interfaces.

6.2   A Route to Supporting Models as Users

The cognitive modeling process is unique in many respects, although the artifacts created by it are similar to products generated during the development of interactive software applications. We examine here the cognitive modeling process and introduce an approach to supporting cognitive models as users.

6.2.1 The Artifacts of the Cognitive Modeling Process

The cognitive modeling process, particularly as applied to the interactive tasks examined here, attempts to produce a cognitive model that performs like a human. The veracity of the cognitive model is tested by comparing its performance with human performance. The differences between the two are analyzed to understand why they occur, and then the cognitive model is appropriately refined, in an iterative cycle (Ritter and Larkin 1994).

The cognitive modeling process can be viewed as producing three artifacts, each of which fulfills a particular purpose. The first artifact is the cognitive model itself, which simulates the cognitive performance and behavior of a human performing the task. As theory, it has primacy.

The second artifact is a task application or its simulation. Simple, static task applications, such as small puzzles like the Tower of Hanoi where the state of the task normally changes only in response to the user's actions, can often be implemented using the cognitive modeling language. Dynamic tasks, however, where the state of the environment can evolve without outside intervention, are best implemented separately. Where the original task is computer based, the simplest and most accurate approach is to allow the model to use the original task environment.

The third artifact is a mechanism that supports interaction between the model and the task simulation. It simulates human perception and action and provides a way for the model and simulation to communicate. The need for this linkage mechanism is most apparent in tasks in which the cognitive model has to interact with a task simulation implemented as a separate program.

There are existing tools that support the development of cognitive models and of task applications. There are few tools, however, that support the creation of the type of linkage mechanism required in cognitive modeling. UIMSs are good candidates to build on.[2]

6.2.2 The Role of User Interface Management Systems

To provide models with access to the same interfaces as users, perhaps the best place to start is to consider tools used to develop user interfaces. In interactive software applications, the communication between the user interface and the underlying application is often implemented as a separate component. This component consists of a set of functions that provide a robust, uniform way of connecting the two. Cognitive models also require a set of capabilities that allow them to interact with the task

---

[2]An alternative linkage mechanism is to recognize objects directly from the screen (Zettlemoyer and St. Amant 1999; St. Amant and Riedl 2001).

simulation but can be modified to approximate human limitations and capabilities. Any initial considerations for a toolkit to support the cognitive modeling process will therefore need to incorporate (1) a tool to create interfaces, (2) a run-time mechanism that lets the cognitive model interact with the task simulation (a model eye and hand), and (3) a communication mechanism that passes information between the cognitive model and the task simulation.

UIMSs provide a similar set of features for the development of interactive applications, supporting interface creation and helping to manage the interaction when the interface is used (Myers 1995). UIMSs can be used to create interfaces and applications in their implementation language or interfaces that are tied to external applications. By definition UIMSs provide a set of features that very closely match our requirements.

UIMSs also offer a way to apply this work widely. They are designed to create multiple interfaces. Working within a UIMS will lead to the models being able to use any interface created with the UIMS.

6.2.3   Cognitive Model Interface Management Systems

The approach we are creating by extending a UIMS to support models as users can be described as a Cognitive Model Interface Management System (CMIMS), a system for managing the interactions of a cognitive model analogous to how a UIMS manages a user's interactions. The name CMIMS reflects the parallels with UIMSs, particularly the parallel needs between (human) users and cognitive models.

Figure 6.1 depicts a CMIMS, showing the functional aspects of tying together a task simulation and a cognitive model. On the left of the figure is the user interface of a task simulation and on the right is the cognitive model. The first step in getting the model to interact with the task simulation is to extend the cognitive model to be a more complete model of the user by adding a simulated eye and a simulated hand to provide the model with capabilities for perception and action. We have found that the simulated eye and hand are best implemented in the same environment as the task simulation. The simulated eye needs access to the visible task objects (to the objects in the display) to create descriptions for the cognitive model, and the simulated hand needs to be able to implement the model's actions in the environment. UIMSs provide facilities that support these functional capabilities. In particular, in UIMSs there are tools to find which objects occlude other objects (such as the simulated eye being over a textual label on the display), the capability to send mouse and keyboard actions to the interface, and the ability to create displays and control panels.

The second step is to link the cognitive model to the simulation, so the model's eye can observe the simulation and pass back information to the cognitive model and the model's hand can pass actions to the simulation. The end result is a model of a user in contact with a task environment, where information about the environment and actions on the environment are conveyed and constrained by the simulated eye and hand.

The resulting configuration is shown in the linked boxes across the middle of Figure 6.1. The model of the user is now split into two parts, with the simulated eye and hand implemented in the same software environment as the simulation, while the cognitive model is separate. Interaction between the model and simulated eye and hand occurs via a communication mechanism. The details of the mechanism will vary depending on implementation language and machine choice. Incorporating the simulated eye and hand into the UIMS potentially allows them to interact with any interface in the UIMS. Thus, it provides models with routine access to interfaces.

The arrows underneath the boxes represent the scope of the various tools. Particularly where the user's task involves interaction with a computer interface, the task simulation is well supported by standard UIMSs. The dashed extension to the UIMS arrow denotes that the facilities needed to implement the eye and hand can usually be based on existing facilities in the UIMS. However, the simulated eye and hand place requirements that not all UIMSs or related systems currently satisfy.

Next, the CMIMS arrow reflects our suggestion for the development of Cognitive Modeling Interface Management Systems. A CMIMS would need to include the simulated eye and hand, as well as the communication mechanism between them and the cognitive model.

Architectures will differ in how they represent and use the results of vision and how they prepare to perform motor output. For all of the architectures, however, visual search is required to find information to examine, the amount of information available at any point is limited, and performing visual search takes time. Similar restrictions apply to the motor output.

In the far left of Figure 6.1, the circle labeled *User* indicates that the cognitive model can work with the same task interface as users. This feature supports gathering data to test the model. This feature also indicates that the user can perform the task, with the model serving as a helper or agent within the user's interface.

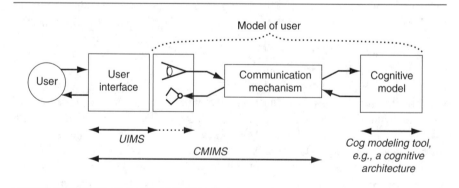

FIGURE 6.1 A cognitive model tied to a user interface of a task simulation, where the model and the simulation may be running in different environments (programming languages, processes, and/or computers). The hand and eye are implemented in the same UIMS as the task simulation.

6.2.4   A Functional Model Eye and Hand

The Sim-eye and Sim-hand[3] are the most important parts of the CMIMS. They bring the model into contact with the interface. We have created an initial set of functional capabilities and empirical regularities on which to base models of interaction (Ritter et al. 2000). With each additional refinement of the implementation, the models have had more capabilities and have exhibited more of the regularities.

These capabilities and regularities, such as the size of visual acuity and the speed of motor movements, were identified as important for an initial model of interaction, based on a literature review (Baxter and Ritter 1996). These capabilities are fundamental necessities to support interaction, and the regularities are the most important constraints on performance.

Models exhibiting a greater number of empirical regularities can be created with these capabilities. This could, for example, include relative recognition rates of different colors. The most important point is first to support the process of providing cognitive models access to interfaces in UIMSs by providing these functional capabilities. Providing functional capabilities first and then modifying the Sim-eye and Sim-hand to match more empirical regularities has proved to be a useful development strategy. For example, by giving the Sim-eye and Sim-hand visible representations, the modeler can observe their behavior on the display screen and use these observations to refine the implementations and use of the Sim-eye and Sim-hand.

The Sim-eye and Sim-hand are controlled by the model through a simple command language. The Sim-eye can be moved around the display using the saccade command to move the eye and can inspect what appears at the current location on the display using the fixate command. The saccade and fixate commands are implemented using functions in the UIMS for handling mouse actions, manipulating display objects, and drawing. Once implemented, the Sim-eye can see (access) every object on interfaces built within that UIMS, provided that the UIMS uses a regular representation of objects that can be accessed at run time. Users and the model see the same display (to the limit of the theory of vision implemented in the Sim-eye).

The Sim-hand also has a set of commands that allow the model to move its mouse around the display and to perform mouse actions, such as press-mouse-button, release-mouse-button, and so on. The Sim-hand implementation will vary based on the UIMS's relationship to its operating system.

In our models, which do not look at very rapid interaction, cognition generates an interaction command and then waits for the perceptual and motor operations to complete. While our models have used these capabilities in a synchronous way, this design allows cognition and interaction to occur in parallel.

---

[3] In order to emphasise the distinction between the model's capabilities and human capabilities, we refer to the model's implementation of visual perception as the Sim-eye, and the model's implementation of motor action as the Sim-hand.

We next examine how this functional model of interaction can support models as users. The case studies presented in the next section show that it is possible to create CMIMSs and the advantages in so doing.

6.3 Example Cognitive Models That Perform Interactive Tasks

We have created a series of cognitive models that interact with task simulations. We present here examples developed using tools that can be described as UIMSs. Two further examples are available that use a Tcl/Tk-based CMIMS to model dialing a variety of telephones (Harris 1999; Lonsdale and Ritter 2000) and exploratory search in interfaces (Ritter et al. 2000). A different set of examples would yield a different set of lessons, but we believe they would be only slightly different. We see many commonalities across this diverse set. We also review some similar systems that model interaction.

6.3.1 A Simplified Air Traffic Control Model

The first task simulation is a simplified air traffic control (ATC) task (Bass et al. 1995). It was designed to explore how to create a general eye and investigate what a model would do with an eye. Such a model could also help support the user by predicting what they would do and then to either assist them or do it for them.

We had access to ATC task simulators but not to one that we could have our model interact with, let alone interact in a psychologically plausible way. A task simulation had to be developed, therefore, to allow the task to be performed both by the cognitive model and by users. The user interface, shown in Figure 6.2, is a simplified version of an air traffic controller's display screen. It includes some of the standard features that would appear on a real controller's screen, such as range rings. The current position of the aircraft is indicated by a track symbol (a solid white square) that has an associated data block depicting the aircraft identifier (cx120), its heading (135°), its speed (150 knots), and its altitude in hundreds of feet (so 200 represents 20,000 feet).

The simulation is a simplified version of approach air traffic control up to the point where aircraft would normally be handed over to ground controllers. So, for example, when an aircraft is directed to change its heading, the turning time is not based on a detailed aircraft model. The task simulation does, however, provide facilities that allow the model to control the behavior of the aircraft by instructing it to change its speed, heading, and altitude. When an aircraft comes close enough to the airport, it is removed from the display and tagged as landed.

The basic task involves learning how to direct a single aircraft to land at an airport located at the center of the display. The choice of flight path is based on finding and reading the wind speed and direction. The aircraft has to be guided along a flight path identified by a number of way markers, which appear on the screen as crosses. A crucial element of the task is that change of heading commands must be issued at the appropriate time, which requires that the cognitive model be able to detect when an aircraft is approaching a way marker.

The simulation was implemented using the Garnet UIMS (Myers et al. 1990), chosen because it was familiar and provides fairly general support for creating interfaces. The model was implemented in Soar (Newell 1990).

6.3.1.1 Visual Perception and Action

The Sim-eye was implemented as part of the user interface developed within Garnet. The visible representation of the Sim-eye's data structure consists of a transparent rectangle outlined in white (representing the area of the screen that would normally project onto the fovea of a real eye, the area of most acute vision). When a fixate command is sent by the model, the details of the objects appearing inside the foveal rectangle are sent back to the cognitive model as symbolic descriptions. This Sim-eye includes a coarse level of vision outside the fovea, only providing to cognition the location of objects that appear outside the fovea. The Sim-eye is moved around the ATC display window (center left in Figure 6.2) by the model placing saccade commands to be processed into the Soar-IO facility. When the Sim-eye saccades, previous visual elements are removed from cognition, a plausible aspect of visual input (Horowitz and Wolfe 1998).

The Sim-hand was initially implemented as simple function calls to the task simulation via the Soar-IO facility. Later, a Sim-hand (Rassouli 1995) was included. The revised version of the ATC cognitive model helped to illustrate two of the difficulties involved in modeling task interaction: (1) Some eye-hand coordination knowledge is needed, and further work needs to be done to explore the best way to gather this from subjects and include it in models, and (2) there is an opportunity to gather and include additional regularities about visual attention, including those relating to mouse movements, such as moving the mouse to a flashing light or object.

6.3.1.2 The Communication Mechanism

The communication mechanism is implemented by a system called MONGSU (Ong 1994), based on UNIX sockets. It allows any pair of Lisp or C-based processes to communicate using list structures and attribute-value pairs.

6.3.1.3 Summary

The ATC model demonstrated that a simple but functional Sim-eye could be created using an existing UIMS. This model used knowledge that has not often been seen in a cognitive model: where to look and how to visually monitor. Knowledge about the ATC display had to be included in the cognitive model because when and where to look at the screen is domain dependent.

Moving the Sim-eye around to see objects on the display slowed down the performance of the model because it had to work to get information—all the problem information was not resident in the model. The model had to find both the wind heading

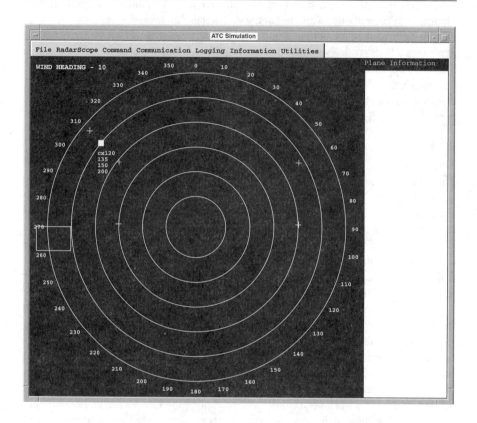

FIGURE 6.2   The ATC simulation display showing the model's fovea (the white rectangle on the left-hand side of the figure) before it moves to the plane labeled "cx120".

and the plane, by using its peripheral vision. Surprising to us at the time, but quite clear in hindsight, is that the eye is not just the fovea. The periphery is needed even for simple search; otherwise the model has tunnel vision and must carefully scan the entire screen with its fovea. So an apparently trivial task became an intricate process, involving its own level of problem solving and search based on the external interface. These behaviors suggest that knowledge acquisition studies of expert performance should not just examine what experts do but must also examine what they look for and where and when they look.

The symbolic descriptions returned upon a fixation are based on the graphical object hierarchy in Garnet. It is easy to create a general Sim-eye when all the objects to be recognized are part of a hierarchy.

The use of sockets as a communication mechanism added an extra layer of complexity because it required the modeler to run two processes instead of one. Establishing a connection that is external in some way is also more prone to human and network errors than working within a single process.

6.3.2   Tower of Nottingham Model

The Tower of Nottingham is a puzzle where wooden blocks are assembled to form a pyramid of five different-size layers, each comprising four blocks of the same size with one pinnacle block. It has been used extensively to study how children's abilities to learn and communicate develop.

The extensive interactive nature of this model and its task, including learning while searching, is a fairly useful, simple way to explore some of the important and common issues in interaction in many screen-based manipulation tasks. The model's and subjects' visual search and object manipulations in service of problem solving are analogous to manipulation in graphical user interfaces and to some aspects of graphic design in drawing and CAD/CAM packages.

The blocks simulation was written in Garnet. The complexity of the task precludes simulating the task with a cognitive modeling language. The model was written using the ACT-R (v. 3.0) cognitive architecture (Anderson and Lebiere 1998), although an earlier model was in Lisp.

6.3.2.1   Visual Perception and Motor Action

The task simulation, shown in Figure 6.3, includes a Sim-eye and a pair of Sim-hands represented graphically, which makes its behavior readily visible. The Sim-eye and Sim-hand are controlled using commands similar to the ATC system's commands, particularly moving the Sim-eye to a location and fixating upon that location, and moving the Sim-hands. The command language was extended to enable the Sim-hands to grasp, release, and rotate blocks. Although this level of representation is more abstract than mouse movements, it represents the atomic cognitive actions in this task, allowing the model and the modeler to represent interaction in an appropriate way.

When the Sim-eye is requested to fixate, it passes back to the model the relevant blocks and block features as moderated by the area of the eye the blocks project onto. There is a small difference between the level of information available from the Sim-eye's fovea and parafovea. The features and sizes of blocks in the fovea are reported accurately, and those in the parafovea are subject to a small, adjustable amount of noise. This mechanism provides a way to mistake blocks that have similar sizes and similar features.

Once an action is completed, the cognitive model is informed. The model can then manipulate the Sim-eye to verify the results. Although actions are currently always completed successfully, it is especially useful for the Sim-eye to fixate when fitting

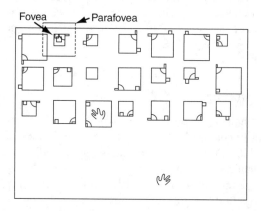

FIGURE 6.3 The Tower of Nottingham. The fovea is the small black outlined square in the center of the block, second from the left in the top row. The parafovea, shown with dashed side lines, extends approximately two fovea widths in each direction beyond the fovea. The left Sim-hand has picked up one of the largest blocks.

blocks together or disassembling block structures because this can change the model's representation of the current state of the task.

The model thus predicts that some mistakes are caught before they are executed. The features of blocks in the parafovea are not always correctly seen. If a block is incorrectly seen as having the target features when it is in the parafovea, the eye will saccade to the block to prepare to pick it up, and the hand will move to the block as well. When the block image is located in the fovea, the features will be seen correctly, and the action abandoned. This behavior of moving hands to blocks but not picking them up seems to occur in adults and suggests there are types of mistakes that are not fully overt. This type of mistake is likely to occur for adults using interfaces as well.

6.3.2.2 The Communication Mechanism

Interaction between the cognitive model and the task simulation uses Lisp function calls because both are based on Common Lisp. The cognitive model sets up a goal in ACT-R for each interaction it wishes to perform. Each goal causes the appropriate function for the Sim-eye or the selected Sim-hand to be called. When the interaction is complete, the relevant goal in the cognitive model is noted as achieved. The model can then terminate the goal and continue its behavior.

6.3.2.3 Summary

This case study further indicates that the Sim-hand and Sim-eye are generally applicable and that they can be used by a different cognitive architecture—in this case, ACT-R. Using a common language for the model and the task simulation makes them easier to implement, test, and run.

The importance of perception in task performance that had been found in the ATC model was confirmed. Explicitly controlling the Sim-eye and Sim-hands changed the model's behavior. Including perception and explicit motor actions forced the model to expend time and effort to find and assemble blocks. The performance of the model matches the performance of adult subjects on the task reasonably well because the whole task was modeled and the necessary learning could occur in visual search, in cognition, and in output. The model spent approximately half of its time interacting with the simulation, suggesting that any model for a task involving interaction requires an external task in order to accurately reflect human behavior.

We were able to examine more closely how problem solving develops. Several important developmental theories were implemented in the model, and their predictions were compared with children's data, showing that a change in strategy choice is the most likely candidate for what develops in children (Jones et al. 2000).

6.3.3   Electronic Warfare Task Model

The final example is a simulated eye and hand in SLGMS, an object-oriented, real-time dynamic UIMS. Tenet Systems, the UK sales agency for SLGMS, developed the Sim-eye and Sim-hand under our direction. They had access to the SLGMS source code, which is necessary for developing a CMIMS. The design and, to the best of our knowledge, the implementation, allows the model to interact with any SLGMS interface.

In the upper window of Figure 6.4 there is a simplified interface that was used to develop and test the Sim-eye and Sim-hand. In the lower window is a control panel based on what we learned from the Tcl/Tk models (Ritter et al. 2000). The control panel displays the current state of the Sim-eye and Sim-hand, making debugging easier because the state is visible and the Sim-eye and Sim-hand can be manipulated prior to programming the model.

6.3.3.1   Visual Perception and Motor Action

The Sim-eye was extended to provide perception of objects located in parafoveal and peripheral vision with several configurable options to facilitate theory development, such as fovea size and how shape and color interact to attract attention. By default, the detail provided for objects appearing in the parafovea is less than that of objects appearing in the fovea but greater than that of objects appearing in the periphery. Only a few features like location and motion are available for peripheral objects, whereas shape, color, orientation, size, and location are available for foveal objects. There were many new types of objects in this task, so this implementation allowed for the eye to be appropriately adjusted based on further relevant experimental or published information. The commands to manipulate the Sim-eye and Sim-hand are the same as in previous examples.

6.3.3.2   The Communication Mechanism

The connection between the cognitive model and the task simulation is based on the ideas in the MONGSU interprocess communication utility that we used in the ATC

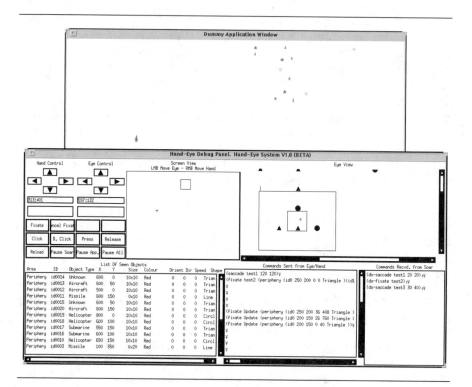

FIGURE 6.4   The Dummy Application Window is a simple test application. The control panel includes controls (upper left of this window) for the Sim-eye and Sim-hand and continuing along its top, two displays showing the current position (screen view) and detailed contents of the fovea (eye view). Along the bottom are listings of objects sent from the eye to the model and the commands in each direction sent through the linkage mechanism. Normally these two windows are displayed on separate monitors.

example. The cognitive model is being implemented in Soar (v. 7.1), which incorporates Tcl/Tk and hence provides built-in commands to manage socket communication.

6.3.3.3 Summary

We have learned several lessons. First, the transfer of the general Sim-eye and Sim-hand design to another development environment provided further evidence of the generality of this design. The Sim-eye and Sim-hand were implemented in SL-GMS in just two weeks, demonstrating that CMIMSs can be quickly understood and implemented by others.

Using two separate display screens, with the simulation (driven by the cognitive model) on one screen and the control panel (driven by the modeler) on the other, solves several problems. During debugging there is a need for the modeler to be able to view the interaction control panel and the task simulation simultaneously. By using a dedicated display screen, the control panel can be extended to incorporate additional debugging facilities. Using separate screens allows the cognitive model to control the Sim-hand's mouse pointer on one screen, while the modeler has control of the mouse pointer for the control panel on the other screen. Without this capability the modeler cannot query the model while it runs, and the model and modeler come into conflict trying to use the same mouse.

An initial model of a corresponding radar task with this display was implemented in Soar before the Sim-eye and Sim-hand implementations became available. None of the model's 70 production rules scan the display or perform interaction. It is clear that interacting with the interface in Figure 6.4 will profoundly change the model's task from a geometry task of computing intercept angles to a scanning and monitoring task with geometry as only a subcomponent.

6.3.4   Related Systems

Other examples where models interact with simulations provide further lessons. The related systems presented here have used three UIMSs and typically can present displays on more than one type of machine. The simulation languages are usually closely tied to the UIMS.

The Soar agent simulations (Jones et al. 1999), which support large-scale military training exercises, and MIDAS (Corker and Smith 1993), which is a design tool for aviation systems that includes a model user, interact directly with simulations without a perceptual/motor filter via function calls for actions and data structures for perception. This approach to interaction has the following advantages: It is easy to implement, it is not tied to a specific cognitive architecture, and, most importantly, it can quickly provide a rich environment and task for the models. Interacting through simple function calls, however, fails to provide as much constraint on cognition as interacting with a Sim-eye and Sim-hand. In this approach as well, humans cannot necessarily use the same systems, which reduces the ability to test and validate the models.

The models and simulations in APEX and Driver-Soar illustrate some of the possible applications and results that are available from employing models as surrogate users. APEX (Freed and Remington 1998; 2000) is a design tool to predict errors in complex domains. It has been applied to air traffic control systems and cockpits. It provides cognitive models in its own architecture, simulated eyes and hands, and a communication mechanism between them. It is not based on a UIMS, but modelers can see the interface. APEX starts to model the effects of interaction, how visual displays can support problem solving, and how errors can arise in air traffic control. It is limited in the types of tasks that can be examined, however.

Driver-Soar (Aasman and Michon 1992) is a detailed model of driving that interacts with a software car to navigate through simulated road intersections. In addition to a simulated eye, Driver-Soar includes interaction modalities not addressed here, including head movements, further hand movements, and feet movements. These interaction modalities are implemented both in a Pascal-based and a Lisp-based simulation. While there are displays for modelers to watch the model's behavior, users cannot interact with the simulation in the same way. Driver-Soar's predictions have been compared with detailed human measurements, showing that such predictions can be quite accurate.

EPIC (Kieras and Meyer 1997) is a system addressing the intricate details of perception and action. Cognitive models are written using EPIC's own production system and communicate directly with a model eye and hand that interact with an interface simulator. Interfaces to be examined are implemented separately using a special production system to provide information to the model at either set times or upon set conditions. Later versions access a visual display shared with users. EPIC can be used to make accurate predictions of interaction behavior such as menu use. Some of EPIC's capabilities and the regularities they support have been used by Soar models (Chong and Laird 1997) and by ACT-R/PM (Byrne and Anderson 1998).

The only other system that we are aware of that could properly be described as a CMIMS is ACT-R/PM (Byrne 1999; 2001). It is a theory of perception and motor behavior realized in Macintosh Common Lisp. It provides an environment in which ACT-R models can interact with task simulations (psychological experiments, for example) that humans can use as well. The interaction is modeled on a detailed level, down to 50 ms (we have neither designed nor tested our functional models for this level of precision). The generality and utility of the ACT-R/PM analysis of perception and action has been demonstrated through multiple use by models (Byrne and Anderson 1998; Byrne 2001; and multiple examples in Taatgen and Aasman 2000).

ACT-R/PM is similar in many ways to the previous models of interaction we have built. We believe that part of the reason for the success of ACT-R/PM is that it provides the facilities required by a basic CMIMS. The ACT-R/PM model of perception is based on graphical objects in Macintosh Common Lisp so it can include a graphic display that can be seen by the modeler and used by subjects. Furthermore, its reuse—the incorporation and adaptation of some of EPIC's results, particularly the general structure (parallel execution of perception and action) and the motor component—are consistent with the approach of theory reuse that we advocate.

The major difference, if there is one, lies in the choice of priorities. ACT-R/PM is more concerned with detailed psychological predictions, but it is not yet positioned to be a tool that can be widely used to develop user interfaces for two reasons: (1) ACT-R/PM was not designed to interact with every interface that can be built in Macintosh Common Lisp (Byrne and Anderson 1998). However, it can already recognize most objects and can be extended by the modeler. (2) ACT-R/PM is not in a major graphic interface tool. In the context of Figure 6.1, it provides a linkage mechanism to a good UIMS but not a common or widely portable UIMS.

Some of these systems are more accurate and allow cognition and interaction to occur in parallel. Often, they have not put development effort into their own usability and have not used more general UIMSs (such as SLGMS, Tcl/Tk, or Visual Basic). With time, these approaches will converge because they only represent different development priorities. None of the developers would argue, we believe, that accuracy or the model's own usability are unimportant.

6.3.5   Limitations of This Approach

There are several limitations to the current generation of systems that could be classed as CMIMSs. The examples presented here cover only a small subset of all possible tasks and interfaces. As a functional model, these implementations of the Sim-eye and Sim-hand intentionally do not cover all that is known about interaction, nor do they include all forms of interaction. These models do not yet include fine-grained behavioral regularities or those that are based on emergent perceptual phenomena—for example, recognizing blank space as a region. When we have used these Sim-eyes and Sim-hands more, we will be in a better position to know where we need to extend the accuracy of perception and motor actions. In certain tasks, having a simpler representation of behavior may be useful (for example, checking the function of an interface, qualitative learning effects) in the way that Newtonian mechanics is compared with quantum mechanics.

The problem most often raised with respect to using models to test interfaces is that the interface must be completely specified before the model can be applied. There are several responses to this limitation. First, the limitation does not appear to be insuperable, but it would be an entirely separate project to apply models to sketchy designs (Szekely et al. 1993). Second, there are many systems and approaches requiring a full design before their analysis can be done. Interfaces may be particularly prone to requiring a full specification before their use and efficiency can be estimated (Gray and Boehm-Davis 2000). Third, our approach will put designers in touch with the limitations of users in testing preliminary designs. With experience, the designers may learn to avoid problems based on their experience with the model user. Finally, tests of the interface are immediately informative and problems can be directly rectified. An unusual advantage of this approach to testing interfaces is that unlike electrical circuits, testing can be done with the actual system.

6.4   Cognitive Models as Users in the New Millennium

Supporting cognitive models as surrogate users is possible. The case studies show that Sim-eyes and Sim-hands can be used by a variety of models interacting with a range of interface tools. It is now possible to routinely apply theoretically grounded cognitive models to real world HCI tasks. In this section we review the approach, noting how it can contribute to the development of cognitive models and what it means for the future of interfaces.

Building a Sim-eye and Sim-hand for each computational cognitive model might be as ad hoc as building each new model in Lisp—you could lose the constraints imposed by an integrated cognitive architecture. Here, eyes and hands have been built in several UIMSs from the same design. This reimplementation of the same approach provides a form of constraint because the design is reused and the capabilities and regularities are noted explicitly. A more important aspect is that the Sim-eye and Sim-hand are now available in several widely used software tools, so reuse should be a real possibility in the future.

Modelers should use these Sim-eyes and Sim-hands to provide their models with an interactive capability. ACT-R/PM's hand is available at www.ruf.rice.edu/~byrne/ RPM/; the Tcl/Tk eye/hand will be available at ritter.ist.psu.edu. Similarly, newer cognitive architectures should provide at least one CMIMS for their models.

Authors of interface design tools and of UIMSs should include support for cognitive models as users. The functional capabilities and experimental requirements noted here and elsewhere (Baxter and Ritter 1996; Ritter et al. 2000) show what is necessary to support cognitive models as a type of user and some of the experimental regularities that can be included. This list will help create models of interaction in other UIMSs.

6.4.1   Implications for Models

The models presented here would not have been possible to develop without access to external simulations. The models are far more complex because they interact with tasks that are too complex to simulate in a cognitive modeling language.

Including a theory of interaction has both provided models with more capabilities and also constrained the speed and abilities of the models in a way approximating human behavior. CMIMSs provide a way to encapsulate these constraints. Interaction has required adding new knowledge and new types of knowledge to the models, including where to look and what to do with what they see. This result suggests that there are types of knowledge (e.g., visual knowledge) that the user has to know that are not often taught or referenced. When users do not know where to look, they have to search through the interface using peripheral vision. The amount of knowledge and effort it typically takes the models to interact suggest that the difficulty of what users have to do has been consistently underestimated. Including interaction thus helps make more complete cognitive architectures and models.

The case studies show that this approach supports several kinds of reuse. Multiple models can use the same interface (for example, through the Sim-eye and Sim-hand with the Tower of Nottingham simulation). The same model can use multiple interfaces (such as the Soar phone model; Lonsdale and Ritter 2000). Models as well as users can work with the same interface (for example, the ATC task). This approach will contribute to the reuse of models envisioned for cognitive architectures (Newell 1990) and provide a further constraint on architectures.

There are several other systems that model interaction. The approach to modeling interactive tasks that we have adopted falls somewhere between the extremes of allowing models to directly access the internals of the task simulation and modeling interaction in full psychological detail. Focusing on functional capabilities has allowed us to apply this technique widely, but the next step will be to incorporate more experimental regularities to model human performance more closely. Enforcing further experimental regularities (as summarized in ACT-R/PM and EPIC) on the functional capabilities we have created in Tcl/Tk would provide a system that both people and Soar could use and one that has numerous existing interfaces and tasks.

6.4.2   Implications for Interfaces

There are at least two significant ways in which CMIMSs can be used to facilitate the improvement of user interfaces. First, cognitive models can be used to evaluate user interfaces. By using cognitive models in place of people, we could start to ask what-if questions about user interfaces, such as changing the interface and examining the effects on task performance. Models of phone interaction are now capable of this (Lonsdale and Ritter 2000; Salvucci 2001). It becomes possible to dynamically evaluate *how* an interface is used and note where important events such as errors may occur (Freed and Remington 1998). Cognitive models of interface use, such as IDXL (Rieman et al. 1996) and the other models of problem solving and task performance we have described, could be developed further and applied. The models can also be used to inform the design of user interfaces by indicating which parts of the interface are used the most or are hard to learn.

Second, the ability to tie more accurate user models to interfaces opens up a range of applications, such as more accurate intelligent assistants to help novices. With the interaction process in hand, it will allow more time to be spent developing the models. Models used as embedded assistants would encapsulate knowledge about a new range of possible behaviors—that is, interaction. This knowledge would then be used to determine what the user should do next and provide appropriate assistance to the user when requested or if the user selected an inappropriate course of action.

Although there is a synergy between the disciplines of HCI and cognitive modeling, it has not yet been fully exploited. Several results and techniques in HCI have been discovered using cognitive modeling (John 1998), but few of the lessons from HCI have been reapplied to increase the understanding and application of the models. We have highlighted one particular area where we believe UIMSs can be exploited to help in the development of cognitive models. It will take time to learn how to take advantage of all the benefits that come through supporting cognitive models as users, but it will provide a new way to test interfaces.

Acknowledgments

Support has been provided by DERA and by the UK ESRC Centre for Research in Development, Instruction and Training. The views expressed in this chapter are those of the authors and should not be attributed to the UK Ministry of Defence. In addition to the authors and those cited, we would like to thank Joe Mertz, Josef Nerb, Sarah Nichols, Gary Pelton, Paul Hall, and David Webb, who have helped implement these examples. We thank Jans Aasman, Erik Altmann, Paul Bennett, Michael Byrne, Wayne Gray, Steve Sawyer, and several anonymous reviewers for comments.

References

Aasman, J., and Michon, J.A. (1992). Multitasking in driving. In J.A. Michon and A. Akyürek (Eds.), *Soar: A cognitive architecture in perspective.* Dordrecht, The Netherlands: Kluwer.

Anderson, J.R., Corbett, A.T., Koedinger, K.R., and Pelletier, R. (1995). Cognitive tutors: Lessons learned. *Journal of the Learning Sciences,* 4, 2, 167–207.

Anderson, J.R., and Lebière, C. (1998). *The atomic components of thought.* Mahwah, NJ: Lawrence Erlbaum.

Bass, E.J., Baxter, G.D., and Ritter, F.E. (1995). Creating cognitive models to control simulations of complex systems. *AISB Quarterly,* 93, 18–25.

Bauer, M.I., and John, B.E. (1995). Modeling time-constrained learning in a highly interactive task. In I.R. Katz, R. Mack, and L. Marks (Eds.), *Proceedings of the CHI'95 Conference on Human Factors in Computer Systems,* 19–26. New York, NY: ACM Press.

Baxter, G.D., and Ritter, F.E. (1996). Designing abstract visual perceptual and motor action capabilities for use by cognitive models (Tech. Report No. 36). ESRC CREDIT, Psychology, U. of Nottingham.

Byrne, M.D. (2001). ACT-R/PM and menu selection: Applying a cognitive architecture to HCI. *International Journal of Human-Computer Studies,* 55, 41–84.

Byrne, M.D. (1999). ACT-R Perceptual-Motor (ACT-R/PM) version 1.0b5: A user's manual. Houston, TX: Psychology Department, Rice University. Available at http://www.ruf.rice.edu/~byrne/RPM/project.html.

Byrne, M.D., and Anderson, J.R. (1998). Perception and action. In J.R. Anderson and C. Lebière (Eds.), *The atomic components of thought.* Mahwah, NJ: Lawrence Erlbaum.

Byrne, M.D., Wood, S.D., Sukaviriya, P., Foley, J.D., and Kieras, D.E. (1994). Automating interface evaluation. In *Proceedings of the CHI'94 Conference on Human Factors in Computer Systems,* 232–237. New York: ACM.

Card, S., Moran, T., and Newell, A. (1983). *The psychology of human-computer interaction.* Hillsdale, NJ: Lawrence Erlbaum.

Chong, R.S., and Laird, J.E. (1997). Identifying dual-task executive process knowledge using EPIC-Soar. In *Proceedings of the 19th Annual Conference of the Cognitive Science Society,* 107–112. Mahwah, NJ: Lawrence Erlbaum.

Corker, K.M., and Smith, B.R. (1993). An architecture and model for cognitive engineering simulation analysis: Application to advanced aviation automation. In *Proceedings of the AIAA Computing in Aerospace 9 Conference.* San Diego, CA: AIAA.

Freed, M., and Remington, R. (2000). Making human-machine system simulation a practical engineering tool: An APEX overview. In N. Taatgen and J. Aasman (Eds.), *Proceedings of the 3rd International Conference on Cognitive Modelling.* 110–117. Veenendaal, The Netherlands: Universal Press.

Freed, M., and Remington, R. (1998). A conceptual framework for predicting error in complex human-machine environments. In M.A. Gernsbacker and S.J. Derry (Eds.), *Proceedings of the 20th Annual Conference of the Cognitive Science Society,* 356–361. Mahwah, NJ: Lawrence Erlbaum.

Gray, W.D., John, B.E., and Atwood, M.E. (1993). Project Ernestine: Validating a GOMS analysis for predicting and explaining real-world task performance. *Human-Computer Interaction,* 8(3), 237–309.

Gray, W.D., and Boehm-Davis, D.A. (2000). Milliseconds matter: An introduction to microstrategies and their use in describing and predicting interactive behavior. *Journal of Experimental Psychology: Applied,* 6, 4, 322–335.

Harris, B. (1999). *PracTCL: An application for routinely tying cognitive models to interfaces to create interactive cognitive user models.* BSc thesis, Psychology, U. of Nottingham.

Horowitz, T.S., and Wolfe, J.M. (1998). Visual search has no memory. *Nature,* 357, 575–577.

Howes, A., and Young, R.M. (1996). Learning consistent, interactive, and meaningful task-action mappings: A computational model. *Cognitive Science,* 20(3), 301–356.

John, B.E. (1998). Cognitive modeling for human-computer interaction. In *Proceedings of Graphics Interface '98,* 161–167. Vancouver, BC: Morgan Kaufman.

John, B.E., and Kieras, D.E. (1996). Using GOMS for user interface design and evaluation: Which technique? *ACM Transactions on Computer-Human Interaction,* 3(4), 287–319.

John, B.E., Vera, A.H., and Newell, A. (1994). Towards real-time GOMS: A model of expert behavior in a highly interactive task. *Behavior and Information Technology,* 13, 255–267.

Jones, G., Ritter, F.E., and Wood, D.J. (2000). Using a cognitive architecture to examine what develops. *Psychological Science,* 11(2), 1–8.

Jones, R.M., Laird, J.E., Nielsen, P.E., Coulter, K.J., Kenny, P., and Koss, F.V. (1999). Automated intelligent pilots for combat flight simulation. *AI Magazine,* 20(1), 27–41.

Kieras, D.E., and Meyer, D.E. (1997). An overview of the EPIC architecture for cognition and performance with application to human-computer interaction. *Human-Computer Interaction,* 12, 391–438.

Lohse, G.L. (1997). Models of graphical perception. In M. Helander, T.K. Landauer, and P. Prabhu (Eds.), *Handbook of Human-Computer Interaction,* 107–135. Amsterdam: Elsevier Science.

Lonsdale, P.R., and Ritter, F.E. (2000). Soar/Tcl-PM: Extending the Soar architecture to include a widely applicable virtual eye and hand. In N. Taatgen and J. Aasman (Eds.), *Proceedings of the 3rd International Conference on Cognitive Modelling,* 202–209. Veenendaal, The Netherlands: Universal Press.

Myers, B.A. (1995). User interface software tools. *ACM Transactions on Computer-Human Interaction,* 2(1), 64–103.

Myers, B.A., Giuse, D.A., Dannenberg, R.B., Vander Zanden, V., Kosbie, D.S., Pervin, E., Mickish, A., and Marchal, P. (1990). Garnet: Comprehensive support for graphical, highly interactive user interfaces. *IEEE Computer,* 23(11), 71–85.

Newell, A. (1990). *Unified theories of cognition.* Cambridge, MA: Harvard University Press.

Olsen, D.R., Foley, J.D., Hudson, S.E., Miller, J., and Meyers, B. (1993). Research directions for user interface software tools. *Behaviour & Information Technology,* 12(2), 80–97.

Ong, R. (1994). *Mechanisms for routinely tying cognitive models to interactive simulations.* MSc thesis, U. of Nottingham. Available as ESRC Centre for Research in Development, Instruction and Training Technical Report #21 and as ftp://ftp. nottingham.ac.uk/pub/lpzfr/mongsu-2.1.tar.Z.

Pew, R.W., and Mavor, A.S. (Eds.). (1998). *Modeling human and organizational behavior: Application to military simulations.* Washington, DC: National Academy Press. http://books.nap.edu/catalog/6173.html.

Rassouli, J. (1995). *Steps towards a process model of mouse-based interaction.* MSc thesis, Psychology, U. of Nottingham.

Rieman, J., Young, R.M., and Howes, A. (1996). A dual-space model of iteratively deepening exploratory learning. *International Journal of Human-Computer Studies,* 44, 743–775.

Ritter, F.E., Baxter, G.D., Jones, G., and Young, R.M. (2000). Supporting cognitive models as users. *ACM Transactions on Computer-Human Interaction,* 7(2), 141–173.

Ritter, F.E., and Larkin, J.H. (1994). Using process models to summarize sequences of human actions. *Human-Computer Interaction,* 9(3), 345–383.

Ritter, F.E., and Major, N.P. (1995). Useful mechanisms for developing simulations for cognitive models. *AISB Quarterly,* 91(Spring), 7–18.

Salvucci, D. (2001). Predicting the effects of in-car interface use on driver performance: An integrated model approach. *International Journal of Human-Computer Studies,* 55, 85–107.

St. Amant, R., and Riedl, M.O. (2001). A perception/action substrate for cognitive modeling in HCI. *International Journal of Human-Computer Studies, 55,* 15–39.

Sears, A. (1993). Layout appropriateness: A metric for evaluating user interface widget layouts. *IEEE Transactions on Software Engineering,* 19(7), 707–719.

Szekely, P., Luo, P., and Neches, R. (1993). Beyond interface builders: Model-based interface tools. In *Proceedings of InterCHI'93,* 383–390. New York: ACM.

Taatgen, N., and Aasman, J. (Eds.). (2000). *Proceedings of the 3rd International Conference on Cognitive Modelling.* Veenendaal, The Netherlands: Universal Press.

Zettlemoyer, L.S., and St. Amant, R. (1999). A visual medium for programmatic control of interactive applications. In *Proceedings of the Conference on CHI'99: Human Factors in Computer Systems,* 199–206. New York: ACM.

7

HCI in the Global Knowledge-Based Economy: Designing to Support Worker Adaptation

Kim J. Vicente

7.1 Introduction

Where is the field of HCI going in the new millennium? Any answer to this question is bound to be a personal one, so I will begin by laying my intellectual cards on the table. For the past 14 years, I have been conducting research on how to support workers in *complex sociotechnical systems* by designing better computer-based tools (see Vicente 1990, 1996, 1999; Vicente and Rasmussen 1990, 1992). These application domains (for example, process control plants, aviation cockpits, engineering design, and medicine) are somewhat different from the domains with which most HCI researchers have been concerned. More specifically, complex sociotechnical systems tend to have many, although not all, of the following characteristics (see Vicente 1999 for a detailed account).

1. Large problem spaces
2. Social
3. Heterogeneous perspectives
4. Distributed
5. Dynamic
6. Potentially high hazards
7. Many coupled subsystems
8. Significant use of automation

©2000 ACM Reprinted with permission from *ACM Transactions on Computer-Human Interaction*, Vol. 7, No. 2, June 2000.

9. Uncertain data

10. Mediated interaction via computers

11. Disturbances

And because different types of problems require different types of solution methods, the work analysis techniques that are suitable for complex sociotechnical systems need to be somewhat different from those in the toolkit of most HCI researchers and designers. The theses of this chapter are that problems of this type will become more prevalent in the new millennium, and they will cause HCI to be increasingly concerned with *designing for worker adaptation.* These points are best made by example.

7.2   Case Study: Hedge Funds in August 1998

In August 1998, the world financial markets experienced a severe setback. One of the interesting events that emerged from this disaster was the catastrophic losses experienced by hedge funds led by Wall Street's "rocket scientists." These funds are based on very complex computer-aided trading strategies and thus are a fascinating (if esoteric) example of HCI in complex sociotechnical systems. The following account of what happened with these hedge funds is based on the insightful article by Coy et al. (1998).

7.2.1   What Are Hedge Funds?

Hedge funds are a high-tech form of financial investment that relies very heavily on quantitative computer models to make trading decisions. Hedge funds are unique because they are purported to be "a clean, rational way to earn high returns with little risk" (Coy et al. 1998, p. 116). They are based on a sophisticated arbitrage strategy that is intended to be "market-neutral," meaning that the funds are designed to make money regardless of whether prices are falling or rising. Before August 1998, hedge funds lived up to these claims. For example, one hedge fund tripled in value between March 1994 and December 1997. Moreover, the fund had never lost more than 3 percent of its value in any one month.

At first glance, hedge funds seem like the financial Holy Grail—excellent returns with minimal risk. How is this possible? The computer models are constructed using historical patterns based on very large amounts of data from many years of market behavior. These historical patterns define a referent for expected market behavior. When prices move outside of the normal relationships defined by this referent, a signal is sent to make a trade, the expectation being that prices will revert to their historical patterns. In addition, other (hedge) trades are made to protect against the anticipated risks that may accompany the initial trade. These investment strategies usually take advantage of very small price discrepancies. As a result, enormous investments are required to generate significant returns. This, in turn, has led to an increasing need for borrowed money to be used as leverage in the trades.

This brief description should make it clear that hedge funds are a very sophisticated form of investment. The highly paid scientists who have developed these models are frequently referred to as "rocket scientists" or "quants" (short for quantitative), and they include two Nobel laureates in economics among their number.

7.2.2   What Happened?

Given their success, hedge funds appeared to be impervious to economic disturbances. However, in August 1998, the claim that high returns could always be obtained with minimal risk was shattered. For example, one hedge fund lost 44 percent of its value ($2 billion) in one month! For some, the losses were worse than those experienced during the 1987 market crash. As one hedge fund newsletter put it at the time, there was a "breakdown in market structure. . . . Something highly unusual is happening" (Coy et al. 1998, p. 118). Financial institutions using similar arbitrage strategies also lost a great deal of money during the same period. For example, Smith Solomon Barney Holdings lost $300 million, and Merrill Lynch lost $135 million.

7.2.3   Why Did It Happen?

How could a seemingly ironclad investment strategy lead to such catastrophic failure? Coy et al. identified a number of related causes.

1. The assumptions that were embedded in the computer models were violated.
2. There was a breakdown in the historical patterns.
3. The computer models were "black box" models that were making automated decisions without the real-time input of seasoned traders.
4. Multiple, unanticipated events occurred all at the same time (for example, Russia experienced a setback on its road to capitalism, the Asian crisis worsened).
5. Many people were making the same kind of bets, and money was being borrowed heavily to finance the bets, thereby amplifying the losses.

As one financial analyst put it, "What occurred . . . was the financial world's equivalent of a 'perfect storm'—everything went wrong at once" (Coy et al. p. 117).

7.2.4   Generalizing the Lessons Learned

What does any of this have to do with HCI? After all, there is no mention of menus, mice, windows, navigation, or the WWW. If we define the field of HCI narrowly as being solely concerned with people interacting *with* computers and *usability* as the only criterion, then there is no lesson to be learned from this case study. However, if we define HCI more broadly as also being concerned with people interacting *through* computers to a complex world teeming with novelty and change and *usefulness* as an important criterion, then there are very important lessons to be learned from this case study.

In fact, for those who are familiar with the details of large-scale industrial disasters, such as the Three Mile Island nuclear power plant incident, the lessons are very familiar ones (Perrow 1984; Reason 1990; Leveson 1995). Complex sociotechnical systems are open systems, meaning that they are subject to disturbances that are unfamiliar to workers and that were not, and in some cases could not have been, anticipated by designers. These unanticipated events can range from the catastrophic—such as the multiple plant failures at Three Mile Island or the multiple financial disturbances during August 1998—to the mundane. As an example of the latter, Norros (1996) conducted a field study of flexible manufacturing systems and found that workers had to cope with an average of three disturbances per hour (events during which the system was functioning in ways that were not anticipated by designers). Because these events are unanticipated, the procedures or automation that designers provide will—by definition—not be directly applicable in these cases. Therefore, to deal with these disturbances effectively, workers must use their expertise and ingenuity to improvise a novel solution. In complex sociotechnical systems, the primary value of having people in the system is precisely to play this adaptive role. Workers must adapt online in real time to disturbances that have not been, or cannot be, foreseen by system designers.

Playing the role of adaptive problem solver to cope with unanticipated events is a challenge. If we expect workers to play such a role effectively, we should provide them with the appropriate support rather than just expect them to play this role on their own, unaided. Specifically, we need to design computer tools that are tailored to help workers perform open-ended intellectual tasks that involve discretionary decision making. In the hedge fund case study, this would involve providing financial analysts with tools that would allow them to take advantage of their domain knowledge to improvise a solution to an unfamiliar and unanticipated set of events like the one that occurred during August 1998.

Note that this conclusion generalizes well beyond the details of this particular case study. I believe that, in the future, HCI will have to be increasingly concerned with systematically designing tools that deliberately support adaptation. The rationale for this claim follows.

7.3 The Global Knowledge-Based Economy and the Demand for Adaptation

Everywhere we look in the media, we see a number of buzzwords appearing with increasing frequency—for example, innovation, knowledge worker, wealth creation, flexible manufacturing, free trade, and global village. What do these terms have in common, and what is their significance for HCI? These terms are symptomatic of a fundamental shift toward a global knowledge-based economy that will lead to an increasing demand for workers, managers, and organizations to adapt in the future.

7.3.1   The Global Knowledge-Based Economy

There are a number of trends that have acted together to transform qualitatively the nature of contemporary industry and economics. These changes, in turn, pose a new set of requirements for success in many workplaces.

Brzustowski (1998), the president of the Natural Sciences and Engineering Research Council of Canada, has identified the following contributors.

- The market is full of products based on recent advances in science and technology.
- These products are made all over the world, regardless of brand name.
- High quality is expected in the market and is frequently achieved.
- Today's new high-tech products become tomorrow's commodity products.
- The market for medium- and low-tech goods is fiercely competitive.
- Commodity prices are low and distance is not a factor even for bulk materials.
- Everybody has to compete on price, so productivity improvement is key.
- Changes in demand and market conditions can be rapid and unpredictable.
- New knowledge appears in new goods and services at an increasing pace.

According to Brzustowski, these factors have led to a global knowledge-based economy that is qualitatively different from the economy of the past.

The speed and connectedness of the global knowledge-based economy is well illustrated by Motorola's manufacturing of electronic pagers (Morone 1993). Seventeen minutes after an order for a pager is received from anywhere in the United States, a bar code is placed on a blank circuit board in a factory. Within two hours of the order, a finished product is shipped, even if the lot size is one. Davis and Meyer (1998) provide additional evidence for the qualitative changes represented by the global knowledge-based economy. What implications do these changes have for success in the workplace and thus for HCI?

7.3.2   The Future Demand for Adaptation

I believe that the trend toward a global knowledge-based economy will increase the need for adaptation. Workers, managers, and organizations will all have to become more flexible and adaptive than in the past. There are a number of arguments from a diverse set of sources that can be put forth in support of this claim.

Workers. The U.S. National Academy of Science / National Research Council Committee on Human Factors issued a report a few years ago, documenting what it believed were the most fertile areas for human factors research in the next few decades (Nickerson 1995). The report was written by a diverse group of experts, spanning the entire range of human factors from physical to psychological to social-organizational aspects. One of the important points made in the report is that computerization will continue to change the nature of work. "Technological change means changes in job requirements. The ability to satisfy changing, and not entirely predictable, job requirements in a complex, culturally diverse, and constantly evolving environment will require a literate workforce that has good problem solving skills and learning skills" (p. 22). Consequently, "a critical aspect of industrial competitiveness will be the ability to adapt quickly to rapid technological developments and constantly changing market conditions" (p. 42). Therefore, in the future, the work force will have to be more versatile and adaptive than in the past.

In his recent monograph on the interaction between engineering and society, Pool (1997) reaches essentially the same conclusion but from a somewhat different path. By reviewing the influence that society has had on technology, Pool noted that there is an increasing social need to "do more with less." This trend will only increase with the demands imposed by the global knowledge-based economy. Because of the premium that is put on increasing efficiency and providing new functionality, engineering systems have become—and will continue to become—more complex. This increase in complexity has had an unintended result, namely a commensurate increase in unanticipated events. In other words, as systems become more complex, they become more open. Unanticipated disturbances are bound to occur. Thus, there is a greater need for worker and organizational adaptation than in the past. By inference, we can expect that the requirement to support adaptation will increase accordingly.

Cannon-Bowers et al. (1997) describe an excellent example of the trend identified by Pool (1997). Because of a tremendous reduction in operating budget, the U.S. Navy is under pressure to greatly reduce costs. As a result, the Navy has set the goal of reducing the manning level on a future generation of ships from the current level of 350 workers to an envisioned level of 95 workers. Clearly, this is a very ambitious target, but the magnitude of the design problem is compounded by the fact that the missions that such ships are expected to play in the future will *increase* in complexity. There will be more missions, they will be more varied in nature, and their nature will be highly unpredictable. Therefore, to meet the challenge to do "more with less" effectively, there will be a greater need to design tools that help workers perform open-ended intellectual tasks that involve discretionary decision making.

Managers. Adaptation is relevant, not just to workers but to managers as well, as evidenced by Morone's (1993) fascinating field studies. He studied corporate general managers that have been successful in turning their companies (Motorola, Corning, and General Electric) into global leaders in high-technology markets. Such markets are particularly affected by the symptoms accompanying the trend toward a global knowledge-based economy, exhibiting a high degree of volatility and uncertainty. Morone learned that successful managers adapted to all of this turbulent change to keep their companies competitive. As one manager put it, "You need a strategic intent—but within that context, you have to be totally opportunistic. . . . You can't know what's around the next corner, so construct an organization that is able to adapt" (p. 119). Morone also observed that some of the successful businesses he studied "followed the general course that had been hoped for, but the specific form they took, the specific market and technological developments to which they had to respond as they followed that general course, were not, and could not have been, anticipated" (p. 190). Yet again we see the need to adapt to unanticipated events. Finally, another manager pointed out, "A lot of people think of product development as involving a lot of planning, but . . . the key is learning, and an organization's ability to learn" (p. 224). The high-tech markets studied by Morone have been particularly volatile in the past and show every sign of continuing to be so. However, as the trends identified by Brzustowski (1998) affect different sectors of the economy, we can expect to see the same strong need for managers to adapt to uncertainty and novelty in other industries as well.

Organizations. Adaptation is also relevant at an organizational level. In his national bestseller, Senge (1990) discussed the importance of organizational learning in the global knowledge-based economy. In many cases, traditional ways of governing and managing have become outdated and are breaking down because of the changes documented by Brzustowski (1998). The static, hierarchical organizational structures that have dominated in the past are no longer as appropriate, given the current pace of change. According to Senge, one path that modern organizations can adopt to succeed and survive in this environment is to learn to accept, embrace, and seek change. This, in turn, would require a decentralized organizational structure whose individuals are committed to continuous learning and adaptation to novelty.

More recently, Davis and Meyer (1998) have identified a similar set of corporate requirements. Because the pace of change has accelerated, the rules that guided corporate decision making in the past are no longer as reliable. As a result, companies might have to give up on the idea of stable solutions to business problems. Instead, they may have to move from relying on prediction, planning, and foresight to building in flexibility, speed, and self-organization. In short, "an enterprise must adapt to its environment. . . . It needs to be every bit as adaptable as the economy in which it participates" (Davis and Meyer, p. 114).

Summary. The global knowledge-based economy will continue to transform the landscape of modern work. Changing and unpredictable circumstances will be the norm. As a result, there is an increasing need for workers, managers, and organizations to become more flexible and adaptive than in the past. These trends suggest that the requirement to design for adaptation will only increase in the future.

7.3.3   The Relationship between Adaptation and Learning

Along with the buzzwords identified earlier, we also frequently encounter others such as lifelong learning, continuous improvement, and learning organization. How does continuous learning fit into the picture I have been drawing?

So far, I have argued that the global knowledge-based economy has created a strong need for adaptation to change. In essence, this is equivalent to a call for *learning to learn*. By adapting to disturbances, workers are, in effect, engaging in opportunities for learning. Hirschhorn (1984) made this point in the context of process control: "Each time operators diagnose a novel situation, they become learners, reconstructing and reconfiguring their knowledge" (p. 95). The connection between adaptation and learning goes well beyond process control, however. Related conclusions have been reached in other research areas, such as psychology, control theory, and cognitive science (Narendra 1986; Gibson 1991; Johannson 1993; Norros 1996).

Nowhere is the robust relationship between adaptation to novelty, action variability, and learning opportunities as well thought out as in the study of human motor control in ecological psychology, thanks to the seminal work of Nicholai Bernstein. This relationship was clearly expressed in a book written approximately 50 years ago but that has only been published much more recently (Bernstein 1996). Bernstein was concerned with a very different problem, so his terminology is different from that used here. For instance, he uses the term "dexterity" to refer to the capability to find "a motor solution for any situation and in any condition" (p. 21). In the terms of this chapter, he is referring to the capability to adapt to unanticipated demands.

According to Bernstein, the need for dexterity (that is, adaptation) increases under the following conditions: (1) the problem to be solved becomes more complex, (2) the problem to be solved becomes more variable, and (3) the number of unique and unexpected problems that need to be solved in real-time increases. Although the content is obviously different for motor control, these generic characteristics are surprisingly similar to those that are associated with the global knowledge-based economy and complex engineering design projects. Demands on workers are becoming more complex; those problems take different forms, rarely repeating themselves; and there is an increasing need to deal with novel, unanticipated situations in a timely fashion. Just as these characteristics lead to an increase in the need for dexterity in motor control, they also lead to an increase in the need for adaptation in complex sociotechnical systems.

These similarities establish the connection between motor dexterity and worker adaptation. How does the relationship with learning fit in? The answer to this question can be found in the rationale behind Bernstein's beautiful phrase, *"repetition without repetition"* (p. 204, emphasis in original). Allowing workers to play the role of adaptive actors means that they will repeatedly have to *generate* a solution to a problem rather than following a prepackaged procedural solution. As Bernstein pointed out in the context of motor control, "During a correctly organized exercise, a student is repeating many times, *not the means for solving* a given motor problem, but *the process of its solution,* the changing and improving of the means" (p. 205, emphasis in original).

But because workers are solving the problem anew each time, opportunities for learning are created. Bernstein explains the process as follows.

> *Repetitions* of a movement or action are necessary in order to *solve a motor problem* many times (better and better) and *to find the best ways* of solving it.

Repetitive solutions of a problem are also necessary because, in natural conditions, external conditions never repeat themselves and the course of the movement is never ideally reproduced. Consequently, it is necessary *to gain experience relevant to all various modifications* of a task, primarily, to all the impressions that underlie the sensory corrections of a movement. This experience is necessary for the animal not to be confused by future modifications of the task and external conditions, no matter how small they are, and to be able to adapt rapidly. (p. 176, emphasis in original)

Bernstein's statements can be generalized to the case of workers in the global knowledge-based economy. Here, too, conditions rarely repeat themselves precisely, so workers should gain experience with solving problems under a wide variety of initial conditions. Supporting workers to be adaptive problem solvers accommodates this need for learning because it recognizes the situated nature of action (Suchman 1987). By accommodating context-conditioned variability in action (Turvey et al. 1978), we can help workers gain valuable experience so that they are not confused if they have to perform the same task in a different way in the future because of a change in context. In other words, designing for adaptation is equivalent to designing for continuous learning.

7.3.4   How Much Have Things Changed?

In this section, I have argued that the characteristics of the global knowledge-based economy put a premium on adaptation and continuous learning and that these trends will increase. The novelty of these work demands is perhaps best illustrated by contrasting them to the Tayloristic approach that was prevalent early in the twentieth century (Taylor 1911). The following quotations from a recent biography of Frederick Taylor by R. Kanigel (1997) make the point in a stark fashion.

The control of work must be taken from the men who did it and placed in the hands of a new breed of planners and thinkers. These men would think everything through beforehand. The workmen—elements of production to be studied, manipulated, and controlled—were to do as they were told. (p. 371)

The work itself might be no more physically demanding, but somehow, by day's end, it felt as if it were. Going strictly by somebody else's say-so, rigidly following directions, doing it by the clock, made Taylor's brand of work distasteful. You had to do it in the one best way prescribed for you and not in your old, idiosyncratic, if perhaps less efficient way. (pp. 209–210)

Clearly, times have changed considerably since Taylor's days. A more flexible approach to work analysis is needed to meet the needs of the global knowledge-based economy.

7.4 Cognitive Work Analysis: A Potential Programmatic Approach

So far, I have described a phenomenon (the global knowledge-based economy) and an associated objective (designing for adaptation, or equivalently, continuous learning). In this section, I briefly describe a potential programmatic approach for achieving that objective. Cognitive work analysis (CWA; Rasmussen et al. 1994; Vicente 1999) is a work analysis framework that can be used to create computer-based tools to support worker adaptation and continuous learning. CWA was developed beginning in the 1960s by researchers at Risø National Laboratory in Roskilde, Denmark (see Vicente 1998, in press, for an introduction to and historical review of this intellectual lineage), and its concepts have been tailored to the properties listed at the beginning of this chapter.

7.4.1 A Constraint-Based Approach

If a work analysis framework is going to support continuous learning and adaptation to novelty and change, then it must be flexible enough to support variability in action that is sensitive to local, contextual details that cannot be, or have not been, anticipated. CWA accomplishes this by adopting a constraint-based approach. Vicente (1999) provides a detailed description of this approach, but the basic idea is illustrated generically in Figure 7.1. Designers identify constraints on action that can be embedded in a computer-based tool. Workers then have the flexibility to adapt within the remaining space of possibilities. Although not shown in the figure, the constraint

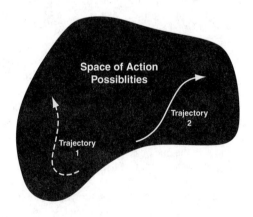

FIGURE 7.1 The constraint-based approach

boundaries, and thus the available degrees of freedom, are situation-dependent and therefore dynamic.

Various layers of goal-relevant constraint can be identified as being pertinent to a particular design problem (see the next section for a more detailed description of the categories of constraint adopted by CWA). These constraints can be integrated to create a dynamic constraint boundary. The resulting constraint space, illustrated in Figure 7.1, defines a set of action possibilities. These possibilities represent the relevant degrees of freedom for productive action. Of course, the constraint boundaries, and thus the constraint space, will change as a function of the context (the task being performed, the strategy being adopted, the competencies of the actor).

By identifying these goal-relevant constraints, designers can generate a set of information requirements that can be used to design a computer-based tool. That tool would provide workers with feedback and decision support as to the constraints that need to be respected, but it would not identify a particular path or trajectory through the constraint space. It would be up to workers to decide which trajectory (that is, which set of actions) to take for a particular set of circumstances. This constraint-based approach thereby provides workers with continual opportunities for learning and the flexibility to adapt within the space of relevant action possibilities. In one circumstance, workers may select one trajectory, whereas in another circumstance, they may have to select a different trajectory to achieve the same task goals. Thus, the constraint space provides the flexibility required to support situated action (Suchman 1987). In addition, the same worker can choose different trajectories, even when the circumstances remain the same. As a result, the constraint space is also flexible enough to support the intrinsic variability frequently observed in human action. Finally, different workers can choose different trajectories to achieve the same outcome in different ways. Therefore, the constraint space is also flexible enough to support individual differences between workers.

In summary, the constraint-based approach illustrated in Figure 7.1 allows workers to respond to unanticipated contingencies and to follow their subjective preferences (by choosing a different trajectory through the constraint space), while at the same time, satisfying the demands of the job (by staying within the constraint boundaries). For an example of an interface and a decision support system designed according to this philosophy, see Vicente (1996) and Guerlain et al. (1999), respectively.

7.4.2   Five Layers of Constraint

The CWA framework is an example of a constraint-based approach that is comprised of five layers of constraint. The first layer of constraint is the work domain that is a map of the environment to be acted upon. The second layer of constraint is the set of control tasks that represents what needs to done to the work domain. The third layer of constraint is the set of strategies that represents the various processes by which action can be effectively carried out. The fourth layer of constraint is the social-organizational structure that represents how the preceding set of demands are allocated among actors, as well as how those actors can productively organize and coordinate themselves. Finally, the fifth layer of constraint is the set of worker competencies that represents the capabilities that are required for success. When the constraints are integrated, the result is a constraint space, as shown in Figure 7.1.

Figure 7.2 illustrates a hypothetical example showing how these five layers of constraint are logically nested. The size of each set in this diagram represents the productive degrees of freedom for actors, so large sets represent many relevant possibilities for action whereas small sets represent fewer relevant possibilities for action. The outer boundary represents the first phase of CWA, work domain analysis, and shows what the controlled system is capable of doing. This level is a fundamental bedrock of constraint on the actions of *any* actor. No matter what control task is being pursued, what strategy has been adopted, what social-organizational structure is in place, or what the competencies of the workers are, there are certain constraints on action that are imposed by the functional structure of the system being acted upon. For example, pilots cannot use engines for functions that they are not capable of achieving. Thus, the work domain delimits the productive degrees of freedom that are available for action.

The second phase, control task analysis, inherits the constraints of the first phase but adds additional constraints as well. For the sake of clarity, only two hypothetical control tasks are illustrated in the example in Figure 7.2. Although the work domain provides a large number of total degrees of freedom, when actors are pursuing a particular control task, only a subset of those degrees of freedom are usually relevant. For

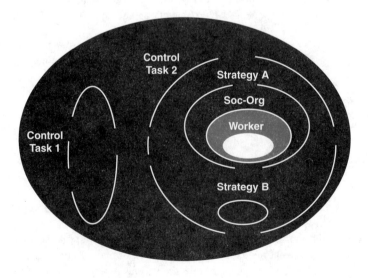

FIGURE 7.2   Nesting of five layers of constraint

example, when pilots are navigating at cruising altitude, the constraints associated with the landing gear and brakes are usually not relevant. Furthermore, there are new constraints that must be respected above and beyond those imposed by the work domain. For example, for some control tasks, it is important that certain actions be performed before others. This constraint is a property of the control task, not the work domain. As shown in Figure 7.2, the net result is a reduction in the relevant degrees of freedom. When workers are pursuing a particular control task, only certain actions are meaningful and require consideration. It is for this reason that the sets depicting Control Tasks 1 and 2 in Figure 7.2 are nested within the set for the entire work domain.

The third phase of CWA is depicted in the figure by two hypothetical strategies, A and B, for Control Task 2 (strategies for Control Task 1 are not shown for the sake of clarity). The strategy phase also inherits the constraints associated with previous phases of analysis. After all, a strategy cannot make a work domain do something that it is not capable of doing. This is why the two sets for Strategies A and B in the figure are subsets of the work domain set. In addition, a strategy must also work within the constraints associated with its corresponding control task; otherwise it will not reliably achieve the required task goals. It is for this reason that Strategies A and B are nested inside the set for Control Task 2. The strategies phase, however, also introduces new constraints of its own. The control task level merely identifies the degrees of freedom associated with achieving a particular goal. There are conceivably many different ways in which Control Task 2, for instance, can be performed. All of these processes are encompassed by the Control Task 2 set. When a particular strategy for performing the control task is identified, some degrees of freedom are usually not relevant because they are only required for other strategies. A specific strategy imposes a certain flow or process that adds constraints on top of those that are imposed by merely achieving the desired outcome. It is for this reason that Strategies A and B are nested within the set for Control Task 2.

The fourth phase of CWA, social-organizational analysis, follows a similar pattern. It too inherits the constraints imposed by previous phases of work analysis, and it too adds a new layer of constraint. There are multiple organizational structures that could conceivably be adopted for any one strategy. To take a very simple example, a strategy may be performed by one worker alone, by two workers in a collaborative manner, by one worker supervising another, or by a worker supervising automation. In each of these cases, the same strategy is being adopted, the same control task is being pursued, and the same work domain is being acted upon. Nevertheless, these different organizational architectures have different constraints associated with them. A worker executing the strategy alone will likely draw on a different, although probably overlapping, set of relevant actions than two workers executing the strategy in a cooperative fashion. Thus, a particular social-organizational structure represents a further narrowing of degrees of freedom. This logic explains why the social-organizational set is nested within the set for Strategy A (analogous constraints for Strategy B are not shown for the sake of clarity).

Finally, the fifth phase of worker competencies reduces the degrees of freedom even further. There are certain things that people are simply not capable of doing.

Consequently, particular ways of working are not feasible. For example, some activities require too much working memory load, too much time, too much knowledge, or too much computational effort for people to perform. These constraints are specifically associated with workers' competencies, not with any of the other preceding phases of analysis alone. This final narrowing down of degrees of freedom is illustrated in the figure by the worker competency set, which is nested within the social-organizational set for Strategy A.

7.4.3 Modeling Tools and Design Implications

The CWA framework is also composed of modeling tools that can be used to identify each layer of constraint (Rasmussen et al. 1994; Vicente 1999). For example, the abstraction hierarchy can be used to conduct a work domain analysis (layer 1), the decision ladder can be used to conduct a control task analysis (layer 2), and the skills, rules, knowledge taxonomy can be used to conduct a worker competencies analysis (layer 5). These modeling tools are used to create models for particular design problems. Each of these models is linked to a particular class of design interventions. This list is merely intended to be illustrative, not definitive or exhaustive.

1. *Work Domain*
   - What information should be measured? (sensors)
   - What information should be derived? (models)
   - How should information be organized? (database)

2. *Control Tasks*
   - What goals must be pursued, and what are the constraints on those goals? (procedures or automation)
   - What information and relations are relevant for particular classes of situations? (context-sensitive interface)

3. *Strategies*
   - What frames of reference are useful? (dialog modes)
   - What control mechanisms are useful? (process flow)

4. *Social-Organizational*
   - What are the responsibilities of all of the actors? (role allocation)
   - How should actors communicate with each other? (organizational structure)

5. *Worker Competencies*
   - What knowledge, rules, and skills do workers need to have? (selection, training, and interface form)

Beginning with the work domain, analyzing the system being controlled provides a great deal of insight into what information is required to understand its state. This analysis, in turn, has important implications for the design of sensors and models (Reising and Sanderson 1996). The work domain analysis also reveals the functional structure of the system being controlled. These insights can then be used to design a database that keeps track of the relationships between variables, providing a coherent, integrated, and global representation of the information contained therein.

The control task analysis deals not with data structures but with control structures. The goals that need to be satisfied for certain classes of situations and the constraints on the achievement of those goals are identified here. This knowledge can then be used to design either constraint-based procedures that guide workers in achieving those goals or automation that achieves those goals autonomously or semi-autonomously. In addition, this analysis will also identify what variables and relations in the work domain may be relevant for certain classes of situations (see Figure 7.2). Those insights can be used to design context-sensitive interface mechanisms that present workers with the right information at the right time (Woods 1991).

The strategies analysis deals not just with what needs to be done but also with how it is to be done. Each strategy is a different frame of reference for pursuing control task goals, each with its unique flow and process requirements. Thus, identifying what strategies can be used for each control task provides some insight into what type of human-computer dialog modes should be designed. Ideally, each mode should be tailored to the unique requirements of each strategy (Pejtersen 1992). The strategies analysis also reveals the generative mechanisms (rules or algorithms) constituting each strategy, which in turn helps specify the process flow for each dialog mode.

The social-organizational analysis deals with two very important and challenging classes of design interventions. Given the knowledge uncovered in previous phases, analysts can decide what the responsibilities of the various actors are, including workers, designers, and automation. These role allocation decisions define the job content of the various actors. In addition, analysts should also determine how the various actors can effectively communicate with each other. That analysis will help identify the authority and coordination patterns that constitute a viable organizational structure.

The final phase is the analysis of worker competencies. Since the work demands have been thoroughly analyzed by this point, the knowledge, rules, and skills that workers must have to function effectively can be determined. This analysis will help develop a set of specifications for worker training and selection (if relevant). In addition, this analysis will also provide some insight into how information should be presented to workers because some competencies may not be triggered unless information is presented in particular forms (Vicente and Rasmussen 1992).

Although this list is not definitive, it shows how—right from the very start—CWA is deliberately geared toward uncovering implications for systems design.

The CWA framework is intended to be a programmatic approach to one large class of HCI problems: how to design computer-based tools that help workers perform open-ended intellectual tasks that require discretionary decision making. These tasks require continuous learning and adaptation to novelty. CWA tries to support these demands by adopting a flexible constraint-based approach, by identifying five categories of goal-relevant constraints, by providing modeling tools that can be used to analyze each layer of constraint, and by linking each layer of constraint to a particular category of systems design interventions.

7.5   The Future: What Can We Be Sure Of?

Prediction is always an uncertain endeavor, but given the analysis presented in this article, there are a few things that appear to be indisputable. As complex sociotechnical systems become more open, change will become the norm, not the exception. Therefore, to be competitive in the global knowledge-based economy, there will be an increasing demand for workers, managers, and organizations to be flexible and adaptive. At the same time, there will be an accompanying need for learning to learn. Accordingly, computer-based tools should be deliberately and systematically designed to help workers effectively fulfill these challenging needs. The CWA framework is intended to be a programmatic approach to this practical problem. But regardless of whether CWA itself succeeds in achieving its objectives, HCI in the new millennium should be, and will be, increasingly concerned with systematically designing for worker adaptation.

Acknowledgments

This research was sponsored in part by a research grant from the Natural Sciences and Engineering Research Council of Canada. I would like to thank Jack Carroll for encouraging me to write this article and the three reviewers for their exceptionally incisive and constructive comments.

References

Bernstein, N.A. (1996). On dexterity and its development. In M.L. Latash and M.T. Turvey (Eds.), *Dexterity and its development,* 1–244. Mahwah, NJ: Erlbaum.

Brzustowski, T. (1998). Engineering design and innovation, what's the connection? Clarice Chalmers' Design Lecture, Department of Mechanical and Industrial Engineering, University of Toronto, Toronto, March 5, 1998.

Cannon-Bowers, J.A., Bost, R., Hamburger, T., Crisp, H., Osga, G., and Perry, A. (1997). Achieving affordability through human systems integration. Paper presented at the Third Annual Naval Aviation Systems Engineering Supportability Symposium. Arlington, VA.

Coy, P., Woolley, S., Spiro, L.N., and Glasgall, W. (1998). Failed wizards of Wall Street. *Business Week,* September 21, 1998, 114–119.

Davis, S., and Meyer, C. (1998). *Blur: The speed of change in the connected economy.* Reading, MA: Addison-Wesley.

Gibson, E.J. (1991). *An odyssey in learning and perception.* Cambridge, MA: MIT Press.

Guerlain, S.A., Smith, P.J., Obradovich, J.H., Rudmann, S., Strohm, P., Smith, J.W., Svirbely, J., and Sachs, L. (1999). Interactive critiquing as a form of decision support: An empirical evaluation. *Human Factors, 41,* 72–89.

Hirschhorn, L. (1984). *Beyond mechanization: Work and technology in a postindustrial age.* Cambridge, MA: MIT Press.

Johannson, R. (1993). *System modeling and identification.* Englewood Cliffs, NJ: Prentice-Hall.

Kanigel, R. (1997). *The one best way: Frederick Winslow Taylor and the enigma of efficiency.* New York: Viking.

Leveson, N.G. (1995). *Safeware: System safety and computers.* Reading, MA: Addison-Wesley.

Morone, J.G. (1993). *Winning in high-tech markets: The role of general management.* Boston, MA: Harvard Business School Press.

Narendra, K.S. (1986). *Adaptive and learning systems: Theory and applications.* New York: Plenum Press.

Nickerson, R.S. (1995). *Emerging needs and opportunities for human factors research.* Washington, DC: National Academy Press.

Norros, L. (1996). System disturbances as springboard for development of operators' expertise. In Y. Engeström and D. Middleton (Eds.), *Cognition and communication at work,* 159–176. Cambridge, England: Cambridge University Press.

Pejtersen, A.M. (1992). The Book House: An icon based database system for fiction retrieval in public libraries. In B. Cronin (Ed.), *The marketing of library and information services 2,* 572–591. London: ASLIB.

Perrow, C. (1984). *Normal accidents: Living with high-risk technologies.* New York: Basic Books.

Pool, R. (1997). *Beyond engineering: How society shapes technology.* New York: Oxford University Press.

Rasmussen, J. (1986). *Information processing and human-machine interaction: An approach to cognitive engineering.* New York: North-Holland.

Rasmussen, J., Pejtersen, A.M., and Goodstein, L.P. (1994). *Cognitive systems engineering.* New York: Wiley.

Reason, J. (1990). *Human error.* Cambridge, England: Cambridge University Press.

Reising, D.V., and Sanderson, P.M. (1996). Work domain analysis of a pasteurization plant: Building an abstraction hierarchy representation. In *Proceedings of the Human Factors and Ergonomics Society 40th Annual Meeting,* 293–297. Santa Monica, CA: Human Factors and Ergonomics Society.

Senge, P.M. (1990). *The fifth discipline: The art and practice of the learning organization.* New York: Doubleday.

Suchman, L.A. (1987). *Plans and situated actions: The problem of human-machine communication.* Cambridge, England: Cambridge University Press.

Taylor, F.W. (1911). *The principles of scientific management.* New York: Harper & Row.

Turvey, M.T., Shaw, R.E., and Mace, W. (1978). Issues in the theory of action: Degrees of freedom, coordinative structures and coalitions. In J. Requin (Ed.), *Attention and performance VII,* 557–595. Hillsdale, NJ: Erlbaum.

Vicente, K.J. (1990). Coherence- and correspondence-driven work domains: Implications for systems design. *Behaviour and Information Technology,* 9, 493–502.

Vicente, K.J. (1996). Improving dynamic decision making in complex systems through ecological interface design: A research overview. *System Dynamics Review,* 12, 251–279.

Vicente, K.J. (in press). Cognitive engineering research at Risø from 1962–1979. In E. Salas (Ed.), *Advances in Human Performance and Cognitive Engineering Research, Volume 1.* New York: Elsevier.

Vicente, K.J. (1998). An evolutionary perspective on the growth of cognitive engineering: The Risø genotype. *Ergonomics,* 41, 156–159.

Vicente, K.J. (1999). *Cognitive work analysis: Toward safe, productive, and healthy computer-based work.* Mahwah, NJ: Erlbaum.

Vicente, K.J., and Rasmussen, J. (1990). The ecology of human-machine systems II: Mediating "direct perception" in complex work domains. *Ecological Psychology,* 2, 207–250.

Vicente, K.J., and Rasmussen, J. (1992). Ecological interface design: Theoretical foundations. *IEEE Transactions on Systems, Man, and Cybernetics,* SMC-22, 589–606.

Woods, D.D. (1991). The cognitive engineering of problem representations. In J. Alty and G. Weir (Eds.), *Human-computer interaction in complex systems,* 169–188. London: Academic Press.

8

A Reference Task Agenda for HCI

Steve Whittaker
Loren Terveen
Bonnie A. Nardi

8.1   The Problems with HCI as Radical Invention

Research in HCI, particularly as embodied in the CHI conference, focuses largely on novel problems and solutions that push the technology envelope. Most publications describe novel techniques or novel applications of existing techniques. Newman (1994) provides quantitative evidence for this. He compared CHI with five other engineering research fields, such as thermodynamics and aerodynamics, using content analysis to classify abstracts of published papers to identify their research contribution. In other engineering disciplines, over 90 percent of published research built on prior work, contributing (1) better modeling techniques (allowing predictions about designs), (2) better solutions (addressing previously insoluble problems), and (3) better tools and methods (to apply models or build prototypes). However, only about 30 percent of CHI papers fitted these cumulative categories. The majority either reported "radical" solutions (new paradigms, techniques, or applications) or described experience and heuristics relating to radical solutions.

8.1.1   Radical Invention Is Not Always Effective

This analysis strongly suggests that CHI differs from other engineering research disciplines. We offer arguments that the current state of affairs is problematic with respect to two different success criteria.

©2000 Lawrence Erlbaum Associates, Inc. Reprinted with permission from *Human-Computer Interaction,* Vol. 15, No. 2/3, September 2000.

One criterion consistent with radical invention is *technology transfer.* One motivation for constant innovation is the example of whole new industries being created by novel user interfaces. Applications like Visicalc and Lotus 1-2-3 drove the early PC market, and Mosaic/Netscape led to the Web explosion. In this view, HCI research is an engine room from which novel interaction techniques are snatched by waiting technology companies. There undoubtedly are some success stories according to this criterion, including collaborative filtering (Communications of the ACM 1997; Goldberg et al. 1992; Hill et al. 1995; Resnick et al. 1994; Shardanand and Maes 1995), UI toolkits and general programming techniques (Rudsill et al. 1996). The early graphical user interfaces developed at Xerox PARC (Smith et al. 1982) successfully combined ideas such as overlapping windows and the mouse that predated the coalescence of the HCI community. These ideas then made their way into the Macintosh and Microsoft Windows systems.

Nevertheless, user interfaces with widespread impact generally originated *outside* the HCI community (Isaacs and Tang 1996). Visicalc was invented by a business student and a programmer. CAD systems developed from Sketchpad (Sutherland 1963) and were also independently invented by engineers at Boeing and General Motors (Foundyller 1984). AOL and Instant Messenger were invented by business people following UNIX and MULTIX precursors. Tim Berners-Lee, the inventor of HTML and the Web, although a computer scientist, was not a member of the HCI community.

The second success criterion is scientific. The radical invention model has not aided the development of a *science* of HCI. This is a controversial area with acrimonious past debate concerning the scientific basis of HCI (Newell and Card 1985; Carroll and Campbell 1986) and extended arguments about the relationship of HCI to psychology and cognitive science. There are isolated pockets of HCI research deriving basic precepts from psychological theories (Card et al. 1983; Gray et al. 1993; Olson and Olson 1990). However, these papers are in the minority (as is evident from Newman's analysis), and they may not have major effects on mainstream HCI practice (Landauer 1995; Newman 1994). The analysis so far should make it clear why this is so. Consolidation is impossible if everyone constantly is striking off in novel directions. While radical invention is vital to making progress, so too is cumulative research. Concepts must be clarified, tradeoffs determined, key user tasks and requirements described, metrics or critical parameters (Newman 1997) identified, and modeling techniques constructed. We are simply not doing enough of this type of work.

8.1.2   What We Don't Know: Requirements, Metrics, and Uses of Everyday Technologies

One significant problem originating from the absence of cumulative research is the lack of clear understanding of *core* user tasks, interactive technologies and techniques. We lack systematic information about tasks that are essential to people's everyday computing activities: browsing, retrieval, and management of Web information; use of e-mail and voice mail; personal information management; and task management.[1] While there are many radical solution attempts in these areas, we lack accepted bodies of knowledge about these everyday computer activities. In many of these areas, while a few initial studies have been conducted, there is no consensus about user tasks, no common view of outstanding issues and problems, and no accepted success metrics. Thus, when addressing these problems, researchers must begin by carrying out their own research to identify requirements, and evaluation metrics. This difficulty is manifest for information retrieval (Amento et al. 1999; Whittaker et al. 1999), asynchronous communication (Whittaker and Sidner 1996; Whittaker et al. 2000), and desktop UIs (Barreau and Nardi 1995). The absence of shared task information makes it difficult to focus research problems, to compare research results, and determine when a new solution is better, rather than simply different (Newman 1997).

A well-known problem with radical invention is that it often is not based on an understanding of user tasks and requirements. Researchers thus find themselves proposing radical solutions to problems that are of little interest to users, while neglecting genuine problems. Barreau and Nardi (1995) studied how users organized desktop information. Most people felt that their computer files were adequately organized and that archiving tasks did not require major support. Nevertheless, much recent technological work has addressed archival support (Fertig et al. 1996; Gifford et al. 1991; Rao et al. 1994). On the other hand, many people experienced problems in transferring information between applications. Here basic empirical investigation uncovered an important task that was not being addressed by the research community. This insight led to work on Apple Data Detectors (Nardi et al. 1998), now a part of the Macintosh operating system. The research also identified a second requirement that desktop organizers should support, namely *reminding*. Users remembered outstanding tasks by simply inspecting folders and files. This research thus discovered two novel user problems (and hence criteria for evaluating new versions of desktop organizers), as well as finding that a commonly addressed problem—archiving— actually didn't deserve as much attention.

In addition to a lack of shared task and requirements descriptions, we also have little systematic data about how people use popular technologies. We lack information about how people actually use e-mail, voice mail, cellular phones, the Windows interface, digital personal organizers, and instant messaging.[2] The popularity of these technologies and their widespread use make it imperative to know how people use them, what they use them for, how successful they are, and where problems lie.

Furthermore, we don't have a good understanding of *why* certain core user interface techniques are successful. GUIs are central to the enterprise of HCI, and although we have successful guidelines for building them (Shneiderman 1982), we lack theoretical understanding of why they are successful (Baecker 1987; Brennan 1990).

---

[1] By systematic bodies of knowledge, we employ the *very weak criterion* that at least two studies have been conducted in a given area. Note that we are not even insisting that the studies agree on their core findings. There are often one or two pioneering studies in a given domain, after which no further research is done.

[2] One complicating factor is that some proprietary research has been conducted into these technologies in industrial contexts. Nevertheless, we still need publicly available data about technologies used by millions of people multiple times a day.

And of course, new radical innovations such as immersive virtual realities, augmented realities, affective computing, and tangible computing make the problem worse. Not only do we not understand these new technologies and their basic operation, we don't have a clear sense of how much innovation is tolerable or desirable. In sum, although we lack basic understandings of current users, tasks, and technologies, the field is encouraged to try out even more radical solutions without pausing to do the analysis and investigation required to gain systematic understanding.

8.1.3 How We Don't Know It: The Dissemination Problem

Even when a useful body of knowledge exists for a core task, the HCI community does not have institutions and procedures for exploiting this knowledge. We advocate workshops for articulating and disseminating knowledge of core tasks and practices. Changes in community standards—for example, reviewing guidelines for the CHI conference and in HCI instruction—are also needed for new practices to take hold. These will allow our suggestions to be institutionalized.

8.2 The Reference Task Solution

To address the overemphasis on radical invention and lack of knowledge about important tasks, we propose a modified methodology for HCI research and practice centered on *reference tasks*. Our proposal has both technical and social practice aspects. We discuss (1) how reference tasks may be represented and used and (2) new practices that the HCI community must adopt in order to develop and utilize reference tasks.

The goal of reference tasks is to capture and share knowledge and focus attention on common problems. By working on common tasks central to HCI, the community will enjoy these benefits.

- Shared problem definitions, datasets, experimental tasks, user requirements, and contextual information about usage situations will allow greater research focus.

- Agreement about metrics (Newman's (1997) critical parameters) for measuring how well an artifact serves its purpose, enables researchers and designers to compare different user interface techniques objectively, and helps determine when progress is being made.

- Advice to designers will be based on a stronger foundation, namely knowledge about core tasks within a domain and the best techniques for supporting the tasks.

- Theory development also will be strengthened; the relationship between core tasks, interface techniques, and critical parameters provides the basis for a predictive model.

Our proposal partly overlaps Roberts and Moran (1983) and Newman (1997). Roberts and Moran argue for the use of standard tasks in evaluating word processing applications. Our proposal differs in being independent of a specific application. Newman suggested using critical parameters to focus design on factors that made critical differences to user interface performance. We are motivated by Newman's original findings (1994) and wish to underscore the importance of critical parameters. However, we offer a broader approach that emphasizes the relationship between requirements, reference tasks, and metrics. Newman's account is unclear about the methods by which critical parameters are chosen. Another concern is that metrics may be task-specific rather than general, as his approach would seem to imply. Finally, we address the institutional processes required for the approach to work, in particular, how researchers can jointly identify reference tasks, collect data, analyze tasks, disseminate, and make use of shared results.

8.2.1   Reference Tasks in Other Disciplines

To motivate our approach, we trace the role of related concepts in speech recognition and information retrieval.

8.2.1.1   Speech Recognition (The DARPA Workshops)

Until the late 1980s, speech recognition research suffered from the same problems as HCI research. Researchers focused on different tasks and datasets, making it difficult to compare techniques and measure progress. Then DARPA organized an annual workshop where researchers meet for a "bakeoff" to compare system performance on a shared dataset (Marcus 1992; Price 1991; Stern 1990; Wayne 1989). A dataset consists of a publicly available corpus of spoken sentences, divided into training and test sentences. The initial task was to recognize the individual sentences in the corpus. There was no dialogue, and there were no real-time constraints. The success metric was the number of correctly recognized words in the corpus.

At each workshop, participating groups present and analyze their system performance. The utility of different techniques can thus be quantified, identifying which techniques succeed with certain types of data, utterances, or recognition tasks. All interested researchers get an annual snapshot of what is working and what isn't, and the overall amount of progress the field is making.

And progress has indeed been made. Initial systems recognized small vocabularies (1,000 words), had response times of minutes to hours, and high error rates (10 percent). Current systems recognize much larger vocabularies (100,000 words), operate in real time, and maintain the same error rate while recognizing increasingly complex spoken sentences. Furthermore, as system performance improves, more difficult tasks have been added to the bakeoff set. Early corpora consisted of high-quality audio monologues, whereas more recent tasks include telephone quality dialogues. More recent developments include attempts to extend these methods to interactive tasks (Walker et al. 1998).

Shared datasets have other benefits independent of the annual bakeoffs. There are now standard ways to report results of research taking place outside bakeoffs. Independent studies now report word error rates and performance in terms of shared datasets, allowing direct comparison with known systems and techniques.

8.2.1.2 *Information Retrieval (The TREC Conferences)*

A core set of tasks and shared data have also successfully driven research in Information Retrieval. The Text REtrieval Conference (TREC) (Voorhees and Harman 1997, 1998), sponsored by the United States National Institute of Standards and Technology (NIST), is analogous to DARPA speech recognition workshops.

A major goal of TREC is to facilitate cross-system comparisons. The conference began in 1991, again organized as a bakeoff, with about 40 systems tackling two common tasks. These were *routing* (standing queries put to a changing database, similar to news clipping services) and *ad hoc queries* (similar to search engine queries). Metrics for evaluation included *precision*—the proportion of documents a system retrieves that are relevant—and *recall*—the proportion of all relevant documents that are retrieved. More refined metrics, such as average precision (for multiple queries at a standard level of recall), also are used.

The field has made major progress over seven years: Average precision has doubled from 20 to 40 percent. Furthermore, the set of TREC tasks is being refined and expanded beyond routing and ad hoc queries. Over the years, new tasks have been added, such as interactive retrieval, filtering, Chinese, Spanish, cross-lingual, high precision, very large collections, speech, and database merging. In each case, participants address a common task with a shared dataset. Common tasks and metrics have made it possible not only to compare the techniques used by different systems but also to compare the evolution of the same system over time (Sparck-Jones 1998a).

Similar approaches have been applied successfully in other disciplines such as digital libraries and machine learning.

8.3   Reference Tasks in HCI

8.3.1   Lessons from DARPA and TREC

The case studies using shared tasks, metrics, and datasets reveal a number of relevant lessons. First, there are a number of positive outcomes.

- They show the essential role of the research community. Researchers defined tasks, produced and shared datasets, and agreed on suitable evaluation metrics. Furthermore, community practices were changed. Groups applied their systems to common tasks and data, then met to present and analyze their results. The bakeoff became a key community event.

- The basic task set is continuously refined. Both sets of workshops have added more tasks, increasing task difficulty and realism. This suggests that discovering "ideal" reference tasks will be an iterative collective process.

- One unexpected outcome is that system architectures and algorithms have become more similar. In consequence, it has become possible to carry out independent "black-box" evaluations of different modules. In the case of IR, this common architecture has also become a de facto decomposition of the overall retrieval task.

- A common architecture and shared datasets allow wider participation. Small research groups can evaluate their techniques on a sub-part of the overall task, without needing to construct complete experimental systems.

Several more problematic issues also arise.

- The workshops rely on a *bakeoff model,* assuming that research results are embodied in working systems that can be evaluated according to objective metrics. But how well will the system bakeoff model work for HCI?

- Are there key HCI results that cannot be implemented and thus cannot be evaluated as part of a system? Are there alternatives to the bakeoff model? Might we extend the bakeoff model to areas of HCI that are not focused on systems—for example, design, methods, or requirements analysis? For methods, does ethnomethodological analysis yield better design data than an experiment? When are different methods, useful (Gray and Saltzman 1998)? Furthermore, the bakeoff itself is not strictly necessary, although it serves an important social function. We can distinguish different elements of the DARPA/NIST process; shared datasets could be provided without bakeoffs to compare performance. Obviously this would decrease social interaction surrounding the meetings, but it would still allow for direct system comparison.

- There are also complex issues concerning *interactivity.* TREC and DARPA have focused mainly on non-interactive tasks. Going from simple tasks (with definable objective metrics) to more difficult and realistic tasks is not straightforward. Doing it may require fundamentally different algorithms and techniques. Both workshops have found difficulty in moving toward interactive tasks with subjective evaluation criteria.

- Previous evaluations allowed researchers to test systems on existing datasets, enabling the calculation of objective success measures such as word error rate, precision, and recall. Bringing humans into the evaluation (as users, subjects, judges) produces a more complicated, costly, and subjective process. If HCI wants to experiment with the bakeoff model, it must begin precisely where other workshops have experienced problems.

- We previously interpreted system convergence positively, but it also may have a negative side. In both workshops, groups sometimes take the strategy of imitating the best system from the previous bakeoff, with additional engineering to improve performance. If this strategy is generally followed, the overall effect is to reduce research diversity, which may mean that techniques do not generalize well to novel problems. It is therefore critical that reference tasks sets are continually modified and made more complex to prevent "overlearning" of specific datasets and tasks.

We do not yet have solutions for these issues. Instead, we view them as cautions that must be kept in mind as we experiment with reference tasks.

8.3.1.1 *Criteria for Selecting Reference Tasks*

How, then, do we choose appropriate reference tasks for HCI? Candidate reference tasks need to be *important* in everyday practice. A task may be "important" for different reasons.

- *Real*—first, tasks must also be "real"—that is, not divorced from actual user practice.
- *Frequent*—a task should be central to multiple user activities so that addressing it will have general benefits. An example here might be processing asynchronous messages. Given the centrality of communication for many user activities, improved ways to manage messages will have widespread benefits.
- *Critical*—other tasks may occur less frequently yet require near-perfect execution. Safety critical applications such as air traffic control are the prime example.

These criteria cannot be determined by researchers' intuitions: significant empirical investigations of user activity are needed. We believe the following areas are worthy of intense study and are likely to yield reference tasks.

- Information browsing, retrieval, and management
- Task management
- Information sharing
- Computer mediated communication
- Document processing
- Image processing and management
- Financial computation

In selecting reference tasks, we also must avoid obsolescence. While radical inventions cannot be anticipated, we should exclude tasks that may become unimportant or be transformed radically through predictable technological progress.

Our goals in defining reference tasks include generating shared requirements, accepted task definitions, descriptive vocabulary, task decomposition, and metrics. Common task definitions are critical for researchers to determine how other research is related to their effort. We will discuss how reference tasks are to be defined and give an illustrative example. First, however, we think it is worthwhile to discuss potential drawbacks of our approach.

8.3.1.2 Potential Objections to Our Proposal

One potential problem is that HCI research may shift from innovation to become merely a "clean up" operation, directed solely at improving existing tasks, techniques, and applications. However, the areas of information retrieval and speech recognition provide hopeful counterexamples. Developments in speech recognition have led to successful applications to novel and important problems, such as searching speech and video archives, and TREC has added tasks in these areas (Voorhees and Harman 1997, 1998).

Furthermore, a shift away from innovation may be necessary: The history of science and technology indicates that many major inventions required a critical mass of innovators producing multiple versions of a given technology before its successful uptake (Marvin 1988). Working in a radical invention mode precisely fails to achieve critical mass and thus the repeated solution attempts needed for adoption. Again, we are not declaring a moratorium on radical invention, just arguing for a different emphasis: HCI needs more "normal science" (Kuhn 1996).

There is also the danger of adopting a faulty paradigm. Progress in a field is severely limited when it is based on commonly accepted assumptions that are flawed. Cognitive Science and Artificial Intelligence have seen much lively debate over foundational assumptions (Dreyfus 1992; Ford and Pylyshyn 1995; Harnad 1990; Searle 1981). The notion of representation that was taken for granted in symbolic AI has been attacked (Bickhard and Terveen 1995). Similar arguments have been offered in the speech community. When non-interactive tasks and the sole performance metric of word error rate were central, techniques based on Hidden Markov models were popular. However, these techniques do not generalize well to "nonstandard" situations such as hyperarticulation (Oviatt et al. 1996) or speech in noisy environments (Junqua 1999). However, we do not believe the reference task approach runs this risk. Instead of proposing new assumptions or a new theory, we are suggesting a modified methodology, with more attention being paid to existing tasks. And note that completely radical *solutions* are consistent with our approach; they just need to be made relevant to a reference task and followed up by systematic analysis. We need a more rigorous understanding of the core conceptual territory of HCI so that we can better understand the role of radical innovations.

A variant of this last argument is that reference tasks induce bias toward the quantifiable and a concurrent blindness to more subtle considerations. Much recent HCI work has shown how factors that are not easily quantified, such as ethical issues (Nardi et al. 1996; Nardi and O'Day 1999) and social relationships among various stakeholders (Grudin 1988; Orlikowski 1992) affect the success of interactive technologies. From a design perspective, aesthetic issues also have a substantial impact on the success of applications (Laurel 1990). Nevertheless, the reference task approach is neutral with respect to such factors. Insofar as factors are crucial to user performance and satisfaction in a given task, successful reference task definitions naturally must incorporate them. Many of these issues also may relate to *subjective user judgments.* Our later discussion on metrics addresses the role of subjective measures such as user satisfaction. Our hope is to discover systematic ways that users make decisions about interfaces. By defining appropriate methods to elicit this information, we can address this problem.

8.4   How to Define a Reference Task

We adopt the activity theory view that a task is a conscious action subordinate to an object (Kaptelinin, 1996). Each action, or task, supports some specific object such as completing a research paper, building a plane, or curing a patient. The object in these cases is the paper, the plane, the patient. The tasks are performed to transform the object to a desired state (complete paper, functioning plane, healthy patient).

The same tasks can occur across different objects; thus, the task of outlining could be useful in writing a book, preparing legal boilerplate, or specifying a product. In studying reference tasks, it is important to determine the object of tasks so that appropriate customizations can be offered. While there might be a generic "outlining engine," outlining a product specification could entail special actions that require customizing the basic engine. Keeping the object in mind will bring designs closer to users' requirements.

We also need empirical work to determine good domains for investigating candidate reference tasks. Of the many tasks involving computers, we must identify tasks satisfying our criteria of frequency and criticality. Defining a reference task may begin with an analysis of prior relevant work. All too often, each individual research effort defines its own problem, requirements, and (post hoc) evaluation metrics. However, by analyzing a broad set of related papers, one can abstract these common elements.

- What are the user requirements in this area? Are they based on solid empirical investigation? Often the answer is no—which means more empirical studies of user activity are needed.

- Is there a common user task (or set of tasks) that is being addressed?

- What are the components of the task(s)? Is a task decomposition given, or can one be abstracted from various papers?

- What is the range of potential solution techniques? What problems do they address, and what problems are unsolved? Are there problems in applying various techniques (do they require significant user input, scaling, privacy, or security concerns)?

- How are solution techniques evaluated? Are metrics proposed that generalize beyond the single originating study? This last issue is crucial—it captures Newman's (1997) "critical parameters" that define the artifact's purpose and measure how well it serves that purpose.

If researchers abstract tasks from related work, they may be personally satisfied with the result. But other researchers may have different perspectives on all task aspects. For this reason, important community practices need to be introduced. Representative researchers and practitioners concerned with a particular area need to meet to discuss, modify, and approve the reference task definition. This would be like a standards committee meeting, although faster and more lightweight. Such groups might meet in the CHI workshops program or in government-sponsored workshops, organized by NIST or DARPA, for example. After a reference task is approved, its definition would be published—perhaps in the *SIGCHI Bulletin* and *Interactions*—with the complete definition appearing on the Web. But agreed reference task definitions also need to be modifiable as researchers and practitioners experiment with them. One might use the NIST TREC model in cases where tasks are discussed annually, with modifications being made in the light of feedback.

Finally, the community must reinforce the important role of the shared knowledge embodied in reference tasks. Educational courses must show how tasks are defined and the benefits from using this knowledge, as well as emphasizing the problems that the reference task approach addresses. And the CHI review process could be modified so that reviewers explicitly rate papers with reference to the reference task model.

8.5   An Example Reference Task: Browsing and Retrieval in Speech Archives

We now discuss an example reference task: browsing and retrieval in speech archives. It is intended to illustrate (1) identifying reference tasks, (2) using them to evaluate and improve user interfaces, and (3) issues arising in this endeavor. We summarize work reported in recent research papers (Choi et al. 1998; Nakatani, et al. 1998; Whittaker et al. 1998a; Whittaker et al. 1998b; Whittaker et al. 1999; Whittaker et al. 2000). Other areas would have served equally well in illustrating reference tasks. We selected this area simply because of our personal expertise in this domain.

8.5.1 Selecting and Specifying Reference Tasks in the Domain of Speech Archives

Two criteria we proposed earlier for selecting a reference task were that the task be either *frequent* or *critical.* So what is the evidence that accessing speech data is an important user task? Conversational speech is both frequent and central to many everyday workplace tasks (Chapanis 1975; Kraut et al. 1993; Whittaker et al. 1994). Voice messaging is a pervasive technology at work and at home, with both voice mail and answering machines requiring access to stored speech data. In the United States alone, there are over 63 million voice mail users. New areas of speech archiving are also emerging, with television and radio programs becoming available online. These observations indicate that searching and browsing speech data meet the criteria of being frequent, general, and real. Furthermore, we will show that the tasks we identify in speech retrieval generalize to retrieval of textual data, making it possible to use them more widely.

But identifying the *area* of speech retrieval does not identify specific user tasks when accessing speech archives. We therefore collected several different types of data concerning people's processing of voice mail. We chose to examine voice mail access rather than other audio data such as news because voice mail is currently the most pervasive speech access application. We collected qualitative and quantitative data for a typical voice mail system, Audix™: (1) server logs, (2) surveys from high volume users, and (3) interviews with high-volume users. We also carried out laboratory tests to confirm our findings on further users.

We found three core speech access tasks: (1) search, (2) information extraction, and (3) message summarization. *Search* is involved in *prioritizing* incoming new messages and for *locating* valuable saved messages. Our working definition of search is, given a set of messages, identify a (small) subset of messages having relevant attributes with certain values (for example being from a particular person or being about a particular topic). *Information extraction* involves accessing information from *within* messages. This is often a laborious process involving repeatedly listening to a message for verbatim facts such as caller's name and phone number. Our definition of information extraction is, given a (set of) message(s) and a set of relevant attributes, identify the values associated with those attributes. A final task at the message level is *summarization:* To avoid repeatedly replaying messages, users attempt to summarize their contents, usually by taking handwritten notes consisting of a sentence or two describing the main point of the message. We define summarization as involving selection of a subset of information from within the document that best captures the meaning of the entire document. For more formal definitions of summarization we refer the reader to Sparck-Jones (1998b).

These three tasks were generated by analysis of voice mail user data. Nevertheless, although they originated from *speech* data, we found analogues in the independently generated TREC *textual* retrieval tasks. The fact that these three tasks are common to searching both speech and text is encouraging for the reference task approach. It argues that there may be general search tasks that are independent of media type.

8.5.2   Defining Metrics

Our data also suggested possible metrics for gauging task success. In the interviews, people oriented to three different aspects of system usage when trying to execute their tasks. First, users wanted to complete their tasks correctly and accurately. People repeatedly accessed voice mail until they had correctly extracted critical information or until they had located a relevant message. We call this criterion *task success.* But people were also focused on *efficiency.* Most users complained that executing the three core tasks was tedious, requiring too many user actions. This led to the metric of *task completion time* (Burkhart et al. 1994; Newman 1997). Finally users made comments about the experiential quality of the interaction, leading to the criterion of *subjective evaluation.*

8.5.3   Task-Oriented Evaluation of a Speech Browsing System

We next applied these task definitions and metrics to a real system that allows users to search and browse recorded news broadcasts.[3] The system applies automatic speech recognition to recorded broadcasts, indexes the resulting errorful[4] textual transcriptions for information retrieval, and provides a user interface to support search and browsing (for a full architectural description, see Choi et al. 1998). Figure 8.1 shows the UI, which is described elsewhere (Whittaker et al, 1998b; Whittaker et al. 1999). The elements of the UI support a new paradigm for speech retrieval interfaces: *"What you see is (almost) what you hear"* (WYSIAWYH).

To evaluate two different versions of the UI (and hence two different UI techniques) we conducted laboratory experiments where users were given three tasks: *search, summarization,* and *information extraction,* corresponding to the three reference tasks we had identified. For search, users had to find the most relevant speech document addressing a given issue. For summarization, they had to produce a six- to eight-sentence summary of a single speech "document" (where documents were about five minutes in length). For information extraction, they had to find a fact in a given speech document *(What were the names of the actors who starred in the Broadway musical* Maggie Flynn*?).* We used three evaluation metrics: *task success, time to solution,* and *perceived utility* of the user interface. To determine task success we had independent judges rank documents for relevance and rate summaries, and to the correctness of factual answers.

We initially used the method to compare two different versions of the user interface. The main problem with browsing speech is that of random access to relevant materials. When browsing *text,* people are able to visually scan exploiting structural cues (formatting, paragraphs, headers) to look for key words, enabling focus on relevant document

---

[3]We are also currently carrying out similar experiments on voice mail data (Whittaker et al. 2000).

[4]The errors arise because ASR performance for this type of data is imperfect: the state of the art is that about 70 percent of words are correctly recognized.

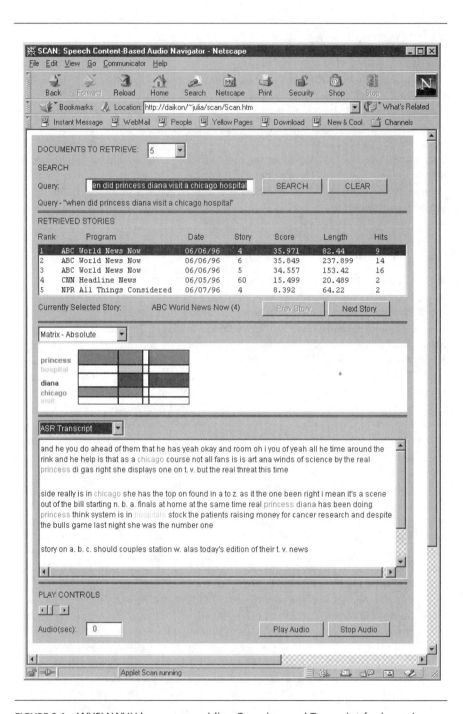

FIGURE 8.1   WYSIAWYH browser providing Overview and Transcript for browsing

regions. One version of the UI attempted to emulate this by providing a visual analogue to the underlying speech, allowing people to visually scan as they would with text (see Figure 8.1). This WYSIAWYH UI provided users with graphical information about how the terms in their query were distributed in a given document, allowing them to "zoom in" on regions containing large numbers of query terms and ignore the parts of the document that weren't relevant to their query. It also provided information about the content of each speech document by presenting the errorful transcript of each story (including highlighted query terms), allowing users to visually scan through stories to identify relevant regions for playing. We compared this with a version of the UI without these browsing features. It allowed users to search for speech documents but provided no browsing support: Users selected audio to play using tape recorder type controls (see Figure 8.2). For all metrics, the more complex UI was better for search and information extraction

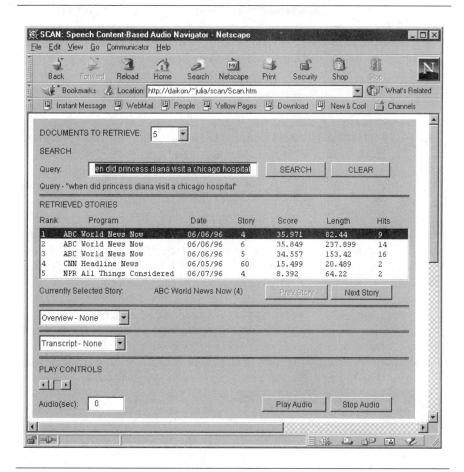

FIGURE 8.2   Basic browser providing play controls for browsing

tasks, but we observed no differences between UI versions for summarization. More details are supplied in Whittaker et al. 1999.

We have since conducted further studies using identical metrics and task sets to evaluate different versions of the UI and also the effects of systematically varying the quality of automatic speech recognition on browsing and search. We found that improving ASR quality beyond 84 percent accuracy made no difference to performance, although users could detect subjective differences qualitatively (Stark et al. 2000).

8.5.4 General Issues Arising from Reference Task-Based Evaluation

While our task-based approach has generally been successful, some issues arose in applying the method. One issue concerns our choice of metrics and the importance we associate with each. We use multiple evaluation metrics, in contrast to approaches, such as the PARADISE method for evaluating interactive spoken language systems (Walker et al. 1998). Our decision was influenced by several factors. Selecting appropriate evaluation metrics is a highly complex process that has generated much previous debate (Gray et al. 1993; Gray and Saltzman 1998; Roberts and Moran 1983; Walker et al. 1998). Prior evaluation work has, for example, shown inconsistencies between *objective* measures (time to solution and task success) and *subjective* measures (user satisfaction) for people doing the same task using the same system (Sellen 1995; Whittaker et al. 1993). This inconsistency may make it impossible to have one metric "stand in" for another. Other evaluation work has made strong claims for the use of *user satisfaction* in evaluating system success (Walker et al. 1998), based on the argument that persistent long-term system use is motivated by *user's perception* of the system's value, rather than externally calculated measures.[5] While acknowledging this argument, there are still outstanding questions concerning the definition and measurement of user satisfaction. Our current (conservative) view is therefore that multiple objective and subjective metrics should be used to measure system success. We regard as research questions the exact relationship between different measures, whether one metric is more useful and predictive than others, and how user satisfaction is defined and measured.

A second issue concerns *reference task selection*. One of our chosen tasks, summarization, was relatively insensitive to different user interface techniques. While our requirements data revealed that summarization was a critical task for users, summarization performance has not proved to be a useful way to distinguish between different user interfaces for any of our metrics. Does this mean that summarization is

---

[5]This is an oversimplification of Walker et al. (1998). They argue that multiple factors contribute to system success (task completion, time to solution, speech recognizer accuracy, use of help prompts), but in modeling the contribution of these factors, their regression analyzes treat user satisfaction as the dependent variable. In other words, they view user satisfaction as the critical metric, and their question is how these other factors affect it.

a poor candidate for a reference task? Closer examination of our data suggests possible reasons for our failure to find effects. Overall performance on the summarization task was low. Our current UI techniques may not have helped with summarization, but better techniques might improve performance and produce observed differences on this task. Another possibility is that our definition of summarization is underspecified, so the task was not well defined for users (Sparck-Jones 1998b). Our experience with summarization has an important implication for the reference task approach. It is not enough to select important tasks by careful analysis of user data. These tasks also must be well operationalized for evaluation purposes. Operationalization itself may be a complex undertaking to achieve plausible instantiations of tasks in experimental settings.

Another problem concerns the relationship between requirements gathering and reference task selection. Most requirements gathering takes place in the context of specific applications. In our case, we gathered information about speech retrieval by investigating voice mail users. But the primary function of voice mail is an asynchronous communications application rather than a speech archive. One decision when selecting reference tasks was therefore whether the observed tasks were relevant to speech retrieval or asynchronous communication. In our requirements gathering for voice mail, we actually identified two further tasks, namely status tracking and archive management. We excluded these from the speech retrieval reference task set because they did not directly concern retrieval. Of course if we were identifying reference tasks for managing asynchronous communications (like e-mail and voice mail), then such tasks would be highly relevant.

We also experienced the problem of *task granularity*. In processing voice mail, users carry out activities that are analyzable at multiple levels of abstraction. At the highest level "processing voice mail" might be an activity that users engage in. Alternatively we might describe low-level acts such as "press button 3" (to delete a message). Neither characterization would be useful as a reference task. The "process voice mail" characterization is too general, and it includes tasks that are not directly relevant to speech retrieval (status tracking and archive management). In contrast the "press button 3" characterization is too specific to a particular implementation. In identifying our three reference tasks we made decisions about abstraction, and our criteria were intuitive. A critical technical issue for our research program concerns principled ways to specify reference task granularity.

We also should be concerned about *task-specificity*. We found different performance for search, summarization, and information extraction tasks. Different user interface techniques may be successful for different reference tasks. Such a conclusion would indeed be consistent with observations about task-specific interfaces (Nardi 1993), and also current theories of situated cognition (Lave 1988; Suchman 1987). Task-specificity highlights the importance of careful task selection. We must choose reference tasks to be critical to our users' everyday computing activities. Careful task selection ensures that we still generate important data to help improve system design for important user problems, even if that design does not generalize to *all* user tasks.

Of course, we hope our approach leads to general principles for UI design, but if not, at least we have data about important user tasks. In the worst case it might mean that the field of HCI splinters into multiple task-based research areas, but at least those areas would be informed by well-researched user needs about critical user problems, along with well-defined evaluation metrics. Furthermore, a number of factors would still unite such task-based communities, including methodologies such as user-centered and participatory design, modeling techniques such as GOMS, broad frameworks such as activity theory, and computational tools such as rapid prototyping environments and interface builders. And as far as application design and development is concerned, having task-specific information may correspond well with common practice: Application development takes place in a task-specific context.

Another issue concerns user population. While we have made every attempt to ensure the representativeness of the people participating in our experiments, specific user groups (such as the elderly or children) may use the technology quite differently. User population also must be included in the reference task analysis.

Another issue concerns inherent limitations of task-based evaluation. In experimental studies people are asked to perform prespecified tasks over a short period of time. We therefore cannot detect ad hoc or creative use of the UI nor how use strategies evolve over time. These phenomena can only be observed in field trials. Of course, field trials also have their drawbacks. Field trial users select their own tasks, making it impossible to draw direct comparisons between different techniques or systems because users are executing different tasks. Extended use in field trials should therefore be used to complement task-based evaluation. The entire evaluation process must be iterative, combining the results of experimental and field-based methods. Field trials may show that critical user tasks have been neglected or that technologies may be developed and used in novel ways. Field trial findings should therefore be used to modify existing task definitions for future evaluations.

Finally, there is a question of novelty. What's new about the reference task speech browsing and retrieval example? After all, isn't the process we just described, good, but standard, HCI practice? Isn't it standard best practice in HCI to interview users to understand their needs, develop a system to meet these needs, and evaluate the system to determine whether it meets their needs? It seems, however, that there are major differences between ideal and actual descriptions of the process of HCI. Although the ideal is to follow the three steps we describe, few actual studies seem to execute all three. Recall also that the reference task agenda involves both technical and social aspects. We diverge from standard technical practice in recommending that we use general evaluation metrics derived from important tasks. However, the more important implications of our example are social. In our domain, we found no set of task definitions or user requirements and no accepted metrics. And in moving toward developing this knowledge, there were no accepted community mechanisms for refining and disseminating that knowledge once we had discovered it. Developing such social mechanisms is the major activity needed to put the reference task approach into practice.

8.6   Conclusions

We identify a problem with the process of HCI research: Emphasis on radical innovation precludes building a common research focus. Without such a focus, people cannot build on the work of others or compare UI techniques to improve them. The lack of common focus also makes it difficult to accumulate the research on common problems needed for theory development. Lack of common knowledge also means that we cannot give informed design advice to builders of new systems. In response to this, we argue that the HCI community focus around reference tasks. We review the advantages and disadvantages of this approach, documenting its use in information retrieval and speech recognition research. We also describe an example reference task for searching and browsing speech archives. We point to a number of outstanding issues arising from applying the approach: choice of metrics, selection and operationalization of tasks, task-specificity of results, user variability, and the need for complementary field trials. We also point to the absence of methods for distributing and sharing data and results within the field.

We outline the necessary steps to execute the reference task research agenda, making both technical and social recommendations. The necessary technical research involves identifying important user tasks by systematic requirements gathering, definition and operationalization of reference tasks and evaluation metrics, and execution of task-based evaluation along with judicious use of field trials. The major technical hurdles are (1) agreeing on common task definitions; (2) developing general templates for describing reference tasks, stating the criteria they must satisfy, including their level of granularity; (3) defining appropriate metrics; and (4) designing appropriate task-based evaluation techniques.

Perhaps more important, we recommend changes in HCI community practice. We must create influential forums for discussion of common tasks and methods by which people can compare systems and techniques. The major obstacle here is to define a process that (1) allows researchers to agree on task definitions and (2) provides methods to disseminate these definitions so that they are broadly used by the HCI community. Only by doing this can reference tasks be incorporated into the process of research and development, helping the field achieve the focus it desperately needs.

Acknowledgments

Thanks to Julia Hirschberg, Candy Kamm, Fernando Pereira, and Marilyn Walker, along with the attendees at HCIC 1999 for useful suggestions and feedback.

References

Amento, B., Hill, W., Terveen, L., Hix, D., and Ju, P. (1999). An empirical evaluation of user interfaces for topic management of Web sites. *Proceedings of CHI'99 Conference on Computer Human Interaction,* 552–559. New York: ACM.

Baecker, R. (1987). Towards an effective characterization of graphical interaction. In R. Baecker and W. Buxton (Eds.), *Readings in Human Computer Interaction.* San Francisco, CA: Kaufmann.

Barreau, D., and Nardi, B. (1995). Finding and reminding: Organization of information from the desktop. *SIGCHI Bulletin, 27,* 39–45.

Bickhard, M.H., and Terveen, L.G. (1995). *Foundational Issues in Artificial Intelligence and Cognitive Science: Impasse and Solution.* New York: Elsevier.

Brennan, S. (1990). Conversation as direct manipulation: An iconoclastic view. In B. Laurel (Ed.), *The art of human computer interface design.* Reading, MA: Addison-Wesley.

Burkhart, B., Hemphill, D., and Jones, S. (1994). The value of a baseline in determining design success. *Proceedings of CHI'94 Conference on Computer Human Interaction,* 386–391. New York: ACM.

Card, S., Moran, T., and Newell, A. (1983). *The psychology of human computer interaction.* Hillsdale, N.J.: Erlbaum.

Carroll, J., and Campbell, R. (1986). Softening up hard science. *Human Computer Interaction, 2,* 227–249.

Chapanis, A. (1975). Interactive human communication. *Scientific American, 232,* 36–42.

Choi, J., Hindle, D., Hirschberg, J., Magrin-Chagnolleau, I., Nakatani, C.H., Pereira, F., Singhal, A., and Whittaker, S. (1998). SCAN—Speech content audio navigator: A systems overview. *Proceedings of International Conference on Spoken Language Processing,* 604–608. Piscataway, NJ: IEEE.

Dreyfus, H.L. (1992). *What computers still can't do.* Cambridge, MA: MIT Press.

Fertig, S., Freeman, E., and Gelertner, D. (1996). Finding and reminding reconsidered. *SIGCHI Bulletin, 28,* 1.

Ford, K.M., and Pylyshyn, Z. (1995). *The robot's dilemma revisited: The frame problem in artificial intelligence.* Norwood, NJ: Ablex Press.

Foundyller, C. (1984). Cad/CAM, *CAE: The contemporary technology* Cambridge, MA: Daratech Associations.

Gifford, D., Jouvelot, P., Sheldon, M., and O'Toole, J. (1991). Semantic file systems. In *Proceedings of 13th ACM Symposium on Operating System Principles,* NY: ACM.

Goldberg, D., Nichols, D., Oki, B.M., and Terry, D. (1992). Using collaborative filtering to weave an information tapestry. *Communications of the ACM, 35,* 51–60.

Gray W., and Salzman, M. (1998). Damaged merchandise? A review of experiments that compare usability evaluation methods. *Human Computer Interaction,* 13, 203–262.

Gray, W.D., John, B.E., and Atwood, M.E. (1993). Project Ernestine: Validating a GOMS analysis for predicting and explaining real-world task performance. *Human-Computer Interaction,* 8, 237–309.

Grudin, J. (1988). Why CSCW applications fail: Problems in the design and evaluation of organizational interfaces. *Proceedings of CSCW'88 Conference on Computer Supported Cooperative Work,* 85–93. New York: ACM .

Harnad, S. (1990). The symbol grounding problem. *Physica D,* 42, 335–346.

Hill, W.C., Stead, L., Rosenstein, M., and Furnas, G. (1995). Recommending and evaluating choices in a virtual community of use. *Proceedings of CHI'95 Conference on Computer Human Interaction,* 194–201. New York, ACM.

Isaacs, E., and Tang, J. (1996). Technology transfer: so much research so few good products. *Communications of the ACM,* 39, 22–25.

Junqua, J-C. (1999). The Lombard Effect: A reflex to better communicate with others in noise. *International Conference on Acoustics Speech and Signal Processing,* 2083–2086. Piscataway, NJ: IEEE.

Kaptelinin, V. (1996). Activity theory: Implications for human-computer interaction. In B. Nardi, (Ed.), *Context and Consciousness: Activity Theory and Human-Computer Interaction.* Cambridge, MA: MIT Press.

Kraut, R., Fish, R., Root, B., and Chalfonte, B. (1993). Informal communication in organizations. In R. Baecker (Ed.), *Groupware and Computer Supported Co-operative Work.* San Francisco: Kaufman.

Kuhn, T.S. (1996). *The structure of scientific revolutions,* third edition. Chicago: University of Chicago Press.

Landauer, T. (1995). Let's get real. In R. Baecker, J. Grudin, W. Buxton, and S. Greenberg (Eds.), *Human Computer Interaction: Towards the year 2000.* San Francisco, CA: Morgan Kaufman.

Laurel, B. (1990). *The art of human computer interface design.* Reading, MA: Addison-Wesley.

Lave, J. (1988). *Cognition in practice.* New York: Cambridge University Press.

Marcus, M. (1992) *Proceedings of speech and natural language workshop.* San Francisco: Kaufmann.

Marvin, C. (1988). *When old technologies were new.* New York: Oxford University Press.

Nakatani, C.H., Whittaker, S., and Hirschberg, J. (1998). Now you hear it now you don't: Empirical studies of audio browsing behavior. *Proceedings of International Conference on Spoken Language Processing,* 1003–1007. Piscataway, NJ: IEEE.

Nardi, B. (1993). *A small matter of programming.* Cambridge, MA: MIT Press.

Nardi, B., Kuchinsky, A., Whittaker, S., Leichner, R., and Schwarz, H. (1996). Video-as-data: Technical and social aspects of a collaborative multimedia application. *Computer Supported Cooperative Work,* 4, 73–100.

Nardi, B., Miller, J., and Wright, D. (1998). Collaborative, programmable intelligent agents. *Communications of the ACM.*

Nardi, B., and O'Day, V. (1999). Information ecologies: Using technology with heart. Cambridge, MA: MIT Press.

Newell, A., and Card, S. (1985). The prospects for psychological science in Human Computer Interaction. *Human Computer Interaction,* 1, 209–242.

Newman, W. (1994). A preliminary analysis of the products of HCI research using Pro Forma abstracts. *Proceedings of CHI'94 Conference on Computer Human Interaction,* 278–284. New York: ACM.

Newman, W. (1997). Better or just different? On the benefits of designing interactive systems in terms of critical parameters. *Designing Interactive Systems (DIS97),* 239–246. New York: ACM.

Olson, J., and Olson, G. (1990). The growth of cognitive modeling in human computer interaction since GOMS. *Human Computer Interaction,* 5, 221–265.

Orlikowski, W. (1992). Learning from Notes: Organizational issues in groupware implementation. *Proceedings of CSCW'92 Conference on Computer Supported Cooperative Work.* New York: ACM.

Oviatt, S.L., Levow, G., MacEachern, M., and Kuhn, K. (1996). Modeling hyper-articulate speech during human-computer error resolution. *Proceedings of the International Conference on Spoken Language Processing,* 801–804. Piscataway, NJ: IEEE.

Price, P. (1991) *Proceedings of speech and natural language workshop.* San Francisco: Kaufmann.

Rao, R., Card, S., Johnson, W., Klotz, L., and Trigg, R. (1994). Protofoil: Storing and finding the information worker's documents in an electronic filing cabinet. *Proceedings of CHI'94 Conference on Computer Human Interaction,* 180–185. New York: ACM.

Resnick, P., Iacovou, N., Suchak, M., Bergstrom, P., and Riedl, J. (1994). GroupLens: An open architecture for collaborative filtering of netnews. *Proceedings of CSCW'94 Conference on Computer Supported Cooperative Work,* 175–186. New York: ACM.

Resnick, P., and Varian, H. (1997). Special issue on recommender systems. *Communications of the ACM,* 26, 56–58.

Roberts, T.L., and Moran, T.P. (1983). The evaluation of text editors: Methodology and empirical results. *Communications of the ACM,* 26, 265–283.

Rudsill M., Lewis C.L., Polson P.G., and McKay T.D. (1996). *Human-computer interface design: Success stories, emerging methods and real-world context.* San Francisco: Kaufmann.

Searle, J.R. (1981). Minds, brains, and programs. In J. Haugeland (Ed.), *Mind Design,* 282–306. Cambridge: MIT Press.

Sellen, A. (1995). Remote conversations: The effects of mediating talk with technology. *Human Computer Interaction,* 10, 401–444.

Shneiderman, B. (1982). The future of interactive systems and the emergence of direct manipulation. *Behavior and information technology,* 1, 237–256.

Shardanand, U., and Maes, P. (1995). Social information filtering: Algorithms for automating "word of mouth." *Proceedings of CHI'95 Conference on Computer Human Interaction,* 210–217. New York: ACM.

Smith, D., Irby, C., Kimball, R., Verplank, W., and Harslem, E. (1982). Designing the Star user interface. *Byte,7.*

Sparck-Jones, K. (1998a). Summary performance comparisons TREC2, TREC3, TREC4, TREC5, TREC6. In E.M. Voorhees and D.K. Harman (Eds.), *Proceedings of the Sixth Text Retrieval Conference (TREC-7),* 1998.

Sparck-Jones, K. (1998b). Automatically summarising: factors and directions. In I. Mani and M. Maybury (Eds.), *Advances in Automomatic Text Summarization.* Cambridge, MA: MIT Press.

Stark, L., Whittaker, S., and Hirschberg, J. (2000). ASR satisficing: The effects of ASR accuracy on speech retrieval. To appear in ICSLP 2000.

Stern, R. (1990*). Proceedings of speech and natural language workshop.* San Francisco: Kaufmann.

Suchman, L. (1987). *Plans and situated actions.* Cambridge, MA: Cambridge University Press.

Sutherland, I. (1963). Sketchpad: A man-machine graphical communication system. *Proceedings of AFIPS 23,* 329–346.

Voorhees, E.M., and Harman, D.K. (1998). Overview of the seventh Text Retrieval Conference (TREC-7). In E.M. Voorhees and D.K. Harman (Eds.), *Proceedings of the Seventh Text Retrieval Conference (TREC-7),* 1998.

Voorhees, E.M., and Harman, D.K., (1997). Overview of the sixth Text Retrieval Conference (TREC-6). In E.M. Voorhees and D.K. Harman (Eds.), *Proceedings of the Sixth Text Retrieval Conference (TREC-6),* 1997.

Walker, M., Litman, D., Kamm, C., and Abella, A. (1998). Evaluating spoken dialogue agents with {PARADISE}: Two case studies. *Computer Speech and Language,* 12, 3.

Wayne, C. (1989). *Proceedings of speech and natural language workshop.* San Francisco: Kaufmann.

Whittaker, S. Davis, R., Hirschberg, J., and Muller, U. (2000). Jotmail: A voicemail interface that enables you to see what was said. *Proceedings of CHI'2000 Human Factors in Computing Systems,* 89–96. New York: ACM.

Whittaker, S., Frohlich, D., and Daly-Jones, O. (1994). Informal workplace communication: What is it like and how might we support it? In *Proceedings of CHI'94 Human Factors in Computing Systems,* 130–137. New York: ACM.

Whittaker, S., Geelhoed, E., and Robinson, E. (1993). Shared workspaces: How do they work and when are they useful? *International Journal of Man-Machine Studies,* 39, 813–842.

Whittaker, S., Hirschberg, J., Choi, J., Hindle, D., Pereira, F., and Singhal, A. (1999). SCAN: Designing and evaluating user interfaces to support retrieval from speech archives. *Proceedings of SIGIR99 Conference on Research and Development in Information Retrieval,* 26–33. New York: ACM.

Whittaker, S., Hirschberg, J., and Nakatani, C.H. (1998a). All talk and all action: Strategies for managing voicemail messages. *Proceedings of CHI'98 Conference on Computer Human Interaction,* 249–250. New York: ACM.

Whittaker, S., Hirschberg, J., and Nakatani, C.H. (1998b). What you see is almost what you hear: Design principles for user interfaces for accessing speech archives. *Proceedings of International Conference on Spoken Language Processing.* Piscataway, NJ: IEEE.

Whittaker, S., and Sidner, C. (1996). Email overload: Exploring personal information management of email. *Proceedings of CHI'96 Conference on Computer Human Interaction,* 276–283. New York: ACM Press.

9

The Maturation of HCI: Moving beyond Usability toward Holistic Interaction

Ken Maxwell

9.1 Introduction

Human-computer interaction (HCI) is a discipline devoted to helping people meet their needs and goals by making computing technology accessible, meaningful, and satisfying. At the beginning of this new millennium the discipline of HCI is developing in earnest to serve the expanding needs of people who live increasingly mobile and interconnected lifestyles with growing expectations of support for their lifestyles from emerging computing technologies. In grappling with the problems of integrating new technologies with new lifestyles, HCI is maturing—but in which directions? What does it mean to have mature HCI? How will it be achieved? What changes in the way HCI is practiced will accompany maturity? This paper presents particular answers to these questions in the context of HCI for personal and business computing. Specialized applications such as HCI in aviation or manufacturing are not directly addressed.

There are several different perspectives from which researchers can assess HCI maturity. From a technology-based perspective, researchers can assess the maturity of interaction technologies. For example, the maturity of speech recognition can be measured quantitatively with respect to several performance factors. From a model-based perspective, researchers can assess the maturity of interaction models with respect to their predictive power. From a process-based perspective, researchers can assess the maturity of methods with respect to their efficiency and effectiveness. For example, the Software Engineering Institute (SEI) has developed the Capability Maturity Model (CMM) to drive software process improvement (Caputo 1998). This model does not specify particular software architectures but instead addresses the maturity of the process of building software by instituting key practices in a staged manner. The model has five levels, and SEI certifies software companies at each level of capability when their respective criteria are satisfied. SEI designed the model so that a company can mature its capabilities and progress to higher-level certification over time. The progression of levels represents greater organizational self-awareness and manageability. Hefley et al. (1995) argue that rigorous processes, methods, and techniques are necessary for an engineering discipline to mature. These researchers further argue that the field of HCI should be working toward making HCI's engineering processes repeatable and well defined. These characteristics are in accordance with moving to higher levels in the CMM. Hefley et al. argue that by making its processes more rigorous HCI will not only mature as a discipline but will also move toward integration with software engineering practices.

Processes and practices are important, and their rigor reflects the maturity of some aspects of the discipline that applies them. However, HCI is primarily a discipline focused on people, and it is about helping to make their relationship with and use of computers easier, more productive, and more fulfilling. The discipline of HCI is only focused on process, models, or technology to the degree that having these facilitates meeting its primary people-oriented goals. Viewed in this way, the maturation of the HCI discipline should represent a progression in the types of human needs and goals that the discipline supports.

Maslow (1962) proposed a model for personal growth consisting of a hierarchy of needs that can serve loosely as an analog for an HCI maturity model. Maslow's hierarchy is most recognizable for the stage of self-actualization. In this model low-level, or more basic, needs in the hierarchy have to be satisfied before higher-level needs can be achieved. Both Maslow's growth model and the CMM share the characteristic of moving from fulfillment of basic requirements toward mastery of greater problems. However, where the CMM focuses on process, Maslow focuses on needs.

Analogously, the work in HCI can be viewed as a progression moving from supporting the basic needs and goals of users toward supporting higher-level human needs and goals with computing technology. Section 9.2 differentiates three levels that illustrate a progression of the character of interaction from people-friendly (past) to people-familiar (present) to people-intimate (future). The human-centered development approach can be used to develop HCI at all three levels. Between levels, the breadth of human needs and goals that are addressed change, as do the methods, techniques, and tools used by system designers to understand people's needs and goals and to create designs that support them. Viewing HCI maturation in this way provides a general compass to assess the directions in which the field will move and a means to assess its progress. Since the third level represents the future, the description of it includes a discussion of possible changes in HCI practice that will help to enable it.

9.2   Present Levels of HCI Maturity

9.2.1   Level 1 HCI: Basic Usability

During the past 20 years, computers have been vigorously transferred from laboratories and central data processing centers, in which only skilled experts used them, to offices and homes, for use by people who need to perform a wide range of tasks that can be assisted by personal computing technologies. However, this expanded group of computer users was not necessarily trained in computer technology. The usability needs of these new computer users propelled the growth of HCI as a discipline of study and focused its primary goal on making computers easier to use. Basic usability, as the term is used here, involves an assortment of support for needs such as ease of use, ease of learning, error protection, graceful error recovery, and efficiency of performance.

The use of graphical user interfaces (GUIs), interaction metaphors, direct manipulation, point-and-click input devices, user interface management systems, GOMS models (Card et al. 1983; Kieras 1988), and design standards to achieve intuitive and visually rich interaction have dominated this stage. HCI at this level is closely associated with engineering models and processes. A goal of many practitioners is to integrate the HCI development process with the overall system engineering process (de Baar et al. 1992; Hefley et al. 1995). Work at level 1 has been ongoing since the beginning of HCI as a discipline. As HCI develops to address people's higher-level needs and goals, work on basic usability issues will continue to be needed. New computing and interaction technologies will require work at this level to make them available and mature enough for application at other levels.

9.2.2   Level 2 HCI: Collaborative, Organizational, and Role-Based Interaction

In more recent years, the rapid proliferation of distributed and networked computing, and its convergence with communication technology has generated an expansion of attention that moves beyond the basic usability issues addressed by level 1 to questions about the sociological, organizational, and cultural impact of computing. Although these questions have been of concern since before home and office computer use became widespread (Tomeski 1976; Wachtel 1976), they had received less emphasis while the need to design usable office and home computer systems was more immediate. The explosive growth of the Internet, enterprise computing systems, decision support systems, and research in computer-supported cooperative work (CSCW) has spawned renewed interest and placed renewed importance in the role HCI plays in organizations and transactions among people.

In particular, HCI's scope of interest has expanded to issues of organizational structure, the nature of work, defining roles in organizations, customization of processes, and teamwork. For example, Grudin and Markus (1997) examined organizational issues influencing both the development and use of HCI. Karsten and Jones (1998) performed a case study to examine the influence of collaborative technology, specifically Lotus Notes, on organizational change within a Finnish computer consultancy. They concluded that, at least for the case studied, collaborative technology can be adopted by individuals to support work in a variety of ways and that a collaborative organizational culture is not necessarily required. Davenport (1998) studied the experiences of several companies in implementing an enterprise computing system. The results indicated that companies that were able to view the introduction of enterprise systems in strategic and organizational terms rather than technological terms had the best success and that the need for top-level management involvement is crucial.

Work on organization and collaboration issues has in part illuminated the users' need for and the value of tailoring the interaction with regard to user roles. One prominent area using this approach is role-based access control (RBAC). Several systems have been developed and are currently used that apply RBAC to ease the tasks associated with user security and authorization. The work in this area has been prolific enough to support an annual conference sponsored by ACM/SIGSAC (Special Interest Group on Security, Audit, and Control). Role-based interaction techniques have also been applied to broader system administration and management tasks (Lupu and Sloman 1997).

The usefulness of role-based interaction has also been illuminated by the increased realization that a one-size-fits-all approach to developing tools for people with different goals, responsibilities, and priorities is ill fated. In the one-size-fits-all approach tools become cumbersome and loaded down with many features, only a handful of which will ever be used by everyone. Customization features embedded in the application provide users with some capability to tailor the interaction to their needs, but these are not extensive and still leave many features that will not be used. Additionally, these complex one-size-fits-all tools tend to be focused on activities such as document preparation rather than on roles.

Shneiderman (1998) views "role-centered design" as a natural progression from interaction designs that are activity-centered. The Personal Role Manager (PRM) he describes is an example of a concept for supporting work with a role-centered lens that permits a focus on tasks, people, schedules, and other activities within a given role. Dertouzos (1998) advocates a role-based approach in arguing that designers should focus on the best way for people in different occupations (such as executives, surgeons, engineers, teachers, and artists) to communicate their indigenous concepts to computers. In related work, the decision support systems and commitment model proposed by Winograd and Flores (1986) is another approach to supporting the needs and goals of individuals within organizations with respect to the roles they occupy.

In some applications of the role-based approach the use of roles is efficient because it reduces the need to handle each user individually. For example, RBAC streamlines the administrative load but allows an individual user's authorizations to be set by assigning that user to a predefined role. This reduces the demand to individually assign authorizations for each user. The role-based approach has not always been successful or liked by users. It can be constraining and can establish barriers to adaptability and flexibility in organizations. However, the role-based approach represents a step away from a one-size-fits-all interaction model toward a more personally tailored interaction model. This step is carried further in the next level of HCI, which places emphasis on a broader set of issues that will drive interaction to become both more individualistic and holistic in nature.

9.3   Future HCI: Level 3: Individualized and Holistic Interaction

9.3.1   The Future Computing Environment

The future computing environment will be ubiquitous, invisible, embedded, tangible, virtual, active, integrated, interconnected, interoperable, and mobile. These characteristics define an environment that is always on, always at hand, pervasive, and blended. They reveal a vision in which the physical and virtual environments are tightly intermingled and much less distinguishable than they are today. In this vision people will communicate with an array of information-based devices using a variety of modalities. They will command clever electronic agents, generate virtual identities, and project their virtual presence to anywhere from anywhere. In this vision communications, media, information resources, commerce, and entertainment converge. In this environment people's bodies are blended with devices that are worn or implanted, and they travel through hybrid physical-virtual spaces populated with active and aware artifacts that behave in symphonic harmony to produce a nearly seamless biophysical-psychosocial-cyber-kinetic reality.

The vision described above is a collective one that emerges from the ideas and work of many researchers in HCI. Weiser (1995) and Norman (1998) both develop compelling arguments for the value of ubiquitous and invisible computing. In the not-too-distant future it is conceivable that we will not think about computers as definable products but rather as critical parts of many varied information-based tools and artifacts. Ubiquitous and invisible computing refers to transferring computing technology from general-purpose machines that incorporate many functional tools to more special-purpose tools that embed computing technology. This approach is intended to create a conceptual shift from thinking about using the computer to performing tasks and activities.

Weiser (1995) imagines computing technology becoming an ubiquitous and integral part of life that disappears into the environment. He describes machines of three scales of size ranging from inches to feet to yards, called tabs, pads, and boards, respectively. These devices can support applications such as smart cards and active whiteboards. Norman (1998) has expounded a concept called information appliances. These embed computing technology in devices designed to perform specific tasks and share information. They are the result of a design strategy to manage complexity by breaking apart unrelated functions into separate devices. Examples of such appliances provided by Norman include a home financial center, active badges, active whiteboards, wearable devices, and implanted health aids. Cerf (1997), in presenting a scenario of future interaction, describes pervasive technology consisting of sensory networks, integrated media, virtual environments, intelligent agents, and highly mobile computing devices.

Ishii (1997), Resnick et al. (1998), and Wrensch and Eisenberg (1998) have all developed imaginative concepts for integrating IT into tangible artifacts that are active, aware, and programmable. Mann (1998) provides descriptions of innovative concepts for assorted wearable computing devices. These researchers, among many others, have addressed the need and benefits of interoperability and interconnectivity of information-based devices.

This vision represents what many forward-looking researchers in HCI see as the path toward resolving persistent problems associated with the human use of advanced computing technology. In the imaginations and work of these researchers, information technology (IT) designed with these characteristics represents a way to harness computing power, manage its complexity, and deliver its benefits. Information technology possessing these characteristics will help people make sense of the world of future technology, realize the productivity improvements that Landauer (1995) and Tenner (1996) have pointed out have so far been marginal and elusive, and make IT serve the human purposes for which it is intended.

9.3.2 Individualized and Holistic Interaction Design

In the ubiquitous computing environment of the future a significant piece of the total environment with which people will interact will consist of information technologies. These technologies will be tightly integrated into the totality of our interaction with and experience of the everyday world around us. In a very real sense the environment created by these technologies will become part of the fabric of the environment and an integral part of our phenomenological field. In this new and augmented reality our psychosocial development and well-being will be affected by our skill in interacting with it and our ability to differentiate a self-concept from it. Holistic interaction is a concept for developing interaction environments that will address people's needs in living in this new, augmented world. Conceptually, holistic interaction is akin to holistic medicine. Holistic medicine is a view of health and healing that accounts for the physical, psychological, social, and environmental factors affecting an individual's wellness, rather than adopting a narrow medical model of disease and healing. It accounts for individual needs and lifestyles, and emphasizes the notions of self-care and self-healing.

A major part of therapy for psychological and social problems is concerned with the manner in which the treated person interacts with and reacts to other people and situations in the world. In the new augmented world, people will be interacting globally with a set of interactive agents, environments, devices, and other people. Their skills, strategies, and effectiveness in interacting with these new pieces of the world will affect their psychosocial and physical well-being. This situation calls for an approach to interaction that accounts for the range of factors addressed by holistic medicine and that emphasizes the subjective nature of successful interaction.

Holistic interaction is a concept for an approach to interaction design that would foster productivity, performance, safety, teamwork, effective habits, and personal growth with respect to an individual's personal needs, goals, and lifestyle. In doing this, the interaction design will need to account for the individual's cognitive and perceptual capabilities, biophysical capabilities, emotional needs, personality traits, and situational factors. As such, holistic interaction design will account for the lower-level HCI design needs and in addition address higher-level needs not considered at the other levels.

Attention to individual needs is an important part of holistic interaction design. Customization through preferences, templates, end-user programming (Eisenberg 1997), and user-level extensions (Alexandrov 1998) are ways in which software and interfaces are individualized today. These techniques provide a way to meet some individual needs, but they do not address the type of customization needed to address the individual higher-level needs addressed by level 3. Research in areas that will be valuable for designing individualized customizations of interaction environments is currently being done. For example, Dillon and Watson (1996) argue that knowledge of differences between people can be valuable in defining interfaces that will differentially assist people based on traits. Smith and O'Brian (1998) present a model to address the need to recouple interfaces that have been subjectively tailored in doing cooperative tasks. Schiano and White (1998) examined the use of virtual identities by participants in LamdaMOO, a social multi-user domain. These are a few examples of the interest in and value of developing HCI that supports individual needs and goals.

Along with a focus on individual needs, holistic interaction design will focus attention on developing an interaction environment that fosters opportunity for personal growth, creativity, teamwork, and promotion of effective habits. Goleman (1998) presents a model of emotional intelligence that includes five components: self-awareness, self-regulation, motivation, empathy, and social skill. Each of these components is further broken down into more specific indicators. Covey (1991) presents seven habits of highly effective people and principle-centered leadership. Both Goleman and Covey agree that these characteristics can be learned. An example design goal of holistic interaction could be to design methods of interaction that would help individuals in developing these characteristics with respect to their individual needs and desire to do so. This aspect of holistic interaction is somewhat akin to the idea of machine "coaching" described by Winograd and Flores (1986) in which new possibilities for interpretations and action are generated through interaction. With reference to computers facilitating thinking and problem solving skills, holistic interaction is also the type of interaction envisioned by Licklidder (1960).

Holistic interaction design would also address issues related to an individual's emotions and motivation. In his recent review of developments in cognitive social psychology Schwartz (1998) reveals renewed interest in models that incorporate the interplay between emotion and cognition. An exercise in holistic interaction design could be to apply these models to design an interaction environment that enhanced both cognitive performance and personal comfort by providing the needed emotional context. Additionally, holistic interaction design would address potential problems that computer use poses for our psychological and social well-being.

Since the computing world of the future will be much more tightly integrated with the physical world than it is today, HCI as a discipline will not be as clearly differentiated as it is today. The design of interaction between people and computing technology will be increasingly concerned with the broader picture of how computing technology is integrated with the total environment and how people interact with the total integrated environment rather than just a piece of it. Some practitioners in the HCI field will continue to work on specific areas and problems. These may lead increasingly to splintered and isolated subdisciplines. However, a group of practitioners will work on the holistic design level and integrate computing interface technologies with the physical world with regard to individual needs. Work at the holistic interaction level will increasingly overlap with work by other disciplines that deal with the interaction of people with other people and the environment. At this point HCI designers, architects, interior designers, fashion designers, business process and organizational specialists, therapists, and other types of counselors and consultants will work together to create new and integrated approaches to holistic interaction design.

9.3.3 Moving toward Holistic Interaction

Progression of HCI design toward holistic interaction will not happen without change. This section describes three major movements that could facilitate the progress toward holistic interaction design. Each movement impacts the manner in which HCI is designed and developed. Together these three movements present an alternative to developing HCI as an integral part of the engineering process and designing interfaces that are optimized across the entire range of users.

9.3.3.1 Moving beyond Engineering

Engineering processes have played a major role in the design and development of human-computer systems. One goal of many HCI practitioners is to more deeply and seamlessly integrate HCI processes with engineering processes. These efforts are appropriate for the lower levels of HCI. However, as the evolution toward an ubiquitous computing environment becomes realized, HCI design will continue to broaden in scope by addressing a wide range of interaction design issues that will increasingly be external to engineering. As the issues that HCI addresses become more distant from engineering solutions and models, these integration efforts become increasingly inappropriate. Furthermore, Pool (1997) demonstrates that the success of products is determined in great part by factors outside of engineering. Consider the relationship between the designers and the engineering disciplines in the following examples.

Fashion Design. The relationship of HCI designers to computer engineering in some respects is akin to the relationship between a fashion designer and materials engineering. Fashion designers rely on materials technology to provide the substance of the design, and clothing design is limited by the material offerings. But the technology involved with producing the materials does not drive the fashion design. Clothing serves many more purposes than its basic utility of protection from the environment. Although the fit of clothes and their appropriateness for different activities is important, clothing conveys status and personality, differentiates cultures, projects power, and builds conformity. In addition, clothing alters perceptions of morality, identity, and privacy. A fashion designer is a human interface designer and relies on materials engineers. Designers may work with engineers to develop new materials that have desired weight, water resistance, breathing quality, and other properties. The design process, however, is distinct from the development of the materials and the process of making the clothes. The more attention the fashion designer gives to people's needs that go beyond basic utility, the wider the gap between what the designer does and the engineers do. In these cases, psychology, sociology, culture, personal taste and style, and many other nonengineering factors drive the design.

Now consider the blending of computing technology with people's bodies and clothing. Researchers have generated many ideas for devices that would be implanted or worn and that perform numerous useful tasks without much intervention by the person wearing or hosting them. The usability of these devices is important, but HCI designers should not be limited to the usability issues concerning these devices and should address questions of how the extra-usability areas of our lives will be impacted by these devices. People's desire to project their individuality or affiliations by the clothes they choose will be extended to wearable computing devices and designers will have to account for these higher-level user needs.

Interior Design. In the ubiquitous computing environment of the future, HCI design in many respects will be more akin to the design of habitat than to mechanism. In this environment, HCI's relationship to engineering is akin to the relationship of architects, interior designers, and landscape architects to civil, electrical, and mechanical engineers. The issues of secure structural and electrical design and the sizing of doors and stairways to accommodate human dimensions are addressed by these designers in close relationship with the engineers and builders. However, issues of personal taste, styles of use, aesthetics, and emotion drive the design externally of engineering.

Information technology is moving toward creating an electronic habitat that will augment and be integrated with the physical habitat. Engineering will provide the basic technologies and infrastructure for building this habitat, but HCI, along with other disciplines, will provide the design of the habitat itself. As the psychological and sociological issues associated with the human experience of ubiquitous computing are addressed, engineering will become less important in influencing the design solutions. Engineering will need to supply many answers. However, just as materials engineers do not design fashions and civil engineers do not design kitchens, computer engineers will not design the virtual habitat.

The issue for HCI is one of self-identity. Is HCI a specialty engineering discipline—that is, another "ility" that should be integrated with a general system engineering process? Alternatively, is HCI a separate type of discipline, neither engineering, social science, nor environmental science? The maturity model presented earlier suggests that it is a bit of both. Which one depends on the level of human needs and goals being addressed and the application domain. In the development of complex human-machine systems, such as commercial aircraft and nuclear power plants, designers model humans as components of the overall system. In the design of such systems, HCI tightly aligns with engineering processes. Concerns of human performance and reliability are paramount.

In the design of automobiles, human-factors designers address driver performance and safety issues using human-machine system models in which the human operator is an integral part of the overall system. Within this realm the system as a whole must be engineered, and human factors are again tightly aligned with engineering. However, many aspects of the automotive human-machine interface design move away from engineering to address issues of style and personal choice. This is a realm sitting between human factors and industrial design. The finished automobile design includes aspects that are driven by electrical and mechanical engineering disciplines, aspects driven by human factors (acting as an engineering discipline), aspects driven by human factors (acting as a psychological and sociological discipline), and industrial design.

As HCI moves to higher levels in the maturation process, the interesting questions that will drive the design of personal and business computing systems are less directed toward software or hardware engineering and more directed toward psychology and sociology. Engineering models and methods cannot address these questions.

9.3.3.2   Uncoupling the Human Interface

The previous section described how the relationship between HCI and engineering varied with the level of user needs that were addressed. As HCI matures toward addressing higher-level needs, there will be greater separation between interaction design and engineering, and a growing part of HCI design will be performed external to engineering. This situation will generate momentum to uncouple the design and development of the human interface from that of the functional technology.

Uncoupling of the human interface from the functional software means that these two pieces of software can, in some ways, be designed and implemented independently from one another. This means that (1) each piece has code that is separable to some degree, (2) the pieces do not have to be developed concurrently, and (3) the pieces do not have to be designed or developed by the same individuals or teams. There can be many instances of human interfaces to the same application software, and these different instances can reflect the individual interaction styles, capabilities, and limitations of the different people who use them.

At the presentation level, human interfaces can be highly customizable. The mechanism used to initiate an action doesn't matter to the underlying functionality. All that matters to the functional software is that the interface incorporates a mechanism to communicate the user's intention to initiate the action. I refer to intention here because it also does not matter to the functionality whether invoking the mechanism actually immediately initiates the action or if it first requires the user to verify that the action should be performed. Of course, this difference matters to overall performance, protection from errors, and other factors. However, it doesn't inhibit the independent modularity that can exist between the human interface and the functional software that will perform the desired action.

Think of purchasing an application program or an operating system that included the needed functionality but did not include a human interface to the functionality. As software has become a commodity, consumers have come to expect that software intended for human use incorporates a human interface. The very idea of software without the interface seems strange. This strong association between functionality and a human interface does not exist with hardware. Consumers are comfortable with viewing keyboards, pointing devices, monitors, and other peripheral devices as interchangeable. The concept of separable human interfaces in hardware extends to many different products. We can replace many parts of a bicycle, put new grips on golf clubs, and use any number of universal remote controls to operate home electronics. In the future consumers may have this same convenience with software, having human interface software developed and marketed as products independent from the software providing the functional services, and becoming what Norman (1998) calls a substitutable commodity.

Hardware products inherit interface separation as a byproduct of component-based architecture and design. Components that adhere to standards are interchangeable and reusable. The analogous concept of developing new software with components has been emerging for several years. Object-oriented technology provides the framework for software component architecture and design. Component-based software development is attractive because it offers the potential for significant gains in productivity realized through reuse (D'souza and Wills 1999; Jacobson et al. 1997).

Components change the manner in which software is developed and the way programmers work. The component development model is a fourth-generation technique in which programmers describe the problem and functions that need to be performed. Building the application amounts to collecting components, customizing them if needed, and connecting them together. To the degree that the needed components already exist, product development is faster and less expensive. Software code is only one type of reusable component. Other components include cost estimates, architectures, designs, test cases, and documentation. Today graphical user interfaces (GUIs) are constructed from various reusable components. Since human interface software can represent more than half the total code for a software product, use of GUI components can produce a significant saving.

Components offer more than just reuse. They present new possibilities for flexible assembly of functionality and interchangeability of parts. Using component building blocks allows for work tools to be assembled in many different ways to meet specific task requirements at hand. In a distributed processing environment, components can be dynamically accessed and used as needed. With the ability to flexibly assemble functionality, we can put together the pieces in ways that make sense for tasks and combinations of tasks being performed in specific situations by specific individuals. Any number of interface components could be designed to interact with a given service component, and any number of components designed to perform the same service could interact with a given interface component. Technologies such as the Common Object Request Broker Architecture (CORBA) provide this interoperability.

This is how component software development is supposed to work in theory, but this ease of development is not yet available. Often the "glue" code that connects the different components is difficult to define and introduces excessive overhead. Also, many of the issues and problems involving making software components interoperable to the degree described here still need to be solved. However, component technology is relatively new, it is growing in popularity, and its future seems promising.

The concept of an uncoupled software interface has potential problems. Wulfman et al. (1988) present examples of the integration discontinuities that can occur when human interfaces are designed and developed before or after the application software. However, these discontinuities do not present an inherent barrier to developing these different pieces nonconcurrently. The primary barrier to effective sequential design of these parts is the degree to which they are designed without complete knowledge or understanding of what the other piece is capable of doing. If the designers of each piece have this requisite knowledge and understanding, then integration discontinuities should be no greater in the sequential design paradigm than they are in the concurrent design paradigm. What is needed is a bridge between interaction components and functional components that provides this knowledge and understanding and reduces the potential for integration discontinuities in the design.

This bridge may be in the form of an abstract task model that could independently guide the development of both human interface and functional components. Much work will be required to determine a workable breakdown of tasks to define the functional components to perform the task and the complementary interface components to control it and receive applicable data. There is much interest in developing modeling techniques that integrate task and work design with software design. Butler et al. (1999) converge the Unified Modeling Language (UML) (Rumbaugh et al. 1999) for object-oriented analysis and design with IDEF3, a language for specifying work processes developed by the U.S. Air Force. Rosson (1999) develops user interaction scenarios as a means to integrate task and object-oriented software design. These user interaction scenarios are expansions of use-case scenarios that include the actor's goals, expectations, and reactions. These research activities provide a basis for establishing a link between the development of human interfaces and the underlying functional software. In establishing this link, these researchers are attempting to place the design of human interaction and the design of software on common ground for the purposes of more tightly integrating them. However, this research could also form the basis for a task description standard that permits human interface and software design to be performed more independently from each other as long as both sides adhere to the standard.

Johnson (1992) describes the use of selectors in the Application Construction Environment (ACE). Selectors provide abstract semantics for describing the functionality required for a human interface separately from the eventual widgets and layouts that will be used. Johnson's intent is that by using selectors, designers will work at a level of application semantics instead of the lower level of individual widgets. Also, because the ACE includes rules for assigning appropriate widgets to selectors, designers will not make inappropriate widget choices. This work demonstrates that designs can be defined with respect to abstract and reusable application semantics. Although Johnson's purposes and goals for selectors are different, the semantics that the selectors represent may provide a basis for the bridge between human interface and functional components.

Object and component strategies of software development combined with distributed architectures and integration technologies work to reduce the need for custom products. Basically, new systems can be built and integrated using heterogeneous and distributed components that are reusable and interoperable if they conform to standards. In one sense these technologies can be viewed as reducing customization because the building blocks are commodities. Viewed from a system level, however, the flexibility inherent in reuse and interoperability of low-level components enables the customization of those systems. System integrators can pick and choose which components to use and integrate them in novel ways. Although the pieces of the system are ready-made, the system being built can uniquely meet the needs of customers. Using standard components to build customized systems has been an approach long valued by buyers of personal computers, bicycles, audiovisual equipment, and houses. When HCI moves beyond engineering, the value of customized human interfaces will drive HCI to meet individual customer's needs more precisely. There is inherent tension between standardization and personalization of human interfaces. However, if decreed at the right level, standardization can stimulate competition by permitting interchangeability of parts from different sources. This substitutability allows system integrators flexibility in defining specific system components and characteristics, thus enabling customized systems to be developed from standard components.

A potential concern for the uncoupled human interface movement is that manufacturers of information devices may decide to develop families of compatible devices that have proprietary interfaces, thus precluding independent vendors from marketing their interfaces to these devices. However, even with proprietary technology, manufacturers may choose to offer customized interfaces developed internally. Additionally, manufacturers could certify and license vendors to create uncoupled interface products specifically for their systems. These approaches would be used to compete with the personalization offered by architectures that are more open.

Uncoupling the human interface is a means to provide greater variety and levels of customization in human interface design. It is a means to achieve mass customization (Pine 1993) of human interaction design. One motivation driving customization will be the fragmentation of customer demand across the wide range of information-based devices and services that will be available in the future. A second motivation will be the increased need and desire for individual expression stemming from the seamless integration of computing technology into the environment and everyday experience.

9.3.3.3 *The Information-Interaction Counselor*

In the ubiquitous computing environment, integrated computing, communication, media, commerce, and entertainment technologies will be delivered through many information-based devices that will be highly connectable and interoperable. In this scenario, many different forms of devices and services will be available from competing vendors. Functionality will be packaged together in many different ways to try to meet the fragmented demands of different people. In this situation, personality, lifestyle, and aesthetics as well as functional requirements matter. How will individuals, families, and businesses determine what combination of these products and services best meets their needs? One possibility is that their needs will be met by using information-interaction counselors (IICs) who would work with clients to match products and services to their particular needs and create customized interaction environments for them. The various services provided by the IICs may be performed by more than one person in a consulting firm. Performing the IIC functions would require expertise in information products and services, and fitting the available technology to the client's needs. Clients could be individuals, families, businesses, or other organizations, both small and large. IICs would provide a mechanism to achieve mass customization of interfaces while avoiding incompatibilities or discontinuities in the design because they would have the requisite design expertise. IICs would provide expertise and services to relieve their clients of the burden of making uninformed decisions just like consultants and counselors in other domains do today.

Some forms of such support activity exist in organizations today. One example, from studies on collaborative work practices with computer-aided design (CAD) users, is the role of "gardeners" (Gantt and Nardi 1992; Nardi 1993). Gardeners serve a formal support role focused on providing expertise and services to improve the productivity of a group of end users that employ the same system or program in their job. In the context of CAD work, gardeners assume responsibility for writing CAD macros and programs, researching new tools for end users, and mediating between end users and system administrators. Gardeners help end users with hardware and software configuration, maintenance, and upgrades. These are similar to the activities that IICs might perform in a broader context.

The functions performed by IICs are envisioned to be multifaceted. In some respects, they would be analogous to independent insurance agents or financial planners. The growth of new types of investment instruments and strategies has complicated personal investment choices. With the need to tailor these choices to specific circumstances, individuals have sought out financial planners to assist them in customizing investments that reflect their future and current needs, abilities, and level of risk-taking. The IIC would perform comparable tasks in designing a personalized "portfolio" of information products and services for their clients. The IIC would resemble a combination of consultant, planner, and broker of corporate and personal information products and services.

The IIC might also perform functions analogous to those performed by interior designers, architects, and counselors in organizational and time-management skills, who work toward personalizing their client's environment. In this context, IICs would be working with clients to achieve greater levels of productivity along with a deeper sense of image, style, and comfort. At a deeper level, IICs might perform functions analogous to those performed in personal growth, coaching, and clinical counseling. At this level, IICs would examine the personal goals and problem areas of clients. They would use this information to construct and tailor a personal interface that would promote the goals of the individual client and respond in ways that assist the client in meeting specific needs. Psychological assessment instruments may be developed to assist IICs in identifying a client's needs and goals to guide the construction of personalized custom interfaces. At this level, IICs would design interfaces to motivate, amuse, or sympathize with clients. Some existing interaction concepts seem to have the potential to incorporate these characteristics. For example, learner-centered systems have enormous potential to foster self-esteem and a sense of accomplishment.

9.4   Summary and Conclusions

This paper describes the maturation of HCI as a progression from support of basic usability needs to support of higher-level human needs and goals. The field of HCI has already moved significantly beyond issues of basic usability. Work in collaborative and organizational interaction has received increasing interest for the past several years. As the evolution toward an ubiquitous computing environment becomes realized, HCI design will continue to broaden in scope by addressing a wide range of interaction design issues. Addressing this broad set of issues will move HCI toward holistic and individualized interaction designs. Holistic interaction designs will provide interaction environments that foster motivation, personal growth, and emotional health; address individual differences; and promote effective habits, as well as meet basic usability needs.

The progression to holistic interaction entails change. Major movements in the manner in which HCI is practiced may facilitate this progress. The broadening set of issues addressed by HCI will increasingly be external to engineering, and, consequently, a large part of HCI design will be performed external to engineering. This separation from engineering will generate momentum toward uncoupling the design and development of the human interface from that of the functional technology. Object, component, and distributed computing technology provides a step toward achieving this uncoupling. This capability combined with the large array of information device, service, and content choices, and the demand to satisfy individual needs and preferences will spawn a new industry of information-interaction counselors

(IICs). The IICs will address the broad range of factors needed for holistic interaction design. They will advise individual and business clients on their information needs and generate customized interfaces to meet these needs. Two factors will drive the demand for customization. One will be the fragmentation of customer demand across the wide range of available information-based devices and services. The second will be the increased need and desire for individual expression stemming from the seamless integration of computing technology into the environment and everyday experience.

In the future, information-based technology will be highly integrated with the rest of the environment. As such, the work of the IICs will tend to overlap with other disciplines that deal with how people can better interact with and experience other people, the environment, or situations. These disciplines will work together to broaden holistic interaction design beyond a discipline specific to interacting with computing technology. A general holistic interaction design approach will emerge in which people's interaction with the totality of the environment, of which computing technology is only a part, is considered.

The maturation of HCI presented in this paper is a progression toward meeting increasingly higher-level human needs and goals with computing technology and with respect to people's individuality. As our reliance on computers has increased, their effect on our individuality has been a prominent factor in the evolution of our fears and trust in them. Consider the following change in perspective.

Following the introduction of computers, people increasingly worried about becoming "just another number" in an impersonal electronic database contained within an unapproachable machine that was employed by uncaring bureaucrats. Within this database individuality would be meaningless and personal identities would be lost in a sea of arcane numbers, decipherable only to an unforgiving authority. Computers would foster impersonal relationships, and the characteristics that made us unique would be overlooked, creating an anonymous and highly depersonalized society.

Today we are faced with data warehouses, data mining, and marketing techniques that are designed to exploit our individuality and individual preferences for goods and services. These technologies have enabled our individual choices to be heard and respected—and to be influential in establishing product, service, and lifestyle trends. The data that we thought would depersonalize us has instead defined us. Today we are concerned that too much individual knowledge and data about us are available and that the machine has invaded our individuality rather than stripped us of it.

In a broader context, Nehamas (1997) describes Heidegger's beliefs about technology's impact on each individual's reach as follows. "Technology turns what had been prerogatives of the few into the necessities for the many. The power over nature that technology gives each individual is translated, in political terms, into the power within society that democracy allows us. Both technology and democracy place individual human beings in the center of the world."

References

Alexandrov, A.D., Ibel, M., Schauser, K.E., and Scheiman, C.J. (1998). Ufo: A personal global file system based on user-level extensions to the operating system. *ACM Transactions on Computer Systems,* 16, 3, 207–233.

Butler, K.A., Esposito, C., and Hebron, R. (1999). Connecting the design of software to the design of work. *Communications of the ACM,* 42, 1, 38–46.

Caputo, K. (1998). *CMM implementation guide.* Reading, MA: Addison-Wesley.

Card, S.K., Moran, T.P., and Newell, A. (1983). *The psychology of human-computer interaction.* Hillsdale, NJ: Lawrence Erlbaum.

Cerf, B.G. (1997). When they're everywhere. In P.J. Denning and R.M. Metcalfe (Eds.), *Beyond Calculation,* 33–42. New York: Copernicus.

Covey, S. (1991). *Principle-centered leadership.* New York: Simon and Schuster.

Davenport, T.H. (1998). Putting the enterprise into the enterprise system. *Harvard Business Review,* July–August, 12–131.

de Baar, D.J.M.J., Foley, J.D., and Mullet, K.E. (1992). Coupling application design and user interface design. *Human Factors in Computing Systems, CHI'92,* 259–266. New York: ACM Press.

Dertouzos, M. (1997). *What will be.* New York: HarperCollins.

Dillon, A., and Watson, C. (1996). User analysis in HCI: Historical lessons from individual differences. *International Journal of Human-Computer Studies,* 45, 6, 619–637.

D'souza, D.F., and Wills, A.C. (1999). *Objects, components, and frameworks with UML.* Reading, MA: Addison-Wesley.

Eisenberg, M. (1997). End-user programming. In M.G. Helander, T.K. Landauer, and P.V. Prabhu (Eds.), *Handbook of Human-Computer Interaction,* 1127–1146. Amsterdam: North-Holland.

Gantt, M., and Nardi, B.A. (1992). Gardeners and gurus: Patterns of cooperation among CAD users. *Human Factors in Computing Systems, CHI'92,* 107–117. New York: ACM Press.

Goleman, D. (1998). What makes a leader. *Harvard Business Review,* November–December, 93–102.

Grudin, J. and Markus, M.L. (1997). The organizational contexts of development and use. In A.B. Tucker Jr. (Ed.), *The Computer Science and Engineering Handbook,* 1424–1439. Boca Raton, FL: CRC Press.

Hefley, W.E., Buie, E.A., Lynch, G.F., Muller, M.J., Hoecker, D.G., Carter, J., and Roth, J.T. (1995). Integrating human factors with software engineering practices. In G. Perlman, G.K. Green, and M.S. Wogalter (Eds.), *Human Factors Perspectives on Human-Computer Interaction.* 359–363. Santa Monica, CA: Human Factors and Ergonomics Society.

Ishii, H., and Ulmer, B. (1997). Tangible bits: Towards seamless interfaces between people, bits, and atoms. *Human Factors in Computing Systems, CHI'97,* 234–241. New York: ACM Press.

Jacobson, I., Griss, M., and Jonsson, P. (1997). *Software reuse.* New York: ACM Press.

Johnson, J. (1992). Selectors: Going beyond user interface widgets. *Human Factors in Computing Systems, CHI'92,* 273–279. New York: ACM Press.

Karsten, H. and Jones, M. (1998). The long and winding road: Collaborative IT and organizational change. *Proceedings ACM Conference on Computer Supported Cooperative Work,* 29–38. New York: ACM Press.

Kieras, D. (1988). Towards a practical GOMS model methodology for user interface design. In M. Helander (Ed.), *Handbook of Human-Computer Interaction,* 135–157. Elsevier Science Publishers, Amsterdam.

Landauer, T.K. (1995). *The trouble with computers: Usefulness, usability, and productivity.* Cambridge, MA: MIT Press.

Licklider, J.C.R. (1960). Man-computer symbiosis, 4–11. *IRE Transactions on Human Factors in Electronics.*

Lupu, E.C., and Sloman, M. (1997). Towards a role-based framework for distributed systems management. *Journal of Network and Systems Management,* 5, 5–30.

Mann, S. (1998). Humanistic computing: "WearComp" as a new framework and application for intelligent signal processing. *Proceedings of the IEEE,* 86, 11, 2123–2151.

Maslow, A.H. (1962). *Toward a psychology of being.* Princeton, NJ: D. Van Norstrand.

Nardi, B.A. (1993). *A small matter of programming: Perspectives on end user computing.* Cambridge, MA: MIT Press.

Nehamas, A. (1997). Foreword to A. Renaut. *The era of the individual.* Translated by M.B. DeBevoise and F. Philip. Princeton, NJ: Princeton University Press.

Norman, D.A. (1998). *The invisible computer.* Cambridge, MA: MIT Press.

Pine. B.J. II (1993). *Mass customization.* Boston, MA: Harvard Business School Press.

Pool, R. (1997). *Beyond engineering: How society shapes technology.* New York: Oxford University Press.

Resnick, M., Martin, F., Berg, R., Borovoy, R., Coletta, V., Kramer, K., and Silverman, B. (1998). Digital manipulatives: New toys to think with. *Human Factors in Computing Systems, CHI'98,* 281–287. New York: ACM Press.

Rosson, M.B. (1999). Integrating development of task and object models. *Communications of the ACM,* 42, 1, 49–56.

Rumbaugh, J., Jacobson, I., and Booch, G. (1999). *The unified modeling language reference manual.* Reading, MA: Addison-Wesley.

Schiano, D.J., and White, S. (1998). The first noble truth of cyberspace: People are people (even when they MOO). *Human Factors in Computing Systems, CHI'98,* 352–359. New York: ACM Press.

Schwarz, N. (1998). Warmer and more social: Recent developments in cognitive social psychology. *Annual Review of Sociology,* 24, 239–264.

Shneiderman, B. (1998). *Designing the user interface,* Third Edition. Reading, MA: Addison-Wesley.

Smith, G., and O'Brien, J. (1998). Re-coupling tailored user interfaces. *Proceedings 11th Annual Symposium on User Interfaces and Software Technology,* 237–246. New York: ACM Press.

Tenner, E. (1996). *Why things bite back.* New York: Vintage Books.

Tomeski, E.A. (1976). The social impact of computers. *Proceedings: The Role of Human Factors in Computers,* 12–22. Symposium sponsored by Metropolitan Chapter of the Human Factors and Ergonomics Society and Baruch College, NY.

Wachtel, J.A. (1976). The computer generation: Options, at what cost? *Proceedings: The Role of Human Factors in Computers,* 107–129. Symposium sponsored by Metropolitan Chapter of the Human Factors and Ergonomics Society and Baruch College, NY.

Weiser, M. (1995). The computer for the 21st century. In R.M. Baecker, J. Grudin, W.A.S. Buxton, and S. Greenberg, (Eds.), *Readings in Human-Computer Interaction: Toward the Year 2000,* 933–940. San Francisco, CA: Morgan Kaufmann.

Winograd, T., and Flores, F. (1987). *Understanding computers and cognition.* Reading, MA: Addison-Wesley.

Wrensch, T., and Eisenberg, M. (1998). The programmable hinge: Toward computationally enhanced crafts. *Proceedings 11th Annual Symposium on User Interfaces and Software Technology,* 89–96. New York: ACM Press.

Wulfman, C.E., Isaacs, E.A., Webber, B.L., and Fagan, L.M. (1988). Integration discontinuity: Interface users and systems. *Proceedings of Architectures for Intelligent Interfaces: Elements and Prototypes,* 57–68. Monterey, CA.

PART III

User Interface Software and Tools

10

Past, Present, and Future of User Interface Software Tools

Brad Myers
Scott E. Hudson
Randy Pausch

10.1   Introduction

There is no question that research in the area of user interface software tools has had an enormous impact on current practices of software development. Virtually all applications today are built using window managers, toolkits, and interface builders that have their roots in the research of the 1970s, 1980s, and 1990s.

These tools have achieved a high level of sophistication due in part to the homogeneity of today's user interfaces, as well as the hardware and software platforms they run on. Whereas the 1970s saw a tremendous amount of experimentation with a variety of input devices and user interface styles, much of the diversity is now gone from user interfaces. Almost all applications on Windows, UNIX, or Macintosh look and work in a very similar fashion, primarily using a small set of constructs invented 15 or more years ago. Further, the hardware platform has largely stabilized on the now familiar desktop machine—one with a large (typically color) bitmap screen, a keyboard, and a mouse (with between one and three buttons).

This stability has had important positive benefits. For end users, the consistency of interfaces now available makes it possible for them to build skills that largely transfer between applications and platforms—knowing one graphical user interface provides skills that apply to many others. For tool builders this relative lack of change has also allowed them to go through significant refinement of concepts. In many respects tools have been able to mature and "catch up" with an otherwise moving target.

However, many feel that significant opportunities for improved interfaces are being lost to stagnation. In addition, conventional GUI (Graphical User Interface) techniques appear to be ill-suited for some of the kinds of interactive platforms now starting to emerge, with *ubiquitous computing* devices (Weiser 1993) having tiny and large displays, *recognition-based user interfaces* using speech and gestures, and requirements for other facilities such as end-user programming.

As predicted by Mark Weiser at Xerox PARC, the age of ubiquitous computing is at hand. Personal Digital Assistants (PDAs), such as the Palm Pilot, and personal organizers, such as the Sharp Wizard, are already popular. Digital cell phones are merging with digital pagers and PDAs to form portable, wireless communication devices that support voice, along with electronic mail, and personal information such as schedules and contact lists. Wall-size displays are already available as projection devices, such as the SMART Technologies SmartBoard, or as large plasma panels, such as ImageSite from Fujitsu, which is 42 inches wide. It is inevitable that the costs of hardware will continue to drop and that new computational opportunities will arise. For example, connectivity will become easier due to new wireless technologies such as the BlueTooth in-room radio network (Haartsen et al. 1998).

Interfaces on these very large and very small displays cannot typically use the standard desktop model, and people will not necessarily expect these devices to act like "regular" computers. Reviews comparing the 3Com Palm Pilot with Windows CE devices often make the point that the Windows user interface style created for the desktop does not work well on palm-size devices. And it clearly does not work for a tiny display on a phone. Similarly, the standard Windows widgets such as pull-down menus are not appropriate on large wall-size displays, since, for example, the menus may be literally too high for short users to reach. Furthermore, people will be interacting with multiple devices at the same time so the devices will need to communicate and coordinate their activities.

The implication of these changes is that we can expect a dramatic increase in the diversity of both the types of computing devices in use and the task contexts in which they operate. This in turn implies that we are poised for a major change in user interfaces, and with it dramatic new needs for tools to build those interfaces. It is especially important to explicitly consider the effects our tools will have on what we can and will build and to create new tools that have the properties needed to meet a new generation of demands. There are many examples that show that tools have significant impact on the styles of interfaces that are created. For example, in the World Wide Web, it is actually easier to use pictures as buttons rather than to use "real" button widgets. Therefore, designers created elaborate, animated user interfaces with rich visual design and high production values.

Why are tools so important and successful? In general, tools help reduce the amount of code that programmers need to produce when creating a user interface, and they allow user interfaces to be created more quickly. This, in turn, enables more rapid prototyping and therefore more iterations of iterative design that is a crucial component of achieving high-quality user interfaces. Another important advantage of tools is that they help achieve a consistent look and feel, since all user interfaces created with a certain tool will be similar.

This paper briefly discusses the history of successes and failures of user interface software tool research to provide a context for future developments. It then discusses the implications of the impending changes on tools. Finally, it examines the requirements for the underlying operating system to support these tools.

10.2 Historical Perspective

10.2.1 Themes in Evaluating Tools

In evaluating past and future tools, we have identified some themes that seem to be important in determining which are successful.

- *The parts of the user interface that are addressed.* The tools that succeeded helped (just) where they were needed.

- *Threshold and ceiling.* The "threshold" is how difficult it is to learn how to use the system, and the "ceiling" is how much can be done using the system. The most successful current systems seem to be either low threshold and low ceiling or high threshold and high ceiling. However, it remains an important challenge to find ways to achieve the highly desirable outcome of systems with both a low threshold and a high ceiling at the same time.

- *Path of least resistance.* Tools influence the kinds of user interfaces that can be created. Successful tools use this to their advantage, leading implementers toward doing the right things and away from doing the wrong things.

- *Predictability.* Tools that use automatic techniques that are sometimes unpredictable have been poorly received by programmers.

- *Moving targets.* It is difficult to build tools without having significant experience with, and understanding of, the tasks they support. However, the rapid development of new interface technology and new interface techniques can make it difficult for tools to keep pace. By the time a new user interface implementation task is understood well enough to produce good tools, the task may have become less important or even obsolete.

10.2.2 What Worked

User interface tools are an area where research has had a tremendous impact on the current practice of software development (Myers 1990). Of course, window managers and the resulting "GUI style" come from the seminal research at the Stanford Research Institute, Xerox Palo Alto Research Center (PARC), and MIT in the 1970s. Interface builders were invented in research laboratories at BBN, the University of

Toronto, Xerox PARC, and others. Now, interface builders are widely used for commercial software development. Event languages, as widely used in HyperTalk and Visual Basic, were first investigated in research laboratories. The current generation of environments, such as Microsoft's OLE (Object Linking and Embedding) and Java Beans, are based on the component architecture that was developed in the Andrew environment (Palay et al. 1988) from Carnegie Mellon University. The following sections discuss these successes in more detail. A more complete history appears elsewhere (Myers 1998) and another reference contains a comprehensive survey and explanation of user interface tools (Myers 1995).

10.2.2.1 Window Managers and Toolkits

Many research systems in the 1960s, such as NLS (English et al. 1967), demonstrated the use of multiple windows at the same time. Alan Kay (1969) proposed the idea of overlapping windows in his 1969 University of Utah Ph.D. thesis, and they first appeared in 1974 in his Smalltalk system from Xerox PARC. Many other research and commercial systems picked up the idea from there, notably the Apple Macintosh and Microsoft Windows.

Window managers provide a basic programming model for drawing and screen update (an *imaging model*) and for accepting user input (an *input model*). However, programming directly at the window manager level tends to be time consuming and tedious. Further, when each programmer creates all interface components from scratch, it is practically impossible to provide much widespread consistency for the user. To address these issues, user interface toolkits were developed on top of the abstractions provided by window managers. Toolkits typically provide both a library of interactive components and an architectural framework to manage the operation of interfaces made up of those components. Employing an established framework and a library of reusable components makes user interface construction much easier than programming interfaces from scratch. As first demonstrated by the Apple Macintosh toolbox (Apple Computer Inc. 1985), the fact that a toolkit makes the programmer's job much easier can be used as leverage to achieve the difficult goal of maintaining consistency. Thus, by achieving the goal of making the programmer's job simpler, toolkits provide a path of least resistance to also achieve the goal of supporting widespread interface consistency.

10.2.2.2 Event Languages

With *event languages,* the occurrence of each significant event—such as manipulation of an input device by the user—is placed in an *event record* data structure (often simply called an *event*). These events are then sent to individual event handlers that contain the code necessary to properly respond to that input. Researchers have investigated this style in a number of systems, including the University of Alberta User Interface Management System (Green 1985) and others. This led to very popular uses of the event language in many commercial tools, such as the HyperTalk language of Apple's HyperCard, Microsoft's Visual Basic, and the Lingo scripting language in Macromedia's Director.

Event languages have been successful because they map well to the direct manipulation graphical user interface. These systems generate events for each user action with the mouse and keyboard, which are directed to the appropriate application that then must respond. Event languages also help encourage the mode-free style of interfaces, since the user is in charge of generating events that the application handles. However, as will be discussed later, the recognition-based user interfaces that are emerging for modalities, such as gestures and speech, may not map well to this event-based style, so we may need a new paradigm.

10.2.2.3 Interactive Graphical Tools

Another important contribution of user interface research has been the creation of what has come to be called *interface builders.* These are interactive tools that allow interactive components to be placed using a mouse to create windows and dialog boxes. Examples include Visual Basic and the "resource editors" or "constructors" that come with Microsoft's Visual C++ and most other environments. Early research on this class of tools includes Trillium from Xerox PARC and MenuLay from the University of Toronto (Buxton et al. 1983). The idea was refined by Jean-Marie Hullot while a researcher at INRIA, and Hullot later brought the idea with him to NeXT, which popularized this type of tool with the NeXT Interface Builder.

An important reason for the success of interface builders has been that they use graphical means to express graphical concepts (for example, interface layout). By moving some aspects of user interface implementation from conventional code into an interactive specification system, these aspects of interface implementation are made available to those who are not conventional programmers. Even the programmers benefited, as the speed of building was dramatically reduced. These properties of interface builders can be thought of as providing a low threshold to use and avoiding making it difficult to learn (at least initially). In these systems, simple things can be done in simple ways.

10.2.2.4 Component Systems

The idea of creating applications by dynamically combining separately written and compiled *components* was first demonstrated in the Andrew system (Palay et al. 1988) from Carnegie Mellon University's Information Technology Center. Each component controlled its rectangle of the screen, and other components could be incorporated inside. For example, a drawing inside a text document would be controlled by a drawing component, which would be independent of the text editor component. This idea has been adopted by Microsoft's OLE and ActiveX, Apple's OpenDoc, and Sun's Java Beans (JavaSoft 1996). One reason for the success of the component model is that it addresses the important and useful aspect of application building: how to appropriately modularize the software into smaller parts, while still providing significant capabilities and integration to users.

10.2.2.5 Scripting Languages

It is no accident that the first toolkits were developed using programming languages that were interpreted: Smalltalk (Tesler 1981) and then Dlisp (Teitelman 1979), which were developed by researchers at Xerox PARC, had small toolkits. The interpreted language enables the developer to rapidly prototype different user interface ideas and immediately make changes, which provides fast turnaround. With the rise of C and C++, most user interface development migrated to compiled languages and these capabilities were lost. Researchers have investigated ways to bring back these advantages, resulting in scripting languages such as tcl/tk (Ousterhout 1991), Python (Lutz 1996) and Perl (Wall and Schwartz 1992). Now, these research languages are seeing increasing commercial use, and popular languages such as Visual Basic and Javascript are providing interpreted capabilities.

Combining scripting capabilities with components and an interface builder has proven to be a particularly powerful approach. For example, there are thousands of components for Visual Basic available from third-party vendors. Using the interface builder of Visual Basic for the layout and the Visual Basic language for scripting the "glue" that holds everything together enables people who are not professional programmers to create sophisticated and useful interactive applications. Visual Basic shows that a little programming—if packaged properly—can make it possible for domain experts to create interfaces that reflect their domain and task knowledge.

10.2.2.6 Hypertext

The World Wide Web is another spectacular success of the research on user interface software and technology. It is based on the *hypertext* idea. Ted Nelson coined the term "hypertext" in 1965 and worked on one of the first hypertext systems called the Hypertext Editing System at Brown University. The NLS system (Engelbart and English 1968) also had hypertext features. The University of Maryland's Hyperties was the first system where highlighted items in the text could be clicked on to go to other pages (Koved and Shneiderman 1986). HyperCard from Apple was significant in helping popularize the idea for a wide audience. For a more complete history of Hypertext, see Nielsen (1995).

Hypertext did not attain widespread use, however, until the creation of the World Wide Web system by Berners-Lee in 1990 and the Mosaic browser a few years later. Some of the elements of the success of the WWW are the ease of use of Mosaic, the simplicity and accessibility of the HTML language used to author pages, the ease of making pages accessible on the Web, and the embedding of pictures with the text. The WWW provided a low threshold of use for both viewers and authors. Viewers had a simple mechanism that provided access to many of the existing network resources (such as ftp, telnet, gopher, etc.) within a hypertext framework, and authors used the very simple HTML textual specification language. This allowed the system to be used by content providers with a minimum of learning. Second, the success of the Mosaic browser clearly demonstrated the power and compelling nature of visual images (and more generally, rich content with high production values).

10.2.2.7 Object-Oriented Programming

Object-oriented programming and user interface research have a long and intertwined history, starting with Smalltalk's motivation to make it easy to create interactive, graphical programs. C++ became popular when programming graphical user interfaces became widely necessary with Windows 3.1. Object-oriented programming is especially natural for user interface programming, since the components of user interfaces (buttons, sliders, etc.) are manifested as visible objects with their own state (which corresponds to instance variables) and their own operations (which correspond to methods).

10.2.3 Promising Approaches That Have Not Caught On

In addition to the lessons learned from successes, a great deal can also be learned from looking at ideas that initially seemed to show great promise but did not succeed in the end (or at least have not *yet* succeeded) in delivering on that promise. Many of these succumbed to the moving-target problem: As these systems were being researched, the styles of user interfaces were changing toward today's standard GUI. Furthermore, many of these tools were designed to support a flexible variety of styles, which became less important with the standardization. This section considers several such examples, including the concept of a User Interface Management System (UIMS), language-based approaches, constraints, and model-based systems.

10.2.3.1 User Interface Management Systems

In the early 1980s, the concept of a *user interface management system* (UIMS) was an important focusing point for the then forming user interface software community. The term "user interface management system" was coined (Kasik 1982) to suggest an analogy to database management systems. Database management systems implement a much higher and more usable abstraction on top of low-level concepts such as disks and files. User interface management systems were to abstract the details of input and output devices, providing standard or automatically generated implementations of interfaces and generally allowing interfaces to be specified at a higher level of abstraction.

However, this separation has not worked out well in practice. For every user interface, it is important to control the low-level pragmatics of how the interactions look and feel, which these UIMSs tried to isolate from the designer. Furthermore, the standardization of the user interface elements in the late 1980s on the desktop paradigm made the need for abstractions from the input devices mostly unnecessary. Thus, UIMSs fell victim to the moving-target problem.

10.2.3.2 Formal Language-Based Tools

A number of the early approaches to building a UIMS used techniques borrowed from formal languages or compilers. For example, many systems were based on state transition diagrams (for example, Jacob 1986) and parsers for context-free grammars (for example, Olsen and Dempsey 1983). Initially these approaches looked very promising. However, these techniques did not catch on for several important reasons that can serve as important lessons for future tools.

The use of formal language techniques was driven in part by an early emphasis in UIMS work on the task of *dialog management*. At the time that these early user interface management systems were being conceived, the dominant user interface style was based on a conversational metaphor (in which the system and user are seen as conversing about the objects of interest). In this setting, dialog management takes on a very central role, and in fact, a number of formal language-based systems did a very good job of supporting that central task. Unfortunately, just as these early systems were being developed, the direct manipulation style of interface (Shneiderman 1983) was quickly coming to prominence. In direct manipulation interfaces, the role of dialog management is greatly reduced because structuring of the dialog by the system is typically detrimental to the concept of directness. As a result, these early user interface tools quickly became ones that had done a very good job of solving a problem that no longer mattered, thus falling victim to the moving-target problem.

There are other problems with this class of tools. In these systems it is very easy to express sequencing (and hard to express unordered operations). As a result, they tend to lead the programmer to create interfaces with rigid sequences of required actions. However, from a direct manipulation point of view, required sequences are almost always undesirable. Thus, the path of least resistance of these tools is detrimental to good user interface design. Another reason that some systems did not catch on is that they had a high threshold for using them because they required programmers to learn a new special-purpose programming language (in addition to their primary implementation language such as Pascal, C, or C++). Even though the dramatically improved power of the tools seemed to justify allowing it to be difficult to learn, many potential users of these systems did not adopt them simply because they never got past initial difficulties.

10.2.3.3 Constraints

Many research systems have explored the use of *constraints,* which are relationships that are declared once and then maintained automatically by the system for implementing several different aspects of a user interface. Examples include Sketchpad (Sutherland 1963), ThingLab (Borning 1981), HIGGENS (Hudson and King 1986), Garnet (Myers et al. 1990), Amulet (Myers et al. 1997), and subArctic (Hudson and Smith 1996). With constraints, the designer can specify, for example, that a line must stay attached to a rectangle or that a scroll bar must stay at the right of a window. Once these relationships have been declared, a constraint solving system responds to changes anywhere in the system by updating any values needed to maintain the declared constraints.

Constraint systems offer simple, declarative specifications for a capability useful in implementing several different aspects of an interface. Further, a range of efficient algorithms has been developed for their implementation. However, constraint systems have yet to be widely adopted beyond research systems. One of the central reasons for this is that programmers do not like that constraint solvers are sometimes *unpredictable.* Once a set of constraints is set up, it is the job of the solver to find a solution—and if there are multiple solutions, the solver may find one that the user did not expect. If there is a bug in a constraint method, it can be difficult to find. Furthermore, the declarative nature of constraints is often difficult to master for people used to programming in imperative languages. It requires them to think differently about their problems, which also contributes to having a high threshold.

One area of user interface design for which constraints do seem successful is the *layout* of graphical elements. Systems such as NeXTStep provided a limited form of constraints using the metaphor of "springs and struts" (for stretchy or rigid constraints) that could be used to control layout. This and other metaphors have found wider acceptance because they provided a limited form of constraints in a way that was easier to learn and more predictable for programmers.

10.2.3.4 Model-Based and Automatic Techniques

Another thread of user interface research that has shown significant promise but has not found wide acceptance is the investigation of automatic techniques for generating interfaces. The goal of this work is to allow the designer to specify interfaces at a very high level, with the details of the implementation to be provided by the system. Motivations for this include the hope that programmers without user interface design experience could just implement the functionality and rely on these systems to create high-quality user interfaces. The systems might allow user interfaces to be created with less effort (since parts would be generated automatically). Further, there is the promise of significant additional benefits such as automatic portability across multiple types of devices and automatic generation of help for the application.

Examples include *model-based* systems such as Mike (Olsen 1986), Jade (Vander Zanden and Myers 1990), UIDE (Sukaviriya et al. 1993), and ITS (Wiecha et al. 1990). These systems used techniques such as heuristic rules to automatically select interactive components, layouts, and other details of the interface.

Automatic and model-based techniques have suffered from the problems of unpredictability. Programmers must also learn a new language for specifying the models, which raises the threshold of use. In addition, model-based systems have a low ceiling. Because automatically generating interfaces is a very difficult task, automatic and model-based systems have each placed significant limitations on the kinds of interfaces they can produce. A related problem is that the generated user interfaces were generally not as good as those that could be created with conventional programming techniques. Finally, an important motivation for model-based techniques was to provide independence of the input-output specification from the details of the specific user interface characteristics, but with the standardization of the user interface elements, this separation became less important. As we will discuss later, a new requirement for device independence is emerging, which may raise the need for model-based or related techniques in the future.

10.3 Future Prospects and Visions

The next sections discuss some of our predictions and observations for the future of user interface tools. It is impossible to discuss the tools without including the user interface changes that will require the new tools. Therefore, these sections are organized around the new user interface paradigms that we see emerging. We see important implications from computers becoming a commodity, ubiquitous computing, the move to recognition-based and 3D user interfaces, and end-user customization.

10.3.1 Computers Becoming a Commodity

As Moore's law continues to hold, computers available to the general public have become fast enough to perform anything that researchers' computers can do. The computer science researchers' trick of buying expensive, high-performance computers to investigate what will be available to the public in five or ten years no longer works, since the computers available to the public are often as fast or faster than the researchers'. This may have a profound impact on how and what computer science research is performed. Furthermore, the quantitative change in increased performance makes a qualitative change in the kinds of user interfaces possible. For example, it has now enabled the production of inexpensive palm-size computers and single chip microprocessors the power of a 68000 that cost only about 30 cents and can be embedded in various devices. Another impact of the high-performance computers is that user interfaces are becoming more *cinematic,* with smooth transitions, animation, sound effects, and many other visual and audio effects.

10.3.2 Ubiquitous Computing

The idea of ubiquitous computing (Weiser 1993) is that computation will be embedded in many different kinds of devices on many different scales. Already we are seeing tiny digital pagers and phones with embedded computers and displays, palm-size computers such as the Palm Pilot, notebook-size panel computers, laptops, desktops, and wall-size displays. Furthermore, computing is appearing in more and more devices around the home and office. An important next wave will appear when the devices can all easily communicate with each other, probably using radio wireless technologies like BlueTooth (Haartsen et al. 1998). What are the implications of these technologies on the tools that will be needed? The next sections discuss some ideas.

10.3.2.1 Varying Input and Output Capabilities

Virtually all of today's interaction techniques have been highly optimized over the last 20 years to work with a fairly large display and a mouse with one to three buttons. Virtually none of the devices envisioned for ubiquitous computing has a mouse, some have no true pointing devices at all, and many have different kinds of displays. The first important issue is how the interaction techniques should change to take these varying input and output hardwares into account.

The most obvious impact is that developers will now have to create user interfaces that work with vastly different sizes and characteristics of displays. Whereas screens on desktop machines have only varied from 640 × 480 to 1280 × 1024 pixels (a factor of 4), and their screens vary from about 8 inches to about 20 inches in diagonal (a factor of 2.5), in the future, screens will be from cell phone displays (60 × 80 pixels at about 2 inches in diagonal) to wall-size displays (a wall-size display at Stanford is using a screen that is 3796 × 1436 pixels and 6 feet × 2 feet [Winograd 1998]). These variations are factors of about 625 in resolution and 100 for size. Current techniques have often made implicit assumptions about device characteristics. For example, standard widgets like pull-down menubars cannot generally be used, since they may not fit on small screens, and on large screens, they might be too high for some short users (Pier and Landay 1992).

Also, the input modalities differ: Cell phones have a numeric keypad and voice, palm-size displays have touch-sensitive screens and a stylus but no keyboard, other PDAs have tiny keyboards, and wall-size displays can often be touched or pointed at. Changing from a mouse to a stylus on a touchpad requires different interaction techniques. Some devices will also provide high-quality speech, gesture, and handwriting recognition. Many tools cannot handle a different number of mouse buttons, let alone the change from a mouse to a stylus, and the move to new input modalities such as speech, gestures, eye tracking, and video cameras is completely out of the question for such tools.

Thus, the same user interfaces obviously cannot be used on all platforms. If a developer is creating an application that should run on a variety of platforms, it becomes much more difficult to hand-design the screens for each kind of display. There is not yet even standardization within devices of the same class. For example, different kinds of PDAs have quite different display characteristics and input methods.

This may encourage a return to the study of some techniques for device-independent user interface specification so that developers can describe the input and output needs of their applications, vendors can describe the input and output capabilities of their devices, and users can specify their preferences. Then the system might choose appropriate interaction techniques taking all of these into account.

10.3.2.2 Tools to Rapidly Prototype Devices, Not Just Software

An important consideration for the new devices is, unlike desktop machines that all have the same input and output capabilities (mouse, keyboard, and color screen), there will be a great variety of shapes, sizes, and input-output designs. Much of the user interface will be built into the hardware itself, such as the physical buttons and switches. Therefore, the designer will have to take into account not only the software but also the physical properties of the devices and their capabilities. Thus, we will need tools that support the rapid design and prototyping of the hardware. It will not be sufficient to use screen-based techniques for prototyping the hardware, since the pragmatics and usability cannot be evaluated solely from a simulation on a screen.

10.3.2.3 Tools for Coordinating Multiple, Distributed Communicating Devices

With the rise in Internet and World Wide Web use, the computer is becoming a technology for *communication* more than for *computation*. This trend will significantly increase with the rise of ubiquitous computing. Many of the devices (cell phones, pagers) are already designed for communication from one person to another, and the computation is bringing added functionality and integration. As room-area wireless networks increasingly enable multiple devices to communicate, it will be more important that computers no longer are used as islands of computation and storage but rather as part of an integrated, multimachine, multiperson environment. Furthermore, as people increasingly distribute their own computation across devices in their office, their home, their car, and their pocket, there will be an increasing need for people to communicate with themselves on different devices. Supporting collaboration with other people will be more complicated than with current multi-user applications such as GroupKit (Roseman and Greenberg 1996) or Microsoft NetMeeting, since it can no longer be assumed that all the people have comparable computers. Instead, some users might be on a cell phone from a car, while others are using PDAs on the train or wall-size displays at home. Sometimes, users may have multiple devices in use at the same time. For example, the Pebbles project is investigating how PDAs can be used effectively at the same time as PCs (Myers et al. 1998). Devices and people will have different levels of connectedness at different times, from disconnected to connected with slow links, to being on a high-speed network. Decisions about what information is to be sent and shown to the user should be based on the importance and timeliness of the information and the capabilities of the current connection and devices. Furthermore, the user's interaction will need to take into account information from the Internet and information generated by sensors and people from all over the world. The status from the environment should also be taken into account (some call these "context-aware" user interfaces [Dey et al. 1998]).

The implications of all this on tools are profound. It will be important for tools to provide facilities to manage data sharing and synchronization, especially since it must be assumed that the data will go out of date while disconnected and need to be updated when reconnected. Since data will be updated automatically by the environment and by other people, techniques for notification and awareness will be important. Furthermore, the tools will be needed to help present the information in an appropriate way for whatever device is being used. If the user has multiple devices in use at the same time, then the content and input might be spread over all the active devices. All applications running in this future environment should be cognizant of multiple people and sharing so that group work can be easily accommodated. This implies that security issues will become increasingly important, and better user interfaces for monitoring, specifying and testing security settings will be crucial.

Since these capabilities should be available to *all* applications, it will be important for them to be provided at a low level, which suggests that the supporting capabilities be included in the underlying operating system or toolkits.

10.3.3   Recognition-Based User Interfaces

Whereas most of today's tools provide good support for widgets such as menus and dialog boxes that use a keyboard and a mouse, these will be a much smaller proportion of the interfaces of the future. We expect to see substantially more use of techniques such as gestures, handwriting, and speech input and output. These are called *recognition-based* because they require software to interpret the input stream from the user to identify the content.

These new modalities will fundamentally change how interfaces are developed. For example, to create speech user interfaces today requires learning about vocabularies, parsers, and Hidden-Markov-Models. Tools will be needed that hide all of this complexity and provide an easy-to-use interface to programmers.

Recognition-based interfaces have a number of fundamental differences from today's interfaces. The primary difference is that the input is uncertain; the recognizer can make errors interpreting the input. Therefore, interfaces must contain feedback facilities to allow the user to monitor and correct the interpretation. Furthermore, interpreting the input often requires deep knowledge about the context of the application. For example, to interpret "move the red truck to here," the system needs access to the objects in the application (to find the red truck) along with timing information about pointing gestures (to find "here").

There are significant implications for tool design. First, a conventional event-based model may no longer work, since recognition systems need to provide input continuously, rather than just in discrete events when they are finished. For example, when encircling objects with a gesture and continuing to move, the objects should start moving immediately when the boundary is closed, rather than waiting for the end of the gesture. Similarly, in speech, the interpretation of the speech should begin immediately, and feedback should be provided as soon as possible. Temporal coordination with other modalities (such as pointing) requires that the continuous nature of the input be preserved.

Another issue is the separation of knowledge about the application's contents. Today's user interface tools work without any deep knowledge about what the application is doing—they only need to know the surface widgets and appearance. To support the new modalities, this will no longer work. We believe an appropriate architecture is for the tools to have access to the main application data structures and internals. Otherwise, each application will need to deal with its own speech interpretation, which is undesirable. Increasingly, future user interfaces will be built around standardized data structures or "knowledge bases" to make these facilities available without requiring each application to rebuild them. The current trend toward "reflection" and the "open data model" is a step in this direction, but this is a deep unsolved problem in artificial intelligence systems in general, so we should not expect any solutions in the near term.

10.3.4 Three-Dimensional Technologies

Another trend is the migration from two-dimensional presentation space (or a 2_ dimensional space, in the case of overlapping windows) to three-dimensional space. Providing tools for 3D is a very difficult problem. Researchers are still at the stage where they are developing new interaction techniques, gestures, and metaphors for 3D interfaces. We predict the need to settle on a set of 3D interaction techniques and 3D widgets before high-level tools for interactive behaviors will be possible. Some research systems, such as Alice, are exploring how to hide the mathematics, which will be increasingly important in the tools of the future. Providing support in a 3D toolkit in 1999 suffers from the problems that 2D toolkits had 15 years ago. First, the need for performance causes the underlying implementation details to be visible. Second, we are not sure what applications will be developed with this new style. In this regard, 3D interfaces are probably in worse shape than 2D interfaces were because 2D interfaces were able to adopt many paper conventions, for example, in desktop publishing. Until a breakthrough occurs in our understanding of what kinds of applications 3D will be useful for, it will be extremely difficult for toolkits to know what abstractions to provide.

10.3.5 End-User Programming, Customization, and Scripting

One of the most successful computer programs of all time is the spreadsheet, and the primary reason for its success is that end users can program (by writing formulas and macros).[1] However, *end-user programming* is rare in other applications, and where it exists, usually requires learning conventional programming. An important reason that the World Wide Web has been so successful is that everyone can create his or her own pages. However, for "active" pages that use forms, animations, or computation, again programming is required, usually by a professional programmer using a programming language like PERL or Java. "Productivity applications" are becoming increasingly programmable (for example, by writing Visual Basic scripts for Microsoft Word) but only to those with some affinity for programming. Other systems use what are called *scripting languages,* such as Lingo for MacroMedia Director, but these are often fairly conventional programming languages.

End-user programming will be increasingly important in the future. No matter how successful interface designers are, systems will still need to be customized to the needs of particular users. Although there will likely be generic structures that can be shared, such systems and agents will always need to be tailored to meet personal requirements. Better interfaces and understandings of end-user programming are needed. Furthermore, these capabilities should not be built into individual applications as is done today, since this means that the user may need to learn a different programming technique for each application. Instead, the facilities should be provided at the system level and therefore should be part of the underlying toolkit.

The important research problem with scripting and customization is that the threshold is still so high that it is too difficult to learn how to program. The threshold and ceiling issue is illustrated by the research on "Gentle Slope Systems," (Myers et al. 1992) which are systems where for each incremental increase in the level of cus-

---

[1]It is interesting to note that spreadsheet formulas are a form of constraint and are tremendously successful, whereas constraints for programmers have not been successful. We conjecture that this is because constraints fit with the business person's mental model, who just needs a computation and an answer, but not with the programmer's, who needs more control over performance and methods. A key for any tool is to fit with the user's model.

tomizability, the user only needs to learn an incremental amount. This is contrasted with most systems that have "walls" where the user must stop and learn many new concepts and techniques to make further progress (see Figure 10.1).

Figure 10.1 shows how hard it is to use the tools to create things of different levels of sophistication. For example, with C, it is quite hard to get started, so the Y intercept (threshold) is high up. The vertical walls are where the designer needs to stop and learn something entirely new. For C, the wall is where the user needs to learn the Microsoft Foundation Classes (MFC) to do graphics. With Visual Basic, it is easier to get started, so the Y intercept is lower, but Visual Basic has two walls—one when you have to learn the Basic programming language, and another when you have to learn C. Click and Create is a menu-based tool from Corel, and its line stops (so it has a low ceiling) because it does not have an extension language, and you can only do what is available from the menus and dialog boxes.

10.3.6 Further Issues for Future Tools

In addition to the preceding issues, we see some additional trends in the near future that will contradict assumptions built into today's tools.

- *Skill and dexterity levels of users.* Most current interfaces assume an average level of dexterity and manual skill on the part of the user. However, based on current demographics, we know that as time passes there will be many more older adults using interactive systems (not to mention younger but disabled persons). With aging comes an inevitable decline in motor,

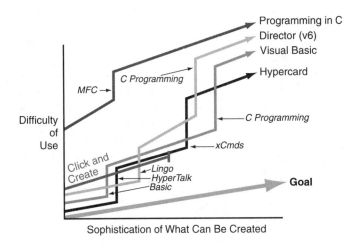

FIGURE 10.1   The Gentle Slope System

memory, and perceptual skills. This may require redesign of many accepted interactive techniques and the tools that support them.

- *Non-overlapping layout or rectangular and opaque interactive components.* Early toolkits (such as the Macintosh toolbox) assumed that interactive widgets such as buttons and text fields would not overlap. Other toolkits (most notably those coming with the X-windows system and systems that were heavily influenced by it such as the Java AWT) instead assumed that overlap was possible but that all components were rectangular and opaque. These assumptions worked well for early GUI interfaces. However, they have more recently become rather limiting, and they typically preclude techniques such as translucency and Magic Lens interactions (Bier et al. 1993) that show great promise and are now technically feasible.

- *Using fixed libraries of interactive components.* Most toolkits have long assumed that a fixed library of interactive components covered the vast majority of interfaces that were to be built. As a result, they have placed an emphasis on making components from the library easy to employ while generally neglecting the issue of making it easy to create new interactive components. The implicit or explicit assumptions made by a system significantly limit the kinds of things that can be (easily) accomplished with it.

- *Interactive setting.* Much of current user interface design knowledge (and hence the supporting tools) also implicitly makes assumptions about the setting in which a user acts. For example, most interfaces assume that the user is sitting, has two hands available, and can look at the interface while operating it. However, some of these properties do not hold in many situations in the world where computational support could be valuable (such as while driving or lying under a machine being repaired).

- *Requiring the user's full attention.* Almost all current interfaces assume that they have the user's full attention. They typically do very little unless the user pays attention to them and acts upon them. However, with ubiquitous computing, the number of devices for each user is multiplying. If each of these demands a small piece of the user's attention, the aggregate result may be quite unpleasant. As a result, there is a clear need for new interaction paradigms that minimize the amount of attention demanded. With these interfaces will be a need for tools that explicitly consider human attention as part of the design criteria. This may require a strong integration of cognitive science knowledge that to date has not been directly employed in user interface tools.

- *Support for evaluation.* Today's tools focus on the design and implementation of user interfaces. However, achieving the general goal of supporting rapid iteration of designs requires rapid evaluation as well as rapid implementation. Unfortunately, few tools have provided explicit support for evaluation. This is partially because tools that have tried, such as MIKE (Olsen and Halversen 1988), discovered that there are very few metrics that can be applied by computers. A new generation of tools is trying to evaluate how people will interact with interfaces by automatically creating cognitive models from high-level descriptions of the user interface (Kieras et al. 1995), but this work is very preliminary and much more research is needed.

- *Creating usable interfaces.* Going even further, tools might enforce or at least encourage user interfaces that were highly usable, rather than today's stance that tools should be neutral and leave the design mostly to the human designer.

10.4   Operating System Issues

What is the "Operating System" in today's systems? Does the Window Manager count as part of the operating system? What about the toolkit that provides access to the standard drawing capabilities and widgets (like Win32 and the Microsoft Foundation Classes)? Today, there is even a legal debate about whether the Web browser can be considered part of the operating system. Furthermore, the distinction between the design-time tools (used for creating the user interface) and the run-time tools (to execute the interface) blur as more services are used by both. It seems clear that the facilities that are provided by the "operating system" will continue to expand, and many of the features and tools that this article discusses will be included in what is called the operating system, for good or ill.

Some of the capabilities *must* be provided at a very low level. For instance, access to information about the input, output, and communication capabilities of devices must be provided to the application software so it can make intelligent choices about the user interface. For instance, Windows CE for palm-size devices seems to make it impossible to find out what kinds of hardware buttons are available on the PDA. Another example is that none of today's networking interfaces makes it possible for an application to decide how fast a connection is available. In fact, it is usually impossible to find out if you are connected *at all,* so applications freeze up for minutes waiting to see if the network might respond when the operating system could easily tell that the machine is disconnected. This is unacceptable. Interfaces of the future will need to make intelligent choices based on knowledge about the current capabilities of the device and its connections to the environment.

Other capabilities might be provided on top of the operating system but alternatively might be part of it. For applications to run on a variety of devices, a portable infrastructure must be provided, possibly like the Java run-time library. There will also need to be high-level protocols for accessing information on distributed files.

End-user programming support will be needed across multiple applications, so this should be provided in a universally applicable form. Ideally, all of these required capabilities will be available but not bundled with the operating system. More progress will be made if multiple vendors and research groups can compete to provide the best possible tools.

10.5   Conclusions

Generally, research and innovation in tools trail innovation in user interface design, since it only makes sense to develop tools when you know for what kinds of interfaces you are building tools. Given the consolidation of the user interface on the desktop metaphor in the last 15 years, it is not surprising that tools have matured to the point where commercial tools have fairly successfully covered the important aspects of user interface construction. It is clear that the research on user interface software tools has had enormous impact on the process of software development. However, we believe that user interface design is poised for a radical change in the near future, primarily brought on by the rise of ubiquitous computing, recognition-based user interfaces, 3D, and other technologies. Therefore, we expect to see a resurgence of interest and research on user interface software tools in order to support the new user interface styles.

We believe that these new tools will be organized around providing a rich context of information about the user, the devices, and the application's state, rather than around events. This will enable end-user programming, recognition-based user interfaces and the data sharing needed for ubiquitous computing. It will be important to have replaceable user interfaces for the same applications to provide different user interfaces on different devices for ubiquitous computing and to support customization. This will include having a procedural interface to everything that can be performed by the user. We recommend that tools aim to have a low threshold so they are easy to use but still provide a high ceiling. Predictability seems to be very important to programmers and should not be sacrificed to make the tools "smarter." All of these challenges provide new opportunities and research problems for the user interface tools of the future.

Acknowledgments

The authors wish to thank Brad Vander Zanden, Dan Olsen, Rob Miller, Rich McDaniel, and the referees for their help with this article.

References

Apple Computer Inc. (1985). *Inside Macintosh.* Reading, MA: Addison-Wesley.

Bier, E.A., Stone, M.C., Pier, K., Buxton, W., and DeRose, T.D. (1993). Toolglass and Magic Lenses: The see-through interface. *Proceedings SIGGRAPH'93: Computer Graphics,* 73–80.

Borning, A. (1981). The programming language aspects of Thinglab: a constraint-oriented simulation laboratory. *ACM Transactions on Programming Languages and Systems,* 3, 4, 353–387.

Buxton, W., Lamb, M.R., Sherman, D., Smith, K.C. (1983). Towards a comprehensive user interface management system. *Proceedings SIGGRAPH'83: Computer Graphics,* 35–42. Detroit, Mich: ACM Press.

Dey, A.K., Abowd, G.D., and Wood, A. (1998). Cyberdesk: A framework for providing self-integrating context-aware services. *Proceedings of the 1998 International Conference on Intelligent User Interfaces (IUI'98),* 47–54. New York: ACM Press.

Engelbart, D., and English, W. (1994). A research center for augmenting human intellect. Reprinted in *ACM SIGGRAPH Video Review.*

English, W.K., Engelbart, D.C., and Berman, M.L. (1967). Display selection techniques for text manipulation. *IEEE Transactions on Human Factors in Electronics,* HFE-8(1).

Green, M. (1985). The University of Alberta user interface management system. *Proceedings SIGGRAPH'85: Computer Graphics.* 205–213. San Francisco, CA: ACM Press.

Haartsen, J., Naghshineh, M., Inouye, J., Joeressen, O., Allen, W. (1998). Bluetooth: Vision, goals, and architecture. *ACM Mobile Computing and Communications Review,* 2, 4, 38–45. Oct. www.bluetooth.com.

Henderson Jr., D.A. (1986). The Trillium user interface design environment. *Proceedings SIGCHI'86: Human Factors in Computing Systems,* 221–227. Boston, MA: ACM Press.

Hudson, S., and King, R. (1986). A generator of direct manipulation office systems. *ACM Trans. on Office Information Systems,* 4, 2, 132–163.

Hudson, S.E., and Smith, I. (1996). Ultra-lightweight constraints. *Proceedings UIST'96: ACM SIGGRAPH Symposium on User Interface Software and Technology,* 147–155. Seattle, WA: http://www.cc.gatech.edu/gvu/ui/sub_arctic/.

Jacob, R.J.K. (1986). A specification language for direct manipulation interfaces. *ACM Transactions on Graphics,* 5, 4, 283–317.

JavaSoft, *JavaBeans.* Sun Microsystems, JavaBeans V1.0, December 4, 1996. http://java.sun.com/beans.

Kasik, D.J. (1982). A user interface management system. *Proceedings SIGGRAPH'82: Computer Graphics,* 99–106. Boston, MA: ACM Press.

Kay, A. (1969). *The reactive engine.* Ph.D. Thesis, Electrical Engineering and Computer Science Department, University of Utah, 327.

Kieras, D.E., Wood, S.D., Abotel, K., Hornof, A. (1995). GLEAN: A computer-based tool for rapid GOMS model usability evaluation of user interface designs. *Proceedings UIST'95: Eighth Annual Symposium on User Interface Software and Technology,* 91–100. Pittsburgh, PA: ACM Press.

Koved, L., and Shneiderman, B. (1986). Embedded menus: Selecting items in context. *Communications of the ACM,* 312–318.

Lutz, M. (1996). *Programming Python.* O'Reilly & Associates. http://www.python. org/.

Myers, B.A. (1995). User interface software tools. *ACM Transactions on Computer Human Interaction,* 2, 1, 64–103.

Myers, B.A. (1998). A brief history of human computer interaction technology. *ACM interactions,* 5, 2, 44–54.

Myers, B.A., Giuse, D.A., Dannenberg, R.B., Vander Zanden, B., Kosbie, D.S., Perrin, E., Mickish, A., Marchal, P. (1990). Garnet: Comprehensive support for graphical, highly interactive user interfaces. *IEEE Computer,* 23, 11, 71–85.

Myers, B.A., McDaniel, R.G., Miller, R.C., Ferrency, A., Faulring, A., Kyle, B.D., Mickish, A., Klimovitski, A., Doune, P. (1997). The Amulet environment: New models for effective user interface software development. *IEEE Transactions on Software Engineering,* 23, 6, 347–365.

Myers, B.A., Smith, D.C., and Horn, B. (1992). Report of the 'end-user programming' working group. *Languages for Developing User Interfaces,* 343–366. Boston: Jones and Bartlett.

Myers, B.A., Stiel, H., and Gargiulo, R. (1998). Collaboration using multiple PDAs connected to a PC. *Proceedings CSCW'98: ACM Conference on Computer-Supported Cooperative Work,* 285–294. Seattle, WA: ACM Press.

Nielsen, J. (1995). *Multimedia and hypertext: The Internet and beyond.* Boston: Academic Press Professional.

Olsen Jr., D.R. (1986). Mike: The Menu Interaction Kontrol Environment. *ACM Transactions on Graphics,* 5, 4, 318–344.

Olsen Jr., D.R., and Dempsey, E.P. (1983). Syngraph: A graphical user interface generator. *Proceedings SIGGRAPH'83: Computer Graphics,* 43–50. Detroit, MI: ACM Press.

Olsen, Jr., D.R., and Halversen, B.W. (1988). Interface usage measurements in a user interface mangement system. *Proceedings UIST'88: ACM SIGGRAPH Symposium on User Interface Software and Technology,* 102–108. Banff, Alberta, Canada.

Ousterhout, J.K. (1991). An X11 toolkit based on the tcl language. *Winter USENIX Technical Conference,* 105–115.

Palay, A.J., Hansen, W.J., Kazar, M., Sherman, M., Wadlow, M., Neuendorther, T., Stern, Z., Bader, M., Peters, T. (1988). The Andrew toolkit—An overview. *Proceedings Winter Usenix Technical Conference,* 9–21. Dallas, TX: WENIX Associates.

Pausch, R., et al. (1995). Alice: A rapid prototyping system for 3D graphics. *IEEE Computer Graphics and Applications,* 15, 3, 8–11.

Pier, K., and Landay, J. (1992). *Issues for location-independent interfaces.* Xerox PARC, Technical Report ISTL92-4, December. Palo Alto, CA. http://www.cs. berkeley.edu/~landay/research/publications/LII.ps.

Roseman, M., and Greenberg, S. (1996). Building real time groupware with Group-Kit, a groupware toolkit. *ACM Transactions on Computer Human Interaction,* 3, 1, 66–106.

Shneiderman, B. (1983). Direct manipulation: A step beyond programming languages. *IEEE Computer,* 16, 8, 57–69.

Sukaviriya, P., Foley, J.D., and Griffith, T. (1993). A second generation user interface design environment: The model and the runtime architecture. *Proceedings INTERCHI'93: Human Factors in Computing Systems,* 375–382. Amsterdam, The Netherlands: ACM Press.

Sutherland, I.E. (1963). SketchPad: A man-machine graphical communication system. *AFIPS Spring Joint Computer Conference,* 329–346.

Teitelman, W. (1979). A display oriented programmer's assistant. *International Journal of Man-Machine Studies,* 11, 2, 157–187. Also Xerox PARC Technical Report CSL-77-3, Palo Alto, CA, March 8, 1977.

Tesler, L. (1981). The Smalltalk environment. *Byte Magazine,* 6, 8, 90–147.

Vander Zanden, B., and Myers, B.A. (1990). Automatic, look-and-feel independent dialog creation for graphical user interfaces. *Proceedings SIGCHI'90: Human Factors in Computing Systems,* 27–34. Seattle, WA: ACM Press.

Wall, L., and Schwartz, R.L. (1992). *Programming perl.* Sebastopol, CA: O'Reilly & Associates.

Weiser, M. (1993). Some computer science issues in ubiquitous computing. *CACM,* 36, 7, 74–83.

Wiecha, C., Bennett, W., Boies, S., Gould, J., Greene, S. (1990) ITS: A tool for rapidly developing interactive applications. *ACM Transactions on Information Systems,* 8, 3, 204–236.

Winograd, T. (1998). *A Human-centered interaction architecture.* Working paper for the Interactive Workplace Project, Stanford University. http://graphics.stanford. EDU/projects/iwork/.

Creating Creativity: User Interfaces for Supporting Innovation

Ben Shneiderman

11.1 Introduction

People have long relied on technology for information preservation and dissemination. Ancient traders recorded contracts on clay tablets, religious scribes hand copied illuminated manuscripts on parchments, and Gutenberg applied his printing press to reproducing Bibles. Print media led to dramatic changes in society, and then modern broadcast media shook the world further with even more rapid and widespread dissemination. Today, even in remote locales, most people have seen TV and heard radio. The World Wide Web is dramatically transforming society by providing greater user control and initiative.

But information preservation and dissemination are only the first two uses of information technologies. A third application is rapid two-way communication among people at ever-greater speed and lower cost. Writing letters was a rare process among the literate members of ancient societies, but making phone calls is now widespread, and sending e-mail is commonplace.

A fourth use for information technologies is to support the creation of knowledge and art. Even into the twentieth century, scientists, inventors, novelists, and painters were seen as specially gifted citizens whose rare creative productions were treasured. Photography shook the art world because it enabled the majority to produce striking images rapidly at low cost. Similarly, information technologies could be harnessed to make creativity more common. Not every artwork, novel, photo, or digital product is creative, but facilitating broad access to powerful tools expands the potential.

Information technologies that allow more people to be more creative more of the time are likely to have profound effects on every institution (Johnson 1997). Education could expand from acquiring facts, studying existing knowledge, and developing critical thinking, to include more emphasis on creating novel artifacts, insights, or performances. Medicine's shift from applying standard treatments to tailoring treatments for each patient reflects the trend to personalization that is already ascendant in marketing and media. Expectations of teachers, lawyers, and designers are likely to rise as creativity is expected on more occasions from more people. These changes will be welcomed by some but resisted by others. The challenge to leaders and participants will be to preserve appropriate elements of existing knowledge work while shaping new technologies and then integrating them into the workplace. Standards for creative work will continue to evolve; computing logarithms by John Napier was a great breakthrough in 1614 but is now seen as merely a mechanical operation that is embedded in calculators.

This paper begins with three perspectives on creativity: inspirationalist, structuralist, and situationalist. Section 11.3 focuses on evolutionary creativity, rather than revolutionary or impromptu creativity. Section 11.4 reviews and refines the *genex* (generator of excellence) proposal, a four-phase integrated framework to support creativity (Shneiderman 1998c). Designers who follow the genex framework can create powerful tools that enable users to be more creative more of the time. This paper's main contribution is the identification of eight activities that support creativity. This list of activities implies a research agenda for human-computer interaction theoreticians, designers, software engineers, and evaluators.

11.2 Three Perspectives on Creativity

The large literature on creativity offers diverse perspectives (Boden 1990; Gardner 1994; Couger 1996; Cave 1999). Some writers—I'll call them *inspirationalists*—emphasize the remarkable "Aha!" moments in which a dramatic breakthrough magically appears. Stories of Archimedes (third century B.C.) jumping from his bath screaming, "Eureka!" as he discovered hydrostatics or Freidrich August Kekule's (1829–1869) dream-given insight about benzene's ring structure emphasize the intuitive aspects of creativity. Most inspirationalists are also quick to point out that "luck favors the prepared mind," thereby turning to the study of how preparation and incubation lead to moments of illumination. The inspirationalists also recognize that creative work starts with problem formulation and ends with evaluation plus refinement. They acknowledge the balance of 1 percent inspiration and 99 percent perspiration—a flash of insight followed by much hard work to produce a practical result.

Those who emphasize this inspirational model promote techniques for brainstorming, free association, lateral thinking (DeBono 1973), and divergence. They advocate strategies to break an innovator's existing mind set and somehow perceive the problem with fresh eyes. Since they want innovators to break from familiar solutions, their recommendations include travel to exotic destinations with towering mountains or peaceful waterfalls.

The playful nature of creativity means that software support for inspirationalists emphasizes free association using textual or graphical prompts to elicit novel ideas. Inspirationalists are often oriented to visual techniques for presenting relationships and for perceiving solutions. They would be sympathetic to information and scientific visualization strategies that helped users understand previous work and explore potential solutions. Developers of tools such as IdeaFisher or MindMapper encourage two-dimensional layouts of loosely connected concept nodes to avoid a linear or hierarchical structure. The casual style and freedom from judgment that is implicit in sketching is encouraged.

A second group of writers on creativity, the *structuralists,* emphasize more orderly approaches (Mayer 1992). They stress the importance of studying previous work and using methodical techniques to explore the possible solutions exhaustively. When a promising solution is found, the innovator evaluates strengths and weaknesses, compares it to existing solutions, and refines the promising solution to make it implementable. Structuralists teach orderly methods of problem solving such as Polya's (1957) four steps in *How to Solve It.*

1. Understanding the problem
2. Devising a plan
3. Carrying out the plan
4. Looking back

For structuralists, libraries and Web sites of previous work are important, but the key software support comes in the form of spreadsheets, programmable simulations, and domain-specific scientific / engineering / analytical / mathematical models. These software tools support "what if" processes of trying out assumptions to assess their impact on the outcomes. They often show processes with visual animations. Structuralists are usually visual thinkers, but their preferred tools are for drawing flow charts, decision trees, and structured diagrams. Since they favor methodical techniques, they are likely to appreciate software support for step-by-step exploration, with the chance to go back, make changes, and try again.

A third group, the *situationalists,* emphasize the social and intellectual context as a key part of the creative process. They see creativity as embedded in a community of practice with changing standards, requiring a social process for approval from scientific journal editors, museum curators, or literary prize juries. For example, Csikszentmihalyi (1996) sees three components to creativity.

1. The domain, such as mathematics or biology, "consists of a set of symbols, rules and procedures."
2. The field, which "includes all the individuals who act as gatekeepers to the domain. It is their job to decide whether a new idea, performance, or product should be included in the domain."

3. The individual person, whose creativity is manifest "when a person using the symbols of a given domain such as music, engineering, business, or mathematics has a new idea or sees a new pattern, and when this novelty is selected by the appropriate field for inclusion in the relevant domain."

Situationalists are most likely to talk about the influence of family, teachers, peers, and mentors. They consider the influence of challenges from memorable teachers, the strong desire to create, and the pursuit of recognition. For situationalists, vital user interfaces are those that support access to previous work in the domain, consultation with members of the field, and dissemination of results to interested members of the field.

These three perspectives on creativity—inspirationalism, structuralism, and situationalism—are all useful in shaping user interfaces to support creative work. With careful design, these perspectives can sometimes be combined. User interface designers can develop tools that stimulate inspiration based on previous work, link to associated ideas, and provide templates for action. Designers can build structured tools for exhaustive exploration, which is already a common strategy in computing. Designers can also facilitate consultation by e-mail and more refined methods to support the social strategies of the situationalists. Section 11.4 expands on these possibilities.

11.3   Levels of Creativity

Only some knowledge work or art products are creative. Much work is merely repetitive application of rules or copying, but it could be competent original work, or it could rise to the level of creative work. A professor's speech may occasionally include rote memorized phrases, but usually it contains original sentences. However, inspired lectures and creative rhetoric, such as Martin Luther King's "I Have a Dream" speech, are rare. Similarly, redrawing a travel map to your home is copying, and doodling on an envelope may be original, but Picasso's drawings in the Vollard Suite reach the level of creative work. The proposals in this paper are intended to support creative, not merely original, work.

The large literature on creativity considers diverse levels of aspiration (Boden 1990). A restricted definition would focus on great breakthroughs and paradigm-shifting innovations (Kuhn 1996). Einstein's relativity theory, Watson and Crick's discovery of DNA's double-helix, or Stravinsky's *Rite of Spring* are often cited as major creative events. Such a definition confines discussion to rare revolutionary events and a small number of Nobel Prize candidates. A looser definition would include what Kuhn referred to as normal science, useful evolutionary contributions that refine and apply existing paradigms (Basalla 1988). Evolutionary acts of creativity include doctors making cancer diagnoses, lawyers preparing briefs, or photo editors producing magazine stories. Their work is important in changing someone's life by medical care, legal practice, or journalist reportage and is public so that it can be assessed by others. Evolutionary creativity is the focus of this paper, in part because it is most likely to be helped by software tools. There is a chance that software tools that support evolutionary creativity may also help produce revolutionary breakthroughs. On the other hand, it is possible that software tools that support evolutionary creativity restrict thinking or even discourage paradigm shifts.

A third, still broader definition of creativity is conceivable—impromptu or personal creativity. Can lively conversation or attentive parenting be considered parts of the creativity spectrum? These more spontaneous and private activities may be creative in a broad sense, but since they seem harder to support and evaluate, they are not considered in this analysis. They are assessed on a personal basis and are less likely to have enduring impact on a wide range of people.

The focus of this paper is not on revolutionary or impromptu creativity but on evolutionary creativity. This still covers a wide range of possibilities. Developing software support tools for evolutionary creativity according to the three perspectives identified in this paper—inspirationalism, structuralism, and situationalism—is a sufficient challenge.

It seems necessary to address in advance the hubris or arrogance of proposing technology to aid human creativity. A critic might scowl that creativity is inherently human and no computer could or should be brought into the process. But technology has always been part of the creative process, whether in Leonardo's paint and canvas or Pasteur's microscopes and beakers. Supportive technologies can become the potter's wheel and mandolin of creativity—opening new media of expression and enabling compelling performances. Creative people often benefit from advanced technology to raise their potential and explore new domains.

My expectations are largely positive, but there are many problems, costs, and dangers in anything as ambitious as a tool and framework to support creativity. An obvious concern is that many people may not want to be more creative. Many cultures encourage respect for the past and discourage disruptive innovations. Promoting widespread creativity raises expectations that may change employment patterns, educational systems, and community norms. Introducing computer supports for creativity may produce greater social inequality as it raises the costs for those who wish to participate. Finally, these tools may be used equally by those who have positive and noble goals as well as by dictators or criminals who seek to dominate, destroy, or plunder.

These fears are appropriate, and reasonable cautions must be taken, but support for innovation could lead to positive changes to our world. However, the moral dilemma of a technology innovator remains troublesome: How can I ensure that the systems I envision will bring greater benefits than the negative side effects that I dread and those that I fail to anticipate? Widespread access to effective user interfaces for creativity support could help with major problems such as environmental destruction, overpopulation, poor medical care, oppression, and illiteracy. It could contribute to improvements in agriculture, transportation, housing, communication, and other noble human endeavors. The path from high expectations to practical action is not easy, but examples of how information technologies helped identify ozone depletion by remote sensing, improve medical diagnosis with computer-aided tomography, and enable bans on nuclear tests are encouraging. Ensuring more frequent positive outcomes and minimizing negative side effects remain challenges, but a framework that provides for substantial consultation and broad dissemination may help. Participatory design methods and Social Impact Statements may be effective because they promote discussion and expand the range of options for decision makers (Greenbaum and Kyng 1991; Muller et al. 1993; Shneiderman and Rose 1997).

11.4   Genex: A Four-Phase Framework for Generating Excellence

This paper combines and extends two previous efforts. The genex framework (Shneiderman 1998c) was a first attempt to build on Csikszentmihalyi's (1996) approach, by supporting access to the domain and consultation with the field. The name genex (generator of excellence) was chosen to echo Vannevar Bush's (1945) memex (memory extender). The original genex framework had four phases: collect, create, consult, and disseminate. This paper refines the genex framework by expanding its scope and being more precise about what user interface tools are needed. The second source for this paper is the educational philosophy, relate-create-donate (Shneiderman 1998b), which emphasized collaborative teams working together to produce something ambitious for use by someone outside the classroom. This service-oriented approach, using Web-based technologies, leads to innovative artifacts or performances. It emphasizes creativity to support learning, and learning to support creativity.

The foundational beliefs that led to genex's four phases were the following.

1. New knowledge is built on previous knowledge.
2. Powerful tools can support creativity.
3. Refinement is a social process.
4. Creative work is not complete until it is disseminated.

However, the social processes that were characterized narrowly as a support for refinement can also be helpful at early, middle, and late stages of the creative process. This paper more clearly defines the powerful tools that can facilitate creative acts. Furthermore, the close relationship of learning and creativity is more apparent now. Combining the strategies in these two papers leads to a revised four-phase genex framework.

- Collect: Learn from previous works stored in libraries, the Web, and so forth.
- Relate: Consult with peers and mentors at early, middle, and late stages.

- Create: Explore, compose, evaluate possible solutions.
- Donate: Disseminate the results and contribute to the libraries.

These four phases are not a linear path. Creative work may require returning to earlier phases and much iteration. For example, libraries, the Web, and other resources may be useful at every phase. Similarly, discussion with peers and mentors may take place repeatedly during the development of an idea. The phases are also meant to be cyclical, in that the dissemination of results should support future users who seek to learn from previous work.

This four-phase genex framework has much in common with previous characterizations and methodologies, but there are important distinctions. Couger (1996) reviews 22 "creative problem-solving methodologies" with simple plans such as Poincaré's classic recipe.

- Preparation
- Incubation
- Illumination
- Verification

It is striking that so many of the plans limit themselves to the narrow perspective of the inspirationalists and structuralists. Problem solving and creativity are portrayed as lonely experiences of wrestling with the problem, breaking through various blocks, and finding clever solutions. The descriptions of even early phases rarely suggest contacting previous workers on this problem or exploring libraries for previous work. Consultation with others and dissemination of the results is minimally mentioned. Some reconsideration of such methodologies is in order because of the presence of the World Wide Web (Berners-Lee et al. 1994). It has already dramatically reduced the effort of finding previous work, contacting previous workers, consulting with peers and mentors, and disseminating solutions (Kiesler 1997).

Of course, there are costs and dangers in reading previous work or consulting with others (Shneiderman 1998c). The time might detract from exploration and the knowledge might be misleading. There are satisfactions in solving a problem on your own, but when dealing with difficult problems, the benefits of building on previous work and consulting with peers and mentors can be enormous. The genex framework builds on the situationalists' perspective by embracing the expanded opportunities offered by the World Wide Web.

However, the need for improvements to the current World Wide Web was revealed in a study of support for idea generation (Massetti et al. 1999). Twenty-three MBA students were asked to generate as many ideas as they could on three topics—robotics, societal change, and business opportunities in Ireland. In this within-subjects design, each subject was asked to use the World Wide Web, categorical cues (five suggested categories), and no support. Subjects using the Web did no better in generating ideas and did not have higher satisfaction.

The goal of genex framework is to suggest improvements for Web-based services and personal computer software tools. By reducing the distraction caused by poorly designed user interfaces, inconsistencies across applications, and unpredictable behavior, users' attention can be devoted to the task. In an effective design for a genex, the boundaries between applications and the burdens of data conversions would disappear. Data representations and available functions would be in harmony with problem-solving strategies.

My suggestion of a close link between supporting creativity and generating excellence is a hope, not a necessity. Creativity support tools may be used to pursue excellence, high quality, and positive contributions, but I am sadly aware that this will not always be the case. The genex framework could tighten the linkage because of its emphasis on consultation and dissemination. I repeat my belief (from the end of Section 11.3) that making creativity more open and social through participatory processes will increase positive outcomes while reducing negative and unanticipated side effects.

11.5   Integrating Creative Activities

The revised genex framework calls for integrated creativity support tools. Some of these tools already exist, but they could be enhanced to better support creativity (Candy 1997; Candy and Edmonds 1997). However, the main challenge for designers is to ensure smooth integration across these novel tools and with existing tools such as word processors, presentation graphics, e-mail, databases, spreadsheets, and Web browsers (Shneiderman 1998a).

Smoother coordination across windows and better integration of tools seem possible. Just as word processors expanded to include images, tables, equations, and more, the next generation of software is likely to integrate additional features. Some aspects of the integration can be accomplished by creating compatible data types and file formats (possibly standardized objects). A second aspect of integration has to do with compatible actions and consistent terminology, such as cut-copy-paste or open-save-close. Higher levels of actions that are closer to the task domain might be candidates such as annotate-consult-revise or collect-explore-visualize. A third aspect of integration is the smooth coordination across windows (Dey et al. 1997; Derthick et al. 1997; North and Shneiderman 2000). For example, if users see an unfamiliar term, they should be able to click on it and get an English definition, a French translation, or a medical dictionary report, all in a predictable screen location. Similarly, if users find a personal name in a document, they should be able to get a biography, e-mail address, or contact information. Other coordinations include synchronized scrolling of related documents to facilitate comparisons and hierarchical browsing of a table of contents and a chapter to enable easy navigation of large resources.

These improved user interfaces will benefit many users for many tasks, but this paper focuses on the genex framework as a means to support creativity. The three perspectives—inspirationalism, structuralism, and situationalism—each lead to useful suggestions for eight activities during the four genex phases.

1. Searching and browsing digital libraries
2. Consulting with peers and mentors
3. Visualizing data and processes
4. Thinking by free associations
5. Exploring solutions—"what if" tools
6. Composing artifacts and performances
7. Reviewing and replaying session histories
8. Disseminating results

Genex's integrated creativity support tools should offer at least these eight activities. Figure 11.1 indicates how these activities are primarily related to the genex phases, but these activities could take place during any phase. For example searching libraries, the Web, or other resources is primarily associated with the collect phase, but searching may occur in order to find consultants or to decide on candidate communities for presenting results. Visualizing objects and processes is the activity that seems most pervasive and could appear in every genex phase.

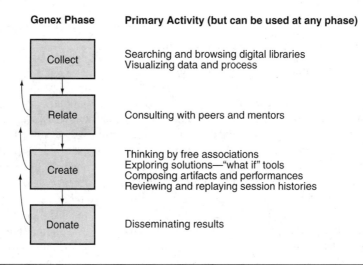

FIGURE 11.1   Genex phases and their related primary activities

11.5.1 Searching and Browsing Digital Libraries

Traditional libraries offer rich resources, but digital libraries provide dramatic capabilities that support searching, browsing, and filtering. Existing Web search engines and digital library interfaces could be much improved, and refinements to support creativity are possible. Situationalist users who want to steer the search to resources about previous work will want more control over the relevance ranking, range of sources, and the presentation of the results (Marchionini 1995; Koenemann and Belkin 1996; Shneiderman et al. 1997). For example, it should be easy for users to restrict a legal search to recent New York, New Jersey, or Connecticut court cases on tenants rights for heating. The result set should be grouped by claims (civil rights, contract violation, etc.) and ordered by date with green or red stars indicating the strength of the results for or against tenants. Extraction of plaintiff's or defendant's lawyers should also be convenient. This may sound like a tall order, but detailed search request specification while maintaining comprehensibility is possible. Since searching is part of a larger creative process, the result set should be easy to save into a spreadsheet for further manipulation, include in an e-mail note for consultation, or paste into a notebook for later referral.

In addition to searching, inspirationalists will want rapid browsing to more effectively support exploration, similar to what many people do in bookstores or physical libraries. Web sites with high branching factors (many links per page) support exploration by making what is available more visible. Yahoo's (www.yahoo.com) 200+ links on the home page are helpful in getting an idea of what is available and what is not. Browsing textual menus supports exploration when specific terms or concepts are not known, but varying interpretations of category names still result in user confusion.

11.5.2 Consulting with Peers and Mentors

E-mail, listservs, newsgroups, and threaded discussions are excellent asynchronous tools for situationalists' inquiries about previous work and for discussing new ideas. The capacity to find people who have a shared interest and are at work on similar problems is one of the greatest gifts of the Internet. Synchronous tools, such as phone calls, videoconferencing, and software sharing (for example, Netmeeting), enrich the possibilities for early, middle, and late stage consultations (Olson and Olson 1997).

For early stage consultations, innovators are likely to search widely, finding diverse information resources and broad communities. At this preparatory stage, innovators are forming questions, finding out about current workers who might be collaborators, and choosing directions. During middle stage consultations, the tasks are to propose potential solution strategies and develop evaluation methods. As solutions are created and refined, late stage consultations are directed at confirming the innovation, refining it to accommodate criticisms, and then disseminating it to appropriate parties (National Research Council 1993).

Consultations might involve continuing dialogs by e-mail, phone calls, or personal visits. While these may often be collegial and friendly, some discussions might be tense, since other workers may be competitors who are pursuing similar goals. Either party might withhold some knowledge or ideas, or probe the other to gauge their intentions. Nondisclosure or noncompetitive agreements might be discussed or signed as part of a corporate consultation. University researchers are often more open, but the competition for solution of important problems and battles to promote reputations can suppress discussion.

These concerns greatly influence the design and use of technologies, since the appropriate balance of privacy protection and easy access to information is vital. Researchers' early notes and explorations need to be kept private, but claimed break-throughs need rapid and broad dissemination. Appropriate credits for articles, patents, or software products are often the source of conflicts, so improved record keeping of the consultations that contribute to an innovation could resolve some questions and maybe encourage more cooperation.

11.5.3 Visualizing Data and Processes

While inspirationalists are likely to propose visual approaches, structuralists will also appreciate the thoroughness and rapidity with which alternatives can be reviewed using visualization. The field of pharmaceutical drug discovery involves review of thousands of compounds for their efficacy, shelf life, solubility, acidity, cost, allergic reactions, interactions with other medications, and so on. Scrolling lists in spread-sheets are useful, but two-dimensional visual presentations with color and size coding are proving to be enormous benefits for this task. Early work on a FilmFinder (Ahlberg and Shneiderman 1994) led to a successful commercial product called Spotfire (http://www.spotfire.com) (see Figure 11.2). A wide range of one-, two-, three- and multidimensional visualizations plus temporal, tree, and network presentations have been proposed (Card et al. 1999).

Visualization of digital library contents (Hearst 1999), financial information (Wright 1995), scientific data (Bryson et al. 1999), medical histories (Plaisant et al. 1996), and so on is growing, but increasing its benefits to creativity requires smooth integration. The results of a Web or database search should be easily imported (for example, by cut and paste) into a visualization. Then users should be able to filter the data appropriately and adjust the visualization features, such as x,y-axes, color, size, or other codings. Then when an interesting group of items is found, users should be able to select them and paste them into a spreadsheet or statistics package for further processing. Then the visualization and processed items should be embeddable in a written report, slide presentation, or e-mail note. E-mail recipients should be able to manipulate the visualization or report still further (Roth et al. 1996). Situationalists should also find use for visualizations in exploring digital libraries, locating key people, and presenting their findings to others.

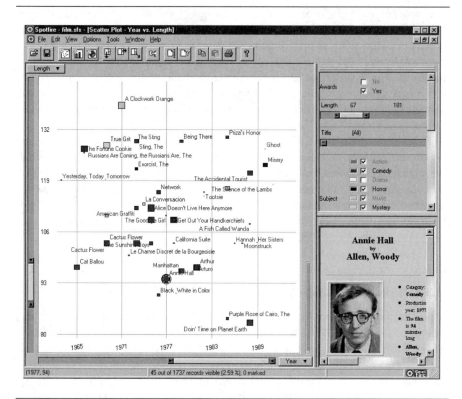

FIGURE 11.2   Multidimensional film database viewed with a two-dimensional starfield display in Spotfire. The x-axis is the years, and the y-axis is the popularity of the film. Color coding is film type (action, drama, mystery, etc.), and larger dots indicate longer movies.

11.5.4 Thinking by Free Associations

Inspirationalists seek to liberate the mind by making free associations to related concepts. This Gestalt psychology approach (Mayer 1992) has led to innovative software that is meant to facilitate association of ideas by presenting related concepts. Idea-Fisher (www.ideafisher.com) claims "to create a new method of generating ideas in a way similar to the workings of the human mind . . . by associations, or links. A thought like food leads to associations such as apple, cooking, cafe, washing dishes, and so on. When a creative new idea is born, it usually consists of associations linked together in a way that has not been thought of before. This is the heart of IdeaFisher technology—a dictionary of associations." Users apparently enjoy using IdeaFisher, but its benefits are still being assessed with empirical studies (Massetti 1996). Support for the benefits of guiding associations with object names was found in a study of ten designers who were asked to design an innovative stool for a Parisian cyber-café. Subjects in the guided condition produced many more concepts during their thinking aloud session than those in the free condition (Bonnardel 1999).

Computerized thesauri may also be helpful textual exploration tools, since varied associations such as synonyms, antonyms, homonyms, rhymes, or even anagrams can be retrieved rapidly. Alternatively, random word presentations are also proposed as a method for stimulating fresh thoughts and breaking through creative blocks.

Other products enable users to produce thought-provoking visual representations of relationships among words or concepts. Examples include The Brain (www.thebrain.com), which taps "the power of association" by "visualizing information flow" and MindManager (www.mindman.com/), which allows users to "create relationships among information easily" and "identify relationships between items or branches." The Axon Idea Processor (www.singnet.com.sg/%7Eaxon2000/) is promoted as "a sketchpad for visualizing and organizing ideas" that "exploits visual attributes such as: color, shape, size, scale, position, depth, link, icon, etc. Visual cues facilitate recall, association, and discovery. Diagrams and pictures help you to represent and solve complex problems." Typical mindmaps show a main idea in a central node and then branches in all directions showing related ideas (Figure 11.3). As the

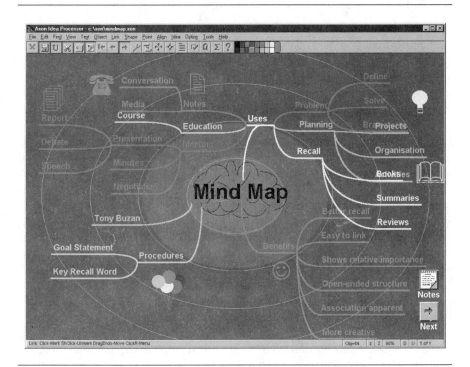

FIGURE 11.3 MindMap produced with the Axon Idea Processor

diagram spreads out, the nodes and font sizes decrease, so that many small details are shown. A popular alternative is to have the main idea at the top or left and then have a branching tree structure going down or to the right.

Mindmaps, concept maps, semantic networks, and other drawing strategies may be helpful to some people. Appropriate visual presentations, such as the periodic table of elements, help in problem solving because they compactly present substantial information and show important relationships. Geographic maps, architect's drawings, and electronic circuit diagrams are other examples of the great power of visual presentations for learning and problem solving. The gift of the computer is the capacity to quickly create and easily manipulate such diagrams. The same attributes are often celebrated in penciled diagrams and sketches that have a similar capacity to invite discussion, exploration, and revision.

The genex framework reminds us that such textual lists and diagrams should be easily shared with others, annotatable, linkable, and searchable. It should be possible to import and export from these programs so that related tools can be employed—for example, to translate terminology in a diagram into a foreign language or to link diagram nodes to Web sites.

11.5.5   Exploring Solutions—"What If" Tools

A large family of software tools already supports methodical exploration of solutions in the structuralist style (Elam and Melissa 1990). Electronic spreadsheets are described as "what if" tools that allow business planners and analysts to quickly try out a variety of scenarios. Such explorations are possible with paper and pencil, but they are far faster with electronic spreadsheets. However, there is still opportunity to support methodical exploration through macros that provide orderly tours of multidimensional attribute spaces. For example, stepping through business scenarios for ranges of expenditures on production, quality control, direct marketing, and advertising might identify creative solutions. These grand tour strategies are appealing but difficult to carry out in high-dimensional spaces.

Similarly, flight simulators, traffic flow models, weather models, and thousands of scientific, engineering, economic, and other modeling tools allow users to explore alternatives safely, economically, and rapidly. Simulators have been largely custom built, but simulation-building software is growing from domain specific to broader coverage. These simulation models are also becoming more richly featured to support explanatory text, collaborative usage, history keeping, and more (Rose et al. 1998; Jones and Schneider 1996). A popular class of home computer software includes simulation games, such as SimCity, that enable users to try out urban planning scenarios. Also popular with personal computer users are flight, driving, and battle simulators that provide various levels of realistic experiences. These applications are enjoyable and also educational, but they are special purpose and standalone applications that are not part of an integrated framework.

The genex framework and the situationalist perspective remind us of the importance of integration to support creativity. Having run a simulation, can users save the whole session and replay it later to study their performance or discuss it with a peer or mentor? Can they send the session to someone by e-mail, annotate steps, or search for key events or actions? Can excellent sessions be stored in a digital library to allow future researchers or problem solvers to build on the best work?

11.5.6 Composing Artifacts and Performances

Another large family of software tools already supports creation of artifacts and performances (Nakakoji et al. 1997). The ubiquitous word processor is the premier example of a flexible tool that enables many users to create diverse high-quality printed documents using a relatively low-cost laser or inkjet printer. Only a few decades ago such high production quality required advanced typesetting skills that were available only to publishing professionals. The word processor enables businesspeople to produce elegant newsletters and professional advertising. It allows individuals to produce high-quality resumes and elaborate full-length books. But word processors do more than facilitate quality appearance—they may also contribute to improved contents. The capacity to easily cut and paste, change terminology, or add references enables more people to create stronger scientific papers, legal briefs, or business proposals. It enables novelists, playwrights, and poets to easily accommodate suggestions from peers and mentors.

But even the word processor can be improved by thinking about creativity support in the genex framework. How might advanced visualization of a document help authors? How can consultation be facilitated? How can users locate appropriate previous work and build on it to suit their current needs? The basic notions of exemplars, templates, and processes have already begun to appear. Authors of business letters can purchase thousands of exemplars that they can adapt in their own word processor. Then some of these authors might be able to contribute or sell their improved or specialized exemplars through growing digital libraries, available through the World Wide Web.

A more flexible strategy is to prepare templates, as is done for business documents such as invoices or travel expense reports. These are supplied with many word processors. Templates differ from exemplars in that they are somewhat more flexible, may include computational capabilities, and can have instructional guidance. Processes, such as Windows Wizards, extend the flexibility and allow richer variations.

Making a wider range of exemplars, templates, and processes available and a mechanism to create a market in new ones are still needed. Microsoft Office contains templates for word processed newsletters, slide presentations, sales reports, spreadsheet invoices, photo library databases, and so forth (Figure 11.4). The structured processes of users' choices, embedded in the Microsoft Wizards, show overviews of the steps for generating an initial version of a personal resume or a legal pleading.

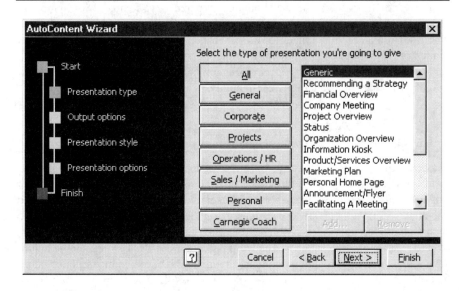

FIGURE 11.4   The overview of steps in the process helps guide users in choosing the components of a slide presentation in Microsoft PowerPoint.

Adobe PhotoDeluxe provides an excellent example of the range of support tools for the complex transformations in getting, cropping, editing, annotating, and sending images. In addition, it offers impressive transformations for images to give them the appearance of Van Gogh's bold brushstrokes, Seurat pointillism, or other styles. Music composition programs also provide transformations for a motif to generate New Orleans jazz or rhythm and blues pieces (www.pgmusic.com). Templates for fugues or sonatas and the strategies to recast motifs in the style of Beethoven or Joplin or other composers are realizable (Cope 1996).

Composition support tools should also provide evaluations. Modern word processors offer spelling and grammar checking, word counts, and sometimes reading difficulty indexes. More advanced evaluation and critiquing tools are possible, especially if the domain of application is kept narrow. For example, tax preparation tools provide continuous feedback on the refund amounts as changes are made to the tax forms.

11.5.7   Reviewing and Replaying Session Histories

Reflecting on work is a central notion in quality improvement, creativity, and education methods. The metacognitive processes that promote self-awareness are learnable, but software support to capture the history of all user actions would seem to be a good foundation for many services. We have come to expect that Web browsers record the history of our site visits so that we can return to them. One study of World Wide Web users showed that 58 percent of all URLs visited by users during a session were return visits (Tauscher and Greenberg 1997). Even in this simple case controversies abound because the strategy for producing a compact, meaningful list (in a linear, tree, or network format) is not apparent. Another problem is that Web sites may change over time, so older histories may no longer produce the same results.

Producing histories of command lines in UNIX or information retrieval programs is relatively easy, but understanding the meaning of each command may depend on the context (for example, the current directory). In richer graphical user interface environments such as simulators, image manipulators, legal information retrieval, or geographic information systems, recording each user step is feasible. However, success requires careful user interface and software design to ensure that the results are compact, comprehensible, and useful. Once these basics are accomplished, structuralists will especially like to manipulate session histories and replay the steps on another set of data or go back to change a step before replaying. Saving a sequence of steps for later use creates a basic macro, and by adding conditional and looping constructs, quite ambitious programs could be built (Figure 11.5). For example, in a simulation of computer chip fabrication, it should be possible to rerun the simulation changing the temperature by single degree increments from 100° to 200° Centigrade. If histories are first-class objects, then users should be able to send them to peers or mentors for comment or assistance with problems. Histories might also be searchable, so that a set of hundreds of directories could be searched to see if any were done at a temperature above 200° C. Users should be able to post or sell exemplars of excellence or processes that might be helpful to others.

11.5.8 Disseminating Results

E-mail, listservs, digital libraries, and the World Wide Web provide an excellent foundation for disseminating results, but these also could be improved by thinking of the genex framework. The first circle of people who should receive an announcement of an innovation include previous and current workers. While digital libraries and online resources may make previous work accessible, extracting e-mail (or mailing) addresses and ensuring that they are current is tedious at best. Finding current workers in a domain is sometimes possible by listservs, newsletters, or Web sites of relevant communities.

A second circle of interest might be readers of papers or viewers of Web sites with related materials. Finding the identity of Web site viewers is not usually possible, but registration strategies might be developed to enable visitors to request information about future developments. The commercial bookseller Amazon.com offers a service that will send you e-mail when books on a topic or by a given author appear. Obviously, such registration lists have great commercial value, but publicly available variants are likely to emerge and be appealing because of their narrow focus. These are modern versions of what information retrieval professionals call selective dissemination of

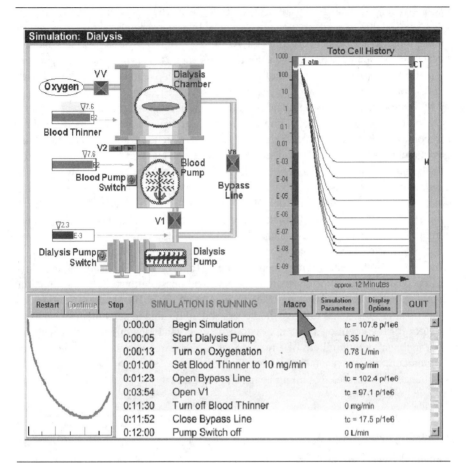

FIGURE 11.5 History keeping in the SimPLE environment (Rose et al. 1998). The user has run a simulation and produced a history, then rerun the history macro eight times to produce the eight outputs on the upper right.

information (SDI), a policy by which users are informed on a regular basis about new publications on topics they have selected.

Digital libraries are being reconceived of as digital library communities by extensive use of online community software to turn every object into the focus of a discussion group (Brothers et al. 1992). Anyone retrieving a novel, scientific paper, legal precedent, or classical music score could register to participate in a discussion of that item. Such online discussion groups can stimulate creative work in many disciplines if appropriate usability design and sociability policies are developed (Preece 2000).

Additions to scientific journals, music libraries, or art galleries would require review by editors, collections managers, and curators. Modern technologies not only speed up the process but also facilitate review from multiple sources. Maybe more importantly, the complexity and cost of establishing online journals, libraries, and galleries is substantially less than physical institutions, thereby lowering the barrier. Having more diverse institutions that create digital libraries is also likely to stimulate creativity.

11.6   Architectural Scenario

The genex framework and the eight activities could reshape many forms of evolutionary creative work. Earlier genex examples included education, medicine, and legislation (Shneiderman 1998c). The following scenario has some elements of wishful thinking, but it exemplifies how the genex phases (collect, relate, create, and donate) and the eight activities (search, consult, visualize, think, explore, compose, review, and disseminate) might be supported. This scenario assumes that genex tools would enable an architect to have a broader range of decision-making power. This reverses the decentralized and fragmented approach of contemporary practice by restoring control and responsibility in one individual. However, this is possible only if powerful consultation tools are available to coordinate and supervise tasks that are often delegated to many others.

Imagine an architect, named Susan, who is chosen to design a hotel at a national park because of her reputation for flexible designs. Her winning proposal was to break away from the uniform array of hotel rooms at many resorts and allow flexible modules that can accommodate couples or be reconfigured for families and groups of up to 12. She searches an architectural library for exemplars of hotels from around the world, such as Swiss chalets, Austrian lodges, or Rocky Mountain log cabins (collect and search). She flips through 300 possibilities to open up her mind to a broad range of roof designs and sidings (collect and think). She visualizes the data on heating requirements, heat loss, and energy consumption patterns for these 300 possibilities to find strategies that are energy efficient (collect and visualize). Susan chooses a log cabin design and pays the creator a modest fee, then wrestles with the problems of adding more windows, movable modules, and solar heating panels. Her composition tools allow her to manipulate the underlying architectural model so she can resize the building to accommodate the required number of rooms (create and explore). After choosing a cedar shingle roof and redwood siding, she superimposes the images on the backgrounds of two potential sites: on the hillside and at the base (create and compose).

The park managers and concessionaires who will run the hotel prefer the hillside site because of the wonderful views, rather than the base site. After consulting electronically with park commissioners and travel industry advisors, they accept the log cabin style since it fits local and tourist tastes (relate and consult). A videoconference directly with the client using dual 3D displays leads to immediate decisions about the reception desk, a commons area with a fireplace, and a gift shop (relate and consult). The distinctive plan for flexible modules to accommodate couples, families, and groups of hikers meets resistance, but Susan perseveres. She adds further flexibility, allowing those who wish to cook their own meals to share a communal kitchen/dining area and offering fine dining and maid service for those who want a more pampered experience. The steep incline of the hillside site presents a formidable challenge, but after an all-night session playing with the engineering models, Susan finds an innovative structural design that costs only 8 percent more than the base site (create and explore, compose). Susan reflects on how the traditional fragmented approach would have killed the flexibility theme because independent contractors would not risk novelty.

Susan collaborates with specialists who conference over her plans for the electric wiring, plumbing, phones, and Internet connections. The same groupware gets her rapid advice from other consultants but preserves her control over wall decorations, flooring, and furniture styles (create and explore, compose). She does in hours what would have taken weeks when these tasks would have been sent out to consultants. After a virtual walk through, the client requests larger windows, which is handled by reviewing the design history and increasing the window sizes (relate and review). This change causes rerouting of wiring and stronger structural supports, but Susan's flexible design is preserved (create and compose).

At this point, consultations begin with potential builders (relate and consult). Susan reviews the capabilities of builders, and she receives bids electronically. She uses her software to generate bill-of-materials lists for suppliers and a construction schedule for discussion by all parties (relate, create, and compose).

Susan decides to break with tradition and insists on supervising construction. She has to replace a slow-working subcontractor, but opening day is on schedule. There is already a waiting list of couples, families, and groups who are attracted to the beautiful setting and the flexible accommodations. Susan registers her design with the architectural society's digital library and sends a description to interest managers of similar parks around the world (donate and disseminate). Her flexible approach is copied by others, for which she collects a fee, and she receives a resort industry award for architectural innovation. Susan appreciates how the software tools enabled creative designs and new business processes but has a list of upgrades she wants before her next project.

11.7 Conclusion

Ambitious visions can be helpful in shaping more concrete research agendas. For example, Engelbart's goal of augmenting human intellect (Engelbart and English 1968) led to innovations such as the mouse and windows. Later, Brooks's (1996) belief in the importance of toolmaking led to innovations such as haptic feedback in 3D graphical environments. These inspirational visions were important catalysts for genex.

The ambition to support evolutionary creativity led to the four phases of genex:

- Collect: Learn from previous works stored in libraries, the Web, and so on.
- Relate: Consult with peers and mentors at early, middle, and late stages.
- Create: Explore, compose, and evaluate possible solutions.
- Donate: Disseminate the results and contribute to the libraries.

These four phases and the eight activities described in this paper (Figure 11.1) are major challenges, but the integrated combination of them could produce an environment that greatly facilitates creativity. The eight activities and their integration form a research agenda for human-computer interaction and user interface design.

The goal of supporting more creativity by more people more of the time is attractive, but there is the danger that the genex framework might be ineffective or even limit creativity. By making easy access to previous work and current workers, there is a risk that more exotic ideas will be suppressed. Similarly, using creativity supports such as simulations and composition tools may restrict imagination to only what is possible with these tools. Consultations are time consuming, and discouraging advice for novel ideas is a possible outcome. Fear that others will plagiarize compositions or steal inventions is another legitimate concern. An understanding of the dangers is important in pursuing the positive possibilities.

Between the lofty ambitions and troubling fears lies the practical path of careful research and detailed design for the eight activities described in this paper. They need development, testing, and refinement to make them successful, find their flaws, and pursue alternatives. At every stage, widespread participation in design reviews increases the possibility that the resulting technologies will serve human needs in constructive and positive ways.

Acknowledgments

I am grateful for thoughtful comments from Charles Cave, Harry Hochheiser, Ross Malaga, Kent Norman, Catherine Plaisant, Jenny Preece, Richard Salter, Susan Schneider, and the anonymous reviewers. This work was supported in part by IBM Research's University Partner Program and the U.S. Census Bureau.

References

Ahlberg, C., and Shneiderman, B., (1994). Visual information seeking: Tight coupling of dynamic query filters with starfield displays. *Proceedings of the CHI'94 Conference: Human Factors in Computing Systems,* 313–321 + color plates. New York: ACM.

Basalla, G. (1988). *The evolution of technology.* United Kingdom: Cambridge University Press.

Berners-Lee, T., Cailliau, R., Luotonen, A., Nielsen, H.F., and Secret, A. (1994). The World Wide Web. *Communications of the ACM, 37,* 8, 76–82.

Boden, M. (1990). *The creative mind: Myths and mechanisms.* New York: Basic Books.

Bonnardel, N. (1999). Creativity in design activities: The role of analogies in a constrained cognitive environment. *Proceedings of the 3rd Creativity and Cognition Conference,* 158–165. New York: ACM.

Brooks, F., Jr. (1996). The computer scientist as toolsmith II. *Communications of the ACM, 39,* 3, 61–68.

Brothers, L., Hollan, J., Nielsen, J., Stornetta, S., Abney, S., Furnas, G., and Littman, M. (1992). Supporting informal communication via ephemeral interest groups: Innovations in e-mail. *Proceedings of the CSCW'92 Conference on Computer-Supported Cooperative Work,* 84–90. New York: ACM.

Bryson, S., Kenwright, D., Cox, M., Ellsworth, D., and Haimes, R. (1999). Visually exploring gigabyte data sets in real time. *Communications of the ACM, 42,* 8, 82–90.

Bush, V. (1945). As we may think. *Atlantic Monthly, 76,* 1, 101–108. Also at http://www2.theAtlantic.com/atlantic/atlweb/flashbks/computer/tech.htm.

Candy, L. (1997). Computers and creativity support: Knowledge, visualisation and collaboration. *Knowledge-Based Systems, 10,* 3–13.

Candy, L., and Edmonds, E. (1997). Supporting the creative user: A criteria-based approach to interaction design. *Design Studies, 18,* 185–194.

Card, S., Mackinlay, J., and Shneiderman, B. (1999). *Readings in information visualization: Using vision to think.* San Francisco, CA: Morgan Kaufmann Publishers.

Cave, C. (1999). Creativity Web Site, http://www.ozemail.com.au/~caveman/Creative/.

Cope, D. (1996). *Experiments in musical intelligence.* The Computer Music and Digital Audio Series, No. 12. Madison, WI: A-R Editions.

Couger, D. (1996). *Creativity and innovation in information systems organizations.* Danvers, MA: Boyd & Fraser Publishing Co.

Csikszentmihalyi, M. (1996). *Creativity: Flow and the psychology of discovery and invention.* New York: HarperCollins.

DeBono, E. (1973). *Lateral thinking: Creativity step by step.* New York: Harper Colophon Books.

Derthick, M., Kolojejchick, J.A. and Roth, S.F. (1997). An interactive visual query environment for exploring data. *Proceedings of the ACM Symposium on User Interface Software and Technology (UIST'97),* 189–198. New York: ACM Press.

Dey, A., Abowd, G., Pinkerton, M., Wood, A. (1997). CyberDesk: A framework for providing self-integrating ubiquitous software services. *Proceedings of the ACM*

Symposium on User Interface Software and Technology (UIST'97), 75–76. New York: ACM Press.

Elam, J.J. and Melissa, M. (1990). Can software influence creativity? *Information Systems Research,* 1, 1–22.

Engelbart, D.C., and English, W.K. (1968). A research center for augmenting human intellect. *AFIPS Proceedings of the Fall Joint Computer Conference 33,* 395–410. Montvale, NJ: AFIPS Press.

Gardner, H. (1994). *Creating minds: An anatomy of creativity seen through the lives of Freud, Einstein, Picasso, Stravinsky, Eliot, Graham, and Gandhi.* New York: Basic Books.

Greenbaum, J., and Kyng, M. (Eds.). (1991). *Design at work: Cooperative design of computer systems.* Hillsdale, NJ: LEA Publishers.

Hearst, M. (1999). User interfaces and visualization. In R. Baeza-Yates and B. Ribeiro-Neto (Eds.), *Modern Information Retrieval.* Reading, MA: Addison-Wesley.

Johnson, S. (1997). *Interface culture: How new technology transforms the way we create and communicate.* New York: HarperCollins.

Jones, P.M., and Schneider, K.J. (1996). Learning environment for magnetic resonance spectroscopy (LEMRS): Supporting apprenticeship learning in operational environments. *Journal of Educational Multimedia and Hypermedia,* 5, 2, 151–177.

Kiesler, S. (Ed.). (1997). *Culture of the Internet.* Mahwah, NJ: Lawrence Erlbaum Assoc., Inc.

Koenemann, J., and Belkin, N. (1996). A case for interaction: A study of interactive information retrieval behavior and effectiveness. *Proceedings of the CHI'96 Human Factors in Computing Systems,* 205–212. New York: ACM Press.

Kuhn, T.S. (1996). *The structure of scientific revolutions,* 3rd Edition. Chicago: University of Chicago Press.

Marchionini, G. (1995). *Information seeking in electronic environments.* United Kingdom: Cambridge University Press.

Massetti, B. (1996). An empirical examination of the value of creativity support systems on idea generation. *MIS Quarterly,* 20, 1, 83–97.

Massetti, B., White, N.H., and Spitler, V.K. (1999). The impact of the World Wide Web on idea generation. *Proceedings of the 32nd Hawaii International Conference on System Sciences.* Los Alamitos, CA: IEEE Computer Society Press.

Muller, M., Wildman, D., and White, E. (1993). Taxonomy of PD practices: A brief practitioner's guide. *Communications of the ACM,* 36, 4, 26–27.

Mayer, R.E. (1992). *Thinking, problem solving, cognition,* 2nd Edition. New York: W.H. Freeman.

Nakakoji, K., Suzuki, K., Ohkura, N., and Aoki, A. (1997). A framework to support creativity in multimedia information design. *Proceedings of the Human-Computer Interaction INTERACT'97,* 212–219. London: Chapman & Hall.

National Research Council—Committee on a National Collaboratory (1993). *National collaboratories: Applying information technology for scientific research.* Washington, DC: National Academy Press.

North, C., and Shneiderman, B. (2000). Snap-together visualization: Coordinating multiple views to explore information. *Proceedings of Advanced Visual Interfaces 2000.* New York: ACM.

Olson, G.M., and Olson, J.S. (1997). Research on computer supported cooperative work. In M.G. Helander, T.K. Landauer, and P.V. Prabhu (Eds.), *Handbook of Human-Computer Interaction,* Second Edition, 1433–1456. Amsterdam: Elsevier.

Plaisant, C., Rose, A., Milash, B., Widoff, S., and Shneiderman, B. (1996). Life-Lines: Visualizing personal histories. *Proceedings of the ACM CHI'96 Conference: Human Factors in Computing Systems,* 221–227, 518. New York: ACM.

Polya, G. (1957). *How to solve it: A new aspect of mathematical method,* Second Edition. Garden City, NY: Doubleday Anchor Books.

Preece, J. (2000). *Thriving online communities: Usability and sociability.* New York: John Wiley & Sons.

Rose, A., Eckard, D., and Rubloff, G. (1998). An application framework for creating simulation-based learning environments. University of Maryland Dept. of Computer Science Technical Report CS-TR-3907.

Roth, S.F., Lucas, P., Senn, J.A., Gomberg, C.C., Burks, M.B., Stroffolino, P.J., Kolojejchick, J.A. and Dunmire, C. (1996). Visage: A user interface environment for exploring information. *Proceedings of Information Visualization '96,* 3–12. Los Alamitos, CA: IEEE Computer Society Press.

Shneiderman, B. (1998a). *Designing the user interface: Strategies for effective human-computer interaction,* Third Edition. Reading, MA: Addison-Wesley.

Shneiderman, B. (1998b). Relate-create-donate: A teaching philosophy for the cyber-generation. *Computers & Education,* 31, 1, 25–39.

Shneiderman, B. (1998c). Codex, memex, genex: The pursuit of transformational technologies. *International Journal of Human-Computer Interaction,* 10, 2, 87–106.

Shneiderman, B., Byrd, D., and Croft, B. (1997). Clarifying search: A user-interface framework for text searches. *D-Lib Magazine.* http://www.dlib.org/dlib/january97/01contents.html.

Shneiderman, B., and Rose, A. (1997). Social impact statements: Engaging public participation in information technology design. In B. Friedman (Ed.), *Human Values and the Design of Computer Technology,* 117–133. Stanford, CA: CSLI Publications and Cambridge University Press.

Tauscher, L., and Greenberg, S. (1997). How people revisit web pages: Empirical findings and implications for the design of history systems. *International Journal of Human-Computer Studies,* 47, 1, 97–137.

Wright, W. (1995). Information animation application in the capital markets. *Proceedings of IEEE Information Visualization '95,* 19–25, 136–137. Los Alamitos, CA: IEEE Computer Society Press.

Interaction Spaces for Twenty-First-Century Computing

Terry Winograd

12.1 Introduction

Computing environments of the late twentieth century have been dominated by a standard desktop/laptop configuration. A single user sits in front of a screen with a keyboard and pointing device, interacting with a collection of applications, some of which use resources from the Internet. As many researchers have pointed out, computing today is moving away from this model in a number of ways (for example, see Weiser 1991).

- Information appliances, such as PDAs, computers integrated with cell phones, and small specialized information devices of diverse kinds (see Norman 1998)

- Multi-user information and work environments, which occupy room-size or building-size spaces, making use of large display areas, sound, environmental control, and so forth

- Immersive environments, both head mounted and shared (such as CAVES)

- Deviceless interaction, in which people's normal movements, gestures, vocalizations, and even physiological parameters are observed and interpreted by the computer system

Each of these changes to today's standard computer interaction modes raises its own technical difficulties and specialized areas of research. Taking a broader view, we need to reexamine some fundamental assumptions about the structure of interactive systems and integrated environments. Today's conventional model of interaction architecture and device communication has served us well up until now but will have to evolve toward a different architecture, focused on multiple users in an interaction space rather than focusing on systems as a network of processors and devices.

This chapter describes a conceptual framework for the development of a new architecture that is oriented toward integrated interaction spaces. It gives brief examples from a research project on interactive workspaces and poses some research issues for the future.

12.1.1 Scenario

Our research group in Graphics and HCI at Stanford University is one of several groups building an *interactive workspace,* which integrates a number of computer displays and devices in a single room (Rekimoto 1998; Streitz 1998). Our workspace includes large high-resolution displays (wall mounted and tabletop), personal and mobile devices (PDAs, tablet computers, laser pointers, etc.), and environmental sensors (cameras, microphones, floor pressure sensors, etc.). The space is designed to support joint work by multiple users, who move from device to device and use multiple interaction modalities appropriate to the task and materials. Many of the activities involve more than one physical device (for example, the large display, pointers, voice, and one or more handheld devices).

As a motivating example, consider a group of people in this interactive workspace working together to develop a complex Web site. A large wall-mounted display contains items such as graphs representing the structure of the site, detailed work plans and schedules, pieces of text, and images. There will be a variety of other devices and modalities, but for purposes of illustration we will focus on an interaction with this display.

1. Jane places her two index fingers on one of the images and slides them apart and together. As she does, the image expands and shrinks accordingly. She stops when it is the right size.

2. She touches the screen with one index finger and draws a circle around a few of the images. The images change appearance to indicate selection.

3. She says aloud, "Hold for product page."

4. The scaled selected images are now available for later retrieval under the category "product page."

This scenario is clearly feasible today, and we can expect the hardware to soon reach a price where the required devices will be commonplace. Each piece of the functionality has been available for some time: the recognition of freehand gestures (Maes et al. 1993), gesture-based interaction with whiteboard contents (Moran et al. 1997), dynamic zooming of images (Bederson and Hollan 1994), and voice-driven commands (Bolt 1980). However, each of the existing systems that provides some of these capabilities is a research system, in which integration is limited and a large amount of specialized coding was required to achieve the desired results.

Consider in contrast an analogous scenario in which the display is on a standard workstation with a graphical user interface (GUI).

1. Jane clicks the mouse over one of the images. The image displays a set of associated handles. She drags one of the handles until it reflects a new desired size and lets up. The image is resized.

2. Jane drags her mouse along the diagonal of a rectangle that encloses several images, holding down the left button. When she lets up on the button, the images within the rectangular area change appearance to indicate selection.

3. She uses the mouse to activate the "Hold" menu in the menu bar at the top of the screen, which contains an item for each of the current categories, and selects "product page."

4. The selected images, in the specified size, are now available for later retrieval under the category "product page."

This second scenario could be programmed fairly easily by anyone skilled in the use of any of a variety of interface building tools (such as Visual Basic, TCL/TK, and various Java tool kits). It is not far beyond what HyperCard made available more than a decade ago to a wide population of programmers from elementary school age up. All of the interaction elements (selection, positioning, command invocation) are available in the basic operating system or in the form of widgets, toolkits, and standard libraries.

So why can't we program the first scenario this easily? One answer might simply be that it takes time for technologies to reach maturity. Because there are not yet many integrated interaction spaces, there have not yet been sufficient resources to develop the corresponding mechanisms for new kinds of interaction. This is, of course, true. But there is a deeper problem as well. The needed mechanisms are not just new features and widgets but require a shift in the way we think about input-output interactions with computer: a shift to a new architecture for interaction spaces.

12.2   Architecture Models

Three obvious elements are needed for human-computer interaction: a person, a computer, and one or more physical devices that operate in the person's physical space and exchange signals with the computer. In the early days of computing, the structure was simple, as shown in Figure 12.1.

A programmer who built an interactive application needed to know about the specific devices (we will refer to sensors and actuators jointly as "devices") and the details of their data structures and signals in order to write code that used them appropriately. The code could be carefully tailored to the specific devices to gain maximum efficiency and/or to take advantage of their special characteristics.

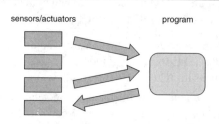

sensors/actuators   program

FIGURE 12.1   Elementary input/output architecture

This arrangement worked, but it had some obvious shortcomings.

1. Each new program had to have code to deal with the specifics of the devices.
2. Each new device (or modification to an existing device) could require reprogramming of pre-existing applications.
3. If a computer supported multiple processes, then conflicts could arise when two processes communicated with the same device.

12.2.1 Decoupling Devices from Programs

Over the first few decades of computing, a more complex architecture emerged to deal with these problems, using *indirection* to decouple programs from device inter-action details, as illustrated in Figure 12.2.

This architecture provides two fundamental levels of indirection between devices and programs.

First, the operating system provides for device drivers, which are coded to deal with the specifics of the signals to and from the device, and which provide a higher-level interface to programmers. Drivers can unify abstractions for different devices

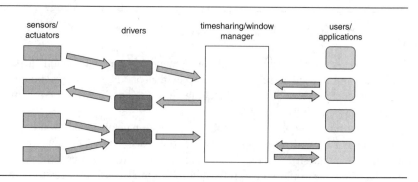

sensors/   drivers   timesharing/window   users/
actuators   manager   applications

FIGURE 12.2   Conventional input/output architecture

(for example, different physical pointing devices can provide the same form of two-dimensional coordinate information) or can provide multiple abstraction levels for a single physical device (for example, both interpreted handwriting and digital ink for a pen device). An operating system can also provide higher-level drivers, which further interpret events. For example, the basic motions of a pointing device can be accessed by programs in terms of an event queue whose events are expressed as high-level window and menu operations. Application programs can use libraries with program interfaces that provide higher-level events and descriptions while accessing lower-level drivers provided by the operating system.

The second level of indirection is in the linking of devices to programs. The operating system provides a time-sharing manager and/or window manager (details have evolved over time), which allocates connections dynamically. For example, the same keyboard may be interpreted as sending keystrokes to different programs at different moments, depending on which window is the current focus. It is possible for this function to be distributed among multiple processes and processors, but for the purposes of this discussion we will simply represent it as a single "Manager" component.

These mechanisms are all at play in making it easy to write a program that implements the workstation GUI scenario just presented. Selection, object sizing, menus, the tracking of position as a mouse moves, displaying a cursor at the location, and so on are all handled by the drivers, libraries, and toolkits, so the programmer can deal with the events at a level that is closer to the user-oriented description of what is happening.

12.2.2 Decoupling Devices from Phenomena

The problem in trying to support the programming of our interactive workspace scenario is not just one of writing more drivers and APIs. There are some fundamental conceptual shifts.

The first problematic question is, "What are the devices?" In the GUI example, there was a mouse and a graphical display. In the interaction space example, the most obvious candidate devices are "the display, Jane's fingers, and Jane's voice." But the latter of these are not devices in the sense of Figures 12.1 and 12.2. Although the user (and the application programmer) may think of them as devices, they are not attached to the computer through direct signals. Their activity is interpreted through devices such as cameras, trackers, and microphones. The programmer needs to deal with fingers and words at an appropriate level of abstraction, just as the GUI programmer deals with selection and menus. But this cannot be done by simply providing higher-level programming interfaces to the "real" devices such as camera and microphone.

The tracking of a user's finger may involve the integration of inputs from multiple visual and proximity-detection devices, along with modeling of the physical dynamics of the body. This integration is not associated with specific devices, nor is it associated with an individual program or application. An integrated "person watcher" would provide information for any number of different programs, just as the windowing system provides keyboard and pointing information for multiple programs.

Even for simpler objects, we are beginning to see a separation between the devices as viewed by a user and those designed into the computer system. For example, "tangible user interfaces" (Fitzmaurice et al. 1995) incorporate passive or semipassive physical objects into computer systems as though they were virtual devices. Sensors such as cameras are used by programs that track these objects and model their behavior and then provide a higher-level interface to them.

The architecture of Figure 12.3 adds an explicit layer of "observers": processes that interact with devices and with other observers to produce integrated higher-level accounts of entities and happenings that are relevant to the interaction structure.

The layer of observers has replaced, rather than being added to, the previous layer of drivers. Device drivers and single-device-based program interfaces in current systems can be thought of as simple observers, efficient for phenomena that are close to the device structure. In general, some observers will have a close relationship to the devices they interact with (for example, a pointing device will be associated with an observer that reports its position). A single device may be used by many different observers (for example, a camera or microphone that is being used to monitor people and their voices, track objects, detect environmental sounds and lighting, and so forth). Some observers may maintain elaborate models (for example, the detailed position and motion of a person's body parts).

Each observer provides an interface in terms of a specific set of objects, properties, and events. These can range from low-level ("the laser pointer is at position 223, 4446") to high-level interpretations ("Jane made a 'select' gesture on the screen"). Some observers will be "translators" or "integrators," which do not deal directly with any perceptual or motor devices but take descriptions in terms of one set of phenomena and produce others (for example, a gesture recognition observer taking hand position information from a physical body motion observer, which in turn may take information from a visual observer based on camera input). The observer processes may operate at different places in the computation structure, some on separate machines (such as a specialized vision or person-tracking processor), some within the operating system, and some installed as specialized libraries in the code of individual application processes.

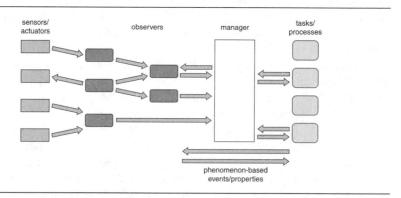

FIGURE 12.3 Architecture with a network of observers

To summarize this step of expanding the architecture, it separates three distinct conceptual elements that are often conflated or put into simple one-to-one correspondence:

1. *Devices:* Sensors and actuators and the signals they accept and produce
2. *Phenomena:* A space of things and happenings that are relevant to a program
3. *Observers:* Produce a particular interpretation of the phenomena using information from devices

12.3 Robust Dynamic Configuration and Communication

Figure 12.3 contains dozens of arrows, representing communication paths between various system components. The arrows are intentionally abstract, not specifying whether communication is between parts of a single program, programs on the same machine, or across a network. In fact, for most systems there will be a mixture, and the resulting complexity creates great problems for building robust systems. Many systems are built today using a mixture of component-to-component connections, which require different kinds of configuration steps (for example, for adding a new observer process on a machine or adding a new processor to the network). The result is brittle rather than flexible—it is difficult to make changes and difficult to recover from the failures of individual components.

Modern network-based software is moving toward another model, in which communication connections are virtual and dynamic rather than explicitly represented in configuration files, routing tables, and the like. In our research we have developed a system called the Event Heap (Johanson 2000), based on an underlying model that has often been referred to as a "blackboard." Rather than creating explicit communication paths between individual components, each component can post information to a shared server and subscribe to receive information that has been posted that matches a chosen pattern. An observer, for example, can subscribe to events posted by particular sensors and can then publish events based on an interpretation of what it received. The person writing the code for the observer does not need to know anything about how the sensors communicate (they post their results on the blackboard) or which other observers will use what this one produces. Of course, there must be agreed-upon data formats so that the posted events can be meaningfully interpreted by receivers, but these are separated from communication protocols.

The basic blackboard idea was proposed many years ago in systems such as LINDA (Ahuja et al. 1986), and has been widely used in Artificial Intelligence programs, in which each source of information is likely to be partial and even unreliable (Engelmore and Morgan 1988; Martin et al. 1999). As we move toward distributed, ubiquitous computing environments, the independence (mutual ignorance), partiality,

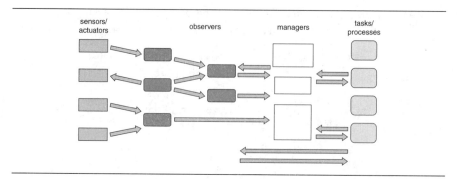

FIGURE 12.4   Distributed communication and management

and unreliability of individual components is becoming a fact of life for systems that make no claims to intelligence. At the same time, advances in computation and communication speed have made it practical to use an architecture that adds an extra stop in the middle of the communication process. It is inherently slower for one component to post to a server and a second component to then read the data rather than communicating directly from one to the other. We are now reaching the stage where for most communication paths this overhead is acceptable. (For exceptions, see the following discussion of perception-action coupling.)

In addition to decoupling communication, robustness can be improved by distributing management. In conventional systems there is a single "Manager" that maintains information about the overall system and coordinates activities across the components. For the traditional single-user, single-computer environment, this is an excellent architecture. The user wants to interact with a variety of applications and devices in an intermixed sequence, and the manager keeps track of what is going on (the current application, the window focus, the open files, the network connections, and so forth). Since the communication paths all go through a single processor, it is a natural place for integration.

In the distributed environment, with communication via a shared blackboard, it makes sense to distribute management functions as well. We still require programs that coordinate other components, but they need not be glued into a monolithic structure that mimics current windowing systems.

Figure 12.4 illustrates the removal of the explicit communication paths and the splitting up of the Manager. There are still implicit communication paths that determine the flow from one component to another, but they are implemented in the components' use of the blackboard, not requiring explicit configuration and recording.

12.4   Context-Based Interpretation

The use of higher-level observers leads to a problem of interpretive context. An application may need to interpret a certain hand motion as a gesture or a sequence of sounds as a voice saying a particular phrase. The purpose of providing a level of indirection through observers is to be able to add general capabilities such as word and gesture recognition to the overall system (not just to one application). But the interpretation of a sequence of motions or sounds will differ depending on what the application (and the user) is doing, how the particular person moves and talks, and so on. A circular wave of the hand may be a selection gesture in one activity and a circle-drawing gesture (or a meaningless motion) in another. The way that Jane moves her hand in pointing may be consistent over time but different from Jim's.

Many programs today apply context models to interpretation. In speech systems, for example, speaker-based models are tuned to the characteristics of a particular speaker. In addition, task-based vocabularies and grammars set dynamically by applications can provide a context in which the interpretation of utterances is shaped by expectations of what would likely be said.

In separating the observer from specific applications, we do not want to create a context-blind interpretation. In monolithic system structures, the "Manager" is the place where context is stored and distributed as needed to components. In our architecture there still needs to be a stable shared place for storage and retrieval of contextual information, but it is separated from the processes that use it, just as data files are separated from the processes that read and write them. A *context memory* can be introduced as a separate component, as shown in Figure 12.5.

The context memory provides persistent storage (beyond the scope of a particular application or interactive session) for context models, which are produced and used by the other components. Some context models deal with the current context (e.g., who is currently where in the physical environment). Others are based in applications (e.g., task-specific vocabularies and grammars). Others belong to a person in general (e.g., preferences or speech and handwriting characteristics). We can imagine each person having an extended kind of "home page" that provides these models along with other information about preferences or resources, such as bookmark collections.

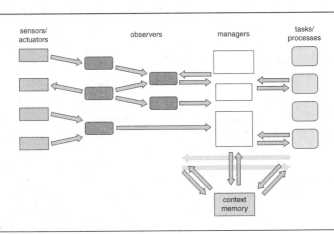

FIGURE 12.5 Providing interpretive context

As applications programs run, they provide models for use by the observers and potentially receive updated models from them. There is no sharp distinction between the kinds of information to be passed directly and the kinds to be stored and retrieved from the memory, but they represent different points in the communication tradeoff space. The memory is persistent with large storage capacity and has relatively slow latency, so it is less appropriate for short-term events (like selecting an object) and more appropriate for slowly changing persistent information (such as user preferences). For example, a speech model for a user would be stored in the memory and downloaded once to the relevant observer during a session. The speech events being interpreted would be passed directly as data, although they might also be saved in memory for replay, logging, and so on.

Although the context memory can be thought of as a single conceptual entity, it spans a space of data sizes and speed requirements that make it best thought of as a multilevel memory. In our implementation, large data objects (such as images) are stored in a conventional file structure, while small data objects (such as information about the location of a particular device in the interaction space) are stored as entries in an XML-structured database. The XML database is also used to store metadata about the objects in file storage so that they can be retrieved by a match of their characteristics.

12.5 Action and Perception

Anyone with experience in writing interactive systems is likely to wonder whether it is practical to make general use of all the levels of indirection and interpretation that have been described so far. There are two primary effects of adding a level of indirection to any computing system.

1. Consistent levels of indirection make possible a cleaner separation of concerns, which makes systems easier to write, modify, integrate, and understand.

2. Consistent indirection requires additional processing across the entire program, potentially hampering performance.

Whether the structural benefit is worth the efficiency cost is determined by the specifics of the situation. The world is full of examples of successful indirection (how many programs today deal directly with the arrangement of sectors and tracks on a disk?) and examples of failed indirection in systems where the gain in generality simply wasn't worth the performance penalty (as has been the case with many generalized GUI builders).

Many aspects of human-computer interaction have been subject to ever-higher levels of abstraction and indirection, with satisfactory performance results. Consider, for example, the level at which a programmer specifies what is to be displayed on a screen. We have progressed from individual vectors to shaded, textured, three-dimensional objects with controlled lighting and viewpoint. Processing power has expanded to make this possible.

The cases where performance has continued to be a deep problem are those with a tight coupling between action and perception. As a prime example, consider virtual reality using a head-mounted display. In order to maintain the perception of immersion in a three-dimensional world, the visual rendering needs to be updated to reflect changes in head position with no perceptible lag. As a more mundane example, we require tight action-perception coupling in simple cursor positioning with a mouse. If the motion of the cursor lags too far behind the movement of the hand, effectiveness is greatly decreased. To operate at action-perception coupling speeds (a latency in the milliseconds), system architectures need to pay special attention to coupling.

Many systems today (from head-mounted VR to the cursor tracker in every GUI OS) achieve satisfactory action-perception coupling by wiring it in specially, rather than using the more general interaction mechanisms provided for less time-sensitive processes. This makes it difficult to extend these programs, as discovered, for example, by anyone who has tried to extend a standard GUI system to handle multiple users each with a cursor (Myers et al. 1998). Some such problems are solved in distributed windowing systems (such as X-Windows) by providing specific coupling mechanisms in the server for operations such as dragging. On the other hand, if the programmer wanted to provide live rotation instead of translation of an object, this would not work, since the server does not provide sufficient tools for a rotation coupling. Specialized platforms for applications, such as live-action games and music playing, provide for coupling within their specialized domains.

A somewhat more general approach was taken in the Cognitive Coprocessor (Robertson et al. 1989), which had a manager dedicated to maintaining interaction coupling between a task queue and a display queue. This can be generalized in tools for action-perception coupling . To be effective, the following conditions must be met.

1. The input observers can provide observations at a guaranteed rate that meets the timing conditions (for example, the sampling rate of a positioning device)

2. The output observers can guarantee an update rate that meets the timing conditions (for example, guaranteed frame rate for visual rendering)

3. The data that needs to be transmitted to and from the manager is small enough to be transmitted in sufficiently short time (for example, sending a new set of coordinates, versus sending an entire image for each change)

4. The computation done by the manager for each iteration of the action-perception loop can be done within the timing conditions. In general this will not allow for a callback to the process that created the coupling.

Not all desired action-perception couplings will be able to meet these conditions. Time characteristics are dependent on the level of control that is available. For example, in current graphical interface systems, dragging of objects with the mouse can be done in a coupled way (rather than dragging an outline), since image translation can be achieved with sufficient update rates. On the other hand, real-time image zooming is not generally possible, since image scaling is not integrated in a sufficiently fast way. Systems such as Pad++ (Bederson and Hollan 1994) use special purpose programming to achieve live zooming.

12.5.1 Examples

The overall model described in this chapter is being developed in conjunction with our project to develop an interactive workspace. That work is still in its early stages and is proceeding by developing components that meet the needs of an integrated space and using the technical demands of those components as a driving function to develop the interaction architecture. The following examples are in the process of being integrated into the structures just described, and their development is helping to flesh out the details of those structures.

12.5.1.1 Barehands

The scenario with which this chapter started was motivated by our observations of people using our prototype interactive workspace, which includes three wall-mounted, touch-sensitive, back-projected displays (SMART board™). The other displays in the room are not touch-sensitive and require the use of some kind of pointing device. People immediately were attracted to the touch-screen interaction and found it natural and convenient. In fact, they often get frustrated when they attempt unsuccessfully to interact with the room's other displays (including a projection on a bare wall) by touching them.

However, our touch screens are limited in the kinds of interaction they support. The hardware can identify only a single point of touch at any time (multiple or large area touches are signaled as a single touch at their center), and there is no simple way to augment a touch with the kind of information provided by the buttons on standard pointing devices. In effect, every touch is interpreted as though the left mouse button is being clicked at a single point.

For the user, the device being used is not the touch screen but the hand that touches it. A hand has much more variability than a single point of touch. It can be held in various postures (such as touching with two fingers at once), can move in complex ways (gestures, rolling, etc.), and can exert complex pressure patterns. By adding additional observers, we can take advantage of the larger space. In our experiments we have added a camera-based observer that enables the system to identify hand posture. By combining this with the information provided by the touch-screen driver, we have designed interaction modes that use posture to modify touch. In one mapping we have experimented with, a single-finger touch is interpreted as a left button, a two-finger touch as a right button, the palm of the hand as an eraser, and the side of the hand as a highlighter. In another mapping, a touch of the side of the hand held vertically against the board does a Copy command, and a touch with the hand held horizontally does a Paste. The user does not think about the devices but about using hands in new ways (Ringel et al., 2000).

12.5.1.2 PointRight

Touch works well for interacting with a screen when a person is right next to it, but there are also uses in which a person seated at a table or standing across the room wants to interact with what is being displayed on a wall-mounted screen. Since our prototype space includes five large displays (including the front-projected wall and a bottom-projected table), each of which can run an independent GUI desktop, the most direct way to support interaction would be to have a pointing device and keyboard for each. An alternative would be to use some kind of monitor switcher that allows users to switch the use of a single pointing device and keyboard among the different desktops.

As with the previous example, this device-centric view does not correspond to the user's view of the world. If there is a single mouse and keyboard, the result of moving the mouse should be oriented to the space as a whole, not to the underlying computational system. When the cursor reaches the edge of a screen, it should continue moving onto the adjacent screen (as it does in multimonitor single-desktop systems), without regard to which processor is displaying on that screen. This includes moving across different kinds of devices—from the back-projected touch screens, onto a front-projected wall, onto the bottom-projected table, and even onto screens of laptops sitting on that table. The keyboard should go along, sending its input to whatever display currently displays the cursor.

The PointRight system we have developed provides this space-oriented interaction, allowing any pointing device (the standard one is a wireless GyroMouse) to point anywhere in the workspace. This example, as mentioned in the section on action-perception coupling, demands a low latency so that the user has the experience of directly moving the cursor, not of operating a pointing device that then gives motion instructions to a cursor. This has required ongoing development of the architecture to combine the desired speed with the generality of communication paths.

12.5.1.3 Room Controller

In any physical environment there will be devices that can be explicitly controlled by users (as well as possibly being automatically controlled for other purposes). The first obvious examples in our interactive workspace were the ceiling lights (controlled by an X10 interface) and the projectors (which are often switched off to preserve bulb life and which can be switched among alternative input sources). It was immediately clear that the simple direct route (physically operating switches on each device and using the X10 remote control) was inconvenient. It required going to the relevant devices and demanded a device-centered operation (in other words, there was no way to turn on all the projectors, just switches for each projector). We developed a series of interactive controllers that could be displayed on any of the devices in the room (including a Clio tablet with wireless connections). These controllers provide the user with higher-level operations (dealing with more than one device) and with a natural mapping for device-specific actions (displaying a geometrical map of the room, with switch-like icons next to each device for the actions it supports).

From the user's point of view, this controller operates directly on the physical devices, without regard to the actual sequence of events that are communicated among various components to achieve the effect. From the system-builder's point of view, the initial controllers were inflexible, requiring reprogramming whenever the physical situation in the space was modified. This provided a need for a context memory. Information about the devices in their room and their physical layout is stored in this memory and updated when the space is changed. The application that provides room-control interfaces to users can make use of this data dynamically to produce a controller that is specific to the setting (Ponnekanti et al. 2001).

12.6 Research Issues

In order to make use of an architecture for interactive spaces, a number of additional problems need to be addressed.

12.6.1 Person-Centered Interaction

One of the basic shifts from today's systems to interactive workspaces is letting go of the conventional assumption that each device is associated with a particular user who is logged onto it at a given moment. Shared wall-based displays, for example, need to be usable by anyone at any moment, without going through a separate login or identification step. However, the sharing needs to respect individual information spaces: When Jane is at the board, she should be able to access her private files, but at the very next moment when Jim walks up to it, he should have access to his instead.

This capability requires observers that can identify which person makes an action using any device. For some observers (such as ones that respond to voice control) this will require specialized programs that do things like speaker recognition. For many devices, it is sufficient to identify the person who is in physical proximity. A variety of methods are possible, including visual observation of people in the space and wearable infrared badges or radio frequency tags that can be tracked. Although experiments have been done, there are not yet reliable, sufficiently accurate means to do this, and there are additional concerns to be addressed about users' privacy and desire to wear tracking devices.

12.6.2 Dealing Efficiently with Incomplete and Unreliable Information

Much of the research on multimodal interaction has made use of artificial intelligence techniques to infer information from multiple sources, each of which might provide only part of the relevant information or that might be inaccurate. Both rule-based and probabilistic techniques (such as Bayes nets) have been applied. Our experiments, on the other hand, have come from the opposite direction, building upward from conventional system architectures and being constrained by the traditional demands on performance. In an interactive space, the power of inferential techniques will need to be reconciled with the performance demands that come from depending on them for the main stream of user interactions, not just for specialized tasks or demonstrations.

12.6.3 Variable Quality Guaranteed Response Rate

One of the criteria for implementing an action-perception coupling is that the observers can provide guaranteed timing for their activities. The conservative way to achieve this is to program for the worst case, limiting capabilities to those that can always be achieved. A more flexible strategy is to have varying levels of capacity that can be achieved at different speeds. This has been explored in the area of visual rendering, where a lower-quality rendering may be perfectly adequate for rendering an object that is in motion, to be replaced by a higher-quality one when it is static. It is possible to design variable-quality actions, both for input and output, which make it possible to maintain guarantees of responsiveness by trading off other resource/quality dimensions. In many cases, the properties of human perception will aid the programmer, since rapid change reduces sensory acuity. In other cases this may not be true (such as a system using force feedback in conjunction with a fingertip motion over a virtual object). Both technical and psychophysical questions need to be explored to make a variable quality strategy effective.

12.6.4 Multiperson, Multidevice, Interaction Modes

One of the key motivations for the generalizations in this architecture is the desire to support integrated applications with multiple users and multiple devices in an interaction structure that is many-to-many (one person may use several devices; several people may share one). There has been a good deal of work on shared-workspace applications, primarily for remotely linked participants. We have not dealt with questions of telepresence in this chapter, but clearly the design of interaction spaces will extend across more than one physical location. The issues in coordinating multiple activities at any degree of copresence are both technical and social, and as we expand the space of possible participant-device configurations, we need to better understand and design the ways that people work together.

12.6.5 Standard Models

Today's GUI systems have a relatively mature and stable model for visual objects, windows, menus, and so forth. This makes possible the ease of programming mentioned in our initial GUI scenario. There are no corresponding models for human physical activities, such as speech, gesture, and freehand drawing. These will be more complex to develop, since they need to deal with inputs that can be ambiguous and uncertain and that may require combining information from multiple modalities. We expect models to emerge for specific aspects of human behavior as the research proceeds and to evolve through experience to become sufficiently general.

12.7 Conclusion

This chapter has proposed a conceptual framework for the design of interactive spaces. It will take an ambitious research program to develop a general-utility system in accordance with this perspective, and there are many open research questions. There are several shorter-term actions that can be effective in solving some of the problems that motivated the approach presented here.

First, in building new systems that implement parts of a general mechanism, we can use structures that are compatible with the larger architecture and open to extension within the framework. In our own work on the interactive workspace, we are taking this approach. We are developing and integrating capabilities using a bottom-up strategy, with the larger-scale view as background. Second, the conceptual distinctions here can be useful in sorting out problems and confusions in designing special purpose systems. This will become increasingly important as more applications begin to make use of broad, rich input devices (such as cameras and microphones) with their attendant problems of person identification and context-based interpretation of the phenomena of relevance to the user and computing system. Finally, a shift of perspective may be a catalyst to help provoke new ideas about what to try and what can be done in improving the ways in which computers and people interact.

Acknowledgments

Thanks to Michelle Baldonado, Henry Berg, François Gumbretiere, and Debby Hindus for helpful comments on earlier drafts. Also, thanks to Pat Hanrahan, Armando Fox, and the students in the Interactive Workspace project for discussions and an environment that raises the right questions.

References

Ahuja, S., Carriero, N., and Gelernter, D. (1986). Linda and friends. *IEEE Computer,* 19, 8, 26–34.

Bederson, B., and Hollan, J.D. (1994). *Pad++:* A zooming graphical interface for exploring alternate interface physics. *UIST'94. Seventh Annual Symposium on User Interface Software and Technology. Proceedings of the ACM Symposium on User Interface Software and Technology,* 17–26. New York: ACM.

Bolt, R.A. (1980). Put-that-there: Voice and gesture at the graphics interface. *ACM SIGRAPH Comput. Graph.,* 14, 3, 262–270.

Engelmore, R.S., and Morgan, A. (Eds.). (1988). *Blackboard systems.* Reading, MA: Addison-Wesley.

Fitzmaurice, G., Ishii, H., and Buxton, W. (1995). Bricks: Laying the foundations for graspable user interfaces. *CHI'95,* 442–449. Denver, CO.

Fox, A., Johanson, B., Hanrahan, P., and Winograd, T. (2000). Integrating information appliances into an interactive workspace. *IEEE Computer Graphics and Applications* 20:3, 54–65.

Maes, P., Darrell, T., Blumberg, B., and Pentland, A. (1993). ALIVE: Artificial Life Interactive Video Environment. *Visual Proceedings of SIGGRAPH'93.* Anaheim, CA.

Martin, D.L., Cheyer, A.J., and Moran, D.B. (1999). The open agent architecture: A framework for building distributed software systems. *Applied Artificial Intelligence,* 13, 91–128.

Moran, T., Chiu, P., and van Melle, W. (1997). Pen-based interaction techniques for organizing material on an electronic whiteboard. *UIST'97,* 45–54. Banff, Alberta, Canada.

Myers, B.A., Stiel, H., and Gargiulo, R. (1998). Collaboration using multiple PDAs connected to a PC. *Proceedings CSCW'98: ACM Conference on Computer-Supported Cooperative Work,* 285–294. Seattle, WA: ACM Press.

Norman, D.A. (1998). *The invisible computer.* Cambridge, MA: MIT Press.

Ponnekanti, S.R., Lee, B.A., Fox, A., Hanrahan, P., and Winograd, T. (In press). ICrafter: A Service Framework for Ubiquitous Computing Environments. *Proceedings of UBICOMP 2001.* Atlanta, GA: ACM Press.

Rekimoto, J. (1998). A multiple device approach for supporting whiteboard-based interactions. *CHI'98,* 344–351. Chicago, IL.

Ringel, M., Berg, H., Jin, Y., Winograd, T. Barehands: Implement-free interaction with a wall-mounted display. *Proceedings of CHI2001,* Seattle, WA. Extended Abstracts, 367–368.

Robertson, G., Card, S., and Mackinlay, J. (1989). The cognitive coprocessor architecture for interactive user interfaces. *UIST'89,* 10–18. Williamsburg, VA.

Streitz, N., Geißler, J., and Holmer, T. (1998). Roomware for cooperative buildings: Integrated design of architectural spaces and information spaces. In N. Streitz, S. Konomi, H. Bunchardt (Eds.), *Cooperative buildings—Integrating Information, organization and architecture;* Proceedings of CoBuild'98, Darmstadt, Germany. Lecture Notes in Computer Science, Vol. 370, 4–21. Heidelberg: Springer.

Weiser, M. (1991). The computer for the twenty-first century. *Scientific American,* 265, 3, 94–104.

PART IV

Groupware and Cooperative Activity

13

Computer-Mediated Communications for Group Support: Past and Future

Murray Turoff
Starr Roxanne Hiltz
Jerry Fjermestad
Michael Bieber
Brian Whitworth

13.1 Introduction

The new millennium marks more than 30 years since the first computer-mediated group communication system became operational in 1969 (Turoff 1970). What seems to have occurred in this time is the creation of the environment and resources (in terms of equipment, networking, and large user populations) that make widespread implementation of the simpler elements of group communication possible. However, many of the originally envisioned more complex features of group communication have yet to be implemented widely, and they only appear to a limited degree in certain research systems.

Computer-mediated communication (CMC) embodies the concept developed in the early 1970s that one could use the processing and storage capabilities of computer networks to support communication processes within a group, as well as tailor those processes to the requirements of the application and the nature of the group (Hiltz and Turoff 1993). This chapter will discuss some of the many challenges still facing this field. It focuses on asynchronous CMC (anytime, anywhere via the Internet and its predecessors and successors) and on the over 25 years of system development and extensive research on social impacts carried out at NJIT, involving thousands of users who have been studied using various types of features for a diversity of tasks. There is a large body of research and development on "decision room" systems (synchronous, same time CMC for Group Decision Support), with central work by faculty and graduates of the Universities of Arizona and Minnesota; this has been reviewed elsewhere (Fjermestad and Hiltz 1999, 2000). And certainly, there have been other notable efforts in the area of asynchronous CMC. We note with special admiration the explorations of structures to deal with information overload in CMC by Malone and his colleagues at MIT (Malone et al. 1987; Ackerman and Malone 1990) and by Jacob Palme and colleagues in Sweden (Palme 1992). Many of these systems are described by Rapaport (1991). While a substantial number of examples of this non-NJIT work will be referred to in this paper, within the limited scope of a short chapter, we will mainly emphasize the prior and ongoing work with which we have been personally involved.

The chapter covers several advanced research areas for CMC, with the hope that future research and resulting systems will be more comprehensive. The features we will discuss are tailoring the communication process, discourse structures, collective intelligence, coordination methods, and various challenges and opportunities for collaborative model building. These features are particularly relevant for the support of large, dispersed groups, working on complex problems over an extended period of time. This has been one of our major foci in the design and study of CMC at NJIT. We then discuss applying these to the next generation of electronic commerce environments. This leads us to consider the opportunities of multimedia interaction and virtual reality. We conclude with a call for open CMC modules, which developers could use to implement the features we describe in the chapter. However, first we will review some of the earliest CMC work, showing that many originally proposed features are still relevant today.

13.2   Early Roots and Insights

Our approach to group communications had its philosophical foundation in the development of the Delphi method (Linstone and Turoff 1975; Turoff 1970; Turoff and Hiltz 1995), which was a paper-based communication system designed to allow large groups to communicate about complex problems. Delphi exercises have typically included 30 to 300 respondents who are expert or knowledgeable about the topic and typically involve a three- to five-round process.

The original computerized Delphi Conference System and its derivative EMISARI (Emergency Management Information System and Reference Index), used by the Executive Office of the President to monitor and coordinate the response to various national crises over a 15-year period (Turoff 1970; Hiltz and Turoff 1993), still today illustrate features that are yet to be incorporated into commercial systems. The foremost example is tailorability. Other examples of features included in EMISARI but not found in most current "groupware" systems are quantitative communication structures, content-based communication, indirect communication, roles, and notifications.

13.2.1 Quantitative Communication Structures

We use the term "computer conference" to refer to a structured group communication space that accumulates a permanent transcript of the discussion. People can communicate with and about numbers, not just with words. A monitor of an EMIS-ARI conference could establish data structures that were single numeric values, columns (vectors), or tables (matrices). A single member of the conference could be made responsible for reporting the specific numeric values, vectors, or tables and build vectors and tables out of them. Whenever anyone retrieved the data items they could see who reported them and when. Members could also ask for a history of the values over time. In addition, one could enter certain alpha codes that would indicate things such as something is wrong with the value this reporting period, the data are not yet available, and so forth. No one needed to know who was interested in the discussion, since those who were interested in retrieving the data relevant to their concerns would find the discussion associated with the data.

13.2.2 Content-Based Communication

By content-based communication we mean that the content of the communication item determines where it is delivered. For example, an EMISARI user could send a message to an individual data item so that they would be notified of any changes to, or new comments on, that item. A single data item could thus be the nucleus for a discussion thread. The important observation is the generality that this facility provides in terms of the philosophy of design. The content of a communication item is able to determine the "address" or ultimate recipients of communication from that item. This seems at the heart of the current revolution in group communication processes and their impacts on social and societal processes. Associated with this property is the need for a communication node tool that can be attached to any quantitative or qualitative data item (like a Post-it™ note can be), which allows a discussion thread to take place associated with that item, whatever it is and wherever it is. This opens the door for any user to add group communications to any item that needs a possible discussion by those accessing that item. The ability of any customer in Amazon.com to review a given book is a current example of content-based communication, since these reviews are tied to the book and available to anyone who is seeking the book. As another example, a future meeting in a group calendar could have an agenda attached, and group members could initiate a discussion on a particular agenda item before the meeting.

13.2.3 Indirect Communication

By indirect communication we mean communications generated by the system but based indirectly on the actions of the users. EMISARI tracked what words or phrases people were using to search for items in what were called notebooks. These were group communication spaces that could be publicly read by any member but only written to by a specified subset of members. These notebooks were used for things like policy interpretations being made by select staff. The computer would make available to the people able to write into the notebook the list of words that people were searching for *but not finding.* This indirect communication channel allowed the writers to determine what was missing from the material and could be used to schedule the discussions leading to new interpretations.

In any organizational context there is a tremendous potential for utilizing the behavior of members in their retrieval patterns to provide information to others that will dynamically improve the flow of meaningful information by identifying needs that may be changing. For example, in Answer Garden (Ackerman and Malone 1990), users first searched for answers to questions in an information database, but if they could not find it, they asked questions that were routed to human experts. Then the question and answer might be added to the database.

Currently Amazon.com provides a form of indirect communications with the records of the set of books that people buy, so if a person is interested in one book, others are recommended. Most of the current generation of recommender systems also demonstrates the concept of indirect communication—for example, collaborative filtering of USENET in GroupLens (Konstan et al. 1997) or recommendations of Web resources by PHOAKS (Terveen et al. 1997).

13.2.4 Roles

By roles we mean behavioral expectations that individuals take on with the group of which they are a part. In most group interaction, people fulfill roles within the group, such as chairperson or secretary. Often it is necessary to provide them with special functionality to carry out that role, which a group interaction computer system must respect. One of the few mass-market examples of this is the role of the instructor in just about all of the group communication systems designed specifically for remote education (Hiltz 1994; Harasim et al. 1995). As groups develop social structures of increasing complexity there will be an increasing need for software to support group member roles.

13.2.5 Notifications

By notifications we mean system messages dedicated to informing people of what they need to know as a result of the action of other members of the group. Simple examples are letting people know when there are sufficient votes gathered for an item for the votes to be viewable. Another example is when a votable item has been changed to let everyone know that they might want to change their vote. These automated notifications are extremely important in minimizing premature or unnecessary actions. They are very useful in cutting down the amount of communication traffic. For example, in educational systems they notify students when a new grade set has been entered, thereby eliminating unnecessary inquiries.

13.3   Tailoring Communications

The concepts of structures for specific types of group tasks and of user tailorability are the most fundamental principles for optimizing group support though CMC. However, since we have treated this topic extensively in previous publications (see Turoff 1991, Hiltz and Turoff 1985; Turoff et al. 1993), we will provide only a brief overview here.

With the emergence of the Web and Internet there are currently hundreds of group systems commercially available. However, very few of them provide any ability of the user or group to self-tailor the communication process. The demonstration of that concept is still largely limited to R&D systems.

The discussion or conference part of a CMC system may be represented as a specific structure of relationships (links) among the objects (nodes) that characterize the system. Most current systems can be described using the basic CMC objects and relationships listed in Table 13.1. It is important to note that both elements of discourse and the individuals or members linked to content objects (by privileges associated with their human roles) are objects in CMC systems (Turoff et al. 1999).

There is significant additional functionality possible with respect to such objects as the different roles and associated software powers a person can have in a given conference. However, the basic discourse structure is usually some combination of temporal occurrence, comment/reply hierarchies, and keyword association of comments.

An example of tailoring that goes beyond these basics is the Virtual Classroom™ (Hiltz 1994; Harasim et al. 1995), where a number of communication options exist on top of a basic computer conferencing structure. For example, an instructor can ask a discussion question and choose whether a student (1) can immediately see all the other discussion answers, (2) cannot see other answers until he or she has answered the question, or (3) cannot see other answers at all. The user can control what the system does,

TABLE 13.1   Common CMC Object and Relationship Structures

	Comment	Reply	Person	Keywords
Comment	Later/earlier than (temporal)	In response to	Author of/ editor of/ reader of	Relevant material
Reply		Additional/ alternative	Author of/ editor of/ reader of	Relevant material
Person			Member of same conference	Interests of
Keywords				Related to

rather than this being defined by the system designer or programmer. Other examples of tailoring that have been included in systems we have designed and/or studied at NJIT include the following. (Topics, tours, and reports are described in Turoff et al. 1993).

- Group membership under the control of the group leader (or open to the public)
- Contributions being anonymous or not, or use of pen names as alternatives to signatures
- Delegation of specialized communication and modification privileges, such as joint editing of the same entry ("Reports")
- Users creating discourse structures, building hypertext-oriented relationships between idea contributions ("Tours")
- Ability to attach executable processes to conference items (for example, a gradebook, voting routines, surveys, etc.) (Virtual Classroom, Hiltz 1994)
- Groups themselves being able to define and change their internal roles (for example, monitors, editors, observers, and indexers) ("Topics")

13.3.1 Next Generation Systems

In an ongoing study of technology adoption for the U.S. Navy, Briggs et al. (1999) reported that infrequent ad hoc use hinders self-sustenance. Furthermore, they suggested that in order for a Group Support Systems (GSS) to be continually used, it had to support a specific continual process. Early asynchronous research (Hiltz 1982, 1984) also demonstrated groups that were self-sustaining over a period exceeding seven months. The groups were involved with operational tasks, such as the following.

- Design and agree on new product standards to be recommended for official adoption by ballot
- Provide scientific information to state legislators, on request
- Update and validate by consensus contents of a National Library of Medicine database ("knowledge bank") on viral hepatitis, including reviews of 850 new papers

The next generation of CMC systems thus needs to be designed to be used with tailorable repeatable processes for supporting "routine" tasks. When group members have integrated routine uses into their work patterns, they can then easily use other features of the system to support short-term or sporadic needs, such as annual planning.

Task groups using future systems should also be able to turn on and off features at will. An initial meeting for a distributed ad hoc software design team might use videoconferencing to establish a social presence and then proceed over the next few weeks with a series of asynchronous CMC and audio sessions. Then, somewhere near the one-third to one-half mark, they should get together for a GSS-supported face-to-face meeting. The project would then resume with any combination of asynchronous CMC session, audio, and/or video sessions. Such "seamless" transitions among various modes can occur only with multimedia software that allows synchronous interactions that include audio or video to be recorded and available for use by the group in an asynchronous mode.

13.4   Discourse Structures

The challenge of allowing ever-larger groups to engage in collaborative problem solving in group communications has always run up against the information overload limit (Hiltz and Turoff 1985). In our view, the key to the problem is the limitation of the current generation discourse structures used in group communications, which are basically a comment and response format. The solution for the future is to allow the group to formulate and utilize problem-dependent discourse structures.

An example of a discourse structure that applies to any topic (a meta discussion structure independent of problem domain) is the process of scientific debate (such as the Hegelian Inquiry Process) that has also been used in policy studies via the Delphi Method and for software requirement formulation (Conklin and Begeman 1989; Fjermestad 1995; Schweiger 1989).

Argumentation and discourse systems such as Aquanet (Marshall et al. 1991), gIBIS (Conklin and Begeman 1989), SEPIA (Streitz et al. 1992), Virtual Notebook (Shipman et al. 1989), and Design Intent (Girgensohn et al. 1996) employ shared views to allow groups to develop shared understandings through semantic hypertext representations. The gIBIS system to handle argumentation can be considered as a graphics-oriented version of the original Delphi Conference (Turoff 1970) without the same richness of voting present in the Delphi design.

Such a group communication activity can be specified by a semantic hypertext structure as shown in Table 13.2 and Figure 13.1. In a given situation, an option could be almost anything: actions, goals, criteria, requirements, solutions, decisions, and so forth. In essence these are structures to organize a constructive debate about a topic, and the results sought are collective group insights into such things as alternative desirable resolutions and feasible actions to take.

TABLE 13.2   Argumentation Template Relationships (link types in table and nodes define rows and columns)

From/To Link	Argument	Option
Argument	Opposing	Pro or con
Option		Alternative
Voting Scales	Importance	Desirability
	Validity	Feasibility

In a typical argument a member can enter a proposition or alternative that in different applications can be actions, goals, solutions, decisions, and so forth. Any other member can enter either a pro or con argument associated with one or more of the proposition nodes, with either pro or con links. Certain arguments might be further linked together by being in opposition to one another. The monitor of the discussion (in some implementations) can choose if the entries are anonymous with pen names, real names, or the choice of the individual writers. Part of the writer's task of creating an argument is indicating which items should have pro/con or alternative links to the one he or she is creating. Since others might disagree with some of the link choices, we need human roles and/or voting tools to resolve such disagreements. Anyone can vote for the degree of desirability and feasibility of the resolution and relative importance and validity of each argument. One may think of this as one of a number of domain-independent general meta-discussion structures that will also be available as tools to link to the appropriate items in a domain-dependent conceptual map.

While the debating/argumentation structure seems rather simple and straightforward, consider a very common planning structure used in many successful corporate planning Delphi exercises. One starts with a trend that could be highly quantitative, such as the amount of a product's sales over the past five years or the number of terrorist actions yearly in the United States. The participants are asked to make a forecast for the trend and to indicate the assumptions they are making about the future that will influence the trend. They are also asked to express any uncertainties (things they don't think will occur but that would change their projection if they did). All these are taken as potential assumptions that the group votes on for degree of validity.

The validity vote is used to distinguish all assumptions into five basic categories: very likely, likely, uncertain, unlikely, very unlikely. The uncertain assumptions are focused on to distinguish between those that can be controlled by actions the organization can take and those that cannot. The group then proposes actions to influence the controllable assumptions and measures or future observations that will determine the occurrence of the other assumptions (Figure 13.2). Note all node types usually

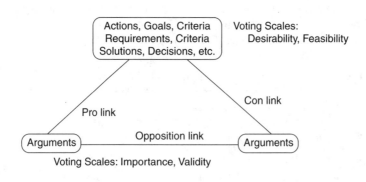

FIGURE 13.1   A discourse structure for debating and argumentation

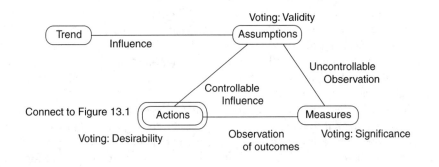

FIGURE 13.2   Planning Delphi discourse structure

have self-links (Table 13.3) that are used as well. For example, assumptions fall into similar categories (such as economic, technology), which results in "membership links" to categories for organizing a large list of assumptions.

There are many such discourse structures that can combine to become more complex structures and as such represent a potential toolkit for collaborative Hypertext. We note the debating structure (Figure 13.1) links quite naturally to the problem of deciding which action to choose. The total communication process involves the combination of two structures. Instead of the sequential nature of carrying on this process in a face-to-face discussion, the advantage of using this template in an asynchronous CMC environment is that any member can bring up any idea or thought dealing with any aspect of the problem at any time and participate in a much more parallel form of group interaction. Such a group process frees individuals from the group temporal regulation of their activities and problem-solving process. The computer can impose a meaningful organization on the contributions that makes it clear what has transpired since a given member last interacted.

TABLE 13.3   Forecasting/Planning Delphi Relationships

From/To Link	Trend	Assumption	Actions	Measures
Trend	Correlated			
Assumptions	Influences	Membership in similar category		
Actions		Controllable Influence	Dependency and arguments template	
Measures		Uncontrollable observation	Observation of outcomes	Related to
Voting Scales	Significance	Validity	Desirability	Significance

The current popularization of the Web as hypertext is a very limited interpretation of the preceding concepts, but it is an integral component of communications and the knowledge creation process (Bieber 1995; Bieber and Kimbrough 1992; Bieber et al. 1997; Nelson 1965; Bush 1945). This is one reason why the integration of hypertext functionality into collaborative model building (Turof et al. 1991) holds a great deal of promise for the integration of qualitative and quantitative aspects of model building.

The specific discourse structures that we have shown are illustrative of a much richer set of potential structures. What is important is the objective of providing tools that allow the users to set up a discourse structure of their own for a given discussion and to evolve over time the discourse structures that they judge are useful for their problem.

13.5   Collective Intelligence

While Computer-Mediated Communication allows individuals to engage in communication at any time or place that is individually convenient for them, these systems also promote "collective intelligence." The objective here is to integrate individual problem-solving abilities using a computer-mediated group process. Different members of the group may address the part of the problem about which they have the most insight or information, each making their contribution to the group. The structure and communication protocols provided by the computer system should integrate group member contributions into a group result. This integration of individual contributions provides the promise of "collective intelligence."

Many of the controlled experiments on face-to-face groups have shown that collective intelligence is a rare occurrence. Often the collective result of the group at the end of the meeting is worse than what the member having the best solution would have done acting alone. In our first controlled experiment comparing face-to-face and asynchronous group communications we showed that a majority of the CMC groups achieved collective intelligence (Hiltz et al. 1986). Content analysis showed that this seemed to occur because of the elimination of process losses due to the blocking of alternative opinions and views, which was more prevalent in face-to-face than CMC. While collective intelligence is a relatively easy thing to measure, it is rare that GDSS studies have examined it; it is an important variable to try to maximize in future research.

The future of this technology is that groups can be formed from anywhere in the world, regardless of place, and possibly even of time. However, we need to recognize that designing human communication systems is, in effect, the designing of social systems. Consequently, such systems must address roles, social structures, and organizational and other issues on a social level.

13.5.1 Collaborative Model Building

Collaborative model building has been a real world activity for quite some time. It provides a good example of how collective intelligence can be applied to a given type of problem. In the late sixties and early seventies it was augmented by terminals brought into meeting rooms and by direct decision support software for individual contributors.

There is a long history of sophisticated techniques and methods that support the development of various types of models. The real world is a "many body problem," and modeling it can rarely be done exactly for social and industrial systems. As a result, most modeling methods are approximations to the real world, and those facilitating the collaborative modeling effort should have an ethic of understanding the limitations of the methods that are employed.

In the early days of linear programming input formats were developed that allowed individuals with no mathematical understanding of linear programming to create models. The results were that many nonlinear situations were modeled and often resulted in misleading decision support information (Isakowitz et al. 1995).

One of the earliest truly collaborative efforts was by John Warfield (1974, 1976) and his development of Interpretive Structural Modeling (ISM) as an approach to the group modeling of the relationships among goals, subgoals, and objectives. This relied on the ability of the contributors to estimate whether a relationship (0 or 1) existed between two goals. The resulting graph can then be analyzed to develop a linear hierarchy of clusters of nodes from the original graph based on cycles in the graph. Warfield would bring a teletype terminal to meetings, and the computer analysis would be supplied as the group worked. Clearly individuals can answer the simple question of whether two items are related, but when one puts together a resulting graph of hundreds of items, it is impossible for the average human to make any sense of it. This is why various forms of modeling and network analysis tools (ISM, cluster analysis, multidimensional scaling, cluster analysis methods (Anderberg 1973), cross impact (Linstone and Turoff 1975), decision payoff and association/similarity matrices, etc.) can and do play such key roles in the collaborative process.

However, each method has its specific limitations and criteria that govern its appropriateness to a given situation. The ISM method can be demonstrated to have a great deal of sensitivity to the existence or nonexistence of a particular link in the graph. This points to the need for incorporating the ability to do sensitivity analysis on any result in order for the individual estimator or the group to test the range of validity for their results.

Methods such as Cross Impact Analysis (the relationships among one-time events utilizing subjective probability estimates) were evolved to function as integral parts of a Delphi process. Cross Impact Analysis has also been extensively used as a collaborative model-building tool in face-to-face meetings.

Many of the modeling approaches may be viewed as special cases of the general area of "structural modeling"—the formulation of model structures can be utilized to build general purposes models without having to learn to program. Structural modeling concepts underlie many individual model building tools that allow users to develop their own models, but little has been done to incorporate these concepts into collaborative systems, perhaps because of what can be called consistency problems.

13.5.2   Consistency Problems

There are three types of consistency problems inherent in collaborative model building. The first is the problem of a single estimator being consistent in the totality of the estimates and judgments needed to build an individual view of the world situation. This leads to the fact that one has to provide the individual whatever decision support tools are needed to aid in arriving at a consistent model.

The second problem is consistency in the estimates made by the respondents. For example, if two people say a certain event is "very likely," does one mean .7 probability and the other mean .9 probability? In the classical area of the analysis of subjective judgments this is the problem of "scaling," and the collaborative model builder has to be very cognizant of what types of scaling methods may be needed to ensure the mutual understanding among the collaborators. There are also qualitative forms of ambiguity that may occur in the collaborative design of the model structure.

We support Torgerson's (1958) view that the purpose of scaling (the science of developing measuring instruments for human judgment) is to make human judgment more "visible." Most scaling theory was evolved to aid the process of measuring psychological variables and consumer impressions. The idea of using scaling methods for the elimination of ambiguity and as a dynamic feedback mechanism for groups is relatively new and unexplored (Reagan-Cirincione 1994). The more multidisciplinary the group and the larger the group, the greater the need for these methods. Unfortunately most scaling methods evolved for one-time survey applications and not for iterative feedback in a group communication process. There is still considerable adaptation and tailoring of the methods required for this application area.

Even when groups are very homogenous there are major consistency problems. In a Delphi on the future of the steel industry (Linstone and Turoff 1975) involving about 45 planners in the industry, the respondents were given a flow model developed by three experts and were asked to fill in the missing estimates for the flows in the industry the prior year. Instead of doing this as asked, about 25 of the respondents redrew the model because they *did not agree* with what the initial three experts had conceived. Model building in real world situations is not a straightforward process of collecting known knowledge from a given domain.

13.5.3   Arrow's Paradox

The fact that no consistent collective judgment function is mathematically possible does not prevent us from utilizing various voting and subjective estimation functions. However, one of the causes of misguided results is illustrated by Arrow's Paradox

(Arrow 1951), where averaging hides (and ignores) unresolved and significant disagreements among group members, yielding group results that no one wants rather than results that everyone wants. Polarized distributions in votes and estimates and the lack of adequate scaling or anchoring of estimates can also cause spurious results (Raiffa 1968; Bell et al. 1988), as can strategic voting by group members. As a result, one has to be particularly concerned with the exposure and the treatment of disagreement in collaborative groups. This further suggests that the quantitative aspects of model building must be linked into social and interpersonal processes and structures that serve to create consensus and develop interpersonal relationships so important in everyday life.

It is necessary to explore and exhibit lower-level inconsistencies in both qualitative and quantitative views to the group, and to provide them mechanisms for visualizing the relationships and impacts that the conflicting judgments have on the total problem being considered. There is no simple technique to do this, implying that fairly sophisticated systems that take time to learn and master are promising for the future. Even such complex scaling techniques as multidimensional scaling can be used as a feedback process for showing group visualizations of views on complex problems. CMC systems that are used every day as part of the regular business process are necessary to allow this evolution of group learning.

13.6 Multimedia Communication Systems

Users of future CMC systems are not going to settle for only one mode of communication but are going to use a mix of media. In addition they are going to seek integration of data, analysis, and communication media. Driven by escalating travel and decreasing technology costs, many organizations have been attempting to integrate audio/videoconferencing into computer-mediated interaction. Given this reality of the next decade and that multimedia decision support systems have been a hot topic in the 1990s, it is interesting that there have been only a very limited number of evaluation efforts for multimedia group systems. Table 13.4 shows the results of the only nine published experiments in multimedia group support systems (out of 238 computer-supported experiments we could locate) (Fjermestad and Hiltz 1999). From the point of view of many businesses, the results are very interesting: In seven out of eight cases where it was measured, there was no difference in quality of performance between face-to-face decision groups and distributed videoconferencing groups, at least on simple tasks using students as subjects. In the four studies where it was measured, meeting time was greater via distributed modes, but this does not count the time spent traveling to meetings. These results suggest that organizations may be able get the same quality from remote groups using Web-based audio- and videoconferencing plus text-based CMC, as from proximate groups, and save transportation and other related meeting costs.

TABLE 13.4 Videoconferencing Experiments

Authors	Independent Variable Communication Modes	Results	Comments/Conclusions
Burke et al. 1999	Videoconferencing (VC), Audioconferencing (AC)	Social presence: VC > AC Comm effectiveness: VC > AC Performance: Not Significant (NS)	Communications effectiveness and social presence improved over time. However, there were no differences between VC and AC groups.
Chidambaram and Jones 1993	Face-to-Face (FtF), Audioconferencing	Decision Quality: NS Number of Alternatives: NS	Augmenting audioconferencing with GSS improves perceptions of communication effectiveness without lowering the social presence of the medium.
Galegher and Kraut 1993	FtF, CMC, CMC + phone	Quality: NS Impression of quality: FtF > CMC	All CMC groups worked harder than the FtF groups and were less committed and satisfied.
Graetz et al. 1998	FtF, CMC, Teleconferencing (T)	Decision quality: FtF, T > CMC Decision time: CMC > FtF, T	Cognitive workloads were significantly higher in CMC groups than in FtF or teleconferencing groups.
Kinney and Dennis 1994	Audio/Video (AV), CMC	Decision time: CMC > AV > FtF Decision Quality: NS Satisfaction: NS	The richer media led to faster decisions (FtF, Audio/Video).
Kinney and Watson 1992	FtF, Audio (A), CMC	Decision time: CMC > A > FtF Satisfaction: NS	Decision time is a function of medium.
Olson et al. 1995	GSS + Audio, GSS + Video	Decision Quality: NS Process Satisfaction: GSS + Video > GSS + Audio	Distributed groups can produce work that is indistinguishable from FtF groups. Video appears to add more value than just audio.
Suh 1999	CMC, Audio, Video, FtF	Decision quality: NS Decision time: CMC > V; FtF > A Process satisfaction: FtF, V > CMC, A Solution satisfaction: NS	Decision quality was the same for the intellective and negotiation task. Audio was the most efficient medium but not the most satisfying.
Valacich et al. 1994	FtF, Phone, Videophone, CMC	Decision Quality: NS Satisfaction: NS	The added technology (phone or video) did not add any benefit to the groups.

13.6.1 Multi-Mode Experiments

In a series of laboratory experiments (Ocker and Fjermestad 1998; Ocker et al. 1995, 1996, 1997) exploring the impact of communication mode on group creativity, quality and satisfaction, experimental groups worked on a collaborative task to specify software requirements for a two-week period. There were two experimental manipulations: Groups either communicated completely asynchronously via CMC or used a combination of face-to-face and asynchronous communication (combined). Results show that asynchronous groups were rated higher in terms of creativity. However, combined groups were rated higher on satisfaction. No differences were found between conditions in terms of quality. Until we can clarify the causes of such communication mode differences, and predict their occurrence, our ability to design multimedia CMC systems will remain limited.

13.6.2 Graphics and Collaborative Model Building

The greater the number of people who must bring their expertise to bear on a single plan, the more difficult it is to communicate adequately using a textual mode. Only recently has the average personal computer offered two- and three-dimensional graphics as possible tools for the communication process. The early literature on Delphi and Nominal Group Techniques provides many examples of graphic-oriented group communication structures that have yet to be computerized (Delbecq et al. 1975). Task groups need to make future projections of variables, construct spatial layouts, create flow diagrams of goods or information, develop organizational and software component charts, and so on, to mention only a few examples. Given the fact that moving a communication design to a computer environment usually requires significant modification, evaluation, and evolution of the design, this is a relatively undeveloped area of application.

Group agreement and standardization is very important in this regard. Most scientific fields develop symbol sets or icons that represent standard objects and understandings in the field. If our software allowed groups to achieve consensus on the use of alternative proposed graphical elements or symbols, then we could conceive systems that would allow the development of new methods of graphical analysis and descriptive representation. Computer-mediated analysis would aid the group in determining the aspects of a graphical representation about which there is collective agreement or disagreement. Being able to visualize the resulting plan in a number of different ways, and being able to vote on these alternatives, will be key elements in this process. Without visualization, trying to coordinate 10 to 20 different attempts to textually represent the same situation will be very difficult. Likewise, without some form of computer-mediated standardization and analysis aids, we will end up with a large number of pretty pictures but no agreed group result.

We may be at last at the point where a combination of graphical and collaborative techniques is possible, allowing large groups to deal with complex problems in an understandable way.

13.6.3 Virtual Reality

Adding multimedia objects to computer-mediated systems provides a sound foundation for making imagination a reality. Until recently, the majority of such virtual realities were isolated—bereft of any social interaction, precluding joint manipulation of 3D objects among World Wide Web users. Today, one can create virtual communities (towns, villages, etc., with all the needed infrastructure) over the Web and allow citizens to own property and build living or work quarters on their "land" and interact with others. Literally thousands of users (actually their avatars) can be seen busy at work translating their creative talents by constructing larger structures from smaller ones. This goes on around the clock on widely available virtual reality environments such as AlphaWorld (www.worlds.net), Community Place, Worldsaway (www.worldsaway.com), and Cyberhub (www.blacksun.com).

The Internet is a virtual system and as such it has the property of "virtuality" (Turoff 1997)—that is, it has the potential to take on properties that are independent of systems constrained by the physical world. Social and economic systems in the virtual environment can be entirely new, different, and, hopefully, will evolve to be better than their physical world counterparts. This may be what is happening with the transition of commerce to the Internet and the gradual evolution to a global marketplace. For example, there is now at least one e-commerce company that will collect and publish student evaluations of courses, instructors, and degree programs of any college or university. Currently the Internet is destroying the geographical oligopolies that existed for institutions of higher education (Turoff 1999, 2000).

However, for dynamic group interaction to occur in virtual worlds, it will be necessary for those worlds to become social worlds. Graphical representation alone is not enough. Internet software will have to be extended to achieve the flexibility and group structures necessary for group activities. The current virtual realities on the Web deal with manipulation and creation of physical objects. They provide for real-time (synchronous) interaction among the users. In addition they will need to incorporate some of the features we have discussed earlier, such as the following.

- Persistence and synchronicity for group communication processes
- The ability to build visible two- and three-dimensional representations of complex models and complex discussion structures
- The ability to notify users dynamically of changes in these structures
- The ability to allow groups to reach consensus regarding items in these structures, using voting and scaling techniques
- Self-tailoring by users of group process and entities
- The support of group member roles and social structures

13.6.4 Pervasive/Mobile CMC Systems

These are systems that allow people to work with information anywhere, at any time. Just as the PC transformed both business and personal life in the 1990s, a new generation of information appliances will transform both the workplace and the home in the next decade. These new systems will be much more powerful than today's mobile devices. They will blur the distinction between computation and communication by both transmitting data and by transforming it. For example, smart sensors detect when the proper person has come into the room and notify the appropriate people. They will allow collaboration between people as well as access to databases. They will be much more portable—either handheld or sufficiently cheap that they can be scattered around the workplace and the home, in your clothes, in your cars, in the walls of your house, in your appliances, on or in your body. . . .

These systems will not be simple extensions of existing devices; they will

- Require radical rethinking at all levels of abstraction, from user interfaces to algorithms to architectures
- Use multiple modes of information: text, audio, video
- Process those inputs to recognize important features
- Integrate information from many sources in order to make smart decisions and simplify the life of the user; and, most notably
- Require careful user-centric design to ensure that these complex systems are, in fact, usable by real people

Future research at NJIT is focusing on some of these key issues related to the use of pervasive/mobile devices for CMC. The first step is to gain a better understanding of when text-only communication (which is easy to accommodate on mobile devices) is sufficient in terms of task types, group size, and the phase of group work; and when and in what form it makes a significant difference to add video, audio, or simulated environments with visual elements (a form of "virtual reality.") A second issue is how to best "fit" the most valuable multimedia functionality for collaborative work onto mobile/pervasive computing devices. This will involve testing the usability and functionality of alternative input/output devices and interface strategies.

13.7 Conclusion

We have suggested that in collaborative systems the communication process must be tailored to respond to the requirements of the application and the nature of the group. The corollary is that there will arise such a wide diversity of possible variations in design that control of the tailoring process needs to be delegated, or devolved, from the system designer/programmer to the level of the user or user group. In effect, this means a shift from centrally controlled systems to systems that allow distributed control. The advantages of turning over the design features of the collaborative system to the users of that system have so far only been illustrated in some prototype systems (Whitworth 1997). The implementation of such group interaction systems is still hampered by the inadequacy of operating systems to support their requirements—for example, in defining which persons can apply which processes to what data elements. As a result the development of flexible role privileges and localized item sharing within objects must be developed as an inherent part of the CMC system itself.

CMC systems also need vendors willing to design open systems into which tools developed by others can be easily integrated. Too many companies are relying totally on proprietary vendor products for CMC and Groupware, which inevitably operate as closed systems for economic reasons. We conceive of vendor-independent components that can be used and combined by organizations and tailored to the nature of their collaboration problems. Once a company employs a CMC system that is open in architecture and adequately deals with the roles and privileges problems in an object-oriented approach, it will be comparatively easy to use "visual" type development packages to add the voting, scaling, structuring, and analysis tools that are needed. Such components, to the degree they are tailored around organizational specific planning and decision analysis, have the potential for being of sizable strategic value.

The modularization of the group communication process itself is also another fundamental desirable advance. This will be slower in coming than open CMC systems because it would be more difficult to do and it would greatly undermine the current vendor market. It is fortunate that the success of the Internet has brought about increased open systems architectures and standards. In many cases it seems like the vendors have been brought kicking and screaming to the global Web environment. Many packages started with their own proprietary clients, and many still have closed toolkits that can only be modified from within the given system.

Why haven't commercial products added many of the special features and tailorability that were present in some of the early research systems described? We can only speculate, but our guess is that it has to do with the evolution of user behavior in CMC (Hiltz and Turoff 1981). New users are focused on replacing means of communication with which they are already familiar, such as person-to-person surface mail with e-mail. They are concerned also with ease of learning and use of a new medium, and the more functionality one has, generally the more usability suffers due to increased learning time and complexity. However, once they have spent several months using CMC and beginning to engage in group projects online, they appreciate advanced features tailored to support their group work. Up until the present, the vendors have probably been focused on the new users flooding onto the Net, literally millions of them. As the "market" becomes saturated and these millions of users become adept at using CMC and dependent on it for their work in "virtual groups" and "virtual organizations" (Mowshowitz 1997), they will appreciate and desire the kinds of features that have been described in this chapter.

There is also the tendency of vendors to seek the single "Model T" or "black telephone" that every user will buy. Trying to convince vendors of the need for a wide variety of systems and tailorable functionality in a product with a limited market is quite difficult when it is so easily confused with e-mail (Turoff 1989). Instead we have vendors extending e-mail systems to try and make them look like group communication systems. However, the recent success of distance education has seen the emergence of a number of very successful CMC systems that include the tailoring necessary for that market.

The Web should be viewed as a massive group communication system (Turoff and Hiltz 1998). The CMC products that are going to succeed are the ones that will allow complete open integration of facilities developed for the Web environment. The benefits of cooperation on a global level will, we predict, gradually become apparent. The situation is similar to that which in the past has driven villages to combine into states, and states into nations. The next combination we suggest will be a global one. The major lesson of the Internet seems to be to illustrate the benefits of global, *or human-wide,* cooperation.

However, within the context of the organization, there will be a significant learning curve and a gradual evolution of CMC tools with greater and greater sophistication and general applicability. In such an environment there has to be an integrated evaluation program that will feed back into the further evolution of the technology. Individuals and groups will come to know that the foundation of their performance rests on communication, and there will be no worse situation than when communication fails or when the communication facilities provided fail to meet their evolving expectations. It is an area of computer applications that will be driven by user requirements.

The coming decade may be the one when CMC finally matures and participates not only in our business lives but also our social and personal lives. CMC communications are changing, and will change, the basic nature of organizations, commerce, education, and politics at all levels of society.

Acknowledgments

Partial funding for this research was provided by the National Science Foundation (NSF 9015236 and CISE-ITO 9732354), the New Jersey Center for Multimedia Research, and the New Jersey Center for Pervasive Information Technology. The opinions expressed are solely those of the authors.

References

Ackerman, M.S., and Malone, T.W. (1990). Answer garden: A tool for growing orga- nizational memory. *Proceedings of the ACM Conference on Office Information Systems,* COIS 90, 31–39.

Anderberg, M.R. (1973). *Cluster analysis for applications.* New York: Academic Press, Inc.

Arrow, K.J. (1951). *Social choice and individual values.* New York: Wiley.

Bell, D.E., Raiffa, H., Tverskey, A. (1988). Decision making: Descriptive, normative and prescriptive interactions. Cambridge (UK) University Press.

Bieber, M. (1995). On integrating hypermedia into decision support and other sys- tems. *Decision Support Systems,* 14, 251–267.

Bieber, M., and Kimbrough, S.O. (1992). On generalizing the concept of hypertext. *MIS Quarterly,* 16, 1, 77–93.

Bieber, M., Vitali, F., Ashman, H., Balasubramanian, V., and Oinas-Kukkonen, H. (1997). Fourth generation hypermedia: Some missing links for the World Wide Web. *International Journal of Human Computer Studies,* 47, 31–65.

Briggs, R.O., Adkins, M., Kruse, J., and Nunamaker, J. (1999). Lessons learned using a technology transition model with the U.S. Navy. *Proceedings of the 32nd HICSS.* Washington, DC: IEEE Press.

Burke, K., Aytes, K., Chidambaram, L., and Johnson. J.J. (1999). A study of partially distributed work groups: The impact of media, location, and time on perception and performance. *Small Group Research,* 30, 4, 453–490.

Bush, V. (1945). As we may think. *Atlantic Monthly,* 176, 101–108.

Chidambaram, L., and Jones, B. (1993). Impact on communication medium and computer support on group perceptions and performance: A comparison of face- to-face and dispersed meetings. *MIS Quarterly,* 17, 4, 465–491.

Conklin, J., and Begeman, M.L. (1989). gIBIS: A tool for all reasons. *Journal of the American Society for Information Science,* 40, 3, 200–213.

Delbecq, A.L., Van de Ven, A.H., and Gustafson, D.H. (1975). Group techniques for program planning: A guide to nominal group techniques and Delphi processes. Glencoe, IL: Scott, Foresman.

Fjermestad, J. (1995). Group strategic decision making: Asynchronous GSS using structured conflict and consensus approaches. *HICSS,* 4, 222–231. IEEE.

Fjermestad, J., and Hiltz, S.R. (1999). An assessment of group support systems experimental research: Methodology and results. *Journal of Management Infor- mation Systems,* 15, 3, 7–149.

Fjermestad, J., and Hiltz, S.R. (2000). Case and field studies of group support sys- tems: An empirical assessment. *Proceedings of the Hawaii Int. Conf. on System Sciences,* Maui, Hawaii. Washington, DC: IEEE Press.

Galegher, J., and Kraut, R.E. (1994). Computer-mediated communication for intellectual teamwork: An experiment in group writing. *Information Systems Research,* 5, 2, 110–138

Girgensohn, A., Lee, A., and Schlueter, K. (1996). Experiences in developing collaborative applications using the World Wide Web 'Shell.' *Hypertext '96 Proceedings,* 246–255. New York: ACM Press.

Graetz, K.A., Boyle, E.S., Kimble, C.E., Thompson, P., and Garloch, J.E. (1998). Information sharing in face-to-face, teleconferencing, and electronic groups. *Small Group Research,* 29, 6, 714–743.

Harasim, L., Hiltz, S.R., Teles, L., and Turoff, M. (1995). *Learning networks: A field guide to teaching and learning online.* Cambridge, MA: MIT Press.

Hiltz, S.R. (1994). *The virtual classroom: Learning without limits via computer networks.* Norwood, NJ: Ablex Publishing Corp.

Hiltz, S.R. (1982). The impact of a computerized conferencing system on the productivity of scientific research communities. *Behavior and Information Technology,* 1, 185–195.

Hiltz, S.R. (1984). *Online communities: A case study of the office of the future.* Norway, NJ: Able, Human-Computer Interaction Series. (Currently available from Intellect at www.intellect-net.com.)

Hiltz, S.R., and Turoff, M. (1981). The evolution of user behavior in a computerized conferencing system. *Communications of the ACM,* 24, 11, 739–751.

Hiltz, S.R., and Turoff, M. (1985). Structuring computer-mediated communication systems to avoid information overload, *CACM,* 28, 7, 682–689.

Hiltz, S.R., and Turoff, M. (1993). *The network nation,* Revised Edition. Cambridge, MA: MIT Press.

Hiltz, S.R., Turoff, M., and Johnson, K.J. (1986). Experiments in group communication via computer, 1: Face-to-face vs. computer conferences. *Human Communication Research,* 13, 2, 225–252.

Isakowitz, T., Schocken, S., and Lucas, H.C. (1995). Toward a logical/physical theory of spreadsheet modeling. *ACM Transactions on Information Systems,* 1–37.

Kinney, S., and Dennis, A. (1994). Reevaluating media richness: Cues, feedback, and task. *Proceedings of the Twenty-Seventh Hawaii International Conference on Systems Sciences,* 4, 21–30. Washington, DC: IEEE Press.

Kinney, S.T., and Watson, R.T. (1992). The effect of medium and task on dyadic communication. *Proceedings of the Thirteenth International Conference on Information Systems,* 107–117.

Konstan, J.A., Miller, B.N., Maltz, D., Herlocker, J.L., Gordon, L.R., and Reidl, J. (1997). GroupLens: Applying collaborative filtering to Usenet news. *Communications of the ACM,* 40, 3, 77–87.

Linstone, H., and Turoff, M. (Eds.). (1975). *The Delphi method: Techniques and applications.* Reading, MA: Addison-Wesley.

Malone, T.W., Grant, K.R., Lai, K.Y., Rao, R., and Rosenblitt, D. (1987). Semi-structured messages are surprisingly useful for computer-supported coordination. *ACM Transactions on Office Information Systems,* 5, 2, 115–131.

Marshall, C.C., Halasz, F.G., Rogers, R.A., and Janssen, Jr., W.C. (1991). Aquanet: A hypertext tool to hold your knowledge in place. *Hypertext T91 Proceedings,* 261–275. San Antonio. New York: ACM Press.

Moshowitz, A. (1997). Virtual organization. *Communications of the ACM,* 40, 9, 30–37.

Nelson, T.H. (1965). A file structure for the complex, the changing and the indeterminate. *ACM 20th National Conference Proceedings,* 84–99.

Ocker, R., and Fjermestad, J. (1998). Web-based computer-mediated communication: An experimental investigation comparing three communication modes for determining software requirements. *Proceedings of the Thirty-First Hawaii International Conference on Systems Sciences,* 1, 88–97. Washington, DC: IEEE Press.

Ocker, R., Fjermestad, J., Hiltz, S.R., and Turoff, M. (1997). An exploratory comparison of four modes of communication for determining requirements: Results on creativity, quality and satisfaction. *Proceedings of the Thirtieth Hawaii International Conference on Systems Sciences,* 2, 568–577. Washington, DC: IEEE Press.

Ocker, R., Hiltz, S.R., Turoff, M., and Fjermestad, J. (1995–1996). The effects of distributed group support and process structuring on software requirements development teams: Results on creativity and quality. *J. Management Information Systems,* 12, 3, 127–153.

Ocker, R., Hiltz, S.R., Turoff, M., and Fjermestad, J. (1995). Computer support for asynchronous software design teams: Experimental results on creativity and quality. *Proceedings of the Twenty-Eighth Hawaii International Conference on Systems Sciences,* 4, 4–13. Washington, DC: IEEE Press.

Olson, J.S., Olson, G.M., and Meader, D.K. (1995). What mix of video and audio is useful for remote real-time work? *Proceedings of the ACM Conference on Computer Human Interaction,* 362–368. New York: ACM Press.

Palme, J. (1992). SuperKOM-design considerations for a distributed, highly structured computer conferencing system. *Computer Communications,* 15, 8, 509–538.

Raiffa, H. (1968). *Decision analysis: Introductory lectures on choices under uncertainty.* Cambridge, MA: Harvard University Press.

Rapaport, Matthew. (1991). *Computer mediated communications: Bulletin boards, computer conferencing, electronic mail, and information retrieval.* New York: Wiley.

Reagan-Cirincione, P. (1994). Improving the accuracy of group judgment: A process intervention combining group facilitation, social judgment analysis, and information technology. *Organizational Behavior and Human Decision Processes,* 58, 246–270.

Schweiger, D.M., Sanberg, W.R., and Rechner, P.L. (1989). Experimental effects of dialectical inquiry, devils advocacy, and consensus approaches to strategic decision making. *Academy of Management Journal, 32,* 4, 745–772.

Shipman, F., Chaney, R., and Gorry, T. (1989). Distributed hypertext for collaborative research: The virtual notebook system. *Hypertext '89 Proceedings,* 129–135. New York: ACM Press.

Streitz, N., Haake, J., Hannemann, J., Lemke, A., Schuler, W., Schtt, H., and Thring, M. (1992). SEPIA: A cooperative hypermedia authoring environment. *Proceedings of the ACM Conference on Hypertext,* 11–22. Milan. New York: ACM Press.

Suh, K.S. (1999). Impact of communication medium on task performance and satisfaction: An examination of media-richness theory. *Information and Management, 35,* 295–312.

Terveen, L., Hill, W., Amento, B., McDonald, D., and Creter, J. (1997). P:HOAKS: A system for sharing recommendations. *Communications of the ACM, 40,* 3, 59–62.

Torgerson, W.S. (1958). *Theory and Methods of Scaling.* New York: Wiley.

Turoff, M. (2000). An end to student segregation: No more separation between distance learning and regular courses. *On the Horizon, 8,* 1, 1–7.

Turoff, M. (1997). Virtuality. *CACM, 40,* 9, 38–43.

Turoff, M. (1991). Computer-mediated communication requirements for group support. *Journal of Organizational Computing, 1,* 1, 85–113.

Turoff, M. (1990). Education, commerce, and communications: The era of competition, *WebNet Journal: Internet Technologies, Applications & Issues, 1,* 1 (January-March), 22–31.

Turoff, M. (1989). The anatomy of a computer application innovation: Computer mediated communications (CMC). *Journal of Technological Forecasting and Social Change, 36,* 107–122.

Turoff, M. (1970). Delphi conferencing: Computer-based conferencing with anonymity. *Journal of Technological Forecasting and Social Change, 3,* 2, 159–204.

Turoff, M., and Hiltz, S.R. (1998). Superconnectivity. *CACM.*

Turoff, M., and Hiltz, S.R. (1995a). Software design and the future of the virtual classroom. *Journal of Information Technology for Teacher Education, 4,* 2, 197–215.

Turoff, M., and Hiltz, S.R. (1995b). Computer-based Delphi processes. In M. Adler and E. Ziglio (Eds.), *Gazing into the oracle: The Delphi method and its application to social policy and public health,* 56–88. London: Kingsley Publishers.

Turoff, M., Hiltz, S.R., Bahgat, A.N.F., and Rana, A. (1993). Distributed group support systems. *MIS Quarterly,* 399–417.

Turoff, M., Hiltz, S.R., Bieber, M., Rana, A., Fjermestad, J. (1999). Collaborative discourse structures in computer mediated group communications. *HICSS, 32.*

Reprinted in *Journal of Computer Mediated Communications,* 4, 4. http://www.ascusc.org/jcmc/vol4/issue4/.

Turoff, M., Rao, U., and Hiltz, S.R. (1991). Collaborative hypertext in computer mediated communications. *Proceedings of the Twenty-Fourth Hawaii International Conference on Systems Sciences,* 4, 357–366. Washington, DC: IEEE Press.

Valacich, J.S., Mennecke, B.E., Wachter, R.M., and Wheeler, B.C. (1994). Extensions to media richness theory: A test of task-media fit hypothesis. *Proceedings of the Twenty-Seventh Hawaii International Conference on Systems Sciences,* 4, 11–20. Washington, DC: IEEE Press.

Whitworth, B. (1997). Generating group agreement in cooperative computer mediated groups: Towards an integrative model of group interaction. University of Waikato, Ph.D. thesis. Hamilton, New Zealand. UMI Publication Number: AAT 9821071.

Warfield, J.N. (1976). *Societal systems.* New York: John Wiley and Sons.

Warfield, J.N. (1974). Toward interpretation of complex structural models. *IEEE Transactions on Systems, Man and Cybernetics,* (SMC-4), 405–417.

14

The Intellectual Challenge of CSCW: The Gap between Social Requirements and Technical Feasibility

Mark S. Ackerman

14.1 Introduction

Over the last ten years, Computer-Supported Cooperative Work (CSCW) has identified a base set of findings. These findings are taken almost as assumptions within the
field. Indeed, many of these findings have been known and have been debated within
Computer Science, Information Science, and Information Technology for over 20
years. The findings will be discussed at length here, but in summary, they argue that
human activity is highly flexible, nuanced, and contextualized and that computational entities such as information transfer, roles, and policies need to be similarly
flexible, nuanced, and contextualized.

Simply put, we do not know how to build systems that fully support the social
world uncovered by these findings. I argue here that it is not from lack of trying. Nor
is it from lack of understanding by technical people. Numerous attempts have been
made, not only within CSCW but within many other subfields of computer science to
bridge what will be called here the *social-technical gap*, the great divide between
what we know we must support socially and what we can support technically. Technical systems are rigid and brittle—not only in any intelligent understanding but also
in their support of the social world.

Researchers and computer professionals have edged toward a better understanding
of this social-technical gap in the last ten years, and CSCW systems have certainly
become more sophisticated. We have learned to construct systems with computer-
mediated communication (CMC) elements to allow people enough communicative

suppleness; yet, these systems still lack much computational support for sharing information, roles, and other social policies. Important CSCW technical mechanisms (for example, floor or session control) lack the flexibility required by social life. The social-technical gap still exists and is wide. Exploring, understanding, and hopefully ameliorating this social-technical gap is the central challenge for CSCW as a field and one of the central problems for HCI. Other areas of computer science dealing with users also face the social-technical gap, but CSCW, with its emphasis on augmenting social activity, cannot avoid it. I also argue that the challenge of the social-technical gap creates an opportunity to refocus CSCW as a Simonian science of the artificial (where a science of the artificial is suitably revised from Simon's strictly empiricist grounds).

This article proceeds in three parts. First, the paper provides an overview of CSCW, briefly reviewing the major social and technical findings of the field, particularly with regard to the construction of computational systems. Next, I argue that there is an inherent gap between the social requirements of CSCW and its technical mechanisms. This is demonstrated through a discussion of a particular CSCW research problem: privacy in information systems. Finally, potential resolutions for the social-technical gap are examined. In Section 14.4.4, the requirements for a science of the artificial are evaluated, along with the need for such a viewpoint for CSCW.

14.2   A Biased Summary of CSCW Findings

Most of this section will be obvious to CSCW researchers, but its contents will be a useful overview for non-CSCW researchers. This does not attempt to be a complete summary of CSCW assumptions and findings; rather, the emphasis is on those social aspects most germane to the social-technical gap.

While March and Simon's (1958) limited rational actor model (Simon 1957) underlies CSCW, as it does for most of computer science, CSCW researchers also tend to assume the following.

- Social activity is fluid and nuanced, and this makes systems technically difficult to construct properly and often awkward to use. A considerable range of social inquiry has established that the details of interaction matter (Garfinkel 1967; Strauss, 1993) and that people handle this detail with considerable agility (Garfinkel 1967; Heritage 1984; Suchman 1987). (In this paper, following Strauss 1991 and others, I will use "nuanced" narrowly to denote the depth of detail as well as its fine-grained quality. Connotations to the term include agility and smoothness in the use of the detail.) People's emphases on which details to consider or to act upon differ according to the situation (Suchman 1987). Yet, systems often have considerable difficulty handling this detail and flexibility.

For example, Goffman (1961, 1971) noted that people have very nuanced behavior concerning how and with whom they wish to share information. People are concerned about whether to release this piece of information to that person at this time, and they have very complex understandings of people's views of themselves, the current situation, and the effects of disclosure. Yet, access control systems often have very simple models. As another example, since people often lack shared histories and meanings (especially when they are in differing groups or organizations), information must be recontextualized in order to reuse experience or knowledge. Systems often assume a shared understanding of information.

One finding of CSCW is that it is sometimes easier and better to augment technical mechanisms with social mechanisms to control, regulate, or encourage behavior (Sproull and Kiesler 1991). An example is the use of chat facilities to allow norm creation and negotiation in commercial CSCW systems.

- Members of organizations sometimes have differing (and multiple) goals, and conflict may be as important as cooperation in obtaining issue resolutions (Kling 1991). Groups and organizations may not have shared goals, knowledge, meanings, and histories (Heath and Luff 1996; Star and Ruhleder 1994).

  If there are hidden or conflicting goals, people will resist concretely articulating their goals. On the other hand, people are good at resolving communicative and activity breakdowns (Suchman 1987).

  Without shared meanings or histories, meanings will have to be negotiated (Boland et al. 1994). As well, information will lose context as it crosses boundaries (Ackerman and Halverson 2000). Sometimes this loss is beneficial, in that it hides the unnecessary details of others' work. Boundary objects (Star 1989) are information artifacts that span two or more groups. Each group will attach different understandings and meanings to the information. Boundary objects let groups coordinate, since the details of the information use in one group need not be understood completely by any other group.

  An active area of CSCW research is in finding ways to manage the problems and tradeoffs resulting from conflict and coordination (Malone and Crowston 1994; Schmidt and Simone 1996).

- Exceptions are normal in work processes. It has been found that much of office work is handling exceptional situations (Suchman and Wynn 1984). Additionally, roles are often informal and fluid (Strauss 1993). CSCW approaches to workflow and process engineering primarily try to deal with exceptions and fluidity (Katzenberg et al. 1996).

- People prefer to know who else is present in a shared space, and they use this awareness to guide their work (Erickson et al. 1999). For example, air traffic controllers monitor others in their workspace to anticipate their future workflow (Bentley et al. 1992; Hughes et al. 1994). This effect has also been found in other control room settings (Heath and Luff 1992) and trading floors (Heath et al. 1994). An active area of research is adding awareness (knowing who is present) and peripheral awareness (low-level monitoring of others' activity) to shared communication systems. Recent research is addressing the tradeoffs inherent in awareness versus privacy and in awareness versus disturbing others (Hudson and Smith 1996).

- Visibility of communication exchanges and of information enables learning and greater efficiencies (Hutchins 1995b). For example, copilots learn from observing pilots work (in other words, situated learning, learning in a community of practice). However, it has been found that people are aware that making their work visible may also open them to criticism or management; thus, visibility may also make work more formal and reduce sharing. A very active area of CSCW is trying to determine ways to manage the tradeoffs in sharing. This is tied to the issue of incentives, discussed below.

- The norms for using a CSCW system are often actively negotiated among users. These norms of use are also subject to renegotiation (Strauss 1991). CSCW systems should have some secondary mechanism or communication back-channel to allow users to negotiate the norms of use, exceptions, and breakdowns among themselves, making the system more flexible.

- There appears to be a critical mass problem for CSCW systems (Markus 1990). With an insufficient number of users, people will not use a CSCW system. This has been found in e-mail, synchronous communication, and calendar systems. There also appears to be a similar problem with communication systems if the number of active users falls beneath a threshold (called the "melt-down" problem in Ackerman and Palen 1996b). Adoption of CSCW systems is often more difficult than for single-user systems, since CSCW systems often require initial buy-in from groups of people, rather than individuals, as well as continued buy-in.

- People not only adapt to their systems, they adapt their systems to their needs (coevolution) (Orlikowski 1992a; O'Day et al. 1996). These adaptations can be quite sophisticated. People may use systems in ways completely unanticipated by the designers. One CSCW finding is that people will need to change their categories over time (Suchman 1994). System designers should assume that people will try to tailor their use of a system.

- Incentives are critical. A classic finding in CSCW, for example, is that managers and workers may not share incentive or reward structures; systems will be less used than desired if this is true (Grudin 1989). Another classic finding is that people will not share information in the absence of a suitable organizational reward structure (Orlikowski 1992b). Even small incremental costs in collaborating must be compensated (either by reducing the cost of collaboration or offering derived benefits). Thus, many

CSCW researchers try to use available data to reduce the cost of sharing and collaborative work.

Not every CSCW researcher would agree with all of the above assumptions and findings, and commercial systems (such as workflow systems) sacrifice one or more of them. The preceding list provides an ideal type of what needs be provided. Since some of the idealization must be ignored to provide a working solution, this tradeoff provides much of the tension in any given implementation between "technically working" and "organizationally workable" systems. CSCW as a field is notable for its attention and concern to managing this tension.

14.3   The Social-Technical Gap in Action

Attempts to deal with online privacy nicely demonstrate the gap between what we need to do socially and what we can do technically. I will use the example of the Platform for Privacy Preferences Project (P3P) of the World Wide Web Consortium. P3P is an attempt to create a privacy standard for the Web. It is inherently a CSCW system and an HCI problem, since it deals with how people manage their private information with regard to other people, companies, and institutions.

> The goal of P3P is to enable users to exercise preferences about Web sites' privacy practices. P3P applications will allow users to be informed about Web site practices, delegate decisions to their computer agent when they wish, and tailor relationships with specific sites. (Cranor and Reagle 1998, p. 209).

It is important to detail at some length how P3P works and what its initial design goals were. Regardless of whether one believes in the efficacy of such protocols for ameliorating privacy issues per se, P3P aims at a common collaborative problem, sharing information. As such, it must tackle the social-technical gap just discussed. With regard to P3P, the gap is large. In the following description, it is not important to grasp the details as much as understand the information space under consideration.

> P3P is designed to help users reach agreements with services (Web sites and applications that declare privacy practices and make data requests). As the first step towards reaching an agreement, a service sends a machine-readable P3P proposal in which the organization responsible for the service declares its identity and privacy practices. . . .

> Proposals can be automatically parsed by user agents such as Web browsers and compared with privacy preferences set by the user. . . . Users should be able to configure their agents to reach agreement with, and proceed seamlessly to, services that have certain types of practices; users should also be able to receive prompts or leave when encountering services that engage in potentially

objectionable practices. Thus, users need not read the privacy policies at every Web site they visit. (Cranor and Reagle 1998, p. 49)

Note that the desire is to deal with this information space automatically, with the exact mechanism determined by those writing P3P clients. The necessity to handle this appropriately was raised with the additional goal of automatically transferring data if the agreement is made between the service and the user's agent. This part of P3P has been shelved for version 1, partially because no one was confident that it could be done well. However, the original intention is worth noting.

> Some P3P implementations will likely support a data repository where users can store information they are willing to release to certain services. If they reach an agreement that allows the collection of specific data elements, such information can be transferred automatically from the repository. (Cranor and Reagle 1998, p. 50)

Even a cursory examination shows a wicked problem (in the computer science sense of "wicked," meaning an ill-formed, intractable problem). If we follow Goffman (1961), a user would wish to control the release of his private information on an ongoing basis to the various individuals and institutions within the environment. Roughly, this translates to allowing the user to customize information transfer in two dimensions—by the recipient (that is, all potential recipients, perhaps including any interaction effects among recipients) and by the datum itself (that is, all possible pieces of private information, as defined by the user).

There are insoluble user interface problems here; users must be able to handle essentially an infinite information space. However, this is not merely a user interface problem; the problem is conditioned by the underlying social requirements. By the findings just explicated (going back to Goffman), people do this every day. Except in unusual circumstances, we do not have to deliberate about these information spaces in detail. Nor do we need to laboriously click and switch modes within everyday information dissemination. To require users to do anything else than the apparently seamless change between "faces" (Goffman 1961) is to place users of P3P within a social-technical gap.

One technical solution might be to allow users to group potential information recipients together into roles or other collections. For example, I may wish to hide my telephone number from all students but not from professional colleagues. Unfortunately, again, by the findings explicated above, in everyday life I move people seamlessly among those groupings (especially roles). Furthermore, exceptions are common and must be accounted for—I may wish to give a prized honors undergraduate my home phone number for a consultation. Again people do this every day in a nuanced and apparently seamless manner. While considerable work goes into accomplishing this everyday activity, people still manage to do it in a manner quite unlike the awkwardness afforded and required by current systems.

The online privacy problem is even more complex than previously stated. The protocol currently allows for the expression of eight dimensions. Still others, such as consequence (what might happen) and duration (how long the data might be kept), were discarded as being nearly intractable technically, socially, or politically.

With some important exceptions, these eight dimensions within P3P incorporate most of the details of everyday life. Yet, one can easily assert that no one knows how to construct a suitable user interface for such a protocol. Without a completely accurate grouping mechanism (or some manner of collapsing categories in a meaningful way), few users will be able to correctly categorize a situation without errors. Fewer yet may take the time to categorize, since normal social activity does not require this explicit categorization. Moreover, one of the CSCW findings was that such categorization (and especially how categories are collapsed into meta-categories) is inherently political. The preferred categories and categorization will differ from individual to individual.

To summarize, there are no current HCI mechanisms to straightforwardly mechanize the naturally occurring, everyday social activity of handling personal information in its entirety. We must necessarily restrict the problem from what we know is appropriate to the social circumstances. This is the social-technical gap.

Within the privacy problem, one can see that the social-technical gap inherent in P3P results from three aligned issues.

1. Systems do not allow sufficient nuance. People make very fine-grained distinctions, often based on contextual or historical knowledge. Systems do not do this, and when they attempt to do so, they either lack the requisite background knowledge or they simplify the number of states.

2. Systems are not socially flexible. People switch among states gracefully. For example, people fluidly move among their "faces" as social settings require. People do not make these switches explicitly, whereas systems require people to explicitly switch states (for example, with their roles).

3. Systems do not allow sufficient ambiguity. In most settings, people are inherently ambiguous about, for example, which role they are currently playing or the import of the information they are disclosing. People do not inhabit the discrete states of a decision or action graph; they inhabit states that are only partially determined and seldom made explicit.

While P3P agents are only one possible collaborative application (and the problems are partially interface and individual-use problems), they demonstrate the social-technical gap. The next section surveys some technical work squarely within the CSCW field and attempts to show that this gap is fundamental.

14.3.1 Technical Research in CSCW

Until the last two or three years, it was not uncommon to read CSCW papers analyzing some aspect of system use or workplace activity that essentially argued that system designers just do not sufficiently understand the social world. The problem, then, was centered by social scientists in the process of design. Certainly, many studies in CSCW, HCI, Information Technology, and Information Science at least indirectly have emphasized a dichotomy between "designers," "programmers," and "implementers" on the one hand and the social analyst on the other.

Indeed, early collaborative systems were awkward. In the 1980s, many researchers made roles, rules, and even floor control necessarily explicit when using a system. The Coordinator (Flores et al. 1988) has been much maligned over its explicit roles and rules; one necessarily had to respond to requests for action. However, one can see explicitness as a design criterion in other CSCW systems, including gIBIS (Conklin and Begeman 1988) and MPCAL (Greif and Sarin 1987). There were notable exceptions: Other systems, especially computer-mediated communication systems (such as CRUISER in Root 1988), were constructed with flexibility and social nuance as critical design factors. That they were partially successful led to considerable additional research.

Social nuance and flexibility were slowly added to all CSCW systems, as the undesirability of being explicit became an assumption within CSCW. For example, the original Answer Garden system (Ackerman 1994; Ackerman and Malone 1990) allowed only two basic roles: the information seeker who asked a question and the expert who answered. (There were tiers of experts, but all were explicit roles, such as help desk provider.) In real life, everyone has expertise about some topics, and everyone asks questions. Answer Garden 2 (Ackerman and McDonald 1996a) attempted to close this false dichotomy in roles by providing for ranges of expertise. People were assumed to be both seeking and providing information at different times. Flexibility was provided through the use of computer-mediated communication (CMC) components and through escalation among the different CMC components. I claim no particular intelligence here in creating better social fidelity over these several versions. Through the decade, all CSCW systems became more sophisticated, as technical researchers better understood the social requirements.

The understanding that CSCW technical researchers bring to the problem is well shown in Marwood and Greenberg (1994). Their paper both demonstrates the social-technical gap again and shows the sophistication that CSCW technical researchers now have in understanding the gap.

Marwood and Greenberg (1994) authoritatively argue that concurrency control (an aspect of which is floor control) is different for CSCW systems than it is for standard distributed systems.

> In particular, concurrency control problems arise when the software, data, and interface are distributed over several computers. Time delays when exchanging potentially conflicting actions are especially worrisome. If concurrency control is not established, people may invoke conflicting actions. As a result, the group may become confused because displays are inconsistent, and the groupware document corrupted due to events being handled out of order. (p. 207)

However, they add the following.

> Most concurrency control approaches are designed for non-interactive computer systems. Groupware is quite different, because the distributed system includes not

only computers but people as well. People can be both more and less tolerant of concurrency problems than computers. (p. 210).

The article discusses locking, serialization, and optimism policies in detail. The article makes it clear that fine-grained locking is difficult to implement well.

> The coarser the lock, the more difficult it is for people to work closely together. Noticeable delays, however, will interfere with the flow of inter-action. For example, selecting a circle and moving it, or moving a text cursor forward and then typing should both be enacted as continuous operations. (p. 211)

Other technical researchers have also argued extensively that aspects of the social-technical gap must be satisfied in CSCW systems. For example, Rodden (1996) argued that systems must consider the ambiguity of awareness and privacy. Kaplan et al. (1992) and Dourish et al. (1996) argued that social protocols are considerably more flexible than technical systems. Clearly CSCW technical researchers are not only aware of the gap but understand its nature.

However, it is not quibbling to question the efficacy of proposed solutions. Kaplan et al.'s (1992) solution was to require writing "social protocols" in Lisp. Rodden (1996) provided a welcome formal evaluation of awareness but provided for only part of what people would consider peripheral awareness and privacy.

14.3.2 Arguments against the Significance of the Gap

Section 14.3.1 suggested one argument against the significance of the social-technical gap: that this gap resulted merely from ignorance or habit by software designers and researchers. However, as Section 14.3.1 pointed out, CSCW software researchers and designers are indeed aware of the need for nuance, flexibility, and contextualization.

There are other arguments against the importance of any social-technical gap to be examined before a reader should be satisfied. There are two major arguments remaining. First, one could argue that the social-technical gap will be solved shortly by some new technology or software technique. Second, one could argue that the gap is merely a historical circumstance and that we will adapt to the gap in some form. This section examines each argument briefly and shows why neither is a strong argument against suggesting plans of action to ameliorate the gap.

First, it could be that CSCW researchers merely have not found the proper key to solve this social-technical gap and that such a solution, using existing technologies, will shortly exist. In this view, Computer Science will learn how to do machine learning, user modeling, or some other technique properly. This paper cannot disprove that a technical solution is imminent. It may be. However, I would argue that such a technical solution is unlikely, since Computer Science, AI, Information Technology, and Information Science researchers have attempted to bridge the gap without success for at least 20 years. It is time to consider that the gap is likely to endure and that we should consider what to do about it.

A logically similar argument is that the problem is with the entire von Neumann machine as classically developed, and new architectures will ameliorate the gap. As Hutchins (1995a) and others (Clark 1997) have noted, the standard model of the computer over the last 30 years was disembodied, separated from the physical world by ill-defined (if defined) input and output devices. In this view, the von Neumann machine came to be socially inflexible, decontextualized, and explicit. Moreover, in this view, the existing von Neumann architecture led to programming practices that in turn led to explicit and inflexible systems using data that was far too simplified over the natural world. Some proponents of this argument suggest that newer architectures, such as the neural network, may hold more promise. It is believed that neural systems or similar architectures will have greater flexibility, being able to learn. It is hoped that these systems could mimic human activity. However, the efficacy of neural networks or other architectures has not yet been proven. While it is possible that some future neural network system could solve the social-technical gap, again this remains unknown. Again, we should consider the gap as enduring until proven otherwise, since the solution may or may not arrive.

A second argument against the significance of the gap is historically based. There are several variants: that we should adapt ourselves to the technology or that we will coevolve with the technology. In its more deterministic and mechanistic form, this argument can be seen as neo-Taylorism—we should adapt ourselves efficiently and effectively to the machine. It has been argued within the software engineering community, for example, that people should fit the necessities of process descriptions. The most famous form of this argument is Osterweil 1987. Osterweil argues that software engineering processes are software, and by extension, software engineers should function according to rule.

The coevolutionary form of this argument is that we adapt resources in the environment to our needs. If the resources are capable of only partial satisfaction, then we slowly create new technical resources to better fit the need. An example in Hutchins (1995a) is the slow evolution of navigational tools. For example, the Mercator projection for maps simplifies navigation calculations, and its creation was an act of tool adoption and coevolution. Moreover, if the resources are important enough, we may slowly change social practice to adapt.

The suggested outcome of the historically based variants is the same: Our culture will adapt itself to the limitations of the technology, so the technical limitations are not important. Admittedly, the variants have differing moral authorities; the neo-Taylorist version argues that we should change to be more rational, explicit, and predictable, while the coevolutionary version suggests evolutionary and progressive forces at work. One might even consider the neo-Taylorist to be a peculiar solution to the gap, arguing the gap's inherent benefit to society.

The coevolutionary argument is difficult to dismiss outright. It is hard to imagine that our culture would not adapt to any technology, and if this gap continues to exist, our culture will adapt to it. However, while coevolution will occur, the gap is still important to consider as a CSCW problem. It would be best to "round off the edges" of coevolution. As Postman (1992) argues, technologies have previously affected our culture in profound ways, especially when just assumed. Postman points to invisible technologies, or technologies chosen and so adopted as to become invisible to societal members, have profound and long-lasting effects. Grading is one such invisible technology. Grading student papers began with William Farish at Cambridge University in 1792, and Postman argues that numerically ranking individuals' work is a technology so assumed and valued by our society that it is largely invisible. Indeed, merely the invisibility of the technology leads to significant social problems (such as overuse of standardized intelligence tests).

As an intellectual discipline, HCI and CSCW should not allow unconscious decisions about technology features and adoptions. Postman argued the following in a journalistic piece.

> What I'm interested in is having people take these questions seriously. . . .
> Technology is not an unmixed blessing. We also need for them to talk about
> what new technologies can undo. . . . I just don't think we can go into these
> things anymore with our eyes closed. (McCreary 1993, p. 84)

As Heilbroner (1994) and others have argued, technological trajectories are responsive to social direction. This paper makes the case that they may also be responsive to intellectual direction.[1] Indeed, a central premise of HCI is that we should not force users to adapt.

14.4 What to Do?

If the social-technical gap is real, important, and likely to remain, then as a field, HCI and CSCW must consider what to do with the gap. We can consider it a black hole in the middle of our discipline or construe it to be an important finding of our field. The argument here is that CSCW's vitality results from its understanding of the fundamental nature of the gap. Indeed, although the gap is often hazily assumed in the CSCW literature, we should make it an explicit intellectual focus.

Centralizing the social-technical gap as a necessary problematic in CSCW's intellectual mission is a major, first step. However, this is not to say that CSCW should continue to state and restate aspects and results of the gap—it may be time to move on. The HCI and CSCW research communities need to ask what one might do (1) to ameliorate the effects of the gap and (2) to further understand the gap.

---

[1]Conceptually, coevolutionary effects lend themselves to an overly pessimistic reading of the situation as follows: If coevolutionary effects are inevitable and largely unforeseeable, then what intellectual guidance can be provided? Perhaps it is inevitable that we will merely continue to blunder our way forward with designs no matter what we know. This reading is contrary to the HCI tenet of providing guidance to design (at some level), and most HCI researchers would reject this pessimistic view. Assuming belief in some level of guidance, the gap still needs to be understood and dealt with.

I believe an answer—and a future HCI challenge—is to reconceptualize CSCW as a science of the artificial. This echoes Simon (1981) but properly updates his work for CSCW's time and intellectual task.[2] The remainder of this section discusses what this would entail.

14.4.1 A Return to Simon: The Science of CSCW

Thirty years ago, Herbert Simon produced his seminal book *The Sciences of the Artificial* (1981, first edition 1969). In his autobiography (Simon 1991), Simon admits that *The Sciences of the Artificial* was thrown together from lectures, and many people feel the book lacks coherence. Yet Simon's book became an anthem call for artificial intelligence and computer science. The book argued for a path between the idea for a new science (such as economics or artificial intelligence) and the construction of that new science (perhaps with some backtracking in the creation process). This argument was both characteristically logical and psychologically appealing for the time.

The book's basic premise is that engineering and design are fundamentally different from the sciences. The key to Simon's argument is his distinction between the artificial (as in "artifice") and the natural. In a famous example, Simon notes that farms are artificial in that they are created and maintained through human design and agency. Science, then, is about the analysis of the natural, but engineering is about the synthesis of the artificial.[3] In this view, engineering and design are synonymous, and new sciences are possible for understanding the nature of design. For Simon, the new sciences of the artificial include economics, organizational science, computer science, and artificial intelligence.

One might expect such an argument would be challenging to existing academic programs and appealing to new intellectual areas. Indeed, for many years, Simon's work was extremely influential, often indirectly, in U.S. programs of computer science and artificial intelligence. Yet, his call to create a science of design per se has gone largely unheeded.

Looking back, one can see a certain naivete about the complexities involved in creating new sciences concerned with the constructed world, whether technical or

---

[2] I have found, through talks and reviews, that mentioning Simon was occasionally tantamount to waving a giant red cape in front of some social researchers. Simon was such a large figure, with such strong views about positivist methods, that he was extremely emblematic and problematic for many CSCW researchers. Indeed, until recently, he was for me as well. In the following sections, I caution the reader to try to separate Simon's overall goal from the particulars of his method.

Simon was contemporary, but we commonly do this with prior theorists. No one today would leap to take Vico or Comte at face value; their methods and specific social insights are dated. Yet, their overall call to a science of the social is still very important. We should do the same for Simon's work; his call to a new type of science is also very important.

[3] Simon raised an important caution about engineering education as opposed to engineering practice. In his opinion, academic programs of engineering were not about design. In his view, they were schools of applied mathematics; design had vanished from their curricula and research programs.

social. This naivete arose from at least two sources. First, Simon confused the task of identifying fundamental intellectual issues in his sciences of the artificial with specific technical ideas and implementations. It is clear that he thought his particular methods would lead to new sciences (he does not separate the intellectual problem of how people examine options from the specific use of his General Problem Solver). Second, Simon did not confront long-term, systemic incapability as an intellectual possibility. Simon was (and is) a Progressive optimist.[4] At a simple level, CSCW's intellectual context is framed by social constructionism and ethnomethodology (Berger and Luckmann 1966; Garfinkel 1967), systems theories (Hutchins 1995a), and many large-scale system experiences (such as American urban renewal, nuclear power, and Vietnam). All of these pointed to the complexities underlying any social activity, even those felt to be straightforward. Simon's book does not address the inevitable gaps between the desired outcome and the means of producing that outcome for any large-scale design process, but CSCW researchers see these gaps as unavoidable. The social-technical gap should not have been ignored by Simon.

Yet, CSCW is exactly the type of science Simon envisioned, and CSCW could serve as a reconstruction and renewal of Simon's viewpoint, suitably revised. As much as was AI, CSCW is inherently a science of the artificial, as Simon meant the term: CSCW is at once an engineering discipline attempting to construct suitable systems for groups, organizations, and other collectivities, and at the same time, CSCW is a social science attempting to understand the basis for that construction in the social world (or everyday experience).

CSCW's science, however, must centralize the necessary gap between what we would prefer to construct and what we can construct. To do this as a practical program of action requires several steps—palliatives to ameliorate the current social conditions, first-order approximations to explore the design space, and fundamental lines of inquiry to create the science. These steps should develop into a new science of the artificial. In any case, the steps are necessary in order to move forward intellectually within CSCW, given the nature of the social-technical gap.

14.4.2 Palliatives: Ideological, Political, and Educational

Centralizing the social requirements in a science of the artificial obliges us to address current conditions. Over the last 20 years, people have worked out a number of ideological, political, or educational initiatives in an ad hoc manner. This chapter has little to add to the actions of these many people; this section merely notes how centralizing the gap leads to the logical coherence of these ideological, political, and educational initiatives.

---

[4]Progressivism was an American political movement in the early twentieth century that optimistically espoused progress through educational, political, and economic reform. It was a sporadic third party at the national level but a very strong political movement in the U.S. Midwest. Simon was raised in Wisconsin in the late 1910s and 1920s, both geographically and temporally the center of Progressivism in the United States.

Ideological initiatives include those that prioritize the needs of the people using the systems. For example, stakeholder analysis in Information Technology is a method that brings into a project the voices of all stakeholder parties. Participatory design is a similar method, actually employing important stakeholder parties in the design. Both methods address the inability to solve the social-technical gap by bringing forth a solution that is open and known to all important parties. The so-called Scandinavian approach to information systems design, where trade union participation is mandated, unequivocally addresses the political implications of the social-technical gap. Stakeholder analysis, participatory design, and the Scandinavian approach, as well as standard HCI techniques, provide users with the ability to block troublesome impacts. Knowing that such political initiatives will be logically necessary, as resulting from viewing the gap as an inevitable concern, may be an important step in ameliorating conditions.

Similarly an educational perspective would argue that programmers and users should understand the fundamental nature of the social requirements. Moving past the naive perspective that additional education or training would bring software engineers the insights for effectively building programs that fit the social world, software engineers could be suitably trained to understand the organizational and social impacts that could result from their designs. If computer science does not know how to build systems that fully support the social world, then a computer science education should teach students what can and cannot be done. However, palliatives by themselves do not create a science nor lead to intellectual coherence in a research area. I next turn to those steps.

14.4.3 Beginning Systematic Exploration: First-Order Approximations

First-order approximations, to adopt a metaphor from fluid dynamics, are tractable solutions that partially solve specific problems with known tradeoffs. They can be constructed from experimentation, although in mature sciences they should result from theoretical extensions. These first-order approximations essentially try to find workarounds for the social-technical gap, to edge around it in ways that are not extremely odious and to do so with known effects. CSCW needs a set of these approximations, with suitable examples and an understanding of why they succeed. I will discuss later how these approximations might gather into a science.

CSCW already has a set of potential first-order approximations. One approximation is to provide systems that only partially address the social requirements. Extremely successful CSCW systems, such as e-mail or chat systems, do not satisfy all social requirements. (Problems with electronic mail often result from contextual problems.) Much CSCW research is centered around knowing which social arrangements need to be satisfied for what tasks and settings; that is, the field is determining what the approximation tradeoffs are. Considerable recent work examined the differences in communication media in providing the necessary social cues for computer-mediated communicative activity (Olson and Teasley 1996; Kraut et al. 1996; Ackerman et al. 1997).

Providing CMC components, such as chat, within a system is another approximation. As previously mentioned, communication through these components allows people to make necessary social adjustments. For example, they can fluidly repair task breakdowns, such as determining which drawing stroke to keep in a shared drawing surface. The use of CMC components allows people to work out arrangements without making their roles or information explicit. They are an approximation, rather than a solution, since they exclude designs that wish to computationally augment communication (such as with routing), role structures (such as with workflow), and information processing (such as with privacy).

Another approximation incorporates new computational mechanisms to substitute adequately for social mechanisms or to provide for new social issues (Hollan and Stornetta 1992). An intriguing example of this is found in Hudson and Smith (1996). In this paper, distorted video images or audio are used to denote presence but not provide the details of activity. In a video link, one can tell that someone is present in the room but not what he or she is doing. In an audio space, one can hear that two people are conversing but not what they are saying. There are, of course, similar mechanisms in natural social activity. For example, muffled voices heard through office walls imply presence. However, similar distortions of visual or aural information would be impossible in normal social activity. The potential privacy disruptions (a form of explicitness) have been ameliorated by a new computational mechanism.

The final first-order approximation is the creation of technical architectures that do not invoke the social technical gap; these architectures do not require action nor delegate it. Instead, these architectures provide supportive or augmentative facilities, such as advice, to users. If users could judge the quality of the support, the systems would serve as merely another resource in their environment (Hutchins 1995a), rather than trying to mechanize elements of their social environment. Such architectures include collaborative filtering that provide ratings for services (Shardanand and Maes 1995; Resnick et al. 1994), recommender systems that facilitate sharing of information profiles (Starr et al. 1996; Terveen et al. 1997), and critic systems that make suggestions to users about design choices (Fischer et al. 1990).

As an example of an approximation that attempts to address the social-technical gap in an augmentative manner, I return to the P3P example used earlier in the paper. One workaround to the social-technical gap with P3P is to avoid the gap itself and merely augment the natural social facilities of the user. In the case of P3P, the approximation is provide privacy critics, small agents that make suggestions to users about impending privacy problems (Ackerman and Cranor 1999). These critics do not take action on behalf of the user; instead, they might offer warnings to the user. Furthermore, this architecture has the capability of having hundreds of different critics. There would not need to be one accurate user agent; many critics would work with the user to provide assurances of privacy. Users could, of course, turn these critics off or on.

These critics watch over the shoulder of the user. One such privacy critic could check a third-party database for consumer complaints about a Web site. For example, a Better Business Bureau database might report sites that have privacy or consumer reports against them. Privacy advocacy groups might have databases that report sites participating in known data scams or even nonstated transfers of personal data. Another privacy critic could watch for sites requesting combinations of personal data that could lead to the user being uniquely identifiable.

In more theoretical terms, we are actively exploring critic-based architectures because each critic is a separate resource for the user. If each resource is relatively small in functionality, users can pick and choose the resources they wish in order to create new ways of engaging in social activity (such as work or social interaction).

In summary, these architectures and the other approximations mentioned explore the dimensions of the social-technical gap in more detail. To create a science, however, it still remains to organize these explorations and demark the fundamental questions and issues.

14.4.4 Toward Making CSCW into a Science of the Artificial

The most formidable task for CSCW is determining systematic methods for designing around the gap. We do not wish to explore blindly. Yet, at first, a fledgling science, such as CSCW, may have only illustrative cases and heuristics for design. It is easy to forget how existing engineering sciences laboriously constructed their repertories of knowledge. Petroski (1994) discusses the Romans' problem of moving enormous blocks of stone over poor roads. One way to do this is to make the columns and slabs into axles for oxen to pull. Trial and error (and suitable reflection) was required to determine how to steer these giant axles. Petroski, citing Vitruvius, describes one effort with a single pull line wrapped around the center of the axle. It is obvious to us that this design will continuously wander off the road; yet, this had to be learned by the Romans. Similarly, no less a genius than Galileo determined that the strength of materials was not geometrically proportional to size (Petroski 1985). That is, if you want to build a ship twice as long as previous ships, you cannot merely use double-sized beams. Again, scientific knowledge in an engineering discipline is slow in coming; yet, failures and successes contribute to a greater understanding over time only if systematically examined.

Nonetheless, determining guiding research principles is difficult when a potential science is still seeking approximations to its problem. This section can make only a general attempt at finding general questions, and it is necessarily preliminary. Nonetheless, several guiding questions are required based on the social-technical gap and its role in any CSCW science of the artificial.

- When can a computational system successfully ignore the need for nuance and context?

- When can a computational system augment human activity with computer technologies suitably to make up for the loss in nuance and context, as argued in the approximation section above?

- Can these benefits be systematized so that we know when we are adding benefit rather than creating loss?
- What types of future research will solve some of the gaps between technical capabilities and what people expect in their full range of social and collaborative activities?

These guiding questions must also address evolving technical capabilities and infrastructures. In addition to the standard learning circle (established within HCI), CSCW (and perhaps HCI as well) actually have a technical spiral over time. No research group can thoroughly explore all design possibilities (and study them systematically). Moreover, one wishes to redo systems designs as the studies progress, based on the analysis from previous designs and on new technological possibilities. A five-year program to thoroughly study the design space of the original Answer Garden system (Ackerman 1994), built with its own underlying hypermedia system, would have been foolhardy, since within that timeframe the Web emerged.

14.5 Conclusion

The title of this paper suggests that the social-technical gap is *the* fundamental problem of CSCW. CSCW, like HCI, clearly has multiple intellectual problems. CSCW shares problems of generalizability from small groups to a general population (as do all of the social sciences), prediction of affordances (as does HCI), and the applicability of new technological possibilities (as does the rest of computer science).

Nonetheless, it has been argued here that the unique problem of CSCW is the social-technical gap. There is a fundamental mismatch between what is required socially and what we can do technically. Human activity is highly nuanced and contextualized. However, we lack the technical mechanisms to fully support the social world uncovered by the social findings of CSCW. This social-technical gap is unlikely to go away, although it certainly can be better understood and perhaps approached.

The gap is also CSCW's unique contribution. CSCW exists intellectually at the boundary and interaction of technology and social settings. Its unique intellectual importance is at the confluence of technology and the social, and its unique potential lies in its recognition of and attention to both. CSCW has an opportunity to become a true science of the artificial, updating and revising Simon's classic call so as to be appropriate for CSCW's time and task.

Indeed, an understanding of the social-technical gap lies at the heart of CSCW's intellectual contribution. If CSCW (or HCI) merely contributes "cool toys" to the world, it will have failed its intellectual mission. Our understanding of the gap is driven by technological exploration through artifact creation and deployment, but HCI and CSCW systems need to have at their core a fundamental understanding of how people really work and live in groups, organizations, communities, and other forms of collective life. Otherwise, we will produce unusable systems, badly mechanizing and distorting collaboration and other social activity.

Acknowledgments

Many people in the CSCW field have contributed toward my understanding of the needs of groups, organizations, and other social collectivities, as well as the technical possibilities for supporting them. In particular, conversations with participants at the Human Computer Interaction Consortium workshop and the IRIS'99 Conference, as well as with members of various Platform for Privacy Preferences Project working groups were invaluable. Any misunderstandings are, of course, mine. Additional conversations with John King and Julian Feldman were helpful in understanding Simon.

This work has been funded, in part, by grants from the National Science Foundation (IRI-9702904) and the U.S. Navy (N66001–97-M-0157).

References

Ackerman, M.S. (1994). Augmenting the organizational memory: A field study of Answer Garden. *Proceedings of the Conference on Computer-Supported Cooperative Work (CSCW'94)*, 243–252.

Ackerman, M.S., and Cranor, L. (1999). Privacy critics: UI components to safeguard users' privacy. *Proceedings of the ACM Conference on Human Factors in Computing Systems (CHI'99)*, 258–259. New York: ACM Press.

Ackerman, M.S., and Halverson, C. (2000). Re-examining organizational memory. *Communications of the ACM*, 43, 1, 58–63.

Ackerman, M.S., Hindus, D., Mainwaring, S.D., and Starr, B. (1997). Hanging on the 'wire: A field study of an audio-only media space. *ACM Transactions on Computer-Human Interaction*, 4, 1, 39–66.

Ackerman, M.S., and Malone, T.W. (1990). Answer Garden: A tool for growing organizational memory. *Proceedings of the ACM Conference on Office Information Systems*, 31–39. New York: ACM Press.

Ackerman, M.S., and McDonald, D.W. (1996a). Answer Garden 2: Merging organizational memory with collective help. *Proceedings of the ACM Conference on Computer-Supported Cooperative Work (CSCW'96)*, 97–105. New York: ACM Press.

Ackerman, M.S., and Palen, L. (1996b). The Zephyr Help Instance: Promoting ongoing activity in a CSCW system. *Proceedings of the ACM Conference on Human Factors in Computing Systems (CHI'96)*, 268–275. New York: ACM Press.

Bentley, R., Rodden, T., Sawyer, P., Sommerville, I., Hughes, J., Randall, D., and Shapiro, D. (1992). Ethnographically-informed systems design for air traffic control. *Proceedings of the ACM Conference on Computer-Supported Cooperative Work (CSCW'92)*, 123–129. New York: ACM Press.

Berger, P.L., and Luckmann, T. (1966). *The social construction of reality: a treatise in the sociology of knowledge.* New York: Anchor.

Boland, Jr., R.J., Tenkasi, R.V., and Te'eni, D. (1994). Designing information technology to support distributed cognition. *Organization Science, 5, 3,* 456–475.

Clark, A. (1997). *Being there: Putting brain, body, and world together again.* Cambridge, MA: MIT Press.

Conklin, J., and Begeman, M.L. (1988). gIBIS: A hypertext tool for exploratory policy discussion. *Proceedings of the CSCW'88,* 140–152. New York: ACM Press.

Cranor, L., and Reagle, J. (1998). The platform for privacy preferences. *Communications of the ACM, 42, 2,* 48–55.

Dourish, P., Holmes, J., MacLean, A., Marqvardsen, P., and Zbyslaw, A. (1996). Freeflow: Mediating between representation and action in workflow systems. *Proceedings of the ACM Conference on Computer-Supported Cooperative Work (CSCW'96)*, 190–198. New York: ACM Press.

Erickson, T., Smith, D.N., Kellogg, W.A., Laff, M., Richards, J.T., and Bradner, E. (1999). Socially translucent systems: Social proxies, persistent conversation, and the design of 'babble.' *Proceedings of the ACM Conference on Human Factors in Computing Systems (CHI'99)*, 72–79. New York: ACM Press.

Fischer, G., Lemke, A.C., Mastaglio, T., and Morch, A.I. (1990). Using critics to empower users. *Proceedings of ACM CHI'90 Conference on Human Factors in Computing Systems,* 337–347. New York: ACM Press.

Flores, F., Graves, M., Hartfield, B., and Winograd, T. (1988). Computer systems and the design of organizational interaction. *ACM Transactions on Office Information Systems, 6, 2,* 153–172.

Garfinkel, H. (1967). *Studies in ethnomethodology.* Englewood Cliffs, NJ: Prentice-Hall.

Goffman, E. (1961). *The Presentation of self in everyday life.* New York: Anchor-Doubleday.

Goffman, E. (1971). *Relations in public.* New York: Basic Books.

Greif, I., and Sarin, S. (1987). Data sharing in group work. *ACM Transactions on Office Information Systems, 5, 2,* 187–211.

Grudin, J. (1989). Why groupware applications fail: Problems in design and evaluation. *Office: Technology and People, 4, 3,* 245–264.

Heath, C., Jirotka, M., Luff, P., and Hindmarsh, J. (1994). Unpacking collaboration: The interactional organisation of trading in a city dealing room. *Computer Supported Cooperative Work Journal,* 3, 2, 147–165.

Heath, C., and Luff, P. (1992). Collaboration and control: Crisis management and multimedia technology in London underground line control rooms. *Computer Supported Cooperative Work Journal,* 1, 1, 69–94.

Heath, C., and Luff, P. (1996). Documents and professional practice: "Bad" organizational reasons for "good" clinical records. *Proceedings of the ACM Conference on Computer-Supported Cooperative Work (CSCW'96),* 354–363.

Heilbroner, R.L. (1994). Technological determinism revisited. In L.M. a. M.R. Smith (Ed.), *Does Technology Drive History?,* 67–78. Cambridge, MA: MIT Press.

Heritage, J. (1984). *Garfinkel and ethnomethodology.* Cambridge: Polity.

Hollan, J., and Stornetta, S. (1992). Beyond being there. *Proceedings of ACM CHI'92 Conference on Human Factors in Computing Systems,* 119–125. New York: ACM Press.

Hudson, S.E., and Smith, I. (1996). Techniques for addressing fundamental privacy and disruption tradeoffs in awareness support systems. *Proceedings of the ACM Conference on Computer-Supported Cooperative Work (CSCW'96),* 248–257. New York: ACM Press.

Hughes, J., King, V., Rodden, T., and Andersen, H. (1994). Moving out from the control room: Ethnography in system design. *Proceedings of the ACM Conference on Computer supported cooperative work,* 429–439. New York: ACM Press.

Hutchins, E. (1995a). *Cognition in the wild.* Cambridge, MA: MIT Press.

Hutchins, E. (1995b). How a cockpit remembers its speeds. *Cognitive Science,* 19, 3, 265–288.

Kaplan, S.M., Tolone, W.J., Bogia, D.P., and Bignoli, C. (1992). Flexible, active support for collaborative work with ConversationBuilder. *Proceedings of the ACM CSCW'92 Conference on Computer-Supported Cooperative Work,* 378–385. New York: ACM Press.

Katzenberg, B., Pickard, F., and McDermott, J. (1996). Computer support for clinical practice: Embedding and evolving protocols of care. *Proceedings of the ACM Conference on Computer-Supported Cooperative Work (CSCW'96),* 364–369. New York: ACM Press.

Kling, R. (1991). Cooperation, coordination and control in computer-supported work. *Communications of the ACM,* 34, 12, 83–88.

Kraut, R.E., Miller, M.D., and Siegel, J. (1996). Collaboration in performance of physical tasks: Effects on outcomes and communication. *Proceedings of the ACM Conference on Computer-Supported Cooperative Work (CSCW'96),* 57–66. New York: ACM Press.

Malone, T.W., and Crowston, K. (1994). The Interdisciplinary study of coordination. *ACM Computing Surveys,* 26, 1, 87–119.

March, J.G., and Simon, H.A. (1958). *Organizations.* New York: Wiley.

Markus, M.L. (1990). Toward a 'critical mass' theory of interactive media. In J. Fulk and C. Steinfield (Eds.), *Organizations and Communication Technology,* 194–218. Newbury Park, CA: Sage.

Marwood, B., and Greenberg, S. (1994). Real time groupware as a distributed system: Concurrency control and its effect on the interface. *Proceedings of the Computer Supported Cooperative Work,* 207–217. New York: ACM Press.

McCreary, L. (1993). Postman's progress. *CIO Magazine,* 7, 3, 74–84.

O'Day, V.L., Bobrow, D.G., and Shirley, M. (1996). The social-technical design circle. *Proceedings of the ACM Conference on Computer-Supported Cooperative Work (CSCW'96),* 160–169. New York: ACM Press.

Olson, G.M., and Olson, J.S. (1997). Research on computer supported cooperative work. In M. Helander (Ed.), *Handbook of Human Computer Interaction,* 1433–1457. Amsterdam: Elsevier.

Olson, J.S., and Teasley, S. (1996). Groupware in the wild: Lessons learned from a year of virtual collocation. *Proceedings of the ACM Conference on Computer-Supported Cooperative Work (CSCW'96),* 419–427. New York: ACM Press.

Orlikowski, W.J. (1992a). The duality of technology: Rethinking the concept of technology in organizations. *Organization Science,* 3, 3, 398–427.

Orlikowski, W.J. (1992b). Learning from notes: Organizational issues in groupware implementation. *Proceedings of the ACM Conference on Computer Supported Cooperative Work (CSCW'92),* 362–369. New York: ACM Press.

Osterweil, L.J. (1987). Software processes are software too. *Proceedings of the International Conference on Software Engineering (ICSE'87),* 2–13. New York: ACM Press.

Petroski, H. (1994). *Design paradigms: Case histories of error and judgment in engineering.* New York: Cambridge University Press.

Petroski, H. (1985). *To engineer is human: The role of failure in successful design.* New York: St. Martin's Press.

Postman, N. (1992). *Technopoly.* New York: Vintage.

Resnick, P., Iacovou, N., Suchak, M., Bergstrom, P., and Riedl, J. (1994). GroupLens: An open architecture for collaborative filtering of Netnews. *Proceedings of the ACM Conference on Computer-Supported Cooperative Work,* 175–186. New York: ACM Press.

Rodden, T. (1996). Populating the application: A model of awareness for cooperative applications. *Proceedings of the ACM Conference on Computer-Supported Cooperative Work (CSCW'96),* 87–96. New York: ACM Press.

Root, R.W. (1988). Design of a multi-media vehicle for social browsing. In *Proceedings of ACM CSCW'88 Conference on Computer-Supported Cooperative Work,* 25–38. New York: ACM Press.

Schmidt, K., and Simone, C. (1996). Coordination mechanisms: Towards a conceptual foundation of CSCW systems design. *Computer Supported Cooperative Work Journal,* 5, 2/3, 155–200.

Shardanand, U., and Maes, P. (1995). Social information filtering. *Proceedings of the ACM Conference on Human Factors in Computing Systems (CHI'95),* 210–217. New York: ACM Press.

Simon, H.A. (1991). *Models of my life.* New York: Basic Books.

Simon, H.A. (1981). *The sciences of the artificial.* Cambridge, MA: MIT Press.

Simon, H.A. (1957). *Administrative Behavior.* New York: Macmillan.

Sproull, L., and Kiesler, S. (1991). *Connections: New ways of working in the networked organization.* Cambridge, MA: MIT Press.

Star, S.L. (1989). The structure of ill-structured solutions: Boundary objects and heterogeneous distributed problem solving. In L. Gasser and M. Huhns (Eds.), *Distributed Artificial Intelligence,* 37–54. San Mateo: Morgan Kaufmann.

Star, S.L., and Ruhleder, K. (1994). Steps toward an ecology of infrastructure: Complex problems in design and access for large-scale collaborative systems. *Proceedings of the ACM Conference on Computer Supported Cooperative Work (CSCW'94),* 253–264. New York: ACM Press.

Starr, B., Ackerman, M.S., and Pazzani, M. (1996). Do-I-Care: A collaborative Web agent. *Proceedings of the ACM Conference on Human Factors in Computing Systems (CHI'96),* short papers, 268–275. New York: ACM Press.

Strauss, A. (1991). *Creating sociological awareness: Collective images and symbolic representations.* New Brunswick: Transaction.

Strauss, A.L. (1993). *Continual permutations of action.* New York: Aldine de Gruyter.

Suchman, L. (1994). Do categories have politics? *Computer Supported Cooperative Work Journal,* 2, 177–190.

Suchman, L., and Wynn, E. (1984). Procedures and problems in the office. *Office: Technology and People,* 2, 133–154.

Suchman, L.A. (1987). *Plans and situated actions: The problem of human-computer communication.* New York: Cambridge University Press.

Terveen, L., Hill, W., Amento, B., McDonald, D., and Creter, J. (1997). PHOAKS: A system for sharing recommendations. *Communicatons of the ACM,* 40, 3, 59–62.

Social Translucence: Designing Systems That Support Social Processes

Thomas Erickson
Wendy A. Kellogg

15.1 Introduction

We are concerned with designing systems to support communication and collaboration among large groups of people over computer networks. We are particularly interested in the question of how to design such systems so that they support communication that is deep, coherent, and productive.

It seems evident that our digital tools are primitive and cumbersome. Most of the communication and collaboration tools in daily use could be implemented, with little loss of functionality or usability, on the time-shared mainframe and character-based terminal systems of three decades ago. This is not because we managed to get things right on the first try: E-mail, mailing lists, chat rooms, discussion databases, and so forth all have substantial shortcomings. There are a host of problems: addressing, managing threads, bringing other people into the middle of a conversation, keeping a conversation on track, knowing who (or whether) anyone is listening, getting people to respond in a timely manner, finding old messages with crucial information in them. It is difficult to conduct a long-running, productive conversation through the digital medium, especially if there are more than a few people involved. Yet we do not believe that these shortcomings are inherent in digital systems.

The difficulty of digital communication and collaboration stands in stark contrast to our ability to communicate and collaborate with one another in the physical world. Consider these ordinary situations.

In another town on business, you and a few colleagues are looking for a place to have dinner. You notice a small restaurant. Through its window you see a cozy room with waiters bustling about. You hear the murmur of conversation, and the clink of glasses and cutlery. You head for the entrance. . . .

You've arrived at the opening reception for a convention. You look around for someone to talk to and see someone you recognize gesturing excitedly as others listen intently. Curious, you wander over. . . .

You're shopping for wine to bring to dinner. As you browse the racks, you hear a muttered, "Aha!" and watch another shopper grab two bottles out of a nearly empty bin. You get a bottle for yourself. . . .

These examples are unremarkable. Every day we make countless decisions based on the activity of those around us. As social creatures, we are immersed in a sea of social information. We've evolved an exquisite sensitivity to the actions and interactions of others. Whether it's wrapping up a talk when the audience starts fidgeting or deciding to forego the grocery shopping because the parking lot is jammed, social information like this provides the bases for inferences, planning, and coordination of activity.

In all of this, the only thing that is remarkable is how radically things change when we move from the ordinary world into the world of digital systems. Digital systems are generally opaque to social information. Most of our knowledge about people, most of our attunement to their interactions, most of our facility for improvising in a changing situation goes unused. In the digital world we are socially blind.

In this chapter our principal goal is to make some progress in redressing this blindness. We begin by describing the notion of social translucence, an approach to designing digital systems that emphasizes making social information visible within the system. Next, to focus and motivate the concept of social translucence, we apply it to knowledge management and sketch the outlines of what we call knowledge communities. Then we ask what it means to actually implement social translucence in a digital system and describe relevant work within HCI and our own implementation efforts. Finally, we describe some of the most pressing research issues raised by a socially translucent approach to systems design.

15.2   Foundations: Social Translucence

As designers of communication and collaboration systems, we find ourselves taking inspiration from work in the areas of architecture and urban design. This is not surprising, since, like architects and urban designers, we are concerned with creating contexts that support various forms of human-human interaction. What architecture and urbanism have to offer is long experience in exploring the interrelationship between physical spaces and social interaction. The interested reader should see Alexander et al. (1977), Gehl (1980), Jacobs (1961), Lynch (1990), and Whyte (1988). In what follows, we primarily draw upon our own examples. Although we have learned much from architecture and urbanism, the fact is that designers in those domains can assume the existence of a consistent and unquestioned physics that underlies social interaction. There is no such constancy in the digital world, and so our goal in this section is to look deeply at social interaction as it is embedded in physical space and try to extract principles that are sufficiently abstract that they might be transposed to the digital realm.

15.2.1 Visibility, Awareness, and Accountability

In the building where our group works there is a door that opens from the stairwell into the hallway. This door has a design problem: Opened quickly, it is likely to slam into anyone who is about to enter from the other direction. In an attempt to fix this problem, this sign was placed on the door: "Please Open Slowly." As you might guess, the sign is not a particularly effective solution.

Let's contrast this solution with one of a different sort: putting a glass window in the door. The glass window means that the sign is no longer required. As people approach the door, they see whether anyone is on the other side and, if so, they modulate their actions appropriately. This is a simple example of what we call a socially translucent system. While it is obvious why this solution works, it is useful to examine the reasons behind it carefully. We see three reasons for the effectiveness of the glass window.

1. First, the glass window makes socially significant information *visible*. That is, as humans, we are perceptually attuned to movement and human faces and figures. We notice and react to them more readily than we notice and interpret a printed sign.

2. Second, the glass window supports *awareness*. I don't open the door quickly because *I know* that you're on the other side. This awareness brings our social rules into play to govern our actions. We have been raised in a culture in which slamming doors into other people is not sanctioned.

3. There is a third, somewhat subtler reason for the efficacy of the glass window. Suppose that I don't care whether I hurt others. Nevertheless, I'll open the door slowly because *I know that you know that I know* you're there, and therefore I will be held *accountable* for my actions. (This distinction is useful because while accountability and awareness usually co-occur in the physical world, they are not necessarily coupled in the digital realm.) It is through such individual feelings of accountability that norms, rules, and customs become effective mechanisms for social control.

We see these three properties of socially translucent systems—visibility, awareness, and accountability—as building blocks of social interaction. Notice that, as exemplified by our other examples, social translucence is not *just* about people acting in accordance with social rules. In socially translucent systems we believe it will be easier for users to carry on coherent discussions; to observe and imitate others' actions; to engage in peer pressure; to create, notice, and conform to social conventions. We see social translucence as a fundamental requirement for supporting all types of communication and collaboration.

15.2.2 Translucence: Visibility and Privacy

There is one other aspect of social translucence that deserves mention. Why is it that we speak of socially *translucent* systems rather than socially *transparent* systems? Because there is a vital tension between privacy and visibility. What we say and do with another person depends on who and how many are watching. Note that privacy is neither good nor bad on its own—it simply supports certain types of behavior and inhibits others. For example, the perceived validity of an election depends crucially on keeping certain of its aspects very private and other aspects very public. As before, what we are seeing is the impact of awareness and accountability. In the election, it is desirable that the voters *not* be accountable to others for their votes but that those who count the votes be accountable to all.

15.3 Application Domain: Knowledge Management

What might it mean to have social translucence in a digital system? How might making social information more visible actually change the way digital systems are used? Why might this be a desirable thing? To answer these questions, let's look at knowledge management from a socially translucent perspective.

15.3.1 Knowledge Management as a Social Phenomenon

Knowledge management is a currently popular term for the attempt to provide organizations with tools for capturing, retrieving, and disseminating information about their own activities to their own employees. In a sense, it is an attempt to make organizations self-conscious, to enable them to tap their own experience in solving problems rather than having to reinvent solutions to recurring problems. Knowledge management is often seen as a problem of putting useful information into databases and providing schemes for organizing and retrieving the information. This perspective leads people to think in terms of data mining and text clustering and databases and documents. This isn't wrong, but it's only part of the picture.

The production and use of knowledge is deeply entwined with social phenomena. For example, one of us once interviewed accountants at a large accounting company about how they would use a proposed database of their company's internal documents. A surprising theme emerged: The accountants said that they'd love to access the documents so that they could find out who wrote them. As one explained, "Well, if I'm putting together a proposal for Exxon, I really want to talk to people who have already worked with them. They'll know the politics, the history, and other information that usually doesn't get into the reports." Of particular import was the fact that someone who had worked with the prospective client could give referrals, thus saving the accountant from having to make a "cold call." The ability to say "so-and-so said I ought to call" was of great value to the accountants (and illustrates yet another function of accountability). Having a referral, however tenuous the connection, is a valuable *social resource* that can only be directly conveyed from one person to another. Saying "I found your name in the corporate knowledge database" is not the same. It was only through the people—and the social networks they were part of—that the accountants could get the knowledge and social resources they needed.

Even as documents may serve as indices into social networks, so may social networks serve as pointers to documents. One of the authors follows an area of research known as genre theory. Giving a search engine a query like "+ genre + theory" will generate about fifty thousand hits, most of which are not very relevant. In contrast, the query "+ genre + yates + bazerman" generates 20 mostly relevant hits. What is happening is that the query effectively selects for papers that mention "genre" and that also have bibliographies that include both "Yates" (a reference frequently cited by those who study genres in digital documents) and "Bazerman" (a rhetorician and scholar of "classical"—that is, nondigital genre, typically cited by other classical genre theorists). Thus, the query selects for scholarly papers that draw on the work of two largely divergent research communities. Of course, this is really a trick: The search engine knows nothing of people or scholarly communities or even of the difference between a scholarly paper and other texts. The query works because of the bibliographic conventions of research papers and takes advantage of the co-occurence of two relatively uncommon names. But it is interesting to think about the possibilities of a system that was designed to "know" about the notions of authorship, citation, and research communities.

This sort of situation—the production and use of knowledge in a social milieu—is not the exception; it is the rule. A variety of research programs—social studies of science, critical theory, the sociology of knowledge, and ethnographies of the work place—all point to the deep connections between knowledge and social and cultural contexts. Knowledge, whether it be of bugs in the Java Virtual Machine or of how to begin negotiations with an executive from another culture, is discovered, shared, and used in a social context, not just for its own sake but to construct the identities and advance the agendas of the individuals, groups, and institutions involved. Having the information in a database isn't as useful as we would hope, unless it also provides an *entree* into the social networks that produced the data. It is from the social networks—not from the information itself—that social resources can be recruited.

15.3.2 From Knowledge Management to Knowledge Communities

Imagine a knowledge management system that was designed from a social perspective, a system predicated on the assumption that knowledge is distributed throughout a network of people and that only a small proportion of it is captured in concrete form. As the previous vignettes suggest, such a system would, along with its data and documents, also provide a rich set of connections back to the social network of people who produced the information. But if we think in terms of making socially significant activity visible, considerably more possibilities suggest themselves. Imagine that the knowledge management system provided access not only to authors but to people who were accessing and using the knowledge. Suppose that—just as we look for crowded restaurants, eye fellow shoppers, or look for engaging conversations—we could see similar traces of those making use of information in a knowledge management system. After all, some of the knowledge users might have to go to considerable work to apply the knowledge to their own ends, thereby developing an understanding of its shortcomings and particularities, as well as building on it. If we could capture traces of this knowledge work, others with similar needs might find as much value in talking with users as with the original authors. Such a system would not be just a database from which workers retrieved knowledge, it would be a *knowledge community,* a place within which people would discover, use, and manipulate knowledge and could encounter and interact with others who are doing likewise.

A knowledge community of this sort has a formidable social problem to overcome: Why should those who produce and use knowledge take the time to engage in such interactions? Why should they wish to? What benefits would they gain that might compensate them for their efforts (Grudin 1989)? This is a deep and difficult research problem. However, we are optimistic that the problem has a solution (after all, such large-scale interaction occurs in the physical world in a wide array of communities and social collectivities). We suggest that the solution to the problem arises as a direct result of social translucence: Making knowledge work visible (thus allowing people to observe and contact one another) also enables those who are skilled at unearthing, applying, and adapting knowledge to receive credit for what is all too often an invisible form of work. If knowledge work is made visible it can be recognized and rewarded by the organization (awareness and accountability at the organizational level), and it can permit knowledge work to shift from something that takes time away from "real work" to being "real work" in and of itself.

This discussion brings us to an important question: Through what mechanism can knowledge work be made visible? How can it leave traces so that not only can others see it occurring but that those who were not present can gain value from it at a later time? We believe that the answer to this lies in conversation.

15.3.3 Conversation: Knowledge Work Made Visible

Conversation is essential. We use conversation as a medium for decision making. It is through conversation that we create, develop, validate, and share knowledge. When systems—computational or bureaucratic—freeze, or simply prove too rigid, we pick up the phone to figure out appropriate workarounds. While e-commerce allows transactions without conversations, it's likely that customers will often want to question, clarify, and negotiate during the purchase of anything other than a commodity. And with all our advances in information retrieval, the preferred method for obtaining information is still to ask a colleague.

Why is this? We suggest that conversation has two characteristics that are central to its power and ubiquity. One vital characteristic of talk is that it is a deeply interactive intellectual process (see Clark 1996 for a detailed exposition). As we talk we refer to a common ground of already established understandings, shared experiences, and past history. As the conversation proceeds, we are continuously attempting to interpret what is said, verify that we have been understood, and offer new contributions. Sometimes misunderstandings occur, and so we attempt to fix them by rephrasing our words or "debugging" the previous conversation to reveal that what we thought were shared understandings were not, in fact, shared. What all this amounts to is that conversation is a superb method for eliciting, unpacking, articulating, applying, and recontextualizing knowledge.

Conversation is more than simply an intellectual endeavor. It is a fundamentally social process (for example, see Goffman 1963, 1967, and Kendon 1990). Conversation is social in two ways. First, people speak *to* an *audience*. Speakers notice how their audience is reacting and steer their remarks appropriately: Nods and eye contact convey one message; questions and furrowed brows another; yawns and fidgeting still another. Second, conversation is social in that people portray themselves through conversation. They advance their personal agendas, project their personal style, take credit, share blame, and accomplish other social ends through their talk, often with a great deal of subtlety. The social nature of talk is not an undesirable side effect but rather the heart of it. Personal motivations fuel conversation and provide the energy for the considerable intellectual work it takes, whether the conversation in question is banter over morning coffee or about the composition of a journal article.

In addition, conversation within the digital medium has a property of great importance for our purposes: It *persists*. Instantiated as text, whether typed in or spoken and recognized, persistence expands conversation beyond those within earshot, rendering it accessible to those in other places and at later times. Thus, digital conversation may be synchronous or asynchronous and its audience intimate or vast. Its persistence opens the door to a variety of new uses and practices. Persistent conversations may be searched, browsed, replayed, annotated, visualized, restructured, and recontextualized, with what are likely to be profound impacts on personal, social, and institutional practices.

15.3.4 The Vision: Conversationally Based Knowledge Communities

While considerably more remains to be said, we will stop here and sketch an outline of the sort of system we have in mind. Our sketch will be rough because our purpose is not to define a system in detail but simply to provide a framework in which to position existing research and to raise new research questions, the subjects of the final two sections of this chapter.

We see several types of needs, each of which suggests a layer of functionality.

- *Activity Support.* First, it is necessary to support the initiation and conduct of social activity via digital media. In particular, we want to support long-running, deep, coherent conversations that can be steered by their participants. In such an environment we believe that knowledge can be constructed through reflective conversations among a community engaged in a shared set of tasks.

- *Conversation Visualization and Restructuring.* The knowledge embedded in conversations should be reusable. That is, we want to move from today's state, where conversation is of value primarily as it occurs, to a situation in which the comments that make up a conversation can serve as a useful work product. It should be possible for members of a knowledge community to search, navigate, and visualize their conversations. Similarly, participants should be able to add structure to conversations: summarizing, highlighting, linking, and otherwise annotating them.

- *Organizational Knowledge Spaces.* Our experience suggests that knowledge production and use will proceed most easily in a semiprivate environment—a relatively small community where knowledge workers feel "safe" enough to venture tentative interpretations and conjectures. At the same time, the *raison d'être* of a knowledge community is to share knowledge with the organization within which it is embedded. One resolution to this tension between privacy and visibility is to support an organizational space within which semiautonomous knowledge communities can exist, each exercising control over the ways and means through which its knowledge is shared with the larger organization.

15.4   Implementation: Social Translucence in Digital Systems

So far we have discussed social translucence as a general approach to designing systems for computer-mediated communication and collaboration and have described how it might map onto the domain of knowledge management and why that might be desirable. In the remainder of the chapter we ask how these ideas might be converted to practice. In this section we review some of the work that is applicable to designing socially translucent systems and describe a prototype system that we have implemented that illustrates a socially translucent approach to supporting conversational activity. In the final section we discuss some of the research issues that remain to be addressed.

15.4.1 Making Activity Visible

While the perspective we've developed—social translucence—is unique, we are certainly by no means the first to be concerned with making the activities of users of digital systems visible to others. First, in addition to our architectural examples, there are a number of ethnographic studies of physical workplaces such as transportation control rooms (Heath and Luff 1991) and office environments (Bellotti and Bly 1996), which reveal the role of visibility and mutual awareness in supporting coordinated activity. A concern for making other users visible in digital systems dates back to at least the Finger program on UNIX. More recently, a considerable body of work begins with research in video-mediated communication (see Finn et al. 1997 for a collection of work), which has since been generalized and is often referred to under the rubric "awareness" (Dourish and Bellotti 1992; Gutwin et al. 1996). A number of investigators have also explored ways of portraying socially salient information in human computer interfaces. Ackerman and Starr (1995) have argued for the importance of social activity indicators, particularly in synchronous CMC systems. Hill and his colleagues (1992) have discussed the creation of persistent traces of human activity. And a considerable number of researchers have constructed systems that attempt, in various ways, to provide cues about the presence and activity of their users (for example, Benford et al. 1994; Gutwin et al. 1996; Hill et al. 1995; Isaacs et al. 1996).

This raises the question of how social cues might best be portrayed in a digital system. We see three design approaches to answering this question: the realist, the mimetic, and the abstract. The realist approach involves trying to project social information from the physical domain into or through the digital domain. This work is exemplified in teleconferencing systems and media space research; see Finn et al. 1997 for many examples.

The mimetic approach tries to re-represent social cues from the physical world, as literally as possible, in the digital domain. The mimetic approach is exemplified by graphical MUDs and virtual reality systems and uses virtual environments and avatars of various degrees of realism to mimic the physical world. Work here ranges from attempts to implement a virtual physics (such as the work of Benford and his colleagues 1994) to the considerably looser re-presentations of social information found in the 2D and 3D avatars found in various graphical MUDs and 3D VRML worlds.

The abstract approach involves portraying social information in ways that are not closely tied to their physical analogs. Exemplars of the abstract approach include AROMA (Pedersen and Sokoler 1997), the Out to Lunch system (Cohen 1994), which uses abstract sonic cues to indicate socially salient activity, and Chat Circles (Donath et al. 1999), which uses abstract visual representations. This approach also includes the use of text to portray social information. Text has proved surprisingly powerful as a means for conveying social information, as can be seen in studies of MOOs (Bruckman 1997; Cherny 1999) and textual chat rooms (Danet et al. 1998).

While we think all these approaches are promising, we're particularly interested in the abstract approach. First, we believe that systems that attempt to leverage social processes need to be developed through a process of creating and deploying working systems and studying their use in ordinary work contexts. This intent to deploy, in and of itself, is a strike against the realist and mimetic approaches, both of which face substantial pragmatic barriers (for example, expense, infrastructure, support) to deployment outside of research institutions. Second, and more importantly, we believe that the abstract approach has not received sufficient attention from designers and researchers, particularly with respect to graphical representations. Text and simple graphics have many powerful characteristics: They are easy to produce and manipulate; they persist over time, leaving interpretable traces (helpful to those trying to learn the representation); and they enable the use of technologies such as search and visualization engines.

15.4.2 Abstract Representations of Social Information: The Babble Prototype

As the first step toward designing an infrastructure for knowledge communities, our group designed, implemented, and deployed a system intended to provide an environment for supporting smooth, long-running, productive conversations among members of small to medium-sized groups. Here we describe the prototype, called Babble, focusing on the way in which it uses textual and graphical representations to make socially salient information visible (see Erickson et al. 1999 for more information).

15.4.2.1 Portraying Social Information in Babble

In designing Babble, we used two tactics to make social information visible: a persistent textual representation of the conversation and a synchronous representation of the activity of participants.

In Babble, a conversation is represented as a single, persistent document (Figure 15.1). Each comment is preceded by a header that has a time stamp and the participant's name; new comments are appended to the end of the document; and the entire conversation is shown in a single window. This approach is employed by some types of asynchronous bulletin boards, and we believe it has significant advantages over other forms of textual representation. Unlike chat, where conversation is ephemeral, or like mailing lists, where the past becomes buried in message archives, accessing the conversation's history is just a matter of scrolling. This visibility of the conversation's history can support the emergence and enforcement of conversational norms (Erickson 1999).

```
===Friday 12 Dec 97 3:43:44 From: Bill
Hi Steven!
===Friday 12 Dec 97 3:44:49 From: Steven
Hellooo Bill. A little guidance please?
Is the […] summary we're preparing for […]
supposed to be an exercise in feeling
good, or are we supposed to be giving
him hard-headed guidance?
===Friday 12Dec 97 3:56:55 From: Bill
yes :-)
```

FIGURE 15.1   A segment of conversation displayed as a single, shared, persistent document

This type of representation has a number of advantages both for readers and for writers. Readers, whether they are newcomers or simply infrequent participants, can get an overview of social norms that govern a conversation by skimming through it. For example, the length of comments is apparent, as is the informality of the conversation (inferable from the simplified syntax and the absence of punctuation) and degree of humor and politeness. In short, the persistent trace left by textual conversation is a rich source of socially salient information (awareness), and its power is enhanced because participants know that the representation is shared and thus that everyone is privy to the same set of cues (accountability). The persistence of the conversation has consequences for authoring as well. Another important element of this representation is its shared sequential structure: Everyone sees the same order of remarks and can therefore count on that as a resource for structuring their interaction. Thus, participants can and do participate with short, indexical utterances like "Yes!," "Thank you," and "Great idea!" This type of response is less likely to occur in a mailing list where the absence of shared, sequential structure requires participants to quote the message to which they are responding (and because participants are often annoyed at opening a message and finding only an "insignificant" comment in it). While such indexical comments may not extend the conceptual bounds of the conversation, they can make it more convivial and inviting by providing an easy way for participants to signal agreement, encouragement, and empathy.

A novel aspect of Babble is the *social proxy,* a minimalist graphical representation of users that depicts their presence and their activities (Figure 15.2). The social proxy portrays the conversation as a large circle and the participants as colored dots (shown as small numbered circles in the schematic in Figure 15.2), referred to hereafter as marbles. Marbles within the circle are involved in the current conversation; marbles outside the circle represent those who are logged on but are in other conversations. The marbles of those who are active in the current conversation—either talking (typing) or "listening" (interacting via mouse clicks and movements)—are shown near

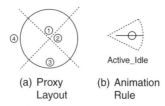

(a) Proxy
Layout

(b) Animation
Rule

FIGURE 15.2 Social proxy schematic. Part (a) shows the layout of the social proxy: Marble 1, 2, and 3, inside the circle, are part of the "current" conversation; marble 4 is in another conversation. Part (b) shows the dot animation: They move abruptly to the center when they are active and slowly drift to the periphery with inactivity. Thus, a tight cluster of dots represents an active conversation.

the circle's center. With inactivity, marbles drift out to the periphery. When people leave the current conversation, their marbles move outside the circle. When they enter the conversation, their marbles move into the circle. When people log onto the system, it creates virtual wedges for their marbles, adjusting the position of all the marbles in the social proxy. When they depart, the wedges are destroyed, and the remaining marbles adjust to uniformly occupy the space. All marble movements are animated, thus making arrivals, movements, and departures visually salient.

Although simple, this social proxy gives a sense of the size of the audience and the amount of conversational activity, as well as indicating whether people are gathering or dispersing and who is coming and going. Also, because the portrayal is graphical, it has a perceptual directness (like the glass window) that a list of written names lacks. Experientially, the social proxy is interesting because it focuses attention on the group as a whole and the coherence (or lack thereof) of its activity.

15.4.2.2 Social Activity in Babble

As of this writing, Babble has been in daily use by its implementers for two years and has been deployed to about eight other groups who have used it for periods of two to six months. Most (though not all) deployments have been to relatively small groups in which most of the members know one another. Babble has proved to be an effective environment for supporting informal group conversations, on a wide range of topics. Here we describe a few of the observed social phenomena that are most relevant to the knowledge communities' vision (see Bradner et al. 1999 for a broader and deeper discussion of usage and adoption issues observed in six deployments).

One social practice we've observed is waylaying, in which a user watches for a particular person to become active on Babble (signaled by the movement of their marble into the center of the social proxy, and then initiates a conversation via private chat, telephone, or other means. Because the movement of the marble occurs when the user has just begun an episode of typing or mousing, it indicates a opportune moment for contact (since the user's attention has just shifted to communication with the group). Waylay is used for purposes ranging from asking questions to initiating casual social chat.

Babble also supports the maintenence of group awareness. For example, when members of a Babble travel, many report reading through conversations that occurred in their absence to "find out what happened." For someone who is a member of the group and understands the context, seemingly trivial comments can convey considerable information about what's going on at the individual, group and organizational levels. Thus, a signoff, "I have to go to the [project] meeting now," reveals that one participant is still involved in a particular project, and a question, "Does anyone know how to do a screen capture," indicates that another participant is beginning to write a paper.

Babble was typically regarded as a semiprivate place, and conversations were often frank and unguarded, since they were produced for a small and well-known audience that shared considerable context. This became apparent when "strangers" (visitors, new members, or, in one case, an unannounced conversational software agent) appeared in various Babbles, their presence and activities being displayed in the social proxy (awareness) along with those of the regulars. In each case, the appearance of strangers provoked concern about how unguarded conversations might be interpreted by those from different contexts (accountability). Sometimes this led to the creation of rules for how new members were admitted into a Babble or for what areas of a group's Babble were appropriate to demonstrate to outsiders.

While one should be cautious about generalizing from a few experiences, these results are not at variance with what has been observed in other online systems (for examples see Bruckman and Resnick 1995; Cherny 1999). In general, we regard Babble as an existence proof that textual and graphical representations of social information can provide a foundation for rich social interaction.

15.5   Some Research Issues

Coming at the design of digital systems from the perspective of social translucence raises a huge number of questions. In this section we describe some of the issues that seem of greatest importance to us with respect to the design of knowledge communities. We do not presume to map out the entire terrain.

15.5.1   Social Proxies: What Should Be Represented?

While the Babble social proxy is simple, we think the concept is promising and can see a variety of ways to extend its scope. The dimensions of this problem include the people and activities represented in the proxy, the spatial scope of the proxy, and the temporal scope of the proxy. For example, in the Babble prototype we show the participants in public conversations, but we do not show who is participating in the private one-to-one chats that the system also supports, or even whether a private chat is taking place. On the one hand, an argument in favor of making private chats visible is that it might increase awareness of the feature and cause others to take up its use. In addition, it can be argued that—just as in shared physical spaces—seeing that two people are chatting (without knowing what is said) can convey useful information without necessarily infringing on their privacy. On the other hand, it is easy to generate negative scenarios. We simply wish to suggest that the tradeoffs are not well understood and that neither a blindly optimistic approach of making everything visible nor a trenchantly pessimistic approach of putting privacy above all else is particularly useful. One approach might be to explore ways of making it evident to all participants which of their actions are visible. This is something that we tend to understand pretty well for physical space but that is not clear how to do effectively in digital systems.

The spatial and temporal scope of the social proxy is another issue. Babble currently shows the synchronous activity of only those participants in the conversation being viewed. Obviously, it could be useful to have a view of several conversations, or the entire knowledge community, so that one could notice activity elsewhere. For example, a community proxy (Figure 15.3) could depict the global structure of a knowledge community, showing the number of topics and the distribution of activity across them. Community members, with an understanding of the semantics of the structure, could make inferences about the meaning of clusters of participants and the distribution of new information.

Similarly, it might be useful to provide a diachronic (longitudinal) view of a conversation. Even in a conversation where people are never simultaneously present, it still makes a difference whether 50 people check in every day or only one person

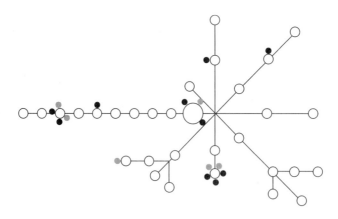

FIGURE 15.3   A social proxy showing the global structure of a knowledge community. Larger circles represent conversation topics, with filled circles indicating new information, and smaller dots represent participants.

checks in every month. In the former case, there will be a lot of social motivation for people to contribute. In the latter, there will be little. Such a proxy could show arrivals and departures, flurries of conversation, and dialog patterns, even in conversations where two people are never simultaneously present. Figure 15.4 shows two examples of diachronic social proxies: The one on the left is based on the model of a ticker tape, with each row representing the activity of an individual (a line indicates presence; a blip indicates speaking) that provides a visualization of global activity across the day (notice the system crash at 10:30 A.M.). The proxy on the right is a schematic of a Babble-like social proxy in which the marbles leave contrails that gradually fade out. This provides a different view of activity over time within a conversation. In the contrail proxy we can see that although dots 1 and 2 are both active, 2 is a recent arrival. Similarly, we see dot 3 has recently gone idle, whereas dot 4 has been inactive for a longer period. These proxies represent two ways of broadening what Johnson-Lenz (1991) refers to as the "rolling present," the time that constitutes the "now" of a particular interaction. Each of the diachronic proxies makes certain things more or less visible. Thus, for example, the tickertape proxy makes it easy to assess who logs on earliest. Similarly, the "contrail" social proxy makes it easy to see who has recently attended to a particular conversation. In both cases, this information could be used to positive or negative ends, and its presence will likely shape interactions in unexpected ways.

15.5.2 Supporting Coherent Activity

One of the problems with online interaction is that it is often characterized by incoherence and drift (Herring 1999). However, this is not necessarily the case. Erickson (1999) presents a case study of an online limerick-making game among several dozen people that, over the course of a year, succeeded in repeatedly producing coherent results. The coherence of the interaction in question was facilitated by a set of rules

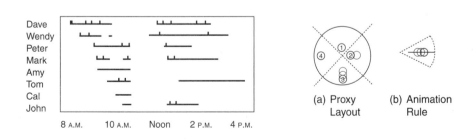

FIGURE 15.4 Two examples of a diachronic (longitudinal) social proxy. The one on the left is modeled after a ticker tape with lines indicating presence and blips indicating talk; the other is a "contrail" proxy in which the dots leave ephemeral trails.

that were shared and mutually enforced by the participants (for example, only one line could be added by a participant at a time). In addition, as the interaction proceeded, new conventions evolved to govern their interactions (for example, the person who completes a limerick is obligated to start the next one). While the case described is unusual in several respects, one important factor is that the combination of the system's interface and the nature of the interaction resulted in many of the conventions being highly visible. That is, when people violated one of the conventions that structured the conversation (such as adding two lines at once), the violation was visible as an interruption in a spatial patterning of text. Because the violation was visible both to the violator and to the other participants, it increased awareness and accountability.

This raises the question of whether social proxies (and other means of portraying social information) might be useful as a way of representing the conventions of an interaction and allowing their enforcement by the participants. For example, the circular form of the Babble version of the social proxy implies an open conversation in which all are allowed to participate. One might redesign the social proxy to make visible the constraints that define different styles of interaction, such as a lecture (Figure 15.5). The "lecture" social proxy is designed in both form and animation dynamics, so when a lecture is proceeding as it ought, it appears well formed. The idea is that a dot is gradually moved toward the apex of the proxy as a function of cumulative talking, so that normally one dot (the lecturer) is all the way at the front, and all the other dots (the audience) are arrayed at the back. However, if the interaction begins to depart from the norm (for example, with multiple members of the audience talking), the proxy will begin to look out of balance, thus supporting awareness and accountability.

15.5.3 Visualizing Conversation

Given a knowledge community that supports fluent conversation, it will very quickly produce a nearly impenetrable mass of text (as the Babble system has). While experienced users may perhaps have some success in navigating it, newcomers or visitors are likely to be overwhelmed. This problem is exacerbated by the fact that the nature of online conversation includes a more casual approach to spelling, abbreviation, and

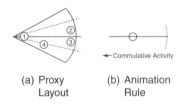

(a) Proxy
Layout

(b) Animation
Rule

FIGURE 15.5   A schematic of a "lecture" social proxy, in which dots move toward the apex of the wedge with cumulative activity

acronyms, thus limiting the usefulness of conventional search techniques. Thus, we see a need for mechanisms that support the visualization of conversation.

Conversations have considerable structure. They vary in their numbers of participants, patterns of participation, dynamics (like the degree of asynchrony), and duration. Contributions may vary in length and formality. Some conversations may be composed primarily of rapid-fire, near synchronous exchanges of short utterances among many people, whereas others may be deliberate, slowly paced, dialogs consisting of long, carefully composed remarks. This structure can be exposed through visualizations. A technique as simple as "greeking" the text down to gray lines, showing boundaries between utterances, and providing a time line can provide an overview of the tempo and rhythms of the conversation. To this visualization can be added information about the participants, commonly used words, the size (and fluctuation thereof) of the audience, and so on. Or one might add an overlay for searching: Figure 15.6 shows a simple textual visualization with an overlay of hits in response to a query for several phrases, each hit highlighted with a color corresponding to its search term. Such tools could help a participant harvest conversation so that it could be cleaned up and made publicly available. We believe that representations of this sort are likely to be meaningful to those who participated in the conversations and can provide a useful structure for browsing and navigating old conversations. To date, little work has been done on this topic (see Donath et al. 1999 and Small 1996).

15.5.4 Restructuring Conversation

While visualization is likely to be helpful for those who have participated in conversations, it will be less useful for visitors and new members. For a knowledge community we envision a core of original conversation, around which has accreted a body of more ordered text—a discourse base that supports the reuse of conversationally produced

FIGURE 15.6   A "greeked" conversation visualization with search hits shown

knowledge. There is a need for tools that support what Johnson-Lenz 1991 calls harvesting: the creation of summaries, indices, and other distillations of conversational content. While some such tools exist, most are designed to work on documents and larger textual corpi, whose volume, stricter conventions, and homogeneity of authorship make them quite distinct from conversations. Whether such tools can be adapted to process conversation is a nontrivial research issue.

15.5.5 Organizational Knowledge Spaces

The creation of discourse bases—productive conversations that have been restructured (or have had new elements like summaries, glossaries, and edited paths added on)—is only part of the solution to making the knowledge produced through conversations accessible. There needs to be a way for members of the larger organization, in which the knowledge community is embedded, to browse its discourse bases and discover useful knowledge. This is not just a benefit for those seeking knowledge; it also provides increased visibility and payoffs for those who do the work of producing, adapting, and distilling knowledge. Even so, this leads to the tension between privacy and visibility observed in the Babble prototype. One area to explore is how to create translucent representations of conversations that allow outsiders to see enough to determine if the conversation is relevant without exposing the jokes, camaraderie, and improprieties that characterize relaxed talk among peers. For example, just as the conversational visualization shown in Figure 15.6 showed search hits without revealing the text of the conversation, so might a community-scale social proxy (as in Figure 15.3) be used to reveal the locus and extent of a particular concept being discussed within a knowledge community without revealing the potentially sensitive surround. Given clues that useful knowledge is present, interested parties could *request* summaries of the topic, *petition* for admission to the community, or simply *converse* with some of the community members. Notice how this strategy blends technical and social mechanisms: Technology is used to locate hot spots without revealing the particulars, and social mechanisms are used to control access. Such an approach has at least two benefits: Explicit requests for information provide a way of documenting the value of the knowledge work, and they could also serve as catalysts for restructuring. More generally, this raises the issue of how one might visualize the knowledge space—contents, structure, activity—of an entire organization.

15.6   Conclusion

Let us return to the tale of the door with the glass window. Although we have focused on designing systems for communication and collaboration, the contrast between the opaque door with its sign and the door with its glass window seems an apt metaphor for a very general problem with technological systems today. In the first case, the system creates a barrier between users. The remedy requires that they do extra work—noticing the sign, interpreting its words, and adjusting their actions just in case. In the second case, the system reveals the presence of those using it, enabling already-established social rules and mechanisms to come smoothly into play.

From our perspective, the digital world appears to be populated by technologies that impose walls between people, rather than by technologies that create windows between them. We suggest that understanding how to design digital systems so that they mesh with human behavior at the individual and collective levels is of immense importance. By allowing users to "see" one another, to make inferences about the activities of others, to imitate one another, we believe that digital systems can become environments in which new social forms can be invented, adopted, adapted, and propagated—eventually supporting the same sort of social innovation and diversity that can be observed in physically based cultures.

Acknowledgments

This work is highly collaborative. Thanks to our colleagues at IBM: David N. Smith for creating the Babble prototype; Mark Laff and Amy Katriel for implementations of the social proxy and Java client; Cal Swart for supporting Babble deployments; and all the members of the Niche Networking and Social Computing groups for conversation, inspiration, and general support. This work also benefited from the efforts of our 1998 summer interns, Erin Bradner who led the deployment studies, and Jason Ellis who designed a number of provocative prototypes, including the lecture social proxy. Thanks to Amy Bruckman, Saul Greenberg, Michael Muller, Charles Taliaferro, and several anonymous reviewers for comments on this work.

References

Ackerman, M.S. and Starr, B. (1995). Social activity indicators: Interface components for CSCW systems. *Proceedings of the ACM Symposium on User Interface Software and Technology* (UIST'95), 159–168. New York: ACM.

Alexander, C., Ishikawa, S., Silverstein, M., Jacobson, M., Fiksdahl-King, I., and Angel, S. (1977). *A pattern language.* New York: Oxford University Press.

Bellotti, V. and Bly, S. (1996). Walking away from the desktop computer: Distributed collaboration in a product design team. *Proceedings of the ACM Conference on Computer-Supported Cooperative Work,* 209–218. New York: ACM Press.

Benford, S., Bowers, J., Fahlen, L., Mariani, J., and Rodden, T. (1994). Supporting cooperative work in virtual environments. *The Computer Journal,* 37, 8, 653–668.

Bradner, E., Kellogg, W.A. and Erickson, T. (1999). The adoption and use of Babble: A field study of chat in the workplace. *Proceedings of the Sixth European Conference on Computer-Supported Cooperative Work,* 139–158. Dordrecht: Kluwer Academic Publishers.

Bruckman, A., and Resnick, M. (1995). The MEDIAMOO project: Constructionism and professional community. *Convergence,* 1, 1, 94–109.

Bruckman, A. (1997). *Moose crossing: Construction, community, and learning in a networked world for kids.* Ph.D. dissertation, Massachusetts Institute of Technology.

Cohen, J. (1994). Monitoring background activities. In G. Kramer (Ed.), *Auditory display,* 439–531. Reading, MA: Addison-Wesley.

Cherny, L. (1999). *Conversation and community: Chat in a virtual world.* Stanford, CA: CSLI Publications.

Clark, H.H. (1996). *Using language.* Cambridge: Cambridge University Press.

Danet, B. Ruedenberg, L., and Rosenbaum-Tamari, Y. (1998). Hmmm . . . where's that smoke coming from?—Writing, play and performance on Internet Relay Chat. In F. Sudweeks, M. McLaughlin, and Rafaeli (Eds.), *Network & Netplay: Virtual Groups on the Internet,* 41–76. Menlo Park, CA: AAAI Press.

Donath, J., Karahalios, K., and Viegas, F. (1999). Visualizing conversation. In J.F. Nunamaker, Jr., and R.H. Sprague, Jr. (Eds.), *Proceedings of the Thirty-Second Hawaii International Conference on Systems Science.* Los Alamitos, CA: IEEE Computer Society Press.

Dourish, P., and Bellotti, V. (1992). Awareness and coordination in shared workspaces. *Proceedings of the Conference on Computer-Supported Cooperative Work,* 107–114. New York: ACM Press.

Erickson, T. (1999) Rhyme and punishment: The creation and enforcement of conventions in an on-line participatory limerick genre. In J.F. Nunamaker, Jr., and R.H. Sprague, Jr. (Eds.), *Proceedings of the Thirty-Second Hawaii International Conference on Systems Science.* Los Alamitos, CA: IEEE Computer Society Press.

Erickson, T., Smith, D.N., Kellogg, W.A., Laff, M.R., Richards, J.T., and Bradner, E. (1999). Socially translucent systems: Social proxies, persistent conversation, and the design of Babble. *Human Factors in Computing Systems: The Proceedings of CHI'99,* 72–79. New York: ACM Press.

Finn, K.E., Sellen, A.J., and Wilbur, S.B. (1997). *Video-mediated communication.* Mahwah, NJ: Lawrence Erlbaum Associates.

Gehl, Jan. (1980). *Life between buildings: Using public space.* New York: Van Nostrand Reinhold.

Goffman, E. (1963). *Behavior in public places: Notes on the social organization of gatherings.* New York: Macmillan Publishing Co.

Goffman, E. (1967). *Interaction ritual.* New York: Anchor Books.

Grudin, J. (1989). Why groupware applications fail: Problems in design and evaluation. *Office: Technology and People,* 4, 3, 245–264.

Gutwin, C., Greenberg, S., and Roseman, M. (1996). Workspace awareness in real-time distributed groupware: Framework, widgets, and evaluation. In R.J. Sasse, A. Cunningham, and R. Winder, (Eds.), *People and Computers XI (Proceedings of the HCI'96),* 281–298. Springer-Verlag.

Heath, C.C., and Luff, P. (1991). Collaborative activity and technological design: Task coordination in London underground control rooms. *Proceedings of the Second European Conference on Computer-Supported Cooperative Work,* 65–80. Dordrecht: Kluwer Academic Publishers.

Herring, S. (1999). Coherence in CMC. In J.F. Nunamaker, Jr., and R.H. Sprague, Jr. (Eds.), *Proceedings of the Thirty-Second Hawaii International Conference on Systems Science,* 8. Los Alamitos, CA: IEEE Computer Society Press.

Hill, W., Hollan, J.D., Wroblewski, D., and McCandless, T. (1992). Edit wear and read wear: Text and hypertext. *Proceedings of ACM CHI'92 Conference on Human Factors in Computing Systems,* 3–9.

Hill, W., Stead, L., Rosenstein, M., and Furnas, G. (1995). Recommending and evaluating choices in a virtual community of use. *Human Factors in Computing Systems: CHI'92 Conference Proceedings,* 194–201. New York: ACM Press.

Isaacs, E.A., Tang, J.C., and Morris, T. (1996). Piazza: A desktop environment supporting impromptu and planned interactions. In M.S. Ackerman (Ed.), *Proceedings of the ACM 1996 Conference on Computer Supported Cooperative Work,* 315–324. New York: ACM Press.

Jacobs, J. (1961). *The death and life of great American cities.* New York: Random House.

Johnson-Lenz, P., and Johnson-Lenz, T. (1991). Post-mechanistic groupware primitives: Rhythms, boundaries, and containers. *International Journal of Man-Machine Studies,* 34, 395–417.

Kendon, A. (1990). *Conducting interaction: Patterns of behavior in focused encounters.* Cambridge, MA: Cambridge University Press.

Lynch, K. (1990). In T. Banerjee and M. Southworth (Eds.), *City sense and city design: Writings and Projects of Kevin Lynch.* Cambridge, MA: MIT Press.

Pedersen, E.R., and Sokoler, T. (1997). AROMA: Abstract representation of presence supporting mutual awareness. *Human Factors in Computing Systems: CHI'97 Conference Proceedings,* 51–58. New York: ACM Press.

Small, D. (1996). Navigating large bodies of text. *IBM Systems Journal,* 35, 3 & 4, 515–525.

Whyte, W.H. (1988). *City: Return to the center.* New York: Anchor Books.

16

Transcending the Individual Human Mind: Creating Shared Understanding through Collaborative Design

Ernesto G. Arias
Hal Eden
Gerhard Fischer
Andrew Gorman
Eric Scharff

16.1 Introduction

Human-computer interaction (HCI) research over the last 20 years has made fundamental contributions to the creation of new paradigms for working, learning, and collaborating in the information age. Its major emphasis has been to develop new technologies, interaction techniques, and design approaches as well as to pioneer socio-technical approaches. In the process, HCI work has progressed from early concerns with low-level computer issues to a focus on people's tasks (Myers 1998; Newell and Card 1985).

Yet, at the threshold of a new millennium, we, along with others, claim that the next major challenges are to move beyond individual task orientation to support for the process of grappling with complex design problems (Landauer 1995). Such problems require more knowledge than any single person possesses because the knowledge relevant to either frame or resolve it is usually distributed among stakeholders. In this context, we claim that bringing different and often controversial points of view together to create a shared understanding among these stakeholders can lead to new insights, ideas, and artifacts. New media that allow owners of problems to contribute to framing and resolving complex design problems can extend the power of the individual human mind.

This chapter (based on Arias et al. 2000b) first identifies a set of challenging problems for HCI based on our past work and study. It then describes our approach to address these challenges by focusing on the Envisionment and Discovery Collaboratory (EDC) as an integrated physical and computational environment and argues that such HCI environment can address some of these challenges by exploiting such concepts as the "symmetry of ignorance" (Rittel 1984). A scenario is introduced that illustrates the current features of the EDC in a specific problem context, which grounds the discussion of the conceptual framework and the specific substrates of the EDC. The chapter then describes how our interaction with user communities has guided us in the assessment and iterative design of the EDC and concludes by articulating some of the many remaining challenges of this approach for HCI in the future.

16.2   Challenging Problems for the Future of Human-Computer Interaction

16.2.1 Transcending the Individual Human Mind

Although the contribution of the individual is critical and the capabilities of the unaided human mind are impressive, cognitive limits often require the use of external artifacts to augment our abilities. As the pace and scope of knowledge continues to expand, the ability of the individual to grasp all aspects of a problem becomes more difficult: the Renaissance scholar no longer exists. Although creative individuals are often thought of as working in isolation, the role of interaction and collaboration with other individuals is critical (Engelbart 1995). Creative activity grows out of the relationship between an individual and the world of his or her work, and from the ties between an individual and other human beings.

Distributed cognition (Norman 1993) emphasizes that the heart of intelligent human performance is not the individual human mind in isolation but the interaction of the mind with tools and artifacts as well as groups of minds in interaction with each other. When a domain reaches a point at which the knowledge for skillful professional practice cannot be acquired in a decade, specialization increases, collaboration becomes a necessity, and practitioners rely on the expertise of others (Galegher et al 1990; Resnick et al. 1991) by making increasing use of artifacts that support distributed cognition such as textbooks, standards, legal constraints, and especially examples from previous practice.

Design (Simon 1996) is a prime example of such a domain. The large and growing discrepancy between the amount of such relevant knowledge and the amount any one designer can possibly remember imposes a limit on progress in design. Overcoming this limit is a central challenge for developers of systems that support collaborative design.

16.2.2 Exploiting the Symmetry of Ignorance

Complexity in design arises from the need to synthesize different perspectives of a problem, manage large amounts of information relevant to a design task, and understand the design decisions that have determined the long-term evolution of a designed artifact. Design problems are wicked (that is, ill defined and ill structured; Rittel and Webber 1984). They are moving targets that have resolutions rather than solutions (Arias and Schneider 1999), and the context in which these problems exist is by nature characterized by change, conflict, and multiple stakeholders (Arias 1995). In many cases, consensus is not achievable, and the best we can strive for is informed compromises emerging from *the symmetry of ignorance* (Rittel 1984)— different aspects of knowledge crucial to the resolution of the problem carried in the minds of individual stakeholders as tacit knowledge. For example, this symmetry might represent different descriptions of the world or reasons behind conflicting arguments and goals among differing agendas in complex design problems.

Rather than viewing the symmetry of ignorance as an obstacle during design, we view it as an opportunity for the creation of new knowledge and new ideas (as observed by C.P. Snow (1993): "The clashing point of two subjects, two disciplines, two cultures ought to produce creative chaos." Having different viewpoints helps one discover alternatives and can help uncover tacit aspects of problems.

Exploiting the symmetry of ignorance requires putting owners of problems in charge (Fischer 1994), which will promote direct and meaningful interaction that involves people in decisions that affect them (Arias 1996). In order to bring important perspectives to the process of design, all stakeholders in the process should be designers and co-developers, not just consumers (Fischer 1998). End-users, as owners of problems, bring perspectives to collaborative design activities that are of special importance for framing problems.

16.2.3 Recognizing the Need for Externalizations in Collaborative Design

The existence of the symmetry of ignorance requires creating spaces and places that serve as *boundary objects* (shared objects to *talk about* and to *think with*) where different cultures can meet and collaborate. Boundary objects serve as externalizations (Bruner 1996) that capture distinct domains of human knowledge. They have the potential to lead to an increase in socially shared cognition and practice (Resnick et al. 1991).

When distributed cognition is at work between an individual human mind and artifacts (such as an address book, a system of e-mail folders, or a file system), it often functions well because the knowledge an individual needs is implicitly distributed between her/his head and the those artifacts. However, in the case of distributed cognition among members of a group, the group has no head, no place for the implicit information about the distribution of knowledge to be available to all members—

therefore externalizations are critically more important for collaborative design. Externalizations (1) create a more complete record of our mental efforts, one that is "outside us" rather than vaguely in memory and (2) represent artifacts that can talk back to us (Schön 1992) and form the basis for critique and negotiation.

Externalizations are used to extend our cognitive abilities (Engelbart 1995; Norman 1993) by allowing all stakeholders to engage in a "conversation with the materials" (Schön 1992). Our research has demonstrated that these "conversations" are very different in physical versus computational environments (Arias et al. 1997). There is a growing interest in blending real-world artifacts with computational media (Eisenberg and Makay 1996; Ishii and Ullmer 1997). Frequently, the design of interactive systems focuses *exclusively* on the capabilities provided by the dynamic nature of computational media. Yet physical models provide certain strengths not found in computational models. Rather than viewing this as a dichotomy—where one must choose between one or the other—HCI needs to explore the creation of combined physical and computational environments that use the strengths of each to augment the weaknesses of the other.

16.2.4 Supporting New Forms of Civic Discourse: From Access to Informed Participation

Another fundamental challenge for HCI in the next millennium is to invent and design a culture in which humans can express themselves and engage in personally meaningful activities. However, a large number of the new media are designed to see humans as consumers only (Fischer 1998). A prominent example of a consumer perspective was articulated by the director of research for Time Warner Entertainment in his closing plenary address at CHI'95. He challenged the HCI community with the task of designing a remote control to browse and efficiently select 500 or more TV channels. Solving this problem is of great commercial interest to industries that regard humans as the ultimate consumers—but is it a focal issue for HCI?

This emphasis on people as consumers is perpetuated in other perceptions of the future as well. The President's Information Technology Advisory Committee's report includes the call that "The Nation must ensure that *access* (italics ours) to the benefits of the information infrastructure are available to everyone in our Nation" [PITAC 1999, p. 10]. While the universality of this vision is important, our claim is that more than *just* access is needed. An example of this broader vision was set forth by the President's Council on Sustainable Development.

> How can more than 261 million individual Americans define and reconcile their needs and aspirations with community values and the needs of the future? Our most important finding is the potential power of and growing desire for decision processes that promote direct and meaningful interaction involving people in decisions that affect them. **Americans want to take control of their lives.** [PCSD 1996, p. 7]

The Council substantiates an increasing trend toward grass-roots, bottom-up efforts to address the impacts of growth (or decline) on the quality of life in U.S. communities. The nature and intensity of these impacts require difficult decisions on how to sustainably manage such growth in the future.

The broad challenge, then, is to move toward and support new forms of *citizen participation* (Arias et al 2000a). Certainly this challenge is not without its difficulties, such as (1) the paradox that citizens cannot really be informed unless they participate, yet they cannot really participate unless they are informed (Brown et al 1994); and (2) that participation has limits that are contingent on the nature of each citizen's situation, the issues, the problems, and the institutional designs (Arias 1989), as well as the available technology and media. One benefit of addressing these challenges is that informed participation leads to *ownership* and a stronger sense of community.

The challenge to the HCI community is to move beyond an emphasis on interaction that is solely focused on information access to one that supports *informed participation*. This rests on the premise that one of the major roles for computational media is not merely to deliver existing and predigested information to individuals but to provide the opportunity and resources for design activities embedded in social debates and discussions in which all people can choose to act as designers rather than being confined to consumer roles.

16.2.5 Moving beyond Closed Systems

If HCI systems are to effectively support collaborative design, they must adequately address not only the problem situations, but also the collaborative activity surrounding the problem. By addressing real-world problems, the system must cope with problem contexts that change over time. In addition to the fluid nature of the problems themselves, the very process of collaboration among stakeholders further increases the ever-changing nature of the problem context. Designing systems to support the constantly evolving problem context as the collaborators work to understand, frame, and address it is an important challenge. Providing *closed systems* with the essential functionality fixed when the system is designed is inadequate for coping with such dynamic problem contexts because many of the issues come out only when a system is used.

Therefore, providing *open systems* with opportunities for significant changes to the system at all levels of complexity is an essential part of supporting collaborative design. By creating these opportunities, the owners of the problems can be involved in the formulation and evolution of those problems through the system. The challenge for these open systems is to provide for extension and modification that are appropriate for the people who need to make changes. This is based on the following principles.

- *Software systems must evolve; they cannot be completely designed prior to use.* System developers cannot anticipate and design for every possible situation. We have discussed this process model for evolution in greater detail previously (Fischer and Scharff 1998).

- *Systems must evolve at the hands of the users.* Giving the *owners* of problems the ability to change systems as they explore their problem leverages the insight into problems that uniquely belongs to those experiencing the problems. Although previous research has explored the notion of end-user programming (Nardi 1993), a broader perspective, which we call end-user modification, is necessary to evolve systems.

- *Systems must be designed for evolution.* Extending an application in an initially closed design may be difficult because of the assumptions implicit in a system designed without extension in mind. A closed system with some extension capabilities will likely restrict what can and can't change. Designing a system for evolution from the ground up, however, can provide a context in which change is expected and can take place.

- *Evolution of systems must take place in a distributed manner.* Systems must acknowledge the fact that users will be distributed both in space and in time. Distributed systems provide a framework for evolution in which all participants have the chance to contribute in a manner appropriate to their ability.

16.2.6 Understanding Motivation and Rewards

Computational support mechanisms are necessary prerequisites but not sufficient conditions to motivate people to become part of a "design culture." People must be motivated and rewarded for investing time and effort to become knowledgeable enough to act as designers. These rewards may range from feeling in control, being able to solve or contribute to the solution of a problem, fulfillment of a passion to master a tool in greater depth, making an ego-satisfying contribution to a group, and/or being a good citizen within a community (Grudin 1994). Motivation is in turn contingent on the nature of the individual's competencies (intellectual, economic, physiological) and needs (the need to learn, socialize, or work), driving the ways in which systems are used: This is therefore central to open systems design since change and evolution takes place through use.

16.2.7 Summary of Challenging Problems for the Future of Human-Computer Interaction

The challenges identified above should be integrated into future HCI agendas. These challenges are opportunities to develop innovative information technologies to support collaborative design and learning in domains characterized by complex problems by providing a basis for understanding *how* and *why* to do the following.

- Support distributed cognition in order to transcend the individual human mind

- Exploit the symmetry of ignorance by constructing shared understanding
- Utilize externalizations to extend our cognitive abilities
- Introduce and support the notion of informed participation because access, although necessary, is not sufficient
- Move beyond closed systems to support open, evolving contexts of complex design problems
- Understand the motivations and rewards necessary to engage people in a design culture

These challenges shift future development away from the computer as the focal point toward efforts that improve our understanding of the human, social, and cultural systems that create the context for use (Greenbaum and Kyng 1991). This vision and its conceptual understanding have guided us in the development behind an integrated environment for learning and design in which users discover and frame problems and construct new visions.

16.3   The Envisionment and Discovery Collaboratory (EDC)

To create a context for our study of shared understanding and informed participation as ways to transcend the individual human mind, our work has centered on developing the EDC as a research prototype. The EDC is a convergence of various systems (as shown in Figure 16.1) to create an integrated environment capable of addressing the following specific challenges: (1) How can we bring a variety of aspects (social, cultural, physical, virtual) together to support the creation of shared understanding (Resnick et al. 1991)? (2) How we can create co-evolutionary environments, in which stakeholders change because they learn, and in which systems change because stakeholders become co-developers and engage in end-user modification and programming (Mackay 1992)? (3) How can we create intrinsically motivating computational environments and open systems, in which stakeholders feel in control and accept the role of active contributors rather than passive consumer (Fischer 1998)? (4) How can stakeholders incrementally construct domain models that do not exist a priori but instead are socially constructed over time by communities of practice (Lave 1988)?

Figure 16.2 shows the current realization of the EDC environment. By using a horizontal electronic whiteboard (referred to in the scenario as the *action space*), participants work "around the table," incrementally creating a shared model of the problem. They interact with computer simulations by manipulating the three-dimensional, physical objects that constitute a language for the domain (Arias 1996; Ehn 1988). The position and movement of these physical objects are recognized by means of the touch-sensitive projection surface. In Figure 16.1, users are constructing a neighborhood through the use of a physical language appropriate for the problem by placing

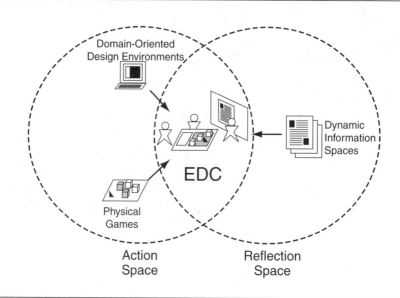

FIGURE 16.1 The EDC as a convergence of systems

FIGURE 16.2 The current prototype of the EDC

objects in the action space. This construction is a description of the setting of concern to the stakeholders and becomes the object through which they can collaboratively evaluate and prescribe changes in their efforts to frame and resolve a problem. In the upper half of Figure 16.1, a second vertical electronic whiteboard (dubbed the *reflection space*) presents information related to the problem-at-hand for exploration and extension. In the figure, a user is filling out a survey constructed from the model presented in the action space. The results of this survey are stored (for future exploration) and are also fed to the simulation, where the ramifications of the decisions specified in the survey can be explored.

16.3.1 A Scenario: Creating Shared Understanding Through Collaborative Design

The most mature EDC prototype application is one developed to support citizens in designing a transportation system for their neighborhood. Although this prototype has not yet been used in a real world setting, its design has been shaped by the feedback we have received during participatory design (Ehn and Löwgren 1997) and demonstration sessions with transportation domain experts, community activists, and peers within the HCI community. We describe in the following scenario, based on actual problem situations in the City of Boulder, how the EDC could be used across multiple design sessions to support citizens in planning a new bus route to service their community. In doing so, we will focus on three important facets of the EDC: (1) how participants interact with the system, (2) how they explore complex design problems, and (3) how they collaboratively construct new knowledge and incrementally create a shared understanding as they frame and resolve these problems.

16.3.1.1 A Neighborhood's Transportation Needs

Traffic and parking have become major problems in and around the city. A local neighborhood group, recognizing their area's contribution to the overall situation, has approached the city transportation planners to develop alternative transportation solutions. Current low-frequency bus routes have had little impact other than to generate comment that the large buses are frequently empty. To study the problem and to open a broader dialog with the neighbors, city planners convene an open meeting of various stakeholders (the concerned neighbors, transportation planners, and other city officials) using the EDC Urban-Planning application.

16.3.1.2 Creating a Language of Objects and Interacting with the System

The EDC Urban-Planning application uses a model and language that allows users to interact with various phenomena relevant to transportation planning. Objects in the system have both physical and computational representations. The physical objects represent language elements from the problem domain—in this setting, a language of colored blocks represents elements important to land use and transportation, such as residences, schools, shopping centers, parks, roads, buses, cars, and bus stops. These are linked to their computational representations through the EDC. The behavior and attributes of the language elements are represented in the computational objects, which can be defined or modified using an end-user, visual programming substrate.

This specific model, previously seeded by a collaboration of domain experts and citizens and evolved through actual use, simulates the dynamics of a bus route and contains specific information pertinent to the City of Boulder, such as population density, walking distances to bus stops, and waiting times. In this way the system is seeded with domain knowledge that will help guide the citizens as they explore transportation issues in their neighborhood. The seed provided will continue to grow and evolve at the hands of the citizens through its use.

The stakeholders begin framing the problem context—collaboratively constructing a description of their neighborhood by placing appropriate physical pieces on the interaction surface. The participants select from a palette of language objects describing elements of their neighborhood, and the touch-sensitive surface recognizes the location of the objects as they are placed. When neighbors place these physical objects on the action space board, the EDC creates a computer representation, which instantiates the object's behavior and default attributes (see Figure 16.3, top). The neighbors then create roads to connect the different elements of their neighborhood. In this example, a road has behavior that automatically adds curves and intersections as necessary (see Figure 16.3, bottom).

16.3.1.3 Exploring Complex Problems

In addition to group construction, the EDC supports collaborative problem solving. Once the model is built, the neighbors indicate how they travel to various destinations by using electronic markers to connect homes, schools, and shopping centers (see Figure 16.4). This allows them to identify where transportation demands are heaviest and lightest and guides informed decisions regarding bus route placement. After the bus route is in place, the EDC's computational model simulates the behavior of the constructed bus system. This provides a dynamic view of the situation—the simulation shows how the model behaves (for example, the neighbors see how the bus *travels* along the route)—situated in a real task that the participants encounter. The resolution grows out of the shared understanding that emerges as neighbors begin to better understand each other's perspectives regarding the neighborhood as they construct the model from *their* own understanding of *their* neighborhood. This is important because each participant may come to the table with different, often tacit (Polanyi 1966) concepts about the neighborhood.

The EDC stores existing constructions so that they can later be retrieved. For example, transportation planners discover that a particular bus route is underutilized, so they set a meeting to solicit input from the community to see if bus stops can be better placed to increase the utilization of the route. To start the design session, the participating citizens focus on the neighborhood in question by selecting the proper section from an orthographic map (see Figure 16.5), which serves as the retrieval mechanism for existing constructions as well as a concrete context during the design session.

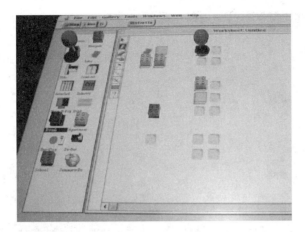

FIGURE 16.3   Constructing the meaning of a neighborhood "around the table." Stakeholders collaboratively describe the problem setting by placing objects (top) and drawing roads (bottom) in the action space that represents their neighborhood.

In this particular simulation the neighbors have modeled the use of the bus system for people traveling to school. The simulation presents different forms of information that may be important in understanding the transportation system. For example, the bus color represents whether it is empty (green), full (red), or in between. By using the "walking distance" tool from the palette, a neighbor concerned that her work-place may be too far from the bus stop sees that, in fact, her office is more than a five-minute walk from the stop. The five-minute walking radius is represented by the "X" marks (see Figure 16.6). She moves the bus closer to the center of the industrial park so that its five-minute radius better covers the area.

Continuing the simulation, another participant notices that the bus remains green most of the time, indicating that the bus is underutilized. After studying the model, he realizes that there is no bus stop serving the major residential area of the neighborhood. The neighbors discuss the problem and agree on a location for a new bus stop to service

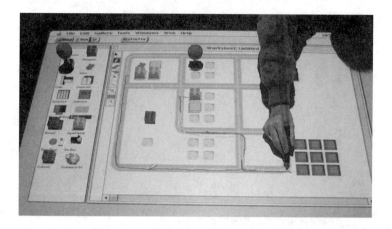

FIGURE 16.4 Making tacit travel preferences explicit to reach informed compromises

the residential area. When they add the bus stop to the model, the EDC automatically generates and displays a Web-based survey contextualized to the area in the reflection space, which solicits ridership behavior data from the participants (see Figure 16.7).

The group discusses the survey and answers the questions in a way that best represents their behavior (for example, they specify how long they will wait for the bus in various situations). The ridership behavior data collected by the survey is then used

FIGURE 16.5 Retrieving constructions from the reflection space to contextualize the design problem in the action space

FIGURE 16.6 Presenting information. In the action space, the bus (circled item, center bottom) and X's surrounding the bus stop (lower right) are visualized using color in the simulation (for publication, these have been accentuated for clarity)

to parameterize the simulation with the neighbors' preferences. While the simulation runs, each bus stop keeps track of how often the bus arrives. If the bus does not arrive often enough, based on the survey information, then people waiting at the bus stop will drive their cars instead of using the bus.

16.3.1.4 Learning on Demand

As cars begin to emerge in the simulation, the EDC displays information about this event in the reflection space. This signals a breakdown in the constructed model (people are not using the bus because it is not arriving frequently enough to suit their needs). The structure of the reflection space provides an avenue for the neighbors to explore and to reflect upon the ramifications of the design choices that they have made in the action space (see Figure 16.8). This is a form of critiquing, linking relevant information to the current breakdown. In the reflection space they see a brief description of the issue, grounding their reflection to the emergent phenomena observed in the action space.

Next, the group explores and learns about the facts supporting different sides of the issue. One of the neighbors points out that increased car use can lead to increased air pollution. She supports her argument with the information she finds in the reflection space. Another participant stresses the convenience and flexibility of taking her car to work. If the buses arrived more frequently, she might consider taking the bus more

FIGURE 16.7 Parameterizing the simulation to the problem context. In the reflection space, a web-based survey allows participants to parameterize the bus stop's attributes, which influences the behavior of the simulation

often. The factual resource material found in this section of the reflection space provides a foundation from which the group members are able to form their own opinions.

Having a better understanding of the issue, the neighbors revisit the model they have constructed. The environmentalist of the group decides the solution is to add a few additional buses to the route. The group sees that this all but eliminates car use. Meanwhile, the EDC continuously calculates the cost of the bus route, and one of the neighbors notices that they have just tripled the cost! Seeing this information, they all agree that this solution is not feasible.

16.3.1.5 Constructing New Knowledge

Faced with this dilemma, one of the neighbors recalls that some cities have implemented a light-rail train system to accommodate their citizens. He wonders if this

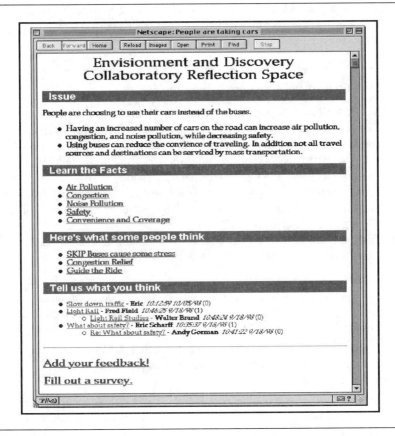

FIGURE 16.8 Supporting Reflection. The Reflection Space combines domain expert knowledge with an extensible discussion forum to provide a mechanism for learning on demand and the construction of new knowledge

would be a cheaper solution to their problem and asks if anyone knows anything about this alternative. None of the neighbors have any direct knowledge about light rail so they post a question to a discussion forum in the reflection space. By doing this, the group documents an open issue that they would like to resolve before they meet again next week.

As the design session comes to a close, the group members agree to explore the light-rail question on their own before they meet again. While at home, each searches the Web for information on light-rail systems. As they find information that supports their individual perspectives, they add comments and URLs as responses to the original light-rail question posted by the group during the previous meeting (see the "Tell us what you think" pane in Figure 16.8). This allows members to collect information that will support their position at the next meeting. Through the face-to-face discussion that took place around the table and comments that each member posted to the discussion forum, the group members begin to understand each other's positions more clearly, and in some cases the perspectives of the members begin to converge.

16.3.2 The Conceptual Principles behind the EDC

The EDC effort is based on our collective prior work integrating the diverse fields of HCI and urban planning. From the HCI perspective we have engaged in the cultivation of conceptual frameworks and the creation of computational systems, such as domain-oriented design environments. The urban-planning contributions include the notions of participation, and the development of physical models and physical-simulation games (Arias 1996) as decision support tools to empower citizens in the framing and resolution of complex planning problems, which by nature exist in a context of change and conflicting objectives (Arias 1995).

Insights from these earlier efforts indicate that supporting a collaborative design process that includes both reflection and action requires a framework that can do the following.

- Allow exploration of design alternatives—supporting design as an argumentative process in which the goal is not to prove a point but to create an environment for dialogue (Ehn 1988; Simon 1996)
- Incorporate an emerging design in a set of external memory structures (Bruner 1996) and record the design process and the design rationale (Fischer et al 1996)
- Generate low-cost, modifiable models that assist stakeholders in creating shared understanding by engaging in a "conversation with the materials"
- Use simulations to engage in "what if" exercises and to replace reliance on assumptions by analysis (Repenning and Sumner 1995)
- Make argumentation serve design (Fischer et al 1996) and support reflection-in-action (Schön 1983) by integrating action and reflection spaces
- Introduce the notion of a common language of design by integrating physical objects with virtual objects (Arias 1996)

16.3.3 The Integration of Action and Reflection

One of the primary theories behind the EDC is that people act until they experience a breakdown, this breakdown leads them to reflect upon their activities, and in this context they are motivated to explore information spaces associated with the activity. Schön calls this approach "reflection-in-action" (Schön 1983), whereas in our own previous work we call it "making argumentation serve design" (Fischer et al. 1996).

The EDC parallels this theory by providing support for action and reflection, along with the mechanisms that blend the two activities. In general, *action activities* (see again left side of Figure 16.2) take place on and around the horizontal table in Figure 16.1, through collaboration using a physical and computational model appropriate for the particular application domain. The scenario presents such a model for the EDC-Urban domain (providing a simulation with physical game pieces appropriate for modeling urban transportation problems), and uses context-dependent information (such as aerial photographs) for the specific application. *Reflection activities* (right side of Figure 16.2) are supported by the vertical whiteboard in Figure 16.1, through the capture, creation, presentation, and modification of hypermedia information (Moran and Melle 1998). This provides a portal to a dynamic, user-extensible, and emergent Web-based information environment. In the scenario, maps, previous constructions, surveys, and critic information are stored and made available to support reflection activities.

The EDC supports ways to blend together these two aspects of reflection-in-action (see Figure 16.9). Critics are active agents that observe the collaborative construction and link to information relevant to the constructed artifact (Fischer et al. 1998), such as when the cars begin to appear in the action space in the scenario. In the reflection space, there are used as generic mechanisms that capture and manipulate Web-based information to contextualize the design activity, as shown with the orthographic map and stored constructions in the scenario.

Both of these forms of activity, along with the mechanisms that support their integration, help make information relevant to the task at hand, support the interaction of multiple stakeholder perspectives, and draw on the various strengths that each brings to the task, resulting in collaborative exploration of the knowledge and the formation of informed compromises that lead to the construction of shared understanding in either framing or resolving the problem.

It is important to understand that there is no strict dividing line between these two types of activity. Reflection can occur directly within the context of action, for example, when feedback from a simulation based on one action triggers several "what if"

Critics

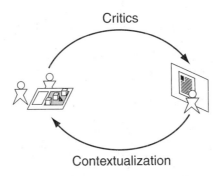

Contextualization

FIGURE 16.9   Blending action and reflection

actions by a participant. The participant then can explore and understand the consequences of decision options without resorting to a separate information space to explain the issue. Action can also take place within the information spaces that support reflection as new information is constructed, externalized, and reorganized. The most important contribution of the EDC is the synergy that is created between the action and reflection activities.

16.3.4 The EDC as an Open System

To support designers in framing and resolving their own problems, the EDC needs to support a dynamic evolving problem context. Exemplifying open principles is important in addressing open-ended problems and collaborative creation of shared understanding in the EDC. In a domain such as transportation planning, no system can completely subsume all information needed to solve a problem. An essential goal of the system is to provide a shared representation that all participants can extend when the need arises. In fact, the extension process itself may play an important role in creating shared understanding by supporting the collaborative activity of extending the realization of the problem.

On the technical level, all of the components used to create the EDC environment are designed to be extensible by users. In the action space, the physical language provides an initial tool to describe a problem, but users might choose to add new objects to the language to represent new kinds of objects. In our current models one might introduce a new object with a different color or shape. The corresponding computational model can be modified as situations arise. AgentSheets (Repenning and Sumner 1995) and Visual AgenTalk (Repenning and Ambach 1996) allow users to quickly add or change the objects that make up a model and experiment with changes they make to the computational model. The dynamic information spaces used in the reflection space are designed to allow users to extend information.

The scenario demonstrated many levels at which extensions might take place in the EDC. Users can add information to a problem situation by entering new or linking existing content into the evolving reflection space. Filling out a survey extends the information available to the computational simulation, in this case altering the parameters of a specific bus stop. Additional parameters are available for every element in the simulation. If existing parameters do not capture the kind of modification that users wish to make, users can change the behavior of individual objects in the simulation.

Although providing support for modification at all levels is an important step toward making the EDC an open system, merely providing opportunities for extension is not enough to truly support evolution. Creating a model for extension tailored to a given situation and created with an understanding of the background of the users is an important future direction. One of the major challenges ahead for evolution in the EDC is to create both a technical and a social context appropriate for evolution, providing a use context in which evolution can be captured through collaborative activity using means that are appropriate for the problem and target audience.

16.4   Assessment

The activities and processes that we want to support with the EDC, as argued in the introduction, take months, years, and decades. We must account for the rich context in which design takes place and create situations grounded in practice. As a result, our goal for the assessment of the EDC effort is to transcend the laboratory and analyze and evaluate our environments in real world settings. While the EDC as a whole has not yet been put into broad practice and evaluated, we have had considerable experience with the assessment of essential parts of our system.

16.4.1   Integrating Assessment with Design and Practice

In our approach to design, assessment is viewed not as the endpoint of a waterfall model but as a process integrated into design and practice. The design of the EDC is based on assessment of our own prior work (as discussed in Arias et al. 1997) as well as a study of the strengths and limitations of other theoretical work, approaches, and systems, including ubiquitous computing (Abowd et al 1998; Weiser 1991), collaboratories (Erickson et al 1999; Olson and Olson 1997), and "Roomware" (Streitz et al. 1999). This is an ongoing activity throughout the design process, not just the starting point for our investigations.

Crucial insights from our prior work that have laid the groundwork for our design of the EDC are based on our use of physical simulations applied to actual community design with specific neighborhoods (Arias 1996). These insights, along with other efforts on how we can create representations that can be shared and understood by all stakeholders, have indicated that physical objects are critically important. This has been borne out at two levels. First, the direct, naive manipulability of physical objects is important for special groups who may not be well versed in technology. Second, we have seen the importance of the innate understanding that comes from manipulation of physical objects. Third, these objects play the role of "boundary objects" by helping stakeholders to articulate and make information relevant to the "task at hand" (Arias and Fischer 2000).

16.4.2   Assessment through Participatory Design

By involving communities of practice in the design of EDC domain prototypes, we have gained considerable insight into how things are (settings, cultures), how they are done (processes, organizations), why they are the way they are, and how they are limited by current practice.

Our work in this area has focused on participatory design efforts based on numerous joint design sessions with the Boulder County Healthy Communities Initiative and the Regional Transportation District in the Denver-Boulder County Region of Colorado. We have gained critical insights into the design and development of the EDC through these interactions, such as the importance of being able to represent multiple perspectives of a problem; the need to support learning as a shared, collaborative activity—particularly in the context of bridging these multiple perspectives; and the need to support interaction and reflection both "around the table" as well as "beyond the table."

16.4.3   Assessment of Open Systems and Emerging Applications

The emergence that takes place in an open system will not take place within the first few days or weeks of use—this makes an experimental psychology approach of hiring subjects and measuring their interaction with the system impossible. We need to understand the long-term use of a system by owners of problems engaged in the cultivation of a rich repertoire of personally and socially meaningful artifacts. We do not expect all users to become Visual AgenTalk programmers or to be interested in making radical changes to the system. Users' contributions will depend on the perceived benefit, which involves the effort needed to make changes and the utility received for effecting changes.

16.4.4   Assessment of the Effectiveness of Interaction Techniques

Although low-level human-technology interaction techniques (Newell and Card 1985) are not the primary focus of our work, nonetheless, they are an important aspect of designing for the activities we want to support. The current touch-screen realization of the action space implicitly creates a turn-taking and modal interaction. We have observed breakdowns when two users try to place objects at once (causing the system to draw objects between the two placements) or place objects that differ from the currently selected object (that is, a user tries to place a home, but because the system is in "school mode," a school gets placed in the simulation instead). People unfamiliar with the technology get confused at these violations of the assumptions they have made about the technology. As we continue to develop the EDC, we will evaluate the effectiveness of interaction through analysis of the breakdowns and successes of the technology through design, demonstration, and use activities.

16.5   Future Work

16.5.1   Assessment of Support for the Creation of Shared Understanding

Supporting "around-the-table" interaction and contextualizing information in design activities are critical elements in creating shared understanding. It is important to discover which social situations are more conducive to the creation of this shared understanding. For example, important aspects to study include determining the utility of a trained facilitator, the efficacy of participant facilitators, and the effect that such interventions would have on "putting the owners in charge" (Fischer 1984). By analyzing how the EDC is utilized during design activities, we will assess the social and technical dimensions of how shared understanding can be created. Important to this end will be tracking long-term effects of the design processes upon the design community, as well as evaluating the design products.

This assessment will take place against a backdrop of experiences with organizational memories and collaborative work that have exposed two barriers to capturing information: (1) individuals must perceive a direct benefit in contributing to organizational memory that is large enough to outweigh the effort (Grudin 1989), and (2) the effort required to contribute to organizational memory must be minimal so it will not interfere with getting the real work done (Carroll and Rosson 1987).

16.5.2 Use of the EDC in Actual Work Situations

Although we have gained a great deal of insight into the design and effectiveness of our approaches through the integrated activities we have already employed, there are still critical perspectives to be gleaned from deployment and study of our systems in use contexts. We will utilize insights from activities such as ethnographic methods "in the wild" (Hutchins 1994), studies of everyday activities (Nardi and Zarmer 1993), and analysis of conversational interaction (Jordan and Henderson 1995).

16.5.3 Beyond Binary Choices

By arguing for the desirability of supporting people as designers, we want to state explicitly that there is nothing wrong with being a consumer and that we can learn and enjoy many things in a consumer role. It is a mistake to assume that being a consumer or being a designer would be a binary choice—it is rather a continuum ranging from passive consumer, to active consumer, to end-user, to user, to power users, to domain designer, to medium designer. Problems occur, for example, when someone wants to be a designer but is forced to be a consumer or when being a consumer becomes a universal habit and mindset dominating one's life completely. We claim that the HCI community should not be content with either (1) restricting its efforts to the user interface or the computational aspects of HCI, or (2) reflecting and evaluating designs developed by other communities (such as the groups who give us 500 TV channels or artifacts over which we have no control). The HCI research community should not confine itself to a consumer role in the process of shaping our future knowledge society (Drucker 1994) in which they focus solely on some technical issues in the context of a world defined by others.

16.6 Conclusion

The EDC is a contribution toward creating a new generation of collaborative human-computer systems that address and overcome current limitations of human-computer interaction. It shifts the emphasis away from the computer screen as the focal point and creates an integrated environment in which stakeholders can incrementally create a shared understanding through collaborative design. It is an environment that is not restricted to the delivery of predigested information to individuals; rather, it provides opportunities and resources for design activities embedded in social debates and discussions in which *all* stakeholders can actively contribute rather than being confined to passive consumer roles.

HCI research and development have made very important contributions over the last decade. The HCI community has acquired a broad understanding of creating computational artifacts fitting better human capabilities and needs by creating theories and innovative systems (Helander et al. 1997). To take the next step forward, the HCI community should accept the challenge of rethinking computational media in broader contexts. Our claim is that computational media can have an impact on our individual lives and our societies similar the fundamental change from oral to literal societies brought about by the introduction of reading and writing. The true contribution of computational media may be to allow all of us to take on or incrementally grow into a designer role in areas that we consider personally meaningful and important such that we are motivated to expend the additional effort. The future of HCI lies in realizing that what we can build is more limited by our imagination, our ability to discover, and our ability to envision than by our system development limitations.

Acknowledgments

The authors thank Taro Adachi, Josh Emhoff, Rogerio dePaula, Christine Giger, Volker Jung, Shigeru Kurihara, Kelli Murphy, Jonathan Ostwald, Alexander Repenning, Kurt Schneider, Stefanie Thies, and Jessica Witter for their help in conceptualizing, implementing, and supporting the EDC as well as with the preparation of this chapter. This work is supported in part by NSF grants CDA-9529549, REC-9631396, and IIS-9711951 and by funding from PFU, Inc, Tokyo.

References

Abowd, G.D., Atkeson, C.G., Brotherton, J.A., Enqvist, T., Gully, P.A., and Lemon, J. (1998). Investigating the capture, integration, and access problem of ubiquitous computing in an educational setting. *Proceedings of CHI'98,* 440–447. New York: ACM Press.

Arias, E.G. (1989). The contingent nature of participation and housing research. *Guru Nanak Journal of Sociology—Special Housing Policy Issue,* 10, 1–2, 81–99.

Arias, E.G. (1995). Designing in a design community: Insights and challenges. In G.M. Olson and S. Schuon (Eds.), *Proceedings of DIS'95 Symposium on Designing Interactive Systems: Processes, Practices, Methods & Techniques,* 259–263. New York: ACM Press.

Arias, E.G. (1996). Bottom-up neighborhood revitalization: Participatory decision support approaches and tools. *Urban Studies Journal—Special Issue on Housing Markets, Neighborhood Dynamics and Societal Goals,* 33, 10, 1831–1848.

Arias, E.G., Eden, H., and Fischer, G. (1997). Enhancing communication, facilitating shared understanding, and creating better artifacts by integrating physical and computational media for design. In *Proceedings of DIS'97: Designing Interactive Systems: Processes, Practices, Methods, & Techniques,* 1–12. New York: ACM Press.

Arias, E.G., Eden, H., Fischer, G., Gorman, A., and Scharff, E. (2000a). Enhancing participation through innovation. In G. Moser (Ed.), *Metropolis: Cities, Social Life and Sustainable Development.* IAPS CD, University of Paris, Paris.

Arias, E.G., Eden, H., Fischer, G., Gorman, A., and Scharff, E. (2000b). Transcending the individual human mind—creating shared understanding through collaborative design. *ACM Transactions on Computer-Human Interaction,* 7, 1, 84–113.

Arias, E.G., and Fischer, G. (2000). Boundary objects: Their role in articulating the task at hand and making information relevant to it. In *Proceedings of ICSC Congress on Intelligent Systems (forthcoming).* University of Wollogong, Australia.

Arias, E.G., and Schneider, K. (2001). Decision support for wicked planning problems. *Journal of Simulations and Games (under revision).*

Brown, J.S., Duguid, P., and Haviland, S. (1994). Toward informed participation: Six scenarios in search of democracy in the information age. *The Aspen Institute Quarterly,* 6, 4, 49–73.

Bruner, J. (1996). *The culture of education.* Cambridge, MA: Harvard University Press.

Carroll, J.M., and Rosson, M.B. (1987). Paradox of the active user. In J.M. Carroll (Ed.), *Interfacing Thought: Cognitive Aspects of Human-Computer Interaction,* 80–111. Cambridge, MA: The MIT Press.

Drucker, P.F. (1994). The age of social transformation. *The Atlantic Monthly,* 53–80.

Ehn, P. (1988). *Work-oriented design of computer artifacts.* Almquist & Wiksell International, Stockholm, Sweden.

Ehn, P., Löwgren, J. (1997). Design for quality-in-use: Human-computer interaction meets information system development. In M.G. Helander, T.K. Landauer, and P.V. Prabhu (Eds.), *Handbook of Human-Computer Interaction,* 299–313. Amsterdam: Elsevier Science B. V.

Eisenberg, M., and Makay, W. (1996). Real meets virtual: Blending real-world arti-facts with computational media. *CHI'96, Human Factors in Computing Systems,* 159–160. New York: ACM Press.

Engelbart, D.C. (1995). Toward augmenting the human intellect and boosting our collective IQ. *Communications of the ACM,* 30–33.

Erickson, T., Smith, D.N., Kellogg, W.A., Laff, M., and Brander, E. (1999). A sociotechnical approach to design: Social proxies, persistent conversations, and the design of babble. In *Proceedings of the ACM Conference on Human Factors in Computing Systems (CHI'99),* 72–79. New York: ACM Press.

Fischer, G. (1994). Putting the owners of problems in charge with domain-oriented design environments. In D. Gilmore, R. Winder, and F. Detienne (Eds.), *User-Centered Requirements for Software Engineering Environments,* 297–306. Heidelberg: Springer Verlag.

Fischer, G. (1998). Beyond "couch potatoes": From consumers to designers. In IEEE (Ed.), *1998 Asia-Pacific Computer and Human Interaction, APCHI'98,* 2–9. IEEE Computer Society. CA: Los Alamitos.

Fischer, G., Lemke, A.C., McCall, R., and Morch, A. (1996). Making argumentation serve design. In T. Moran and J. Carrol (Eds.), *Design Rationale: Concepts, Techniques, and Use,* 267–293. Mahwah, NJ: Lawrence Erlbaum and Associates.

Fischer, G., Nakakoji, K., Ostwald, J., Stahl, G., and Sumner, T. (1998) Embedding critics in design environments. In M.T. Maybury and W. Wahlster (Eds.), *Readings in Intelligent User Interfaces,* 537–559. San Francisco: Morgan Kaufmann Press.

Fischer, G., and Scharff, E. (1998). Learning technologies in support of self-directed learning. *Journal of Interactive Media in Education,* www.jime.open.ac.uk/98/4.

Galegher, P., Kraut, R., and Egido, C. (Eds.). (1990). *Intellectual teamwork.* Hillsdale, NJ: Lawrence Erlbaum Associates, Inc.

Greenbaum, J., and Kyng, M. (Eds.). (1991). *Design at work: Cooperative design of computer systems.* Hillsdale, NJ: Lawrence Erlbaum Associates, Inc.

Grudin, J. (1989). Why groupware applications fail: Problems in design and evaluation. *Office: Technology and People,* 4, 3, 245–264.

Grudin, J. (1994). Groupware and social dynamics: Eight challenges for developers. *Communications of the ACM,* 37, 1, 92–105.

Helander, M.G., Landauer, T.K., and Prabhu, P.V. (Eds.). (1997). *Handbook of Human-Computer Interaction* (Second, completely revised ed.). Amsterdam: Elsevier Science Ltd.

Hutchins, E. (1994). *Cognition in the wild.* Cambridge, MA: The MIT Press.

Ishii, H., and Ullmer, B. (1997). Tangible bits: Towards seamless interfaces between people, bits and atoms. In *Proceedings of ACM CHI'97 Conference on Human Factors in Computing Systems,* 234–241. New York: ACM Press.

Jordan, B., and Henderson, A. (1995). Interaction analysis: Foundations and practice. *Journal of the Learning Sciences,* 4, 1, 39–103.

Landauer, T.K. (1995). *The Trouble with Computers,* Cambridge, MA: MIT Press.

Lave, J. (1988). *Cognition in practice.* Cambridge, UK: Cambridge University Press.

Mackay, W.E. (1992). Co-adaptive systems: Users as innovators. In *CHI'92 Basic Research Symposium.* New York: ACM Press.

Moran, T., and Melle, W.v. (1998). Tailorable domain objects as meeting tools for an electronic whiteboard. *Proceedings of the ACM 1998 Conference on Computer Supported Cooperative Work (CSCW'98),* 295–304. New York: ACM Press.

Myers, B.A. (1998 March). A brief history of human computer interaction technology. *ACM Interactions,* 44–54.

Nardi, B.A. (1993). *A small matter of programming.* Cambridge, MA: The MIT Press.

Nardi, B.A., and Zarmer, C. (1993). Beyond models and metaphors: Visual formalisms in user interface design. *Journal of Visual Languages and Computing,* 4, 5–33.

Newell, A., and Card, S.K. (1985). The prospects for psychological science in human-computer interaction, *Human-Computer Interaction,* 1, 3, 209–242.

Norman, D.A. (1993). *Things that make us smart.* Reading, MA: Addison-Wesley.

Olson, G.M., and Olson, J.S. (1997). Research on computer supported cooperative work. In M.G. Helander, T.K. Landauer, and P.V. Prabhu (Eds.), *Handbook of Human-Computer Interaction,* 1433–1456. Amsterdam: Elsevier Science B.V.

PCSD—President's Council on Sustainable Development. (1996). *Sustainable America: A New Consensus for Prosperity, Opportunity, and a Healthy Environment for the Future.* President's Council on Sustainable Development. Washington, DC.

PITAC—President's Information Technology Advisory Committee. (1999). *Information Technology Research: Investing in Our Future.* National Coordination Office for Computing, Information, and Communications. Arlington, VA. At http://www.ccic.gov/ac/report/pitac_report.pdf.

Polanyi, M. (1966). *The tacit dimension.* Garden City, NY: Doubleday.

Repenning, A., and Ambach, J. (1996). Tactile programming: A unified manipulation paradigm supporting program comprehension, composition and sharing. In *Proceedings 1996 IEEE Symposium on Visual Languages,* 102–109. Los Alamitos, CA: IEEE Computer Society Press.

Repenning, A., and Sumner, T. (1995) Agentsheets: A medium for creating domain-oriented visual programming languages. *IEEE Computer, Special Issues on Visual Programming,* 28, 3, 17–25.

Resnick, L.B., Levine, J.M., and Teasley, S.D. (Eds.). (1991). *Perspectives on socially shared cognition.* Washington, DC: American Psychological Association.

Rittel, H. (1984). Second-generation design methods. In N. Cross (Ed.), *Developments in Design Methodology,* 317–327. New York: John Wiley & Sons.

Rittel, H., and Webber, M.M. (1984). Planning problems are wicked problems. In N. Cross (Ed.), *Developments in Design Methodology,* 135–144. New York: John Wiley & Sons.

Schön, D. (1992). Designing as reflective conversation with the materials of a design situation. *Knowledge-Based Systems Journal, Special Issue on AI in Design,* 5, 1, 3–14.

Schön, D.A. (1983). *The reflective practitioner: How professionals think in action.* New York: Basic Books.

Simon, H.A. (1996). *The sciences of the artificial,* 3rd Edition. Cambridge, MA: The MIT Press.

Snow, C.P. (1993). *The two cultures,* Cambridge, UK: Cambridge University Press.

Streitz, N.A., Geißler, J., Holmer, T., Konomi, S., Müller-Tomfelde, C., Reischl, W., Rexroth, P., Seitz, P., and Steinmetz, R. (1999). I-LAND: An interactive landscape for creativity and innovation. In *Proceedings of the ACM Conference on Human Factors in Computing Systems (CHI'99),* 120–127. New York: ACM Press.

Weiser, M. (1991). The computer for the 21st century. *Scientific American,* 265, 3, 66–75.

The Development
of Cooperation: Five Years
# of Participatory Design
in the Virtual School

John M. Carroll
George Chin
Mary Beth Rosson
Dennis C. Neale

17.1 Introduction

Participatory design—also called cooperative design—is the inclusion of users or user representatives within a development team, such that they actively help in setting design goals and planning prototypes. It contrasts with still-standard development methods in which user input is sought only after initial concepts, visions, and prototypes exist. This approach was pioneered and has been widely employed in Europe since the 1970s, and it now consists of a well-articulated and differentiated set of engineering methods in use worldwide (Greenbaum and Kyng 1991; Muller et al. 1997; Schuler and Namioka 1993).

In 1994, our research group began a design collaboration with two public school teachers. We wanted to investigate whether and how the teachers could contribute to a design collaboration. We were specifically interested in exploring the utility of a scenario-based design approach in this context (Carroll 1995). We were guided by beliefs that the teachers could participate effectively in the design of educational applications, that their expertise in education could be especially critical, and moreover, that the teachers had a right to such participation. Our hypothesis was that the principal obstacles to achieving such an interaction were the culture and professional jargon of software design. Our initial investigation addressed these barriers by creating a cooperative relationship, spanning more than a year, between the teachers and a software developer who worked with them to create several novel educational applications (Laughton 1996).

In 1995, with the support of the U.S. National Science Foundation (NSF), we formed the LiNC project (for "Learning in Networked Communities"), a partnership between Virginia Tech and the public schools of Montgomery County, Virginia. The objective was to develop and investigate a high-quality communications infrastructure to support collaborative science learning. Montgomery County is located in the rural Appalachian region of southwestern Virginia. In March 2000, one of its high schools was listed among the top 100 in the United States by *Newsweek* magazine. However, in others, physics is only offered every other year and to classes of only three to five students. Our initial vision was to give students in this diverse and dispersed school district access to peers through networked collaboration. We developed an ambitious set of objectives with respect to participatory design.

First, we wanted to coordinate participatory design with ethnographically driven design (Bentley et al. 1992). Participatory design is sometimes conflated with approaches that base design concepts on detailed observation of workplace practices. In fact, the two approaches can work well together because they are complementary: Ethnographic field studies can bring to light factors in the background of the user's experience, circumstances of which the users themselves may be unaware. But field studies cannot reveal the perspectives and insights users bring to the development process as participants in that process. We wanted to create an overall participatory design framework with a supplementary role for ethnographic description.

Second, we wanted to create and study a broad framework for participatory design interactions. The NSF program that sponsored our work was directed at producing models for how new computer networking infrastructures could facilitate systemic change in public education (as opposed to producing specific curricular innovations). Thus, an important orienting goal was enhancing the autonomy of teachers with respect to our technology infrastructure. In other words, we assumed from the start that in order to succeed, we must someday fade from the project and leave the teachers to maintain and develop its achievements. This meant that the teachers' involvement could not be limited to requirements interviews, or even to relatively active roles in conceptual design. We needed to think of them as collaborators in implementation, deployment, testing, and refinement, and as leaders in the development of courseware and classroom activities that would exploit the software.

Third, we wanted to inaugurate a very long-term design collaboration. Because the LiNC project was specifically chartered to create new collaborative technology and applications with systemic implications for public education, we could not specify all of its technical goals a priori. The project was intended to be exploratory. We knew from the start that we would be gathering, refining, and developing requirements more or less throughout the project, even as we implemented and evaluated software in the classrooms. We understood from the beginning that we would not be able to achieve our goals, for example, through a brief course of participatory exercises. From the standpoint of pushing the bounds of participation, this was very exciting: We knew that we would need the teachers as design collaborators for years to come.

Public education is a uniquely appropriate domain in which to carry out this sort of methodological investigation. Teachers work in a complex and dynamic context in which measurable objectives and underlying values collide on a daily basis. Traditionally, teachers work in isolation from their peers; individual teachers have well-established personal practices and philosophies of education. Teachers have enormous discretion with respect to what goes on in their classrooms, yet are also routinely interrogated by supervisors, by parents and other community members, and by educational bureaucracies. This has led to an abiding tension in the culture of schools: Teachers' innovative practices are often not adequately acknowledged or valued, and at the same time, teachers often passively resist school reforms that are imposed top-down.

Technology is a particularly problematic element in the culture of schools. The isolation and discretion of the teacher's work environment requires that technology for classroom use be highly appropriate and reliable. Yet it is generally assumed that teachers are to be *trained* on new technologies, not asked to *define* what those technologies should be. From the teacher's standpoint classroom technology often is itself the problem, not the solution. This culture of technology development in the schools has been singularly ineffective—film and radio in the 1920s, television in the 1950s, computer-assisted instruction in the 1980s, among others, have been notable failures (Cuban 1986; Hodas 1993; Tyack and Cuban 1995).

Despite all this, education is strikingly underresearched as a domain for participatory design. The only prior study (Williams 1994) involved customization of off-the-shelf software in which teachers interacted only indirectly with engineers through a "translator." We concluded that the collaborative development of new networking infrastructures for education would be an excellent testbed for extending participatory design.

17.2   Stages of Cooperative Engagement

Looking back at the past five years, we can distinguish four stages in our collaboration with the teachers: At first, the teachers were *practitioner-informants;* we observed their classroom practices and we interviewed them. Subsequently, the teachers became directly and actively involved in the requirements development process as *analysts.* Some two and a half years into the project, the teachers assumed responsibility as *designers* for key aspects of the project. Through the past year particularly, the teachers have become *coaches* to their own colleagues within the public school system.

We use the term "developmental" in the sense of Piaget and Inhelder (1969) and Vygotsky (1978). We believe that the teachers have developed qualitatively different roles through the course of our collaboration. In some cases, these roles were suggested to them, in other cases, they defined and claimed new roles. But in all cases, these transitions exemplified the defining characteristics of *developmental change:* active resolution of manifest conflicts in one's activity, taking more responsibility, and assuming greater scope of action. Each successive stage can be seen as a relatively stable organization of knowledge, skills, and attitudes that resolves the instigating conflict.

In a classic Piagetian example, a child in the preoperational stage perceives single dimensions of quantity. This produces conflicts: A given quantity of liquid poured from a short, wide container into a tall, thin container appears suddenly to be more, but, of course, it cannot be more. These conflicts eventually precipitate a cognitive reorganization called the concrete operational stage, in which constant quantities are perceived as constant regardless of varying shapes and arrangements.

Developmental change in adults is of course more complex. The stages we describe are not singular competencies, but relatively complex ensembles of collaboration, social norms, tool manipulation, domain-specific goals and heuristics, problem-solving, and reflection-in-action. They are social constructions achieved through enculturation, constituted by the appropriation of the artifacts and practices of a community (Vygotsky 1978).

In the Piagetian notion of stages in child development, successive stages build upon the cognitive structures and enabled activity of prior stages but ultimately replace those structures. A child who enters the concrete operational stage can no longer function at the preoperational stage. Adult growth, however, is not static achievement but continual elaboration. The teachers are still practitioners whose classroom practices we regularly observe and whose classroom expertise we still interrogate; they seem to us and to themselves to be representative practitioner-informants. However, they are now *also* analysts and designers, and often coaches. Indeed, effective design coaches probably must be experienced designers, successful designers must be skilled analysts, and analysts must have attained significant domain knowledge.

A third modulation of the developmental perspective in our analysis is our relativistic viewpoint with respect to the nature of expertise. In classic developmental work, it is the child who is developing and indeed doing so by becoming more like the adult. In contrast our situation is one of mutual learning. Through the past five years, the faculty and graduate student researchers in our group have learned a vast amount about the practices, the exigencies, the values, and the politics of public schools. The teachers could present a complementary analysis of the development of *our* capacities to collaborate in the design of educational activities and technologies. Such reflexivity is inherent in any participatory design project. We acknowledge this and thus offer a partial analysis of the long-term development of participatory design, from a single perspective, as a start toward a more complete understanding.

17.3   The Practitioner-Informant

Our project began in the summer of 1994. Stuart Laughton, a Virginia Tech graduate student at the time, initiated an investigation of how teachers could contribute to the participatory design of educational software. He worked with two teachers from the

Montgomery County school division, one a middle school physical science teacher and the other a high school physics teacher. In this investigation we used ethnographic interviews as a means of understanding the teachers' concerns and requirements and scenarios as a means of conveying and developing visions of how the new software could impact teaching and learning interactions. The focus of the research was on bridging the communication gap between classroom expertise and software development expertise.

This effort was successful not only in producing several educational tools for the teachers but in demonstrating that the teachers could play a creative and effective role in the design process. Specifically, it showed how the techniques of ethnographic interviewing and scenario-based design could facilitate cooperative design interactions involving teachers and software developers (Laughton 1996).

The teachers Laughton had worked with also became part of the large team that developed a proposal for the U.S. National Science Foundation (NSF) in 1995. They provided sanity checks for plans to develop a virtual school networking infrastructure that could leverage teachers, students, and other resources in a sparsely populated region in southwestern Virginia. But the teachers' role was somewhat peripheral. There is a revealing irony in this: Although the university researchers could take the initiative to enter the teachers' context and establish a genuine two-way cooperation, the teachers were less able to reciprocate in "our" project-planning and grant-writing activity.

We later learned that at this point in time the teachers were both amazed and shocked by aspects of our virtual school proposal. They could barely believe that computer networking could support real-time collaborative classroom activities effectively, for example, allowing students to jointly carry out simulation experiments and writing projects. Figure 17.1 is the vision scenario for the virtual school that guided the development of our NSF proposal.

Perhaps more significantly, the teachers could barely believe that anyone would *want* to create a virtual school. However, these strong reactions were not conveyed to

---

- Marissa, a 10th-grade physics student, is studying gravity and its role in planetary motion. She goes to the virtual science lab and navigates to the gravity room.

- In the gravity room she discovers two other students, Randy and David, already working with the Alternate Reality Kit, which allows students to alter various physical parameters (such as the universal gravitational constant) and then observe effects in a simulation world.

- The three students, each of whom is from a different school in the county, discuss possible experiments by typing messages from their respective personal computers. Together they build and analyze several solar systems, eventually focusing on the question of how comets can disrupt otherwise stable systems.

- They capture data from their experiments and display it with several visualization tools, then write a brief report of their experiments, sending it for comments to Don, another student in Marissa's class, and Ms. Gould, Randy's physics teacher.

FIGURE 17.1 The Marissa Scenario (fall 1994) was our initial vision of the virtual school.

the university researchers at the time. Instead the teachers continued to serve as supportive domain experts. In part the teachers believed that they had relatively little to contribute, and that the researchers knew what they were doing. Of course, the teachers were confident of their own expertise as public school educators, but they did not see that expertise as a critical determinant in the virtual school vision. In this, they—and implicitly we—reflected the values of contemporary society: somewhat skeptical of public education and public school teachers, while at the same time accepting of computer technology tout court.

The LiNC project ramped up in the spring of 1996 with an influx of graduate student research assistants funded by the NSF grant. We focused a great deal of effort on understanding needs and opportunities in the classrooms. University faculty and students became regular visitors in the classrooms of the four teachers who worked with us, videotaping classroom activities, and interviewing teachers and students. This extensive direct presence in the classrooms was one way in which we hoped to expand upon Laughton's work, which had relied on interviews with teachers outside the context of classroom activity.

We initiated a series of biweekly project meetings involving the teachers, the university faculty, and the central graduate student researchers. The topics of these meetings through the spring of 1996 was always dominated by the ongoing collection of materials and observations from the classrooms. Although our interaction with the teachers became far more regular and intensive in this period, their role was largely the same as it had been from the start: They provided information and interpretations based on their domain expertise and in response to requests from us. The teachers remained very cooperative and responsive, but we had to actively prompt and evoke their expertise. Their primary concern seemed to be that we not diminish learning opportunities for their students. They were interested in the project and willing to talk about trying things out as long as it did not distract from their "real" goals and needs too much.

In the spring of 1996, George Chin—a Virginia Tech graduate student at the time—conducted a series of structured interviews focused on the teachers' practices regarding collaborative activities and their initial attitudes toward the project.

Figure 17.2 presents responses of four teachers to one of the interview items that specifically queried their expectations about project roles. Even after more than a year of working with us to develop the NSF project, which centrally emphasized teachers as designers, and the need for participatory approaches to the design of educational technology, the teachers still felt that their role was chiefly to test, or to facilitate testing with students. This is particularly striking since two of these four teachers are the same people who worked with Laughton. They had already participated in the design, not merely the testing, of new educational technology.

A major and long-lived challenge during this stage in the project and in the teachers' development as designers was to convince them that we truly wanted their ideas and not merely their compliance. One issue was the establishment of trust and mutual understanding. In Figure 17.2, T4 clearly is suspicious about the project's true goals. T4's reaction can be dismissed as extreme, but it is important to recognize that this sort

Prior to the start of the project, what role did you anticipate for yourself on the LiNC project?

T1: I think I was expecting to be more of a guinea pig—you build it and I test it—you pick my brain and leave.

T2: I did not truly understand the LiNC project but thought I would be asked to try out programs with my students written by Tech people.

T3: I thought the programs would be developed and we would test them with the students and evaluate them—make suggestions for changes if need be.

T4: Initial expectations were to function as contact with students. I thought we'd be involved mostly with trial runs of software and possibly some data collection. The possibility that this was a double-blind experiment was also present.

FIGURE 17.2 Responses of four teachers to an interview question (spring 1996)

of reaction is awkward to articulate. Perhaps what is significant is that T4 was willing to say out loud what others might have felt and repressed. At the stage of practitioner-informant, in which the main role of the user is to provide domain information and expert interpretations, it is easy to mistake users who are just "going along" with participatory design for users who are truly engaged and committed to a collaboration.

A second, more prosaic issue was the development of skills that would support critical evaluation of design ideas. In the early stages of our collaboration, the teachers' stance with respect to design proposals can be summarized as positive, with some skepticism about feasibility and effectiveness. For example, they accepted the Marissa scenario (Figure 17.1) and our subsequent design proposal involving a shared lab notebook, but both their support for these ideas and the qualifications of that support were somewhat vague. In retrospect, it seems clear that the teachers were not able to use the textual descriptions to envision these proposals in their own context. None had had much relevant experience; they were tentative, uncertain, and intimidated. When they subsequently had the opportunity to experience the proposals in analysis exercises and classroom prototypes, they were able to critique and extend the design in specific ways.

Although the teachers' interaction with the university researchers was most salient to us, they were at the same time also developing working relationships with one another. We were surprised to learn that including two high school–level physics teachers in our project, in effect included *all* the county's high school physics teachers: There were only two, and one taught physics only part-time. No one in the school system had mentioned this to us during the development of the grant proposal. We were also surprised to find that most of the teachers had not worked closely before and knew one another only casually. This is a further manifestation of our own initial naiveté with respect to the culture of schools.

The teachers exchanged perspectives on teaching styles and pedagogical objectives during the early months of the project. Indeed, this exchange became a central topic in the project as it became clear that it entailed the requirement that our software be sufficiently flexible to support a variety of teaching styles and strategies. More specifically, the teachers had differing perspectives on collaboration among teachers and their classes. None felt that such collaborations would be sufficiently easy for them to manage or beneficial for their students so as to be immediately self-justifying. To varying degrees and in varying ways they were intrigued but not fully convinced or committed to the vision in Figure 17.1.

Later, we learned that two of the teachers had been slightly coerced into joining our project by the school administration. In retrospect, it is hardly shocking to find that expert practitioners might not be champing at the bit to join a technology development project whose objectives would have the effect of discombobulating their own established practices. Indeed, the ambivalence and tension the teachers felt is absolutely appropriate. What was unfortunate is that this issue remained submerged for the most part.

Powerful organizational forces impinged upon our participatory objectives from the start. Laughton's investigation was an independent research project. It was relatively small in scope and depended on the teachers' personal commitment, indeed on their personal time. Our NSF grant provided far better resources; it meant, for example, that part of the teachers' time was compensated. Although several teachers later remarked that this helped them to believe that their participation was really valued, it inevitably also diluted "pure" intrinsic motivation with material rewards. The larger, better-resourced project also had a greater scope and intensity of commitments and responsibilities, with more coordination and management overheads—schedules, dependencies, reminders, requests, meetings, and so on.

The grant comprised a legal relationship between Virginia Tech and the Montgomery County school division. Thus, the teachers, as well as the university faculty who were principal investigators, became institutional representatives, and the work became official work. This reified a power structure: The university faculty and one school administrator were the principal investigators, with financial and technical management responsibility; the teachers were investigators who reported to them. This relationship validated the assumption on the part of the teachers that they were supporting our effort, rather than collaborating in a shared endeavor. Indeed, making project activities part of the teachers' official work emphasized that their role was to meet expectations of the school administration. In our initial euphoria about having significant resources for the project, it was easy to underestimate the downsides of having such resources (Greene and Lepper 1979).

17.4 The Analyst

In July 1996, we held a two-week workshop for all project members. One of the central objectives was to analyze the ethnographic data that had been collected during the preceding spring. In particular, we made a detailed analysis of several videotaped classroom interactions. As a group (four teachers, four human-computer interaction designers, four software developers) we used claims analysis to identify salient features in these scenarios and the desirable and undesirable consequences of these features for students. This kind of work is exciting but demanding. It is directed brainstorming in which lines of causal reasoning are rapidly improvised, questioned, and refined. The teachers, of course, knew a lot already about classroom matters. However, they were not used to explicitly identifying tradeoffs for human activity in classroom situations. As one teacher commented: "It intruded on the way I design activities—I like to brainstorm and think out loud, [but] every time you say something, it gets analyzed." The teachers seemed exhausted after these sessions.

Nevertheless, the teachers were remarkably effective in these participatory analysis sessions. As illustrated in Figure 17.3, they were at least as productive as any other constituency in the project team at identifying teaching and learning issues, key situational features, and tradeoff relations in consequences for students (Chin et al. 1997). An example is a discussion we had about student leadership in groups. We analyzed a group activity in which students measured kinetic energy for collisions involving model trains. One issue we identified was leadership style. We contrasted a consensus-building style, in which the leader ensures that all ideas are considered and enhances group dynamics and the self-esteem of members, with an individual initiative-taking style, which is efficient, challenging, and provides opportunities for group members to play leadership and supporting roles.

Our discussion identified upsides and downsides of each style but was focused on efficiency of initiative-taking in group leadership. At this point, the teachers emphasized that while task-oriented productivity is important, a more critical consideration is that all group members have the opportunity to hypothesize and test their individual ideas and to participate fully in the group activity. This led to a more complete

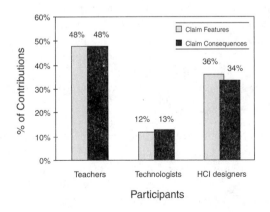

FIGURE 17.3   Contributions to claims analyses by teachers, technologists, and HCI designers (from Chin et al. 1997)

tradeoff analysis of student leadership and had specific ramifications for issues of floor control and group formation in the virtual school environment.

One of the immediate and long-lasting changes in the project dynamics arising from the workshop was that the teachers became more active advocates for the importance of classroom situations. The teachers already believed that understanding and addressing real classroom issues was critical to the project and recognized that they were in the best position to recognize and articulate these issues. What changed in the summer of 1996 is that they became far more willing to proactively share that perspective with other members of the project.

The only way to become an analyst is to analyze. In the workshop, we not only emphasized what we could see happening in a classroom activity but also how we made sense of it. Teachers were confronted by a situation in which they had to transcend the role of informant, to make proposals about *why* some aspect of a learning situation might be good or bad. Analysts value the skills and knowledge of practitioner-informants, but at the same time it is the analysts who are in control. Analysis, not raw data, drives design. By publicly objectifying their own knowledge in the workshop, the teachers appropriated the license not merely to testify about events in the classroom but to make sense of those events with respect to the project's goals.

The teachers were even affected *as teachers* by this analytic work. For example, during the workshop, the teachers articulated some rationale for assigning students to groups—students with complementary skills and leadership styles can be grouped together, known personality conflicts can be avoided, natural mentoring relationships can be set up. Prior to this analytic work, the teachers had been quite relaxed about group formation, allowing students to choose their own partners (generally friends). However, in the year following the workshop, the teachers became much more proactive in creating groups, requesting and using online tools for group assignment.

Both informants and analysts must understand the problem domain. However, analysts must additionally understand the problem domain in the context of system capabilities. Through the course of the project the teachers have learned a great deal about the various networking mechanisms incorporated in the virtual school software (text chat, video conferencing, whiteboards, e-mail, Web pages, shared editors). Structured interviews indicated that through the first three years of the project they also developed an understanding of how computer technology can be used to support their own teaching objectives, and of how students can remotely collaborate (Chin, in preparation).

In the fall of 1996, we designed and carried out a series of classroom collaborative activities. For example, middle school students at different schools used text chat, synchronous audio, and video teleconferencing to collaborate on a melting/freezing point experiment. Each group was given one of two possible substances; collaborating groups compared measurements from their lab experiments in an attempt to determine which group had received which substance. The teachers played a central role in conceiving of and analyzing these activities. For example, they identified the opportunity of pooling data as an appropriate and intrinsically motivating application of networking among classrooms in the virtual school. They led the analysis of how student groups might use various networking mechanisms to collaborate in these activities.

This was a process of reflection-in-action (Schon 1983): The teachers analyzed the technology by "auditioning" it in classroom activities. They tried to predict educational benefits and assess them by formulating activities involving sharing of data, equipment, and expertise.

17.5   The Designer

During the early spring of 1997, the teachers participated in a series of paper prototyping sessions. Scenario descriptions of classroom interactions were used as task-oriented representations that could help to articulate features of the learning environment. This was real design work that actually directed subsequent development of our virtual school software. For example, the teachers prototyped a milestone-tracking capability to help manage student groups. They developed the idea that teachers would provide templates in the collaborative notebook tool to convey assignments to students. They analyzed the problem of student and group authentication and developed a group-logon design. They also designed a folder scheme for partitioning student work. These contributions moved the teachers beyond the analyst role; they were not just articulating the problem, they were suggesting solutions.

In April of 1997, the teachers met on their own and formulated an approach to classroom activity design that they called "projects." They had concluded that the pedagogical value of the relatively brief and technology-oriented classroom activities investigated in fall 1996 was too limited, that the overhead of initiating these activities was too high relative to their value. They urged a different approach for the 1997–1998 school year, one involving activities that extended over several weeks, even months.

This episode is truly a turning point in the LiNC project. This is not because the teachers wanted to focus on long-term, rather than short-term activities. Other members of the team also wanted to focus on more realistic activities and on more ambitious activities that would drive our software ideas more vigorously. What is significant is that the teachers took the initiative to develop and articulate a central design concept to the group as a whole and that this design concept entailed more responsibility and more work *for them*. There is no way to see their proposal as less than fundamental to the project's design strategy. Rather than responding to our visions (such as Figure 17.1), they were contributing a vision. Rather than agreeing to a workplan, they were providing a strategy for the workplan. Perhaps most importantly, through this episode, the teachers embraced the virtual school as a major tool in their own pedagogical planning. This sharply contrasts with the earlier principle of cooperating as long as the project did not diminish learning opportunities for their students.

The teachers' transition to activity designers in the project was a sharp punctuation in the project's course of development. After this point, the teachers regularly met as a subgroup within the larger project. Their efforts to understand one another's teaching styles and pedagogical objectives became far more pointed and considered as they tried to develop an integrated curriculum with common objectives, timing, scale, and grading. It was understood that the design of the classroom activities belonged to them and that this was the primary source of requirements for the software design efforts. To a great extent, the teachers' planning drove other aspects of project activity.

The teachers' paper prototype design work was scaffolded in the sense that their efforts were supported and guided by experienced software designers on the project team. Nevertheless, the ideas came from the teachers. When this design was subsequently presented to the full project team, there was a spirited discussion of the specific features that had been proposed. Afterward, the teachers felt their design had been attacked, that they were put on the defensive. This is not a positive result. Designers should not be defensive about their proposals, and their colleagues should be careful to avoid making them feel defensive. But what is equally notable is that the teachers felt ownership of the design and wanted to defend it. They became embroiled in the typical give and take of design work.

Prior to this point, the teachers, as designers, had been coddled to some extent. Their ideas and perspectives were received with gratitude, generally in design sessions designated for teacher input, like the paper prototyping sessions. After this point, the teachers were treated much more normally; they neither received nor seemed to need or want special handling.

This has led to a productively eclectic design framework. Some members of our project start from architectural considerations about collaborative software, albeit constrained by classroom activity requirements and overall design concepts. Some start from scenarios of project interactions for individual students and groups. The teachers, as designers, tend to start from classroom activities, pedagogical objectives, curriculum plans, and so on. What is true now, and was less true in the past, is that we are able to move convergently toward common goals from these diverse starting points. A key factor seems to be that even though different people take different approaches and represent different knowledge and skill, everyone understands everyone else well enough to see how we complement one another and how things can fit together.

During the 1997–1998 school year, the teachers introduced various innovative classroom activities. In one activity high school and middle school students collaborated on the design of a robot; the middle school students designed a grasping arm, and the high school students designed a mobile base. Many of these longer-term projects involved the development of mentoring relationships by community members in areas such as the optics of photography, mechanics in the context of amusement parks, the astrophysics of black holes, the engineering principles of bridge building, and the aerodynamics of kites and model planes. In some cases, the mentoring was carried out using combinations of videoconferencing, e-mail, and chat, raising many issues for our developing virtual school software and indeed even for the concept of what the virtual school is intended to be. Our original concept had not developed the concept of community participation in the schools, but the teachers' initiatives helped to reemphasize this theme in the project throughout the year.

The software we developed strongly reflects the design concepts championed by the teachers. Our original plan emphasized support for high-bandwidth, real-time interactions. Our vision was of a graphically enhanced multi-user domain (Carroll et al. 1998). Early development work focused on creating a shared whiteboard that would allow students to collaborate on simulation experiments (Koenemann et al. 1999). However, the teachers' emphasis on long-term projects led us to reweigh goals having to do with maintaining work context. Our current virtual school is a Java-based networked learning environment, emphasizing support for the *coordination* of synchronous and asynchronous collaboration, including planning, note taking, experimentation, data analysis, and report writing. The central tool is a collaborative notebook that allows students to organize projects into shared and personal pages. It can be accessed collaboratively or individually by remote or proximal students.

In July 1998, the teachers circulated a detailed specification for a fall collaboration activity, which would last for two weeks and would orient students to the virtual school software. This would be followed by a long-term project that would run from mid-November through late April. In retrospect, this phased use of the virtual school can be seen as a sophisticated response to the ongoing software development process. Through the summer, the overall system had been coming together, and the teachers knew we expected them to use it in their classrooms. Yet at the same time they felt the need to scaffold their use of the software, to be certain that it would effectively support curricular activities.

The specification of major classroom activities for the 1998–1999 school year was generated entirely by the teachers and included several specific new functions they needed in order to carry out the planned activities (see Figure 17.4). For example, the teachers described an "info" button for the collaborative notebook. The button would open a browser on teacher-defined help for using the notebook in the current project. They described a bibliography tool as a notebook page with fields, supporting entry of various sorts of reference materials, as well as student notes derived from the references. They described a planner tool as a notebook page displaying projects' checkpoints and

---

General Functionality

- Long-term projects
- Mentoring by members of the community
- Integration of synchronous and asynchronous collaborative work
- Interaction with virtual school from home as well as school

Specific Features

- Assignment templates presented as notebook pages
- Info button providing access to teacher-generated help
- Structured editor for bibliography entries
- Planning page with project checkpoints and due dates
- Teacher comment tool

FIGURE 17.4 General functionality and specific features introduced by teachers through their design scenarios.

due dates. The teachers also requested software support to allow students (and teachers) to access the virtual school from home.

The teachers described a "message" tool for the collaborative notebook that could be used to attach comments to notebook pages. The tool would be used to approve student work (that is, to convey to groups that they were on track) as well as to answer student queries. It would also convey at a glance to other teachers that a given notebook page had been approved. The teachers were explicit that they would grade student projects as a team and trust one another's assessments. Even planning to try such an arrangement is quite radical from the standpoint of the culture of schools.

We are still in the midst of evaluating the software and activity design outcomes of the LiNC project, a complex matter in itself (Neale and Carroll 1999). However, our design method objectives have been achieved. The teachers all function now as ordinary members of the design team. They are empowered and feel that they have both the capabilities and the right to participate in all facets of design work. One teacher recently summarized this.

> Actually, my role in LiNC has been much more than I expected. I like feeling like I am an expert at something and that my experience is valued. I like feeling comfortable talking to all other players as equals. I like to truly collaborate and I like to be treated with respect. Finally, I like honesty even if I disagree.

This is precisely what we wanted to achieve. It is not a state of user buy-in but a state of mutual respect and engagement.

17.6   The Coach

In August of 1997, the LiNC group organized a training program for middle and high school science and mathematics teachers throughout the Montgomery County school division. This effort was supported by the federal Eisenhower Teacher Development Program administered in Virginia by the State Council of Higher Education. Twelve teachers spent two weeks learning about various networking communication and collaboration mechanisms, and developing ideas and materials for using these resources in their classrooms. The university faculty and graduate students from our project helped to organize and run the training program as lecturers and coaches. Indeed, the program proposal we wrote assumed that the teaching would be handled by the university faculty and graduate students (as is typical for the Eisenhower program).

As we planned the Eisenhower program, the four teachers in the LiNC project assumed more and more responsibility for various aspects. They began by coordinating plans and schedules among the 12 teachers, who, after all, were their colleagues. Soon, though, the teachers were added to the program schedule to share personal classroom experiences from the preceding school year. Finally, their role expanded to include coaching the other teachers during the Eisenhower program and managing the year-long follow-up program during the 1997–1998 school year.

This was not a deliberate plan, though perhaps it should have been. The teachers were clearly able to inspire their colleagues. And they also seemed to benefit from the exercise of externalizing and reconstructing their experience in order to convey it to others. This put them in the interesting role of helping other teachers embark on the same journey they themselves had taken. Participating in the Eisenhower workshop as technology specialists, facilitators and coaches, and ultimately as organizers allowed the LiNC teachers to more vividly appreciate their own development, to reflect upon their new expertise, their changed skills and practices as teachers.

The highest stage of intellectual development in Piaget's developmental theory is the formal operational stage in which people reflect upon their own thinking processes (Piaget and Inhelder 1969). Coaching others is a natural way to evoke reflection on one's experience. As the teachers assumed responsibility for the training and development of their colleagues, they considered their use of collaborative technologies and of LiNC tools in particular. In the two and a half years since the Eisenhower program, there are many examples of the teachers becoming leaders within the Montgomery County schools.

For example, the teachers have helped to recruit and train new teachers for the LiNC project. One veteran teacher (interestingly the one who was least experienced with technology at the outset of the LiNC project) has formed a partnership with two other teachers. In a group discussion in the spring of 1999 (a Web-forum; Carroll et al. 2000), this teacher argued that the time had come for the teachers to take even more responsibility in developing new activities. Subsequently, she identified a set of new activities she felt would be good candidates for collaborative learning (involving Lego constructions), and organized the effort to select and design classroom projects, place materials in virtual school notebooks, and carry out an extensive long-term collaboration during the 1999–2000 school year. Such teacher autonomy is essential to the sustainability of collaboration infrastructures like the virtual school, and indeed it is precisely the kind of outcome one almost never sees in educational technology interventions.

Another veteran teacher initiated contacts with another Virginia school division (Giles County), arranging an activity in which his students would use the virtual school's collaborative notebooks to mentor writing projects of younger students. We went along to the meetings and agreed to play a supportive role, but it was clearly the case that this initiative would have gone forward with or without us. The teacher, at this point, needs only the tools to implement his designs.

To operate at the coach level, people need to see beyond particular applications. They must appreciate the patterns of utility that motivate *types* of examples. Many teachers interested in classroom computing are familiar with word processors and Web browsers and can make creative use of these. However, few are familiar with the potential of computers as collaborative systems. Some of the new teachers joining the LiNC project were sophisticated with respect to the educational potential of multimedia, film, virtual museums, and graphics but did not readily grasp the value of

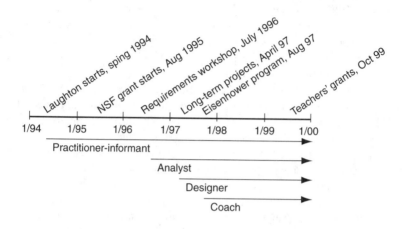

FIGURE 17.5 Timeline of the LiNC project

advanced communication tools and integrated collaboration. The veteran LiNC teachers do see this underlying pattern, which enables them to innovate and lead as coaches. This willingness and ability to conceive of new applications is a critical step in sustainability of a technology infrastructure and systemic reform of practices (as in educational reform). It shows that users have truly appropriated the technology as their own. This creative adaptation can be seen as the highest level of development.

Several of the teachers expressed interest in writing their own grants to continue aspects of the LiNC project. In fall 1999, two teachers, one of the veteran teachers and one of the new teachers, submitted two proposals. Figure 17.5 summarizes the timeline of the LiNC project, indicating the approximate span of each stage.

17.7 Transitions between Stages

Developmental theory explains transitions between stages as resolutions of conflict. Thus, the preoperational child's conflicting perceptions of quantity based on single dimensions, such as height and width, are resolved in the abstraction of quantity as an invariant in the concrete operational stage. For development to take place, the child must have attained the requisite competencies to experience the triggering conflict and then be able to reconceptualize the situation in such a way that the conflict dissolves.

This analytical schema seems to fit the transitions between the stages of cooperation we have described. The general mechanism seems to be that successive increases in knowledge, skill, and confidence empowered the teachers to resolve conflicts by assuming successively greater scope of action and responsibility in the project. In the

July 1996 workshop, the teachers faced the conflict that their pedagogical concerns and perspectives would be adequately represented and fully considered by the group only if they themselves represented those concerns. This went beyond the role they had played in the project up to then. But they were both motivated and competent to resolve this conflict by assuming the analyst role in the project.

Once the teachers were functioning as analysts in the project team, further conflicts and resolutions arose. In spring 1997, the teachers experienced a conflict between their own analyses of requirements and the current state of the virtual school software and development plans. They resolved these conflicts by formulating their own design proposals, ultimately a radical reorientation of the project's vision of classroom activity. Subsequently, the teachers recognized that they were the best qualified project members to administer the Eisenhower program and, more recently, that they are best qualified to pursue specific curricular extensions of the LiNC project.

The teachers' behavior also reflects development *within* the four general stages we have described. For example, during the requirements analysis workshop, scaffolding (examples, reflective prompts) was needed to engage the teachers in the novel and abstract activity of claims analysis. But as the project progressed, teachers spontaneously presented claims as a way to articulate personal positions and frequently identified "upsides" or "downsides" as part of our design discussions. This, of course, is quite consonant with the general notion of learning as movement through a zone of proximal development (Vygotzky 1978).

The designer stage also reflects several different levels of development. Initially, the teachers were able to collaborate with a research assistant in focused design sessions, cowriting scenarios of technology-mediated activities for their classroom. Later they banded together as a subgroup, pooling their goals and expertise to develop a scenario that specified a new vision of collaborative learning activities. Ultimately, each learned to function as an independent designer, with the result that they can now envision and specify activities optimized for their own teaching styles, objectives, and classroom environments. In their coach role, the teachers again worked first as a group in the Eisenhower workshop but have now begun to recruit and mentor colleagues in a 1:1 fashion.

In sum, it appears that the transitions among stages were triggered by conflicts with respect to the teachers' role in the project. In each case, a series of scaffolded activities enabled them to attain the knowledge, skill, and confidence that led them to expand their role.

One natural follow-up question is whether and how the developmental process we described could be accelerated. Must it take five years for technologists to work effectively with teachers? In the case of cognitive development, the timing of stage transitions cannot be altered substantially because the capacities for resolving the triggering conflicts depend on brain development—in other words, they are governed by sequencing of physical development. In our case, the relevant capacities are not biological, but they are quite fundamental. Trust, empathy, and commitment are critical and cannot be manufactured. They emerge from significant shared experience—joy and insight, as well as confrontation of external threats and resolution of interpersonal conflicts.

Some things we did more or less inadvertently, or at least intuitively, seemed to facilitate teachers' development as autonomous members of the project team. For example, at the outset of the project, one student research assistant took the initiative to identify and articulate teacher concerns to the rest of the group. This clearly helped the teachers to assume this role for themselves. A further technique we think might have been useful, but that we did not employ, would be to designate a "lead teacher." Especially in the early stages of the project, teacher concerns might have come to light too slowly because no one was specifically designated as responsible for representing those concerns to other constituencies.

Further efficiencies are definitely possible. We believe that we could accelerate the practitioner-informant stage by at least one year and possibly a year and a half. However, we are concerned that further compression would compromise the coordination of participatory and ethnographically driven approaches to requirements development—to a great extent a project such as this is tied to the natural rhythms of the school year. Other stages could be structured more deliberately, to ensure that teachers attain prerequisite competencies, and that they directly encounter and resolve role conflicts. In the LiNC project, the transitions among states was more or less organically driven by project needs and by our evolving ideas for how to broaden the framework for participatory development. But trusting fortune in exploratory technology development can be bumpy: We believe that with experience, long-term projects can be managed to better align project needs and human development opportunities as a sort of workplace "curriculum." We can imagine an overall speed-up on the order of a factor of two.

We see this case analysis as positive and hopeful. If technologists and teachers can cooperate more effectively, can develop the knowledge, skills, and sensibilities to combine their different expertise more successfully, perhaps educational technology can become more effective. Perhaps it can have a more positive and profound impact on education. Other recent work seems to support similar themes. Davies (1991) describes the importance of teachers working together to articulate and analyze new strategies for schooling—and receiving stipends for their research efforts. Krasnow (1990) describes the new thinking and reflection produced in schools by empowering teacher-researchers. Shields (1994) emphasizes that research should study comprehensive relationships among parents, communities, and schools, as opposed to quantifying piecemeal relationships (like the correlation between test scores and parental attendance on school council). Wadsworth (1997) emphasizes that the engagement of parents, teachers, and community takes place through action—agreeing on needs, committing to actions, and reporting results, not through new ways to talk about problems.

These themes are not as prominent in the educational research elite. For example, at a June 1999 NSF workshop involving investigators from a wide range of sponsored educational research projects, we were unable to find any other project with significant and long-term roles in design for teachers. An interesting footnote pertains to the objective of sustainability. As mentioned earlier, the NSF program that supported the LiNC project was directed at systemic reform in education. The NSF is aware that most reform efforts do not have a lasting impact and encourages projects to take various actions to help ensure that innovations are sustainable after the project activity—but this often focuses on administrative commitments from school divisions. Our view is that an equally critical factor is development of teachers as autonomous collaborators.

17.8   Conclusion

We originally committed to a long-term participatory design method because we conjectured that such an approach would be appropriate, if not crucial, for success in this educational technology setting. This appears to have been correct. We believe we could not have succeeded to the extent we have had we not made this commitment. Working from the national agenda for school reform, educational technology, science education (American Association for the Advancement of Science 1993; Goals 2000: Educate America Act 1994; National Science Teachers Association 1992), and our own vision of a virtual school (Figure 17.1), we would have built the wrong system, we would not have had effective support from teachers, and little or nothing would have been sustained after the initial project funding ended.

Participatory design is fundamentally a process of mutual learning and thus of personal development for participants. But it is often exemplified by rather singular and ephemeral learning interactions. Our study expands the scope of the design participants' personal development by examining a case of long-term cooperative design interaction and by describing a developmental sequence of roles with constituent capacities and responsibilities.

Much research on participatory design has focused on relatively short-term collaborative relationships. This is especially true in North America. For example, the well-known PICTIVE technique is directed at brief user interface design interactions of perhaps one hour (Muller 1992). Such methods are both effective and democratic, but it seems unlikely that the experience of manipulating a user interface mock-up during a brief participatory session can have a significant developmental effect on a person's knowledge, skills, self-confidence, or other professional capacities.

Our case study is different in that user interface design per se has been a secondary issue. We have used brief participatory exercises since 1994, but this level of engagement is more a starting point than the objective of our work. More specifically, we wanted the teachers to have a significant voice in designing the functionality and the use of the virtual school, not merely its appearance. We needed to learn about pedagogical goals and practices, classroom management, school system politics, the relationship of community and the schools, and so forth.

Where participatory design investigations *have* focused on longer-term interactions, chiefly in Europe, these often involve extremely well-organized user groups with well-defined roles and prerogatives in the design process. In many cases, the users are represented by labor unions whose personnel provide legal representation of user interests in the design process. In these cases there is sometimes a clear demarcation, even conflict, between the user (union) interests and management's technology strategy. Indeed, this is an important element of the context for many of these studies. Because the user role in many of these studies is both specified a priori and representative (versus individual), the personal development of user-designers is not a central issue. These case studies also typically involve situations in which the development and deployment of new information technology is a given, and the challenge is to define appropriate technology for the users and their activities (Bødker et al. 1987).

In the educational domain, the deployment of new information technology is far from a given. Indeed, the introduction of new technology has historically almost always failed in school settings. One of the key questions for us was whether a concept for appropriate technological support could be developed at all.

The users in our domain are very loosely organized. As mentioned earlier, teachers traditionally work in isolation from peers. They manage their own work practices and environments (classrooms). The notion of "user community" in this domain is almost ironic. Teachers' unions in the United States are also extremely weak and play no role in the introduction of classroom technology. Indeed, school administrations in the United States rarely have technology strategies at all. Thus, unlike the European case studies, the issue is almost never one of recognized conflict but rather finding a direction at all.

The teachers in our team do not represent other teachers. They are individuals who, as members of our team, have become teacher-designers. This is precisely why their personal development as designers is a central issue in our study. Of course, we do hope that they are representative teachers—allowing us to generalize our investigation to other teachers participating in similar development projects—but this is a separate issue. The point is that in our project, and unlike many long-term participatory design efforts in Europe, the teachers act as individual professionals, just as university researchers do.

An interesting aspect of the teachers and their development is that the four original teachers are now among the most senior members of the LiNC team: Only the two faculty participants have also been part of the project from the start, with students and post-docs joining and participating for shorter periods of time. Undoubtedly this has increased the teachers' sense of expertise and confidence as they have seen numerous issues and ideas raised, addressed, incorporated, or discarded. More importantly, perhaps, they have seen these issues play out *in the context of their own work*. Thus, these four individuals own a central element of the LiNC project's organizational memory—the activities of the classroom.

The stages we have described here are specific to our project; they emerged through specific things that we did, and are rooted in the specific goals of our project. At the same time, they suggest a schematic program for developing cooperative engagement more generally. Most participatory design work engages users at the practitioner-informant stage. This would seem to be an obvious and general starting point for any participatory design collaboration. In our project, the teachers transitioned to the analyst stage through their inclusion in a requirements analysis workshop and a significant process of iterative requirements development (Carroll et al. 1997, 1998). This is perhaps not typical of participatory design practice, but it is a modest extension. Nevertheless, the teachers found it quite stimulating to be invited to objectify their own experience, to dissect it and not merely describe it.

Teachers' work is "invisible" in the sense that their work organizations (their school divisions) do not explicitly analyze its nature or support (Suchman 1995). However, teaching is even more invisible than that of the legal personnel studied by Suchman because it is only very loosely coupled to organizational workflow. As emphasized by Tyack and Cuban (1995), it is difficult for anyone to see what is happening in a given classroom. The personal control inherent in teachers' work is what makes participation in technology development so important. It is not just a matter of accurately describing the work or even of designing appropriate support. The teachers also must accept and deploy "appropriate" solutions. When users have total discretion throughout the entire development cycle, a long-term participatory approach is essential.

Acknowledgments

We are grateful to Kathy Bunn, Laura Byrd, Peggy Davie, Dan Dunlap, Jim Eales, Mark Freeman, Craig Ganoe, Alison Goforth, Philip Isenhour, Jürgen Koenemann, Stuart Laughton, Suzan Mauney, and Fred Rencsok for bringing such energy and creativity to the LiNC project. This work was partially supported by the Hitachi Foundation and the National Science Foundation (REC-9554206 and DGE-9553458).

References

American Association for the Advancement of Science. 1993. *Benchmarks for science literacy.* New York: Oxford University Press.

Bentley, R., Hughes, J.A., Randall, D., Rodden, T., Sawyer, P., Shapiro, D., and Sommerville, I. (1992). Ethnographically-informed systems design for air traffic control. In *Proceedings of CSCW'92* (Toronto, Canada, October 31—November 4), 123–129. New York: ACM Press.

Bødker, S., Ehn, P., Kammersgaard, J., Kyng, M., and Sundblad, Y. (1987). A utopian experience. In G. Bjerknes, P. Ehn, and M. Kyng (Eds.), *Computers and democracy: A Scandinavian challenge,* 251–278. Brookfield, VT: Avebury.

Carroll, J.M. (Ed.). (1995). *Scenario-based design: Envisioning work and technology in system development.* New York: John Wiley.

Carroll, J.M., Neale, D.C., and Isenhour, P.L. Submitted. The Collaborative Critical Incident Tool: Supporting reflection and evaluation in a Web community.

Carroll, J.M., Rosson M.B., Chin, G., and Koenemann, J. Requirements development: Stages of opportunity for collaborative needs discovery. In *Proceedings of the DIS'97: Designing Interactive Systems: Processes, Methods and Techniques Conference* (August 18–20, Amsterdam, The Netherlands), 55–64.

Carroll, J.M., Rosson, M.B., Chin, G., and Koenemann, J. (1998). Requirements development in scenario-based design. *IEEE Transactions on Software Engineering,* 24, 12, 1–15.

Chin, G. (in preparation). *A methodology for integrating ethnography, scenarios, and participatory design.* Ph.D. Dissertation, Computer Science Department, Virginia Tech, Blacksburg, VA.

Chin, G., Rosson, M.B., and Carroll, J.M. (1997). Participatory analysis: Shared development of requirements from scenarios. In *Proceedings of CHI'97: Conference on Human Factors in Computing Systems,* 162–169. New York: ACM Press.

Cuban, L. (1986). *Teachers and machines.* New York: Teachers College Press.

Davies, D. (1991). Schools reaching out: Family, school, and community partnerships for student success. *Phi Delta Kappan,* 72, January, 376–382.

Goals 2000: Educate America Act. (1994). See http://www.ed.gov/CommInvite/.

Greene, D., and Lepper, M.R. (Eds.). (1979). *The hidden costs of reward.* Hillsdale, NJ: Erlbaum.

Greenbaum, J., and Kyng, M. (Eds.). (1991). *Design at work: Cooperative design of computer systems.* Hillsdale, NJ: Erlbaum.

Hodas, S. (1993). Technology refusal and the organizational culture of schools. *Educational Policy Analysis Archives,* 1, 10, September 14.

Koenemann, J., Carroll, J.M., Shaffer, C.A., Rosson, M.B., and Abrams, M. (1999). Designing collaborative applications for classroom use: The LiNC Project. In A. Druin (Ed.), *The design of children's technology,* 99–122. San Francisco: Morgan-Kaufmann.

Krasnow, J. (1990). Building new parent-teacher partnerships: Teacher researcher teams stimulate reflection. *Equity and Choice,* Spring, 25–31.

Laughton, S. (1996). *The design and use of Internet-mediated communication applications in education: An ethnographic study.* Ph.D. Dissertation, Computer Science Department, Virginia Tech, Blacksburg, VA.

Muller, M.J. (1992). Retrospective on a year of participatory design using the PICTIVE technique. In *Proceedings of CHI'92: Conference on Human Factors in Computing Systems,* 455–462. New York: ACM Press.

Muller, M.J., Haslwanter, J.H., and Dayton, T. (1997). Participatory practices in the software lifecycle. In M. Helander, T.K. Landauer, and P. Prabhu (Eds.), *Handbook of Human-Computer Interaction,* 255–297. Second Edition. Amsterdam: Elsevier.

National Science Teachers Association. (1992). *Scope, sequence and coordination of secondary school science, Volume 1: The content core.* Washington, DC: National Science Teachers Association.

Neale, D.C., and Carroll, J.M. (1999). Multi-faceted evaluation for complex, distributed activities. In *Proceedings of CSCL'99: Computer Supported Cooperative Learning,* 425–433. Mahwah, NJ: Lawrence Erlbaum.

Piaget, J., and Inhelder, B. (1969). *The psychology of the child.* New York: Basic Books.

Schon, D.A. (1983). *The reflective practitioner.* New York: Basic Books.

Shields, P.M. (1994). September. Bringing schools and communities together in preparation for the 21st century: Implications for the current educational reform movement for family and community involvement policies. In *Systemic Reform— Perspectives on Personalizing Education.*

Schuler, D., and Namioka, A. (Eds.) (1993). *Participatory design: Principles and practices.* Hillsdale, NJ: Erlbaum.

Suchman, L.A. (1995). Making work visible. *Communications of the ACM,* 38, 9, 56–64.

Tyack, D., and Cuban, L. (1995). *Tinkering toward utopia: A century of public school reform.* Cambridge, MA: Harvard University Press.

Vygotsky, L.S. (1978). *Mind in society.* Cambridge, UK: Harvard University Press.

Wadsworth, D. (1997). Building a strategy for successful public engagement. *Phi Delta Kappan,* 78, 10, 749–752.

Williams, M.G. (1994). Enabling schoolteachers to participate in the design of educational software. *Proceedings of PDC'94,* Participating Design Conference, 153–157. Palo Alto, CA: Computer Professionals for Social Responsibility.

Distance Matters

Gary M. Olson
Judith S. Olson

18.1   Introduction

In 1898, Arthur Mee stated, "If, as it is said to be not unlikely in the near future, the principle of sight is applied to the telephonc as well as that of sound, earth will be in truth a paradise, and distance will lose its enchantment by being abolished altogether." Ninety-nine years later, Frances Cairncross (1997), a senior editor at *The Economist,* published a book entitled *The Death of Distance.* The dust jacket blurb stated that "Geography, borders, time zones—all are rapidly becoming irrelevant to the way we conduct our business and personal lives. . . ." The book trumpeted the marvels of modern communication technologies.

To paraphrase Mark Twain, the reports of distance's death are greatly exaggerated. Even with all our emerging information and communications technologies, distance affects how humans interact with each other. There are characteristics of face-to-face human interactions that the emerging technologies are either pragmatically or logically incapable of replicating. Cairncross was wrong. Distance is not only alive and well, it is in several essential respects immortal.

There are several broad reasons why distance will persist as an important element of human experience. Differences in local physical context, time zones, culture, and language all persist in spite of the use of distance technologies. Some distance work is possible today, but some aspects of it will remain difficult if not impossible to support even in the future.

©2000 Lawrence Erlbaum Associates, Inc. Reprinted with permission from *Human-Computer Interaction,* Vol. 15, No. 2/3, September 2000.

We will focus in this paper mainly on *same-time,* or synchronous, interactions that take place either in the same place or from different places. Asynchronous interactions are also very important to human collaborative activities. We will look at some of these issues later. But our principal focus will be on the same-time case because it is especially challenging with respect to the role of distance technologies. Also, the issues of context, time zones, culture, and language play out here most acutely.

We will first examine how work is conducted when people are maximally *collocated,* working in project rooms or "warrooms." Second, we examine how work is conducted today when people work on *remote* teams trying to achieve "virtual collocation." Our findings in these settings fall into two categories: behavior that will change for the better when the technology achieves certain qualities that are possible in the next 20 years and behavior that will never change. It is this second category we expand in the third part of the paper, exploring *why distance will continue to matter* even with significant technological advances.

1. *Collocated work.* This is the case where the team members are at the same physical location, either temporarily because they've traveled to a common location or permanently because they are at a common site. By "same location" we mean that coworkers can get to each others' workspaces with a short walk. Additionally, we assume that the coworkers have access to common spaces for group interactions (meeting rooms, lounges) and have mutual access to significant shared artifacts (displays, files, models, whatever they are using in their work).

2. *Distance work today.* Today's distance work is interesting because available technology is changing rapidly, and groups vary enormously in what they have access to. But to support synchronous work we can assume that today the options include the following.
   a. Telephony
   b. Meeting room video conferencing
   c. Desktop video and audio conferencing
   d. Chat rooms
   e. File transfer
   f. Application sharing
   g. Primitive virtual reality options
   There are commercial options emerging for most of these, although lab options have been available for at least 10 to 15 years. All of these vary widely in quality and cost, and even the most expensive have serious limitations.

3. *Distance work in the future.* Good design and more horsepower in the infrastructure will solve a number of the limitations of current distance technologies. Greater bandwidth will solve the disruptive influence of today's delays in audio and video transmission and will allow for larger, smoother, more life-size displays of remote workers. Perhaps even more interesting is the possibility that future tools may provide capabilities that

are in some ways *superior* to face-to-face options (Hollan and Stornetta 1992).

We will try to contrast those aspects of distance work that may have technical solutions with those that may not. This will help us choose the appropriate technologies and craft an organizational design that creates effective remote work.

We integrate research results with these four key concepts.

- Common ground
- Coupling (dependencies) of group work
- Collaboration readiness
- Collaboration technology readiness

These concepts are defined, examples are given, and the concepts are used in our discussion of the future. A more detailed version of this paper can be found in Olson and Olson (2001).

18.2 Collocated Work Today

We have recently observed the work of people who are maximally or radically collocated (Covi et al. 1998; Olson et al. 1998; Teasley et al. 2000). We observed the work of people in nine corporate sites who share office space, typically a large room the size of a conference room, to conduct work like software design, appliance design, organizational redesign, or high-level sales coordination. These rooms were often called "project rooms" or "warrooms." In seven of these nine sites, people working in them had no other office and typically were assigned to only the task at hand for the duration of the project. We conducted interviews and surveys, had people fill out diaries, and observed them at work.

One site collected productivity measures on the six teams that we observed, as they do with all their software-engineering teams (Teasley et al. 2000). The results were remarkable: They produced *double* the function points per unit of staff time[1] compared to the corporate average, and they cut the total time to market (per function point) by two-thirds. Although several things were new to these groups besides collocation, the results suggest that being collocated at least assisted in the productivity gain.

What did these teams have that distant teams do not? The team in Figure 18.1 shows typical activity in the room. They often moved from working in subgroups, sometimes with one or two working alone to having a spontaneous meeting. This fluidity of participation was rated as very important to the timely completion of their work. They could move from one subgroup to another, or to a meeting of the whole by merely overhearing others' conversations and/or seeing what someone was working on.

---

[1]The software profession metrics count function points instead of lines of code as a way of standardizing different levels of complexity.

FIGURE 18.1   The left frame shows a group divided into two subgroups. The right frame shows the two groups moments later merged to solve a particularly difficult problem together.

Figure 18.2 shows a different team embedded in the artifacts of their work. This team generated and repeatedly used 42 flip charts during their project. These depicted the use cases for their software, annotated to show the objects and methods, the object hierarchy, the system architecture, and a to-do list with items ticked off when completed. Particularly important were the *spatiality* and the *stability* of context in these

FIGURE 18.2   A team working using an object-oriented development method, creating, editing, and referring to the material on numerous flip charts.

rooms. A team member could refer to someone's list of ideas on a taped-up flip chart sheet or gauge another's reaction to something being said by making a gesture or glance in its direction that everyone could immediately interpret. Similarly, Whittaker and Schwarz (1995) observed developers using a project-planning wall to extract critical information about their work. Often meetings were held in front of it in order to jointly examine the implications of new events.

These groups came into their projects with established working habits within a corporate culture and had extensive experience working as teams. The room, the flip charts, and, in one case, a printing whiteboard were their collaboration technologies. Their adoption of these technologies was smooth because they constituted small steps from how they worked with earlier tools. When they needed to work intensely solo, they moved to nearby unowned cubicles, reducing the amount of disturbance the collocation engendered. But they were not far away, and when the work had to be collaborative, they rejoined the group. All the surveyed teams reported initial fear that working in the rooms would cause too much interruption of their individual work. Their attitudes changed significantly for the better. They found ways to cope with the disadvantages of collocation and highly valued the advantages.

Table 18.1 lists some of the key characteristics of face-to-face interaction. All of these are examples of how the ordinary ebb and flow of situated cognitive and social activities are exploited for ease of interaction and information extraction in collocated settings. This can be used as a list against which one can compare the sets of current technologies to see how difficult it is to do today's work remotely.

TABLE 18.1   Key Characteristics of Collocated Synchronous Interactions

Characteristic	Description	Implications
Rapid Feedback	As interactions flow, feedback is rapid.	Quick corrections possible.
Multiple Channels	Information from voice, facial expressions, gesture, body posture, and so on flows among participants.	There are many ways to convey a subtle or complex message; also provides redundancy.
Personal Information	The identity of contributors to conversation is usually known.	The characteristics of the person can help the interpretation of meaning.
Nuanced Information	The kind of information that flows is often analog or continuous, with many subtle dimensions (such as gestures).	Very small differences in meaning can be conveyed; information can easily be modulated.
Shared Local Context	Participants have a similar situation (time of day, local events).	Allows for easy socializing as well as mutual understanding about what's on each others' minds.

(continued)

TABLE 18.1   Key Characteristics of Collocated Synchronous Interactions (*continued*)

Characteristic	Description	Implications
Informal "Hall" Time Before and After	Impromptu interactions take place among participants upon arrival and departure.	Opportunistic information exchanges and social bonding.
Coreference	Ease of joint reference to objects.	Gaze and gesture can easily identify the referent of deictic[2] terms.
Individual Control	Each participant can freely choose what to attend to.	Rich, flexible monitoring of how the participants are reacting.
Implicit Cues	A variety of cues as to what is going on are available in the periphery.	Natural operations of human attention provide access to important contextual information.
Spatiality of Reference	People and work objects are located in space.	Both people and ideas can be referred to spatially; "air boards."

18.3   Remote Work Today

In discussing remote work today, we draw on observational studies of five corporate sites and two scientific collaboratories, all with work of teams distributed over long distances, sometimes across continents (Olson and Teasley 1996; Olson et al. 1998; Finholt and Olson 1997; Herbsleb et al. 2000; Rocco et al. 2000; Teasley and Jain 2000). Sites include corporate finance, automobile design, software engineering, and two science collaboratories, one for space physics and one for AIDS researchers.

In addition, we report related findings from comparative laboratory studies. These studies collected quality, process, and satisfaction measures from over 70 groups of three people each who know each other and have worked together before. These groups work on a standard design problem (designing an automatic post office) for 1½ hours. A number of groups work in a standard face-to-face mode using a whiteboard, paper, and pencil; others use a shared editor while working face to face; and others are using the editor while working remotely, connected either by full duplex audio or audio plus high-quality video connections (Olson et al. 1995, 1997; Veinott et al. 1999).

---

[2] "Deictic" are references to objects or ideas made by pointing and gesturing and using the words "this" and "that."

18.3.1 Successes

The Space Physics and Aronomy Research Collaboratory (SPARC) is an example of success. This collaboratory focuses on simultaneous access to real-time data from instruments around the world, allowing scientists to talk about phenomena while they are happening. With such online resources, many more scientists are able to participate in specific research campaigns. This is particularly beneficial to students, junior scientists, scientists at non-elite institutions, and scientists in developing countries. Modelers can predict and alter their models in real time, which in turn inform empiricists about what phenomena to expect. The online campaigns can be saved and replayed later. This has facilitated electronic data analysis workshops in which a wide range of data surrounding upper-atmospheric events of particular interest can be discussed over the Internet.

The design of SPARC was highly user-centered, taking them through small steps in each iteration of the design. The technology has migrated from the early digital embodiment of the original physical devices through a more integrated view capturing the relationships between the data streams. Today they have a side-by-side view of the empirical data superimposed on the map of the globe and the theoretician's model in the same orientation and scale. Furthermore, they began with simple single-stream chat. Today they have "rooms" and "clubs" in which to converse with people with similar interests. When the scientists began, they were only partially fluent in e-mail. They have been taken through a number of steps to get them to tools they are using today—3-D renderings of data and virtual rooms of objects and remote partners.

The use of NetMeeting at Boeing is a similar success (Mark et al. 1999). The technology is a small step from what they had used previously. But further, the meetings using NetMeeting that are most highly rated had a formal structure to them or were facilitated. The ambiguity of the work was removed when the meetings became structured.

A third success is the ongoing work at the telecommunications company doing software maintenance and enhancement (Herbsleb et al. 2000; Rocco et al. 2000). This work involves over 1,000 software engineers in four main sites, working on millions of lines of code. It is supported by a mix of e-mail, video- and audioconferencing, transferred files, and fax. Two things seem to contribute to its success. Although the evolving software is somewhat messy, its structure has remained more or less intact for more than a decade. Everyone knows the boundaries, who owns what, who is allowed to change what, and what sorts of things cause problems. There is a detailed process shared across all sites, allowing the teammates to communicate in a common language about the state of the work, what has been done, and what condition it is in when it is handed off. Most team members have been on the project for many years. It takes a novice about two years to learn what the long-term members know about the structure and process.

18.3.2 Failures

Many of the attempts to use distance technology have either failed outright or have resulted in Herculean efforts to adjust behavior to the characteristics of the communication media. Our laboratory data show that remote groups, though able to get quality work done, change how they work. They engaged in more clarification and more management overhead (Olson et al. 1995; see also Tang and Isaacs 1993; Isaacs and Tang 1994). Remote work is hard to conduct, even with the best of today's technologies.

In the field, we have seen repeatedly the effects of this extra effort. In those situations when people attempted to work closely with remote team members on difficult problems (for example, reconciling reported financial figures, doing software design— [not coding], diagnosing mechanical failures to decide whether they are faults of manufacturing or original design), over time, the remote technologies were used less and less. Work was reorganized so that people could work on hard problems with only local people. For example, the software design effort was reorganized to partition the design work into loosely coupled modules, assigning all the work of each module to one location. Tight interactions conducted remotely are hard to support.

Universally, in all our fieldwork as well as in Tang and Isaacs (1993), people complained about the quality of communication over audio- and videoconferences. Participants in audioconferences had trouble figuring out who is talking or what is being referred to. Videoconferencing tools are hard to set up and "produce." People speaking were off-camera because no one knew how to run the remote camera. People's voices were faint; no one adjusted the volume.

New behaviors emerge to compensate for these shortcomings: always identifying oneself before speaking, more formal protocols for turn taking, specialized vocabularies and discourse rules (as in air traffic control). Effective communication can take place, but the effort is usually quite large (Heath and Luff 1991 and Isaacs and Tang 1994 provide good examples of this). In the Boeing meetings, they created a new role of "virtual meeting facilitator," making sure remote sites were polled occasionally, listening for places things might need clarification and so forth. Although people recognize the greater flexibility and access that such new media provide, they still prefer face-to-face interactions for most purposes (Mark et al. 1999).

It is not yet widely recognized *where* the value of video lies for remote conversation. It is not surprising that if team members are referring to a complex artifact, video of that artifact helps (Farmer and Hyatt 1994; Nardi et al. 1997). Up until recently, empirical literature showed that although there is a consistent effect on satisfaction (see Finn et al. 1997 for a review), there is no effect of video on the quality of the work unless it involves negotiation (Short et al. 1976). Video has been shown to add nothing to the outcome performance of people engaged in a variety of tasks: design, service provision, and instruction, among others (Olson and Olson 1997).

These studies, however, used various teams of people who had a lot in common and who were doing fairly unambiguous tasks. More recently, a study showed that pairs of people from different countries speaking English as their second language performing a task with a moderate amount of ambiguity (reconciling two maps that are slightly different) performed significantly better when they had video compared to audio only (Veinott et al. 1999). Figure 18.3 shows what the video medium afforded the team members: The person instructing could add gestures to explain their ideas better. Furthermore, the recipient could understand the spoken word better by seeing the speaker (Krauss and Bricker 1967), and the instructor could see if they had achieved understanding yet. Williams (1997) also reported that native and non-native speakers behaved differently with respect to audio and video channels. And Boyle et al. (1994) have shown that video can help to disambiguate difficult to understand audio.

Motivation (Orlikowski 1992) is another major source of failure in adoption of groupware. In early attempts to develop a collaboratory for AIDs researchers, we spent several years working with scientists, encouraging them to share their ideas and data with others to increase the speed of discovery. Many remained uninterested, however, fearing loss of control over the use of their data, perhaps missing a key discovery that another scientist will get credit for. In contrast, some researchers whose work depended on the talents of others (for example, where one lab is the only place to get a particular analysis done) were eager to collaborate. They became early adopters of distance technology (Teasley and Jain 2000).

18.4 The Findings Integrated: Four Concepts

The results previously described can be synthesized into four key concepts: common ground, coupling of work, collaboration readiness, and collaboration technology readiness. In each of the following sections, we first define the concept, point to examples in the preceding results, and then end with a prescription for success.

FIGURE 8.3 Two people with little common ground, using a video channel well to achieve understanding on an ambiguous task.

18.4.1 Common Ground—A Characteristic of the Players

Effective communication between people requires that the exchange take place with respect to some level of common ground (Clark 1996). Common ground refers to that knowledge that the participants have in common and that they are aware that they have in common. People describe the same event or idea quite differently talking to a spouse, a coworker, a distant relative, a neighbor, a stranger from across the country, and a stranger from overseas.

We establish common ground not just from some general knowledge about the person's background but also through specific knowledge gleaned from the person's appearance and behavior during the conversational interaction itself. If we say something based on an assumption about what someone knows, but their facial expression or verbal reply indicates that they did not understand us, we will revise our assumptions about what common ground we share and say something to repair the misunderstanding. As Clark and Brennan (1991) show, this is often a collaborative process in which the participants mutually establish what they know so conversation can proceed.

We construct common ground from whatever cues we have at the moment. The fewer cues we have, the harder the work in constructing it and the more likely misinterpretations will occur. These misinterpretations in turn require more work to repair, or if the effort required is too high, people will abort the effort and move on knowing they don't have perfect correspondence. Clark and Brennan (1991) described some of the ways distance technologies differ from face to face in their support of common ground, shown in Table 18.3.

Copresence typically implies access to the same artifacts to support the conversation, allowing diectic reference and shared context. *Cotemporality* leads to understanding of the circadian context. *Visibility* and *Audibility* provide rich clues to the situation. *Simultaneity* and *Sequentiality* relieve the person of having to remember the context of the previous utterance when receiving the current one. *Reviewability* and *Revisability* assist people in both formulating carefully what they mean and having several chances to decode the message received.

In our studies, we have seen numerous examples of the effect of failure at establishing common ground. When teams are fully collocated, it is relatively easy. They share not only cultural and local context but also more micro context of who is doing what at the moment and what remains to be done. Those who are remote complain about the difficulty of establishing common ground. When connected by audioconferencing, it is very difficult to tell who is speaking if you don't know the participants well. Offhand reference to some local event (say, the Littleton shooting or the Tour de France) is understood by the locals but makes the remote people feel even more remote. People with video can engage in the subtle negotiation that establishes local common ground—whether what was said was understood or not, whether the conversation can proceed or needs repair. Broad shared knowledge is also important. The people working on the telecommunications project for a long time had common ground. They knew each other and were schooled in the development process to which they all adhered.

TABLE 18.3   The Characteristics for Achieving Common Ground in Various Communication Media

Medium	Copresence	Visibility	Audibility	Cotemporality	Simultaneity	Sequentiality	Reviewability	Revisability
Face-to-Face	•	•	•	•	•	•		
Telephone			•	•	•	•		
Videoconference	•	•	•	•	•			
Two-Way Chat			•	•	•	•	•	•
Answering Machine			•			•		
E-mail							•	•
Letter							•	•

One important feature of collocation that is missing in remote work is awareness of the state of one's coworkers, both their presence/absence and their mental state. This awareness is again an important part of common ground. If you know that someone just returned from a difficult meeting and is stressed, your communication with him/her will be different than if they had just been in the room with you working on the project you are focused on. There have been a number of attempts to recreate this sense of awareness remotely, including the open video link in the Portland experiment (Olson and Bly 1991), desktop glance systems at several Xerox sites (Gaver et al. 1992; Dourish and Bly 1992; Dourish et al. 1996) Cruiser and Videoat Bellcore (Fish et al. 1993), Montage at Sun (Tang et al. 1994), and CAVECAT at Toronto (Mantei et al. 1991). All of these installations had some success in getting people to communicate more easily, though a number of human factors, social, and organizational issues interfered with their ready use. In all cases they were abandoned after a demonstration period, in part because their cost could not be justified by appropriate benefit.

This leads us to our first set of prescriptions, focusing on the importance of common ground. The more common ground people can establish, the easier the communication, the greater the productivity. If people have established little common ground, allow them to develop it, either by traveling and getting to know each other or by using as high a bandwidth channel as possible. People who have little common ground benefit significantly from having a video channel.

18.4.2 Coupling in Work—A Characteristic of the Work Itself

We use the concept of "coupling" to refer to the extent and kind of communication required by the work. Tightly coupled work is work that strongly depends on the talents of collections of workers and is nonroutine, even ambiguous. The work typically requires frequent, complex communication among the group members, with short feedback loops and multiple streams of information. In contrast, loosely coupled work has fewer dependencies or is more routine. For example, the routing of a travel voucher from originator through approval and finally accounting and payment has a number of dependencies (it cannot be paid until it is approved), but the work is routine enough to not require clarification or reconciliation. In loosely coupled work, there is common ground about the task goal and procedure. It merely needs to be played out. Loosely coupled work requires either less frequent or less complicated interactions.

Coupling is based on the nature of the task and the common ground of the participants. The greater the number of participants, the more likely aspects of the task are ambiguous to some. Tasks that are by nature ambiguous are tightly coupled until clarification is achieved. The more common ground the participants have, the less interaction required to understand the situation and what to do.

In our research, we have seen that tightly coupled work is very difficult to do remotely. Technology, at least today, does not support rapid back and forth in conversation or awareness and repair of ambiguity. Consequently, we saw numerous occasions where the work was reorganized so that the tightly coupled work was assigned to people who were collocated. In short, the work was reorganized to fit the geography.

The various success cases were all examples of loosely coupled work. The space physicists did their detailed work typically by themselves and their local cohort group. When they are online, they are not dependent on each other. The pace of the unfolding science was slow, and though discovery was ambiguous, some of the data gathering and analysis techniques they shared were not.

The second prescription thus is to design the work organization so that ambiguous, tightly coupled work is collocated. Long-distance dependencies have to be straightforward and unambiguous to succeed. Furthermore, the more formal the procedure to enact the communication, the more likely the success.

18.4.3 Collaboration Readiness

Using shared technology assumes that the coworkers value sharing. Different fields and work settings engender a willingness to share. The space physicists had a long tradition of collaboration before they began using the Internet to support their long-distance interactions. On the other hand, several biomedical communities failed because the players were not willing to share what they knew. People at the computer company did not learn TeamRoom (a Lotus Notes application) because it was unclear to them what they would get out of it. Those benefiting were different from those having to do the work in entering what they knew (fitting Grudin 1988).

The third prescription is that one should not attempt to introduce groupware and remote technologies in organizations and communities that do not have a culture of sharing. If the organization needs to collaborate more, then the incentive structure has to be aligned with the desired behavior.

18.4.4 Technology Readiness

Some organizations are sufficiently collaborative to be good candidates for successful adoption of the appropriate technologies for distance work. Their habits and infrastructure, however, are not. Those organizations that have not adopted e-mail, for example, will not be ready adopters of NetMeeting. The more advanced technologies require a technical infrastructure (networking to desktops and meeting rooms, as well as projection equipment in meeting rooms). But more importantly, they require the habits, particularly those of preparation (such as meeting setup), regular access (such as reading Notes every day), attention given to others' need for information (thinking whether one's current work could be useful to others, then taking the time to make it accessible), and so forth. Poor alignment of technology support, existing patterns of everyday use, and the requirements for a new technology are major inhibitors of successful adoption (Star and Ruhleder 1994).

The space physicists are good examples of evolving collaboration technology readiness. When they began this effort, only some were users of e-mail. All used telephone and fax. Indeed their major collaboration activity was attending conferences or sitting together in a remote site chatting about a phenomenon that was unfolding. The earliest collaboration technology we offered them allowed similar behavior but at a distance. Data from the upper atmosphere were displayed in views like the instruments they would read at the site, and they chatted about it. Early behavioral data show that the content and style of the conversations were very similar in face-to-face situations and those now held remotely (McDaniel et al. 1996).

Later incarnations of the collaboration technology for the space physicists evolved with their general technical sophistication. When the Web became popular, others started putting relevant instruments online. Those who had already participated in the project began to demand access to these sites as well, and the entire project became Web-based. As experience grew, they became more and differently Technology Ready. The interface they have now would not likely have been accepted at the outset.

The Boeing teams had experienced video- and audioconferencing, even putting shared objects on camera so that they could be viewed (albeit poorly) at both local and remote sites. It was an easy step to adopt NetMeeting; they were appropriately Technology Ready (Mark et al. 1999). However, while they were ready for such technology, frustrations with the audio and the limited usefulness of the video resulted in declining use of NetMeeting. It appears the users were ready for a technology that was unable to deliver on its promise. This, of course, can cause major problems with subsequent attempts to introduce similar tools, since such failure experiences are often very memorable. Once burned, twice shy.

The fourth prescription is that advanced technologies should be introduced in small steps. It is hard to see far in the future where not only are technologies available but they fit an entirely new work form.

18.5   Distance Work in the New Millennium

Could the technology ever get good enough to fully mimic the ease of interaction we see in face-to-face settings? Yes and no. We believe there is room for improvement over today's technologies. But even with high-bandwidth, display of appropriate size and distance dues, access to shared objects, and so on, there will always be things about the remote situation that make it qualitatively different than collocation. These include aspects of common ground and context, the effects of different time zones, cultural differences, and various interactions of these with technology.

One way to think about what might be possible in the future is to take our earlier list of characteristics of face-to-face interactions and imagine what is the best we could ever hope for. Again, we are mindful of arguments that in thinking about distant interactions we should not fall into the trap of singling out face-to-face interactions as the gold standard. There may be a number of ways in which distant interactions may have properties that are better than "being there" in terms of how a collaborative activity unfolds (Hollan and Stornetta 1992). But this exercise will help us think about what the distinctive characteristics of value of face-to-face and remote interactions might be.

Table 18.4 presents an initial cut at such an analysis. As technologies evolve, more and more of these characteristics will be amenable to technical solutions. However, we feel that several key elements of interactivity, mostly having to do with context, the locality and spatiality of individual participant's situation, will be very resistant to support. Let us look in a little more detail at some of the characteristics of distance that will continue to be resistant to technological support.

TABLE 18.4   How Well Today's and Future Technologies Can Support the Key Characteristics of Collocated Synchronous Interactions

Characteristic	Today	Future
Rapid Feedback		●
Multiple Channels	O	●
Personal Information	O	●
Nuanced Information	O	●
Shared Local Context		
Informal "Hall" Time Before and After	O	O
Coreference		O
Individual Control		O
Implicit Cues		O
Spatiality of Reference		O

● = well supported; O = poorly supported

18.5.1 Common Ground, Context, and Trust

People who are born and live in entirely different countries, with their local political and sports events, holidays, and so forth, will always have to take extra effort to establish common ground. For example, in a videoconference between London and Chicago in March, the entire conference was delayed for 45 minutes out of the allotted hour because of a huge snowstorm in Chicago that prevented people from coming in on time. Participants in London knew only that the remote partners were absent, not the reason why. It became clear only when the first participant straggled in and was completely drenched from melting snow. It would have taken extra effort on the Chicago end to inform the London participants of the reason for the delay.

Establishing common ground is also an important precursor to trust. Trust is defined as the condition in which one exhibits behavior that makes one vulnerable to someone else, not under one's control (Zand 1972). People will trust others who make a sincere effort to fulfill commitments, are honest in negotiating commitments, and do not take advantage of another when the opportunity arises (Cummings and Bromiley 1996). Remote teams have been reported to be less effective and reliable than face-to-face teams, based on the observation simply stated as "trust needs touch" (Handy 1995).

Trust is very fragile in the world of electronic communication. As Rocco (1998) showed, trust and cooperation is developed in face-to-face situations. When people communicate by text only, they develop more self-serving stances. Fortunately, this self-serving behavior is diminished if the teammates meet each other face-to-face before working remotely.

18.5.2 Different Time Zones

A second difficulty is that remote participants arc often working in different time zones. The more time zones you cross, the fewer the number of hours when people are at work at the same time. At the automobile site we saw a very different work pace during the hours in the day when "France was still awake" or "When the United States woke up" and the hours of nonoverlap. There was high tension when things could be communicated in real-time long distance, hoping to get things resolved with quick turnaround. When there was nonoverlap there was a more relaxed pace, a resignation that nothing could be resolved until the next overlap.

The positive side of the time zone difference, of course, is that if properly coordinated, work can proceed 24 hours a day. This requires loosely coupled work and firm communication about the status of pieces of work that need to be coordinated and any other "color commentary" about the situation to make the next shift of work productive.

The second effect of different time zones is that during the overlap, the participants at various sites are at different points in their circadian rhythms. Videoconferences between the United States and France saw sleepy morning stragglers at the

U.S. site and alert afternoon workers at the French site. Later in the day, the U.S. site had the prelunch agitated workers, and France had tired people ready to close things down and go home.

18.5.3 Culture

We have observed remote teams misunderstand each other because of cultural differences. Such simple things as different local conventions about dress can lead to improper attributions about motivation in videoconferences. We witnessed Silicon Valley engineers in T-shirts and blue jeans and Big Five consultants in their formal corporate wear make incorrect attributions about each other.

There are also differences in process (Hofstede 1980, 1991). It is well known that the American culture is very task oriented and being parts of ad hoc, short-term teams is common. Southern and Eastern Europeans as well as Asians are known to value personal relationships more than the task at hand. They will sacrifice promptness when a previous interaction with a valued colleague is not deemed finished (Hall and Hall 1990). They will spend whole meetings in social interaction where American business people will at most have a few sentences asking about the family or noting the weather before "getting down to business." When remote meetings mix these cultures, there is high likelihood of misunderstandings.

Another important characteristic is "power distance" (Hofstede 1980, 1991). This refers to the relationship between a manager and his or her direct reports. In Europe and Asia, workers respect authority. There is a large power distance between them. Managers make directives. They do not need to spend time getting workers to buy in. In contrast, in the United States, managers need to review plans and actions with direct reports so that "everyone is on board." In the United States, there is less power distance; people at different levels communicate freely. Misunderstandings emerge when a U.S. manager has European or Asian direct reports. The manager expects a consideration and discussion about actions he or she proposes. The direct reports will merely take the directive and enact their part. The opposite happens with European or Asian managers directing U.S. direct reports. They are surprised when their directives are countered or not carried out because the workers have not been consulted.

18.5.4 Interactions among These Factors and with Technology

We have seen instances when culture, time zones, and technology interact. At the automobile company, we witnessed two such interactions of culture. At one, routine videoconference meetings were scheduled for Friday morning, U.S. time. To accommodate the French local time, these were scheduled first thing, 7:30 A.M. in the United States. Unfortunately for the French, who traditionally work a 35-hour week, Friday afternoon is outside of normal work time. The French, respecting the authority of the manager, did not complain. Their behavior during the meeting, however, was irritated and short, intolerant of expansion, clarification, or discussion episodes.

The French had one-word responses to almost all agenda items. This, of course, could be corrected by better knowledge of the local situations in scheduling such conferences. But it is difficult to anticipate all dimensions of such differences, particularly for three or more sites participating.

The most egregious misunderstanding we witnessed occurred as an interaction of culture and the distance technology. Videoconferencing is expensive. Americans, being task focused and cost conscious, begin a videoconference when everyone is in the room. As soon as the video is on, the first agenda item is discussed, and at the end of the last item, the video is terminated. At one particular meeting we witnessed a typically abrupt beginning and end by the Americans to a three-way conference between the United States, France, and Germany. Unfortunately, one of the French engineers was experiencing his last day on the job, having been forced into retirement after a misunderstanding about a rule for certain workers. The Americans had said nothing to him about this unhappy situation nor did they say a personal good-bye. They cut the video connection as usual right after the last agenda item. The Germans stayed on the videoconference a full 15 minutes after the Americans left, wishing him well and kidding him affectionately about what he was going to do in retirement. The French and Germans were embarrassed by the Americans' apparent affront.

Perhaps these remote technologies are so new that we just haven't yet had time to adapt to them. We established rules of behavior to accommodate these cultural differences to fit fast travel. "When in Rome, do as the Romans do." When we travel, we adapt to the manners of the site traveled to. But in a videoconference, where is "Rome"? There is no default location to which the parties accommodate. No one even thinks that they are experiencing a foreign culture and that misunderstandings might abound.

18.6 Conclusion

Collaborative work at a distance will be difficult to do for a long time, if not forever. There will likely always be certain kinds of advantages to being together. However, as a wide range of collaborative tools emerges, we will find useful ways to use them to accomplish our goals. If at some point in the past we had written a similar article about telegraphy, the telephone, radio, television, or fax machines, we would have had tables that catalog their shortcomings. However, in their own ways, all of them have turned out to have been useful for a variety of purposes, and they worked their ways into social and organizational life in enduring fashion. Indeed, some of the most profound changes in social and organizational behavior in this century can be traced to these tools. The rich repertoire of present and future collaborative technologies will have a similar fate. We will find uses for them, and descriptions of collaborative work in the future will enumerate the emergent social practices that have put these technologies to useful ends. But it is our belief that in these future descriptions distance will continue to matter.

Acknowledgments

The research described in this paper was generously supported by the National Science Foundation (research grant numbers IIS-9320543, IIS-9977923, and ATM-9873025, and cooperative agreement number IRI-9216848), Steelcase Corporation, Ford Motor Company, IBM, and Sun Microsystems. We are grateful to Wendy Kellogg, Paul Resnick, and three anonymous reviewers for useful comments on an earlier draft.

References

Boyle, E., Anderson, A., and Newlands, A. (1994). The effects of visibility on dialogue performance in a cooperative problem solving task. *Language and Speech,* 37, 1, 1–20.

Cairncross, F. (1997). The death of distance: How the communications revolution will change our lives. Boston, MA: Harvard Business School Press.

Clark, H.H. (1996). *Using language.* New York: Cambridge University Press.

Clark, H.H., and Brennan, S.E. (1991). Grounding in communication. In L. Resnick, J.M. Levine, and S.D. Teasley (Eds.), *Perspectives on Socially Shared Cognition,* 127–149. Washington, DC: APA.

Covi, L.M., Olson, J.S., and Rocco, E. (1998). A room of your own: What do we learn about support of teamwork from assessing teams in dedicated project rooms? In N. Streitz, S. Konomi, and H.J. Burkhardt (Eds.), *Cooperative Buildings,* 53–65. Amsterdam: Springer-Verlag.

Cummings, L.L., and Bromiley, P. (1996). The organizational trust inventory (OTI): Development and validation. In R.M. Kramer and T.R. Tyler (Eds.), *Trust in organizations: Frontiers of theory and research,* 302–330. Thousand Oaks, CA: Sage Publications.

Dourish, P., Adler, A., Bellotti, V., and Henderson, A. (1996). Your place or mine? Learning from long-term use of audio-video communication. *Computer-Supported Cooperative Work,* 5, 1, 33–62.

Dourish, P., and Bly, S. (1992). Portholes: Supporting awareness in a distributed group. *Proceedings of the 1992 Conference on Computer-Human Interaction,* 541–547. New York: ACM Press.

Farmer, S.M., and Hyatt, C.W. (1994). Effects of task language demand and task complexity on computer-mediated work groups, *Small Group Research*, 25, 3, 331–336.

Finholt, T.A., and Olson, G.M. (1997). From laboratories to collaboratories: A new organizational form for scientific collaboration. *Psychological Science*, 8, 1, 28–35.

Finn, K., Sellen, A., and Wilbur. S. (Eds.). (1997). *Video Mediated Communication*. Mahwah, NJ: Lawrence Erlbaum Associates.

Fish, R.S., Kraut, R.E., Root, R., and Rice, R.E. (1993). Video as a technology for informal communication. *Communications of the ACM*, 36, 8–61.

Gaver, W.W., Moran, T., MacLean, A., Lovstrand, L., Dourish, P., Carter, K.A., and Buxton, W. (1992). Realizing a video environment: EuroPARC's RAVE system. *Proceedings of the ACM Conference on Human Factors in Computing Systems (CHI'92)*. New York: ACM Press, 27–35.

Grudin, J. (1988). Why CSCW applications fail: Problems in the design and evaluation of organizational interfaces. *Proceedings of the ACM Conference on Computer Supported Cooperative Work (CSCW'88)*, 85–93. New York: ACM Press.

Hall, E.T., and Hall, M.R. (1990). *Understanding Cultural Differences: Germans, French and Americans*. Yarmouth, ME: Intercultural Press.

Handy, C. (1995). Trust and the virtual organization. *Harvard Business Review*, 73, 3, 40–50.

Heath, C., and Luff, P. (1991). Disembodied conduct: Communication through video in a multi-media office environment. *Proceedings of CHI'91*, New York: ACM Press. 99–103.

Herbsleb, J.D., Mockus, A., Finholt, T.A., Grintner, R.E. (2000). Distance, dependencies, and delay in global collaboration. *CREW Technical Report*, University of Michigan.

Hofstede, G. (1980). *Culture's Consequences*. Newbury Park, CA: Sage Publications, Inc.

Hofstede, G. (1991). *Cultures and Organizations: Software of the Mind*. London: McGraw-Hill International.

Hymes, C.M., and Olson, G.M. (1992). Unblocking brainstorming through use of a simple group editor. *Proceedings of the ACM Conference on Computer Supported Cooperative Work (CSCW'92)*, 99–106. New York: ACM Press.

Hollan, J., and Stornetta, S. (1992). Beyond being there. *Proceedings of CHI'92*, 119–125. New York: ACM Press.

Isaacs, E.A., and Tang, J.C. (1994). What video can and cannot do for collaboration: A case study. *Multimedia Systems*, 2, 63–73.

Krauss, R., and Bricker, P. (1967). Effects of transmission delay and access delay on the efficiency of verbal communications. *Journal of the Acoustical Society of America*, 41, 286–292.

Mantei, M.M., Baecker, R.M., Sellen, A.J., Buxton, W.A.S., and Mulligan, T. (1991). Experiences in the use of a media space. *Proceedings of the 1991 Conference on Computer-Human Interaction,* 203–208. New York: ACM Press.

Mark, G., Grudin, J., and Poltrock, S.E. (1999). Meeting at the desktop: An empirical study of virtually collocated teams. *Proceedings of ECSCW'99.* Boston: Kluwer Academic, 159–178.

McDaniel, S.E., Olson, G.M., and McGee, J.C. (1996). Identifying and analyzing multiple threads in computer mediated and face-to-face conversations. *Proceedings of the Conference on Computer Supported Cooperative Work, CSCW'96,* 39–47. New York: ACM Press.

Mee, A. (1898). The pleasure telephone. *The Strand Magazine,* 16, 339–345.

Nardi, B.A., Kuchinsky, A., Whittaker, S., Leichner, R., and Schwarz, H. (1997). Video-as-Data: Technical and social aspects of a collaborative multimedia application. In K. Finn, A. Sellen, and S. Wilbur (Eds.), *Video Mediated Communication.* Mahwah, NJ: Lawrence Erlbaum Associates.

Olson, G.M., Atkins, D.E., Clauer, R, Finholt, T.A., Jahanian, F., Killeen, T.L., Prakash, A., and Weymouth, T. (1998). The Upper Atmospheric Research Collaboratory. *Interactions,* 5, 3, 48–55.

Olson, J.S., and Olson, G.M. (1997). Face-to-face group work compared to remote group work with and without video. In K. Finn, A. Sellen, and S. Wilbur (Eds.), *Video Mediated Communication.* Hillsdale, NJ: Lawrence Erlbaum Associates.

Olson, G.M., and Olson, J.S. (In press). Distance matters. *Human Computer Interaction.*

Olson, J.S., Covi, L., Rocco, E., Miller, W.J., and Allie, P. (1998). A room of your own: What would it take to help remote groups work as well as collocated groups? *Short Paper the Conference on Human Factors in Computing Systems (CHI'98),* 279–280. New York: ACM Press.

Olson, J.S., Olson, G.M., and Meader, D.K. (1995). What mix of video and audio is useful for remote real-time work? *Proceedings of the Conference on Human Factors in Computing Systems (CHI'95).* Denver, CO: ACM Press.

Olson, J.S., Olson, G.M., and Meader, D. (1997). Face-to-face group work compared to remote group work with and without video. In K. Finn, A. Sellen, and S. Wilbur (Eds.), *Video Mediated Communication.* Hillsdale, NJ: Lawrence Erlbaum Associates.

Olson, J.S., and Teasley, S. (1996). Groupware in the wild: Lessons learned from a year of virtual collocation. *Proceedings of the Conference on Computer Supported Cooperative Work,* 419–427. New York: ACM.

Olson, M.H., and Bly, S.A. (1991). The Portland experience: A report on a distributed research group. *International Journal of Man-Machine Studies,* 34, 211–228.

Orlikowski, W. (1992). Learning from notes: Organizational issues in groupware implementation. *Proceedings of the Conference on Computer Supported Cooperative Work,* 362–369. New York: ACM Press.

Rocco, E. (1998). Trust breaks down in electronic contexts but can be repaired by some initial face-to-face contact. *Proceedings of the Conference on Human Factors in Computing Systems CHI'98,* 496–502. New York: ACM Press.

Rocco, E., Finholt, T.A., Hofer, E.C., and Herbsleb, J.D. (2000). Designing as if trust mattered. *CREW Technical Report,* University of Michigan.

Short, J., Williams, E., and Christie, B. (1976). *The social psychology of telecommunications.* London: Wiley.

Star, S.L., and Ruhleder, K. (1994). Steps towards an ecology of infrastructure: Complex problems in design and access for large-scale collaborative systems. *Proceedings of ACM 1994 Conference on Computer Supported Cooperative Work (CSCW'94),* 253–264. New York: ACM Press.

Tang, J.C., and Isaacs, E.A. (1993). Why do users like video? *Computer Supported Cooperative Work,* 1, 163–196.

Tang, J.C., Isaacs, E.A., and Rua, M. (1994). Supporting distributed groups with a Montage of lightweight interactions. *Proceeding of the ACM Conference on Computer Supported Cooperative Work (CSCW'94),* 23–34. New York: ACM Press.

Teasley, S., and Jain, N. (2000). Scientists apart working together: A collaboratory for AIDS research. *CREW Technical Report,* University of Michigan.

Teasley, S., Covi, L., Krishnan, M.S., and Olson, J.S. (In press). How does radical collocation help a team succeed? *Proceedings of the Conference on Computer Supported Cooperative Work. CSCW'00,* 339–346. New York: ACM Press.

Veinott, E., Olson, J.S., Olson, G.M., and Fu. X. (1999). Video helps remote work: Speakers who need to negotiate common ground benefit from seeing each other. *Proceedings of the Conference on Computer Human Interaction,* 302–309. New York: ACM Press.

Whittaker, S., and Schwarz, H. (1995). Back to the future: Pen and paper technology supports complex group coordination. *Proceedings of CHI'95,* 495–502. New York: ACM Press.

Williams, G. (1997). Task conflict and language differences: Opportunities for video-conferencing. *Proceedings of ECSCW'97.*

Zand, D.E. (1972). Trust and managerial problem solving. *Administrative Science Quarterly,* 17, 229–239.

PART V

Media and Information

19

Designing the User Interface for Multimodal Speech and Pen-Based Gesture Applications: State-of-the-Art Systems and Future Research Directions

Sharon Oviatt   Josh Bers

Phil Cohen   Thomas Holzman

Lizhong Wu   Terry Winograd

John Vergo   James Landay

Lisbeth Duncan   Jim Larson

Bernhard Suhm   David Ferro

19.1   Introduction to Multimodal Speech and Gesture Interfaces

The growing interest in multimodal interface design is inspired largely by the goal of supporting more transparent, flexible, efficient, and powerfully expressive means of human-computer interaction. Multimodal interfaces also are expected to be easier to learn and use, and are preferred by users for many applications. They have the potential to expand computing to more challenging applications, to be used by a broader spectrum of everyday people, and to accommodate more adverse usage conditions than in the past. This class of systems represents a relatively new direction for computing that draws from the myriad input and output technologies currently becoming available.

Since Bolt's (1980) original "Put That There" concept demonstration, which processed multimodal speech and manual pointing during object manipulation, considerable strides have been made in developing more general multimodal systems that process complex gestural input other than just pointing, examples of which will be outlined in Section 19.4 of this chapter. Since Bolt's early inspiration, the basic architectural components and framework needed to support more general multimodal systems have become better established, as will be described in Section 19.3. In contrast to Bolt's initial concept, which was a limited prototype, significant progress also has occurred in building a variety of real applications, four of which are illustrated in Section 19.4. In addition, during the past decade, proactive empirical work has contributed predictive information on human-computer multimodal interaction, which has provided a foundation for guiding the design of new multimodal systems that are still in the planning stages.

In a more general vein, major advances in new input technologies and algorithms, hardware speed, distributed computing, and spoken language technology in particular all have supported the emergence of more transparent and natural communication with this new class of multimodal systems. During the past decade, due largely to progress inspired by the DARPA Speech Grand Challenge project and similar international efforts, there has been significant progress in the development of spoken language technology (SLT). Spoken language systems now are implemented extensively for telephony applications and on workstations, and they are beginning to appear on small palm computers. These new technical capabilities, along with advances in natural language processing, are leading to increasingly conversational query-and-answer systems. Spoken language systems also are supporting new training systems for learning foreign languages and basic reading skills, as well as the commercialization of automated dictation systems for applications such as medical charting, legal records, and word processing.

Like spoken language technology, steady advances have occurred in pen-based hardware and software capabilities, which currently provide handwriting and gesture recognition on handhelds, small pocket-sized computers, and recently on mobile phones. Typically, these pen-based applications are used to automate telephony or to extend personal memory during management of calendars, contact information, and other personal information. Pen computing also supports visual-spatial applications involving map-based interaction, as well as specialized sketching applications for the design of flow charts, user interface designs, circuit designs, and the like. These strides in pen technology, spoken language systems, and the development of increasingly general and robust multimodal systems all are clear landmarks of progress since Put That There's initial demonstration of combined speech and manual gesturing in the user interface.

In this chapter, we begin in Section 19.2 by introducing multimodal speech and pen-based gesture interfaces, with a focus on their primary advantages and optimal uses. To date, multimodal systems that combine either speech and pen input (Oviatt et al. 2000) or speech and lip movements (Rubin et al. 1998) constitute the two major research areas within the field. Although many of the issues discussed for multimodal systems incorporating speech and 2D pen gestures also are relevant to those involving continuous 3D manual gesturing (such as Bolt's system), the latter type of system presently is less mature. This is primarily because of the significant problems associated with segmenting and interpreting continuous manual movements compared with a stream of x,y ink coordinates. As a result of this difference, the multimodal subfield involving speech and pen-based gestures has been able to explore a wider range of research issues and to advance more rapidly in its multimodal architectures and applications.

In Section 19.3, we summarize the architectural approaches currently being used to interpret dual input signals—including early and late fusion approaches and a new hybrid symbolic/statistical approach to speech and pen-based gesture interpretation. In Section 19.4, we then illustrate four diverse state-of-the-art multimodal systems that support challenging applications. These include map-based and virtual reality systems for engaging in simulations and training (Sections 19.4.1 and 19.4.3), text-editing that has the potential to reshape daily computing for everyday users (Section 19.4.2), and mobile field-medic systems for documenting trauma care while ambulance crews work in noisy and chaotic multiperson settings (Section 19.4.4). Finally, in Section 19.5 we discuss several key multimodal research challenges that remain to be addressed.

19.2   Advantages and Optimal Uses of Multimodal Interface Design

As applications generally have become more complex, a single modality does not permit the user to interact effectively across all tasks and environments. A multimodal interface offers the user freedom to use a combination of modalities or to switch to a better-suited modality, depending on the specifics of the task or environment. Since individual input modalities are well suited in some situations and less ideal or even inappropriate in others, modality choice is an important design issue in a multimodal system. In this section, we discuss the strengths of speech and pen input as individual modalities, as well as issues specific to their benefits within a combined multimodal interface.

Among other things, speech input offers speed, high-bandwidth information, and relative ease of use. It also permits the user's hands and eyes to be busy with a task, which is particularly valuable when users are in motion or in natural field settings. Users tend to prefer speech for functions like describing objects and events, sets and subsets of objects, out-of-view objects, conjoined information, past and future temporal states, as well as for issuing commands for actions or iterative actions. During multimodal pen/voice interaction, users tend to prefer entering descriptive information via speech, although their preference for pen input increases for digits, symbols, and graphic content.

While also supporting portability, pen input has a somewhat different and multifunctional range of capabilities. Although the pen can be used to write words that are analogous to speech, it also can be used to convey symbols and signs (digits, abbreviations), gestures, simple graphics and artwork, and to render signatures. In addition, it can be used to point, to select visible objects like the mouse does in a direct manipulation interface, and as a means of microphone engagement for speech input. From a usage standpoint, pen input provides a more private and socially acceptable form of input in public settings and a viable alternative to speech under circumstances of extreme noise. In architectural and similar domains, sketching and drawn graphics are a particularly rich and generative capability. In addition, pen input to maps and other graphic displays can easily and efficiently convey spatial information about precise points, lines, and areas. In brief, the pen offers critical capabilities for interacting with any form of graphic application, and it potentially can provide a very versatile and opportune base system, especially for mobile tasks.

As forms of human language technology, spoken and pen-based input have the advantage of permitting users to engage in more powerfully expressive and transparent information-seeking dialogues. Together, the speech and pen modes can easily be used to provide flexible descriptions of objects, events, spatial layouts, and their interrelation. This is largely because spoken and pen-based input provide complementary capabilities. For example, analysis of the linguistic content of users' integrated pen/voice constructions has revealed that basic subject, verb, and object constituents almost always are spoken, whereas those describing locative information invariably are written or gestured (Oviatt et al. 1997). This complementarity of spoken and gestural input also has been identified as a theme during interpersonal communication (McNeill 1992).

Compared with speech-only interaction, empirical work with users during visual-spatial tasks has demonstrated that multimodal pen/voice interaction can result in 10 percent faster task completion time, 36 percent fewer task-critical content errors, 50 percent fewer spontaneous disfluencies, and also shorter and more simplified linguistic constructions with fewer locative descriptions (Oviatt 1997). This constellation of multimodal performance advantages corresponds with a 90 to 100 percent user preference to interact multimodally (Oviatt 1997). In large part, people's performance difficulties during visual-spatial tasks are due to their error-proneness and reluctance to articulate spatially oriented information. During multimodal interaction, people instead prefer to use pen input to point or create graphics, since it generally is a more effective and precise way to convey locations, lines, areas, and other inherently spatial information. Likewise, when people are manipulating 3D objects, a multimodal interface that permits them to speak and gesture while handling objects manually is both preferred and more efficient.

A particularly advantageous feature of multimodal interface design is its ability to support superior error handling, compared with unimodal recognition-based interfaces, both in terms of error avoidance and graceful recovery from errors (Oviatt and vanGent 1996; Oviatt 1999; Rudnicky and Hauptmann 1992). There are both user-centered and system-centered reasons why multimodal systems facilitate error recovery. First, in a multimodal interface users will select the input mode that they judge to be less error prone for particular lexical content, which leads to error avoidance. Second, users' language is simplified when interacting multimodally, which reduces the complexity of natural language processing and thereby reduces recognition errors. Third, users have a strong tendency to switch modes after system errors, which facilitates error recovery. The fourth reason why multimodal systems support more graceful error handling is that users report less subjective frustration with errors when interacting multimodally, even when errors are as frequent as in a unimodal interface. Finally, a well-designed multimodal architecture can support *mutual disambiguation* of input signals. Mutual disambiguation involves recovery from unimodal recognition errors within a multimodal architecture, because semantic information from each input mode supplies partial disambiguation of the other mode—thereby leading to more stable and robust overall system performance (Oviatt 1999). To reap these error-handling advantages fully, a multimodal system must be designed so that the speech and pen modes provide parallel or duplicate functionality, which means that users can accomplish their goals using either mode.

Since there are large individual differences in ability and preference to use different modes of communication, a multimodal interface permits users to exercise selection and control over how they interact with the computer. In this respect, multimodal interfaces have the potential to accommodate a broader range of users than traditional graphical user interfaces (GUIs) and unimodal interfaces—including users of different ages, skill levels, native language status, cognitive styles, sensory impairments, and other temporary or permanent handicaps or illnesses. For example, a visually impaired user may prefer speech input and text-to-speech output, as may a manually impaired user (for example, somebody with repetitive stress injury or an arm in a cast). In contrast, a user with a hearing impairment, strong accent, or a cold may prefer pen input. Likewise, a young preschooler using an educational application can use *either* speech or graphical pen input well before a keyboard is a viable input device. A multimodal interface also permits alternation of individual input modes, which can be critical in preventing overuse and physical damage to any single modality, especially during extended periods of computer use.

Interfaces involving spoken or pen-based input, as well as the combination of both, are particularly effective for supporting mobile tasks, such as communications and personal navigation. Unlike the keyboard and mouse, both speech and pen are compact and portable. When combined, people can shift these input modes from moment to moment as environmental conditions change. There is a sense in which mobility can induce a state of "temporary disability," such that a person is unable to use a particular input mode for some period of time. For example, a user carrying a child may be temporarily unable to use pen or touch input at a public information kiosk, although speech is unaffected. In this respect, a multimodal pen/voice system permits the alternation needed to cover a wider range of changing environmental circumstances that may be encountered during actual field use.

In summary, it has been demonstrated that combined multimodal speech and gesture interfaces do the following.

- Permit flexible use of input modes, including alternation and integrated use
- Support improved efficiency, especially when manipulating graphical information
- Support less disfluent, shorter, and more linguistically simplified constructions than a speech-only interface, which results in more robust natural language processing
- Support greater precision of spatial information than a speech-only interface, because pen input conveys rich and precise graphical information
- Satisfy higher levels of user preference
- Support enhanced error avoidance and ease of error resolution
- Accommodate a wider range of users, tasks, and environmental situations
- Are adaptable during the continuously changing environmental conditions of mobile use
- Accommodate individual differences, such as permanent or temporary handicaps
- Prevent overuse of any individual mode during extended computer usage

19.3   Architectural Approaches to Multimodal Integration and Systems

As an introduction to the multimodal system descriptions that follow in Section 19.4, in this section we summarize the main architectural requirements and components of multimodal systems. In particular, the main architectural approaches are outlined for interpreting multimodal speech and pen-based gestures in a robust manner—including primarily late semantic fusion approaches, but also the introduction of a new hybrid symbolic/statistical approach that illustrates the future direction of multimodal architectures.

19.3.1   Introduction to Multimodal Architectural Requirements

Many early multimodal interfaces that handled combined speech and gesture, such as Bolt's Put That There system (Bolt 1980), were based on a control structure in which multimodal integration occurred during the process of parsing spoken language. When the user spoke a deictic expression, such as "here" or "this," the system would search for a synchronized gestural act that designated the spoken referent. While such an approach suffices for processing a *point-and-speak multimodal integration pattern,* unfortunately less than 20 percent of all users' multimodal commands are of this limited type (Oviatt et al. 1997; McNeill 1992). For this reason, multimodal pen/ voice systems must be able to process richer pen-based input than just pointing— including gestures (arrows, delete marks), digits, symbols, simple graphic marks (square to designate a building), and so forth. To support the development of broadly functional multimodal systems, a more general processing architecture clearly is needed. Ideally, such an architecture should handle both (1) a variety of multimodal speech-and-gesture integration patterns and (2) the interpretation of unimodal gestural or spoken input, as well as combined multimodal input. Such an architecture would support the development of multimodal systems with multiple modalities that are used and processed individually as *input alternatives* to one another, as well as those designed to support *combined multimodal input* from two or more modes.

For multimodal systems designed to handle joint processing of input signals, there are two main subtypes of multimodal architectures—ones that integrate signals at the *feature* level ("early fusion") and others that integrate information at a *semantic* level ("late fusion"). Systems that utilize the early feature-fusion approach generally are based on multiple Hidden Markov Models or temporal neural networks.[1] In a feature-fusion architecture, the recognition process in one mode influences the course of recognition in the other. Feature fusion generally is considered more appropriate for closely coupled and synchronized modalities, such as speech and lip movements (Rubin et al. 1998), for which both input channels provide corresponding information about the same articulated phonemes and words. However, such a system tends not to apply or generalize as well if it consists of modes that differ substantially in the information content or time-scale characteristics of their features. This is the case, for example, with speech and pen input, for which the input modes provide different but complementary information that is typically integrated at the utterance level. Modeling complexity, computational intensity, and training difficulty are typical problems associated with the feature-fusion integration approach. For example, a large amount of training data is required to build this type of system. Unfortunately, multimodal training corpora rarely have been collected and currently are at a premium.

Generally, multimodal systems using the late semantic fusion approach include individual recognizers and a sequential integration process. These individual recognizers can be trained using unimodal data, which are easier to collect and already publicly available for modalities like speech and handwriting. This type of architecture also can leverage from existing and relatively mature unimodal recognition techniques and off-the-shelf recognizers. Such unimodal systems often can be integrated directly or changed when necessary without retraining. In this respect, systems based on semantic fusion can be scaled up more easily, whether in the number of input modes or the size and type of vocabulary set.

---

[1]Hidden Markov Modeling (HMM) is a state-of-the-art statistical modeling technique that has been widely applied to problems such as large-vocabulary continuous speech recognition and handwriting recognition. Neural networks (NNs) are an alternative pattern recognition technique, and temporal neural networks (TNNs), such as time-delay neural networks and recurrent neural networks, are those capable of modeling the temporal structure of input signals.

Multimodal systems that are designed to process combined input from two or more modes also require an architecture that supports fine-grained time stamping of at least the beginning and end of each input signal. Since users' multimodal speech and gesture constructions can involve either *sequentially integrated* or *simultaneously delivered* signal pieces, a multimodal architecture also must be prepared to handle input signals that may or may not be overlapped in their temporal delivery (Oviatt et al. 1997). Empirical work on speech and gesture input has established that users' written input precedes speech during a sequentially integrated multimodal command (Oviatt et al. 1997), and it also has clarified the distribution of typical intermodal lags. This type of information has been useful in determining whether two signal pieces are part of a multimodal construction or whether they should be interpreted as unimodal commands. In addition, data on intermodal lags has been used to establish the temporal thresholds for joining signal pieces in multimodal architectures (see Section 19.4.1).

One major design goal of multimodal systems is the selection of complementary input modes that are capable of forging a highly synergistic overall combination. In theory, a well-designed multimodal system should be able to integrate complementary modalities such that the strengths of each modality are capitalized upon and used to overcome weaknesses in the other (Cohen et al. 1989). This general approach can result in a more broadly functional system, as well as a more reliable one, in part due to *mutual disambiguation*. In fact, empirical work has demonstrated that a well-integrated multimodal system can yield significant levels of mutual disambiguation between input signals (with speech disambiguating the meaning of gesture, and vice versa). Mutual disambiguation generates higher overall recognition rates and more stable system functioning than either component technology can as a standalone (Oviatt 1999, 2000).

In summary, to create useful and general multimodal pen/voice architectures that are capable of processing both separate and combined input modes in a robust manner ideally requires the following.

- Parallel recognizers and interpreters that produce a set of time-stamped meaning fragments for each continuous input stream
- A common framework for representing meaning fragments derived from multiple modalities
- A time-sensitive grouping process that determines when to combine individual meaning fragments from each modality stream
- Meaning fusion operations that combine semantically and temporally compatible meaning fragments
- A data-driven statistical process that enhances the likelihood of selecting the best joint interpretation of multimodal input
- A flexible asynchronous architecture that permits multiprocessing, keeps pace with user input, and potentially handles input from multiple simultaneous users

- A multimodal interface design that combines complementary modes in a synergistic manner, thereby yielding significant levels of mutual disambiguation between modes and improved recognition rates

---

19.3.2 Multi-Agent Architectures and Multimodal Processing Flow

Before discussing the motivation and specifics of multimodal speech and pen-based gesture architectures, it is important to identify the primary ways in which emerging multimodal architectures are distinct from those of standard graphical user interfaces (GUIs). First, GUIs typically assume that there is a single event stream that controls the underlying event loop. For example, most GUIs will ignore typed input while a mouse button is depressed. However, for many multimodal interfaces the need to process *simultaneous input* from different streams will be the norm. Second, GUIs assume that the basic interface actions, such as selection of an item, are atomic and unambiguous events. In contrast, multimodal systems are being designed to process natural human input modes via recognition-based technologies, which must handle uncertainty and therefore are based on *probabilistic* methods of processing. Third, GUIs often are built to be separable from the application software that they control, but the interface components themselves usually reside together on the same machine. In contrast, recognition-based user interfaces typically have larger computational and memory requirements, which can make it preferable to *distribute the interface* over a network such that separate machines handle different recognizers. For example, cell phones and networked PDAs may extract features from speech input and transmit them to a recognizer that resides on a server. In light of these new architectural requirements, multimodal research groups currently are rethinking and redesigning basic user interface architectures.

Figure 19.1 depicts the basic information flow needed to process multimodal speech and gesture input.[2] In such an architecture, speech and pen-based gestures are recognized in parallel, and each is processed by an understanding component. The results are meaning representations that are fused by the multimodal integration component, which also is influenced by the system's dialogue management and interpretation of current context. During the integration process, alternative lexical candidates for the final multimodal interpretation are ranked according to their probability estimates on an n-best list. The best ranked multimodal interpretation then is sent to the application invocation and control component, which transforms this information into a series of commands to one or more "back end" application system(s). System output typically is presented via either a graphical, auditory (such as for telephony), or multimedia display. Both system context and dialogue management typically are altered during user input, as well as during system output generation.

---

[2]Note that the most common variant of this information processing flow for multimodal pen/voice systems is cases in which gesture functionality is limited to deictic pointing. For such systems, speech dominates the natural language processing (NLP), and deictic points are filled into the speech frame before NLP occurs. No separate language processing is performed on the pen-based pointing gestures.

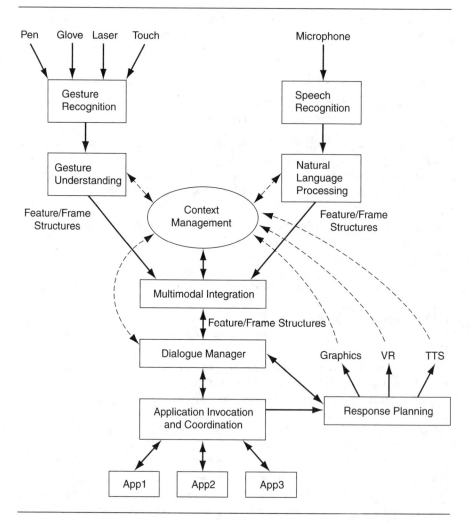

FIGURE 19.1   Typical information flow in a multimodal architecture

There are numerous ways to realize this information processing flow as an architecture. One well-understood way is to pipeline the components via procedure calls or, if the system is distributed but homogeneous in its programming language, remote procedure calls. However, if the system is heterogeneous (for example, in programming languages, operating systems, or machine characteristics), the preceding method may prove difficult. To provide a higher-level layer that supports distributed heterogeneous software, while shielding the designer from the details of communication, a number of research groups have developed and employed *multi-agent architectures,* such as the Open Agent Architecture[3] (Cohen et al. 1994) and Adaptive Agent Architecture (Kumar and Cohen 2000).

In a multi-agent architecture, components may be written in different programming languages, on different machines, and with different operating systems. Each component is "wrapped" by a layer of software that enables it to communicate via a standard language over TCP/IP. The resulting component-with-communication-layer is termed an *agent*. The agent communication language often uses message types reminiscent of speech act theory, but ones extended to handle asynchronous delivery, triggered responses, multicasting, and other concepts from distributed systems. In some multi-agent architectures, agents communicate directly with other components about which they have knowledge (such as component's name, API). This design has the advantage of no intermediaries, but it can be brittle in the face of agent failure.

As an alternative design, many architectures have adopted a *facilitated* form of communication, in which agents do not need to know to whom they are making requests or supplying answers. Instead, these agents communicate through a known facilitator, which routes messages to the interested and capable receivers. This becomes a *hub-and-spoke architecture*, with all agents communicating via the central facilitator. The facilitator provides a place for new agents to connect at run time, and they then can be discovered by other agents and incorporated into the ongoing distributed computation. The hub also becomes a locus for building collaboration systems, since the facilitator can route communications to multiple agents that may be interested in the same messages.

Figure 19.2 illustrates the same basic components as Figure 19.1 but now arrayed around a central facilitator. When that facilitator also has a global area in which to store data, it is sometimes referred to as a *blackboard system*. Note that a facilitator/hub can be a bottleneck, possibly impeding high-volume multimedia data transfer (speech). It also is a single point of failure, which can lead to a lack of system robustness. Recent research has developed fault-tolerant multiagent architectures (Kumar and Cohen 2000), which employ a team of facilitators that can share the load in case of individual facilitator failure. Such architectures now support both facilitated and point-to-point communication.

Within this type of facilitated architecture, speech and gesture input can arrive in parallel or asynchronously via individual modality agents, and they then are recognized and the results are passed to the facilitator. These results, typically an n-best list of conjectured lexical items as well as time stamp information, then are routed to agents that have advertised the capability of handling this type of data. Next, sets of meaning fragments derived from the speech and pen signals arrive at the multimodal integrator. This agent decides whether and how long to wait for recognition results from other modalities, based on the system's temporal thresholds. It then attempts to fuse the meaning fragments into a semantically and temporally compatible whole interpretation before passing the results back to the facilitator. At this point, the system's final multimodal

---

[3]The Open Agent Architecture (OAA) is a trademark of SRI International.

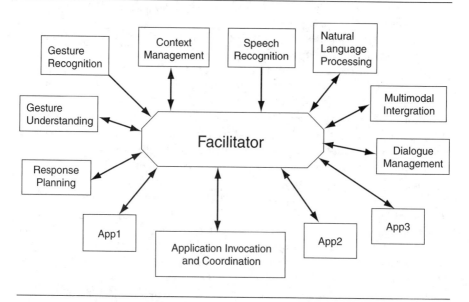

FIGURE 19.2   Facilitated multimodal architecture

interpretation is confirmed by the user interface and executed by any relevant applications. Meanwhile, new input that may have arrived from the same user or other users is processed asynchronously. Processing within this kind of a multi-agent framework is usually bottom-up and asynchronous, with an emergent control flow.

19.3.3 Frame-Based and Unification-Based Multimodal Integration

The core of multimodal integration systems based on semantic fusion comprises algorithms that integrate meaning representations derived from speech, gesture, and other modalities into a combined overall interpretation. As mentioned earlier, the semantic fusion operation requires that there be a meaning representation framework that is common among modalities, and a well-defined operation for combining partial meanings. During the initial development of multimodal speech and gesture systems, each system had its own meaning representation framework and an idiosyncratic algorithm for multimodal integration. However, in recent years a data structure called *frames* or *feature structures* has de facto become accepted to represent meaning. These structures represent objects and relations as consisting of nested sets of attribute/value pairs. Feature structures go beyond frames in their use of shared variables to indicate common substructures.

   In order to fuse information derived from multiple modalities, various research groups have independently converged on a strategy of recursively matching and merging attribute/value structures, although details of the algorithms differ. However, the most well-developed literature on this topic comes from computational linguistics, in which formal logics of typed feature structures have been developed (Carpenter 1992; Calder 1987). These structures are pervasive in natural language processing and have been used for lexical entries, grammar rules, and meaning representations. For feature structure logics, the primary operation is *unification*—a more general approach that subsumes other frame-merging strategies. Unification-based architectures have only recently been applied to multimodal system design (Cohen et al. 1997; Johnston et al. 1997; Wu et al. 1999).

Typed-feature-structure unification is an operation that determines the consistency of two representational structures and, if they are consistent, combines them into a single result. Feature-structure unification is a generalization of term unification in logic programming languages, such as Prolog. A feature structure (FS) consists of a type, which indicates the kind of entity it represents and an associated collection of feature-value or attribute-value pairs. Feature structures are partial in that if no attributes from FS1 correspond to a given attribute (ATTR) in FS2, then the resulting unified FS simply will contain ATTR and its value. If the values are themselves feature structures, the unification operation is applied recursively. Importantly, feature-structure unification can result in a directed acyclic graph structure when more than one value in the collection of feature/values pairs makes use of the same variable. Whatever value is ultimately unified with that variable therefore will fill the value slots of all the corresponding features. Most of the frame-merging integration techniques do not include this capability.

Feature-structure unification is ideally suited to the task of multimodal speech and gesture integration, because unification can combine complementary input from both modes or redundant input, but it rules out contradictory input (Johnston et al. 1997). The basic unification operations can be augmented with constraint-based reasoning to operate declaratively in a multimodal integrator. Given this foundation for multimodal speech and gesture integration, more research still is needed on statistical ranking and filtering of the feature structures to be unified, and on the development of canonical meaning representations that are common across input modes and research sites.

19.3.4 New Hybrid Architectures: An Illustration

When statistical processing techniques are combined with a symbolic unification-based approach that merges feature structures, then the multimodal architecture that results is a *hybrid symbolic/statistical* one. Hybrid architectures represent one major new direction for multimodal system development.[4] Such architectures are capable of achieving very robust functioning, compared with a late-fusion symbolic approach alone. In this section we illustrate the general nature and advantages of a hybrid

---

[4]Multimodal architectures also can be hybrids in the sense of combining Hidden Markov Models (HMMs) and Neural Networks (NNs). This can be an opportune combination in the case of a pen/voice system, since speech is processed well with HMMs and NNs handle pen input well.

approach by describing the first such architecture developed for a pen/voice multi-modal system (QuickSet), which utilizes the Associative Map and Members-Teams-Committee techniques (Wu et al. 1999). QuickSet will be discussed more fully in Section 19.4.1.

For a multimodal speech and gesture system with a semantic fusion architecture, the primary factors that influence recognition performance include (1) recognition accuracy of the individual modes, (2) the mapping structure between multimodal commands and their speech/pen constituents, (3) the manner of combining posterior probabilities, and (4) the prior distribution of multimodal commands. The Associative Mapping and Members-Teams-Committee (MTC) techniques introduced in this section provide a statistical approach to developing and optimizing the second and third factors, respectively.

For a given application, the *Associative Map* is an architectural component that defines all semantically meaningful mapping relations that exist between the set of speech constituents and the set of pen-based gesture constituents for each multimodal command, since a constituent in one mode typically associates with only a limited number of constituents in the other mode. During multimodal recognition, the defined Associative Map supports a simple process of table lookup. This table can be defined directly by a user, or it can be built automatically using labeled data. The Associative Map basically functions to rule out consideration of those speech and gesture feature structures that cannot possibly be unified semantically. As such, it provides an efficient means of quickly ruling out impossible semantic unifications.

Members-Teams-Committee (MTC) is a novel hierarchical recognition technique, the purpose of which is to weight the contributions derived from speech and gesture recognizers based on their empirically derived relative reliabilities, and in a manner that optimizes system robustness. As illustrated in Figure 19.3, the MTC is composed of a three-tiered divide-and-conquer architecture with multiple members, multiple teams, and a committee. The *members* are the individual recognizers that provide a diverse spectrum of recognition results in the form of local posterior estimates.[5] Member recognizers can be on more than one team. Members report their results to their recognizer *team* leader, which then applies various weighting parameters to their reported scores. Furthermore, each team can apply a different weighting scheme and can examine different subsets of data. Finally, the *committee* weights the results of the various teams and reports the final recognition results. The parameters at each level of the hierarchy are trained from a labeled corpus. The MTC technique serves two purposes within the QuickSet multimodal system. It is used as a gesture recognizer, and in this case the members are recognizers for the 190 possible gestures. It also is being integrated into QuickSet as the statistical mechanism for combining recognition scores from the unifiable speech and gesture feature structures.

The Associative Map and MTC techniques provide an approach to refining the multimodal integration process so that different weights are assigned to different

---

[5]A local posterior estimate is an estimate of the conditional probability of a specific recognition result, given the input.

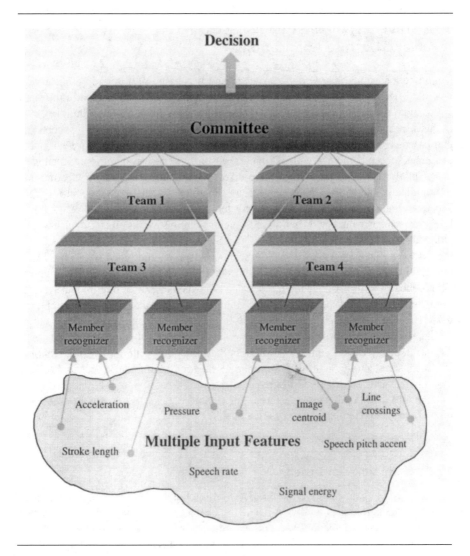

FIGURE 19.3 The three-tiered bottom-up MTC architecture, composed of multiple members, multiple teams, and a decision-making committee

modes and different constituents, thereby enhancing overall system robustness. The multimodal hybrid architecture summarized in this section recently has been evaluated using a multimodal corpus and the QuickSet system and has achieved 95.26 percent correct recognition performance—or within 1.4 percent of the theoretical system upper bound (for further details see Wu et al. 1999).

19.4   Diversity of Emerging Speech and Gesture Applications

Multimodal systems that recognize speech and pen-based gestures represent a very new field. This type of multimodal system first was designed and studied in the early 1990s, with the original QuickSet system prototype (see Section 19.4.1) built in 1994. In this section, we describe three research-level systems that process users' speech and pen-based gestural input, as well as one example of a prototype (in Section 19.4.3) that processes speech combined with 3D manual gesturing. These systems represent a variety of platforms, and they illustrate the diverse and challenging nature of emerging multimodal applications. With respect to functionality, the Human-centric Word Processor and Field Medic Information System (see Sections 19.4.2 and 19.4.4) both integrate spoken words with pen-based deictic pointing events (that is, selection of words or graphic objects), whereas the QuickSet and VR Aircraft Maintenance Training Systems (Sections 19.4.1 and 19.4.3) process speech combined with varied gestures. With the exception of the Field Medic Information System, which supports alternative recognition of one input mode at a time, the other three multimodal systems time stamp the parallel speech and gesture input streams and then jointly interpret them based on a late semantic fusion approach. In most cases, signal fusion within multimodal systems is performed using a frame-based method, although QuickSet relies on a statistically ranked unification process that functions within a hybrid symbolic/statistical architecture. Figure 19.4 summarizes the four multimodal speech and gesture systems that will be described in greater detail in this section, as well as their main functionality and architectural features. For a more detailed discussion of these and other multimodal applications, see Oviatt et al. 2000.

19.4.4   OGI's QuickSet System

QuickSet is an agent-based, collaborative multimodal system that enables a user to create and position entities on a map with speech, pen-based gestures, and direct manipulation (Cohen et al. 1997). These entities then are used to initialize a simulation. The user can create entities by speaking their names and distinguishing characteristics, while simultaneously indicating their location or shape with an electronic pen. For example, a medical unit could be created at a specific location and orientation by saying "medical company facing this way <draws arrow>." The user also can control entities in a simulation, for example, by saying "Jeep 23, follow this evacuation route <draws line>" while gesturing the exact route with the pen. The QuickSet interface is illustrated in Figure 19.5 running on a handheld PC. In addition to multimodal input, commands can be given just using speech or gesture as individual input modalities.

When used together, speech and gesture input are interpreted by parallel recognizers, which generate a set of typed-feature-structure meaning-fragments for each

Multimodal System Characteristics	QuickSet	Human-Centric Word Processor	VR Aircraft Maintenance Training	Field Medic Information
Recognition of simultaneous or alternative individual modes	Simultaneous and individual modes	Simultaneous and individual modes	Simultaneous and individual modes	Alternative individual modes[1]
Type and size of gesture vocabulary	Pen input, Multiple gestures, Large vocabulary	Pen input, Deictic selection	3D manual input, Multiple gestures, Small vocabulary	Pen input, Deictic selection
Size of speech vocabulary[2] and type of linguistic processing	Moderate vocabulary, Grammar-based	Large vocabulary, Statistical language processing	Small vocabulary, Grammar-based	Moderate vocabulary, Grammar-based
Type of signal fusion	Late semantic fusion, Unification, Hybrid symbolic/ statistical MTC framework	Late semantic fusion, Frame-based	Late semantic fusion, Frame-based	No mode fusion
Type of platform and applications	Wireless handheld, Varied map and VR applications[3]	Desktop computer, Word processing	Virtual reality system, Aircraft maintenance training	Wireless handheld, Medical field emergencies
Evaluation status	Proactive user-centered design and iterative system evaluations	Proactive user-centered design	Planned for future	Proactive user-centered design and iterative system evaluations

[1]The FMA component recognizes speech only, and the FMC component recognizes gestural selections or speech. The FMC also can transmit digital speech and ink data, and can read data from smart cards and physiological monitors.

[2]A small speech vocabulary is up to 200 words, moderate 300-1,000 words, and large in excess of 1,000 words. For pen-based gestures, deictic selection is an individual gesture, a small vocabulary is 2-20 gestures, moderate 20-100, and large in excess of 100 gestures.

[3]QuickSet's map applications include military simultation, medical informatics, real estate selection, and so forth.

FIGURE 19.4 Functionality, architectural features, and general classification of different multimodal speech and gesture systems.

input stream. QuickSet then is able to fuse this partial information from these two modes by unifying any temporally and semantically compatible meaning fragments (Johnston et al. 1997). QuickSet then ranks the final joint interpretations statistically (Wu et al. 1999) and selects the best joint interpretation from the n-best alternatives

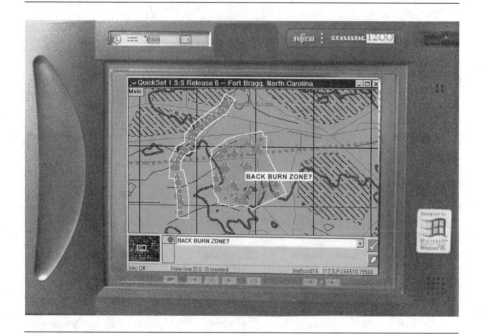

FIGURE 19.5 Quickset system running on a wireless handheld PC, showing user-created entities on the map interface

to confirm to the user. During this process, individual modes can disambiguate one another, which effectively suppresses errors (Oviatt 1999, 2000). In this respect, QuickSet permits the strengths of each mode to assist concretely in overcoming weaknesses in the other mode.

QuickSet has been developed as a set of collaborating agents using the Open Agent Architecture as its infrastructure (Cohen et al. 1994), as illustrated in Figure 19.6. Agents can be written in Java, C, C++, Prolog, Visual Basic, Common Lisp, and other languages, and can reside anywhere on the Internet. These agents communicate with a Horn Clause language through a centralized facilitator, which routes queries, responses, requests, and so on to agents that have advertised relevant capabilities. The facilitator also supports triggering, thereby enabling asynchronous communication.

Among the agents that comprise QuickSet's main components[6] are (1) continuous speaker-independent speech recognition,[7] which for different applications have used recognizers such as IBM's Voice Type Application Factory, Microsoft's Whisper, and

---

[6]Unless stated otherwise, the agents described here were written at OGI.

[7]For QuickSet's military simulation application, the speech vocabulary is approximately 660 words, and the gesture vocabulary is 190 gestures.

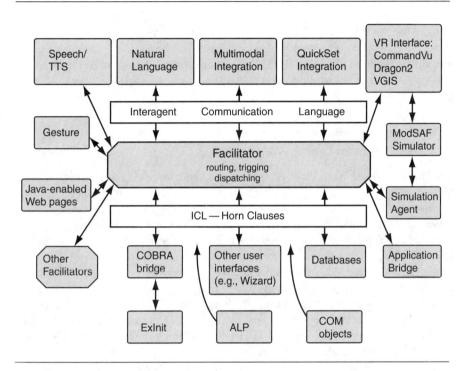

FIGURE 19.6   The OGI Quickset system's facilitated multi-agent architecture

Dragon Systems Naturally Speaking, (2) the Members-Teams-Committee gesture recognizer (Wu et al. 1999), (3) a multimodal natural language parser (Johnston et al. 1997), (4) a unification-based multimodal integration component (Johnston et al. 1997), and (5) a map-based user interface. Other agents shown in Figure 19.6 also can support text-to-speech output, bridges to other software integration frameworks (such as Corba and KQML), and so forth. Most of these agents can run standalone on a handheld PC, or they can be distributed over a network. The agent architecture also enables the system to scale from handheld to wallsize interfaces, and to operate across a number of platforms (PCs, UNIX workstations) and operating systems (Windows CE, Windows 95/98 and NT, versions of UNIX).

The QuickSet system has functioned favorably during extensive user testing (Cohen et al. 1998; Oviatt 1999, 2000), in part because of the proactive user-centered empirical work that provided the foundation for its design (Oviatt 1997; Oviatt et al. 1997). QuickSet has been used for several map-based and VR applications, including military simulations, training systems, 3D virtual-terrain visualization systems, a community disaster management system, a medical informatics system, and so forth (Cohen et al. 1997; Cohen et al. 1998; Oviatt 1999). The componential nature of

QuickSet's agent architecture has resulted in relatively easy reuse and integration of QuickSet's agents with other systems, including a mobile augmented reality application and the Naval Research Laboratory's 3D Dragon 2 virtual-reality system (Cohen et al. 1999). Additional research based on QuickSet currently is examining multimodal interaction in virtual worlds, in mobile environments (Oviatt 2000), and also multimodal interfaces that support flexible interaction with tangible everyday objects (McGee et al. 2000).

19.4.2 IBM's Human-Centric Word Processor

The Human-Centric Word Processor (HCWP) combines speech recognition and natural language understanding (Papineni et al. 1997) with pen-based pointing and selection gestures to create a multimodal word processing system. It is designed to solve one of the main usability problems of typical speech dictation systems—the need to correct, manipulate, and format text in a facile manner *after* it has been dictated. This need for postdictation corrections is motivated by the fact that (1) people do not always dictate well-organized, grammatically correct text, (2) speech recognition systems are imperfect, so not all words are transcribed correctly, and (3) most people find it easier to edit and format their text *after*, rather than during, dictation. The HCWP system aims to support error correction and postdictation manipulation of text by permitting flexible multimodal interaction using spoken language, an electronic stylus, and natural language processing.

Text editing is basically a spatial task, which requires manipulation and movement of text elements. The vast majority of users, or nearly 100 percent, prefer to interact multimodally when functioning in a visual-spatial domain. Here are some typical examples of multimodal constructions handled by HCWP.

Example 1: "Delete this word <points to word>."

Example 2: "Change this date to the third <points to date>."

Example 3: "Underline from here to there <points to start and end of text line>."

Example 4: "Move this sentence here <points to sentence and new location>."

Examples 1 and 2 are accompanied by a single pointing event for selection, whereas Examples 3 and 4 are accompanied by two pointing events to designate a text line or text movement. In Example 2, the user only needs to point in the vicinity of a date for the system to understand which text elements are involved. Spoken language also can be used to specify the scope of an operation, as in "Delete this paragraph <points to vicinity>." Example 4 in particular illustrates the power of multimodal interaction in the text editing domain, since executing this same command with the standard GUI entails selecting the source text, cutting it, identifying the destination and, finally, pasting it in place. In all four examples, the ability to express these requests multimodally results in reduced task completion time, compared with either traditional GUI techniques or a speech-only dictation system.

In HCWP, the speech recognition vocabulary size is approximately 64,000 words, which is available for commands and dictation but primarily utilized during dictation mode. With this large vocabulary, the user can phrase action requests in an unconstrained manner, in contrast with a dynamic vocabulary or grammar-based approach to speech recognition. The interpretation of multimodal input to HCWP uses a statistical engine to interpret the natural language and gestural input, which was based on wizard-of-Oz experiments (Vergo 1998). The HCWP system also uses an LCD tablet with a stylus for gestural input. At present, the only gesturing supported by the system is pointing. These deictic gestures are detected as asynchronous events and are stored in the deictic gesture history along with context-dependent information, as illustrated in Figure 19.7.

The HCWP system maintains a notion of the context of the conversation, which can change as a result of any input modality specified by the system designer. A set of heuristics was developed to govern the determination of system context, with the following rules applied in priority order.

1. If there are pointing events associated with the spoken command, use them to determine the object of the command.

2. If there is selected text on the screen, it has the highest priority.

3. If there is no selected or otherwise indicated text, then the word(s) at the current cursor position are the object of the command.

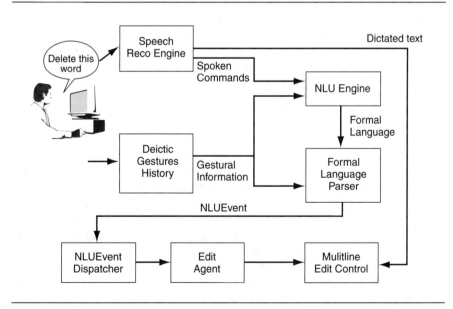

FIGURE 19.7 Architectural flow of signal and language processing in IBM's Human-Centric Word Processor (HCWP) system

4. When a command is given unimodally using speech (for example, "Underline the date") then, following the execution of the action, the cursor is left at the end of the affected string.

5. After a command is executed, any text selections are unselected.

The above rules permit the following natural sequences of interaction to be interpreted correctly.

- "Underline this sentence <pointing>. Make it red." (Uses principles 1, 5, and 3)
- <select some text> "Make it red." (Uses principle 2)
- "Move this sentence over here <points to sentence and new location>. Underline it." (Uses principles 1, 5, and 3)
- <select text ABC> "Underline it. Underline EFG." (Uses principles 2 and 5)

During spoken language processing, any pointing events are considered a "feature" that the statistical translator takes into account when evaluating conditional probabilities associated with formal language statements. Basically, the NLU engine receives information about whether and how many pointing events were associated with the natural language statement, and the NLU engine responds by selecting an appropriate formal language statement. Time-stamped pointing events stored in a deictic history buffer then are aligned with the time-stamped subelements of formal language statements. Formal language statements produced by the NLU engine are flat text representations, which are transformed by the parser into top-level NLUEvent objects that reflect the language's domain/task dependent structure. The parser then sends NLUEvents to one of the application agents, which carries out the corresponding actions. The dispatcher decides where to send NLUEvents based on the event, its dialogue context, and the application's input focus, as summarized in Figure 19.7.

19.4.3 Boeing's Virtual Reality Aircraft Maintenance Training Prototype

Boeing's Virtual Reality (VR) Aircraft Maintenance Training prototype is intended for use in assessing the maintainability of new aircraft designs and training mechanics in maintenance procedures using virtual reality (Duncan et al. 1999). A large percentage of the life cycle cost of an airplane is associated with maintenance, so making airplanes cheaper to maintain is a high priority. Since VR interfaces permit a user to perceive and interact with 3D objects directly, mechanics can use such interfaces to "walk through" and assess the maintainability of an aircraft design in the planning stages. Once a maintainable and cost-effective design is established, VR interfaces also can provide a simulated training environment for mechanics to both learn and practice procedures without taking an actual aircraft out of service.

The model scenes shown in Figure 19.8 illustrate the prototype VR maintenance training system. Figure 19.8 represents the main equipment center beneath the cockpit

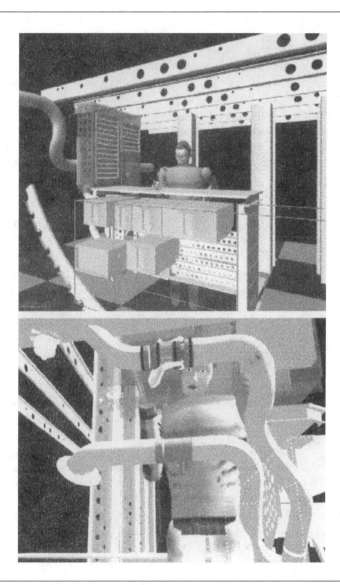

FIGURE 19.8   Boeing 777 aircraft's main equipment center

of a Boeing 777 airplane. The system prototype features an avatar driven by magnetic trackers attached to a human actor, so that the avatar's motions in the virtual environment shadow a human's motions in the real physical environment. The prototype task involves replacing a supplemental cooling check valve behind the P210 power maintenance panel in the VR scene.

Current VR interfaces are gesture-based and tend to be unnatural, frustrating to learn, and generally difficult to use. Besides the lack of haptics in most VR interfaces, the major shortcoming of prevailing gesture-based VR interfaces is that they fail to utilize the power of speech, or to accommodate the fact that human communication is multimodal. As an alternative to the standard approach, Boeing's system employs speech understanding and generation as part of the VR interface. When working in the VR environment, the user can decide when to gesture and when to speak and can use these modes alone or in combination. For example, the user can point to an object and say, "Give me that." Alternatively, if the object is distant, occluded, or otherwise out of view she might say, "Hand me the socket wrench." In another case, the user might say, "Take me to the E4 table rack" to fly to that location. Once there, she can physically walk slightly to the left or right to position her avatar body more precisely, use a flying gesture, or simply say, "Fly forward " to reposition herself.

To handle speech recognition, the system uses the IBM ViaVoice98 speaker-independent large-vocabulary speech recognizer and integrates its results with recognition of manual gestures. It uses a Cyberglove gesture input device from Virtual Technologies and the GesturePlus 3D-gesture recognizer, which was programmed to recognize seven gestures. The graphics rendering is done using the Division system, which handles inverse kinematics, detailed collision detection, and interprocess communication. As an example of gesture recognition, the user can hold her palm flat with fingers extended to request a "flying" action through the VR environment. Since the Cyberglove is not nimble at fine-motor tasks, the user can select speech for tasks like removing small capitals.

The natural language technology used to understand spoken commands is the same that supports other Boeing NLU applications (Wojcik and Holmback 1996). As illustrated in Figure 19.9, it includes a syntactic parser and grammar interleaved with a semantic interpretation module. The output for each sentence-level representation is integrated into a discourse representation using reference resolution algorithms and other discourse-level processing. Although this NLU technology originally was developed to handle text-processing applications, it is being adapted and extended for use in multimodal speech/gesture interfaces.

As illustrated in Figure 19.10, while the NLU subsystem interprets speech input using linguistic and domain knowledge, the gesture system simultaneously interprets gestures from the Division virtual reality system's "gesture actor." Although speech is the primary driver of language interpretation, with gestural information used to fill in slots in the speech event frame (such as object identification, location), gesture input alone also can drive the downstream application. When the system's temporal constraints are met, the integration subsystem combines time-stamped spoken language and gestural frames. The integration subsystem sends these integrated frames to the command generation subsystem, which builds final commands that the system's "visual actor" can render.

The system configuration depicted here is realized as a distributed architecture using heterogeneous platforms (such as SGI Onyx, PCs, special-purpose hardware) and languages (such as Lisp, C++, Visual Basic), with components communicating

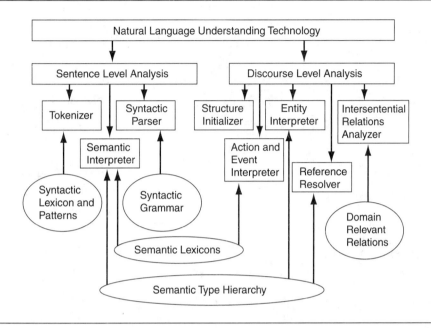

FIGURE 19.9   Boeing's natural language understanding technology

via TCP/IP. To implement the VR elements, Division's immersive dvMockup software was used, along with a head-mounted display and Ascension's Motion Star body tracking system.

Compared with a standard gesture-based VR interface, this prototype provides a more satisfactory way for users to engage in natural command and control in a VR world. Future work on the VR training application will extend the present prototype's limited domain functionality, add more discourse capabilities, and conduct formal usability testing with the second system prototype now under construction.

19.4.4 NCR's Field Medic Information System

The Field Medic Information System prototype was developed by NCR Corporation in collaboration with the Trauma Care Information Management System Consortium (Holzman 1999). The system permits medical personnel (ambulance crews) to document patient care as it occurs in the field, including the entry of information about means of injury, patient assessment, treatment, triage and evacuation priority, and patient profile (identification, age, gender). This information is then forwarded electronically to a hospital in preparation for the patient's arrival. The system was designed to address field medics' current difficulty using paper forms to document patient care rapidly and accurately, especially under emergency circumstances when

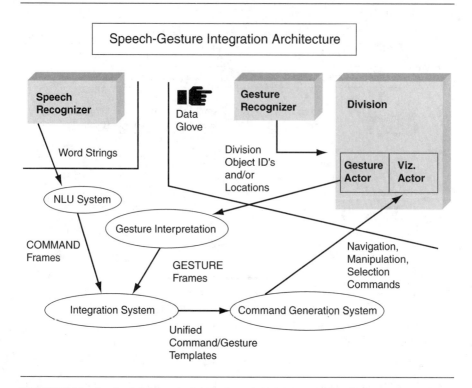

FIGURE 19.10 Boeing's integrated speech and gesture system architecture

their eyes and hands must be devoted to assessing and treating the patient. More than 100 members of the medical community participated in knowledge engineering and system evaluation sessions that led to the current Field Medic Information System prototype. The system is composed of two major hardware components—the Field Medic Associate (FMA) and the Field Medic Coordinator (FMC).

The FMA is a flexible computer worn around the waist or in a vest, which uses a headset with earphones and a noise-reducing microphone for entering speech, as illustrated in the bottom of Figure 19.11. As the medic speaks into the microphone, the FMA recognizes this input as data associated with specific fields in an electronic patient record. When the medic speaks to the patient record, the system confirms with a "ping" sound as audio feedback whenever the recognizer judges that speech input is consistent with its vocabulary and syntax, but with a "click" if not recognized as a valid entry. The user also can query the electronic record, for example, by saying "Play back record," which produces synthesized speech readout of the record. In the future, the FMA's interface will permit querying and editing specific fields. For example, the medic will be able to request "Play back triage priority" and then say "Delete" to edit that part of the record.

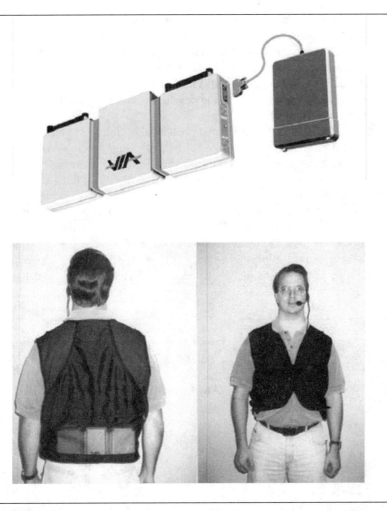

FIGURE 19.11   The NCR Field Medic Associate's (FMA) flexible hardware components (top); FMA inserted into medic's vest while speaking during field use (bottom)

The FMA uses a speaker-independent speech recognition system, which has a 425-word vocabulary and the ability to accommodate approximately 8,700 phrases. Many of these phrases are alternative means of expressing the same information (for example, "abrasion left lower arm" and "abrasion lower left arm"). The vocabulary and grammar were derived from various medical sources and were iterated during field testing. Civilian and military medical users judged the vocabulary and grammar to be sufficiently large and flexible to permit them to complete varied field patient forms with little or no training on the speech system.

The current FMA speech recognition system does not permit entry of the patient's name, which would be out of vocabulary, nor free-form entry of descriptive information such as patient complaints. However, it supports patient identification via numbers (for example, Social Security or other ID number), and both the FMA and FMC can read identification and medical history from a smart card carried by the patient. The FMA architecture also accommodates digital recording, but not recognition of freeform input.

The Field Medic Coordinator (FMC) is a handheld tablet computer. It displays the patient record illustrated in Figure 19.12 and permits the medic to modify it, either through the same speech-audio user interface incorporated in the FMA or by a series of quick pen taps to select items on lists that describe the patient's condition and treatment. Medics also can make freeform notations on the record using pen input to transmit electronic ink. Alternatively, they can quickly create speech annotations, which are associated with specific fields or graphics of the human body, by simply speaking while holding their pen on that area (tapping on neck graphic while speaking a description of the injury). The FMC also has a touch screen with a pop-up keyboard for typing information (patient name and complaints) into fields that otherwise can't be completed via selection from predefined lists.

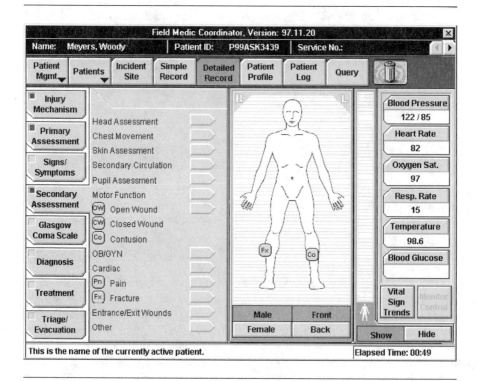

FIGURE 19.12 The NCR Field Medic Coordinator's (FMC) visual interface

The FMC can share data with the FMA via a wireless local area network (LAN) that operates over distances of hundreds of meters, and it also can receive data over the LAN from patient physiological monitors. A single FMC can simultaneously track patient data transmitted from multiple FMAs (thus the term Field Medic "Coordinator"), and it can relay those records to a hospital via cellular telephone, satellite, or radio, while simultaneously maintaining availability for local field use.

Typically, medics will use speech input with the FMA while initially assessing and stabilizing a patient at a point when they need to keep their eyes and hands free. Once the patient is stabilized and on the ambulance, medics then have more time to work with the pen-based visual interface of the FMC. Like the FMA, the FMC is not designed to recognize speech and pen input signals simultaneously, nor does it entail a fusion-based architecture. Rather, the speech and pen input modes are provided as *alternative* input modes in this application, with spoken input recognized by the FMA, and either speech or pen selection recognized by the FMC. Both speech and pen input are particularly compatible with the mobile field use needed for this application domain.

19.4.5 Limitations of Current Speech and Gesture Multimodal Systems

All of the multimodal speech and gesture systems outlined above have been built since the mid-1990s, and they still are research-level systems. However, in some cases they have developed well beyond the prototype stage and are beginning to be integrated with a variety of other software at both academic and federal sites (Cohen et al. 1999). Therefore, although the field is developing rapidly, there are not yet commercially available systems of this type. To reach this goal, more general, robust, and scalable multimodal architectures will be needed, which are just now beginning to emerge. In addition, substantially more evaluation will be needed to guide the iterative development and optimization of these systems.

In addition, although it is well known that users have a strong preference to interact multimodally, and multimodal interaction offers many performance advantages that have been outlined in Section 19.2, nonetheless not all system design is necessarily best approached with a multimodal interface. Empirical work has documented that the largest performance gains for multimodal pen/voice systems occur in visual/spatial domains (Oviatt et al. 1997). If an application is developed that has little or no spatial component, then it is far less likely that users will communicate multimodally. In such a case, a unimodal interface may be appropriate. Finally, although a multimodal pen/voice combination is an attractive interface choice for next-generation systems due to the mobility, transparency, and expressive power of these particular input modes, nonetheless other modality combinations also need to be explored and will be preferred by users for certain applications. Section 19.5 presents several of the major research directions that will need further work before new multimodal systems can be developed fully and eventually commercialized but for a fuller discussion of future directions see (Oviatt et al., in press).

19.5 Future Research Directions for Multimodal Interfaces

Advancing the state of the art of multimodal speech and gesture systems has depended on hardware advances in new media, the construction of new concepts for multimodal prototype systems, substantial empirically oriented research with human subjects, and the development of appropriate metrics and techniques for evaluating alternative multimodal system designs. However, to develop successful and varied multimodal systems of the future, ones with better performance characteristics than unimodal interfaces or GUIs, many fundamental scientific issues and multidisciplinary research challenges remain to be addressed. In this section, we discuss a few of these key research challenges.

19.5.1 New Multimodal Interface Concepts

Although the main multimodal subliteratures have focused on either speech or pen input and speech and lip movements (Rubin et al. 1998), recognition of other human input modes also is beginning to mature and be integrated into new types of multimodal systems. In particular, there is growing interest in designing multimodal interfaces that incorporate vision-based technologies, such as tracking and interpretation of gaze, head position, body location and posture, facial expressions, and manual gesturing. These kinds of vision-based technology, recently referred to as "perceptual user interfaces" (Turk and Robertson 2000), unobtrusively monitor user behavior. That is, they involve *passive* human input that requires *no explicit user command to the computer at all.* This contrasts with *active* input modes, such as speech, pen-based gestures, or other manual input, which the user *intends as a command issued to the system.* While passive modes may be less obtrusive, active modes generally are more reliable indicators of user intent.

As vision-based technology and perceptual interfaces mature, one future direction for multimodal interface design is the development of a *blended interface style* that combines both a passive and active mode. A blended multimodal interface can be temporally cascaded such that advance information arriving from the passively tracked mode (for example, eye gaze) is used to improve the multimodal system's prediction and interpretation of the active mode that follows (manual or speech input). This type of hybrid multimodal interface potentially can perform more reliably than a pure passive-tracking system because the active input mode is available to clarify ambiguous user intentions. Early information from the passive mode can also provide predictive power that enhances system robustness and delivers usability advantages, compared with an active mode alone. In the future, this kind of blended multimodal interface may provide the user with greater transparency, better control, and an improved usability experience, while also supporting broader application functionality.

Finally, as new types of multimodal systems proliferate in the future, they also are increasingly likely to include more than two input modes. This trend has already been initiated within the field of biometrics research, which has combined multiple behavioral modes (voice recognition, handwriting recognition) with physiological ones (fingerprints, retinal scans) using sensor fusion technologies (Pankanti et al. 2000). The driving goal behind this trend to add modes has been improvement of the reliability of person identification and verification tasks within a wider range of realistic usage conditions. As research progresses in the demanding area of biometric security applications, future work will be needed to transfer the more promising new techniques and architectures to other types of interactive multimodal systems.

19.5.2 Error Handling Techniques

Fragile error handling currently remains the number one interface problem for recognition-based technologies like speech and pen (Karat et al. 1999; Oviatt, 2000; Rhyne and Wolf 1993). However, as discussed earlier in Section 19.2, multimodal interface designs that combine two input modes tend to have superior error handling characteristics (Oviatt and vanGent 1996; Oviatt 1999; Rudnicky and Hauptmann 1992). Future research needs to continue to investigate strategies for developing graceful error handling in multimodal systems. In particular, research should explore issues such as (1) methods for designing multimodal architectures that support higher levels of mutual disambiguation between signals, (2) the impact of incorporating a third input mode on error avoidance and system stability, (3) the impact of new language and dialogue processing techniques on error avoidance and resolution, and (4) adaptive architectures that reduce errors and stabilize system performance in noisy mobile environments and other challenging contexts.

19.5.3 Adaptive Multimodal Architectures

The future research agenda for developing adaptive multimodal speech and gesture architectures subsumes the problems of what and when to adapt, as well as how to adapt multimodal systems so that their robustness can be enhanced. Adaptive multimodal architectures will increase the ease with which users can interact with a system by continually adjusting to a user and her surroundings. Two primary candidates for system adaptation are *user-centered* and *environmental* parameters. With respect to environmental parameters for adapting multimodal pen/voice systems, background noise and speech signal-to-noise ratio (SNR) are two widely used audio dimensions that have an impact on system recognition rates. To design robust mobile pen/voice systems for field use, future research will need to experiment with adaptive processing that tracks the background noise level and dynamically adjusts the system's weightings for speech and gesture input from the less to more reliable input mode (Rogozan and Deleglise 1998). In general, the quality of speech and pen input signals can be estimated by relative recognition uncertainty, which some system recognizers produce along with posterior probabilities. The MTC approach outlined in Section 19.3.4 estimates signal-level uncertainty, and potentially could be used to provide a base architecture for developing successful adaptive processing. Finally, most existing adaptive multimodal architectures were developed for audiovisual recognition of speech and lip movements. A major area in need of further investigation is the application of these adaptive processing methods specifically to pen/voice multimodal input.

19.5.4 Multimodal Research Infrastructure

Multimodal systems still are very new and hard to build. In order for the fledgling multimodal research community to develop high-performance multimodal systems and eventually commercialize them, considerable research will be needed to develop appropriate infrastructure, including (1) semiautomatic simulation methods for empirical data collection and prototyping new systems, (2) automated tools for collecting and analyzing multimodal corpora during realistic usage contexts, (3) novel metrics for evaluating multimodal systems, and (4) automated corpus collection and analysis tools for iterating new multimodal systems in order to steadily expand and improve their performance. Before multimodal systems can proliferate, the community also will need (5) software tools that support the rapid creation of next-generation multimodal applications.

19.6 Conclusion

Multimodal systems that process users' speech and pen-based gestural input have become a vital and expanding field, especially within the past five to eight years, with demonstrated advances in a growing number of research and application areas. Among the benefits of multimodal interface design are general facilitation of the ease, flexibility, and power of computing, support for more challenging applications and forms of computing than in the past, the expanded use of computing while mobile and in natural field settings, and a potentially major increase in the accessibility of computers to a wider and more diverse range of users. In particular, since multimodal systems support relatively natural interaction without special training, they will make computing and information services available to field workers, business and service people, students, travelers and other mobile users, children, the elderly, permanently and temporarily disabled users, and computer-illiterate and casual users.

In this chapter, we have summarized both the prevailing and newly emerging architectural approaches that are available for interpreting dual input signals in a robust manner—including early and late semantic fusion approaches, as well as a new hybrid symbolic/statistical architecture for processing pen/voice input. We also have described four state-of-the-art multimodal systems that are capable of processing users' spoken and gestural input—ranging from map-based and virtual reality systems for engaging in simulations and training, to field medic systems for mobile use in noisy environments, to standard text-editing applications that will reshape daily computing tasks. We have indicated several key research challenges that remain to be addressed before successful multimodal systems can be realized fully. Among these challenges are the development of new multimodal interface concepts and error handling techniques. While the rapid maturation of spoken language technology has contributed directly to recent advances in multimodal systems, nonetheless further strides will be needed in other component technologies and hardware before existing multimodal systems can be diversified and optimized fully. In addition, new and more sophisticated architectures will be needed, as will more intelligently adaptive and robust multimodal systems. Before this new class of systems can proliferate, multimodal research infrastructure and software tools also will be needed to support the development of both simulated and fully functioning systems.

Finally, some of the requirements for advancing innovative multimodal systems are not intellectual ones but rather social, political, and educational in nature. The development of state-of-the-art multimodal systems of the kind described in this chapter also requires multidisciplinary expertise in a variety of areas, such as speech and hearing science, perception and graphics, linguistics, psychology, signal processing, pattern recognition, statistics, engineering, and computer science. The multidisciplinary nature of this research makes it unlikely that a single group can conduct meaningful research across the entire spectrum. As a result, collaborative research and "community building" among multimodal researchers will be critically needed to forge the necessary relations among those representing different component technologies and key disciplines. In addition to cross-fertilization of ideas and perspectives among these diverse groups, there also is a critical need for cross-training of students and junior researchers. Like spoken language systems, multimodal technology does not fit neatly into a traditional academic departmental framework. To make the appropriate educational opportunities and resources available to future students, new academic programs certainly will need to be formulated that encourage and reward researchers who successfully reach across the boundaries of their narrowly defined fields.

Acknowledgments

We would like to thank Dana Director, Gwen Brake, and Bridget Adams for their expert assistance with graphics and manuscript preparation. The preparation of this chapter has been supported in part by Intel Corporation, by NSF grant IRI-9530666, and NSF Special Extension for Creativity (SEC) grant IIS-9530666 to the first author. Additional support has also been provided by DARPA contracts DABT63-95-C-007 and N66001-99-D-8503, as well as ONR grants N0014-95-1164, N00014-99-1-0377, and N00014-99-1-0380 to the second author. This book chapter is an abridged version of an article that originally was published in the December 2000 issue of the Journal of Human Computer Interaction.

References

Bolt, R.A. (1980). Put-that-there: Voice and gesture at the graphics interface. *Computer Graphics,* 14, 3, 262–270.

Calder, J. (1987). Typed unification for natural language processing. In E. Klein and J. van Benthem (Eds.), *Categories, Polymorphisms, and Unification,* 65–72. Center for Cognitive Science, University of Edinburgh.

Carpenter, R. (1992). *The logic of typed feature structures.* Cambridge, UK: Cambridge University Press.

Cohen, P.R., Cheyer, A., Wang, M., and Baeg, S.C. (1994). An open agent architecture. *AAAI '94 Spring Symposium Series on Software Agents,* 1–8. AAAI Press. (Reprinted in Huhns and Singh (Eds.). (1997). *Readings in Agents,* 197–204. San Francisco: Morgan Kaufmann Publishers, Inc.)

Cohen, P.R., Dalrymple, M., Moran, D.B., Pereira, F.C.N., Sullivan, J.W., Gargan, R.A., Schlossberg, J.L., and Tyler, S.W. (1989). Synergistic use of direct manipulation and natural language. *Proceedings of the Conference on Human Factors in Computing Systems (CHI'89),* 227–234. New York: ACM Press. (Reprinted in Maybury & Wahlster (Eds.) (1998). *Readings in Intelligent User Interfaces,* 29–37. San Francisco: Morgan Kaufmann.)

Cohen, P.R., Johnston, M., McGee, D., Oviatt, S.L., Clow, J., and Smith, I. (1998). The efficiency of multimodal interaction: A case study. *Proceedings of the International Conference on Spoken Language Processing,* 2, 249–252. Sydney: ASSTA, Inc.

Cohen, P.R., Johnston, M., McGee, D., Oviatt, S., Pittman, J., Smith, I., Chen, L., and Clow, J. (1997). Quickset: Multimodal interaction for distributed applications. *Proceedings of the Fifth ACM International Multimedia Conference,* 31–40. New York: ACM Press.

Cohen, P.R., McGee, D., Oviatt, S., Wu, L., Clow, J., King, R., Julier, S., and Rosenblum, L. (1999). Multimodal interaction for 2D and 3D environments. *IEEE Computer Graphics and Applications,* 19, 4,10–13. IEEE Press.

Duncan, L., Brown, W., Esposito, C., Holmback, H., and Xue, P. (1999). *Enhancing virtual maintenance environments with speech understanding.* Boeing M&CT TechNet.

Holzman, T.G. (1999). Computer-human interface solutions for emergency medical care. *Interactions,* 6, 3, 13–24.

Johnston, M., Cohen, P.R., McGee, D., Oviatt, S.L., Pittman, J.A., and Smith, I. (1997). Unification-based multimodal integration. *Proceedings of the 35th Annual Meeting of the Association for Computational Linguistics,* 281–288. San Francisco: Morgan Kaufmann.

Karat, C.-M., Halverson, C., Horn, D., and Karat, J. (1999). Patterns of entry and correction in large vocabulary continuous speech recognition systems. *Proceedings of the International Conference for Computer-Human Interaction (CHI'99)*, 568–575. New York: ACM Press.

Kumar, S., and Cohen, P.R. (2000). Towards a fault-tolerant multi-agent system architecture. *Fourth International Conference on Autonomous Agents 2000*, Barcelona, Spain, June 2000, 459–466. New York: ACM Press.

McGee, D.R., Cohen, P.R., and Wu, L., (2000). Something from nothing: Augmenting a paper-based work practice with multimodal interaction. *Proceedings of the Designing Augmented Reality Environments Conference 2000*, 71–80. Copenhagen, Denmark: ACM Press.

McNeill, D. (1992). *Hand and mind: What gestures reveal about thought.* Chicago, IL: University of Chicago Press.

Oviatt, S.L. (1997). Multimodal interactive maps: Designing for human performance. *Human-Computer Interaction* (special issue on *Multimodal Interfaces*), 12, 93–129.

Oviatt, S.L. (1999). Mutual disambiguation of recognition errors in a multimodal architecture. *Proceedings of the Conference on Human Factors in Computing Systems (CHI'99)*, 576–583. New York: ACM Press.

Oviatt, S.L. (2000). Taming recognition errors within a multimodal interface, *Communications of the ACM,* 43, 9, 45–51.

Oviatt, S.L., Cohen, P.R., Wu, L., Vergo, J., Duncan, L., Suhm, B., Bers, J., Holzman, T., Winograd, T., Landay, J., Larson, J., and Ferro, D. (2000). Designing the user interface for multimodal speech and pen-based gesture applications: State-of-the-art systems and future research directions. *Human Computer Interaction,* Vol. 15, no. 4, 263–322.

Oviatt, S.L., DeAngeli, A., and Kuhn, K. (1997). Integration and synchronization of input modes during multimodal human-computer interaction. *Proceedings of Conference on Human Factors in Computing Systems (CHI'97)*, 415–422. New York: ACM Press.

Oviatt, S.L., and vanGent, R. (1996). Error resolution during multimodal human-computer interaction. *Proceedings of the International Conference on Spoken Language Processing,* 2, 204–207. University of Delaware Press.

Pankanti, S., Bolle, R.M., and Jain, A. (Eds.). (2000). Biometrics: The future of identification (special issue), *Computer,* 33, 2, 46–80.

Papineni, K.A., Roukos, S., and Ward, R.T. (1997). Feature-based language understanding. *Proceedings of the 5th European Conference On Speech Communication and Technology,* 3, 1435–1438. Rhodes, Greece: European Speech Communication Association.

Rhyne, J.R., and Wolf, C.G. (1993). Recognition-based user interfaces. In H.R. Hartson & D. Hix (Eds.), *Advances in Human-Computer Interaction,* 4, 191–250.

Rogozan, A., and Delegise, P. (1998). Adaptive fusion of acoustic and visual sources for automatic speech recognition. *Speech Communication,* 26, 1–2, 149–161.

Rubin, P., Vatikiotis-Bateson, E., and Benoit, C. (1998). Special issue on audio-visual speech processing. *Speech Communication,* 26, 1–2. North Holland.

Rudnicky, A., and Hauptman, A. (1992). Multimodal interactions in speech systems. In M. Blattner and R. Dannenberg (Eds.), *Multimedia Interface Design,* 147–172. New York: ACM Press.

Turk, M., and Robertson, G. (Eds.). (2000). Perceptual user interfaces (special issue), *Communications of the ACM,* 2000, 43, 3, 32–70.

Vergo, J. (1998). A statistical approach to multimodal natural language interaction. *Proceedings of the AAAI'98 Workshop on Representations for Multimodal Human-Computer Interaction,* 81–85. AAAI Press.

Wojcik, R., and Holmback, H. (1996). Getting a controlled language off the ground at Boeing. *Proceedings of the First International Workshop on Controlled Language Applications,* 22–31.

Wu, L., Oviatt, S., and Cohen, P. (1999). Multimodal integration—A statistical view. *IEEE Transactions on Multimedia,* 1, 4, 334–341.

Technologies of Information: HCI and the Digital Library

Andrew Dillon

20.1 Introduction

Though not precisely defined in current usage, the term *digital library* is frequently employed to describe any organized and networked collection of information that is stored, accessed, and presented electronically. The term commonly refers to large repositories incorporating some combination of text, graphics, animation, and even video, accessible either locally or over the Internet, so we might reasonably conclude the size and mixed media are further elements to throw into the definition pot. But these are largely computing requirements. As Fox et al. (1995) notes, the term *digital library* connotes various images: the digitization of existing libraries, a collection of distributed information services, networked multimedia, or even collaborative work environments, depending on who is imagining it. Thus, DLs occupy and indeed create a social space for users and producers of information, the design of which raises significant human factors issues that lie at the core of HCI's contribution to knowledge.

To understand the excitement of Digital Libraries and the interest they hold for the field of HCI, one needs only to consider what users can or might do with such resources. No longer dependent on the physical artifacts of information such as books, journals, pictures, and so forth, users might access from their immediate environment information that only exists in another country. Rapid reproduction of the information enables copies to be made instantly, perhaps for little or no cost, and subsequently modified, marked up, or dissected to suit the needs and preferences of the user (as opposed to the intentions of the author or the requirements of the publishers). Beyond access, users can exploit the technology to search, analyze, and extract patterns from the information before reporting the results of such analyzes instantaneously to a worldwide audience of interested fellow users. Multimedia configurations can enable modeling and simulations explorable by learners on demand. Filtering software might tailor both delivery and format of information for you, regardless of your point of access. In short, Digital Libraries hold forth the promise that information can be stored, accessed, manipulated, and moved in ways and at speeds that were heretofore impossible. The implications for designers and users of information technology are profound. Indeed Marchionini (1999) considers the term *digital library* to be too constraining for what is on offer and suggests that *Sharium* as a better conveyer of the potential for such technologies to create shared workspaces for information exploration and collaborative work. For the remainder of this chapter it is worth keeping such visions in mind whenever the more standard term digital library occurs.

The present chapter is concerned with the application and impact of HCI theories and methods on the design, use, and acceptance of digital libraries. It is not a review of existing digital libraries nor even an explanation of how digital libraries work. Instead it is an examination of how HCI can contribute to the development of better information technologies, with DLs as the focus of examples. Also, since we are discussing HCI, my treatment of DLs is user-focused, not technological, which places this work in sharp relief to most of the DL literature that has emerged to date. As I will attempt to show, the emergence of DL systems is both a boon and a threat to the field. The technology's importance makes HCI central, while the nature and presentation of HCI as a discipline threatens to sideline our findings and methods. My intention is to point to a future for HCI that maximizes the boon side while overcoming (not just minimizing) the threats.

While digital libraries are at the forefront of technological advances, the HCI concerns are more familiar. Indeed, there are many parallels between the role of HCI in this domain and the issues faced 20 years ago by HCI researchers seeking to shape and understand the impact of desktop computing by nonspecialist users. I will return to this theme later as I look ahead to HCI in the twenty-first century, but for now we need to establish a context. For digital libraries, that means reflecting back briefly to the days before digital computing and the roots of the shift from paper to alternative information technologies.

20.2 Antecedents of Digital Libraries: The Ideas and the Evidence

20.2.1 The Major Thinkers

The article most often cited when discussing the origins of the digital library is Vannevar Bush's (1945) "As We May Think." Bush has been described by many as a visionary who foresaw the increasing specialization of knowledge workers and a commensurate need to access an ever-growing collection of information. For Bush, a means of representing and accessing this information was essential if knowledge was to be organized and nurtured. He presented a conceptual design of a system to support the location, use, and addition of information, which he termed the *memex*—a mechanized workstation that would enable retrieval and linking of information.

There are innumerable references and accounts of Bush's work in the literature on digital libraries (McKnight et al. 1991; Nielsen 1995) though nothing really improves on reading the paper itself. I shall not recount more of Bush's memex here except to point out that the idea of linking information based on personal meaning to form "trails" was a striking idea that is now accepted as standard by Web users. Indeed as Lesk (1997) notes, for 40 years Bush's ideas of personal associative linking seemed out of fashion in a worldview dominated by the application of statistical analyses of language to computer-based information retrieval. The emergence of the Web and the demonstrable willingness of users to exploit its linking functions shows how attractive personal association is to the user community, vindicating Bush's original argument.

While the conception of the digital library is attributed widely to Bush, he really was not thinking in digital terms. Others more directly saw the computer as the leverage for new forms of information technology, among them Ted Nelson and Doug Engelbart. Nelson is credited with coining the term "hypertext" to refer to the linking and direct access of information nodes, foreseeing the possibility of networks of information, accessible from any computer, incorporating everything ever written. He sought the creation of a "docuverse," an information structure in which the entire literature of the world could be linked (Nelson 1988). Calling his dream system "Xanadu," Nelson argued that nothing ever needed to be written twice, since a document could be built up of original bytes and links from other documents. In many details, Nelson clearly envisaged a worldwide network that has many parallels to our current technology.

Engelbart's emphasis has always been on augmenting or amplifying human intellect. He envisaged technology as a means of empowering users to perform tasks that would prove difficult or impossible for them to perform on their own. From the DL perspective, Engelbart is key, since he envisages knowledge workers interacting online, with the computer providing the means of storing, accessing, and presenting a wealth of information on demand. What makes him unique is his recognition that the exploitation of such a technology might require training or new skill acquisition on the part of the user.

Writing more directly about hypertext than digital libraries, McKnight et al. (1991) argued that we can see Bush, Nelson, and Engelbart as representing three different views of information technology that continue to attract adherents today. Bush advocates information storage and presentation through associative mechanisms that reflect in some sense the underlying structure of the human mind. Nelson most directly seems to have envisaged the Web, with users able to access any document from their own workstations. Engelbart seeks an augmentation environment; the users of information technologies should be able to achieve more through using information technology, even if they required some learning or training.

Each of these views resonates with HCI concerns, such as providing direct access and building tools that are user-centered and cognitively compatible. However, these ideas could not be directly tested until the technology emerged that more fully embodied them. The interaction underlying digital library design and use only began to emerge once the technology took a form that was amenable to user testing (a common criticism of the traditional HCI perspective on design also was that it routinely becomes involved only after a design has been built). For digital libraries, that technology was hypermedia (a term that I use generically here to include hypertext and multimedia, the technology that enabled the Web)—the emergence of applications that enabled the active linking and direct accessing of information nodes within a larger document or document set.

20.2.2 HCI Enters the Digital Library

Hypermedia technologies emerged dramatically in the late 1980s amid claims for the death of the book, the advancement of interactive instructional technologies, and the emergence of a new digital age. I have written elsewhere about the precise myths underlying hypermedia use (Dillon 1996), but in a nutshell these include the following arguments.

- Information could be modeled on the cognitive structures of human memory.
- Users would be liberated from the tyranny of paper's linear forms.
- Rapid access to information would automatically lead to better use and/or learning from hypermedia than from paper.
- Future gains in speed and storage would render any current problems obsolete (the classic deterministic argument so pervasive in utopian views of information technology).

HCI researchers immediately began to test many of these emerging applications. Over the next ten years a stream of empirical investigations compared hypermedia with paper documents, tested various alternative hypermedia formats, and analyzed user performance with numerous hypermedia features. Summing up these findings in 1994, I concluded that the experimental findings centered on five basic outcome differences—speed, accuracy, comprehension, fatigue, and preference—and two major process differences—navigation and manipulation. It became clear from these experiments that the claims made for the superiority of hypermedia technologies for information tasks were frequently inaccurate. In truth, users, depending on their tasks, frequently experienced tremendous difficulties with this technology and routinely performed faster or more accurately with paper. (See Dillon 1994 or Muter 1996 for detailed reviews of important human factors findings on user performance with digital documents.)

Just as it might have seemed that HCI was beginning to understand some of the important variables in digital information design and would be able to impart recommendations to designers, hypermedia creation and use exploded with the emergence of the World Wide Web. With an uptake rate that outpaced all expectations, Nelson's "docuverse" was given form, and Bush's "trails" began to emerge. What might have been once viewed as a standalone technology became a worldwide network, and the user response indicated a huge demand for the tools to create, search, and link large dispersed multimedia resources.

As we enter the twenty-first century, the interest in digital libraries is reflected in major international funding initiatives, well-attended annual conferences worldwide, and the emergence of dedicated academic journals on the subject. Digital libraries are being created across the globe, covering subject domains as varied as musical composition (such as VARIATIONS at Indiana University) to the history of the United States (such as the Making of America Project jointly developed by Cornell University and the University of Michigan). But such examples constrain as much as they illuminate, since a simple search of "digital library" on the Web will likely result in more output than any user could usefully exploit on topics one barely believed existed.

From an HCI perspective, much of the literature on DL research is highly techno-centric. Papers report on how a DL was constructed, how image files were treated, or how knowledge-based metadata can be extracted, using specific projects as examples. Users only occasionally raise their heads in such a literature—for example, being studied in less than a third of the papers published in the latest ACM Digital Library Conference Proceedings (DL00). However, such a statistic can be misleading. The power of this technology imparts concerns with ownership, copyright, privacy, accessibility, authenticity, transfer, and permanence—issues that extend beyond the technical to the psychological, social, economic, and legal domains. Literatures are growing up around each of these topics so rapidly that one can hardly hope to gain and keep perspective through a single journal or conference proceedings. Though the labels might be different, concern with digital information pervades a range of conferences from educational technology to geographic information systems and from medical informatics to literary theory. Among the issues raised by DLs, usability and the human response to digital information remain key, and for the remainder of this chapter, it is the contribution of HCI theories and methods to DL design, development, and use that will be my focus.

20.3   HCI Research: From Enabling to Envisioning

In reviewing the last 20 years of HCI research on information design and its application to digital library design, and in speculating where current initiatives in might take us, it seems to me that the field of HCI can be dissected into three somewhat distinct research emphases. For the present purpose let us call them stages of research, each embodying a set of assumptions, emphases, and methods about what questions are most important to answer and how we might proceed to answer them. In the sense that I am speculating on HCI in the twenty-first century, stage three is clearly less developed, although the future seems to call for answers to some of the first questions raised by the earliest thinkers in digital libraries. In the present section I outline these stages and discuss their various emphases and contributions to shaping our understanding of interaction and HCI's creation of knowledge.

20.3.1 Stage 1—Interface Design and the Methodological Tradition

What quite rightly identifies HCI as a distinct emphasis in systems design is its strong empirical tradition forged in the earliest work of people like Shackel (1959), Shneiderman (1980), and others who advocated user testing as the best means of improving the usability of the human-computer interface. Since the 1970s, HCI researchers have routinely run experimental trials of interface features and published the results in mainstream HCI journals and conference proceedings, creating en route a resource for designers and other researchers seeking answers to questions on such topics as optimum menu depth, screen size, input device, response rate, image quality, and so on. Like the classic human engineering tradition from which it sprang, this emphasis embodies the experimental paradigm and research methods of psychology and related behavioral sciences, treating interface features as experimental variables to be manipulated and their impact measured. Such work provides the bedrock for better design, and DL research is still sadly lacking in such formal user studies (though see Shneiderman et al. 2000).

While feature comparisons have often proved illuminating, a research stream focused primarily on features is always going to be partial in its coverage, and in the mid-1980s, a move to couple the approach of user testing to the iterative design of new systems led to the emergence of "usability engineering" (Gould and Lewis 1985). Advocating an operational definition of usability (usually incorporating effectiveness, efficiency, and satisfaction as dependent variables), usability engineers set measurable criteria for user performance that any interface must support. User testing is advocated as early and as frequently in the design process as is required to either confirm performance goals are met, to provide clues as to how the interface might be redesigned to meet them, or as happens more often, to confirm that the appropriate scenarios of use are being envisaged and supported.

Usability engineering has proved extremely powerful as a means of bringing HCI into the design process early on, a classic problem for the field. Yet it would not be too harsh to describe the approach as fundamentally empirical in nature, eschewing theory in favor of performance data. As such, usability engineering is concerned less with *why* an interface design works than with demonstrating that it *does*. Landauer (1991 and 1995) is the most articulate proponent of this methodological approach to HCI, and he makes an eloquent case for why HCI should pursue the empirical route. While the pragmatics of his case are seductive, it is my view that we cannot be atheoretical as a field, even if we so wished, since the very artifacts we design must embody theoretical assumptions no matter how weakly articulated (Carroll 2000; Dillon 1995). Failing to attend to these theoretical assumptions weakens the initial prototype and renders interpretation of test findings problematic. Furthermore, HCI has always sought be more than just about interface design but about interaction. It is against this backdrop that Stage 2 research in HCI has gained a foothold.

20.3.2 Stage 2—Modeling Interaction: The Theoretical Tradition

It is not yet possible to talk of a complete theory of interaction, and many believe we will never have such an all-embracing theory. However, as findings on user performance accumulated, attempts have been made in the HCI community to broaden and generalize these data, interpreting them in the light of theoretical positions, usually incorporated from psychology but also in the 1980s and early 1990s from sociology, anthropology, and related fields.

While part of this approach has been driven by concerns about collaboration and distributed cognition and the potential limitations of a narrow cognitivist approach, theoretical efforts also sprang directly from interface analysts seeking generalized principles and laws of interaction. This approach has worked best where it has been constrained to explain specific interactive phenomena rather than the full range of user responses to information technology. Space precludes a detailed examination of the range of HCI theories here, but examples of specific phenomena that are theoretically explicable include the reading speed differences for digital and paper media (Gould et al. 1987), expert performance speeds for routine (nondecision making) cognitive tasks (Card et al. 1983), and user performance in menu navigation tasks (Norman 1992). Even the supposedly complicated dynamics of user acceptance of new technologies show signs of being partially predictable with current models (Davis et al. 1989; Dillon and Morris 1996).

While none of these theoretical explanations constitutes more than a localized model of some facet of human-computer interactions, their emergence and application represents a level of maturation in HCI that should not be dismissed. Of course, I am emphasizing theoretical positions that both predict and explain interactive phenomena. There exists a multitude of theoretical positions that can be brought to bear, each offering a plausible explanation for some form of human-computer interaction. But it is the more thorny issue of prediction that separates the useful from the potentially informative or the post hoc rationalization. We are a long way from having sufficient theoretical power to predict many of the user issues that are important to usable systems design, but we are no longer completely dependent on user testing to determine the design alternatives we consider. All of the previous examples could usefully be applied to some aspect of DL design and implementation. Furthermore, weaker, but no less valuable, predictive power can be derived from case studies and involvement in design processes, whereby the importance of HCI professionals' roles as facilitators, early testers, scenario-generators and task analysts can be confidently established and used as estimators of a successful design outcome. It is not difficult to imagine that twenty-first century HCI will extend and improve its theoretical base to cover other facets of interaction. In so doing, the move from being an evaluative to a prescriptive discipline should provide a push for HCI to move on to Stage 3.

20.3.3 Stage 3—Beyond Usability: Enhancement and the Design of Augmenting Technologies

While the field continues to seek theoretical explanations of greater power and generalization, there exists a third level of emphasis, one that the field has not yet truly attained but that remains a goal. I call this stage "enhancement." By enhancement I mean to describe HCI's ability to lead the design of technologies that truly empower users, to support them in the performance of tasks that would be impossible otherwise, or to enable users to overcome limitations in their own capabilities that hinder their development. The term is a very deliberate reference to Engelbart's call for augmentation, which has largely been ignored in the years since he first advocated it by HCI's resultant focus on usability.

While I do not wish to play down the importance of usability, it strikes me that on its own, usability is really not a sufficiently ambitious goal for this field. If it were, we should be content to remain an interface design speciality expending effort either refining our methodological tools to speed up the collection of reliable and valid data on interactions or devising more localized models of tasks. Certainly this is not a bad goal, but determining and measuring usability is neither representative of everything HCI researchers wish to do nor does it encapsulate all that I believe the field can offer. In a context where technology permeates both work and leisure activities, traditional notions of effectiveness and efficiency are rightly questioned as potentially limiting.

As it evolved, HCI sought ways of studying human performance and working practices at a deep level, trying to understand how tools are embedded more in our collective practices and how technology might empower users to attain performance and knowledge gains that are beyond their reach without technical support. While the plurality of approaches at work here makes it appear to a casual observer that perhaps such work is either too diffuse or is not really HCI, I would counter that the analysis of interaction cannot be so neatly bounded to interface concerns, especially if we are to serve HCI's primary aim of supporting the design of more humanly acceptable information technologies.

To grow, the field needs to be more predictive than evaluative in its scope, capable of contributing to the identification and analysis of usage scenarios where new technological forms might be envisaged to enhance human capabilities in all spheres. At this time, it is clear that enhancement is not where HCI has made its major contribution, and it is difficult to point to examples of research that embody this level of issue. I remain hopeful, however, that this is the way forward for the field, and writers reviewing HCI, if it exists at the end of the next century, are likely to see enhancement as a defining characteristic of such a field. What is exciting about digital library technologies is the power they offer ordinary users (who I believe will be the primary drivers of information technology designs in the next century), and it is this power that I believe can promote the study of HCI to a new stage.

20.4   Problems with HCI's Role in Digital Library Design

While I have avoided placing too rigid a timeline on the three stages of research, it should be apparent that they have followed a relatively sequential path, from interface analysis to theoretical models toward, hopefully, the enhancement stage, with large overlaps. Though, worryingly, each new technology seems to induce a recycling of these stages with minimal attention given to cumulative findings in the study of HCI. What is exciting about digital libraries is the obvious attraction of such tools to most users who are exposed to them. People have always been excited by technologies that bring images, sounds, animation, and text to us, but the ability to explore a huge reservoir of such information in a manner seemingly unconstrained by cost and distance is very seductive, and the growth of the Internet is testimony to this fact. The convergence of the information technology, entertainment, and communications industries promises a potentially seamless web of information access via the home, the office, or public space.

The consequences of this attraction are important. Perhaps more than any other application in the relatively short history of information technology, digital libraries are truly a technology for the masses. The challenges, then, are enormous. We have here writ large the familiar problem of gaining resources for interaction issues, while there are competing demands for resources to address the technical issues of copyright, bandwidth, cost, service provision, and so on. But there is reason for optimism here. HCI is accepted as important by anyone who sees a digital library, who watches others try to formulate a search query or try to navigate a large document space, or who examines the behavior of people in cyberspace. The potential difficulty for the field is making the transition from being seen as studying issues of importance to being seen as capable of offering the theoretical and methodological means of addressing these issues in a manner that yields answers (if provided with the resources).

The field's value, we might thus argue, is self-evident. But doubts remain. The excitement with which the Web has been received has resulted in a lot of attention being given to usability and interface design. Yet much of this attention is from people unwilling to learn about the more than two decades of work this field has accumulated on interaction. Even where a Web specialist expresses interest in the history of HCI, it is not uncommon to hear comments to the effect that while those findings and data are interesting, they reflect interaction with technologies from pre-Web times, and their relevance is therefore questionable since a new technology needs new methods. I receive e-mails regularly asking me if any of the work on hypermedia has been replicated for Web environments, as if the findings on user navigation and comprehension of linked nodes in standalone documents are not relevant if the documents are now part of the Internet! In extreme cases it is argued that the very concept of usability is of little value in world where browsing and exploration render task effectiveness measures elusive. Colleagues report similar experiences. An examination of commercial and personal Web sites confirms that most of the HCI findings on screen layout, color combinations, and readability have been ignored or violated by many designers. In some very real senses, therefore, the Web has returned the study of HCI to the 1970s, where all new interface features were considered potentially useful and in need of comparison. In such a climate we must recognize the problems we face in translating our findings to practice and learn from the mistakes we have made in not transferring HCI knowledge adequately to design practice.

20.4.1 Do We Really Know Our Users?

To move forward the field of HCI must package itself in a way that matters to design. This is not a new issue for HCI, but the stakes have never been this high. There are many ways we can do this, and some of these we are already doing, such as increasing the opportunities for people to receive education and training in the field and by publicizing more the importance of usability to technology acceptance, but these are slow and somewhat passive activities. I am more concerned with how HCI constructs itself as an intellectual field and, primarily, how it carves up the process of interaction because it is in this that I believe we face a serious challenge to our wish to have greater impact.

If we consider, for example, the notion of the user as she exists in HCI texts and is presented in HCI conferences, we see a disjointed picture. In HCI terms, users are conceptualized at one of four levels: the physical or psychophysiological, the perceptual, the cognitive, and the social. Each level of user response represents a particular granularity of analysis, with associated theoretical frameworks and methodological practices. Some have argued this distinction reflects the basic information processing characteristics of humans (Newell 1993), with each level necessitating different disciplinary analyses to be fully understood. Most obviously, the cognitive level is considered as covering the range of human actions in the timeframe of 0.1 to, at most, 10 seconds. Anything above the upper limit is more appropriately studied by sociological than psychological methods. Anything below the lower limit is the purview of psychophysiology.

While few HCI professionals take such limits seriously, there is a real division in HCI practice that seems to follow these divisions closely. Interface designers tend to concern themselves with task analysis and feature design, employing cognitive psychology's methods in so doing. Researchers interested in collaborative work are similarly wrapped up in frameworks that draw more on social psychology and anthropology than individual cognition. While there are many exceptions to this rule, it would seem as if Newell's carve-up of human activities into time slots really does reflect some deep division in the ways we conceptualize and study users, even though such divisions appear arbitrary and prove unhelpful to many designers who seek HCI advice and input.

Such boundaries are apparent in the way in which HCI research has progressed and is applied. If we consider the research most obviously applicable to digital library design, for example, we find rigid partitions. Gould et al. (1987) showed that reading speed differences between the media were at least partially explicable by perceptual factors, and one might think this finding would be relevant to designers and DL analysts. However, many studies of digital library design, while advocating the HCI mantra of being user-centered, adopt a social constructivist view where interpretation and negotiated meaning are considered primary, and interface variables such as image quality are captured only through the comments of participants, not through any objective assessment of the interface. Indeed, such objective tests of interface usability are rare in DL work and have even been labeled "positivistic" (Kilker and Gay 1998). The costs of such stereotyping are high. Poor interface design will limit access, and collaboration will fail to materialize. But a narrow focus, on say, physical or cognitive ergonomics can blinker the HCI analyst to simple but profound issues of access that prevent interaction in the final context. In both cases, the user's cause is being advocated, and the designers could certainly claim to be user-centered in their approach, but the results fail to deliver the usable and useful technology we all desire because the HCI input has conceived only partial views of the user.

To be effective, HCI must overcome this problem. And it will only overcome it by developing a more holistic view of users and their interactions that does not treat each level of processing, be it cognitive, social, or perceptual, as if it represented all the important user issues in full. We must be aware of the embodiment of all levels in any one user—that is, any user exists at each of these levels in one organism and does not herself make such distinctions in a fixed manner. While there is always a need for specialist attendance on certain levels, the majority of issues we face in DL design entail a response from HCI that is multileveled. The divided user perspective is a natural outcome of our history but, as we move into the twenty-first century, HCI should rightly be seeking its own representations. Such user analyzes must find room for user learning and development, the perception of aesthetics, and the role of motivation—all attributes of users and interactions that tend to be factored out of current conceptualizations. As the hottest technology in town, digital libraries provide a medium that is open to such an HCI input, and we should grasp that opportunity for holism. Digital Library users are physical beings, they are certainly behaving cognitively, and they invariably are engaged in social contexts as they use the tools. Piecemeal inputs will not yield significant results, and it is the results of our efforts by which HCI will be judged.

20.4.2 Variables in HCI Research and Measurement

A second problem we face is the limited range of dependent variables that HCI considers part of its conceptual structure. We have become reasonably successful at selling usability as an operational and dynamic construct that has certain observable indices: effectiveness, efficiency, and satisfaction (although within DL circles even this is not fully understood and usability is often treated not as a dynamic property of interaction but as a fixed value measured in terms of how many errors a novice user makes). Usability testers who are trained in HCI analyzes routinely capture these behavioral and affective measures, aware, for example, that usability cannot be reduced to one simple data point such as time to complete task or rating of the interface on a Likert scale. While this is certainly an improvement over matching an interface to a set of design heuristics or asking users to state what they like about a new interface, the operational approach also induces a certain blinkering, leading us to think always in terms of performance and preference measures for specific tasks.

Where in HCI do we find people measuring variables that answer questions people outside HCI are asking of us, such as how do we attract users to our resources, and once there, what might make them stay and use it? What will bring a user back to our resource again? How do I build an interface that not only allows access but supports a richer comprehension or appreciation of the contents? These are very real design concerns, which tax us to answer some fundamental questions. What role do aesthetics play in the interactive experience? What makes material more learnable by users? Does long-term use of a digital resource affect a user's ability to read and use paper documents? Can novices learn from viewing an expert's construction of an information space? How do we determine validity or authority in shared, dispersed, and perhaps chaotic information networks? The list of interesting questions is practically endless, but what is most important, it seems to me, is that questions of this kind are central to any study of interaction but are not easily answered with the currently operationalized effectiveness, efficiency, and satisfaction metrics. Within hypermedia, for example, there is an important difference between satisfaction with an interface and satisfaction with information content, and these may measure very differently in a test, but few (if any) of the standard satisfaction inventories in existence enable the discovery of this distinction. Furthermore, studies of usability tend not to take long-term measures either. Yet what faith can we place in data that reflects only early learning or exposure to an interface? We know users change over time, but our experiments and usability tests are dominated by a once-off assessment of performance. While current measures are useful, they are not the only measures we could take, and they are not the only measures that would be useful to us as we seek to exploit the potential of digital technologies.

The role HCI plays in the future of DLs is partly dependent on our own ability to step outside and see ourselves as contributors. Regardless of when we start the clock, any review of HCI's twentieth-century contribution to technology design can only be seen as piecemeal and reactionary. I believe it could not have been otherwise, but I also believe it can be different in the future. In the final section I wish to outline a somewhat more ambitious plan for HCI and to point to at least several paths that might lead us to make an improved contribution to information systems design and implementation.

20.5   Extending HCI's Remit with DLs

While I have no doubts that HCI is vital for the future exploitation of DL technologies, I am equally sure that DLs are important for the development of HCI. One reason for my optimism on this front is the sheer necessity of studying interaction in DL environments. The ubiquity of Web technologies alone ensures that attention from all quarters is focused on what people do online. We can extend this to concerns with technology in the classroom, the ability of cranks and extremists to access, share, and proliferate information and viewpoints, the value of digital information to organizations, the shifting nature of mediated communication over time and distance and so forth. Everywhere we look the impact of information technology on some human endeavor is of interest. In such a climate, HCI is pushed center stage, and even if the label "HCI" is not attached, the issues that define our field will remain crucial. In the twenty-first century, people will be studying HCI regardless of whether they call themselves usability engineers, information architects, or user experience analysts. As a field we are likely to find our approaches, theories, and methods sidelined unless we engage such issues head on.

In this section I outline several specific research questions that HCI is called upon to answer in the domain of DLs. This is clearly not an exhaustive set but a sampling of issues. What I attempt to show with each one is that not only could HCI make a difference here but that each issue affords HCI a chance to extend its analysis beyond usability to enhancement and, in so doing, to extend the remit of the field to the full range of human issues surrounding information technology.

20.5.1 The Multimedia Mix and Match

At a basic level, DL interfaces require the smooth blending of multimedia. There is an inevitable HCI challenge here to understand the best means of incorporating video with text or sound with images. These are classic HCI issues that we have the methods to tackle and resolve. However, embedded in this topic is a set of concerns that relate to more than layout or screen real estate (important as such topics are in determining the quality of the interactive experience).

If we accept that layout and interlinking are important issues, then it is but a short step to recognizing that information design impacts the ability of the user to comprehend the display, to recognize patterns and relationships in the material being presented, and to explore these relationships with tools for filtering, exploding, and reconfiguring the display. It is not enough that we think about efficient access to a digital resource. As HCI professionals we need to be at the forefront of envisioning means of manipulating information that enable users to extract meaning. To do that requires us to examine seriously the manner in which users learn and comprehend. And it is not enough that we draw on the existing models we have of text and graphics processing. The power of this new technology to mix multimedia in real time introduces the possibility of creating information forms that have never existed for users such as immersive environments linking sound, graphics, video, and text in instantly reconfigurable forms from heterogeneous sources. Might we want to consider preconfigurations for user types? Are there information overload concerns to address? Again, the questions are potentially endless, and people will turn to HCI for guidance. Our current approach to usability engineering will not be sufficiently able to guide us here, and we will need to extend the range of variables we measure to include deeper measures of active cognition.

20.5.2 Digital Genres and the Perception of Information Shape

As we start to examine meaning and representation of content, it becomes harder to think only in terms of individual users. We know that human communication is patterned and regular, even when it appears chaotic, and humans learn the complex rules of communication over time in both general and specific contexts. These rules are shared across users through discourse communities who evolve shared representations that support access, location, comprehension, creation, and linking of information structures. Communication is full of subtle cues that participants attune to over time, and it is only in their absence that we tend to notice the importance such cues have for successful interaction. We see the emergence of these cues in such e-mail protocols as not shouting (using all capitals) or the liberal use of quotation marks as contextualizers for new comments. Future HCI is likely to study how such rules and patterns give rise to communicative acts that are comprehensible, and this could unlock clues to what renders information spaces navigable by meaning as much as by physical landmarks, since we must inevitably break down the division between semantics and spatiality.

The new technologies will give rise to new genres of information that only exist digitally. Indeed, it seems to have already done so (Dillon and Gushrowski 2000). We may be able to influence the form of such genres so as to optimize their value to users and to speed up their emergence. Tools that support the reconstruction of documents tailored to the reader depending on their knowledge and interests might derive various genre forms from the same underlying information units (Graham 1999). Where genres reflect sociocognitive compatabilities of communities of practice, they might provide clues to future designs, thereby serving an enhancement role in our design activities rather than an evaluative one.

20.5.3 Learning, Education, and Instruction

One unfortunate characteristic of twentieth-entury studies of HCI has been the partitioning of the field and the resultant exclusion of certain key topics from the direct concern of HCI. I consider the domain of instructional technology to be central to any informed study of human-computer interaction, addressing as it must issues related to information layout, sequencing, formatting, and mixing for user comprehension.

The poor showing of educational technology in much of the research on learning outcome is in part due, I believe, to the shortcomings inherent in most instructional technology designs (see Dillon and Gabbard 1998 for a review) Not only could the field of HCI prove highly applicable to instructional technology design, but by opening HCI up to the concerns of instructional designers we will surely address core issues of concern to users and designers of much twenty-first-century information technology. Furthermore, DL initiatives demand this of us. It is not acceptable to those funding or implementing large DL initiatives that we partition their problems into issues that fit our existing strengths—that is, HCI professionals cannot just say, "We only deal with usability." The positive impact of DLs on user learning is a major promise of this new technology. In a culture that is increasingly seeking new ways of improving education, of providing training and lifetime learning opportunities to greater numbers of people in dispersed locations, HCI needs to be able to tackle this topic directly. I believe there is tremendous scope for HCI to study and impact designs for instruction, and, indeed, the work has already started (see Carroll 1998 on minimalist instruction), and the payback for us will not only be increased involvement but a richer domain of inquiry that affords intriguing possibilities for new theoretical directions.

20.5.4 "Intelligent" IR

In an ocean of information, the ability to retrieve information on demand is undoubtedly important. While this is in many ways an old concern of information scientists, it is only a relatively new one for HCI researchers. Users will not formulate complex Boolean searches, and they will be completely frustrated by hit rates that fail to discriminate among search results. The technology for filtering is improving, and associated issues of user modeling might enable us to create profiles and search engines that are more personalized and relevant. If nothing else, this is a rich vein for HCI to mine, but I suspect that the future will require even more imaginative responses from this field.

The opportunity to devise technologies that tailor their delivery to our needs, be it through know-bots, agents, filters, or search engines, challenges the field to understand user requirements for information over extended periods of time. In a world of ever-expanding information availability and ever-improving technical capabilities to locate, present, and indeed modify information, how do we deal with the inherent desire of users to limit and filter? Will we end up with the level of specialization that first worried Bush into conceiving the memex, while at the same time enabling the free access to information as and when desired? Are we able to reconcile these two apparently contradictory demands in a single technology? Any answers to such questions, it seems to me, rely on better understanding of HCI.

20.5.5 Ubiquity (or "We Want Information Where We Are")

The desktop is not dead, but it has spawned a family of alternative workspaces that augment it, sometimes replace it, and certainly transform it. The revolution in personal digital assistants (PDAs) had its birth pangs but seems to have found a trajectory that people enjoy. The argument is less about desktops and locations but is better understood as information access. That is, we want information where we are (less "wysiwyg" and more "wwiwwa"). Why own a home theater, an audio system, a home PC, a laptop, and a PDA (not to mention a watch—all that hardware just to tell the time!—a calculator, cell phone, etc.)? How about using walls as screens, spectacles as navigation systems, and access to e-mail from public resources as common as fast-food restaurants on the noninformation superhighway?

The point here, of course, is that HCI has always advocated technology as a means, and the greatest liberations will come from freeing us from the need for multiple workstations with their commensurate physicality. The ideal might be something like an accessible DL that could be voice activated from anywhere, using whatever physical hardware is present to project a screen, offering a personal portal to the online world, shareable on demand, and, of course, suffering no download lags or "out of range" messages. Or the ideal might be something very different, but one thing is sure: It will be different than what we have now. Do we allow enough space for such tools to emerge from our analyses of users, tasks, and work contexts? If not, that might tell us something about what we should be asking as HCI specialists.

20.6 Conclusion

These are just some of the interesting challenges for HCI. Personalization, portability, and ubiquitous access hold promises and problems for us. Induced by developments in DL technology, HCI is invited to influence information systems design on a scale that is unprecedented. The challenges to provide reliable, valid, and timely inputs throughout the development life cycle of these technologies are exciting, but what we may create, as a result of this work, can only be imagined. HCI will thus need visionaries as much as evaluators or, ideally, both tendencies wrapped up in the one professional. Am I falling prey to millennium optimism with this view of a new HCI—theoretically rich, ethically aware, engaged openly and repeatedly in the conception, design, and implementation of information technologies that enhance human capabilities to learn, locate, and synthesize information? Of course I am, but the reality might just be closer than it seems.

Acknowledgments

The author wishes to thank Cliff McKnight, Elaine Toms, Javed Mostafa, Jack Carroll, and a further anonymous reviewer for insightful comments on earlier drafts of this chapter.

This work was partly funded through the Digital Libraries Phase II program, with support from the National Science Foundation and the National Endowment of the Humanities (Anard #9909068).

References

Bush, V. (1945). As we may think. *Atlantic Monthly, 176*, 1, 101–108.

Card, S.K., Moran, T.P., and Newell, A. (1983). *The psychology of human-computer interaction.* Hillsdale, NJ: Lawrence Erlbaum Associates.

Carroll, J. (Ed.). (1998). *Minimalism beyond the nurnberg funnel.* Cambridge, MA: MIT Press.

Carroll, J. (2000). *Scenario-based design.* Boston: MIT Press.

Davis, F., Bagozzi, R., and Warshaw, P. (1989). User acceptance of computer technology: A comparison of two theoretical models. *Management Science, 35*, 8, 982–1003.

Dillon, A. (1994). *Designing usable electronic text: An ergonomic analysis of human information usage.* Bristol, PA: Taylor and Francis.

Dillon, A. (1995). Artifacts as theories: Convergence through user-centered design. *Proceeding of the 58th Annual ASIS Conference,* 208–210. Medford, NJ: ASIS.

Dillon, A. (1996). Myths, misconceptions and an alternative view of information usage and the electronic medium. In J. Rouet, J. Levonen, A. Dillon, and R. Spiro (Eds.) *Hypertext and Cognition,* 25–42. Mahwah, NJ: Lawrence Erlbaum Associates.

Dillon, A., and Gabbard, R. (1998). Hypermedia as an educational technology: A review of the quantitative research literature on learner comprehension, control and style. *Review of Educational Research, 68*, 3, 322–349.

Dillon and Gushrowski, B. (2000). Is the home page the first digital genre? *Journal of the American Society for Information Science, 51*, 2, 202–205.

Dillon, A., and Morris, M. (1996). User acceptance of information technology: Theories and models. In: M. Williams (Ed.), *Annual Review of Information Science and Technology,* 1, 31, 3–32. Medford, NJ: Information Today Inc.

Fox, E. ,Akscyn, R., Furuta, R., and Leggett, J. (1995). Digital Libraries. *Communications of the ACM,* 38, 4, 23–28.

Gould, J., and Lewis, C. (1985). Designing for usability: Key principles and what designers think. *Communications of the ACM,* 28, 300–311.

Gould, J.D., Alfaro, L., Finn, R., Haupt, B., and Minuto, A. (1987). Reading from CRT displays can be as fast as reading from paper. *Human Factors,* 29, 5, 497–517.

Graham, J. (1999). The reader's helper: A personalized document reading environment. *Proceedings of the ACM SCIGCHI Conference (CHI'99),* 481–488. New York: ACM.

Kilker, J., and Gay, G. (1998). The social construction of a digital library: A case study examining implications for evaluation. *Information Technology and Libraries,* 17, 2, 60–70.

Landauer, T. (1991). Let's get real: A position paper on the role of cognitive psychology in the design of humanly useful and usable systems. In J. Carroll (Ed.), *Designing Interaction,* 60–73. Cambridge, UK: Cambridge University Press.

Landauer, T. (1995). *The trouble with computers.* Cambridge, MA: MIT Press.

Lesk, M. (1997). *Practical digital libraries: Books, bytes and bucks.* Morgan Kaufmann.

Marchionini, G. (1999). Augmenting library services: Toward the sharium. Paper presented at the International Symposium on Digital Libraries. http://www.ils. unc.edu/~marchsharium/ISDL.pdf.

McKnight, C., Dillon, A., and Richardson, J. (1991). *Hypertext in context.* Cambridge, UK: Cambridge University Press.

Muter, P. (1996). Interface design and optimization of reading of Continuous Text. In H. van Oostendorp and S. de Mul (Eds.), *Cognitive Aspects of Electronic Text Processing,* 161–180. Norwood NJ: Ablex.

Nelson, T.H. (1988). Managing immense storage. *Byte,* January, 225–238.

Newell, A. (1993). *Unified theories of cognition.* Cambridge MA: Harvard University Press.

Nielsen, J. (1995). *Multimedia and hypertext: The Internet and beyond.* Boston: AP Professional.

Norman, K (1992). *The psychology of menu selection. Designing cognitive control at the human-computer interface.* Norwood, NJ: Ablex.

Shackel, B. (1959). Ergonomics for a computer. *Design,* 120, 36–39.

Shneiderman, B. (1980). *Software psychology: Human factors in computer and information systems.* New Jersey: Winthrop.

Shneiderman, B., Feldman, D., Rose, A., and Ferre Grau, X. (2000). Visualizing digital library search results with categorical and hierarchical axes. *Proceedings of DL00, the Fifth ACM Conference on Digital Libraries,* 57–68. New York: ACM.

21

Interfaces That Give and Take Advice

Henry Lieberman

21.1   Introduction: Advance-Based Interfaces

Why is almost every kind of input by a human to a computer referred to as a "command"? This strikes up the image of the user as a military commander issuing orders, and the computer as an obedient soldier. But perhaps this is not the best kind of relationship that we can envision between a person and a computer to collaborate in problem solving.

The challenge for the new millenium will be to evolve the human computer relationship from a "command" structure to a more flexible and collaborative stance. I propose that a key idea in achieving this will be the development of computer interfaces based on the idea of *advice*.

Computer systems will act in an advisory role to give people suggestions, help and assistance. People will utilize advice as a means of affecting the computer's operation without the rigidity of "commands." In this paper, we will explore the notion of advice, give a few examples, and point to prospects for the future.

The idea of the computer relating to people as both advisor and advisee is becoming increasingly important as applications get more and more advanced. Sophisticated media interfaces are accruing more and more functionality, and soon the bottleneck will not be how to get our computers to do more for us but how to let them know what we would like them to do. Intelligent software will have the capability to do more and more problem solving for us, but there is also the danger that the machine may take unwanted actions or we may distance ourselves too far from the problem-solving process. The best solution may sometimes be to set up the computer in an advisory capacity, leaving critical decisions and top-level control to the human.

Too much of today's human-computer interaction is couched in terms of *commands*. This is evidenced by the fact that the word "command" has almost come to mean any input whatsoever to a computer. The human "commands" the computer through icons and menu operations. Traditional computer interfaces tend to leave users feeling "commanded" by their rigid and inflexible nature, which accounts for much of the hostility the general public feels toward computers.

The best theories of management in business are moving away from viewing managers as autocratic "bosses" of passively obedient workers to a more cooperative model where managers act as advisors to help empower their workers. Similarly, we hope to abandon the military command-and-control view of the user-computer relationship and move toward a more cooperative model. The route to this is through the notion of advice.

Advice is softer. It needn't be as exact as commands. It need not specify everything the advisee must do but only address some aspect or part of the advisee's behavior. It can suggest action or modify action rather than specify action. It need not solve the whole problem—only part of it. It does not need to be given or received in a strict sequential order. It can critique past behavior or serve as guidelines for future behavior. In these qualities advice differs from what we ordinarily think of as "programming" computers.

Advice is ongoing. Although advice may be in the form of a conversation between the advisor and advisee, it assumes that both the advisor and advisee are active simultaneously. This is quite unlike traditional query-response computer interfaces that assume that either the human is working or the computer is working but not both at the same time. Advice assumes that both the advisor and the advisee will continue to operate even in the absence of the advice, and the goal of the advice is improvement of the advisee's behavior.

The necessity of advice in computer interfaces was recognized as early as 1959, when John McCarthy proposed as a goal a machine that could act as an *Advice Taker* (McCarthy 1959). He defined "common sense" as the knowledge that would enable a human or machine to meaningfully accept advice. McCarthy viewed advice-taking as a stepping-stone toward a fully autonomous artificial intelligence, but advice-taking interfaces have value of their own that is yet to be fully appreciated.

21.1.1 Agents and Advice

Intelligent software agents have recently become a popular movement for extending the human interface beyond traditional direct manipulation interfaces. Not all agents are advice-givers or advice-takers, but the role of advice as a means of communication between an agent and a user is a central component of agent competence.

In many agent projects, the user is encouraged to think of the agent as serving the role of a butler or secretary (Negroponte 1995). Someone in such a role can often provide services that are personalized to an individual's needs and desires, and they are often most appreciated when the agent can provide them without even being asked. When the agent is simply providing a service to the user, the issue of advice may not come into play at all.

But the user's relationship with the agent consists of more than having the agent do things for the user. First of all, if the agent is to act according to the user's desires and preferences, the agent must first *learn* what it is that the user wants, likes, and dislikes. The most natural way for the user to express desires and preferences to the agent is in the form of advice to the agent. As the agent performs services (or fails to in a situation where it really should), the user can *critique* the performance of the agent, acting as advice for future behavior. Finally the user may turn to the agent for advice in deciding what action to take which is one of the ways in which agents can be of the most helpful to the user.

Advice-giving and advice-taking agents can be a way of responding to critics who oppose the whole idea of agents. They argue that humans are abdicating responsibility to software agents and that there is a danger that the agent will autonomously take harmful actions. Advice gives the user an avenue of control without being burdensome and enables the user to benefit from the agent's work while retaining responsibility for decisions.

21.2   Examples of Advice in Interfaces

What would advice really look like in a computer interface?

I'll illustrate two examples from my own work, one in which the computer gives advice and another where it takes advice from the user. In both cases, the original goal of the project was not solely to explore the notion of advice, but as these projects developed, they convinced me of the importance of the advisory nature of the interaction.

21.2.1 Letizia: A Web Browser That Gives Advice

One way that an agent can advise the user is for the agent to try to accomplish the same task as it perceives the user to be doing. It can make its attempt while the user is idle or while working on the same or perhaps another task. When the agent feels it has accomplished something that might interest the user, it gives the benefit of its efforts to him or her as advice. It is up to the user to accept, reject, or ignore the advice.

Letizia is a user interface agent that assists a user browsing the World Wide Web (Lieberman 1997). It treats browsing as a cooperative venture between the human user and the agent. As the human is surfing [in the left window in the illustration], the agent also surfs, and continuously shows its advice to the user in the windows on the right.

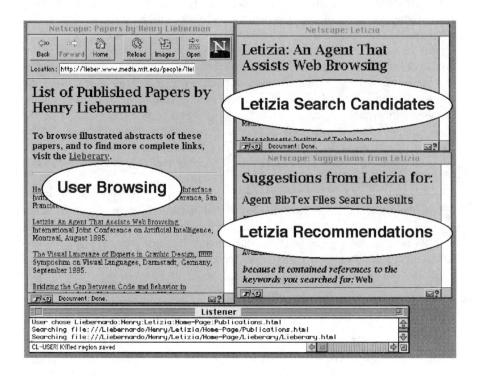

Letizia's advice has the following qualities.

- *It is personalized.* It watches the user's actions and compiles an interest profile, which it uses to filter its search.

- *It is ongoing.* Letizia operates continuously, making use of the user's idle time, and displays a continuous, "channel surfing" display of its recommendations. It reacts immediately to changes in the user's browsing behavior.

- *It is non-coercive.* The user may, at any moment, choose to browse the pages that Letizia recommends or simply ignore it.

Right now, Letizia doesn't really accept explicit advice from the user, except in the form of observing the user's actions and making decisions based on them. However, explicit advice could be incorporated in a number of ways.

Users could give both feedback on the specific choices or criteria for determining those choices, all in real time as the program is running. Speech (see the next section) would also be a particularly useful modality for accepting advice, since the user is otherwise occupied by the browsing process. Users could supply commentary on both their own behavior and that of the agent and the relationship between them. Users could also explicitly advise and modify the profile that Letizia forms of them.

21.2.2 Mondrian: A Graphical Editor That Takes Advice

Mondrian (Lieberman 1995a) is a learning agent for an object-oriented graphical editor that learns new procedures demonstrated by the user by example. Mondrian takes advice from the user about how to learn new graphical procedures. Since the domain is graphical, often the advice comes in contextual forms.

Advice can be *demonstrative*. In the beginning of the demonstration, specific objects can be designated as being examples, and that action advises Mondrian that any further operations involving these examples may be generalized in the future.

Advice can be *graphical*. The user draws a diagram that shows Mondrian about part-whole relationships. In my experiments in a technical procedure domain, I allow the user to annotate selected frames of video by outlining images of parts and grouping them into part-whole relationships. This means that when Mondrian records an action involving that part, it is described in terms of its relationship in the object's structure.

Advice can be *verbal*. A speech recognition system is trained to recognize a set of visual relations, constraints, and predicates that modify the actions the user is taking or objects that the user is manipulating. When the user gives verbal advice, that changes how Mondrian is interpreting the user's actions (Stoehr and Lieberman 1995).

This gives the interaction a natural "show and tell" feel. In many speech applications, spoken commands simply replace typed or mouse commands. However, speech

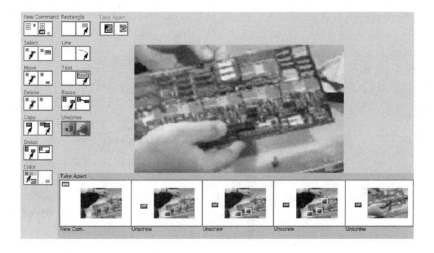

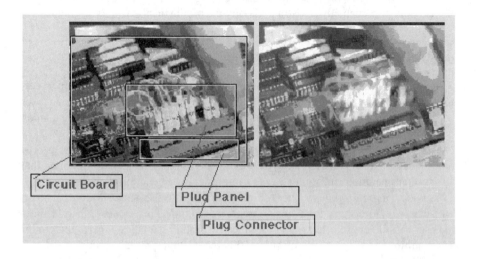

is more appropriate as a medium for giving advice, since the hands and eyes are already occupied with interacting with the graphical interface.

Mondrian represents a class of interfaces where advice is given *by example.* The user uses concrete, visual examples to explain what is expected, together with actions that tell the system how to interpret the examples. Using examples is often easier for people than preparing advice in the abstract and less prone to error. An outstanding problem is achieving some sort of integration between the kind of advice-giving interfaces represented by Letizia and the kind of advice-taking interfaces represented by Mondrian.

21.3   Advice-Based Interfaces in AI and HCI

While advice-based interfaces are not yet widespread, many investigators are tackling conceptual problems that provide important capabilities that will enable such interfaces. Some of these come from the field of Artificial Intelligence (AI), where the basic representation and reasoning processes are studied, and some from the traditional field of Human-Computer Interaction (HCI), where the interaction issues such as feedback, learnability, and convenience are addressed. A true synthesis has not yet been fully achieved, but the beginnings and recent developments can be observed in the growing subfield of Intelligent User Interfaces (IUI), as evidenced the annual conferences of this subfield. Information on these conferences can be found at http://www.iuiconf.org/. The following sections discuss some of the important trends.

21.3.1 More Flexible Planning and Reasoning

Planning (determining a sequence of actions that is aimed at achieving a desired goal in a certain situation) has long been an important topic in AI. However, classical planning assumes that all the steps are worked out in advance before execution of the problem-solving steps starts, that all steps will have their desired effect, and that the world is relatively static between steps. Systems that will give and take advice often do not satisfy these assumptions, so that more flexible notions of planning and reasoning become more applicable to advice-based interfaces. Mixed-initiative planning allows some of the goals and actions to be specified by the machine and others by the user in an integrated fashion.

Collagen (Rich and Sidner 1998) is a good example of how such a mixed-initiative user interface can accept advice from the user. In their system, the user and an agent cooperate to plan a travel itinerary. Advice from the user enables dynamic recognition of plan patterns and incremental replanning on the part of the system. Either party can take the initiative ["Let's work on <goal>"] or cede initiative ["What next?"].

21.3.2 Resource-Limited Reasoning

Some characteristics of human reasoning that are often not shared by formal systems are that humans get tired or frustrated, have limited attention, and have competing demands on their attention. These characteristics, far from being flaws, are actually important mechanisms for the control of problem-solving processes, as Minsky (1988) pointed out in his Society of Mind theory.

Many kinds of advice that a user would like to give to a system are about how to deal with these kinds of limitations on resources. We've already seen how Mondrian accepts advice from the user on what to pay attention to, thereby short-circuiting an otherwise potentially intractable computation about how to generalize an example.

Systems also need to consider the user's limitations when they are providing advice for that advice to be useful to the user. Systems that assume that the user has infinite attention, complete knowledge of the system, and infinite patience quickly become annoying. Horvitz (1999) describes a system that dynamically adjusts its advice according to a user model describing the user's attention in a situation-dependent manner.

21.3.3 Anytime Algorithms

A related recent development in theoretical AI is emphasis on so-called *anytime algorithms* (Zilberstein 1996). These algorithms for planning and problem solving, rather than insisting on running to completion, can be paused at any time [or at sufficiently frequent intervals] and can return the "best answer so far." Making algorithms used by software agents incremental in this fashion facilitates the dynamic adjustment of resources mentioned above. It also facilitates accepting advice, since the user can be assured of being able to interrupt the system before it gets too far "off track."

21.3.4 Critics

In the Letizia example cited previously, advice from the system to the user takes the form of suggestions. Another role for the system's advice is to take the form of criticizing proposals from the user. This, of course, is a delicate manner, as users might react badly to what they judge as negative feedback from the system. However, users might appreciate well-presented reminders if they are overlooking important domain constraints. A classic example is Fischer's kitchen-design critic (Fischer and Nakakoji 1993), where the system informs the user if a given kitchen design violates the heuristic of minimizing the distance of the triangle between the kitchen, the sink, and the refrigerator.

21.3.5 Programming by Example

There are many kinds of advice lying along a spectrum from very explicit, almost procedural advice, to general hints and suggestions. At the explicit end, advice borders on programming. As programming becomes more high level, it starts looking more like advice. Lieberman and Maulsby (1996) refer to this as the "spectrum of instructibility." A middle ground that is gaining popularity is populated by systems, that, like Mondrian, take their advice in the form of demonstrations on specific examples, possibly along with a conversation between the human and the machine about how those examples are to be generalized. Such systems, referred to as Programming by Example or Programming by Demonstration systems, are a "sweet spot" in the inevitable tradeoff between convenience and control. A survey of the state of the art of such systems appears in Lieberman (2001).

21.3.6 Context-Sensitivity

An important aspect of good advice is that it is always sensitive to the context in which it is given, and making use of good advice depends crucially on the context in which it is received. Computer science in general has had trouble with the idea of context because it goes against the grain of computer science's constant search for abstraction. Computer science, in the tradition of mathematics, is always trying to make things more abstract, and the only way you can make rules or assertions more abstract is to take them out of context, ignoring details of particular situations. Now, though, in order to make intelligent agent software and embedded devices more useful to their users, we have to swing the pendulum back to taking more seriously the idea of context sensitivity. The problem for advice-giving and advice-taking interfaces is that identifying the relevant portions of the context and communicating them between the human and the machine puts too much burden on the user if it needs to be done explicitly. Thus, systems will have to figure out automatically what parts of the context (time, place, history of interaction, etc.) are relevant and automatically take them into account. This argument is fully developed in Lieberman and Selker (2000).

21.4 The Future of Advice-Oriented Interfaces

Letizia and Mondrian are two examples of the current state of the art in advice-giving and advice-taking interfaces. Current trends in interface development point toward the increasing need for such interfaces and some of the directions in which they might develop.

21.4.1 Internet Applications

The vastness and lack of organization of the Internet cries out for interfaces that advise users on how to look for, provide, and use information. Letizia is just one example of a wide class of such advisors. In the future, people will not be content with simply browsing and consuming information as in today's "surfing." Net-based information will be integrated in with other software applications that process information, use it for problem solving, transcode it, and redistribute it. All these processes can be supported by advisory agents and benefit from the ability to accept advice.

Many people currently look to the Net for advice by searching for information "content" to advise their activities, either for work or play. People also use the net to make connections with people who may be able to serve as advisors or to offer advice to others. Advice-based interfaces could be developed to assist this process.

21.4.2 Physically Based Interfaces

A primary function of personal information devices such as PDAs, wearable computers, and computers embedded in household and office devices is that they will serve as reminders to people in their daily activities. In this role they are acting as advice givers, and care must be taken in designing these interfaces so that the user perceives them as helpful rather than annoying. Many of these devices will be so small that they will be unable to provide traditional display and mouse interfaces and have to accept advice from the user primarily by speech recognition and automatic observation and sensing of the user's activities. Understanding interfaces that give and take advice will be essential in integrating these devices into our daily lives.

21.4.3 Speech, Natural Language, and Gesture Interfaces

A large part of making users feel that their computers are acting intelligently is to make the communication between people and computers more like the interaction between people. This involves not only direct commands given via speech recognition but also indirect advice such as that accepted by Mondrian. Clues to the user's desires can be given by tone of voice and gestures or facial expressions recognized by a vision system. These secondary inputs act to advise the primary interaction specified by the surface commands. Theories of discourse, speech acts, and multi-agent communication can inform the advice-taking process so as to make use of this implicit advice in the human-computer dialogue. This can streamline the communication process, requiring less explicit communication from the user, and make the computer seem more responsive and personalized.

21.4.4 Advice and the Design of Visual Communication

An important component of visual design in interactive interfaces, publishing on the Web, and other contexts is the relation between visual and textual information. Often the visual information serves as advice to the reader in how to interpret textual information, or vice versa. Problem-solving expertise in visual design is often communicated through the use of concrete visual examples that serve as advice about how to visually represent information (Lieberman 1995b, 1996).

21.4.5 Advice as a Tool for Helping People Learn

Seymour Papert (1980) has long advocated "teaching the computer" through programming as a path for people, especially children, to become better problem solvers themselves. With more intelligent learning and programming environments, this can be extended to "advising the computer." Advising has the advantage that it is less dependent on the precision of instruction and the exact of order of sequencing of events—precisely those aspects of learning programming that are most troublesome to beginners.

21.5 Conclusion

While there have been many specific examples of computer applications acting as advisors and advisees, the central role of advice in human-computer interaction has not yet been fully appreciated. Artificial intelligence may contribute commonsense knowledge and learning algorithms, but traditional AI has been more focused on the idea of a computer as a standalone problem solver. Human interface research offers more sensitivity to user needs, but it currently seems stuck on the direct-manipulation paradigm, which needs to be transformed into an advisor-advisee relationship. It is this relationship that we need to build the foundation of the digital future.

Take my word for it.

References

Fischer, G., and Nakakoji, K. (1993). Embedding critics in design environments. *The Knowledge Engineering Review Journal, Special Issue on Expert Critiquing,* 8, 4, 285–307.

Horvitz, E. (1996). Principles of mixed-initiative user interfaces. *ACM SIGCHI Conference on Human Factors in Computing Systems* (CHI'99), 159–166. New York: ACM Press.

Lieberman, H. (1995a). A demonstrational interface for recording technical procedures by annotation of videotaped examples, *International Journal of Human-Computer Studies,* 3, 383–417, 1995.

Lieberman, H. (1995b). The visual language of experts in graphic design. *IEEE Symposium on Visual Languages.* Darmstadt, Germany.

Lieberman, H. (1996). Intelligent graphics: A new paradigm. *Communications of the ACM,* 8.

Lieberman, H., and Maulsby, D. (1996). Instructible agents: Software that just keeps getting better, *IBM Systems Journal,* 35, 3/4.

Lieberman, H. (1997). Autonomous interface agents. *CHI'97.* Atlanta.

Lieberman, H., and Selker, T. (2001). Out of context: Computers systems that adapt to, and learn from, context. *IBM Systems Journal.*

Lieberman, H. (Ed.). (2001). *Your wish is my command: Programming by example.* San Francisco: Morgan Kaufmann.

McCarthy, J. (1959). Programs with common sense. In V. Lifschitz (Ed.), *Formalization of Common Sense, Papers by John McCarthy.* Ablex.

Minsky, M. (1988). *The society of mind.* Simon and Schuster.

Negroponte, N. (1995). *Being digital.* A. Knopf.

Papert, S. (1980). *Mindstorms.* Basic Books, Inc.

Rich, C., and Sidner, C.L. (1998). COLLAGEN: A collaboration manager for software interface agents. *User Modeling and User-Adapted Interaction,* 8, 3/4, 315–350.

Stoehr, E., and Lieberman, H. (1995). Hearing aid: Adding verbal hints to a learning interface. ACM Multimedia Conference. San Francisco.

Zilberstein, S. (1996). Using anytime algorithms in intelligent systems. *AI Magazine,* 17, 3, 73–83.

22
Beyond Recommender Systems: Helping People Help Each Other

Loren Terveen
Will Hill

22.1 Introduction

The new millennium is an age of information abundance. The 1990s have seen an explosion of information and entertainment technologies, and thus of choices a person faces. People may choose from dozens to hundreds of television channels, thousands of videos, millions of books, CDs, and multimedia, interactive documents on the World Wide Web, and seemingly countless other consumer items presented in catalogs or advertisements in one medium or another. The Web in particular offers myriad possibilities—in addition to interactive documents, there are conversations to join and items to purchase. Not only is there a vast number of possibilities, but they vary widely in quality. Evaluating all these alternatives, however, still takes about the same time and effort it always has. Our attention remains as it was—the information explosion has not been accompanied by a leap in human evolution. Therefore, individuals cannot hope to evaluate all available choices by themselves unless the topic of interest is severely constrained.

So what can we do? When people have to make a choice without any personal knowledge of the alternatives, a natural course of action is to rely on the experience and opinions of others. We seek *recommendations* from people who are familiar with the choices we face, who have been helpful in the past, whose perspectives we value, or who are recognized experts. We might turn to friends or colleagues, the owner of a neighborhood bookstore, movie reviews in a newspaper or magazine, or Consumers Union product ratings. And we may find the social process of meeting and conversing with people who share our interests as important as the recommendations we receive.

Today increasing numbers of people are turning to computational *recommender systems*. Emerging in response to the technological possibilities and human needs created by the World Wide Web, these systems aim to mediate, support, or automate the everyday process of sharing recommendations.

We explore the field of recommender systems in the remainder of this chapter. The main goal is to identify challenges and suggest new opportunities. We begin by developing a conceptual framework for thinking about recommender systems that builds on everyday examples of recommendation and identifies basic concepts and design issues. The bulk of this chapter is devoted to surveying several distinct approaches to recommender systems and analyzing them in terms of the design issues they address and how they do so. Finally, we suggest a number of challenges and opportunities for new research and applications. Two main challenges are (1) assisting people in forming communities of interest while respecting privacy concerns and (2) developing recommendation algorithms that combine multiple types of information.

22.2   Recommendation: Examples and Concepts

Everyone can bring to mind examples of recommendation. You might think of reading movie reviews in a magazine to decide which movie to see. Or you might recall visits to your local bookstore, where you've talked to the owner about your interests and current mood, and she then recommended a few books you'd probably like. Finally, you might remember walking through your neighborhood and noticing that a particular sidewalk cafe is always crowded. You think that its popularity must be a good sign, so you decide to give it a try.

Reflecting on these examples helps to clarify the concept of recommendation. A person is faced with a *decision,* which for our purposes is a choice among a universe of alternatives. The universe typically is quite large, and the person probably doesn't even know what all the alternatives are, let alone how to choose among them.[1] If the person doesn't have sufficient personal knowledge to make the choice, he or she may seek recommendations from others. Recommendation, therefore, is a communicative act.

Recommendation is based on the *preferences* of the recommender (and perhaps of the seeker and other individuals). For our purposes, a preference is an individual mental state concerning a subset of items from the universe of alternatives. Individuals form preferences based on their experience with the relevant items, such as listening to music, watching movies, tasting food, and so on. For example, I might prefer vanilla or strawberry ice cream (among ice cream flavors); Bach, Mozart, and Haydn (among classical composers); and Joel Coen and Kevin Smith (among contemporary film directors). Of course, preferences can be more complicated: I might prefer one item over another (*The Simpsons* over *The X-Files*) or even think in terms of some scoring system ("On a scale of 1 to 10, Bob Dylan's 'Highway 61 Revisited' is a 10").

---

[1]Some researchers have characterized a user's path through a space of alternatives as a process of *navigation. Social Navigation of Information Space,* edited by Munro, Höök, and Benyon (1999), collects a set of papers written from this perspective. Dourish's chapter (1999) discusses the navigation metaphor clearly.

A recommendation may be directed to specific individuals or "broadcast" to anyone who's interested. For the person who receives it, a recommendation is a resource that helps in making a choice from the universe of alternatives. The recommendation serves as a view or filter onto the whole, often inaccessible, universe. A recommendation may be based not just on the recommender's preferences but also on those of the recommendation seeker. For example, in recommending books to you, I might find out which genres you like (for example, science fiction) and even which books you've really enjoyed (like Robinson's *Mars* trilogy). I then can recommend books that are both good (in my opinion) and will meet your preferences. I even can recommend books based on the preferences of others. Maybe *I'm* not a science fiction fan, but I have friends who are, so I can make recommendations based on what they like. Further, I may put you in touch with people who share your interests. Maybe there's a science fiction reading group you might like to join. Finally, a recommendation may include explanatory material that helps the recommendation seeker evaluate it (why you'd like the *Mars* trilogy, what's good about *The Simpsons,* and why it's better than *The X-Files*).

22.3   A Model of the Recommendation Process

Figure 22.1 summarizes these concepts and situates them in a general model of recommendation. A recommendation seeker may ask for a recommendation, or a recommender may produce recommendations with no prompting. Seekers may volunteer their own preferences, or recommenders may ask about them. Based on a set of known preferences—his/her own, the seeker's, and those of other people, often people who received recommendations in the past—the recommender recommends items the seeker probably will like. In addition, the recommender may identify

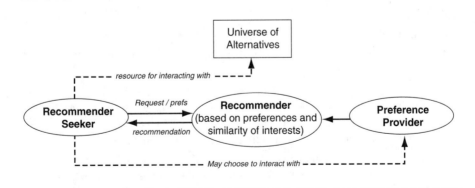

FIGURE 22.1   Model of the recommendation process

people with similar interests. The seeker may use the recommendation to select items from the universe or to communicate with like-minded others.

This model is intended to be general enough to cover a broad range of recommendation activities. Real activities may vary significantly; in particular, they may not instantiate some aspects of the model. For example, movie reviewers publish their reviews based on their own preferences, without any specific knowledge of reader preferences or explicit requests. In a case like the crowds at the sidewalk café example, the recommendation activity itself may seem to disappear. The preferences of a group of people (the diners) are directly visible to all who pass by and thus can be used to select restaurants to visit. (As we shall see, in computational analogues, the recommender can't quite disappear. Computation plays a vital, though perhaps hidden, role in making preferences visible.) Sometimes seekers aren't interested in communication with others—all they want is a good book to read—while in other cases, that's the whole point. Finally, the structure and content of recommendations vary from quite complex like the movie reviews in *Entertainment Weekly* that consist of a few hundred words of text, a letter grade, and sometimes ratings on specific features such as "language," "violence," and "nudity)" to quite simple (a list of recommended movies.)

22.3.1 Issues for Computational Recommender Systems

A computational recommender system automates or supports part of the recommendation process. An automated recommender system assumes the recommender role: It offers recommendations to users based on their preferences (and perhaps also based on the preferences of other people). A recommendation support system makes it easier for people to create and share recommendations.

We can identify four main issues to characterize the design space for recommender systems. The issues concern preferences, roles and communication, algorithms, and human-computer interaction. We introduce each briefly at this point.

22.3.1.1 Preferences

Recommendation is based on preferences. Thus, an automated recommender system must obtain preferences from people concerning the relevant domain. This raises a number of questions.

- Whose preferences are used? Those of the person seeking the recommendation? Those of previous users of the system? Or perhaps the preferences expressed by people in an altogether different context, such as a public forum (such as a chat room, bulletin board, or newsgroup)?

- How are preferences obtained? For example, do recommendation users have to express their own preferences as part of the process of seeking a recommendation? Are preferences expressed explicitly or implicitly (as with the popular restaurant example)?

- What incentives are there for people to offer preferences?
- What is the form of a preference? How are preferences represented?

22.3.1.2 Roles and Communication

- Is the recommender role filled by a computational system or a person? If the latter, what role does computation play in supporting the recommendation process?
- Do people play distinct roles, or do all users of a system play the same role? Are roles fixed, or do they evolve?
- How is the interaction between the recommendation user and the recommender initiated? Who initiates it? Is the recommendation directed to a specific person, or is it broadcast to anyone who's interested? Is there opportunity for recommendation users to give feedback to the recommender?
- What information about the people whose preferences are used in computing a recommendation is revealed to the recommendation user? Is there an opportunity for communities of like-minded people to form? If information about preference providers is revealed, are any measures taken to safeguard privacy?

22.3.1.3 Algorithms for Computing Recommendations

- How does an automated recommender system determine whose preferences to use in computing a recommendation? If we think of all the people who have expressed their preferences for a given domain as being placed in a large, multidimensional space, this is the problem of finding *neighbors* in that space for the person seeking a recommendation.
- How are recommendations computed? For example, given that a set of neighbors for the recommendation seeker has been determined, how are the preferences of these neighbors weighted and combined?

22.3.1.4 Human-Computer Interaction

- How are recommendations presented to the person who sought them? The most simple and common example is an ordered list. More complicated examples include 2D and 3D visualizations, as well as visual annotations of existing information spaces.

22.3.2 Major Types of Recommender Systems

Many different recommender systems were developed during the 1990s. Terminology proliferated, too, with labels such as "collaborative filtering," "social filtering," and "social navigation" used to describe various bodies of work. We attempt to make sense of the field by characterizing different approaches in terms of the four issues just introduced. The approaches[2] can be distinguished by which of the four main issues they focus on and how they address the issues.

- *Content-based* systems use only the preferences of the seeker. They attempt to recommend items that are similar to items the user liked in the past. Their focus is on algorithms for learning user preferences and filtering a stream of new items for those that most closely match user preferences.

- *Recommendation support* systems do not automate the recommendation process. Thus, they do not have to represent preferences or compute recommendations. Instead, they serve as tools to support people in sharing recommendations, helping both those who produce recommendations and those who look for recommendations.

- *Social data mining* systems mine implicit preferences from computational records of social activity, such as Usenet messages, system usage history, citations, or hyperlinks. These systems also have focused on the HCI issues involved in visualizing the results. These visualizations often have been presented to aid the navigation of information spaces like the World Wide Web. This helped motivate the term *social navigation.*

- *Collaborative filtering* systems require recommendation seekers to express preferences by rating a dozen or two items, thus merging the roles of recommendation seeker and preference provider. These systems focus on algorithms for matching people based on their preferences and weighting the interests of people with similar taste to produce a recommendation for the information seeker.

Table 22.1 summarizes the four main approaches and the issues they focus on. We consider the four main approaches in more detail in the remainder of the chapter. We characterize the different ways they support the recommendation process and identify challenges and opportunities for future work.

---

[2]The proliferation of approaches has meant that there is no accepted clustering of approaches nor accepted names for the approaches (*content-based* systems are the exception to this rule). With *recommendation support* and *social data mining,* we chose descriptive terms that accurately characterized the approach. With *collaborative filtering,* we chose a term that originally was used more generally to refer to *all* (social) recommender systems. However, gradually the term *recommender system* has become preferred, perhaps at the urging of Resnick and Varian (1997). The term collaborative filtering still is used, typically in a narrower sense; it is this narrower sense that we use.

TABLE 22.1   Recommender Systems Issues and Approaches

		Approaches		
Issues	**Content-Based**	**Recommender Support**	**Social Data Mining**	**Collaborative Filtering**
Preferences	Seeker's preferences only		Mines preferences; seeker's preferences typically not used	Seekers must state preferences
Roles and Communication	System automates	System supports human recommenders and seekers	System automates High potential for community; raises significant privacy concerns	
	Role asymmetry		Role asymmetry vs. role uniformity	
Algorithms	Machine learning, information retrieval		Data mining	Preference matching and weighting
HCI			Visualization; visual annotation	Explanation

22.4   Content-Based Recommenders

Content-based recommenders (Lieberman 1997; Maes 1994) build on the intuition "find me things like I have liked in the past." They *learn* preferences through user feedback. The feedback may be *explicit*—for example, users may rate items as "good" or "bad." Or the feedback may be *implicit*—for example, based on whether users choose to read a recommended document and how much time they spend reading the document. Preferences are represented as a *profile* of user interests in particular types of content, often expressed as a set of weighted keywords. Techniques from machine learning and information retrieval are applied to learn and represent user preferences.

Content-based recommenders are not the primary concern of this chapter. However, they serve as a point of contrast that helps clarify the type of system we are interested in: *social* recommender systems. Social recommender systems create a mediated (perhaps indirect) interaction between a person seeking a recommendation and a set of people who previously have expressed relevant preferences.

Content-based and social recommenders have complementary strengths. For example, if in the past you have liked books about the exploration of Mars, you're likely to be interested in a new book about Mars, independent of a recommendation from anyone else. (In other words, this book can be recommended based on its *content.*) On the other hand, a friend may recommend a book on a completely new subject, say, on the role of disease in deciding the outcome of battles throughout history. If you take the recommendation and like the book, you may find yourself developing a completely new interest. This potential for serendipity is very important, since it may help people break out of a rut and broaden their horizons.

There also is a crucial difference from a systems point of view. Content-based recommender systems must be able to represent and manipulate the content of items. This is technically challenging even in the most well-understood case—that is, for text—and currently is virtually impossible for nontext items such as music or images. However, social approaches have no such problem, since they don't (have to) process content at all. Instead, they work with user preferences, opinions, and behaviors. Because of the complementary aspects of content-based and social recommenders, an attractive research tactic is to create hybrid systems. We discuss this type of work later.

22.5   Recommendation Support Systems

Recommendation support systems are computational tools to support people in the natural activity of sharing recommendations, including both producing and finding them.

Researchers at Xerox PARC developed Tapestry, the first recommendation support system[3] (Goldberg et al. 1992). Tapestry was an electronic messaging system that allowed users to either rate messages ("good" or "bad") or associate free text annotations with messages. Messages were stored in a database and could be retrieved based not only on their content but also on the opinions of others. For example, one could retrieve documents rated highly by a particular person or persons or could retrieve documents whose annotations contained particular keywords.

Maltz and Ehrlich (1995) further developed this approach. They observed existing practice within organizations and noticed that a few individuals always played a very active role in making recommendations. They built a system designed expressly to support the two distinct roles of recommendation producer and user (or seeker). Their system enabled people to create recommendations consisting of pointers to documents, which could be organized into "digests." The recommendations then could be directed to specified colleagues. The system also supported recommendation users in reading these digests.

---

[3]Tapestry usually is considered the first recommender system of any sort.

Similar ideas have been popular on the World Wide Web since its origin—the early incarnation of the personal home page, with its "Cool Links," was the prime example. More recently, however, this activity has matured and evolved. As it has done so, it gained a new name—*weblogs*—and much attention (Barrett 1999; Katz 1999). More and more people are creating annotated logs of links. They select links and write annotations to reflect their unique interests and perspectives. Many weblogs are updated daily, so content is naturally ordered chronologically, but some also offer topical categorizations of links. Some weblogs are done entirely by a single individual, some are a group effort, and others fall somewhere in the middle. Some have thousands of readers, while others have only a few. Some are strongly focused on a single topic (for example, new media), but most tend to be fairly eclectic (not surprisingly, since they tend to encompass whatever their editors find interesting, and most people have more than one interest).

About.com commercializes a related notion, that of a human topic guide. The About.com site hosts hundreds of topic-specific areas, each maintained by a human topic expert. The content in each topic area includes organized and annotated collections of Web links, news, polls, FAQs, and other "community" features, as well as commercial features.

Recommendation support systems follow existing practice quite closely. They don't posit new roles or new activities. Rather, they build on a well-attested, naturally occurring division of labor: A few people are highly motivated to produce recommendations, while most people, most of the time, prefer to use them.

Recommendation support systems are effective when there are enough people who are willing to put in the effort of finding and recommending information. People almost never are paid to do this; usually, it's a labor of love. Additionally, the needs of both recommenders and users must be met. For recommenders, primary needs are recognition and feedback; eliciting grateful, encouraging, or provocative responses often is all (and just what) recommenders want. For users, the recommendations they receive must be relevant and interesting. To have your mailbox flooded with messages that a friend finds interesting but you don't is just a personalized version of spam.

People such as weblog editors who go into the "recommendation business" have several needs. First, keeping their weblogs useful over periods of time confronts them with a significant information management task. They need to check for stale links. They also need to provide a nonchronological organization of content—for example, developing content categories into which links can be placed or indexing the content and providing a search engine. Second, they may need recommender systems to suggest new and interesting items that fit their theme. Finally, techniques to help recommenders find the right audience are crucial. The proliferation of viewpoints, as represented in the growing number of weblogs, almost seems to guarantee that every recommender can find an audience and every information seeker can find a like-minded guide. However, the familiar specter of information overload soon appears: With more and more choices, how do people find each other?

22.6 Social Data Mining

The motivation for this approach goes back at least to Vannevar Bush's (1945) *As We May Think* essay. Bush envisioned scholars blazing trails through electronic repositories of information and realized that these trails subsequently could be followed by others. Everyone could walk in the footsteps of the masters. In our work, we have formulated a similar intuition using the metaphor of a path through the woods. However, this metaphor highlights the role of collective effort rather than the individual. A path results from the decisions of many individuals, united only by where they choose to walk, yet still reflects a rough notion of what the walkers find to be a good path. The path both reflects history of use and serves as a resource for future users.

Social data mining approaches seek analogous situations in the computational world. Researchers look for situations where groups of people are producing computational records (such as documents, Usenet messages, or Web sites and links) as part of their normal activity. Potentially useful information implicit in these records is identified, computational techniques to harvest and aggregate the information are invented, and visualization techniques to present the results are designed. Thus, computation discovers and makes explicit the "paths through the woods" created by particular user communities.

The "history-enriched digital objects" line of work (Hill et al. 1992; Hill and Hollan 1994) was a seminal effort in this approach. It began from the observation that objects in the real world accumulate *wear* over the history of their use and that this wear—such as the path through the woods or the dog-eared pages in a paperback book or the smudges on certain recipes in a cookbook—informs future usage. *Edit Wear* and *Read Wear* were terms used to describe computational analogues of these phenomena. Statistics such as time spent reading various parts of a document, counts of spreadsheet cell recalculations, and menu selections were captured. These statistics were then used to modify the appearance of documents and other interface objects in accordance with prior use. For example, scrollbars were annotated with horizontal lines of differing length and color to represent amount of editing (or reading) by various users.

The World Wide Web, with its rich content, link structure, and usage logs, has been a major domain for social data mining research. A basic intuition is that a link from one Web site to another often indicates both similarity of content between the sites and an endorsement of the linked-to site. Various clustering and rating algorithms have been designed to formalize this intuition. Kleinberg's algorithm (Kleinberg 1998) is a well-known example. In the commercial world, the Google search engine (www.google.com) uses a similar link analysis algorithm to group and order URLs. Other work has focused on extracting information from Web usage logs. Footprints (Wexelblat and Maes 1990) records user browsing history, analyzes it to find commonly traversed links between Web pages, and constructs several different visualizations of this data to aid user navigation through a Web site. For Chalmers et al. (1998) the activity *path*—for example, a sequence of URLs visited during a browsing session—is the basic unit. They have developed techniques to compute similarities between paths and to make recommendations on this basis—for example, to recommend pages to you that others browsed in close proximity to pages you browsed. Other techniques extract information from multiple sources. For example, Pitkow (1997) and Pirolli et al. (1996) combined Web links with Web usage data and text similarity to categorize and cluster Web pages.

Other work has focused on extracting information from online conversations, such as Usenet. PHOAKS (Hill et al. 1996) mines messages in Usenet newsgroups looking for mentions of Web pages. It categorizes and aggregates mentions to create lists of popular Web pages for each group. Viegas and Donath (1999) have harvested information from Usenet newsgroups and chats and have used them to create visualizations of the conversation. These visualizations can be used to find conversations with desirable properties, such as equality of participation or many regular participants.

22.6.1.1 Discussion

Social data mining systems do not require users to engage in any new activity; rather, they seek to exploit user preference information implicit in records of existing activity. Like recommendation support systems, they work in situations where people naturally take on different roles—that is, a few produce and share opinions and preferences, while most people are content to use this information when they have a need for it.

Systems can preserve and transmit information about the activity context from which preferences were extracted. This can lead to more informative and potentially more useful recommendations. It also creates opportunities for community building—people can be put in touch with others who share their preferences. However, unlike recommendation support systems, which assist people who *intend* to share recommendations, social data mining systems extract preference data from contexts where the providers may have had no such intention. Thus, the opportunities for community building must be balanced against a consideration of the privacy of the people who produced the preferences in the first place. We discuss this challenge later.

Most social data mining systems create "broadcast" recommendations; that is, the recommendations are made available (perhaps as visualizations and navigation aids) to anyone who uses the system. However, nothing about the approach forces this: If preferences are extracted and associated with the people who produced them, an algorithm can match users based on their preferences and thus compute personalized recommendations. The system of Chalmers et al. (1998) is one example of a system that does this.

22.6.1.2 Issues

The first set of issues concern the data that is mined and the mining algorithms. We refer to our experience with the PHOAKS and TopicShop systems to illustrate the issues.

- *Are there useful data (preferences) hidden in the activity records?* Experiments we ran as part of the PHOAKS project in 1996 showed that about one quarter of all Usenet messages contained mentions of URLs, and about 20 percent of the time people mentioned a URL, they were expressing a preference for it. This means that there are many thousands of URL recommendations in Usenet every day. Therefore, the next challenge is the following.

- *Can the data be extracted accurately and efficiently?* In the PHOAKS experiments, we showed that our rules for classifying mentions of URLs as recommendations were nearly 90 percent accurate (in both precision and recall).[4]

- *Is the extracted data of high quality?* We wanted to know whether the URLs PHOAKS recommended for a given topic actually were good recommendations. Specifically, we asked whether our ordering metric—which assigned one vote to a URL for each distinct person who recommended it—accorded with human judgments of quality. We showed a positive correlation between this metric and the probability that a given URL was included in an FAQ (Frequently Asked Question) list for the relevant newsgroup. In other words, the more people who recommended a URL, the more likely an individual topic expert was to have included it in a list of relevant resources.

    We also investigated this question for the TopicShop system (Amento et al. 1999; Terveen et al. 1999). TopicShop mines information from Web pages and links, and its interface provides users easy access to this interface. Experiments showed that TopicShop subjects were able to select about 80 percent more high-quality sites, while taking less time and considering fewer sites than users who did not have access to this data.

Other issues arise when recommendation seekers are interested as much or more in finding a person as in finding information. ReferralWeb (Kautz et al. 1997) analyzes Web documents, processes co-occurrence of names within documents to create a social network, and associates people with their expertise. It can answer queries like "Find documents on collaborative filtering written by people who are socially close to Loren Terveen." McDonald and Ackerman's system (1998) analyzes software artifacts and documents to associate individuals with specific code modules. Help desk personnel can then be directed to people who are likely to have expertise about specific aspects of the code. Other systems like PHOAKS, the Designer Assistant (Terreen et al. 1995), and Answer Garden (Ackerman 1994; Ackerman and McDonald 1996) present information first but then allow users to get in touch with the people responsible for the information.

---

[4]Precision and recall are well-known information retrieval metrics. Precision is the proportion of items that a system classifies as being in a given category that actually do belong to that category (according to prior human judgement). Recall is the proportion of items known to belong to a given category that the system classifies as being in that category.

This issue relates to the large body of work on *awareness* in collaborative systems (Dourish and Bly 1992). Recommender systems can address the issue of *who should be made aware of whom*—that is, how to form communities. Maglio et al. (2000) identified a number of different techniques for defining communities or "places" on the Web. Communities can be formed that consist of people from the same organization, users who are browsing the same or closely related pages, or users with similar browsing histories (Chalmers et al. 1998).

22.7   Collaborative Filtering

You would expect to get the best recommendation from someone with similar taste. The problem, though, is how to find such a person. You may have to engage in many interactions with lots of different people, through which you slowly learn about each others' preferences, before you start to receive recommendations you are confident in.

Collaborative filtering explores techniques for matching people with similar interests and then making recommendations on this basis. Three pillars of this approach are (1) many people must participate (making it likely that any given person will find others with similar preferences), (2) there must be an easy way for people to represent their interests to the system, and (3) algorithms must be able to match people with similar interests.

Collaborative filtering has made the user task quite simple: You express your preferences by rating items (like books or movies or CDs) that the system presents to you. These ratings then serve as an approximate representation of your taste in this domain. The system then matches these ratings against ratings submitted by all other users of the system. The result is the set of your "nearest neighbors"; this formalizes the concept of people with similar taste. Finally, the system recommends items that your nearest neighbors rated highly that you have not rated (and presumably are thus not familiar with); a key issue is how to combine and weight the preferences of your neighbors. You can immediately rate the recommended items if they do not interest you. Therefore, over time, the system acquires an increasingly accurate representation of your preferences.

Seminal collaborative filtering systems included GroupLens (Resnick et al. 1994), the Bellcore Video Recommender (Hill et al. 1995), and Firefly (Shardanand and Maes 1995). The systems varied in how they weighted the ratings of different users (that is, determined who your neighbors were and how close they were) and how they combined the ratings.

Collaborative filtering has found many applications on the Web. Electronic commerce sites such as Amazon.com and CDNow feature recommendation centers, where, in addition to expert reviews, users can rate items and then receive personalized recommendations computed by a collaborative filtering engine. User preference also is inferred from site usage. For example, purchasing a book may be taken as evidence of interest not just in that book but also in the book's author.

22.7.1.1 Discussion

The primary strength of collaborative filtering is that recommendations are *personalized*. To the extent that your nearest neighbors really have similar taste, you can find out about items you wouldn't have thought of on your own that you are quite likely to find interesting. Second, you don't have to go looking for a recommendation or recommender—you simply state your preferences and receive recommendations. Finally, from a computational view, the data representation is simple and uniform—a user-item matrix whose cells represent ratings—and thus is amenable to many different computational manipulations.

Collaborative filtering does not simply support an existing activity. Instead, it requires users to engage in a somewhat novel computationally mediated activity. This activity has a single combined role, the recommendation seeker/preference provider. We describe this as *role uniformity*. Everyone does the same work (rates items) and receives the same benefits (gets rated items as recommendations). We might describe rating items as an "ante"—to get recommendations, you have to give them. This leads naturally to growth in the system's knowledge (and thus to better recommendations), since using the database leads to the database being updated (Hill et al. 1995).

Role uniformity has both good and bad aspects. On the one hand, observed practice suggests that most people don't want to offer recommendations. Instead, they just want to make use of them. On the other hand, rating items is not particularly onerous work, and you do this work precisely when you want a recommendation.

Finally, collaborative filtering separates out personal contact from the recommendation process (Hill et al. 1995)—there need be no contact between recommendation producer and receiver. Of course, if the system designers wish, the results of the matching algorithm can be used to introduce people to their nearest neighbors. Indeed, this is an excellent technique for community formation, since people can be linked automatically with others who share their interests.

22.7.1.2 Issues

There are several technical challenges for collaborative filtering algorithms, including the "first rater" and "sparsity" problems (Balabanoric and Shoham 1997; Good et al. 1999). No recommendation for an item can be offered until someone has rated it. Further, if the number of people who have rated items is relatively small compared to the number of items in the database, it is likely that there won't be significant similarity between users. This in turn means that nearest neighbors really won't be all that near, so recommendations won't be all that good. These problems become more urgent as the number of items increases.

One major tactic for addressing these problems is to combine collaborative filtering with content-based recommenders. A simple example can illustrate the benefits of such hybrid systems. For example, suppose one user has rated the NBA page from

ESPN.com favorably, while another has rated the NBA page from CNNSI.com favorably. Pure collaborative filtering would find no match between the two users. However, content analysis can show that the two items are in fact quite similar, thus indicating a match between the users. The Fab (Balabanovic and Shoham 1997) system builds on this intuition. It analyzes the content of items that users rate favorably to build content-based profiles of user interest. It then applies collaborative filtering techniques to identify other users with similar interests. In another effort, the GroupLens research group is experimenting with using collaborative filtering as a technique to combine the opinions of other users and personal information filtering agents (Good et al. 1999).

Other researchers have analyzed the problem of incentives (a generalization of the "first rater" problem) theoretically. Again, the issue is why I should rate first and get no benefit when I can wait for others to rate so I do benefit. Avery et al. (1999) carried out a game theoretic analysis of incentive systems to encourage optimal quantity and order of ratings.

Billsus and Pazzani (1998) took another approach to addressing problems with collaborative filtering. They observed that the task of predicting items a user would like based on other users' ratings for these items can be conceptualized as *classification,* a well-investigated task within the machine learning community. They take the singular value decomposition of the initial ratings matrix to extract features, then apply a learning algorithm such as a neural network. By exploiting "latent structure" in the user ratings (as Latent Semantic Analysis [Deerwester et al. 1990] exploits latent structure in text), the system greatly reduces the need for users to rate common items before one user can serve as a predictor for another. Experiments showed that this approach significantly outperformed previous collaborative filtering algorithms.

Recently Aggarwal et al. (1999) invented a new graph-theoretic approach to collaborative filtering that appears to avoid some of the limitations of previous algorithms. In particular, it can compute more accurate recommendations given sparse data.

Like any system that offers results to people on the basis of significant computational processing, a collaborative filtering system faces the issue of *explanation*—why does the system think I should like this item? Herlocker (2000) described techniques for explaining recommendations computed by a collaborative filtering system and presented results of experiments that evaluated the efficacy of the explanations.

A final important issue concerns the notion of *serendipity.* Stated informally, I want a recommender system to "tell me something I don't already know." Many current systems fail this test. For example, one of the authors of this chapter, Terveen, uses Amazon.com's recommendation center. After Terveen rated a number of items, the system recommended Shakespeare's *MacBeth,* which he rated positively (by indicating "I own it"). At this point, the system began to recommend more Shakespeare plays, such as *King Lear, Hamlet,* and *Twelfth Night.* It seems unlikely that someone who is familiar with *any* of Shakespeare's work will be unaware of the rest of his plays. Thus, these recommendations carried no new information.

Such situations are common. To generalize the Shakespeare example, it may seldom be useful to recommend books by an author to someone who already has rated books by that author highly. An analogous argument can be made for CDs and artists.

In fact, the argument can even be strengthened. If someone rates CDs by Nirvana highly, that person is highly likely to already have an opinion about CDs by Hole and Foo Fighters (because of overlap and/or relationships between members of these groups).

Thus, a system can be improved through knowledge of correlations in user opinions about items. That is, if a user has an opinion about item X, it is quite likely that he or she already has an opinion about item Y. One approach to this problem is to build in knowledge about the items, essentially creating a hybrid content-based and collaborative system. Aggarwal et al.'s (1999) algorithm incorporates a hierarchical classification structure that can be used to make so-called "creative" recommendations that span categories. Perhaps this scheme also could serve as the basis for making serendipitous recommendations, too. A more challenging (but ultimately more scalable) approach is to invent algorithms that can determine these sorts of correlations automatically. Experimenting with the technique of Billsus and Pazzani (1998) may be a promising place to start.

22.8   Current Challenges and New Opportunities

We close by considering several current challenges for recommender systems. The first set of challenges concerns issues of bringing people together into communities of interest. A major concern here is respecting people's privacy. The second challenge is to create recommendation algorithms that combine multiple types of information, probably acquired from different sources at different times.

22.8.1   Forming and Supporting Communities of Interest

22.8.1.1 Naturally Occurring Communities as Laboratories

A first challenge is to study, learn from, and better support naturally occurring communities. For example, where we have spoken of only a few roles—recommendation seeker, recommender, and preference provider—and have treated them as distinct, neither of these assumptions may hold in real communities. Observations of weblogs illustrate this.

Slashdot.com is a well-known weblog/web community, whose slogan is "News for Nerds." Topics such as Linux, Java, and open source software are core interests. Slashdot was started by a few people as a place to collect and discuss information they found interesting. It grew rapidly and soon fell prey to the very problems of information overload a weblog tries to avoid. Dozens of stories and thousands of comments are posted each day—too much for anyone to read.

Slashdot's editor has developed an interesting moderation mechanism (see http://slashdot.com/moderation.shtml) to cope with the problem. "Good" Slashdot participants are given limited moderation powers. For a limited amount of time, they can rate a few comments as good or bad, thus incrementing or decrementing a score. Readers can set filters to see only content with a certain score.

Slashdot is a community with multiple, transient, and shifting roles. Rather than a set of recommendations produced by a few people and consumed by others, it serves as a community notebook, a medium in which all participants can propose and comment on ideas. Communities like Slashdot should serve as laboratories for researchers to study and conduct experiments.

Human participants in such communities may need recommender systems. If you want to maintain an FAQ or if you contribute to a weblog, it does not matter how motivated you are—it is impossible for you to read and evaluate all the information on the Web for any reasonably broad topic. You—a human recommender—need a recommender system.

Different types of recommender systems could be used to suggest content. A content-based recommender could observe the documents an editor considers for inclusion, note which ones he or she selects and rejects, and gradually evolve a filter to capture these preferences. A social data mining systems can mine relevant newsgroups or continuously crawl and analyze relevant Web localities for new or popular items. With a social recommender systems, the editor gets access to the opinions of many different individuals; this is a sort of "community pulse." Thus, he or she might come across new ideas and information. With the content-based recommender, on the other hand, the editor will get suggestions for items that are like items he or she has selected in the past. This may lead to a more coherent but narrow and static offering of information.

22.8.1.2 Forming Communities Automatically—While Respecting Privacy

Recommender systems can link people based on shared interests. Systems that mine preferences from activity records can choose to convey the identity of people who produced preferences. Collaborative filtering systems may communicate the set of "neighbors" that were used to compute a recommendation. In either case, users of the system have the opportunity to contact and form a community with others who share their interests. However, this opportunity raises significant privacy concerns.

These concerns are more acute for social data mining systems, since they extract information from its original context. Consider PHOAKS as an example: It extracts preferences concerning Web pages from newsgroup messages and aggregates these preferences into recommendations that are made available on a Web site. Presumably, most of the people who view the Web site were not participants in the original newsgroup. Neither the way in which the information was processed nor the new audience that can access the results was intended or foreseen by the original producers of the information.

A system designer has various choices for balancing individual and group privacy against opportunities for expanded contacts between people. First, one can "play it safe"—that is, present only information that has been aggregated and decontextualized. For PHOAKS, this could mean presenting only ordered lists of recommended URLs, with no information about the recommending messages or the persons who posted the recommenders. However, this both results in less rich and informative recommendations and gives up on the opportunity for people to make new contacts with others who share their interests. Second, one can make it all explicit. For example, we could have designed PHOAKS to make the identity of recommenders prominent and make it technically easy to contact a recommender (by including mailto: links). We chose not to go this far. We included the e-mail addresses of recommenders but not at "top-level." If PHOAKS users want to find this information, they have to dig around a bit, and if they want to e-mail recommenders, they must explicitly cut and paste e-mail addresses.

More generally, we are interested in middle-ground solutions that lie between the extremes of complete disclosure and complete anonymity. A good place to start is with techniques used in places such as online "personals" or dating services. In these cases, the system is a trusted intermediary, mediating interaction between people. Participants can progressively reveal more about themselves, perhaps beginning only with their system login, then adding their personal e-mail address, then revealing other information as they become comfortable.

22.8.2 Combining Multiple Types of Information to Compute Recommendations

22.8.2.1 Authority/Expertise, Not Just Similarity of Taste

The basis of collaborative filtering algorithms is matching people based on similar interests. While getting recommendations from somebody with similar tastes is a good start, you might also want something else: that the person making the recommendation is an *expert* on these topics. You might prefer getting a recommendation based on the opinions of one expert, rather than 10 other people, even if the 10 others actually have interests somewhat closer to yours.

This raises multiple challenges, including obtaining expertise information, qualifying the information, and combining it with information about similarity of preferences to compute a recommendation. Various techniques for getting information about expertise may be explored. For example, in an online conversation, metrics such as the amount of messages a person contributes and the number of responses these messages receive could be used to assess a participant's expertise. In academic contexts, citation indexing methods could be used. A further consideration is that expertise is topic specific—for example, in the music domain, one person might be an expert on baroque music, another on big band swing, and a third on punk rock. Several techniques may help categorize a person's expertise. If a system has categorical information about items (for example, their genre), then if a person rates items from one category more often (and more highly) than other genres, this may indicate expertise in this category. And in a conversational application, the messages an individual produces may be analyzed to extract topics that he or she discusses frequently. (We realize that discussing a topic a lot doesn't necessarily make one an expert, but this is a good place to begin experimenting.) The final issue is how to combine expertise and taste information. Existing collaborative filtering algorithms could simply be tweaked with another term that weights neighbors' influence on a recommendation by their expertise. However, how much weight to assign is not clear a priori; experiments are necessary, and perhaps different combinations will be appropriate in different circumstances.

22.8.2.2 Combining Multiple Sources of Preferences

Thinking about combining expertise and preference information leads to another realization: Preferences can be obtained from different sources, and algorithms should be able to combine different types of preferences appropriately. For example, the preferences in PHOAKS were obtained by mining and aggregating opinions from Usenet messages. However, PHOAKS users were able to rate the recommended URLs, and the system captured usage history (that is, how often each URL was browsed). Thus, in the end, we had three sources of preferences about URLs: mentions in newsgroup messages, usage history, and explicit ratings. How to combine the three types of preferences is a challenge: As above, it is not clear how much weight to assign to a given type. The analysis of usage history, in particular, requires some thought. For example, simply counting the number of times users clicked on each URL as a preference measure is an obvious strategy. However, one should expect users to click more often on URLs that were higher in the display list. Building on this intuition, deviation from the expected pattern—that is, URLs that were clicked on significantly more or less frequently than expected—probably needs to be considered.

This example also illustrates an interesting general point: *Using* a recommendation to make a decision also may yield additional preference data that can be used to *evolve* the recommendation. And a single user may play multiple roles—recommendation seeker and preference producer—simultaneously.

22.9   Conclusion

Recommender systems have developed in response to a manifest need: helping people deal with the world of information abundance and overload. Further, it has become clear that they can link people with other people who share their interests, not just with relevant information. We identified a set of four major issues for recommender systems: (1) how preference data is obtained and used, (2) the roles played by people and by computation and the types of communication involved, (3) algorithms for linking people and computing recommendations, and (4) presentation of recommendations to users. We then identified four major approaches to recommender systems, which can be distinguished in large part by which of the issues they address and how they address them. Finally, we closed by suggesting several challenges that raise important opportunities for new research and application.

Acknowledgments

We thank Brian Amento for his participation in the PHOAKS and TopicShop projects. We thank Paul Resnick, Bonnie Nardi, Steve Whittaker, and anonymous reviewers for valuable comments on earlier drafts of this chapter.

References

Ackerman, M.S. (1994). Augmenting the organizational memory: A field study of answer garden. *Proceedings of CSCW'94*, 243–252. New York: ACM Press.

Ackerman, M.S., and McDonald, D.W. (1996). Answer garden 2: Merging organizational memory with collaborative help. *Proceedings of the Conference on Computer-Supported Cooperative Work (CSCW'96)*, 97–105. New York: ACM Press.

Aggarwal, C.A., Wolf, J.L., Wu, K-L., and Yu, P.S. (1999). Horting hatches an egg: A new graph-theoretic approach to collaborative filtering. *Proceedings of ACM SIGKDD International Conference on Knowledge Discovery and Data Mining.*

Amento, B., Hill, W., Terveen, L., Hix, D., and Ju, P. (1990). An empirical evaluation of user interfaces for topic management of web sites. *Proceedings of the CHI'99 Conference on Human Factors in Computing Systems*, 552–559. New York: ACM Press.

Avery, C., Resnick, P., and Zeckhauser, R. (1999). The market for evaluations. *American Economic Review* 89, 3, 564–584.

Balabanovic, M. and Shoham, Y. (1997). Fab: Content-based, collaborative recommendation. In Resnick and Varian (Eds.), 66–72.

Barrett, C. (1999). Anatomy of a weblog. *Camworld,* January 26, 1999. http://www.camworld.com/journal/rants/99/01/26.html.

Billsus, D., and Pazzani, M. (1998). Learning collaborative information filters. *Proceedings of the International Conference on Machine Learning.* San Francisco: Morgan Kaufmann Publishers.

Bush, V. (1945). As we may think. *The Atlantic Monthly.*

Card, S.K., Robertson, G.C., and York, W. (1996). The WebBook and the Web Forager: An information workspace for the World Wide Web. *Proceedings of the CHI'96 Conference on Human Factors in Computing Systems*, 111–117. New York: ACM Press.

Chalmers, M., Rodden, K., and Brodbeck, D. (1998). The order of things: Activity-centred information access. *Proceedings of 7th International Conference on the World Wide Web*, 359–367. Brisbane, Australia.

Deerwester, D., Dumais, S.T., Landauer, T.K., Furnas, G.W., and Harshman, R.A. (1990). Indexing by latent semantic analysis. *Journal of the Society for Information Science,* 41, 6, 391–407.

Dourish, P., and Bly, S. (1992). Portholes: Supporting awareness in a distributed work group. *Proceedings of CHI'92 Conference on Human Factors in Computing Systems,* 541–547. New York: ACM Press.

Dourish, P. (1999). Where the footprints lead: Tracking down other roles for social navigation. In Munro, Höök, and Benyon (Eds.), *Social Navigation of Information Space,* 15–34. Springer.

Goldberg, D., Nichols, D., Oki, B.M., and Terry, D. (1992). Using Collaborative filtering to weave an information tapestry. *Communications of the ACM,* 35, 12, 51–60.

Good, N., Schafer, J.B., Konstan, J., Borchers, A., Sarwar, B., Herlocker, J., and Riedl, J. (1999). Combining collaborative filtering with personal agents for better recommendations. *Proceedings of the Sixteenth National Conference on Artificial Intelligence* (AAAI-99).

Herlocker, J.L., Konstan, J.A., and Riedl, J. (2000). Explaining collaborative filtering recommendations. *Proceedings of ACM 2000 Conference on Computer-Supported Collaborative Work,* 241–250. New York: ACM Press.

Hill, W.C., Hollan, J.D., Wroblewski, D., and McCandless, T. (1992). Edit wear and read wear. *Proceedings of the CHI'92 Conference on Human Factors in Computing Systems,* 3–9. New York: ACM Press.

Hill, W.C., and Hollan, J.D. (1994). History-enriched digital objects: Prototypes and policy issues. *The Information Society,* 10, 2, 139–145.

Hill, W.C., Stead, L., Rosenstein, M. and Furnas, G. (1995). Recommending and evaluating choices in a virtual community of use. *Proceedings of the CHI'95 Conference on Human Factors in Computing Systems,* 194–201. New York: ACM Press.

Hill, W.C., and Terveen, L.G. (1996). Using frequency-of-mention in public conversations for social filtering. *Proceedings of ACM 1996 Conference on Computer Supported Cooperative Work.* 106–112. New York: ACM Press.

Katz, J. (1999). Here come the weblogs. *Slashdot,* May 24, 1999. http://www.slashdot.org/features/99/05/13/1832251.shtml.

Kautz, H., Selman, B., and Shah, M. (1997). The hidden Web. *AI Magazine,* 18, 2, 27–36.

Kleinberg, J.M. (1998). Authoritative sources in a hyperlinked environment. *Proceedings of 1998 ACM-SIAM Symposium on Discrete Algorithms.* New York: ACM Press.

Konstan, J.A., Miller, B.N., Maltz, D., Herlocker, J.L., Gordon, L.R., and Riedl, J. (1997). GroupLens: Applying collaborative filtering to usenet news. In Resnick and Varian (Eds.), 77–87.

Lieberman, H. (1997). Autonomous Interface Agents. *Proceedings of the CHI'97 Conference on Human Factors in Computing Systems,* 67–74. New York: ACM Press.

Mackinlay, J.D., Rao, R., and Card, S.K. (1995). An organic user interface for searching citation links. *Proceedings of the CHI'95 Conference on Human Factors in Computing Systems,* 67–73. New York: ACM Press.

Maes, P. (1994). Agents that reduce work and information overload. *Communications of the ACM,* 37, 7, 31–40.

Maglio, P.P., Farrell, S., and Barrett, R. (2000). How to define "place" on the Web. In K. Höök, A. Munro, and Wexelblat, A. (Eds.), *CHI 2000 Workshop, Social Navigation: A Design Approach?*

Maltz, D., and Ehrlich, K. (1995). Pointing the way: Active collaborative filtering. *Proceedings of the CHI'95 Conference on Human Factors in Computing Systems,* 202–209. New York: ACM Press.

McDonald, D., and Ackerman, M. (1998). Just talk to me: A field study of expertise location. *Proceedings of ACM 1998 Conference on Computer Supported Cooperative Work,* 315–324. New York: ACM Press.

Munro, A.J, Höök, K., and Benyon, D (Eds.) *Social Navigation of Information Space.* Springer, 1999.

Pirolli, P., Pitkow, J., and Rao, R. (1996). Silk from a sow's ear: Extracting usable structures from the Web. *Proceedings of the CHI'96 Conference on Human Factors in Computing Systems,* 118–125. New York: ACM Press.

Pitkow, J., and Pirolli, P. (1997). Life, death, and lawfulness on the electronic frontier. *Proceedings of the CHI'97 Conference on Human Factors in Computing Systems,* 383–390. New York: ACM Press.

Resnick, P., Iacovou, N., Suchak, M., Bergstrom, P., Riedl, J. (1994). GroupLens: An open architecture for collaborative filtering of netnews. *Proceedings of ACM 1998 Conference on Computer Supported Cooperative Work,* 175–186 New York: ACM Press.

Resnick, P., and Varian, H.R (Guest editors). (1997). *Communications of the ACM.* Special issue on Recommender Systems, 40, 3.

Resnick, P. and Varian, H.R. (1997). Recommender systems. In Resnick and Varian (Eds.), 56–58.

Shardanand, U., and Maes, P. (1995). Social information filtering: algorithms for automating "word of mouth." *Proceedings of the CHI'95 Conference on Human Factors in Computing Systems,* 210–217. New York: ACM Press.

Terveen, L.G., Selfridge, P.G., and Long, M.D. (1995). Living design memory: Framework, implementation, lessons learned. *Human-Computer Interaction,* 10, 1, 1–38.

Terveen, L.G., Hill, W.C., and Amento, B. (1999). Constructing, organizing, and visualizing collections of topically related web resources. *ACM Transactions on Computer-Human Interaction,* 6,1, 67–94.

Viegas, F.B., and Donath, J.S. (1990). Chat circles. *Proceedings of the CHI'99 Conference on Human Factors in Computing Systems,* 9–16. New York: ACM Press.

Wexelblat, A., and Maes, P. (1990). Footprints: History-rich tools for information foraging. *Proceedings of the CHI'99 Conference on Human Factors in Computing Systems,* 270–277. New York: ACM Press.

PART VI

Integrating Computation and Real Environments

Charting Past, Present, and Future Research in Ubiquitous Computing

Gregory D. Abowd
Elizabeth D. Mynatt

23.1 Introduction

Weiser introduced the area of ubiquitous computing (ubicomp) and put forth a vision of people and environments augmented with computational resources that provide information and services when and where desired (Weiser 1991). For the past decade, ubicomp researchers have attempted this augmentation with the implicit goal of assisting everyday life and not overwhelming it. Weiser's vision described a proliferation of devices at varying scales, ranging in size from hand-held "inch-scale" personal devices to "yard-scale" shared devices. This proliferation of devices has indeed occurred, with commonly used devices such as hand-held personal digital assistants, digital tablets, laptops, and wall-sized electronic whiteboards. The development and deployment of necessary infrastructure to support continuous mobile computation is arriving.

Another aspect of Weiser's vision was that new applications would emerge that leverage off these devices and infrastructure. Indeed, ubicomp promises more than just infrastructure, suggesting new paradigms of interaction inspired by widespread access to information and computational capabilities. In this paper, we explore how this applications perspective has evolved in the decade since the start of the Ubiquitous Computing project at Xerox PARC. Specifically, we review the accomplishments and outline remaining challenges for these three themes.

- We desire *natural interfaces* that facilitate a richer variety of communications capabilities between humans and computation. It is the goal of these natural interfaces to support common forms of human expression and leverage more of our implicit actions in the world.

- Ubicomp applications need to be *context-aware,* adapting their behavior based on information sensed from the physical and computational environment.

- Finally, a large number of ubicomp applications strive to automate the *capture* of live experiences and provide flexible and universal *access* to those experiences later on.

Undertaking issues of scale is implicit in the definition of ubicomp research. Weiser defined the notion of scale as a broad space of *computational devices* (Weiser 1991). Likewise, scaling systems with respect to distribution of computation into *physical space* reinforces the desire to break the human away from desktop-bound interaction. Requirements for critical mass acceptance and collaboration imply scaling with respect to *people.* A final dimension, *time,* presents new challenges for scaling a system. Pushing the availability of interaction to a "24 by 7"[1] basis uncovers another class of largely unexplored interactions that will also push ubicomp research into the next century. To address scaling with respect to time, in Section 23.5, we introduce a new theme, called *everyday computing,* that promotes informal and unstructured activities typical of much of our everyday lives. These activities are continuous in time, a constant ebb and flow of action that has no clear starting or ending point. Familiar examples are orchestrating tasks, communicating with family and friends, and managing information.

The structure of this paper follows the evolutionary path of past work in ubiquitous computing. The first step in this evolution, demonstrated by the PARCTab and Liveboard, is computers encased in novel form factors. Often these computational appliances push on traditional areas in computer science such as networking and operating systems. Since these new form factors often do not work well with traditional input devices such as the keyboard and mouse, developing new, and more natural, input capabilities is the next step. An example of this work is the pen-based shorthand language Unistroke for the PARCTab. After some initial demonstrations, infrastructure is needed to deploy these devices for general use. It is at this point that application designers begin working with these new systems to develop novel uses, often focusing on implicit user input to minimize the intrusion of technology into everyday life. The objective of this application-centered research is to understand how everyday tasks can be better supported and how they are altered by the introduction of ubiquitous technologies. For example, ubicomp applications in support of common meeting tasks at PARC (through the Tivoli project) have resulted in new ways to scribe and organize materials during meetings. Capture environments in educational settings have provided more opportunities to understand the patterns of longer-term reviewing tasks over large multimedia records. Applications of wearable computers initially empha-

---

[1] 24 hours a day, 7 days a week.

sized constant access to traditional individual tasks, such as accessing e-mail. More recent applications have attempted to augment an individual's memory and provide implicit information sharing between groups. The direction of applications research, what Weiser himself deemed the ultimate purpose for ubicomp research, is deeply influenced by authentic and extended use of ubicomp systems.

Today we are just starting to understand the implications of continuous immersion in computation. The future will hold much more than constant availability of tools to assist with traditional, computer-based tasks. Whether we wear computers on our body or have them embedded in our environment, the ability of computers to alter our perception of the physical world, to support constant connectivity to distant people and places, to provide information at our fingertips, and to continuously partner with us in our thoughts and actions offers much more than a new "killer app"—it offers a killer existence.

23.1.1 Overview

In this chapter, we investigate the brief history of ubiquitous computing through exploration of the above-mentioned interaction themes—natural interfaces, context-aware computing, and automated capture and access for live experiences. We outline some of the remaining research challenges for HCI researchers to pursue in the new millennium. We then explain the necessity for ubicomp research to explore continuous everyday activities. This area of research motivates applications that build off of the three earlier themes and moves ubicomp more into the realm of everyday computing characterized by continuously present, integrative, and unobtrusive interaction. Inherent in all of these interaction themes are difficult issues in the social implications of ubiquitous computing and the challenges of evaluating ubiquitous computing research. We conclude with our reflections on these issues and description, via case studies, of our current strategies for evaluation of ubicomp systems.

23.2 Computing with Natural Interfaces

Ubiquitous computing inspires application development that is "off the desktop." Implicit in this mantra is the assumption that physical interaction between humans and computation will be less like the current desktop keyboard/mouse/display paradigm and more like the way humans interact with the physical world. Humans speak, gesture, and use writing utensils to communicate with other humans and alter physical artifacts. These natural actions can and should be used as explicit or implicit input to ubicomp systems.

Computer interfaces that support more natural human forms of communication (like handwriting, speech, and gestures) are beginning to supplement or replace elements of the GUI interaction paradigm. These interfaces are lauded for their learnability and general ease of use, and their ability to support tasks such as authoring and drawing without drastically changing the structure of those tasks. Additionally, they can be used by people with disabilities for whom the traditional mouse and keyboard less accessible.

There has been work for many years in speech-related interfaces, and the emerging area of perceptual interfaces is being driven by a long-standing research community in computer vision and computational perception. Pen-based or free-form interaction is also realizing a resurgence after the failure of the first generation of pen computing. More recently, researchers have suggested techniques for using objects in the physical world to manipulate electronic artifacts, creating so-called graspable or tangible user interfaces. PARC researchers attached sensors to computational devices in order to provide ways for physical manipulations of those devices to be interpreted appropriately by the applications running on those devices. Applications that support natural interfaces will leverage off of all of these input and output modalities. Two issues must be addressed to make progress in natural interface research, as discussed in the next sections.

23.2.1 First-Class Natural Data Types

To ease the development of more applications with natural interfaces, we must be able to handle other forms of input as easily as keyboard and mouse input. The raw data or signals that underlie these natural interfaces, audio, video, ink, and sensor input, need to become first-class types in interactive system development. As programmers, we expect that any user interface toolkit for development provides a basic level of support for "fundamental" operations for textual manipulation, and primitives for keyboard and mouse interaction. Similarly, we need basic support for manipulating speech—such as providing speaker pause cues or selection of speech segments or speaker identification—as well as for video and ink and other signals, such as physical device manipulations detected by sensors.

Take, for example, free-form, pen-based interaction. Much of the interest in pen-based computing has focused on recognition techniques to convert the "ink" from pen input to text. However, some applications, such as personal note-taking, do not require conversion from ink to text. In fact, it can be intrusive to the user to convert handwriting into some other form. Relatively little effort has been put into standardizing support for free-form, pen input. Some formats for exchanging pen input between platforms exist, but little effort has gone into defining effective mechanisms for manipulating the free-form ink data type within programs.

What kinds of operations should be supported for a natural data type such as ink? The Xerox PARC Tivoli system provided basic support for creating ink data and distinguishing between uninterpreted, free-form ink data and special, implicitly structured gestures. Another particularly useful feature of free-form ink is the ability to merge independent strokes together as they form letters, words, and other segments of language. In producing Web-based notes in Classroom 2000 (discussed in more detail shortly), for example, a temporal and spatial heuristic was used to merge pen-strokes together and assign them a more meaningful, word-level timestamp. This kind of structuring technique must become standard and available to all applications developers who wish to create free-form, pen-based interfaces.

23.2.2 Error-Prone Interaction for Recognition-Based Interaction

When used for recognition-based tasks, natural interfaces come with a new set of problems—they permit new and more kinds of mistakes. When recognition errors occur, the initial reaction of system designers is to try to eliminate them—for example, by improving recognition accuracy. However, research has shown that a reduction of 5 to 10 percent in the absolute error rate is necessary before the majority of people will even notice a difference in a speech recognition system.

Worse yet, eliminating errors may not be possible. Even humans make mistakes when dealing with these same forms of communication. As an example, consider handwriting recognition. Even the most expert handwriting recognizers (humans) can have a recognition accuracy as low as 54 percent. Human accuracy increases to 88 percent for cursive handwriting, and 96.8 percent for printed handwriting, but it is never perfect. This evidence all suggests that computer handwriting recognition will never be perfect.

On the other hand, recognition accuracy is not the only determinant of user satisfaction. Both the complexity of error recovery dialogues and the value-added benefit for any given effort affect user satisfaction. For example, Frankish found that users were less frustrated by recognition errors when the task was to enter a command in a form than when they were writing journal entries. He suggests that the payback for entering a single word in the case of a command is much larger when compared with the effort of entering the word in a paragraph of a journal entry.

Error handling is not a new problem. In fact, it is endemic to the design of computer systems that attempt to mimic human abilities. Research in the area of error handling for recognition technologies must assume that errors will occur, and then answer questions about the best ways to deal with them. Several research areas for error handling of recognition-based interfaces have emerged.

Error reduction This involves research into improving recognition technology in order to eliminate or reduce errors. It has been the focus of extensive research and could easily be the subject of a whole paper on its own. Evidence suggests that its Holy Grail, the elimination of errors, is probably not achievable.

Error discovery Before either the system or the user can take any action related to a given error, one of them has to know that the error has occurred. The system may be told of an error through explicit user input and can help the user to find errors through effective output of uncertain interpretations of recognized input.

Reusable infrastructure for error correction Toolkits provide reusable components and are most useful when a class of common, similar problems exists.

Interfaces for error handling would benefit tremendously from a toolkit that presents a library of techniques error-handling of recognition-based input. Such a toolkit would have to handle the inherent ambiguities that arise when multiple interpretations are generated for some raw input.

23.3 Context-Aware Computing

Two compelling early demonstrations of ubicomp were the Olivetti Research Lab's Active Badge and the Xerox PARCTab, both location-aware appliances. These devices leverage a simple piece of context, user location, and provide valuable services (automatic call forwarding for a phone system, automatically updated maps of user locations in an office). Whereas the connection between computational devices and the physical world is not new—control systems and autonomously guided satellites and missiles are other examples—these simple location-aware appliances are perhaps the first demonstration of linking implicit human activity with computational services that serve to augment general human activity.

Location is a common piece of context used in application development. The most widespread applications have been GPS-based car navigation systems and handheld "tour guide" systems that vary the content displayed (video or audio) by a handheld unit given the user's physical location in an exhibit area. Another important piece of context is recognizing individual objects. Earlier systems focused on recognizing some sort of barcode or identifying tag while recent work includes the use of vision-based recognition. Rekimoto and Nagao's NaviCam (see Figure 23.1) recognized color barcodes overlaying additional information about objects on a hand-held video display.

Although numerous systems that leverage a person's identity and/or location have been demonstrated, these systems are still difficult to implement. One of the main reasons for this is a lack of separation of context sensing and storage from application-specific reaction to contextual information. An appropriate separation of concerns along these lines would facilitate the construction of context-aware applications.

In many ways, we have just scratched the surface of context-aware computing with many issues still to be addressed. Here we will discuss challenges in incorporating more context information, representing context, ubiquitous access to context sensing and context fusion, and the coupling of context and natural interaction to provide effective augmented reality.

23.3.1 What Is Context?

There is more to context than position and identity. Most context-aware systems still do not incorporate knowledge about time, history (recent or long past), other people than the user, as well as many other pieces of information often available in

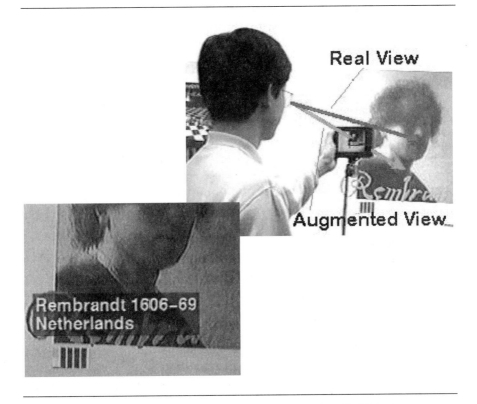

FIGURE 23.1   In Rekimoto and Nagao's NaviCam system, a handheld device recognizes tagged objects and then overlays context-sensitive information.

our environment. Although a complete definition of context is illusive, the "five W's" of context are a good minimal set of necessary context.

Who: Current systems focus their interaction on the identity of one particular user rarely incorporating identity information about other people in the environment. As human beings, we tailor our activities and recall events from the past based on the presence of other people.

What: The interaction in current systems either assumes what the user is doing or leaves the question open. Perceiving and interpreting human activity is a difficult problem. Nevertheless, interaction with continuously worn, context-driven devices will likely need to incorporate interpretations of human activity to be able to provide useful information.

Where: In many ways, the "where" component of context has been explored more than the others. Of particular interest, is coupling notions of "where" with other contextual information, such as "when." Some tour guide systems have theorized about learning from a history of movements in the physical world, perhaps to tailor information display based on the perceived path of interest by the user. Again these ideas need fuller exploration.

When: With the exception of using time as an index into a captured record or summarizing how long a person has been at a particular location, most context-driven applications are unaware of the passage of time. Of particular interest is understanding relative changes in time as an aid for interpreting human activity. For example, brief visits at an exhibit could be indicative of a general lack of interest. Additionally, when a baseline of behavior can be established, action that violates a perceived pattern would be of particular interest. For example, a context-aware home might notice when an elderly person deviated from a typically active morning routine.

Why: Even more challenging than perceiving "what" a person is doing is understanding "why" they are doing it. Sensing other forms of contextual information that could give an indication of a person's affective state, such as body temperature, heart rate and galvanic skin response, may be a useful place to start.

23.3.2 Representations of Context

Related to the definition of context is the question of how to represent context. Without good representations for context, applications developers are left to develop ad hoc and limited schemes for storing and manipulating this key information. The evolution of more sophisticated representations will enable a wider range of capabilities and a true separation of sensing context from the programmable reaction to that context.

23.3.3 The Ubiquity of Context Sensing—Context Fusion

An obvious challenge of context-aware computing is making it truly ubiquitous. Having certain context, in particular positioning information, has been shown useful. However, there are few truly ubiquitous, single-source context services. Positioning is a good example. GPS does not work indoors and is even suspect in some urban regions as well. There are a variety of indoor positioning schemes as well, with differing characteristics in terms of cost, range, granularity, and requirements for tagging, and no single solution is likely to ever meet all requirements.

The solution for obtaining ubiquitous context is to assemble context information from a combination of related context services. Such *context fusion* is similar in intent to the related, and well-researched, area of sensor fusion. Context fusion must handle seamlessly handing off sensing responsibility between boundaries of different context services. Negotiation and resolution strategies need to integrate information from competing context services when the same piece of context is concurrently provided by more than one service. This fusion is also required because sensing technologies are not 100 percent reliable or deterministic. Combining measures from multiple sources could increase the confidence value for a particular interpretation. In short, context fusion assists in providing reliable ubiquitous context by combining services in parallel, to offset noise in the signal, and sequentially to provide greater coverage.

23.3.4 Coupling Context-Aware and Natural Interaction— Augmented Reality

The goal of many context-aware applications is to allow the user to receive, in real time, information based on actions in the physical world. The tour guide systems are a good example—the user's movements in an exhibit triggered the display of additional, context-sensitive information. These applications typically used separate, albeit portable, devices that require attention away from the rest of the physical world. The best metaphor to describe these interactions is that the user is "probing the world with a tool," similar to tools such as electronic stud-finders and geiger counters.

By incorporating augmented vision and augmented hearing displays, as well as natural input such as voice and gesture, we will more closely integrate context-aware interaction with the physical world in which it resides. In these interactions, the system is modifying how a user perceives the physical world. This tighter integration of information and perception should allow for more natural, seamless, hands-busy, and serendipitous interaction (see Figure 23.2).

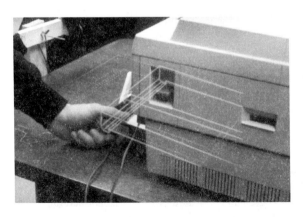

FIGURE 23.2 In the KARMA system (on the left) augmented views required heavy, clunky, head-mounted displays. Now lightweight glasses, such as the ones shown on the right above from MicroOptical, provide similar display capabilities.

23.4 Automated Capture and Access to Live Experiences

Much of our life in business and academia is spent listening to and recording, more or less accurately, the events that surround us, and then trying to remember the important pieces of information from those events. There is clear value, and potential danger, in using computational resources to augment the inefficiency of human record-taking, especially when there are multiple streams of related information that are virtually impossible to capture as a whole manually. Tools to support automated capture of and access to live experiences can remove the burden of doing something humans are not good at (recording) so that they can focus attention on activities they are good at (indicating relationships, summarizing, and interpreting).

There has been a good deal of research related to this general capture and access theme, particularly for meetingroom/classroom environments and personal note-taking. These systems focus on the capture of a public, group experience. Other capture systems focus on capture for the individual or even a mixture of public and personal experiences. Most of these systems produce some sort of multimedia interface to review the captured experience. By focusing on this postproduction phase, some systems provide automated support for multiple camera fusion, integration of various presentation media, and content-based retrieval mechanisms to help search through a large repository of captured information. The postproduction results can then be accessed through a multimedia interface, typically distributed via the Web. In all of these cases, the emphasis on ubiquity is clearly seen in the separate capture and access phases. Electronic capture is moved away from traditional devices, like the keyboard, and brought closer to the user in the form of pen-based interfaces or actual pen and paper. Input in the form of voice and gesture is also accepted and is either treated as raw data or further interpreted to provide more understanding of the captured experience.

23.4.1 Challenges in Capture and Access

Despite substantial research and advances in automated capture systems, there are a number of open research issues, which we summarize here. We separate out issues primarily associated with capture from those primarily associated with access.

23.4.1.1 Capture

We have mentioned earlier the importance of having a good driving application for ubicomp research. In the capture domain, the main compelling applications have been for meeting support and education/training. These are indeed compelling application areas. In particular, our evidence in Classroom 2000 points to overwhelming acceptance of capture from the student perspective (Abowd 1999). There are many more possibilities, however, for exploring capture in equally compelling domains.

- Many of us record the special events in our lives—vacations, birthday parties, visits from relatives and friends—and we often spend time, years later, reflecting and remembering the events through the recordings on film and in diaries. How many times have we wished we had a camera at a particularly precious moment in our lives (a child's first steps) only to fumble for the recording device and miss the moment?

- In many collaborative design activities, the critical insights or decisions are often made in informal settings and are usually not documented properly. Technical exchanges often flow quite freely in opportunistic encounters. Even in more formal design meetings, the rich exchange of information and discussions around artifacts, such as storyboards or architectural recommendations, is often very poorly captured.

- Maintenance of a building might be better supported if we captured a record of the actual construction of the building—in contrast to the building plans. When repairs are needed, the appropriate technician could "replay" the construction and maintenance history of the relevant building artifact in order to determine the right course of repair.

There has been little work on capturing artifacts in the physical world and making them easily accessible in the access phase. The emergence of low-cost capture hardware, such as the CrossPad™ and the mimio™ from Virtual Ink, will lead more researchers to work in this area.

Much of the capture currently being done is for what we would call raw streams of information that are captured mainly for the purpose of direct playback. No further analysis on those streams is done. However, it is often useful to *derive* additional information from a simple stream to provide a greater understanding of the live event. An audio signal can be processed to segment the audio stream into topical segments, based on results from discourse analysis. Other computational perception techniques can be used to analyze the simple audio, ink, or video signals.

Another application of signal analysis is to improve the recording of raw streams. How can we automate certain well-known production practices that merge multiple camera feeds into a single, coherent, and high-quality video that can be viewed later? Single, fixed camera angles are not sufficient to capture the salient parts of a live experience, but when we scale a system like Classroom 2000 to an entire campus, we cannot afford to pay technicians to sit in each of the classrooms. The single biggest challenge here is being able to determine the focus of attention for the group, and more difficult, for each individual at a live event.

23.4.1.2 Access

In the access phase, we need to provide a number of playback capabilities. The simplest is to playback in real time, but there are often situations in which this is inappropriate or overly inefficient. In reviewing a lecture for an exam, a student does not always want to sit through an entire lecture again, but he or she might want to pinpoint a particular topic of discussion and replay only that portion. Alternatively, a summarization of the experience that gleans salient points from across an entire captured session might be more appropriate.

Synchronization of multiple captured streams during playback is vital. Commercial streaming products, such as RealNetworks G2/SMIL™ and Microsoft's MediaPlayer/ASF™, are emerging standards to allow for powerful synchronization of programmer-defined media streams. However, it is not clear that any of these products will support the foreshadowing of streams so that a user can see what lies ahead in reviewing a stream. Such foreshadowing can help a user skim more quickly to a point of interest.

In most of the systems, the captured material is static upon reaching the access phase. Of course, there are often cases where annotating or revising captured material is appropriate, as well as then revising revised notes and so on. Although versioning is not a new problem to computer scientists, there are numerous challenges in providing an intuitive interface to multiple versions of captured material, especially when some of the material is already time-based such as audio and video. A timeline is an effective interface for manipulating and browsing a captured session, but when the time associated with a captured artifact is split up into a number of noncontiguous time segments, the usefulness of the timeline is at least questionable.

Finally, and perhaps most challenging, as these systems move from personalized systems to capturing events in more public settings, privacy concerns for the capture and later access of this material increase. Although these issues must be addressed in the specific design of each system, we still need general techniques for tagging material and authenticating access. We will discuss these issues later.

23.5   Toward Everyday Computing

Earlier, we describe an emerging area of interaction research, *everyday computing,* which results from considering the consequences of scaling ubiquitous computing with respect to time. Just as pushing the availability of computing away from the traditional desktop fundamentally changes the relationship between humans and computers, providing *continuous* interaction moves computing from a localized tool to a constant presence. Our motivations for everyday computing stem from wanting to support the informal and unstructured activities typical of much of our everyday lives. These activities are continuous in time, a constant ebb and flow of action that has no clear starting or ending point. Familiar examples are orchestrating tasks, communicating with family and friends, and managing information.

Designing for everyday computing requires addressing these features of informal, daily activities.

They rarely have a clear beginning or end. Either as a fundamental activity, such as communication, or as a long-term endeavor, such as research in human-computer interaction, these activities have no point of closure. Information from the past is often recycled. Although new names may appear in an address book or new items on a to-do list, the basic activities of communication or information management do not cease. When designing for an activity, principles such as providing visibility of the current state, freedom in dialogue, and overall simplicity in features play a prominent role.

Interruption is expected. Thinking of these activities as continuous, albeit possibly operating in the background, is a useful conceptualization. One side effect is that resumption of an activity does not start at a consistent point but is related to the state prior to interruption. Interaction must be modeled as a sequence of steps that will, at some point, be resumed and built upon. In addition to representing past interaction, the interface can remind the user of actions left uncompleted.

Multiple activities operate concurrently. Since these activities are continuous, the need for context-shifting among multiple activities is assumed. Application interfaces can allow the user to monitor a background activity, assisting the user in knowing when they should resume that activity. Resumption may be opportunistic, based on the availability of other people or on the recent arrival of needed information. To design for background awareness, interfaces should support multiple levels of "intrusiveness" in conveying monitoring information that matches the relative urgency and importance of events.

Time is an important discriminator. Time is a fundamental human measuring stick although it is rarely represented in computer interfaces. Whether the last conversation with a family member was last week or five minutes ago is relevant when interpreting an incoming call from that person. When searching for a paper on a desk, whether it was last seen yesterday or last month informs the search. There are numerous ways to incorporate time into human-computer interfaces. As we try to regain our working state, interfaces can represent past events contingent on the length of time (minutes, hours, days) since the last interaction. As applications interpret real world events, such as deciding how to handle an incoming phone call or to react to the arrival at the local grocery store, they can utilize timing information to tailor their interaction.

Associative models of information are needed. Hierarchical models of information are a good match for well-defined tasks, while models of information for activities are principally associative since information is often reused on multiple occasions, from multiple perspectives. For example, assume you have been saving e-mail from colleagues, friends, and family for a long time. When dealing with current mail, you may attempt to organize it into a hierarchy of folders on various topics. Over time, this organization has likely changed, resulting in a morass of messages that can be searched with varying degrees of success. Likewise, interfaces for to-do lists are often failures given the difficulty in organizing items in well-defined lists. Associative and context-rich models of organization support activities by allowing the user to re-acquire the information from numerous points of view. These views are inherent in the need to resume an activity in many ways, for many reasons. For example, users may want to retrieve information based on current context such as when someone enters their office or when they arrive at the grocery store. They may also remember information relative to other current information, for example, a document last edited some weeks ago or the document that a colleague circulated about some similar topic.

As computing becomes more ubiquitously available, it is imperative that the tools offered reflect their role in longer-term activities. Although principles in everyday computing can be applied to desktop interfaces, these design challenges are most relevant given a continuously changing user context. In mobile scenarios, users shift between activities while the computing resources available to them also vary for different environments. Even in an office setting, various tools and objects play multiple roles for different activities. For example, use of a computer augmented whiteboard varies based on contextual information such as people present. Different physical objects such as a paper file or an ambient display can provide entry points and background information for activities. This distribution of interaction in the physical world is implicit in the notion of everyday computing, and thus clearly relevant to research in ubiquitous computing.

23.5.1 Research Directions in Everyday Computing

Everyday computing offers many challenges to the HCI research community. In our current and future work, we are focusing on the following challenges.

Design a continuously present computer interface. There are multiple models for how to portray computers that are ubiquitous although none of these models are wholly satisfying. The notion of an information appliance typically reflects a special-purpose device that sits dumbly in the background without any knowledge of ongoing activity. These interfaces often borrow from traditional GUI concepts and from consumer electronics. Computational systems that continue to operate in the background, perhaps learning from past activity and acting opportunistically, are typically represented as anthropomorphized agents. However it is doubtful that every interface should be based on dialogue with a talking head or human-oriented personality. Research in wearables explores continually worn interfaces, but these are limited by the current input and display technologies and are typically rudimentary text-based interfaces.

Presenting information at different levels of the periphery of human attention. Despite increasing interest in tangible media and peripheral awareness, especially in computer-supported collaborate work (CSCW) and wearable computing, current interfaces typically present a generic peripheral backdrop with no mechanism for the user, or the background task, to move the peripheral information into the foreground of attention. Our current design experiments are aimed at creating peripheral interfaces that can operate at different levels of the user's periphery.

Connecting events in the physical and virtual worlds. People operate in two disconnected spaces: the virtual space of e-mail, documents, and Web pages and the physical space of face-to-face interactions, books, and paper files. Yet human activity is coordinated across these two spaces. There is much work left to be done to understand how to combine information from these spaces to better match how people conceptualize their own endeavors.

Modifying traditional HCI methods to support designing for informal, peripheral and opportunistic behavior. There is no one methodology for understanding the role of computers in our everyday lives. However, combining information from methods as different as laboratory experiments and ethnographic observations is far from simple. In our research and classroom projects, our goal is to learn by doing, by interrogating the results we derive from different evaluation strategies. We have consciously chosen a spectrum of methods that we believe match the questions we are asking. Learning how these methods inform each other and how their results can be combined will be an ongoing effort throughout our work. We continue this discussion in the next section on evaluating ubicomp systems.

23.6   Additional Challenges for Ubicomp

Two important topics for ubicomp research—evaluation and social implications— cut across all themes of research, and so we address them here.

23.6.1 Evaluating Ubicomp Systems

In order to understand the impact of ubiquitous computing on everyday life, we navigate a delicate balance between prediction of how novel technologies will serve a real human need and observation of authentic use and subsequent coevolution of human activities and novel technologies. Formative and summative evaluation of ubicomp systems is difficult for several reasons, which we will discuss. These challenges are why we see relatively little published from an evaluation or end-user perspective in the ubicomp community. A notable exception is the work published by Xerox PARC researchers on the use of the Tivoli capture system in the context of technical meetings. Since research in ubiquitous computing will have limited impact in the HCI community until it respects the need for evaluation, we have some advice for those wishing to undertake the challenges.

23.6.1.1 Finding a Human Need
The first major difficulty in evaluating a ubicomp system is simply having a reliable system to evaluate. The technology used to create ubicomp systems is often on the

cutting edge and not well understood by developers, so it is difficult to create reliable and robust systems that support some activity on a continuous basis. Consequently, a good portion of reported ubicomp work remains at this level of unrobust demonstrational prototypes. This kind of research is often criticized as being technocentric, but as we will show, it is still possible to do good user-centered feasibility research with cutting-edge technology.

It is important in doing ubicomp research that a researcher build a compelling story, from the end user's perspective, on how any system or infrastructure to be built will be used. The technology must serve a real or perceived human need, because, as Weiser (1993) noted, the whole purpose of ubicomp is to provide applications that serve the humans. The purpose of the compelling story is not simply to provide a demonstration vehicle for research results. It is to provide the basis for evaluating the impact of a system on the everyday life of its intended population. The best situation is to build the compelling story around activities that you are exposed to on a continuous basis. In this way, you can create a living laboratory for your work that continually motivates you to "support the story" and provides constant feedback that leads to better understanding of the use.

Designers of a system are not perfect, and mistakes will be made. Since it is already a difficult challenge to build robust ubicomp systems, you should not pay the price of building a sophisticated infrastructure only to find that it falls far short of addressing the goals set forth in the compelling story. You must do some sort of feasibility study of cutting-edge applications before sinking substantial effort into engineering a robust system that can be scrutinized with deeper evaluation. However, these feasibility evaluations must still be driven from an informed, user-centric perspective—the goal is to determine how a system is being used, what kinds of activities users are engaging in with the system, and whether the overall reactions are positive or negative. Answers to these questions will both inform future design as well as future evaluation plans. It is important to understand how a new system is used by its intended population before performing more quantitative studies on its impact.

Case Study: Xerox PARC's Flatland: Designing ubiquitous computing applications require designers to project into the future how users will employ these new technologies. Although designing for a currently impossible interaction is not a new HCI problem, this issue is exacerbated by the implied paradigm shift in HCI resulting from the distribution of computing capabilities into the physical environment.

In our design work for Flatland (Mynatt et al. 1999), we employed ethnographic observations of whiteboard use in the office, coupled with questionnaires and interviews, to understand how people used their whiteboards on a daily basis (see Figure 23.3). The richness of the data from the observations was both inspirational in our design work and a useful constraint. For example, the notion of "hot spots," portions of the board that users expect to change frequently, was the result of day-to-day observations of real whiteboard use. The data from the observations was key in grounding more in-depth user studies through questionnaires and interviews. Without this data, discussions would too easily slip into what users think they might do. By

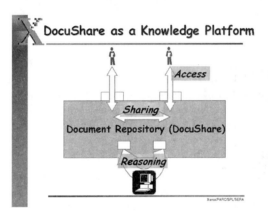

FIGURE 23.3   In the design of Flatland, we used observations of whiteboard use to inform our design. Here whiteboard drawings on two different boards are used as the basis for discussing the complex concepts illustrated with more detail in the bottom slide.

referring to two weeks of observational data, we were able to uncover and examine the details of daily practice.

Although the technology for our augmented whiteboard was not ready for deployment, or even user testing, we were able to gather a wealth of information from observations and interviews that critically informed our design.

Case Study: Audio Aura: The affordances and usability issues of novel input and output technologies are not well understood when they are first introduced. Often these technologies are still unusable for any real, long-term use setting. Nevertheless user-centric evaluations are needed to influence subsequent designs. In the design of

Audio Aura (Mynatt et al. 1998), we were interested in exploring how peripheral awareness of relevant office activities could be enhanced through use of ambient sound in a mobile setting. Our combination of active badges, wireless headphones and audio generation was too clunky for real adoption by long-term users. The headphones were socially prohibitive as they covered the ears with large black shells. The capabilities for the development language, Java, to control sound presentation were too limited for creating rich auditory spaces. Nevertheless we wanted to understand the potential interaction knowing that these technological limitations would be removed in the future.

We employed *scenarios* of interaction, based on informal observations of the Xerox PARC work environment, to guide our design and evaluation. These scenarios incorporated information about how people at PARC work together, including practices such as gathering at the coffee bistro, often dropping by people's offices for impromptu conversations, and even the physical oddities of the building such as the long hallways that are the backbone of the layout. By grounding our scenarios in common practices, potential users could reflect on their daily activities when evaluating our designs. The scenarios also helped us understand a particular interaction issue: timing. In one of our scenarios, the communication path between the component technologies was not fast enough to meet the interaction demands. Although the speed could be increased, this modification required balancing a set of tradeoffs, namely speed vs. scalability, both important for our design goals. In short, the scenarios helped us understand the design space for further exploration.

23.6.1.2 Evaluating in the Context of Authentic Use

Deeper evaluation results require real use of a system, and this, in turn, requires a deployment into an authentic setting. The scaling dimensions that characterize ubicomp systems—device, space, people, or time—make it impossible to use traditional, contained usability laboratories. Effective evaluation, in which users are observed interacting with the system in routine ways, requires a realistic deployment into the environment of expected use.

Case Study: Classroom 2000: In this last case study, centered at Georgia Tech, we demonstrate a much longer-term research project that evolved from early prototyping and feasibility studies into a more mature system that is currently used by a large population in a living classroom laboratory, shown in Figure 23.4. The project began in July 1995 with the intent of producing a system that would capture as much of the classroom experience as possible to facilitate later review by both students and teachers. In many lectures, students have their heads down, furiously writing down what they hear and see as a future reference. While some of this writing activity is useful as a processing cue for the student, we felt that it was desirable from the student and teacher perspective to afford the opportunity for students to lift their heads occasionally and engage in the lecture experience. The capture system was seen as a way to relieve some of the note-taking burden.

We needed to test the feasibility of this hypothesis quickly, so within six months of the project launch, we provided an environment to capture an entire course and

FIGURE 23.4   In the Classroom 2000 project, we have had the ability to learn from long-term actual use in the Georgia Tech educational environment.

observe whether our initial hypothesis was worth testing more vigorously. We learned some very valuable lessons during this first extended experience. The initial experiments included student note-taking devices that were clear distractions to the students (Abowd 1999), so we abandoned that part of the experiment, only to resume it in the past few months when the technology had caught up. We also learned from this initial experience that in order to understand the impact of this capture system on teaching and learning we would have to gather usage data from a larger set of classes. This required significant engineering effort to create a robust and reliable capture system that by the Spring Quarter of 1997 was able to support multiple classes simultaneously. Today, after capturing over 100 courses with 30 different instructors, we have gained significant insight into how the system is used and what future directions to take (Abowd 1999). As a direct result of these deeper evaluations, we know that the system encourages 60 percent of its users to modify their in-class note-taking behavior. We also know that not all of this modified behavior is for the better. Taking no notes, for example, is not a good learning practice to reinforce. We know that it is time to reintroduce student note-taking units that can personalize the capture experience and also encourage better note-taking practices. We also know to facilitate more content-based retrieval and synchronized playback of the lecture experience. These insights have motivated further research efforts and established a long-term research project, eClass, that stands as a model for ubicomp research and automated capture and access.

23.6.1.3 Task-centric Evaluation Techniques Are Inappropriate

Assuming an authentic deployment can occur, when users are comfortable with the service being provided and have developed habits for using the service, there is still the question of how to apply qualitative or quantitative evaluation methods. The majority of usability techniques are task-centric. If the user's tasks are known, then an evaluation is performed to determine the fitness of the system and its interface for completing that task. It is not at all clear how to apply task-centric evaluation techniques to informal everyday computing situations.

23.6.2   Social Issues for Ubiquitous Computing

We are pushing toward making it easier for computation to sense, understand and react to phenomenon in the physical world and to record those phenomena. These enabling technologies carry with them numerous dangers—for example, making it too easy for people to build systems that effectively spy on others without any controlling authority. Ubicomp researchers would be remiss if they undertook their work without understanding these issues. However, the fear of wrongdoing is not a call to cease all work in this area but to work toward technological, design, and social solutions to address these concerns.

A basic concern about any information stored in a computer is knowing who can access and modify the contents. Where are the bits? Are they secure? Security and encryption schemes are part of the technological solutions available especially as information is gleaned from the environment and transported over networks. Alternatively, work in wearable computing emphasizes a design approach—providing security by keeping the bits local (on the body) and removing the risks of transporting them over a public network.

One fear of users is the lack of knowledge of what some computing system is doing or that something is being done "behind their backs." Although the original vision of ubiquitous computing described computing as disappearing into the physical environment, this "invisibility" is counter to informing users about how they are being sensed. To assuage that fear, design solutions can be employed to make this information visible. For example, systems that sense physical phenomena and capture live situations should provide clear indicators that this sensing or recording is occurring. As these sensing and recording capabilities are more commonly found, one challenge for everyday computing is to enable people to be aware of how they are being sensed. Just as people can ascertain their visibility in physical space (How public is this space? Are there windows?) we need cues to convey our visibility in virtual space.

The next step is to allow those being sensed or recorded to have control to either stop this activity or to at least control the distribution and use of the information. This challenge is related to the design of collaborative environments where the actions and roles of collaborators are fluid and difficult to articulate in a static snapshot. The capture, distribution, and use of information will be determined over time by the specific practices of people in workplace and home settings.

There are a number of reactions that system builders can have for handling the sensitive topic of when and what to capture. At Xerox PARC, one solution for capture was to agree to capture only the summary portions of technical meetings. In Classroom 2000, we defaulted to recording all of a lecture but did not attempt to obtain good quality audio or video of anyone except the lecturer in the front of the room. An interesting challenge for collaborative situations is to figure out acceptable policies for "erasing" or "forgetting" some shared memory. A more positive slant on this issue would focus on ways to accommodate heightening awareness of particularly valuable segments of a captured experience in lieu of eliminating or forgetting parts of a captured history.

Although issues surrounding the appropriate use and dissemination of information are as old as the dawn of human communication, specific concerns stem from ubicomp making a new kind of information more generally available. The fact that computers can easily track our daily activities—a feat that previously required a large amount of human effort—is disconcerting at the least. In addition to addressing the above-mentioned concerns of security, visibility, and control, our approach is to create designed examples of appropriate and beneficial uses of this information. For example, one affordance of the low-quality video in early media spaces was that the amount of information conveyed was more socially appropriate. The not-real-time, grainy images met important needs for awareness and feelings of connectivity without violating privacy concerns. In the design of Audio Aura (Mynatt et al. 1998), we took great care in conveying *qualitative* information about the activities of colleagues. When stopping by someone's office, information that could be obtained by the system (e.g., this person has not been in their office for a few hours) was akin to the information that someone in a neighboring office could provide.

There are other social issues as well that are not as directly linked to privacy. For example, recording a meeting or a lecture can have both positive and negative impact on those in attendance. On the positive side, knowledge of recording encourages people to be less reckless in their commentary. On the negative side, this same knowledge can cause people to refuse to contribute to a discussion for fear of saying something that would be regretted in the future. A more subtle problem was noticed in our extensive experience in Classroom 2000. Some students indicated that they chose not to ask questions in class because the answer was likely already discussed and it was up to the student to go back and listen to the lecture.

In general, social and legal practices continue to evolve in concert with technological and design innovations. In each situation people will compare the perceived benefits and costs of the uses of ubicomp technologies. For example, skiers and hikers choose to wear radio transponders so they can be located by rescue personnel. Firefighters benefit from understanding what each of them is doing and where they are located. Recent research details the calendaring practices at Sun Microsystem, where colleagues share extensive information about their daily collaborative activities. As discussed in the previous section on evaluation, our understanding of the social implications of these technologies will often come after people invent new, unforeseen, uses of these technologies. Although the sand is always shifting beneath us, attention to issues of security, visibility, control, and privacy should help ensure a more positive use of these technologies.

23.7   Conclusion

In this paper, we have attempted to outline the trajectory of ubicomp research in the decade since the inspiring work of Weiser and colleagues at Xerox PARC. We have identified three research themes for ubicomp, provided some background on significant achievements in those areas, as well as highlighted some of the remaining challenges. We have done this with the desire to motivate budding ubicomp researchers to attack some important and well-defined problems. We no doubt have left out some other important challenges for ubicomp research, and we look forward to seeing those problems articulated and solved by others.

Weiser (1993) claimed that the whole point of ubiquitous computing was to create compelling applications that would drive the development of devices and infrastructure. We agree in spirit with this claim, but want to promote a broader view that promotes the general purpose utility (and challenge) of ubiquitous interaction with computational resources. The application or task-centric focus has been a fruitful one for HCI research. If we look at successful computing technology, however, it is not the case that a single application has driven critical mass acceptance and deployment. What is the motivating application for the personal computer in our office or home, or for a Palm Pilot™? There are many applications, different for each person. The real goal for ubicomp is to provide many single-activity interactions that together promote a unified and continuous interaction between humans and computational services. The focus for the human at any one time is not a single interface to accomplish some task. Rather, the interaction is more free-flowing and integrative, akin to our interaction with the rich physical world of people, places, and objects in our everyday lives.

Acknowledgments

The authors would like to acknowledge the significant inspiration from the late Mark Weiser, who died somewhat suddenly during initial drafts of this paper. Mark's vision and enthusiasm influenced a countless number of researchers, and we are indebted to his contributions in many ways. We would also like to acknowledge the interactions and influence of a number of colleagues from Xerox PARC and the Georgia Tech's Future Computing Environments Group within the College of Computing. An extended version of this paper, with more complete references, was recently published in the *ACM Transactions on Computer Human Interaction* special issue on HCI Research for the new millennium (March 2000).

References

Abowd, G.D. (1999). Classroom 2000: An experiment with the instrumentation of a living educational environment. *IBM Systems Journal, Special Issue on Human-Computer Interaction: A Focus on Pervasive Computing,* 38, 4, 508–530.

Mynatt, E.D., Back, M., Want, R., Baer, M., and Ellis, J. (1998). Designing audio aura. *Proceedings of the 1998 ACM Conference on Human Factors in Computing Systems (CHI'98),* 566–573. Los Angeles, CA.

Mynatt, E.D., Igarashi, T., Edward, W.K., and LaMarca, A. (1999). Flatland: New dimensions in office whiteboards. *1999 ACM Conference on Human Factors in Computing Systems (CHI'99).*

Norman, D.A. (1998). *The invisible computer: Why good products can fail, the personal computer is so complex, and information appliances are the solution.* Cambridge, MA: MIT Press.

Weiser, M. (1991). The computer of the 21st century. *Scientific American,* 265, 3, 66–75.

Weiser, M. (1993). Some computer science issues in ubiquitous computing. *Communications of the ACM,* 36, 7, 75–84.

24

Situated Computing: The Next Frontier for HCI Research

Kevin L. Mills
Jean Scholtz

24.1 Introduction

Increasingly people work and live on the move. To support this mobile lifestyle, especially as our work becomes more intensely information-based, companies are producing various portable and embedded information devices. Consider, for example, personal digital assistants (PDAs), cellular telephones, pagers, active badges, and intelligent buttons. Cellular phones allow us to receive and place telephone calls anywhere. Personal Digital Assistants let us take calendar information, contact information, and even e-mail messages with us when we leave the desktop. Active badges and intelligent buttons give us ways to track objects and people. Carrying the idea of a mobile information device toward a natural extension, in 1997 Daimler-Benz announced the demonstration of a concept car: Internet Multimedia on Wheels. In this concept, a car would become a node on the Internet, allowing information services to be delivered to the car and back using wireless technology. Interesting wireless technologies, including Bluetooth, IrDA (Infrared Data Association—standards for infrared communications), and HomeRF™ (wireless home networking), promise to outfit portable and embedded devices with high-bandwidth, localized wireless communication that can also reach the globally wired Internet. (Web sites for the technologies discussed in this chapter can be found among the references.)

An impressionist painting emerges of nomadic workers with collections of small, specialized devices roaming among islands of wireless connectivity within a global sea of wired networks. Each wireless island defines a context of available services, embedded devices, and task-specific information. As nomadic workers roam the landscape, the context in which they are working continuously changes. As workers move onto wireless islands of connectivity, their context is merged with the context of the island to automatically compose a computational environment to support their needs. At other times, when not connected, an array of portable devices provides each nomad with a local context for computing. This painting, which relies heavily on Weiser's (1991, 1993) concept of ubiquitous computing and on Suchman's notion of situated computing (Suchman 1987), suggests a future where information and people connect directly and work together across a range of contexts.

Weiser envisioned a future where people would interact continually with computation embedded in physical objects. The computers would be small enough to be invisible inside the physical objects and would enhance, rather than interfere with, the original functionality of the physical objects. In Weiser's vision, people would do their work assisted by computer technology but without having to focus on the computers. This vision continues today in Don Norman's (1998) prospect for the invisible computer. Suchman (1987) goes further, suggesting that not only should the computer step into the background but also that the computer should continuously monitor the situation in order to proactively aid an information user. Aiming to improve our interaction with information, researchers today investigate four main directions: Smart Spaces or Smart Rooms, Wearable Computing, Tangible User Interfaces, and Information Appliances. While each of these directions shows promise along some dimensions of ubiquitous computing, they fail along others. We will discuss these research efforts later in the chapter. First, though, from the shortcomings of this current research, we discern two grand challenges that prevent the universal use of ubiquitous computing.

As a first grand challenge, researchers must alter the inequality of interaction between the two participants: the human and the computer. Currently, the human is responsible both for manipulating and managing the information—that is, locating the information, synchronizing the information, moving the information between devices, and possibly converting the information to a format required by a given device or application. The human is clearly the active player, while the computer assumes a more passive role. This inequality must be altered so that people need only interact with their information, while the computer takes on the ancillary management tasks. As grand challenge two, researchers must find a means to endow cyberspace with a better understanding of the physical and logical world in which people live and work. Moreover, the computer needs to understand and adapt to the user. In order to accomplish this, researchers must give the computer knowledge of the user's context—the task, the environment, the user's emotional and physical states, and the available computing resources. To be truly invisible, the computer needs to gain an understanding of context without relying on the user to supply that information.

In this chapter, we outline specific facets of these two grand challenges. We assert that the human-computer interaction (HCI) research community must meet these challenges before society can reap full benefits from specialized, information appliances. In the sections that follow, we discuss some specific research problems that must be solved to meet each grand challenge. Where applicable, we also point to some ongoing research that appears to be tackling, at an early stage, some aspects of these challenges.

24.2   Grand Challenge #1: Emancipating Information

Today people collect information in spreadsheets, databases, document repositories, and Web sites. In the main, each set of information is captive of a specific application program. The application dictates the format of the information, and provides the means of interacting with the information. To move data between computers in an understandable form, industry has agreed to a uniform approach, based on Multipurpose Internet Mail Extension (MIME) types, which permit an electronic mail message to describe the format of any included attachments. Even when a computer understands the type of specific attachments, appropriate software must exist on the receiving node in order for the data to be useful. For example, to move data between different types of applications (such as spreadsheet to document) or between different products for the same type of application (such as Microsoft Word™ to Lotus Wordpro™), either the information must be exported and imported through compatible filters, or the information must be encapsulated inside information of another type but in a form (such as Microsoft Object Linking and Embedding) that enables the appropriate application to be initiated when a user selects the encapsulated information. In addition to application programs controlling information, the applications themselves are captive within specific computer operating systems. For example, while Microsoft Word will certainly execute on Windows 98™ or Windows NT™, the application will probably not execute on Sun Solaris™. These captivating dependencies will become even more irksome as people begin to use the myriad of specialized devices, such as cell phones, personal digital assistants, pens, pads, and wristwatches, to collect, view, and transport information. The need for information filters and data synchronization programs will increase rapidly. As a result, if the current paradigm continues, then people will be spending more unproductive time managing information—that is, locating data, transforming it to an appropriate format, and sending it to an appropriate device.

In the past, industry has developed standards for describing data for various applications, such as the office document architecture (ODA) and office document interchange format (ODIF) for professional documents. For some reason, these past attempts at uniform data-description languages have failed in the marketplace. Industry continues to explore alternative technologies, such as eXtensible Markup Language (XML™), which can provide more precise information about the structure and format of data. Successful development of XML as a universal data-description language might one day enable every application to provide a single import and export filter, thus removing the current cacophony of filters deployed with each application. Even in the case of XML, competing approaches are emerging for encoding information intended for exchange over wireless communication channels, as distinct from wired Internet channels. Further, assuming that XML is universally deployed to describe data, various applications must still act on the data in order to provide behavior. No widely accepted approach exists to describe behavior appropriate to specific data. Java™ and other platform-independent languages, such as Python and TCL (Ousterhout 1994), show one possible approach to solve the problem of expressing behavior. An alternate possibility envisions treating software behaviors more as a network service. In such cases, once an appropriate description of the data exists, behaviors can be located as services on the network. For example, Microsoft recently unveiled their vision of a next-generation Windows service architecture. Success in such endeavors will require widespread, almost universal, agreement on the techniques for expressing data format. Perhaps XML will achieve this goal. The second requirement for success entails a means to associate behavior with data. One approach requires all nodes and devices to include a run-time environment that can interpret behaviors described in a standard language. Another approach requires data to include references to behaviors that can be located on the network. In the past, these objectives have proven difficult to achieve, though some progress can be discerned.

To understand the extent of the problem better, consider the study that Jun Rekimoto (1997) made of software engineers, arguably among the most advanced users of computer software. Among the software engineers surveyed, Rekimoto found that 54 percent had three or more computers on their desks, 39 percent had two computers, and the remainder had only one. Seventy percent of those engineers transferred data between computers very often and another 25 percent transferred data often. When considering only nearby computers, 28 percent of the engineers moved data very often, 23 percent often, and 36 percent sometimes. Transfer mechanisms included cut-and-paste, shared files, file transfer, e-mail, and floppies. The decisions about what information to transfer and where and the means of transfer were all left to the software engineers. While this data comes from a highly specialized user community, we expect that many users, less skilled than these software engineers, will soon face such problems on a daily basis, concomitant with the increase in specialized information devices.

Aside from the overhead of managing our increasingly scattered information, we are all becoming more mobile in our working lives. For example, Bellotti and Bly (1996) studied the work activities of a product design team in a company with various facilities distributed around a small geographic area. In particular, the study identified the places where designers did their work and measured how much time they spent in each place. For two typical product design engineers, Bellotti and Bly discovered that only 10 to 13 percent of the designer's work was conducted at their desktop computers, while 76 to 82 percent of the work was spread over 11 other locations, and 8 to 11 percent of work time was spent moving between work locations.

For our purposes, two observations are worth nothing from the Belotti and Bly study. First, as workers move among work locations they must carry with them a range of information and portable tools that will be needed at each work site. Second, at each work site, there exists a number of local tools, and perhaps some relevant local information, as well as tools and information brought by others on the design team. The designers must combine the local tools and information with the imported tools and information in order to complete specific design tasks. While these designers probably represent an extreme focus on mobility, we argue that an increasing population of workers spends more time at different locations and traveling among locations. Even within a more typical office environment, workers attend meetings in conference rooms, visit colleagues in their offices, and discuss work over lunch in the cafeteria.

We see new work styles emerging where people will increasingly (1) move among locations to complete work, (2) use a number of specialized, portable, and embedded devices in ad hoc arrangements at each work location, and (3) shuffle information back and forth among work locations and among devices. For such work styles to prove productive, the information technology research community must liberate information from the confines of specific applications and specific computers. We discuss in the following paragraphs some ideas necessary to support these new work styles.

24.2.1 Moving Information to People

One option is to carry all of our information with us. This approach appears feasible, as the miracle of hardware continues to bring us ever-increasing density in disk storage along with cheaper and faster processors. We don't believe, however, that this will prove feasible because human activities continue to produce information at prodigious rates, and not all such information belongs to particular individuals. In fact, much of the information we produce is context-dependent. For example, we typically attend meetings to conduct specific tasks. Before, after, and during these meetings we create information. Some of this information we retain personally, while other information is shared among the meeting attendees and others outside of the group. Only a small fraction of this information is our own personal information. Surely, as we move to the next meeting on the same subject we will wish to have information from the last meeting available.

We argue that context can often be inferred from a combination of user, location, and task. If so, then why should a user be required to ensure that the right information is available at the right place and time? Can't the information itself take on this responsibility? Imagine *active information* objects that can move, that can replicate themselves, and that can communicate as a group. Active information objects should monitor context and remind us of their existence. Wouldn't it be useful to have your information remind your workgroup that you had discussed the same topic several weeks ago and present you with a summary of that discussion? Active information should be able to track the location, state, and trajectory of information users, of object replicas, and of linked objects. In addition, active information objects should be able to plan the movement, replication, and transformation of information to serve the projected needs of its users. Active information objects must also be able to implement consistency, access, and sharing policies among replicated and linked objects.

A combination of commercial and research activities shows some promise that a day will soon appear in which active information becomes both possible and interesting. Clearly mobile code systems, such as Python and Java, hint at the possibility of distributed object systems that can replicate and move. The computer science research laboratory at the University of California, Berkeley (Bindel et al. 2000; McCanne et al. 1997), is developing scalable reliable multicast protocols, beaconing protocols, and transcoding algorithms that distributed objects can use to discover each other, to communicate, and to transform their presentation. Other work at UC Berkeley promises a processing-capable network infrastructure that can provide a platform for mobile distributed objects to reside within a network and to move and copy themselves toward specific situated computing locales as users begin to congregate (Amir et al. 1998). The OceanStores (Bindel et al. 2000) work on persistent storage, also at UC Berkeley, aims to define secure, reliable storage for a ubiquitous computing environment. By using unique identifiers for the data, encrypting the data, and providing multiple paths to locate data objects, a nomadic worker would be able to access data from anywhere, assuming Internet connectivity.

Novel research is still required to investigate information models that will make it possible for information to transform itself for specific contexts, including the applications available, the devices and other resources at hand, and the tasks to be performed. In addition, information objects will need mechanisms to reveal their active properties and to discover the active properties of other information objects in order to permit individual objects or object webs to combine into larger object systems to support specific contexts and tasks. One particular active property must describe the mechanisms through which users can interact with specific information objects, independent of particular devices and applications.

24.2.2 Removing the Tyranny of an Interface per Application per Device

As many specialized devices become available, human-information interfaces can be distributed across devices and interaction modes. In fact, several devices can be networked to support a richer interaction and computing capability than any of the single devices alone. We use the term *multimodal* to refer to interfaces that combine modes of interaction. In today's user interfaces, multimodal most often refers to two modes of input, typically pen and speech. To make interactions in a ubiquitous computing environment truly natural, this capability must be extended to include gestures, facial expressions, gaze, and tactile input, among others. Multimodal should include a combination of multiple modes of interaction, where multiple exceeds two!

Depending on application requirements, user preferences, and knowledge about human awareness, about specific tasks, and about the type of information being conveyed, tomorrow's multimodal interfaces must coordinate interactions across devices and among interaction events. In addition, a model of interaction events will be needed, as well as rules for mapping between the interaction event model and mode-specific interactions. Given a fluid set of devices available in any particular situated computing locale, software mechanisms must support the dynamic composition of interfaces from among software components and information objects. In addition to composition, rules must also be provided for instantiating optimal multimodal interfaces for specific tasks, given available devices and modalities. Naming and identification will be a key issue, along with authentication and access control. Since information and interaction events will likely fly through the air across wireless links, privacy will also become more important. Other issues will arise regarding arbitration of shared access to devices within a situated computing locale.

All of these changes have ramifications for the future of software architectures. First, future software architectures for flexible multimodal interfaces must be constructed from components that will need to discover in real-time a distributed component bus within each specific locality and to configure themselves into the bus. Second, components must be able to discover related components, as well as their capabilities, and to participate in a composition of components into larger services. In many cases, the capabilities must express assumptions and goals regarding performance, and composition techniques must consider the overall performance requirements of the flexible interface when connecting components together. Third, client components must be prepared to operate robustly in the face of missing or suboptimal service components. Fourth, components must expect to interact through loosely coupled communication mechanisms that can exhibit various error properties. Industry is developing several competing technologies (such as Jini and Universal Plug-and-Play) that could serve as a basis on which to construct tomorrow's flexible, component-based interfaces. HCI researchers should investigate how these technologies can be exploited, extended, and improved to provide the capabilities needed to build effective multimodal interfaces.

Some researchers are already looking into a few of these concerns. Multimodal interaction is going beyond speech and pen-based interaction. For example, the Rutgers CAIP (Computer Aids for Industrial Productivity) Center has integrated into a single desktop interface a range of multimodal technologies, including gaze and gesture tracking, voice recognition, and speech synthesis, along with the typical display, mouse, and keyboard (Medl et al. 1998). Visual tracking is also being investigated as an interaction technique (Stiefelhagen 1998). Gestures and facial expressions may soon be used as interaction mechanisms. Wouldn't a confirming nod of the head be even easier at times than saying "Yes?" Novel research is still needed to develop an abstract interaction event model that exists independently from specific HCI hardware. In addition, mappings must be developed between the abstract model and specific HCI hardware, both current commercial hardware and experimental hardware. XML might become a specification language that can be translated to appear on different output devices. XML tags and attributes can be attached to text and then translated at the time that text is to be displayed. Transducers and layout engines are being used to translate Web pages so that users of handheld devices can obtain Web data. More research is needed into the specification of interactions, independent of device and modality. Such specifications would allow one interface to be developed for use with any input modality and any type of output display.

24.2.3 Information Interaction: Making It Real Again

Today we interact with digital information through graphical user interfaces (GUIs) in the WIMP (Windows, Icons, Menus, and Pointers) style. In other words, we use abstract symbols to represent information objects, and we manipulate those abstractions. Meanwhile, people have a long history of using physical information objects—books, photographs, newspapers, unstructured notes, and video recordings to name a few. People manipulate these physical objects separately and then need to execute intermediary translators (such as optical scanners) to bring this "real world" information into the virtual world. Some interesting research seeks to bridge the gap between the real and virtual worlds. Fitzmaurice (1993) investigated using objects in the physical world as anchors for digital information. Using handheld portals, people could move through the environment, viewing digital information based on the spatial characteristics of their handheld. Moving the handheld closer to the physical object might cause a computer to zoom in on the information. In a hands-free approach, Steven Feiner et al. (1999) at Columbia attempt to exploit augmented reality interfaces as a means of relating virtual information with the physical world. At the MIT Media Laboratory, Ishii (Ishii and Ullmer 1997) has been researching tangible user interfaces (TUIs), where physical objects are used to manipulate electronic information with the goal of reducing the cognitive overhead associated with using electronic information. To the extent that tangible user interfaces build on current user expectations of manipulating physical information, TUIs show promise.

Other researchers also investigate the gap between the real and the virtual. For example, Harrison et al. (1998) at Xerox PARC have investigated user interfaces that exploit physical manipulations to control devices, such as PDAs. Rather than using an artificial input device, such as a mouse or track point, manipulation of the device itself is used as a control. Harrison et al. (1999) have also investigated electronic staples, bits of electronic information embedded into physical objects. They have illustrated this technique using books and posters that advertise events. Here, using a reader attached to a portable computer, the information contained in the staple (a URL in the PARC examples) can be captured by mobile users. Arai et al. (1997) also developed technology that allows people to insert electronic links into paper documents. Len et al. (2000) are developing an electronic environment that allows an interface designer to sketch a user interface, a job that is usually done on paper. In the Portolano project, researchers at the University of Washington augment laboratory instruments with a radio-frequency transmitter that sends the instrument's identify (a URL) and timestamp through a user's skin to a wearable computer whenever the user grasps the instrument.

Several products being sold today also address the merger of real and virtual worlds. One example is the Cross Pad™, which combines regular paper and a digital pen with automated capture of digital information. As a user writes on the paper, electronic signals of the strokes made with the pen are stored digitally. After the user returns to a desktop computer, the digital version of the notes can be transferred, as bitmaps, to the desktop. Optical character recognition routines can translate the bitmaps into editable documents.

24.3   Grand Challenge #2: Clueing in Those Clueless Computers

Norman (1998) advocates the use of information appliances, special-purpose computers designed for a particular use. The key principle of an information appliance is simplicity. As the appliance is designed to do one task, that task can be carried out extremely easily. The user does not have to look through many menu options or to supply a variety of information via dialogue boxes. This approach provides a definite improvement over the complexity of our current desktop computer. However, complexity has not vanished—it has merely been pushed to another level. If we want to do more than one task (as most of us must), we now have to decide which appliance to use for which task. Moreover, information for various tasks has to be located and, in some instances, transferred between devices. For example, my pager, my cell phone, my e-mail, and my personal organizer don't know of the existence of each other. If I get an urgent e-mail and don't attend to it within a specified time, wouldn't it be useful if I got paged, or if my cell phone called me and read me the message? When I look up a contact on my personal organizer, shouldn't the phone number automatically move into my cell phone? One solution might be to simply combine devices. But where would this stop? Might we wind up with numerous devices hardwired together, yielding a device now as complex as our desktop computer?

How can this complexity be addressed? During any given period of time, a nomadic worker knows what tasks must be performed. Given the worker's preference and the appropriateness of devices for the tasks to be performed, could an appropriate set of devices be assembled by the worker? Perhaps these devices could be interconnected using wireless technologies. This solution would give the worker a custom "wearable" network of devices. As the selected devices discover each other, they could become aware of the services and information each can provide, and they could combine to support the user's information needs.

At present, such networked-based computing works largely because people carry in their heads a reasonably good model of cyberspace. We know where computers and printers can be found, we know how information can be organized for storage on a disk, and we understand the meaning of the three-character extensions that tag each file name. We know, but just barely, how to locate, download, configure, and execute various plug-ins to display information in specific formats or to convert information between formats. In fact, sometimes we think our computers and networks should pay us because we sure do a lot of work for them. We also have a good understanding of our environment and how to act in it. Most of the time we remember to shut off our cell phones before the movie starts. We turn down the sound on our laptops when we start them up in meeting rooms (don't we?). We sort out the messages on our pagers, we respond to the urgent, and we defer the less urgent. This sorting represents management overhead time—why should we spend so much time dealing with such mundane tasks? Suppose, on the other hand, that our computers and networks had a much better model of the world in which we, and they, live. Would it be possible for our computers and networks to help us more than we help them today?

To achieve such a world, computer software must begin to understand the context of each situated computing locale in which it operates. By context, we mean the connectivity, bandwidth, and services available in a locale, the location of users, devices, and information relative to a locale, and the physical and logical surroundings within and near a locale, as well as the tasks being performed and the environment in which those tasks are performed. If computer software can ascertain contextual information, then programs and active information can adapt to the situation, especially as the situation changes when network resources and services come and go and when people enter and leave a locale. What adaptations might be possible?

Multimodal interfaces could be designed to accommodate a level of uncertainty about the availability of network connectivity and bandwidth and about the availability of specific interaction devices. Active information might be designed to present different information or to present information in different forms, depending on the number of users, the available devices and network bandwidth, and the user task. Active information might also move or replicate itself to situated computing locales toward which its user or users are moving. Such movement or replication can ensure that task-specific information becomes available when and where needed with little cognitive investment by the user. In addition, since the information will be proximate to the user's interface devices, interaction latency can be reduced. A user interface could also be designed to modify its behavior, and an active information object could be designed to present itself differently, depending on sensory information about the user's surroundings and environment.

24.3.1 Adapting Information Delivery Using Knowledge of People, Places, and Devices

We suggest that researchers consider trying to build models that cross the gap between physical and logical space, as we perceive it, and cyberspace, as it exists in our computers and networks. Physical space would include models of the practical geometric limits that humans face in physical spaces. Logical space would include models capturing the way in which we think about concepts. Then models that unify the models of cyberspace, physical space, and logical space are needed to allow computer programs to reason across these spaces. Suppose we could couple sensor data with resource and scene description languages to model within our computers the physical and logical space that people perceive and understand. If we could, then our software might be able to exploit location, proximity, and visibility of both physical and cyber resources to determine where to deliver specific services for us. In addition, our software might be able to adapt information presentation to the specific characteristics of available devices and services. In fact, more generally, if the software has a model of space that appears reasonably consistent with our own, then we might be able to encode, inside a computer, heuristics similar to those that we now use when reasoning on our own about cyberspace.

Think a bit more about this idea. Sensors of all kinds are becoming cheaper and more capable. These include digital still and video cameras, digital sensors, eye-tracking devices, radio-frequency tags, and global positioning system chips. These sensors can be used to determine something about a user's context and to adjust information and its delivery accordingly. Some context-aware applications already exist. The global positioning systems for automobiles show the position of your car on a map. Georgia Tech's CyberGuide (Abowd et al. 1997) uses the location of the user, and other tour sites the user has visited, to present appropriate information about the tourist site the user is currently viewing. Other Georgia Tech context-aware applications have used the identity and activity of users to modify the behavior of applications (Salber et al. 1999). Using hidden Markov models, researchers at the MIT Media Lab have been able to extract context from ambient audio (Clarkson and Pentland 1998).

Researchers at the MIT Media lab have also tried exploiting location to determine a user's information needs. ComMotion (Marmasse 1999) tracks a user via a GPS system and, after having the user identify commonly frequented locations, uses agent technology to monitor incoming messages and queries, delivering the preferred information given the location. Sawhney and Schmandt (1998, 1999) use the audio level of a user's environment to determine a social context and to deliver e-mail messages in an appropriate mode given the social situation. Researchers have also used context as input. For example, a study of an application built for ecology observations showed that adding contextual information automatically created better data with much less manpower (Pascoe 1998).

In addition to simple context information, such as location, researchers are investigating how to account for a user's status when selecting interactions. For example, Picard (1997) and Kelin et al. (1999) are two researchers investigating concepts of affective computing. In affective computing, the emotional state of a user is considered when determining the computer's formulation of a response. The current work uses various sensory inputs to assess the state of the user. Work on user interface adaptation techniques remains to be explored. A project at Microsoft Research (Hornitz et al. 1998) learns about a user's preferences and adapts behaviors accordingly. Still, in the whole, much research remains before guidelines are developed regarding interface adaptation given the various emotional states of a user. Progress on these issues may prove crucial for expanded use of wearable computers.

Wearable computers (Siewiorek et al. 1998; Stein et al. 1998) are just now emerging for use by workers carrying out physical tasks, such as aircraft maintenance and inspection and repairing of oil drilling equipment. Today, wearable computers are designed for a specific task or set of tasks. The form factor for the wearable, the interaction devices, and the information stored on the wearable are all part of the design. If the tasks or the users or the environment in which the task is conducted change significantly, the situation must be analyzed and a redesign might be required. A redesign can prove costly. If, however, the context of the user could be determined and the interactions modified by the system itself, wearable computing might become less costly. In addition, the design of wearable computers might allow for easy customization by individual users. On first order, a user might assemble a computational device, an assortment of preferred input and output devices, an appropriate set of context-sensing devices, a connection to a wireless LAN, and set off to do the job. Just possibly, user customization might improve the productivity of individual workers.

24.3.2 Solving Three Hard Problems

Enabling customization and adaptation among software elements requires that HCI researchers solve three hard problems. *First, what constitutes context?* What aspects of the task, environment, user, and services need to be considered, and in what detail for what duration? Further, do collaborative tasks have a "collaborative" context, or does everyone have a personal view of the context, or must individual and group contexts be mixed together? As sensors become cheaper, we can begin to capture biological data to augment other context information. The issue is not capturing more data but identifying the relevant data to capture for various situations.

Second, how can context be modeled, represented, and reasoned about in a computer interpretable form? Such models might require multiple levels and might also entail associating confidence or uncertainty values with interpretations used to construct specific instantiations of the models. Issues of interest might include who is present, what they are working on, what devices, services, and information resources are nearby, and how these items relate to one another both logically and physically. On a more detailed level, the characteristics and interfaces provided by the available services and devices might also be of use. Researchers will need to devise mechanisms to extract context in both real-time and non-real-time from streams of sensor data, including the ability to derive context when interpreting data across multiple sensor streams.

Once researchers can construct machine-readable models of context, the *third* tough problem must be faced: *How can models of context be exploited to help users get their tasks completed effectively?* Researchers will need to investigate heuristics for deciding what information to present to users, what devices to use, and what presentation form to select. Of specific concern will be the ability to support dynamic generation of multimodal interfaces for particular collections of users working in given locations on assigned tasks under varying environmental conditions.

24.4 Conclusion

Smart Homes, Smart Cars, Smart Rooms (Pentland 1996), and research projects such as i-LAND (Streitz 1999), Oxygen (Dertouzos 1999), Endeavour, Portolano, and Aura promise to lead us toward universal ubiquitous computing. Researchers in these, and other, efforts are attempting to devise techniques for computing systems to recognize user activities and to adapt to user needs. While the promise is large, we have a long way to come. We need more concentrated work on context-dependent, or situated, computing. We need projects building large systems, and we also need smaller projects that focus on recognizing and using context and that look for better ways to bridge the physical-virtual gaps we must currently work around to interact with information. As we build test beds and start living and working in them, we will solve some research issues, but we will also discover others. The initial set of investigations addresses mainly technology issues. While these issues are difficult, the social implications of ubiquitous computing remain largely unknown. What are the implications for our privacy? How will the nature of our work and play change? What are the implications for interaction within and among organizations? Will ubiquitous computing widen or reduce the digital divide?

Today, much of our information-intensive work is carried out at desktop computer workstations. In these settings, the computer is the job. The computing infrastructure supporting our work, including operating systems, applications, and hardware remains relatively stable, and our work location appears mainly fixed. When we adjust our physical environment or when we introduce new applications software or upgrade the operating system or add new networking connections, we expect to spend some amount of our time coping with these changes. Very soon, if not now, we will carry many small information-processing appliances along from place to place as adjuncts to support our jobs. Under such conditions, context changes continuously. If forced to cope with continuous change using the same approach now required for our desktop workstations, we will find that managing our information appliances will become the job. Should that occur, we would cast aside our information appliances. The challenge to the HCI research community is simply this: Portable devices and pico-cellular wireless networks are coming in large numbers and quickly. Can you provide the foundation needed to extract their value? In the United States and overseas, research funding is now being directed toward various aspects of ubiquitous computing. Within the next five years, large-scale research prototypes will become available for experimentation. For ubiquitous computing to succeed commercially, these research prototypes must demonstrate an information-rich environment with few visible computers.

References

Abowd, G.D, Atkeson, C.G., Hong, J., Long, S., Kooper, R., and Pinkerton, M. (1997). Cyberguide: A mobile context-aware tour guide. *ACM Wireless Networks,* 3, 421–433.

Amir, E., McCanne, S., and Katz, R. (1998). An active service framework and its application to real-time multimedia transcoding. *Proceedings of ACM 1998 Conference of the Special Interest Group on Communications,* 178–189.

Arai, T., Aust, D., and Hudson, S. (1997). PaperLink: A technique for hyperlinking from real paper to electronic content. *Proceedings of ACM 1997 Conference on Human Factors in Computing Systems,* 327–333.

Belotti, V. and Bly, S. (1996). *Walking away from the desktop computer: Distributed collaboration and mobility in a product design team. Proceeding of ACM 1996 Conference on Computer Supported Cooperative Work,* 209–218. Cambridge, MA: ACM Press.

Bindel, D., Chen, Y., Eaton, P., Geels, D., Gummadi, R., Rhea, S., Weatherspoon, H., Weimer, W., Wells, C., Zhao, B., and Kubiatowicz, J. (2000). OceanStore: An architecture for global-scale persistent storage. To appear in *ASPLOS'00*.

Birbeck, M. (2000). *Professional XML*. Wrox Press, Inc.

Chawathe, Y., Fink, S., McCanne, S., and Brewer, E. (1998). An active service for reliable multicast in heterogeneous environments. *Proceedings of the Sixth ACM International Multimedia Conference*, 161–169.

Clarkson, B., and Pentland, A. (1998). Extracting context from environmental audio. *The Second International Symposium on Wearable Computers*, 154–155.

Dertouzos, M. (1999). The future of computing. *Scientific American*, 281, 2, 52–56.

Feiner, S., Höllerer, T., Terauchi, T., Rashid, G., and Hallaway, D. (1999). Exploring MARS: Developing indoor and outdoor user interfaces to a mobile augmented reality system. *Computers and Graphics*, 23, 6, 779–785.

Fitzmaurice, G. (1993). Situated information spaces and spatially aware palmtop computers. *Communications of the ACM*, 36, 7, 38–49.

Gessner, R. (1999). Netscape's Gecko. *Web Techniques*, 63–70.

Haarsten, J., Allen, W., Inouye, J., Joeressen, O., and Naghshineh, M. (1998). Bluetooth: Vision, goals, and architecture. *Mobile Computing and Communications Reviews*, 2, 4, 38–45.

Harrison, B., Fishkin, K., Gujar, A., Mochon, C., and Want, R. (1998). Squeeze me, hold me, tilt me: An exploration of manipulative user interfaces. *Proceedings of the ACM 1998 Conference on Human Factors in Computing Systems*, 17–24.

Harrison, B., Fishkin, K., Gujar, A., Portnov, D., and Want, R. (1999). Bridging physical and virtual worlds with tagged documents, objects and locations. *Proceedings of the ACM 1999 Conference on Human Factors in Computing Systems*, 29–30.

Horvitz, E., Breese, J., Heckerman, D., Hovel, D., and Rommelse, K. (1998). The Lumiere project: Bayesian user modeling for inferring the goals and needs of software users. *Proceedings of the Fourteenth Conference on Uncertainty in Artificial Intelligence*.

Bluetooth SIG Web site: http://www.bluetooth.com/default.asp.

Project Aura Web site: http://www.cs.cmu.edu/~aura.

Daimler-Benz Internet on Wheels Web site: http://www.daimler-benz.com/ind_gfnav_e.html?/research/text/70430_e.htm.

An ODIF web site: http://www.dsg.harvard.edu/public/intermed/odif-report.html.

Endeavour Project Web site: http://endeavour.cs.berkeley.edu/.

HomeRF Consortium Web site: http://www.homef.org/tech/.

Infrared Data Association Web site: http://www.irda.org/.

ITU ODA Specification Web site: http://www.itu.int/itudoc/itu-t/rec/t/t411.html.

Portolano Web site: http://portolano.cs.washington.edu.

Java Web site: http://java.sun.com/.

Jini Web site: http://developer.java.sun.com/developer/products/jini/.

Ishii, H., and Ullmer, B. (1997). Tangible bits: Towards seamless interfaces between people, bits and atoms. *Proceedings of the ACM 1997 Conference on Human Factors in Computing Systems,* 234–241.

Kelin, J., Moon, Y., and Picard, R. (1999). This computer responds to user frustration. *Proceedings of CHI '99,* 242–243. New York: ACM Press.

Len, J., Newman, M., Hong, J., and Landay, U. (2000). DENIM: Finding a tighter fit between tools and practice for Web site design. *Proceedings of the ACM 2000 Conference on Human Factors in Computing Systems,* 510–517.

Marmasse, N. (1999). ComMotion: A context-aware communication system. *Proceedings of the ACM 1999 Conference on Human Factors in Computing Systems,* 320–321. New York: ACM Press.

McCanne, S, Brewer, E., Katz, R, Rowe, L., Amir, E., Chawathe, Y., Coopersmith, A., Mayer-Patel, K., Raman, S., Schuette, A., Simpson, D, Swan, A., Tung, T., Wu, D., and Smith, B. (1997). Towards a Common Infrastructure for Multimedia-Networking Middleware. *Proceedings of the 7th Intl Workshop on Network and Operating Systems Support for Digital Audio and Video (NOSSDAV'97).*

Medl, A., Marsic, I., Andre, M., Kulikowski, C., and Flanagan, J.L. (1998). Multimodal man-machine interface for mission planning. *Proceedings of the AAAI Spring Symposium on Intelligent Environments,* 41–47.

Norman, D. (1998). *The invisible computer.* Cambridge, MA: MIT Press.

Ousterhout, J. (1994). *Tcl and the Tk Toolkit.* Reading, MA: Addison-Wesley.

Pascoe, J. (1998). Adding generic contextual capabilities to wearable computers. *The Second International Symposium on Wearable Computers,* 92–99.

Pentland, A. (1996). Smart rooms. *Scientific American,* 274, 4, 68–76.

Picard, R. (1997). *Affective computing.* Cambridge, MA: MIT Press.

Python Language Web site: http://www.python.org/.

Rekimoto, Jun. (1997). *Pick-and-drop: A direct manipulation technique for multiple computer environments. Proceedings of the ACM Symposium on User Interface Software and Technology '97,* 31–39. New York: ACM Press.

Salber, D., Dey, A., and Abowd, G. (1999). The context toolkit: Aiding the development of context-enabled applications. *Proceeding of the ACM 1999 Conference on Human Factors in Computing Systems,* 15–20. New York: ACM Press.

Sawhney, N. and Schmandt, C. (1998). Speaking and listening on the run: Design for wearable audio computing. *Proceedings of the International Symposium on Wearable Computing.*

Sawhney, N., and Schmandt, C. (1999). Nomadic radio: Scalable and contextual notification for wearable audio messaging. *Proceeding of the ACM 1999 Conference on Human Factors in Computing Systems,* 96–103. New York: ACM Press.

Siewiorek, D., Smailagic, A., Bass, L., Siegel, J., Martin, R., and Bennington, B. (1998). Adtranz: A mobile computing system for maintenance and collaboration. *The Second International Symposium on Wearable Computers,* 25–40.

Suchman, L. (1987). *Plans and situated actions.* New York: Cambridge Press.

Stein, R., Ferrero, S., Hetfield, M., Quinn, A., and Krichever, M. (1998). Development of a commercially successful wearable data collection system. *The Second International Symposium on Wearable Computers,* 18–24.

Streitz, N.A., Geißler, J., Holmer, T., Honomi, S., Müller-Tomfelde, C., Reische, W., Rexroth, P., Seitz, P., and Steinmetz, R. (1999). i-LAND: An interactive landscape for creativity and innovation. *Proceedings of the ACM 1999 Conference on Human Factors in Computing Systems,* 120–127. New York: ACM Press.

Weiser, M. (1991). The computer for the 21st century. *Scientific American,* 3, 94–104.

Weiser, M. (1993). Some computer science issues in ubiquitous computing. *Communications of the ACM,* 36, 7, 75–84.

Yan, J., Stiefelhagen, Meier, U., and Waibel, A. (1998). Visual tracking for multi-modal human computer interaction. *Proceedings of the ACM 1998 Conference on Human Factors in Computing Systems,* 140–147.

Universal Plug and Play Forum Web site: http://www.upnp.org/.

25

Roomware: Toward the Next Generation of Human-Computer Interaction Based on an Integrated Design of Real and Virtual Worlds

Norbert A. Streitz
Peter Tandler
Christian Müller-Tomfelde
Shin'ichi Konomi

25.1 Introduction

The next generation of human-computer interaction (HCI) is determined by a number of new contexts and challenges that have evolved during the last five to ten years and will be evolving more rapidly in the next five to ten years. They are rooted in new, emerging technologies as well as in new application areas asking for new approaches and visions of the future beyond the year 2000. It is not the intention of this chapter to give a comprehensive account of all relevant new contexts. We focus on selected areas complementing other contributions in this book. There is no doubt that new developments in the fields of multimedia, hypertext/hypermedia (especially in their popular versions as World Wide Web-applications), three-dimensional representations, and virtual reality technology will have a great impact on the type of issues HCI has to address and on how interfaces will look in the future.

Taken those developments as given, we present an approach and a framework that—at least so far—has not become a mainstream orientation for guiding design and development of the next generation of human-computer interaction. We are aware of the fact that there are related attempts, and we describe them. Nevertheless, there is still an indispensable need for a comprehensive framework. According to our view, the following four areas have to be integrated into an "umbrella" framework:

Computer-Supported Cooperative Work (CSCW), Ubiquitous Computing (UbiCom), Augmented Reality (AR), and Architecture. Note that in this chapter we use the term *architecture* primarily in the sense of real, physical environments—like rooms and buildings—and not in the sense of system architecture or software architecture. These areas are not an arbitrary list but rather the necessary constituents for a framework of designing HCI in the future. Their mutual relationships and dependencies are shown in Figure 25.1.

25.1.1 CSCW

User-interfaces used to be interfaces for single-user applications; now, most applications are multi-user applications supporting cooperative work. This means that user-interfaces have to be built in such a way that they always indicate if people are either working alone, in one of several possible subgroup constellations, or with all members of their team or organization. The interfaces will provide intuitive ways of sharing information synchronously as well as asynchronously. People will be able to move smoothly between the different configurations without having to change applications.

25.1.2 Ubiquitous Computing

While in the past there was a central mainframe computer with terminals for many users, the age of the personal computer follows the guideline of one person and one computer. Now we are moving into an era where one person will have *multiple devices* available in his or her environment. Computational power will be available everywhere, will be ubiquitous, or *ubiquitous computing* (Weiser 1991). People will view and use many of them as rather specialized *information appliances* (Norman 1998). Our extension of this view is that multiple devices are not only available to individuals but to groups. Thus, the cooperative nature of multiple devices will be

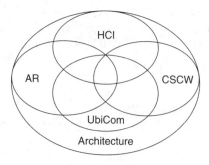

FIGURE 25.1   Our view of the contexts of the future of HCI

more in the foreground than it is currently. The devices are networked in several ways (more and more wireless), allowing to share information between them. People will use them in parallel as individuals as well as in groups. These devices will differ in their characteristics—for example, in terms of size from very small (palm size) to very large (wall size). They will also differ in terms of the functionality they provide in local as well as in distributed settings.

25.1.3 Augmented Reality

In contrast to virtual reality, there are conceptual and technological developments emphasizing that the objects of the real environment should and can be augmented instead of diving into "cyberspace" or immersing into "virtual reality." *Augmented reality* is the result of overlaying and adding digital information to real objects or integrating computational power into them (Wellner et al. 1993). The importance of "tangible bits" conveyed by real objects (Ishii and Ullmer 1997) is a related approach. This direction will be even more relevant in combination with the next area: the architectural environment around us.

25.1.4 Architecture

Finally, HCI and the preceding areas have to be aware of the importance of the real world—that is, the physical, *architectural space around us* in which people interact with the devices. For many HCI applications in the future, the space is constituted by buildings with their range of offices, meeting rooms, cafeterias, hallways, stairways, foyers, gardens, and so on, thus going far beyond the traditional desktop setting. This motivates a more explicit relationship to the field of *architecture*. Our view is that the physical space around us provides rich affordances for interaction and communication that should be exploited. Research in HCI has neglected this larger context by limiting itself for a long time to the desktop computer. More recently, these issues are now being addressed, such as with the notion of cooperative buildings (Streitz et al. 1998a).

We will elaborate on the role of these areas to HCI in more detail as we go along, presenting the design rationale for the development of what we call "roomware" as the constituents of so called "Cooperative Buildings." By *roomware®*, we mean computer-augmented objects resulting from the integration of room elements, such as walls, doors, or furniture with computer-based information devices. Their characteristics require, and at the same time provide, new forms of human-computer interaction and of supporting cooperative work or, more general, cooperative experiences and activities. With *Cooperative Buildings,* we indicate the overall conceptual framework as well as its concrete realization in terms of the envisioned architectural envelope with integrated ubiquitous IT components resulting in smart artifacts so that the world around us is the interface to information and for cooperation. In these settings, traditional *human-computer* interaction will be transformed to *human-information*-interaction and *human-human* communication and cooperation.

The chapter is organized as follows. In Section 25.2, we present three points of departure determining the requirements and challenges for the next generation of human-computer interaction. Related work and technologies are described in Section 25.3. Section 25.4 and 25.5 introduce the basic concepts of our approach: Section 25.4 describes four design perspectives for the workspaces of the future; Section 25.5 introduces the overall framework of "cooperative buildings." Section 25.6 complements the conceptual analysis with requirements taken from an empirical study. Section 25.7 describes the implications for designing new forms of human-computer interaction and cooperation in terms of the "roomware" components and their realization as part of the i-LAND environment. Section 25.8 and 25.9 provide the description of the network infrastructure and the BEACH software. Final conclusions are given in Section 25.10.

25.2   Three Points of Departure

In this section, we present three areas as points of departure in order to determine important requirements for the next generation of human-computer interaction: information and communication technology, work practice and organization, and the architectural setting of the real world around us.

25.2.1   Information Technology: From the Desktop to the Invisible Computer

The introduction of information and communication technology caused a shift from the physical environment as the place for information objects to desktop displays as *the* interfaces to information. In the traditional office environments of the past, information objects were themselves physical objects: paper documents such as books, memos, letters, calendars in the office, announcements on bulletin boards in hallways, flip charts, and whiteboards in meeting rooms. They were created, accessed, and manipulated in a straightforward way via physical operations with appropriate tools and very little overhead. Although the "paperless office" did not become a reality and probably never will, these physical information objects have been replaced to a large degree by digital information objects such as electronic documents. Large and bulky monitors sitting on desktops and being connected to a PC tower under the table became the standard computer equipment in our offices today. Desktop displays became the "holy" entrance to "cyberspace" as the virtual place where one finds information.

As a result, the main focus of research and practice in human-computer interaction was and still is concerned with the issues of designing, creating, and using virtual information spaces to be displayed on desktop computers. But is human-*computer* interaction really the goal? Isn't it human-*information* interaction and human-*human* interaction and cooperation? Shouldn't we get rid of the computer as a device in the foreground? Similar to driving a car and not thinking about the underlying machinery and the fact that one is (at least in modern cars) interacting with 20 or more microprocessors and computers, one should be able to interact with information in an intuitive way and be able to cooperate with other people. The basic underlying idea was expressed by Mark Weiser (1991) in the following way.

> The most profound technologies are those that disappear. They weave themselves into the fabric of everyday life until they are indistinguishable from it.

This vision, although addressed many times in the past, has become again a major concern in recent years. Technology should be moved to the background and turn into "calm technology" where the interface will be invisible (Weiser 1998). The computer will be "invisible"—for example, when using information appliances that are "hiding the computers, hiding the technology so that it disappears from sight" (Norman 1998). We have adopted this perspective but extended it in various directions to be described in the main part of the paper.

25.2.2 Organization: New Work Practices and Team Work

The introduction of information technology in the workplace did not only change the contents of work but also the work processes. These changes effect the organization of work in the office (desk sharing is an example) as well as the place of work. Working from home (telework) or in the hotel, on the train, on the plane, or at the customer's site (mobile work) results in a higher degree of transitions between individual work "on the road" and collaborative work at the office (for example, group meetings) and between asynchronous and synchronous work. In parallel, new organizational forms have changed the business world based on new developments in management sciences and business process (re)engineering efforts. Organizations adopt process and customer-oriented business models resulting in more flexible and dynamic organizational structures. A prominent example is the creation of ad hoc and on demand teams in order to work on a project for a given period of time, solving a specific problem.

On demand and ad hoc formation of teams requires powerful methods and tools for the support of different work phases in teams. When evaluating the meeting support systems we have developed in the past (Streitz et al. 1994), we found in one of our empirical studies (Mark et al. 1997) that the provision of hypermedia functionality facilitates the division of labor in team work. This resulted in better results in the group problem-solving activities. Furthermore, we investigated the role of different personal and public information devices (networked computers, interactive whiteboard) and different combinations of them for meeting room collaboration in another empirical study (Streitz et al. 1997). These results show that groups with a balanced proportion of individual work, subgroup activities, and full team work achieved better results than those groups that stayed most of the time in the full-team work configuration. The degree of flexibility to work in different modes was largely determined by the range and combination of information devices provided to the team.

25.2.3 Architecture: The New Role and Structure of Office Buildings

In the future, work and cooperation in organizations will be characterized by a degree of dynamics, flexibility, and mobility that will go far beyond many of today's developments and examples. It is time to reflect these developments not only in terms of new work practices and use of information technology but also in the design of the physical architectural environment so that the workspaces of the future will be equally dynamic and flexible. While the introduction of information and communication technology has already changed the content of work and work processes significantly, the design of the physical work environments such as offices and buildings has remained almost unchanged. Neither new forms of organizations nor computer-supported work practices have been reflected in relevant and sufficient depth in the design of office space and building structures. This is especially true for the issues related to mobile work. If, in principle, one can work anytime anyplace, one could ask the challenging questions "Why do we still need office buildings? Aren't they obsolete given the possibilities of modern mobile technology?"

It is our point of view that office buildings are still of high value but that their role will change—*must* be changed. They will be less the place for individual work and more the space for planned team work and group meetings as well as for a wide range of social interactions, such as spontaneous encounters, informal communication, and unplanned opportunistic cooperation. We are also convinced that social interactions in co-located settings, as in buildings, are becoming increasingly important for establishing a corporate identity, group feeling, and trust, because teams with changing team members and changing tasks are established at much higher rates than before.

These considerations are the starting points for our framework of *cooperative buildings* (Streitz et al. 1998a). They have to be designed as flexible and dynamic environments that provide cooperative work and experience spaces supporting and augmenting human communication and collaboration.

25.3 Related Work

As indicated earlier, we are trying to offer a comprehensive framework integrating a wide range of approaches. Thus, there are a number of developments that have influenced our thinking. Due to the limitations of space, we concentrate here on two areas of recent developments that are especially relevant: augmented reality and ubiquitous computing. We selected those because they best reflect one of our central beliefs that the real world around us should be the starting point for designing the human-computer interaction of the future. We are also aware that there is a large body of research in the area of CSCW on which we are building, especially work on electronic meeting rooms and/or interactive whiteboards where we also contributed (Stefik et al.

1987; Pederson et al. 1993, Olson et al. 1993; Streitz et al. 1994; Nunamaker et al. 1995; Schuckmann et al. 1996). Due to lack of space, we decided not to describe this work in more detail. For an overview of CSCW, see Baecker (1993). Augmented reality can be understood as the counterpart to virtual reality. Rather than wearing goggles or helmets in order to immerse in a virtual world, augmented reality is concerned with the use of computational devices in order to augment our perception and interaction in the physical world. For an overview of initial work, see Wellner et al. (1993). A well-known example is the DigitalDesk that uses a video projection of a computer display as an overlay on paper documents on a real desk (Wellner et al. 1993). A project that uses front projection techniques is The Office of the Future (Raskar et al. 1998). It is based on computer vision and computer graphics technology utilizing spatially immersive displays (SID's) in order to surround users with synthetic images. Their vision is that "anything can be a display surface," whether it be a wall or a table. Even objects with irregular shapes can be used. Their major application is to build systems for shared telepresence and telecollaboration. Other examples of augmented surfaces were developed by Rekimoto and Saitoh (1999), for creating hybrid environments, and the ZombieBoard by Saund (1999). In order to extend the channels of perception and make use of peripheral awareness, so called "ambient displays" have been proposed. A well-known example is the ambient-ROOM (Wisneski et al. 1998) where, for example, water ripples are projected on the ceiling of a room to indicate different activities.

Another direction is the notion of "graspable" user interfaces with "bricks" (Fitz-maurice et al. 1995) and "tangible bits" (Ishii and Ullmer 1997). This work was also inspired by the "marble answering machine" developed by Bishop (Poynor 1995), where incoming phone calls are indicated by (physical) marbles that can be placed on a specific area for playing the message. We will come back to this idea when we describe our Passage mechanism (Konomi et al. 1999) in Section 25.7.6. Related to this approach is the mediaBlocks system (Ullmer et al. 1998). It uses electronically tagged blocks to store, transport, and sequence online media. Although they realize a certain degree of simplicity and "lightweight" mode of operation, "mediaBlocks" have to be specially crafted before the system is used and can be inserted into dedicated slots.

Ubiquitous computing is in some way a direct consequence when pursuing the approach of augmented reality seriously. It requires having many, loosely spread and networked information devices around, with displays of different sizes, providing functionality everywhere instead of only at the desktop computer. This is the concept of ubiquitous computing (Weiser 1991) and ubiquitous media (Buxton 1997). The size of these devices can range from very small to very large. Some of the devices will stand out and be recognized as computers; others will be "invisible" as they are embedded in the environment. Once the physical space is filled with multiple devices, two sets of issues come up. First, how can you transfer information between them in an intuitive and direct way, and, more generally, how can you interact with them? Second, it is desirable to know the position of the devices and their state wherever they are in a room or a building. The first issue is addressed by the "pick-and-drop" technique (Rekimoto 1997, 1998), and our concepts of "take-and-put" and

"Passage" (Konomi et al. 1999) are described in Section 25.7.6. The second issue requires setting up an infrastructure of sensing and localization technology that determines where the devices are and where users are performing their tasks. (We know this raises a number of controversial issues with respect to privacy considerations, but they are beyond the scope of this paper.)

25.4 Design Perspectives for the Workspaces of the Future

In our vision of the workspaces of the future, we believe *the world around us will be the interface to information,* represented via ubiquitous devices, some visible and others "invisible," in the sense that they are embedded in the physical environment. We anticipate a situation where people interact with each other in ubiquitous and interactive landscapes for interaction and cooperation augmenting our real environments.

In order to develop the workspaces of the future, we follow a human-centered design approach (see Figure 25.2). Since the human is at the center, we first must

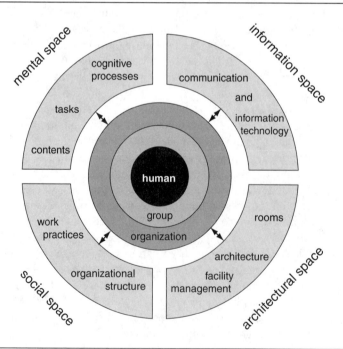

FIGURE 25.2 Four design perspectives for the work spaces of the future

address the *mental space*—considering the potential and the limitations of the human processing system and the individual's cognitive processing of content and tasks. The perspective of designing the *information space* represents the mapping of tasks and contents on corresponding and compatible representations of the information system realized as software and hardware. Human problem-solving activities are mapped on corresponding ways of human-computer interaction and mediated by networked information devices providing the functionality needed for working on the task. However, the human is part of a group or a team, and the team has to be viewed in the context of an organization. This requires consideration of the *social space,* which reflects the role of different work practices and organizational context in the design of corresponding cooperation and communication technology. This is (in a way) the CSCW perspective. Finally, we have to take into account the *architectural space* reflecting the characteristics of the rooms and other architectural components of the building. It is obvious to us that physical objects and their placement in the architectural space provide valuable "affordances" for organizing content information and meta information for the activities of individuals as well as groups.

In summary, we have to consider all four design perspectives or spaces shown in Figure 25.2 where the implicit distinction between real and virtual worlds plays a special role. Although we will come back to this, we want to emphasize here that we argue for a two-way augmentation and smooth transitions between real and virtual worlds. Combining them in an integrated design allows us to develop enabling interfaces that build on the best affordances of everyday reality and virtuality in parallel. As designers of human-computer interaction, or rather human-information interaction, and human-human cooperation, we want to use the best of both worlds.

25.5 Cooperative Buildings

Due to the new role of office buildings in the future, one has to reflect this in the overall design of the workspaces of the future. To this end, we proposed the concept of *Cooperative Buildings* in Streitz et al. (1998a) and established also a series of International Workshops on Cooperative Buildings (Streitz et al. 1998b, 1999b). We used the term *building* (and not *spaces*) to emphasize that the starting point of the design should be the real, architectural environment: Even a person navigating in the chat rooms of cyberspace is sitting somewhere in the real space. By further calling it a "cooperative" building, we wanted to indicate that the building serves the purpose of cooperation and communication. At the same time, it is also "cooperative" toward its users, or rather, inhabitants and visitors, by employing active, attentive, and adaptive components. In other words, the building not only provides facilities but it also (re)acts "on its own" after having identified certain conditions. It is part of our vision that it will adapt to changing situations and provide context-aware information according to knowledge about past and current states or actions and, if available,

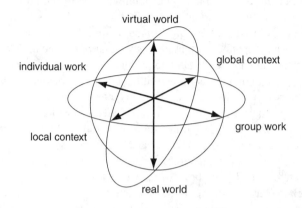

FIGURE 25.3   Three dimensions of cooperative buildings

even about plans of the people. The three dimensions, shown in Figure 25.3, are useful to structure the requirements for the design of cooperative buildings.

First, we address the *"real world vs. virtual world"* dimension or, using a different terminology, the physical or architectural space vs. the digital information space or cyberspace. While each terminology has its own set of connotations, we use them here more or less interchangeably. Our day-to-day living and working environments are highly determined by the physical, architectural space around us constituted by buildings with walls, floors, ceilings, furniture, and so forth. They constitute also rich information spaces due to the inherent affordances either as direct information sources (such as calendars, maps, charts hanging on the walls, books and memos lying on the desks) or by providing ambient peripheral information (such as sounds of people passing in the hallway). Furthermore, nonplanned encounters of people at the copying machine, in the commons, or in the cafeteria are rich opportunities for the exchange of information, either social or task- and goal-oriented.

While the term *building* implies strong associations with a physical structure, our concept of a cooperative building goes beyond this. It is our understanding that a cooperative building originates in the physical architectural space, but it is complemented by components realized as objects and structures in virtual information spaces. In a cooperative building, we augment therefore the informal interaction spaces in addition to the "official" meeting rooms with information technology, so that people can create, retrieve, and discuss information in a ubiquitous fashion. This requires an integration of information spaces and a means of interacting with them in the physical environment, such as walls and furniture (this results in "roomware"— see Section 25.7).

There is another aspect of the "virtual" part of this dimension. People are not only in one physical location but in remote, distributed locations. Associated terms are virtual meetings, virtual teams, and virtual organizations. Our perspective encompasses a distributed setting with remote locations where people work and dwell. The remote location might be an office building at another site of the organization or in a building at a client's site, a teleworker's small office at home, or the temporary hotel room of a traveling salesperson. Within the framework of a cooperative building, people can communicate, share information, and work cooperatively independent of the physical location. In contrast to today's restricted desktop-based videoconferencing scenarios, we envision a seamless integration of information and communication technology in the respective local environment. This results in more transparency and a direct and intuitive way of interaction, communication, and cooperation in distributed environments. This approach is in line with the work on media spaces (Bly et al. 1993) and ubiquitous media (Buxton 1997). If one goes beyond standard desktop videoconferencing, one is faced with challenging design issues for creating a "shared" background setting in which the distributed members are placed (Buxton 1997). Further issues of distributed rooms coupled via videoconferencing are addressed by Cooperstock et al. (1997).

This interpretation of "virtual" is, of course, closely related to the *local vs. global context* dimension. This dimension addresses the issue that we have to design the local environment with respect to the requirements resulting from its two roles. One role is to augment individual work and support group work in face-to-face meetings. The other is to provide an environment that facilitates the global cooperation of distributed people. While there is an intuitive understanding of the meaning of "local vs. global," one has to look at it in more detail. The term "local" is often used synonymously with colocated, or "same place." Think for example of a standard office or meeting room. But what is the scope of the "same place"? Is the hallway part of it when the door is open? Where are the boundaries? In contrast, where does a "remote" place begin? Is the meeting room on the next floor local because it is "nearby" or a remote place? Does the notion of remote location and global context start in another building, another city, or another continent? Using sensors for determining positions facilitates that the information devices know where they are and what their local and global context is. In this way, the cooperative building can be provided with information about the location of people in relationship to the devices. At a more general level, the local vs. global dimension addresses also the differences in social contexts of work arising from different organizational structures, either working in a local team or with other organizational units of a global organization, like a multinational company.

A third relevant distinction is based on the *individual vs. group* dimension. It emphasizes that the type of support should be able to distinguish, for example, between different degrees of coupling shared workspaces. This is based on our earlier work on cooperative hypermedia groupware (Streitz et al. 1994). It should be possible to determine the degree of coupling by the users and provide awareness about who is sharing what and to which degree. This dimension reflects also the implications of different phases of team work: plenary presentation and discussion in the complete group, splitting up in subgroups, working individually on an assigned task, resuming again for the integration of ideas and merging of intermediary results, and so on.

In summary, it is our opinion that the realization of a "cooperative building" has to pay attention to these three dimensions in order to constitute the basis for designing, using, and evaluating the Workspaces of the Future. In our ongoing work of developing the i-LAND environment (see Section 25.7.1), we concentrate especially on two of the three dimensions discussed in the previous section: the real vs. virtual and the individual vs. group dimension.

25.6   Requirements from Creative Teams

While innovative concepts and visionary scenarios as well as advances in basic technologies are important to make progress, we know from the principles of user-centered and task-oriented design that this is not sufficient for the development of new systems. In order to inform our design, we conducted an empirical study investigating the current work situation of teams and their requirements for future environments. Due to limited space, we report only selected results of the study (Streitz et al. 1998c).

We selected five companies from the automobile and oil industry and in the advertising and consulting business. These companies were chosen because they had special groups called "creative teams" working in the areas of strategic planning, identifying future trends, designing and marketing new products, and so on. We interviewed representatives of the teams, visited the project and team meeting rooms, and distributed a questionnaire to all team members. The total number of people in these five teams was 80. They had academic education with various backgrounds: engineering, computer science, business administration, psychology, and design.

The results showed that the meeting facilities were in most cases traditional meeting rooms furnished with standard equipment like large, solid tables and chairs, flip charts, whiteboards, and overhead projectors. In only one case, there were a couple of computers, a scanner, and a printer permanently installed in the meeting room. No active creation of content during the meeting was done with the aid of computers. Different creativity techniques (brainstorming, Metaplan) were used but only in a paper-based fashion. The results on the current state were somehow contrary to our expectations because we had expected more (active) usage of computer-based technology in the meetings.

The situation changed when we asked about the requirements for the future. Usually, a large room was required with a flexible setup and variable components that would allow different configurations. The room should have the character of a marketplace or a landscape providing opportunities for spontaneous encounters and informal communication. The response (translated from German) was "Team meetings are not anymore conducted by meeting in a room but by providing an environment and a situation where encounters happen." The furniture should be multifunctional and flexible.

Although the current situation was rather low-tech, there was a great openness for computer-based support in the following areas.

- Information gathering while preparing meetings in advance by accessing internal and external databases
- "Pools of ideas"—also called "idea spaces"
- A wide range of creativity techniques where the computer-based version should allow for flexible configuration or tailoring of the underlying rules
- Presentation styles deviating from the traditional situation and involving the attendees in an active fashion labeled as "participatory presentation"
- Visualizations inspiring and enhancing the creative process
- Communicating and experiencing content via channels other than only visual: acoustic, tactile

There was less emphasis on videoconferencing than we expected. The teams stressed the importance of personal presence being essential for creating a stimulating and productive atmosphere. While computer-based support was strongly requested, the computer should stay in the background. As they explained (translated from German), "We have the creative potential, not the computers." In summary, the teams wanted to have much freedom in reconfiguring their physical environment and their information environment.

25.7   Roomware® Components

Our approach to meet the requirements of flexible configuration and dynamic allocation of resources in physical and information environments in parallel is based on the concept we call *roomware*®. By roomware, we mean computer-augmented objects resulting from the integration of room elements—walls, doors, furniture—with computer-based information devices. While the term roomware was originally created by Streitz and his Ambiente-Team (Streitz et al. 1997, 1998a) and is now also a registered trademark of GMD, it is also used for a general characterization of this approach and even products in this area.

The general goal of developing roomware is to make progress toward the design of integrated real architectural spaces and virtual information spaces. In the context of supporting team work, roomware components should be tailored and composed to form flexible and dynamic "cooperation landscapes" serving multiple purposes: project team rooms, presentation suites, learning environments, information foyers, and so forth. Also, all these goals involve the development of software that enables new forms of multi-user, multiple-displays human-computer interaction and cooperation. We will present examples as we go along.

25.7.1 The i-LAND Environment

On the basis of our conceptual and empirical work as well as integrating ideas from related work, we created a first visualization and description of the planned environment. Figure 25.4 shows the "vision scribble" in spring 1997. The environment is called i-LAND: an interactive landscape for creativity and innovation. On the one hand, i-LAND is a generic environment consisting of several roomware components that can be used in different ways. On the other hand, its development was also application-driven, especially in terms of the functionality provided by the BEACH software we developed for working with roomware (see Tandler 2000, 2001, and Section 25.9). The original vision scribble showed the following roomware types: an interactive electronic wall *(DynaWall®)*, an interactive electronic table *(InteracTable®)*, and mobile and networked chairs with integrated interactive devices *(CommChairs®)*. This was the initial set of the *first generation of roomware®* and was assembled in the AMBIENTE-Lab at GMD-IPSI in Darmstadt. Together with the BEACH software, this set constituted the first version of the i-LAND environment in 1997 and 1998. In 1999, we developed together with partners from industry—as part of the R&D consortium "Future Office Dynamics" (FOD 1999)—the *second generation of roomware®* where we redesigned the CommChairs® and the InteracTable® and developed a new component called *ConnecTable®*.

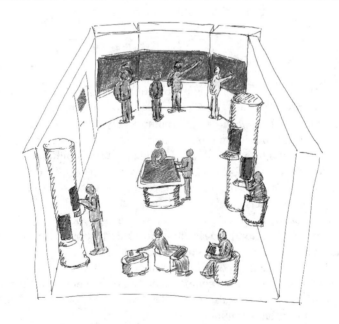

FIGURE 25.4   The vision scribble of the i-LAND environment in early 1997

In our vision scribble (Figure 25.4), we also suggested workplaces for individual work—for example, searching for background information—and called them "columns of knowledge." Furthermore, we think that there will be always paper in one way or the other. Thus, we suggested the mobile "ScanTable" as an integrated device for scanning paper documents so that the content is immediately available for further processing via the network on different roomware components, for example, to be shown and annotated on the DynaWall. Since the latter two components were not so innovative, we built—for the first generation of roomware—the previous three types initially mentioned. Although the focus was on designing workspaces for co-located teams, the i-LAND environment can easily be extended to provide support for global cooperation of distributed teams. Further information on i-LAND can be found in Streitz et al. (1999a). Now we give an overview of the different roomware components.

25.7.2 The DynaWall®

The objective of the *DynaWall®* is to provide a computer-based device that serves the needs of teams for cooperating in project and meeting rooms. It can be considered the electronic equivalent of large areas of assembled sheets of paper covering the walls for creating and organizing information. Teams are now enabled to display and interact with large digital information structures collaboratively on the DynaWall that can be considered an "interactive electronic wall." The current realization consists of three segments with back projections and large touch-sensitive display surfaces. The total display size of 4.50 m (15 ft) width and 1.10 m (3 ft 7 in.) height covers one side of the room completely (see Figure 25.5). Although driven by three computers, the BEACH software provides one large homogeneous workspace with no interaction boundaries between the segments. Two or more persons are able to either work individually in parallel or to share the whole display space.

The size of the DynaWall causes new challenges for human-computer interaction. For example, it will be very cumbersome to drag an object or a window over a distance of more than 4 m by having to touch the DynaWall all the time (similar to holding down the mouse button) while walking from one side to the other. Therefore, we have developed two mechanisms addressing these problems. Similar to picking up an object from a pinboard and place it somewhere else, our "take and put" feature allows us to "take" information objects at one position, walk over (without being in contact with the DynaWall), and "put" them somewhere else on the display. For bridging the distance between several closely cooperating people, "shuffle" allows us to throw objects (even with different accelerations) from one side to the opposite side where they can be caught and used by another team member.

The interaction of creating, moving, and deleting objects and their content is primarily gesture-based and does not require selecting different modes. This mode-less interaction is achieved by using the incremental gesture recognition provided by BEACH. (For more details see Tandler [2000, 2001] and Section 25.9).

FIGURE 25.5   Two people sitting in CommChairs cooperating with a person at the DynaWall (first generation of Roomware)

25.7.3 The CommChairs®

The *CommChairs*® (see Figures 25.5 and 25.6) are mobile chairs with built-in or attached slate computers. They represent a new type of furniture combining the mobility and comfort of armchairs with high-end information technology. The CommChairs allow people to communicate and to share information with people in other chairs, standing in front of the DynaWall or using other roomware components. They can make personal notes in a private space but also interact remotely on shared (public) workspaces—for example, making remote annotations at the DynaWall. The cooperative sharing functionality is provided by the BEACH software. For maximum flexibility and mobility each chair is provided with a wireless network and independent power supply.

In the first roomware generation (see Figure 25.5), we developed two versions. One has a docking facility (on the left side in Figure 25.5) so that people can bring their laptop computers and drop them into the swing-up desk, which is part of the armrest. The other version (on the right side in Figure 25.5) has an integrated pen-based computer built into the swing-up desk.

In the second roomware generation (Figure 25.6), we made a complete redesign resulting in the new version shown in the center of Figure 25.6 in front of the DynaWall and on the right side of Figure 25.7.

25.7.4 The InteracTable®

The *InteracTable®* (see Figure 25.6) is an interactive table that is designed for creation, display, discussion, and annotation of information objects. It is used by small groups of up to six people standing around it. People can write and draw on it with a pen and interact via finger or pen gestures with information objects. There is also a wireless keyboard for more extensive text input if needed. The InteracTable, with its horizontal setup display and people standing around it at each side, is an example of an interaction area with no predefined orientations, such as top and bottom, left and right, as found with vertical displays like monitors of desktop computers. Horizontal and round or oval displays require new forms of human-computer interaction. To this end, we developed in BEACH special gestures for shuffling and rotating individual information objects or groups of objects across the surface so that they orient themselves automatically. This accommodates easy viewing from all perspectives. Furthermore, one can create a second view of an object and shuffle this to the other side so that the opposite team member has the correct view at the same time. Now everybody can view the same object with the correct perspective in parallel and edit and annotate it.

Design: GMD-IPSI, Wiege, Wilkhahn

FIGURE 25.6   Second Generation of Roomware: ConnecTables, CommChair, InteracTable, DynaWall

In the first roomware generation, a stand-up version (115 cm high—not shown) was built using a vertical bottom-up projection unit. A high-resolution image was projected to the top of the table providing a horizontal touch-sensitive display of 65 cm × 85 cm and a diameter of 107 cm (42 in.).

In the second roomware generation, we made a complete redesign resulting in the new version shown on the right side of Figure 25.6. In this version, the projection was replaced by a large touch-sensitive plasma display panel (PDP) with a display size of 65 cm × 115 cm and a diameter of 130 cm (51 in.).

25.7.5 The ConnecTable®

The ConnecTable® (see left side in Figure 25.7) is a new component that was developed as part of the second roomware generation. It is designed for individual work as well as for cooperation in small groups. The height of the display can be quickly adapted in order to accommodate different working situations: standing up or sitting in front of it on an arbitrary chair. The display can also be tilted in different angles to provide an optimal view. By moving multiple ConnecTables together, they can be arranged to form a large display area (see left side in Figure 25.6). Integrated sensors measure the distance between the ConnecTables and initiate the automatic connection of the displays once they are close enough. The cooperative BEACH software enables the resulting large display area to be used as a common workspace where several people can work concurrently and move information objects beyond the physical borders of the individual displays.

FIGURE 25.7 Three configurations of the ConnecTable (left) and the redesigned CommChair (right)

In the same way as for the InteracTable, people can create second views, shuffle them from one ConnecTable to the opposite one, rotate them there, and work on them in parallel with correct perspectives.

The mobility of the ConnecTables and the CommChairs is achieved by employing a wireless network connection and an independent power supply based on Nickel Metal Hydride (NiM) accumulators. The IT components are packaged in a translucent container. Because there are no rotating or inductive consumers (using passive cooling, RAM-disk, etc.), these roomware-components are completely noise free.

25.7.6 The Passage Mechanism

Passage describes a mechanism for establishing relations between physical objects and virtual information structures—that is, bridging the border between the real world and the digital, virtual world. So-called *Passengers* (Passage-Objects) enable people to have quick and direct access to a large amount of information and to "carry them around" from one location to another via physical representatives that are acting as physical "bookmarks" into the virtual world. It is no longer necessary to open windows, browse hierarchies of folders, worry about mounted drives, and so on. Passage is a concept for ephemeral binding of content to an object. It provides an intuitive way for the "transportation" of information between computers/roomware components—for example, between offices or to and from meeting rooms.

A Passenger does not have to be a special physical object. Any uniquely detectable physical object may become a Passenger. Since the information structures are not stored on the Passenger itself but only linked to it, people can turn any object into a Passenger: a watch, a ring, a pen, glasses, or other arbitrary objects. The only restriction Passengers have is that they can be identified by the Bridge and that they are unique. Figure 25.8 shows a key chain as an example of a Passenger placed on a dark area representing the real part of the "Bridge" device embedded in the margin of the InteracTable and the interface area in the front of the display representing the virtual part of the Bridge device.

Passengers are placed on so-called *Bridges,* making their virtual counterparts accessible. With simple gestures, the digital information can be assigned to or retrieved from the Passenger via the virtual part of the Bridge. The Bridges are integrated in the work environment to guarantee ubiquitous and intuitive access to data and information at every location in an office building (Cooperative Building). For example, a Bridge can be integrated into the tabletop of an interactive electronic table (InteracTable®) in the cafeteria or mounted in front of an interactive electronic wall (DynaWall®) in a meeting room.

We developed two methods for the detection and identification of passengers. The first method enables us to use really arbitrary objects without any preparation or tagging. Here, we use a very basic property of all physical objects—weight—as the identifier. Therefore, each Bridge contains an electronic scale for measuring the

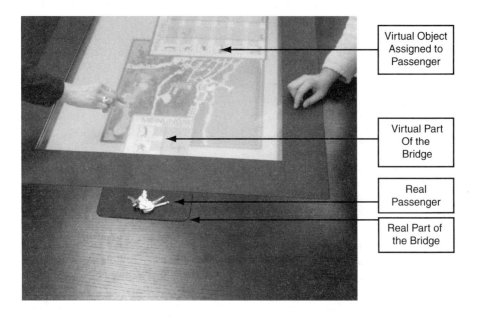

FIGURE 25.8   Passage: a key chain as a Passenger object on the Bridge of the InteracTable

weight of the Passengers (with a precision of 0.1g). This implementation is very different from other approaches in this area using electronic tags as, for example, mediaBlocks (Ullmer et al. 1998). Their approach is similar to our second method because each Bridge is also equipped with a contact-free identification device that uses radio-frequency-based transponder technology. Small electronic identification tags (RFID) that do not need batteries are attached on or embedded in physical objects so that the Passenger can be identified by a unique value. While identification via the weight of an object provides greater flexibility and is used for short-term assignments, the electronic tag method provides higher reliability and is used for long-term assignments, but it requires some preparation of the objects. For a more elaborate description and technical details of the Passage-Mechanism see Konomi et al. (1999).

25.8   Network Infrastructure

While each of these roomware components has a value of its own, the full benefit is only available via a comprehensive integration and combined use. The network infrastructure provides the connectivity between the components, while the software infrastructure provides a wide range of cooperative sharing capabilities. For extending the mobility of team members and roomware components in the whole building, it is necessary to identify them in different locations. This requires an appropriate sensing and localization infrastructure. So far, we are able to identify people in front of the three different segments of the DynaWall: the InteracTable, the ConnecTables, and the CommChairs. Extensions are planned.

In the current implementation, we use a combination of the local area network already installed in the building and an RF-based wireless network. For maximum flexibility, all mobile roomware components are connected to the wireless network. The roomware components are equipped with an antenna that comes along with a PC-Card. The computers of fixed roomware components—for example, the DynaWall—are connected via cables to the LAN. The network connection for the wireless access to the LAN is realized by a two-channel access-point that acts as a bridge between the cable-based and the RF-based Ethernet.

25.9   The Beach Software: Supporting Creativity

As already pointed out, although the design of the roomware components is generic, the development of the i-LAND environment was also application-driven. The main application is the support of team work with a focus on creativity and innovation. We support different types of creativity techniques and related generic functionality as, for example, visualization of knowledge structures. Other application areas can be organizational group memory, cooperative design activities, support for teaching and learning (electronic classroom of the future), and group entertainment environments.

In order to meet the requirements of i-LAND, we developed the BEACH software. BEACH, the *B*asic *E*nvironment for *A*ctive *C*ollaboration with *H*ypermedia, provides an architecture and a user interface adapted to the needs of roomware components, which require new forms of human-computer and team-computer interaction. Furthermore, the roomware components must be connected to allow synchronous collaboration with shared documents distributed over multiple devices. This is also important for large interaction areas like the DynaWall, which is currently realized via three separate segments because of the technical limitations of displays currently available. Other requirements are one user working with multiple devices or composite roomware, dynamic configuration of roomware, modeling also the physical environment, components to be used by different multiple users at the same time, adapting for different orientation and shape of displays, and mode-less user-interface.

BEACH has a layered architecture that is built on top of a core model. A layer with common models defines the basic interfaces for documents, user interface, tools, and interaction styles. On top of these models, a set of generic components is defined that provides the basic functionality necessary in most teamwork and meeting situations. This includes, for example, standard data types like text, graphics, and informal handwritten input (scribbles), as well as private and public workspaces for generic collaboration support. Based on the common models and the generic components modules, specific support can be added, which defines tailored functionality for distinct tasks. For more details on BEACH see Tandler (2000, 2001). BEACH is built on top of the COAST framework (Schuckmann et al. 1996) as a platform for the distribution of objects. COAST was previously developed at GMD-IPSI and was also used for the implementation of the groupware system DOLPHIN (Streitz et al. 1994).

It was a high-level design goal for the user-interface of BEACH to rely as much as possible on intuitive actions people are used to in their day-to-day physical interaction space. As a result, gestures and pen-based input are the major interaction types. Standard input devices like a mouse and a keyboard are also supported but play a minor role. A prominent and convincing example is the provision of the "shuffle" functionality where users can "throw" objects and depending on the momentum provided by the user, objects are flying faster or slower and covering a larger or shorter distance.

In contrast to "normal" mouse input, where the mouse position is always at a single, exact point, the handling of pen input is a little more demanding. Pen input normally consists of strokes touching several view objects (UI elements) on the display. This makes it impossible to use the position of the stroke as a distinct criterion. It is also important to be tolerant of inaccuracy of the input. Furthermore, it has to be decided whether a stroke should be interpreted as a command or data input. When a user has entered a stroke with a pen in the BEACH user interface, the shape of the stroke is continuously analyzed whether it is of a known form or not. The distinction as to whether the stroke is interpreted as a gesture invoking a command or as scribbled information is completely up to the controller handling pen events. It offers the possibility of context-sensitive semantic gestures.

BEACH offers a mode-less user-interface where the user does not have to select different modes before an action. It does not matter if he or she wants to provide handwritten input via a scribble or to make a "command" gesture operating on existing objects or creating new objects. This is achieved by implementing an incremental recognition of gestures: While a stroke is recorded, the current shape is continuously computed. This is then used to give feedback to the user (via different colors of the lines created) and inform him or her in this way about the operation resulting from this action.

25.10 Conclusion

We have presented the design and implementation of roomware components as central constituents of our vision of "Cooperative Buildings" for the workspaces of the future. They are based on an integrated design of real architectural and virtual information spaces going beyond the traditional desktop computer. Our approach is related to and was inspired by different developments in human-computer interaction, augmented reality, ubiquitous computing, and computer-supported cooperative work, in particular meeting support systems.

Our initial experiences are quite promising. In addition to our AMBIENTE-Lab in Darmstadt, we have had two external installations of i-LAND since May 2000 (one at the DASA in Dortmund, one at Wilkhahn in Bad Münder) that are still ongoing. Both were part of registered projects of the world exhibition EXPO 2000 but are still operated. Previous to that, we demonstrated i-LAND at different international fairs (CeBIT 1999 and 2000; Orgatec 2000). In October 2000, the roomware components of the second generation won the International Design Award of the state Baden Württemberg in Germany. More information about our future developments can be found at http://www.darmstadt.gmd.de/ambiente.

A final comment: Considering the affordances of the architectural space as a guiding metaphor for designing environments supporting the cooperation between humans and their interaction with information is a very important perspective for us. Mechanisms like "Passage" employing arbitrary real world objects as "Passengers," interaction forms like "throwing" information objects on large interactive walls, and other activities reported here seem to provide new intuitive forms of cooperation and communication. They are pointing in a similar direction as related developments emphasizing the importance of physical, tangible objects summarized in the section on related work. Nevertheless, it remains to be seen how far the use of these concepts and metaphors will actually carry. In the end, this is an empirical question that has to be answered, and we plan to address it. There is also a need for a more comprehensive approach as it is the objective of the new EU-funded proactive initiative "The Disappearing Computer" (www.disappearing-computer.net).

Notes: The term *roomware*® and the names of the roomware components *DynaWall*®, *InteracTable*®, and *CommChair*® are registered trademarks of GMD. The name *ConnecTable*® is a registered trademark of our cooperation partner Wilkhahn.

Acknowledgments

We would like to thank Jörg Geißler, Torsten Holmer, and Thorsten Prante as well as many of our students for their valuable contributions to various parts of the i-LAND project and in the AMBIENTE division of GMD-IPSI in Darmstadt. Furthermore, we appreciate the cooperation with Heinrich Iglseder, Burkhard Remmers, Frank Sonder, and Jürgen Thode from the German office furniture manufacturer Wilkhahn and Michael Englisch from their design company WIEGE in the context of the R&D consortium "Future Office Dynamics" (FOD), which sponsored part of the work presented here.

References

Baecker, R. (Ed.). (1993). *Readings in groupware and computer-supported cooperative work.* San Mateo: Morgan Kaufmann Publishers.

Bly, S.A., Harrison, S.R., and Irwin, S. (1993). Media spaces: Bringing people together in a video, audio, and computing environment. *Communications of the ACM,* 36, 1, 28–47.

Buxton, W. (1997). Living in augmented reality: Ubiquitous media and reactive environments. In K. Finn, A. Sellen, and S. Wilbur (Eds.), *Video-Mediated Communication,* 363–384. Hillsdale, NJ: Lawrence Erlbaum.

Cooperstock, J., Fels, S., Buxton, W., and Smith, K. (1997). Reactive environments: Throwing away your keyboard and mouse. *Communications of the ACM,* 40, 9, 65–73.

Fitzmaurice, G., Ishii, H., and Buxton, W. (1995). Bricks: Laying the foundations for graspable user interfaces. *Proceedings of the CHI'95 ACM Conference on Human Factors in Computing Systems,* 442–449. New York: ACM Press.

FOD (1999). *"Future Office Dynamics" Consortium.* http://www.future-office.de.

Ishii, H., and Ullmer, B. (1997). Tangible bits: Towards seamless interfaces between people, bits and atoms. *Proceedings of the CHI'97 ACM Conference on Human Factors in Computing Systems,* 234–241. New York: ACM Press.

Konomi, S., Müller-Tomfelde, C., and Streitz, N. (1999). Passage: Physical transportation of digital information in cooperative buildings. In N. Streitz, J. Siegel, V. Hartkopf, and S. Konomi (Eds.). *Proceedings of the Second International Workshop on Cooperative Buildings (CoBuild'99),* 45–54.

Mark, G., Haake, J., and Streitz, N. (1997). Hypermedia use in group work: Changing the product, process, and strategy. *Computer Supported Cooperative Work: The Journal of Collaborative Computing,* 6, 327–368.

Norman, D. (1998). *The invisible computer.* Cambridge, MA: MIT Press.

Nunamaker, J.F., Briggs, R.O., and Mittleman, D.D. (1995). Electronic meeting systems: Ten years of lessons learned. In D. Coleman and R. Khanna (Eds.), *Groupware: Technology and Applications,* 149–193. Upper Saddle River, NJ: Prentice-Hall.

Olson, J., Olson, G., Storrosten, M., and Carter, M. (1993). Groupwork close up: A comparison of the group design process with and without a simple group editor.

In T. Malone and N. Streitz (Eds.), *Special Issue on CSCW. ACM Transactions on Office Information Systems,* 11, 4, 321–348.

Pedersen, E., McCall, K., Moran, T., and Halasz, F. (1993). Tivoli: An electronic whiteboard for informal workgroup meeting. *Proceedings of InterCHI'93 ACM Conference on Human Factors in Computing Systems,* 391–399. New York: ACM Press.

Poynor, R. (1995). The hand that rocks the cradle. *I.D.—The International Design Magazine.* May-June.

Raskar, R., Welch, G., Cutts, M., Lake, A., Stesin, L., and Fuchs, H. (1998). The office of the Future: A unified approach to image-based modeling and spatially immersive displays. *Proceedings of SIGGRAPH98.* New York: ACM Press.

Rekimoto, J. (1997). Pick-and-drop: A direct manipulation technique for multiple computer environments. *Proceedings of the UIST'97 ACM Conference on User Interface Software Technology,* 31–39. New York: ACM Press.

Rekimoto, J. (1998). Multiple-computer user interfaces: A cooperative environment consisting of multiple digital devices. In N. Streitz, S. Konomi, and H. Burkhardt (Eds.), *Proceedings of the First International Workshop on Cooperative Buildings (CoBuild'98),* 33–40

Rekimoto, J., and Saitoh, M. (1999). Augmented surfaces: A spatially continuous work space for hybrid computing environments. *Proceedings of the CHI'99 ACM Conference on Human Factors in Computing Systems,* 378–385. New York: ACM Press.

Saund, E. (1999). Bringing the marks on a whiteboard to electronic life. In N. Streitz, J. Siegel, V. Hartkopf, and S. Konomi (Eds.), *Proceedings of the Second International Workshop on Cooperative Buildings (CoBuild'99),* 69–78.

Schuckmann, C., Kirchner, L., Schümmer, J., and Haake, J. (1996). Designing object-oriented synchronous groupware with COAST. *Proceedings of CSCW'96 ACM Conference on Computer-Supported Cooperative Work,* 30–38. New York: ACM Press.

Stefik, M., Foster, G., Bobrow, D., Khan, K., Lanning, S., and Suchman, L. (1987). Beyond the chalkboard: Computer support for collaboration and problem solving in meetings. *Communication of the ACM,* 30, 1, 32–47.

Streitz, N., Geißler, J., Haake, J., and Hol, J. (1994). DOLPHIN: Integrated meeting support across LiveBoards, local and desktop environments. *Proceedings of CSCW'94 ACM Conference on Computer-Supported Cooperative Work,* 345–358. New York: ACM Press.

Streitz, N., Geißler, J., and Holmer, T. (1998a). Roomware for cooperative buildings: Integrated design of architectural spaces and information spaces. In N. Streitz, S. Konomi, and H. Burkhardt (Eds.), *Proceedings of the First International Workshop on Cooperative Buildings (CoBuild'98),* 4–21.

Streitz, N., Konomi, S., and Burkhardt, H. (Eds.). (1998b). *Cooperative buildings— Integrating information, organization and architecture. Proceedings of the First International Workshop on Cooperative Buildings (COBuild'98).* LNCS 1370. Springer-Verlag, Heidelberg.

Streitz, N., Rexroth, P., and Holmer, T. (1997). Does "roomware" matter? Investigating the role of personal and public information devices and their combination in meeting room collaboration. *Proceedings of ECSCW'97 European Conference on Computer-Supported Cooperative Work,* 297–312. Dordrecht, The Netherlands: Kluwer Academic Publishers.

Streitz, N., Rexroth, P., and Holmer, T. (1998c). Anforderungen an interaktive Kooperationslandschaften für kreatives Arbeiten und erste Realisierungen. In T. Herrmann and K. Just-Hahn (Eds.), *Groupware und organisatorische Innovation. Proceedings of D-CSCW'98,* T237—250. (In German)

Streitz, N., Geißler, J., Holmer, T., Konomi, S., Müller-Tomfelde, C., Reischl, W., Rexroth, P., Seitz, R., and Steinmetz, R. (1999a). i-LAND: An interactive landscape for creativity and innovation. *Proceedings of CHI'99 ACM Conference on Human Factors in Computing Systems,* 120–127. New York: ACM Press.

Streitz, N., Siegel, J., Hartkopf, V., and Konomi, S. (Eds.). (1999b). *Cooperative Buildings—Integrating information, organizations, and architecture. Proceedings of the Second International Workshop (CoBuild'99).* LNCS 1670. Heidelberg: Springer.

Tandler, P. (2000). Architecture of BEACH: The software infrastructure for roomware environments. Workshop presentation at *ACM Conference on Computer-Supported Cooperative Work (CSCW'2000).*

Tandler, P. (2001). Software infrastructure for ubiquitous computing environments supporting synchronous collaboration with multiple single- and multi-user devices. *Proceedings of UBICOMP 2001: Lecture Notes in Computer Science.* Heidelberg: Springer.

Ullmer, B., Ishii, H., and Glas, D. (1998). MediaBlocks: Physical containers, transports, and controls for online media. *Proceedings of SIGGRAPH'98,* 379–386. New York: ACM Press.

Weiser, M. (1991). The computer for the 21st century. *Scientific American,* 265, 3, 94–104.

Weiser, M. (1998). The invisible interface: Increasing the power of the environment through calm technology. Opening keynote speech at the *First International Workshop on Cooperative Buildings (CoBuild'98).* Abstract of the speech available at http://www.darmstadt.gmd.de/CoBuild98/abstract/0weiser.html.

Wellner, P., Mackey, W., and Gold, R. (Eds.). (1993). Computer-augmented environments: Back to the real world. *Special Issue of Communications of the ACM,* 36, 7.

Wisneski, C., Ishii, H., Dahley, A., Gorbet, M., Brave, S., Ullmer, B., and Yarin P. (1998). Ambient displays: Turning architectural space into an interface between people and digital information. In N. Streitz, S. Konomi, and H. Burkhardt (Eds.), *Proceedings of the First International Workshop on Cooperative Buildings (CoBuild'98).* LNCS 1370. Springer-Verlag, Heidelberg. 22–32.

26
Emerging Frameworks for Tangible User Interfaces

Brygg Ullmer
Hiroshi Ishii

26.1   Introduction

The last decade has seen a wave of new research into ways to link the physical and digital worlds. This work has led to the identification of several major research themes, including augmented reality, mixed reality, ubiquitous computing, and wearable computing. At the same time, a number of interfaces have begun to explore the relationship between physical representation and digital information, highlighting kinds of interaction that are not readily described by these existing frameworks.

Fitzmaurice, Buxton, and Ishii took an important step toward describing a new conceptual framework with their discussion of "graspable user interfaces" (Fitzmaurice et al. 1995). Building on this foundation, we extended these ideas and proposed the term "tangible user interfaces" in Ishii and Ullmer (1997). Among other historical inspirations, we suggested the abacus as a compelling prototypical example. In particular, it is key to note that when viewed from the perspective of human-computer interaction (HCI), *the abacus is not an input device.* The abacus makes no distinction between "input" and "output." Instead, the abacus beads, rods, and frame serve as manipulable *physical representations* of numerical values and operations. Simultaneously, these component artifacts also serve as *physical controls* for directly manipulating their underlying associations.

This seamless integration of *representation* and *control* differs markedly from the mainstream graphical user interface (GUI) approaches of modern HCI. Graphical interfaces make a fundamental distinction between "input devices," such as the keyboard and mouse, as *controls,* and graphical "output devices" like monitors and head-mounted displays for the synthesis of visual *representations.* Tangible interfaces, in the tradition of the abacus, explore the conceptual space opened by the elimination of this distinction.

In this chapter, which is based on Ullmer and Ishii (2000), we take steps toward a conceptual framework for tangible user interfaces. We present an interaction model and key characteristics for tangible interfaces (or "TUIs") and illustrate these with a number of interface examples. We discuss the coupling between physical objects and digital information, taken both as individual and interdependent physical/digital elements. In the process, our goal is to identify a distinct and cohesive stream of research including both recent and decades-old examples, and to provide conceptual tools for characterizing and relating these systems under the common umbrella of "tangible user interfaces."

26.2 A First Example: Urp

To provide context for our discussions, we will begin by introducing an example interface: "Urp." Urp is a tangible interface for **ur**ban **p**lanning, built around a workbench that allows the direct manipulation of physical building models to configure and control an underlying urban simulation (Underkoffler et al. 1999a, 1999b). The interface combines a series of physical building models and interactive tools with an integrated projector/camera/computer node called the "I/O Bulb."

Under the mediation of the I/O Bulb, Urp's building models cast graphical shadows onto the workbench surface, corresponding to solar shadows at a particular time of day. The position of the sun can be controlled by turning the physical hands of a clock tool. The building models can be moved and rotated, their corresponding shadows transforming accordingly, to visualize intershadowing problems (shadows cast on adjacent buildings).

A "material wand" can be used to bind alternate material properties to individual buildings. For instance, when bound with a "glass" material property, buildings cast not only solar shadows, but also solar reflections. These reflections exhibit more complex (and less intuitive) behavior than shadows. Moreover, these reflections pose glare problems for urban drivers (roadways are also physically instantiated and graphically augmented by Urp.)

Finally, the "wind tool" is bound to a computational fluid flow simulation. By adding this object to the workbench, an airflow simulation is activated, with field lines graphically flowing around the buildings. Changing the wind tool's physical orientation correspondingly alters the orientation of the computationally simulated wind. A "wind probe" object allows point monitoring of the wind simulation's numerical results (see Figure 26.1).

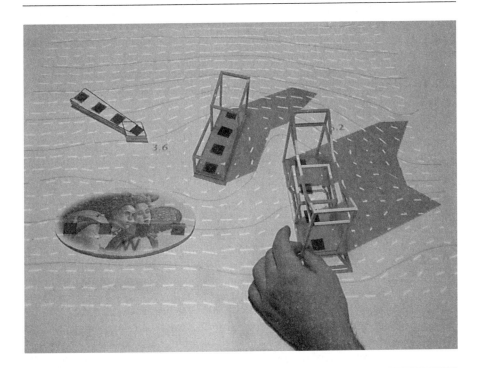

FIGURE 26.1   "Urp" urban planning simulation, with buildings, wind tool, and wind probe (Courtesy John Underkoffler)

26.3   Tangible User Interfaces

As illustrated by the previous example, tangible interfaces give physical form to digital information, employing physical artifacts both as *representations* and *controls* for computational media. TUIs couple physical representations (e.g., spatially manipulable physical objects) with digital representations (e.g., graphics and audio), yielding interactive systems that are computationally mediated but generally not identifiable as "computers" per se.

Clearly, traditional user interface devices such as keyboards, mice, and screens are also physical in form. Here, the role of physical representation provides an important distinction. For example, in the "Urp" tangible interface, physical models of buildings are used as physical representations of actual buildings. The physical forms of Urp's models (representing specific buildings), as well as their position and orientation upon the system's workbench, serve central roles in representing and controlling the state of the user interface.

In contrast, the physical form and position of the mouse hold little "representational" significance. Graphical user interfaces (GUIs) represent information almost entirely in transient visual form. While the mouse mediates control over the GUI's graphical cursor, its function can be equally served by a trackball, joystick, digitizer pen, or other "input peripherals." This invariance differs sharply from the Urp example, where the interface is closely coupled to the identity and physical configuration of specific, physically representational artifacts.

26.4   Interaction Model

As we have discussed, tangible interfaces are centrally concerned with notions about representation and control. "Representation" is a rather broad term, taking on different meanings within different communities. In artificial intelligence and other areas of computer science, the term often relates to the programs and data structures serving as the computer's *internal* representation (or model) of information. In this chapter, our meaning of "representation" centers upon *external* representations—the external manifestation of information directly perceivable by the human senses.

We divide the space of external representations into two broad classes. First, we consider *physical representations* to be information that is physically embodied in concrete, "tangible" form.[1] Alternately, we consider *digital representations* to be computationally mediated displays that are perceptually observed in the world, but are not physically embodied, and thus "intangible" in form. For instance, we consider the pixels on a screen or audio from a speaker to be examples of digital representations, while we view physical chess pieces and chess boards as examples of physical representations.

Our concept of digital representations in some respects approximates audio/visual representations, or perhaps "intangible" representations. Clearly, even the "digital representations" of a CRT or speaker require physical phenomena to be perceptible to humans. By choosing the digital representations term, we seek to identify the transient displays that are products of ongoing computations. As a clarifying heuristic, when the power to a tangible interface is removed, it is the "digital representations" that disappear, and the embodied, persistent "physical representations" that remain. Tangible interfaces are products of a careful balance between these two forms of representation.

Traditional computer interfaces frame human interaction in terms of "input" and "output." Computer output is delivered in the form of "digital representations" (especially screen-based graphics and text), while computer input is obtained from control "peripherals" such as the keyboard and mouse. The relationship between these components is illustrated by the "model-view-controller" or "MVC" archetype—an interaction model for GUIs developed in conjunction with the Smalltalk-80 program-

---

[1] It is worth noting that the "tangible" term derives from the Latin words *tangibilis* and *tangere*, meaning "to touch."

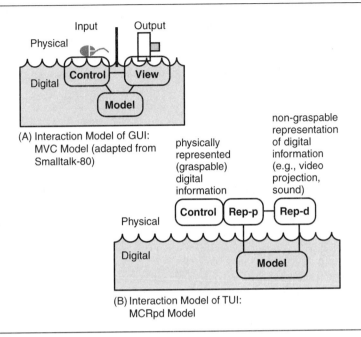

FIGURE 26.2   GUI and TUI interaction models

ming language. We illustrate the MVC model in Figure 26.2(a). MVC highlights the GUI's strong separation between the digital representation (or *view*) provided by the graphical display, and the *control* capacity mediated by the GUI's mouse and keyboard.

Drawing from the MVC approach, we have developed an interaction model for tangible interfaces that we call "MCRpd," for "model-control-representation (physical and digital)." This model is illustrated in Figure 26.2(b). We carry over the "model" and "control" elements from MVC, while dividing the "view" element into two subcomponents: *physical representations* ("rep-p") and *digital representations* ("rep-d").

Where the MVC model of Figure 26.2(a) illustrates the GUI's separation between graphical representation and control, MCRpd highlights the TUI's integration of physical representation and control. This integration is present not only at a conceptual level but also in physical point of fact—TUI artifacts *physically embody* both the control pathway as well as a central representational (information-bearing) aspect of the interface.

In this chapter, we will concentrate on the space of interfaces where each element of the MCRpd model is clearly present, with an emphasis on the role of physical representation. However, it is important to note that a series of interesting interaction regimes are highlighted by relaxing these expectations. For instance, if we relax our *control* expectations, the space of "ambient media" is highlighted, where devices such as spinning pinwheels and rippling water are used as information displays (Ishii and

Ullmer 1997; Wisneski et al. 1998). Alternately, if we relax our expectations of physical state (discussed more in the following section), interfaces such as the synchronized rollers of inTouch (Brave et al. 1998) or the graspable handles of Bricks (Fitzmaurice 1995) are brought to the fore. While we do not intend to exclude these kinds of systems from the larger tangible interface design space, we will focus on interfaces that follow a tighter interpretation of MCRpd.

26.5   Key Characteristics

The MCRpd interaction model provides a tool for examining several important properties of tangible interfaces. In particular, it is useful to consider the three relationships shared by the physical representations ("rep-p") of TUIs.

As illustrated in Figure 26.3, the MCRpd model highlights three key characteristics of tangible interfaces.

1. **Physical representations *(rep-p)* are computationally coupled to underlying digital information *(model)*.**

   The central characteristic of tangible interfaces lies in the coupling of physical representations to underlying digital information and computational models. The Urp example illustrates a range of such couplings, including the binding of graphical geometries (data) to the building objects, computational simulations (operations) to the wind tool, and property modifiers (attributes) to the material wand.

2. **Physical representations embody mechanisms for interactive control *(control)*.**

   The physical representations of TUIs also function as interactive physical controls. The physical movement and rotation of these artifacts, their insertion or attachment to each other, and other manipulations of these physical representations serve as tangible interfaces' primary means for control.

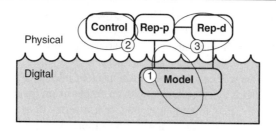

FIGURE 26.3   Key characteristics of tangible interfaces

3. Physical representations are perceptually coupled to actively mediated digital representations *(rep-d)*.

Tangible interfaces rely on a balance between physical and digital representations. While embodied physical elements play a central, defining role in the representation and control of TUIs, digital representations—especially graphics and audio—often present much of the dynamic information processed by the underlying computational system.

Where the preceding three characteristics refer directly to our MCRpd model, a fourth TUI characteristic is also significant.

4. The physical state of interface artifacts partially embodies the digital state of the system.

As illustrated in Figure 26.3, the MCRpd model does not specify whether a TUI's physical representations are composed of one or many physical artifacts. In practice, tangible interfaces are generally built from *systems* of physical artifacts. Taken together, these collections of objects have several important properties. As physical elements, TUI artifacts are *persistent*—they cannot be spontaneously called into or banished from existence. Where a GUI window can be destroyed or duplicated at the touch of a button, the same is not true of Urp's building objects. Also, TUI artifacts frequently may be "read" by both people and computers by their *physical state,* with their physical configurations tightly coupled to the digital state of the systems they represent.

Building from these properties, tangible interfaces often employ systems of multiple objects following one of several major interpretations. In *spatial* approaches, the spatial configurations of physical objects are directly interpreted and augmented by the underlying system. For instance, in the Urp example, the positions and orientations of physical building models map directly into the geographical space of the urban simulation, and are then computationally augmented with graphical shadows, wind interactions, and so forth.

In addition to spatial approaches, several other interpretations are possible. In *relational* approaches, the sequence, adjacencies, or other logical relationships between systems of physical objects are mapped to computational interpretations. In the next section, we will present an example system that was inspired by the Scrabble™ game's tile racks. A third approach involves the *constructive* assembly of modular interface elements, often connected together mechanically in fashions analogous (and sometimes quite literal) to the classic LEGO™ system of modular bricks.

26.6 Example Two: mediaBlocks

Where the Urp simulator provides a spatial interface for manipulating the arrangement of architectural building, the mediaBlocks system provides a relational interface for logically manipulating more abstract digital information (Ullmer et al. 1998).

MediaBlocks are small, digitally tagged blocks that are dynamically bound to lists of online media elements. The mediaBlocks system is a tangible interface for manipulating collections of these physically embodied videos, images, and other media elements.

MediaBlocks support two major kinds of use. First, they function as capture, transport, and playback mechanisms, supporting the movement of online media between different media devices. Toward this, mediaBlock "slots" are attached to conference room cameras, digital whiteboards, wall displays, printers, and other devices. Inserting a mediaBlock into the slot of a recording device (like a digital whiteboard) triggers the recording of media onto a networked computer and couples this media to the physical block as a "dynamic binding." Thus, while the block does not actually contain any information other than its digital ID, the block is linked to online information as a kind of physically embodied URL.

Once it is bound to one or more chunks of digital media, a mediaBlock may be inserted into the slot of a playback device (such as a printer or video display) to activate playback of the associated media. Alternately, inserting the block into a slot mounted on the face of a computer monitor allows mediaBlock contents to be exchanged with traditional computer applications using GUI drag-and-drop.

The system's second major function allows mediaBlocks to function as both media containers and controls on a sequencing device (see Figure 26.4). A media-Block "sequence rack," partially modeled after the tile racks of the Scrabble™ game,

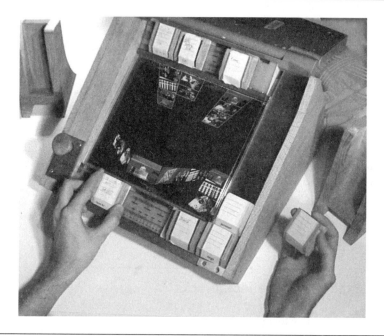

FIGURE 26.4 mediaBlocks and media sequencer *(©ACM)*

allows the contents of multiple adjacent mediaBlocks to be assembled into a single ordered media list and dynamically bound to a new mediaBlock container. Similarly, a "position rack" maps the physical position of a mediaBlock into an indexing operation upon the block's contents. When a mediaBlock is moved to the position rack's left edge, the block's first media element is selected. Moving the block to the rack's right edge accesses the block's last content, with intermediate positions providing access to intermediate elements in the block's internal list of media contents.

26.7 Terminology

In the previous sections, we have somewhat loosely used a number of terms like "object," "artifact," and "container." As is common in rapidly evolving research areas, many of the terms in this chapter have not yet reached widespread consensus (including the "tangible user interface" phrase itself). With such a consensus likely to be slow in coming, it is valuable to consider the terminology currently in use, as the choice of names often reflects important underlying assumptions.

"Objects," in the physical sense of the word, are clearly a central concern of tangible interfaces. At the same time, this term has been broadly interpreted in the computer science and HCI communities to mean many things, most having nothing to do with the physical world. Moreover, most physical objects have no connection with tangible interfaces. Therefore, while we often discuss "objects" in the TUI context, it is a somewhat ambiguous term. The term "physical/digital objects" is sometimes used to clarify this ambiguity, highlighting the dual physical/digital aspect of TUI elements.

"Artifacts," carrying the implication of man-made physical objects, offers an alternate term with less prior use in the computer science and HCI communities. However, naturally occurring objects like stones and seashells have been used in a number of tangible interfaces, leaving this term again useful but imprecise.

The "props" term has been used in several related research systems, including Hinckley et al.'s (1994) influential "doll's head" neurosurgical interface. However, the props term carries the implication of an element that is somehow peripheral to the core (presumably graphical) user interface. We find this somewhat counter to TUI's emphasis on physical objects as central elements of the user interface.

"Physical icons" or "phicons," a name we introduced in Ishii and Ullmer (1997) with reference to the GUI "icon" concept, offers another possible descriptor. However, as we discuss in Ullmer and Ishii (2000), this term also has shortcomings. For one, it faces a dilemma that has been widely discussed in the GUI literature: strictly speaking, many graphical and physical "icons" are not "iconic" but rather "symbolic" in form. For instance, from the perspective of semiotics (the study of signs and symbols), the physical forms of mediaBlocks are symbolic and not iconic.

The "tangibles" term refers specifically to the physical elements of tangible interfaces and to their role in physically representing digital information. Partially inspired by the Marble Answering Machine and other work of Bishop (Crampton Smith 1995), it was used in this context with the development of the LogJam video logging and ToonTown audioconferencing systems at Interval Research (Cohen et al. 1999; Singer et al. 1999). This term has the advantage of brevity and specificity to the TUI context.

For careful consideration of tangible interfaces, we believe the physical elements of tangible interfaces may be usefully described in terms of "tokens" and "reference frames." We consider *tokens* to be the physically manipulable elements of tangible interfaces and *reference frames* to be the physical interaction spaces in which these objects are used. For example, we consider the building, wind, clock, and material artifacts of Urp, along with the blocks of mediaBlocks, to be kinds of "tokens." Similarly, we consider the graphically mediated workbench of Urp and the sequencer and slots of mediaBlocks to be examples of "reference frames."

From an applied perspective, symbolic tokens are often used as "containers" for other media (as in mediaBlocks). Similarly, tokens that are used to represent digital operations or functions often serve as "tools" (as in Urp). Where the token and reference frame terms are relatively new to the discussion of tangible interfaces, the "container" and "tool" terms have seen wider use.

We have developed the token and reference frame terms partly from a study of board games, which share interesting properties with tangible interfaces. Games such as Chess, Go, Backgammon, Monopoly™, and Trivial Pursuit™ all can be seen as systems of tokens and reference frames. Like tangible interfaces, these games also use manipulable physical tokens as representations for underlying systems of abstract rules. The physical forms assumed by these tokens and reference frames are widely varying, highly evolved, and tightly coupled to their respective games, to the extent that none of these games could be played with the physical "equipment" of another. These characteristics illustrate the critical role of physical representation within these games. Several board games also illustrate how tokens can themselves serve as "nested" reference frames, as with the "pies" and "pie wedges" of Trivial Pursuit™.

Several other alternate classifications have been proposed. For instance, Holmquist et al. (1999) suggest the terms "tokens," "containers," and "tools" as classifications for physical/digital objects. Their concept of "containers" and "tools" is similar to our own, while their use of "token" approximates our "iconic tokens" and "phicons." Alternately, Underkoffler and Ishii (1999a) present a "continuum of object meanings," with objects interpreted as reconfigurable tools, verbs, nouns, attributes, and "pure objects." Both of these proposals are useful for their function-oriented classifications.

26.8 Coupling Objects with Digital Information

In the previous sections, we have introduced several TUI examples and presented the beginnings of a conceptual framework centering on the MCRpd model. In this section, we will consider several elements of MCRpd more carefully, focusing on the ways that TUIs couple physical objects with digital information. First, we will consider MCRpd's *model* aspect, discussing the kinds of digital information that can be associated with TUI artifacts. Next, we will explore the *control* issues of how physical/digital bindings are established and invoked. Finally, we will discuss the kinds of *physical representation* that TUIs may employ and some of the technical mechanisms by which they operate.

26.8.1 Kinds of Digital Bindings

The Urp and mediaBlocks examples have illustrated several different kinds of digital associations for TUI artifacts. In Urp, physical building models are coupled to 3D graphical geometries. The material wand is coupled to several material properties ("brick" and "glass"), which may be bound to buildings to invoke graphical shadows and reflections. The wind tool is coupled to a fluid-flow simulation, while the clock tool is coupled to the system's model of time.

The mediaBlocks example introduces several contrasting approaches. The blocks themselves represent a kind of simple data structure—in particular, a list of media elements. The system enables blocks to "contain" lists of images, video, audio, and by implication, any information that can be referenced by a URL. The system also demonstrates blocks embodying "conduits" to remote devices (like a remote printer) and suggests how these conduits might be used as "sources" and "sinks" for live audio, video, and other streaming media. In parallel, physical racks, slots, and pads are mapped to digital operations for connecting mediaBlocks to a variety of media sources and sinks.

As these examples suggest, tangible interfaces afford a wide variety of associations between physical objects and digital information. These associations include the following.

- Static digital media, such as images and 3D models
- Dynamic digital media, such as live video and dynamic graphics
- Digital attributes, such as color or other material properties
- Computational operations and applications
- Simple data structures, such as lists or trees of media objects
- Complex data structures, such as combinations of data, operations, and attributes
- Remote people, places, and things (including other electronic devices)

As a simple example, a TUI might couple a physical token to a simple digital file. For example, we have described how a mediaBlock can "contain" a digital image. In this case, it is clear that the mediaBlocks' "associations" are indeed "digital information."

However, as another example, a TUI token could also represent a remote person, perhaps mediating this at different times through live audio, video, or other means. Technically, the token's audio or video connection is likely to depend on the transfer of "digital information." But conceptually, the user of a successful system may prefer to think of the token as simply representing "John" (or whomever is associated with the object). Such associations, which stretch the notion of "digital information," strike us as some of the most interesting couplings for tangible interfaces.

26.8.2 Methods of Coupling Objects with Information

How does digital information become coupled to physical objects? Again, the Urp and mediaBlocks examples suggest several possibilities. In Urp, building models are statically coupled to building geometries. This basic object/geometry binding cannot be changed within the tangible interface itself; the relationship is assumed to be either specified by the system's designer or assigned in some other fashion "out of band" from the tangible interface's core physical interaction.

Similarly, the assignment of digital functions to Urp's other artifacts (the material, clock, and wind tools) are statically bound by the system's designer. However, interactions between these artifacts are used to establish dynamic bindings. This is most notable with the use of the material wand, but it is also used in other parts of the system (for example, the use of a distance-measuring tool, which is used to link pairs of interface objects).

In contrast, the mediaBlocks system centers upon the establishment of dynamic bindings between digital contents and physical containers. This binding is performed in several ways. As we have described, mediaBlock slots are used both to bind media "into" the blocks (for example, as a recording from a digital whiteboard), as well as to retrieve a mediaBlock's prior associations (for example, as media playback onto a printer or screen). Where these examples illustrate the establishment of bindings without use of a "computer" per se, the monitor slot provides a bridge between mediaBlocks and the drag-and-drop "bindings" of the traditional GUI world. In addition, the sequencer racks provide another mechanism for accessing media contents, as well as expressing new mediaBlock bindings in concert with other TUI elements such as the sequencer's "target pad."

26.8.3 Approaches to Physical Representation

The design and selection of appropriate physical representations is a very important aspect of tangible interface design. The disciplines of graphic design, industrial design, architecture, and even furniture and environmental design all hold strong relevance to this task.

However, relatively few tangible interfaces have been strongly shaped by industrial design and other traditional design perspectives. One common approach involves the use of "found objects"—pre-existing objects that are perhaps embedded with position sensors or ID tags, and recontextualized to take on roles within tangible interfaces. For instance, in Hinckley et al.'s (1994) neurosurgical interface, a doll's head (and later, a rubber ball) was embedded with position trackers and used as a physical representation of the human brain. Manipulation of this object controlled the orientation and zooming of a screen-based neurosurgical visualization. Use of the doll's head/ball in combination with a clear acrylic plane invoked and controlled a cross-section view, while a probe object physically expressed the prospective trajectory of a surgical incision.

Another common TUI approach might be described as engineering-driven design. Unlike the software-centric world of graphical interfaces, tangible interface design often hinges on the engineering of custom electronics and mechanics. Often, the design of tangible interfaces has been driven first by the pragmatics of electronic and mechanical design, with conceptual and aesthetic issues of physical form taking a lower priority. Sometimes, this results in bare electronic or mechanical elements being put forward as completed TUI artifacts, often resulting in interfaces that fall short from the standpoint of physical representation and "good design."

A third approach is to center design around the physical artifacts underlying pre-existing workplace practices. For instance, Mackay et al. (1998) identified the physical "flight strips" used for managing air traffic in European aircraft control towers as compelling artifacts and developed computational interfaces augmenting these objects. Similarly, McGee et al. (2001) have developed PostIt™-based interfaces in military command posts that add computational support to existing command-post practices. While these efforts can also be viewed as augmented reality systems, their usage of physical objects as computationally mediated artifacts also holds much in common with tangible interface approaches.

Some tangible interfaces have been motivated primarily by concerns for physical representation and design. For example, Oba's Environment Audio concept design used elegantly crafted wooden, metal, and plastic tokens as containers for ambient sounds from nature, urban spaces, and the electronic airwaves, respectively (Oba 1990). This work emphasized the use of physical materials and forms to evoke digital contents. Bishop's influential Marble Answering Machine concept sketch illustrated the use of physical marbles as containers and controls for manipulating voice messages (Crampton Smith 1995). This piece, along with Bishop's accompanying studies, provided one of the earliest illustrations for interlinking systems of physical products through a shared physical/digital "language."

All of these design approaches reflect a tension between interface functionality, "legibility," pragmatics, and aesthetics. Speaking of related issues, the *Encyclopedia Britannica* notes that "as with some other arts, the practice of architecture embraces both aesthetic and utilitarian ends that may be distinguished but not separated, and the relative weight given to each can vary widely from work to work" (*Britannica* 2000). We believe that this assessment also applies to the design of tangible interfaces.

26.8.4 Technical Realization of Physical/Digital Bindings

The function of tangible interfaces hinges upon the ability to computationally mediate people's interaction with physical objects. While the technical implementation underlying such capabilities goes well beyond the scope of this chapter, a brief flavor of the relevant technologies is useful. From a sensing standpoint, some of the most long-standing approaches include commercial position trackers (often using technologies targeted at virtual reality applications), computer vision, and custom electronics. Over the past decade, the use of wired and wireless ID tag technologies has grown increasingly popular. In particular, RF-ID tags (wireless radio frequency identification tags) have shown special promise.

From an actuation and display standpoint, some of the earliest approaches have relied upon embedded LEDs, speakers, and traditional computer monitors. Beginning with Wellner's (1993) pioneering DigitalDesk, a growing number of interfaces began to use front- or back-projected graphical workbenches. This trend has been accelerated by the rapid progress of video projector technologies. Similar advances in flat panel display technology have driven increased use of embedded flat panels in TUI designs. Motors and other actuation and force-feedback devices are also making inroads into TUI design.

26.9   Interpreting Systems of Objects

As we have discussed in the context of TUI's fourth key characteristic, tangible interfaces tend to combine systems of physical objects in one (or more) of three major interpretations: spatial, relational, and constructive. In Ullmer and Ishii (2000), we categorized 39 example systems in terms of these approaches. In addition, we identified a number of properties that cluster within these categories.

Here, we will present an overview and illustrative examples of these categories. We do not propose our categories as a formal taxonomy, although they may lend support to such efforts. Instead, our goal is to use these categories as a means for understanding and characterizing diverse systems as part of a cohesive stream of research.

26.9.1   Spatial Systems

In *spatial* approaches, the spatial configuration of physical tokens within one or more physical reference frames is directly interpreted and augmented by the underlying system. For example, the positions and orientations of Urp's physical building models map directly into the geographical space of the urban simulation and are then complemented with graphical shadows, wind interactions, and so forth.

We have also spoken of Hinckley et al.'s (1994) neurosurgical interface, in which brain, cutting plane, and surgical props are used to drive a visualization task. Where Urp's system of tokens remain on its horizontal planar workbench when in use, the neurosurgical props are held in "free space" by the user's two hands. Since the spatial relationships between these props are mapped directly into the system's visualization, we also consider this a spatial interface approach.

26.9.2 Relational Systems

Spatial approaches tend to use distances, orientations, and Cartesian displacements between physical tokens as key interface parameters. In contrast, *relational* approaches map the sequences, adjacencies, and other logical relationships between tokens onto more abstract computational interpretations. For instance, in the mediaBlocks system, we have discussed ways in which the docking of blocks and slots are used to establish dynamic bindings, and in which racks are used to aggregate or disaggregate block "contents" as a function of their sequence or relative position. We have also briefly described Bishop's Marble Answering Machine, a relational interface where marbles are moved between active surfaces to replay marble contents, redial a marble message's caller, or store the message for future reference.

Another particularly interesting relational interface example is the Slot Machine of Perlman, an interface for controlling LOGO's robotic and screen-based "Turtle" (Perlman 1976). In this interface, sequences of physical "action," "number," "variable," and "conditional" cards were configured within several colored horizontal slots to construct LOGO programs. Multiple cards could be stacked upon one another to create composite commands. For example, the number card for "4" could be stacked on the action card for "move forward" to express "move forward 4." Number cards were physically shorter than action cards, allowing all of the card stack's elements to remain visible.

Among many interesting features, the Slot Machine's approach for physically expressing recursion is particularly intriguing. A red "action" card carried the meaning "run the commands in the red slot," and so on for other colored slots and cards. In this way, a red card used within the red slot represented a recursive command. When combined with a variable card, for instance, the procedure for drawing a spiral could be compactly expressed.

These examples suggest the possibilities for rich physical/digital languages, especially for interaction contexts that already depend on collections of physical-world objects or devices. At the same time, such systems require a careful balance between physical and graphical expression to avoid physical clutter and to take advantage of the contrasting strengths of different representational forms. This balance between physical and digital representations stands as one of TUI's greatest design challenges.

26.9.3 Constructive Systems

A third approach involves the *constructive* assembly of modular elements, often connected together mechanically in fashions analogous (and sometimes quite literal) to the classic LEGO™ assemblies of modular bricks. For instance, in the work of Anagnostou et al. (1989) and Frazer et al. (1994) (begun in the early 1980s), a series of interconnecting cubes were used to describe fluid-flow simulations, 3D cellular automata, and other computational simulations.

Even earlier efforts in this area were initiated in 1979 by Aish, who described and later implemented a computational "building block systems" for the architecture domain. Aish imagined that this system might allow lay users to explore and respond to complex factors such as a building's simulated energy consumption early in the architectural design process. More recently, Anderson et al. (2000) have designed new implementations and applications for similar systems of blocks, focusing on the integration of "tangible interaction + graphical interpretation." A number of systems have also been built directly on the LEGO™ bricks platform, including the long-standing work of Resnick et al. (1998).

26.9.4 Mixed Constructive/Relational Systems

The classifications of spatial, relational, and constructive systems are not mutually exclusive. For example, one promising space lies at the intersection between constructive and relational approaches. Like their constructive kin, these systems tend to be composed of modular, mechanically interconnecting elements. Also like relational systems, these modules and the relationships between them are frequently bound with abstract computational semantics.

One early system in this area is AlgoBlock, a system of cubical aluminum blocks that is related in function to Perlman's Slot Machine (Suzuki and Kato 1993). Like the Slot Machine, AlgoBlock was used to physically express a LOGO-like language. Unlike the Slot Machine, AlgoBlock consisted of an array of cubes that dock with each other on a table. Where the Slot Machine stacked "number cards" on "action cards" to express commands like "ROTATE LEFT BY 45°," each AlgoBlock represented a command and offered control of associated parameters through knobs and levers permanently embedded within each block. AlgoBlocks also contained lighted buttons to trigger the execution of each physically embodied command. This execution would propagate onward to other connected blocks, with the lights glowing to indicate the program execution's progression and evolving state.

Another interface with both constructive and relational characteristics is Triangles, a system of triangular acrylic tiles intended for use as a kind of physical/digital interaction toolkit (Gorbet et al. 1998). Triangles interconnect physically and digitally through magnetic hinging connectors. Each contains an embedded microcontroller and unique ID, allowing individual tiles to be associated with specific data or operations. As an example application, "Cinderella 2000" associated Triangles with characters and places from the Cinderella story in a kind of reactive "audio comic book." Connecting the "stepmother" tile to the "Cinderella's home" tile triggered the stepmother's audio recounting of Cinderella's inadequate housework. Attaching Cinderella's tile would then invoke a scripted dialog between Cinderella and the stepmother.

It is worth noting that both the AlgoBlock and Triangles interfaces, along with many other systems in the constructive + relational category, have been oriented toward use by children in educational contexts. The authors of these systems have emphasized the ability of physical artifacts to support collaboration between multiple users and to deliver concrete representations of abstract concepts with special value in educational contexts.

26.10 Application Domains

What kinds of tasks are tangible interfaces good for? Beyond the broad generalizations and point examples we have discussed, several particular applications domains have begun to emerge.

Information storage, retrieval, and manipulation. One of the largest classes of TUI applications is the use of tangibles as manipulable containers for digital media. The mediaBlocks, Marble Answering Machine, LogJam, and ToonTown examples all illustrate this kind of usage. These systems seem to hold special potential for mediating interaction within and among networked "information appliances."

Information visualization. TUIs broadly relate to the intersection of computation and "external cognition." As such, they share common ground with the area of information visualization. TUIs offer the potential for rich multimodal representation and input, often providing increased specialization at the cost of general-purpose flexibility. The Urp and neurosurgical props interfaces both offer good illustrations of this application domain.

Modeling and simulation. Many spatial interfaces and the whole category of constructive interfaces illustrate the use of computationally enhanced cubes, blocks, and tiles as primitive units for modeling and simulating mixed physical/digital systems. Urp, AlgoBlock, the cubes of Frazer and Anagnostou et al., and the bricks of Aish and Anderson et al. illustrate such approaches.

Systems management, configuration, and control. Several tangible interfaces illustrate the broad capacity for manipulating and controlling complex systems such as video networks, industrial plants, and so forth. Example interfaces include mediaBlocks, AlgoBlock, ToonTown, and LogJam.

Education, entertainment, and programming systems. A number of tangible interfaces have demonstrated techniques for programming, most commonly in the context of concretely demonstrating abstract concepts in elementary education. Examples include the Slot Machine, AlgoBlock, Triangles, and the work of Resnick et al. Interestingly, many of these systems are also perceived as holding entertainment value, which perhaps contributes to their prospects for educational use.

While all of these domains represent areas where computers are broadly known to be useful, tangible interfaces are distinguished by a number of special properties. For instance, TUIs are intrinsically well suited to collocated cooperative work by virtue of their many loci of physical control. This contrasts clearly with traditional GUIs, where multiple users must share a single keyboard and pointing device. This property also contrasts with augmented reality and wearable computing systems based on head-mounted displays, which limit the computer's displays to the viewing space of individual users. Tangible interfaces' externalization of information into physical, manipulable forms also has important implications for facilitating communications and "transparency" of interaction between multiple collocated users.

These properties illustrate ways in which tangible interfaces can leverage lessons from distributed cognition, as discussed within Chapter 5. Distributed cognition describes the roles played by physical objects and the physical environment in supporting memory, learning, and interpersonal communications—all properties of direct relevance to tangible interfaces. The related concept of "physical affordances" also speaks to people's ability to creatively combine physical objects in unexpected fashions—for example, to use a bowl for holding soup, peas, rubber bands, or floppy disks, or, more whimsically, as a hat or boat. Despite the flexibility of graphical interfaces, their support for such recombinations is comparatively quite rudimentary and brittle. Building on the strength of their embodied physical affordances, tangible interfaces hold the potential to support truly creative and spontaneous physical/ digital combinations.

26.11 Related Areas

26.11.1 Broad Context

Humans are clearly no newcomers to interaction with the physical world or to the process of associating symbolic function and relationships with physical artifacts. We have referenced the abacus example earlier in this chapter, which we have considered in the context of other historic scientific instruments within Ishii and Ullmer 1997.

We have also discussed traditional games of reasoning and chance as presenting interesting case examples. In prototypical instances such as chess and cribbage, we find systems of physical objects—the playing pieces, boards, and cards—coupled with the abstract rules these artifacts symbolically represent. The broader space of board, card, and tile games, considered as systems of tokens and reference frames, provides an interesting conceptual parallel and grounding for modeling TUIs.

Map rooms, "war rooms," and control rooms offer other examples of the symbolic and iconic uses of physical artifacts. Magnet boards and LEGO boards are sometimes used with reconfigurable tokens for groups to collaboratively track and explore time-evolving processes (we know of such instances in dairies and graduate schools). Within domestic contexts, people use souvenirs and heirlooms as representations of personal histories.

The disciplines of cognitive science and psychology are concerned in part with "external representations." These are defined as "knowledge and structure in the environment, as physical symbols, objects, or dimensions, and as external rules, constraints, or relations embedded in physical configurations" (Zhang 1997). These and other theories and experiments, including analyses of the cognitive role of physical constraints in tasks like the Towers of Hanoi game, seem closely applicable to tangible user interfaces.

As we have discussed, ideas about affordances by Gibson, Norman, and others have long been of interest to the HCI community and hold special relevance to tangible interface design. Related studies of spatial representation and bimanual manipulation (most notably by Guiard) also hold special applicability for TUIs. The doctoral theses of Fitzmaurice and Hinckley have offered both perceptive analyses of this literature, as well as contributing new studies in these areas.

The discipline of semiotics—the study of signs and symbols—is concerned in part with the symbolic role of physical objects. We have discussed Peircian semiotics in the context of GUI icons and TUI phicons within Ullmer and Ishii 2000. Additionally, semioticians Krampen, Rossi-Landi, Prieto, Moles, Boudon, and von Uexkull have considered the relation of physical tools to human language, grammars, and semantics. We believe these studies may bear strong relevance for TUI design.

26.11.2 HCI Context

Shneiderman's (1983) three principles of "direct manipulation," while posed in the context of graphical interfaces, are also directly applicable to tangible interfaces. The first principle—"continuous representation of the object of interest"—knits especially well with the persistent nature of TUI tangibles. As such, the sizable literature relating to direct manipulation, and associated analyses of topics such as perceptual distance, are broadly relevant to TUI design. As with other direct manipulation interfaces, TUIs can be said to cultivate tool-like, rather than language-like, modalities of interaction. At the same time, tangible interfaces are also subject to some of the criticisms that have been directed at direct manipulation approaches, including those discussed in Frohlich (1997).

The area of visual programming languages holds relevance for TUIs. Here, principles such as the "Deutsch Limit," which suggests the implausibility of more than 50 visual primitives in simultaneous use on the screen, may have analogues for TUI systems of physical primitives. At the same time, people's homes and workplaces routinely hold and (at least loosely) structure human interactions with many thousands of objects. While these complex physical environments point to the real challenge of physical clutter and lost objects, they also indicate the richness, power, organizational properties, and flexibility of physical space.

The areas of augmented reality, mixed reality, and ubiquitous computing hold the closest relation to tangible interfaces among existing major research streams. While these areas hold in common a concern for physically contextualized interaction, we believe they inhabit different conceptual and design spaces than tangible interfaces. In particular, where tangible interfaces are centrally concerned with the user interface properties of systems of representational physical artifacts, none of these alternate frameworks share this emphasis.

Different researchers associate widely divergent interpretations of these terms. For instance, where many researchers consider augmented reality to be closely associated with the use of head-mounted displays, others hold a view of augmented reality much closer to our discussion of tangible interfaces. We do not believe these alternate stances are inconsistent but instead offer different conceptual frameworks, different perspectives and insights, and different points of leverage for considering new kinds of physically embodied user interfaces.

The area of ubiquitous computing, as discussed in Chapter 24, also holds common ground with tangible interfaces. Weiser's (1991) vision of ubiquitous computing, and particularly his concern for bringing computation into niche physical contexts, has strongly influenced TUI research. From a user interface standpoint, the individual devices of ubiquitous computing systems have tended to follow traditional GUI approaches. At the same time, UbiComp's more evolutionary user interface trajectory gives it heightened practical relevance in the immediate term.

26.12 Conclusion

In this chapter, we have presented steps toward a conceptual framework for tangible user interfaces. We have introduced an interaction model and key characteristics, and applied these to a number of example interfaces. These have included not only systems explicitly conceived as "tangible interfaces" but more broadly numerous past and contemporary systems that may be productively considered in terms of tangible interface characteristics. While these examples illustrate considerable diversity, we believe they also share a number of basic properties and common approaches, which we have begun to generalize into a unifying conceptual framework.

In discussing a broad topic within limited space, we have necessarily left a great many concerns for future consideration. From an HCI standpoint, these include issues of cognitive engagement and distance, general vs. special purpose approaches, and many others. From an engineering perspective, issues include tagging and tracking technologies, hardware and software architectures, prototyping, toolkits, and beyond. And from a design viewpoint, among a great many particular challenges, there is also a more fundamental one: What makes for good tangible interface design? As Underkoffler et al. (1999b) write, "the future of reactive, real-world graphics will surely have its own Rands and Tuftes, Leacocks and Gilliams." We find this analogy—and even more so, the prospects it raises—highly compelling.

In preparing this chapter, we were both humbled and inspired by Halasz's landmark "Seven Issues" hypermedia paper and "'Seven Issues' Revisited" address. Reflecting on his paper after several years, Halasz (1991) remarked that "the Seven Issues paper, in retrospect, takes a very simple and narrow view of what the world of hypermedia encompasses, what was of interest to us as hypermedia researchers." Expanding on this theme, Halasz reflected on the diversity of the hypermedia community—ranging from the divergent interests of literary and technologist practitioners, to differing notions of what constitutes a link, to the contrasting metrics of success in academia and industry.

Again speaking in 1991, Halasz said, "One of the main selling points of hypermedia (relates to) very large document collections (10K–100K documents). . . . Unfortunately, reality has yet to catch up to the vision." From the perspective of the year 2000, Halasz's words offer a breathtaking reminder of how quickly realities can change and how profoundly long-latent visions can blossom.

While the areas of hypermedia and tangible interfaces are very different in character, Halasz's experiences with unexpected diversity provide an interesting benchmark. For tangible interfaces, who is the community of developers, and what are the dimensions of its diversity?

Our experience suggests this must include practitioners of computer science and cognitive science, mechanical engineering and electrical engineering, art and design, academia and industry. The fusion of physical and digital worlds provides for an extraordinarily rich, and sparsely populated, design space. We look forward to joining with others in exploring the bounds of its potential.

Acknowledgments

We would like to thank James Patten, Ben Piper, John Underkoffler, Rob Jacob, Alexandra Mazalek, Lars Erik Holmquist, and David McGee for valuable feedback on this chapter. We also thank Paul Yarin, Matt Gorbet, Phil Frei, and other students of the Tangible Media group, as well as Bill Verplank, John Frazer, John Maeda, Neil Gershenfeld, Jun Rekimoto, Johan Redström, and Tim McNerney for past and ongoing discussions of many of these ideas. We also thank Joe Marks for introducing us to the works of Frazer and Anagnostou, and Whitman Richards for discussions on the cognitive roles of physical artifacts in nonathletic games. This research was supported in part by IBM, Intel, Steelcase, Canon, and other sponsors of the MIT Media Laboratory's Things That Think and Digital Life consortiums.

References

Aish, R. (1979). Three-dimensional input for CAAD systems. *Computer-Aided Design,* 11, 2, 66–70.

Anagnostou, G., Dewey, D., and Patera, A. (1989). Geometry-defining processors for engineering design and analysis. *The Visual Computer,* 5, 304–315.

Anderson, D., Frankel, J., Marks, J., Agarwala, A., Beardsley, P., Hodgins, J., Leigh, D., Ryall, K., Sullivan, E., and Yedidia, J. (2000). Tangible interaction + graphical interpretation: A new approach to 3D modelling. *Computer Graphics (Proceedings of SIGGRAPH'00),* 393–402.

Brave, S., Ishii, H., and Dahley, A. (1998). Tangible interfaces for remote collaboration and communication. *Proceedings of the ACM 1998 Conference on Computer Supported Cooperative Work,* 169–178.

Architecture. (2000). *Encyclopædia Britannica Online.* <http://members.eb.com/bol/topic?eu=9403&sctn=1>.

Cohen, J., Withgott, M., and Piernot, P. (1999). Logjam: A tangible multi-person interface for video logging. *Proceedings of the CHI'99 Conference on Human Factors in Computing Systems,* 128–135.

Crampton Smith, G. (1995). The hand that rocks the cradle. *I.D.,* May/June, 60–65.

Fitzmaurice, G., Ishii, H., and Buxton, W. (1995). Bricks: Laying the foundations for graspable user interfaces. *Conference Proceedings on Human Factors in Computing Systems,* 442–449.

Frazer, J. (1994). *An evolutionary architecture.* London: Architectural Association.

Frohlich, D. (1997). Direct manipulation and other lessons. *Handbook of Human-Computer Interaction,* 2nd Edition. Amsterdam: Elsevier.

Gorbet, M., Orth, M., and Ishii, H. (1998). Triangles: Tangible interface for manipulation and exploration of digital information topography. *Conference Proceedings on Human Factors in Computing Systems,* 49–56.

Halasz, F. (1991). "Seven issues" revisited. Keynote address. *Hypertext'91 Conference.* http://www.parc.xerox.com/spl/projects/halasz-keynote/ +. http://www.csdl.tamu.edu/~leggett/halasz.html (video).

Hinckley, K., Pausch, R., Goble, J., and Kassel, N. (1995). Passive real-world interface props for neurosurgical visualization. *Proceedings of CHI'94,* 452–458.

Holmquist, L., Redström, J., and Ljungstrand, P. (1999). Token-based access to digital information. *Proceedings of the First International Symposium on Handheld and Ubiquitous Computing (HUC'99),* 234–245. Springer Verlag.

Ishii, H., and Ullmer, B. (1997). Tangible Bits: Towards seamless interfaces between people, bits, and atoms. *Conference Proceedings on Human Factors in Computing Systems,* 234–241.

Mackay, W., Fayard, A., Frobert, L., and Medini, L. (1998). Reinventing the familiar: Exploring an augmented reality design space for air traffic control. *Conference Proceedings on Human Factors in Computing Systems,* 558–573.

McGee, D., and Cohen, P. (2001). Creating tangible interfaces by augmenting physical objects with multimodal language. *Proceedings of the International Conference on Intelligent User Interface,* 113–119.

Oba, H. (1990). Environment audio system for the future. Sony concept video.

Perlman, R. (1976). Using computer technology to provide a creative learning environment for preschool children. MIT Logo Memo #24.

Resnick, M., Martin, F., Berg, R., Borovoy, R., Colella, V., Kramer, K., and Silverman, B. (1998). Digital manipulatives: New toys to think with. *Conference Proceedings on Human Factors in Computing Systems.*

Shneiderman, B. (1983). Direct manipulation: A step beyond programming languages. *IEEE Computer,* 16, 57–69.

Singer, A., Hindus, D., Stifelman, L., and White, S. (1999). Tangible progress: Less is more in Somewire audio spaces. *Proceedings of the CHI'99 Conference on Human Factors in Computing Systems,* 104–111.

Suzuki, H., and Kato, H. (1993). AlgoBlock: A tangible programming language, a tool for collaborative learning. *Proceedings of 4th European Logo Conference,* 297–303.

Ullmer, B., Ishii, H., and Glas, D. (1998). mediaBlocks: Physical containers, transports, and controls for online media. *Computer Graphics (Proceedings of SIGGRAPH'98),* 379–386.

Ullmer, B., and Ishii, H. (2000). Emerging frameworks for tangible user interfaces. *IBM Systems Journal,* 39, 3–4, 915–931.

Underkoffler, J., and Ishii, H. (1999a). Urp: A luminous-tangible workbench for urban planning and design. *Proceedings of the CHI'99 Conference on Human Factors in Computing Systems,* 386–393.

Underkoffler, J., Ullmer, B., and Ishii, H. (1999b). Emancipated pixels: Real-world graphics in the luminous room. *Computer Graphics (Proceedings of SIGGRAPH'99),* 385–392.

Weiser, M. (1991). The computer for the 21st century. *Scientific American,* 265, 3, 94–104.

Wellner, P. (1993). Interacting with paper on the digital desk. *Communications of the ACM,* 86–96.

Wisneski, C., Ishii, H., Dahley, A., Gorbet, M., Brave, S., Ullmer, B., and Yarin, P. (1998). Ambient displays: Turning architectural space into an interface between people and digital information. *Proceedings of International Workshop on Cooperative Buildings (CoBuild '98),* 22–32. Darmstadt: Springer Press.

Zhang, J. (1997). The nature of external representations in problem solving. *Cognitive Science,* 21, 2, 179–217.

PART VII

HCI and Society

Learner-Centered Design: Reflections and New Directions

Chris Quintana
Andrew Carra
Joseph Krajcik
Elliot Soloway

27.1 Introduction

As computers became more powerful and prevalent in the 1980s, the computing community began to realize that the issue of computer usability was becoming more important. No longer was computer use restricted to scientists and other researchers who would persevere through the difficult and arcane computer systems of the day. Computers had begun to enter the home and school, and it was recognized that if computers were to be used successfully by a wider audience, then computer system designers would have to pay more attention to the needs of the computer user. Scientists and engineers would endure computer systems that were difficult to use in order to harness the available computing power for their professional work, but the average consumer would not. Thus, the field of human-computer interaction (HCI) began to explore computer usability and the notion of user-centered design (UCD) (Norman and Draper 1986).

Since then, HCI researchers and practitioners have made many advances toward improving computer usability. In the 2000s, the HCI community is being faced with new challenges. Soloway et al. (1994) identified one challenge for the HCI community that centers around the use of computers to "support individuals and groups of individuals in developing expertise in their professions, in developing richer and deeper understandings of content and practices." This is a key challenge. As computing power and computer ubiquity continue to increase, many environments include a range of computer technologies for the work practices employed in those environments. Thus, one new challenge for HCI is to move beyond usability issues and begin exploring how to design computer systems that support people who are developing expertise in new and unknown work practices. The challenge of using computers to "make people smarter" entails a different design perspective, an evolving *learner-centered design* (LCD) perspective that considers the needs of learners (Soloway et al. 1994).

The notion of designing computer tools centered on the needs of learners has become more popular in recent years, and there are many researchers exploring learner-centered design (see special issues of *Communications of the ACM:* Communications of the ACM 1996a, 1996b). However, while LCD methods are being developed, much learner-centered design is still performed in an ad hoc fashion. In order to continue on the path toward meeting the goals of learner-centered design, more work is needed from the HCI community to develop better design methods, techniques, and examples that can be used by software designers to build learner-centered software.

Seven years after the initial LCD article in Soloway et al. (1994), we now review the effort and take stock to see where LCD has been and where it is going. Specifically, we cover the following in this chapter.

- First, we want to put forth a more detailed description of learner-centered design. Although, many researchers have intuitive definitions of LCD, we want to detail a more structured definition for the community to consider.

- Second, we want to discuss the challenges and open questions involved in learner-centered design. Given traditional HCI design methods, we will discuss what design issues still need to be considered for LCD and identify some open issues in current LCD work in order to lay out new challenges and future research directions for the HCI community to address.

Note that we focus this discussion on issues surrounding software for learners. There are other issues pertaining to supporting materials and the learning environment in which the software will be used. These issues are certainly important, and we briefly touch on them throughout the chapter. However, we focus more on LCD open issues for the HCI community.

27.2 An Overview of Learner-Centered Design

We begin by outlining a more structured definition of learner-centered design. Learner-centered tools address the needs of learners: people who are novices in a given work practice. Essentially, the goal of LCD is to develop tools that mediate the development of new understanding in learners of an unknown work practice. Therefore, learner-centered tools address the conceptual distance that lies between the audience of learners and the work practice in which they are engaged. By developing *scaffolding strategies* informed by constructivist learning theories, a learner-centered tool incorporates support that allows a learner to participate in a new work practice to develop an understanding of the practice.

Given this high-level overview, let us now describe learner-centered design in more detail by considering three different dimensions for our definition.

1. The audience addressed by LCD, specifically, the audience of learners
2. The central design problem being addressed by LCD
3. The underlying approach taken by LCD to address the central design problem

---

27.2.1 Audience: Who Are "Learners"?

As with any design approach, we need to describe the target audience and the activity the target audience is performing. The audience of learners we describe includes novices in some given work practice who are trying to develop a better understanding of that practice. Note that this differs from traditional user-centered design, in which tool usability and "ease-of use" are the central tenets. Any learning that occurs in user-centered tools involves learning the tool or system itself. In learner-centered design, learners are trying to learn a new work practice in addition to the tool or system they are working with. By a "work practice" we meant the following:

> *Work practice:* The responsibilities, tasks, tools, artifacts, terminology, knowledge, and relationships involved in a given work activity.

While the central goal of LCD is to help a learner learn new work, this should not imply that learners are restricted to being students in school. Learning new work can occur at any point in life. While our specific research focuses on designing tools for students in middle school and high school, we do not limit the definition of learners to such an age group. Learners can be students learning new tasks and practices in school, such as beginning business students learning the work of financial analysis. But learners can also be adults in the workforce, such as a new corporate work hire learning her new company's internal consulting practices during a corporate orientation.

In traditional user-centered design, computer users are considered to have more expertise in the target work practice. These users simply need computer tools that help them perform their work easily and efficiently (Mayhew 1999). In contrast, learners are novices in the target work practice and thus need tools that address their lack of expertise in the work and support them in engaging in the new work practice (Figure 27.1). More specifically, we can characterize learners as having the following characteristics (Soloway and Pryor 1996).

> *Learners do not possess a significant amount of expertise in the work practice.*
> Learners (for example, the business student or the new consultant) do not share an understanding of the activities, terminology, and so forth of the work practice with their professional counterparts (like the financial analyst or the corporate manager). More specifically, learners have an incomplete or naive mental model of the work

Lack of Work Knowledge

FIGURE 27.1 Primary learner characteristic

they are trying to perform. It may be the case that learners have an "empty" model of the work practice, not having any idea about what is involved in the work. It may also be the case (and more often than not) that learners have some model of the work practice, albeit a misunderstood or incorrect work model. Regardless, learner-centered tools need to take this lack of expertise into consideration and address the corresponding learner needs. This way, learners can engage in the work to form a more correct and appropriate model of the work practice that they are engaging in.

Learners are heterogeneous. Essentially, user-centered design takes into consideration a homogenous population consisting of a prototypical user due to the fact that users share a common work culture. However, learners do not necessarily share a common culture nor a common body of expertise in the work practice. Thus, learner-centered tools need to consider the wide range of diversity in background, development, gender, age, and learning styles in the learner population.

Learners are not always highly motivated to pursue a new work practice. Experts in the work practice, by the nature of their involvement with their work (professions, labors of love) have an intrinsic motivation that many learners may lack. Furthermore, the motivation of learners further suffers from the obstacles that they face in trying to perform the new work (Hogan et al. 2000). Learners who might have some motivation to learn new work may lose that motivation because of the complexity of the new work. Thus, learner-centered tools need to consider the lack of motivation and incorporate motivational support for learners.

Learners' understanding grows as they engage in and continue to engage in a new work practice. User-centered tools help experts engage in their work easily and do not need to change significantly since work experts are not necessarily learning about their work through the tools. Learners, however, will change as they gain new expertise in the work practice. Thus, learner-centered tools (that is, the learner's window on the work practice) need to grow and change as the learner does.

27.2.2 LCD Problem: The Conceptual Gap between Learner and Work

Given a description of the target population for learner-centered design, we now turn to the next dimension in our definition: the conceptual problem being addressed by LCD. In traditional user-centered design, the central problem being addressed is the conceptual gap between the user and the tool—that is, the gulfs of execution and evaluation (Norman 1986). We cannot ignore these gulfs in LCD, since learners certainly need to be able to use the learner-centered tools designed for them. However, in LCD, the central problem is not the conceptual gap between user and tool. Rather, the central problem is the conceptual gap—a gulf of *expertise*—between the learner and the model of expertise embodied by an expert in the work practice (Figure 27.2).

Lave and Wenger (1991) state that learning and knowledge mastery require that newcomers to the work practice move toward full participation in the practices of the work community. We can describe a work expert as one who can fully participate in

FIGURE 27.2   Conceptual gap and underlying theory for LCD

the work practice. If we consider the learner to be the "newcomer" in the work practice, then the goal for the learner is to change and grow so that they can fully participate in the work. This movement occurs over the gulf of expertise—that is, over the conceptual gap that lies between the newcomer to the community of practice and the full participant in that community of practice.

For a learner to be able to participate in some work practice, the learner needs to understand what kind of activities are in the practice, facts about the practice, knowledge needed to complete the work activities, and so forth. In other words, the learner needs to develop a correct and appropriate conceptual model of the work involved. Thus, we can say that the "size" of the gulf of expertise describes how far a learner is from understanding the work practice. Specifically, the size of the gulf of expertise is proportional to the amount of conceptual change needed in the learner's model of the work practice so that they can fully participate with other experts in the work community.

If we describe the central LCD problem as one of helping learners develop into experts in a work practice, we can describe the central task for LCD: designing tools that support learners in moving across the gulf of expertise. In order to see how to develop such tools, we now move to the third and final dimension of our overall LCD description.

27.2.3 Bridging the Learner-Centered Conceptual Gap: Designing for Learners

Traditional user-centered design is concerned with having users develop an understanding of the tool they are using. As we have now seen, learner-centered design is concerned with mediating the movement of a learner across the gulf of expertise to develop a correct conceptual model of a target work practice. As part of an overall learning environment, learner-centered tools can support the learner in doing new work through the use of *scaffolding*. Scaffolds are software features that support the mindful performance of a given task or activity by someone who is a novice in that task or activity. However, we need an underlying theory to inform the design of scaffolding in learner-centered tools.

In traditional user-centered design, Norman's "theory of action" informed the design of usable tools (Norman 1986). Correspondingly, for LCD, we need a theory that helps us understand the notion of "gaining expertise" so that we can develop learner-centered design principles. For this, we consider the design implications of *constructivist* and *social constructivist* learning theories to help us describe the nature of expertise that we are considering and provide a model to help learners bridge the gulf of expertise (Soloway et al. 1994, 1996).

27.2.3.1 Constructivist Learning Theory

Over the past 15 years, the constructivist theory of learning (Piaget 1954; Papert 1993) has increasingly gained favor in education. The central notion is that understanding and learning involve active, constructive, generative processes. The constructivist approach recognizes that learning is not a simple, passive process of transferring information from expert to novice. Rather, learning is an active process, employing a "learning by doing" approach where the learner must cognitively manipulate the material they are learning in order to create cognitive links from the new material to their own prior knowledge.

A tenet of the constructivist approach is that learning occurs from *active and mindful engagement* in a task. However, many work tasks may be too complex for novice learners. Learners need tools that make complex tasks accessible to them, but in a way that does not oversimplify the task to a point where it is contrived. This way, learners can begin to develop a "foothold" on the work, giving them entry into the work practice.

Let us ground this with a small example. One example of making complex tasks accessible is seen in Model-It, a system dynamics modeling tool for science students (Soloway et al. 1996). Students use Model-It to build models of complex systems, such as ecosystems, in order to explore scenarios and explain the behavior of such complex systems. A complex task in building system models is defining how different factors in the model relate to each other. For example, in an air quality model, students may want to relate car exhaust, pollution levels, wind speed, and citizens' health. Professional modeling programs may require relationships to be defined by writing differential equations, a task much too difficult for students. Instead of using differential equations, Model-It makes relationship definition accessible through a relationship editor, which allows students to define quantitative relationships by *building qualitative sentences* that describe the relationship (Figure 27.3).

In Figure 27.3, students building an air quality model describe how pollution and health are related. By filling in the sentence, students define the relationship by saying "as pollution increases, people's health decreases." When describing how health decreases, students are presented with qualitative choices (a little, more and more, the same, a lot) that they understand but that are still useful for defining a working model. Students still have to think about the relationships in the model that they are building. However, rather than oversimplifying the task, learners can now build relationships using a tool that is simpler (certainly simpler than writing differential equations), but that still requires them to reflect on how they believe factors in their model are related.

27.2.3.2 Social Constructivist Learning Theory

Learning does not occur in a vacuum; rather, learning must occur in some context. As Brown et al. (1989) state, "Knowledge is . . . in part a product of the activity, context, and culture in which it is developed and used." These researchers see knowledge as being contextualized, meaning that learners must build their knowledge within a

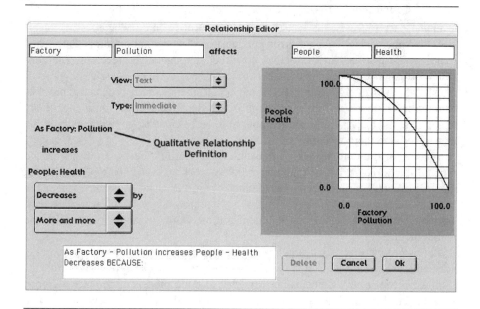

FIGURE 27.3   Model-It relationship editor

community of peers and experts. Thus, gaining expertise involves participating in the context of the professional culture in order to understand the common practices, languages, tools, and values of a professional culture.

A tenet of the social constructivist approach is that learning (that is, enculturation) occurs when learners work within a context that allows them to see and understand the professional work culture. Thus, learner-centered tools should embody the work culture in a manner that the learner can understand. In other words, tools should conceptualize (or visualize) professional work practices in such a way that the learner can engage in and understand the activities, language, terms, and so forth that comprise the new work practice.

Examples of "work process visualization" are found in Symphony (Figure 27.4), a scaffolded integrated tool environment that integrates a range of data collection, visualization, and modeling tools within a framework for conducting scientific investigations (Quintana et al. 1999). Symphony incorporates a variety of process maps to visualize both the range of possible activities that make up a science investigation and the procedures for carrying out certain science activities. Figure 27.4 shows the Symphony main screen with two process maps visible. First, on the left is the central *process wheel* that illustrates to students the space of activities involved in a science investigation. Students can survey the process wheel in order to begin building a plan for their investigation. By showing students the space of possible activities, students can begin to see and understand what kinds of activities comprise the work of science inquiry.

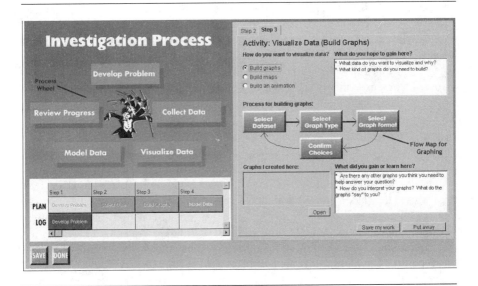

FIGURE 27.4   Symphony process maps

Second, on the right of Figure 27.4 is a directed *flow map* that describes the procedure for performing certain science activities. The flow map shown in Figure 27.4 specifically illustrates the procedure for building a graph. Students step through the flow diagram to build a graph by pressing the buttons in the map, which in turn launch the appropriate portion of the graphing tool. Not only does the flow map make the graph-building task accessible to the student, it also explicitly presents the steps of the process so that the student can internalize the work involved in graph-building and eventually build graphs without needing the flow map.

27.2.3.3 Ramifications of Learning Theory for Design

Given these learning theories, what are the ramifications for the design of learner-centered tools? We can now say that gaining expertise in a new work practice involves *actively engaging in authentic activities* from the work practice. Learning needs to be an active process, one where learners ask questions, collect and organize information, and assess their work, all by engaging in activities from the given work practice. By doing so, learners can begin to develop an understanding of the work practice.

If learners are to participate in the new work practice, they need to have access to and participate in activities similar to those of the work experts. Since learners lack an understanding of the work practice, they will need additional support (scaffolding) to help them perform the new work activity (such as our previous two small scaffolding examples). Of course, learners cannot use the same tools that work experts use because of the difference in their levels of expertise. Thus a learner-centered designer must design tools modeled on expert tools but simplified to be appropriate for learners. These tools should allow learners to participate in activities similar to those of work experts and allow construction of artifacts used in the work practice (Belamy 1996). As learners gain expertise in the work, the scaffolding can "fade" or disappear, leaving the learner with a tool that is more like those used by work experts.

Just as Norman's "theory of action" and other cognitive theory informs the development of heuristics for building user-centered tools, we are now beginning to distill LCD heuristics from constructivist and social constructivist theories. For example, our previous two scaffolding examples embody two LCD heuristics: make complex tasks accessible and visualize the space of possible activities. Other examples of LCD heuristics include (1) show real world representations, (2) support metacognition and reflection (Schoenfeld 1987), (3) provide multiple representations, design task-oriented interfaces, and (4) design task-oriented interfaces, and so on (Soloway et al. 1996; Squires and Preece 1999). As more learner-centered tools are being developed, a wider range of LCD heuristics and scaffolding strategies are coming to light (Squires and Preece (1999) present more LCD heuristics and a review of socio-constructivist principles in software design).

The use of constructivist and social constructivist theories in learner-centered design differs from the past efforts to design software tools for learning. Computer-aided instruction (CAI) (based on behaviorist principles) and intelligent-tutoring systems (ITS) (based on information processing psychology) have attempted to package educational components that can train learners. There are certainly successful CAI and ITS systems. However, many CAI systems use a more information-transfer, passive model of learning. And ITS approaches can be less useful in loosely structured, wide-ranging work practices. While useful in more constrained fields like geometry and algebra, ITS tools can be difficult to implement for less constrained work activity. Certainly there are more aspects of CAI and ITS that can be used for learner-centered tools. The key is that learner-centered tools should scaffold active participation by the learner in new work practices of all kinds.

27.2.3.4 LCD Design Models and Roles

We end this section by describing the range of design models and design roles involved in LCD software development (Figure 27.5). In traditional user-centered design, the end product designed by a design team is called the *system image*. The goal then for a LCD team is to design a system image that a learner can use to engage in the new work practice. As we have seen in our heuristic examples, one way to support learners is to present work activities and terminology in the system image. Therefore, the design team needs to have a detailed understanding of the work practice that they are supporting with the tool. In other words, designers need to have a good *work model*—that is, an articulation of the target work practice and the expertise needed to engage in the practice.

A good work model alone, however, will not suffice for the learner-centered tool. Because the learner is a novice, the work model cannot be presented as it is to the learner because he or she does not understand the work. Rather, the design team needs to conceptualize the work model to the learner in a manner that the learner can understand. Thus, the design team also needs an *educational model* that describes how the work model should be conceptualized to best facilitate the learner's construction of new understanding. So the work and educational models should be used to construct a system image that mediates the development of the learner.

Because of these conceptual models, we need a variety of roles for the LCD process. The learner-centered design team needs *work experts* (such as work professionals) to analyze and articulate the work practice and create a good work model. The LCD team also needs *educational experts* (such as teachers and educational researchers) to articulate ways of communicating with learners and guide them in making the conceptual shift from learner to expert. In our design experience, our educational experts have included both education students and faculty along with public school teachers. We have found it essential to have the researchers' theoretical educational information coupled with the schoolteacher's advice on more "real world" issues, such as how their students learn and how we can design and implement software tools within the context of classrooms.

In the end, the development of work models and educational models are vital. The input made by the work and educational experts is needed early in the design process to assist the designer, who is then responsible for both designing a usable system and realizing the contributions of the work and educational experts.

We end our description of learner-centered design by summarizing the LCD definition that we have described (Table 27.1). Given the description of learner-centered design, we now move to describing some specific issues involved in actually carrying out LCD and detail some open research areas that need to be addressed by the HCI community.

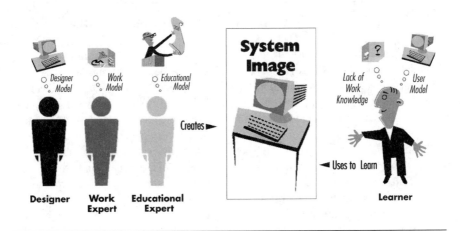

FIGURE 27.5   Conceptual models and roles in LCD

TABLE 27.1 Summarizing the Description of Learner-Centered Design

Dimensions	Learner-Centered Design
Target Audience	Learners: Novices in some work practice
Central Goal	Designing tools that support learners in developing a better understanding of a new work practice
Conceptual Gap to Address	Gulf of expertise between learner and work practice (without ignoring the user-centered gulfs between learner and tool)
Theoretical Approach to Bridging the Conceptual Gap	Using theories of learning: Looking at constructivist and social constructivist theories of how people learn
Tool Requirements	Learner-centered tools need to do the following. ▪ Support learners in engaging and participating in new work practices, by incorporating work-related scaffolding in the tool ▪ Support a diverse audience that considers diverse expertise levels, learning styles, age and gender differences, and so on. ▪ Change and "fade" the scaffolding as a learner's conceptual model of the work changes to one more consistent with that of an expert
Design Implications	Design tools that support learners in actively performing authentic tasks from a work practice and that gradually expose learners to the culture (tools, tasks, and language) of the work practice

27.3 Open Issues in Designing Learner-Centered Tools

Given our description of learner-centered design, we now focus on design issues for LCD. In this section, we will review traditional software design activities and describe issues that need to be addressed within each design phase for learner-centered design. We will see that engaging in learner-centered design raises some questions that still need to be addressed if we are to produce a more concrete methodology for LCD.

Any design process, whether it be building architecture, experimental design, or graphic design, involves the same high-level phases: analysis, synthesis, and evaluation (Lawson 1990). Software design—user-centered or learner-centered—is no different. Software design must employ an iterative design process incorporating specific methods for these phases. While there are different models for software design—for example, the spiral model (Boehm 1988), the star model (Hartson and Hix 1989), the usability engineering lifecycle (Mayhew 1999), we can distill the following high-level design phases for discussion.

- *Task or work analysis:* Analyzing and understanding the work activities that will be supported by the software.

- *Requirements specification:* Determining the functional requirements for the software.

- *Design:* Determining the conceptual strategies to carry out the requirements and determining the physical instantiations of these strategies in software.

- *Evaluation:* Determining the successes and failures of the software design.

While there are many design methods employed in each of these phases for designing user-centered software, there are still questions about what kinds of methods to use in these phases for learner-centered design. Traditional software development techniques are aimed at building usable software. Certainly, many of these techniques can be used in a LCD process to help develop usable LCD tools. However, we also need design methods specific to LCD. We need techniques that will help us uncover the complexities learners will face as they try to engage in the designated work practice. We also need ways of identifying and evaluating the scaffolding strategies that can be used to address the complexities that learners face.

Given our work and the work of other researchers designing learner-centered tools, we are reflecting on our various design experiences to uncover and address the resulting challenges for LCD. Here, we briefly review the different high-level software design phases with respect to LCD and discuss various open issues that arise during each phase.

27.3.1 Issues in Learner-Centered Work and Task Analysis

For LCD, work analysis is paramount because the focus of LCD is to design tools that support participation in a new work practice. Thus, design teams must also have a thorough and detailed understanding of the work practice so they can design appropriate support in the tool for the learner. While the goal is not necessarily to reproduce the work practice for the learner (although in some cases, such an approach may work as in some simulation programs), the design team does need to conceptualize the work practice in a manner that the learner can understand. Even such a conceptualization requires a thorough analysis and understanding of the work practice.

The HCI community is exploring a variety of more expansive work analysis techniques. There are lower-level task analysis such as GOMS (John and Kieras 1994) and cognitive task analysis (Lesgold et al. 1986). There are also a myriad of higher-level analysis methods, including: the ActionWorkflow model (Medina-Mora et al. 1992), scenarios (Carroll 1995), contextual analysis (Beyer and Holtzblatt 1999), process-space analysis (Fitzpatrick and Welsh 1995; Quintana et al. 1999), and activity theory (Leont'ev 1974; Nardi 1992).

Methods for analyzing work are not just needed for learner-centered design but for a variety of design problems in HCI. However, LCD especially needs good formal methods for analyzing a work practice to help designers fully understand the practice they are helping learners engage in. Specifically, an effective work analysis method for LCD should do the following.

- Explicitly represent the various components (tasks, terms, artifacts, etc.) that make up the work practice. Process space analysis, activity theory, scenarios, and contextual analysis can help us analyze and articulate the overall structure and components of a work practice.

- Explicitly represent the relationships between the work components and the members of the work community. The ActionWorkflow model and other workflow models can help us analyze the flow of information between the different roles in a work practice.

- Explicitly represent the implicit knowledge that experts have "in their heads" to do their work. Lower-level task analysis methods like GOMS and cognitive task analysis can help us identify the "hidden" cognitive knowledge needed to perform different tasks in the work practice.

We find that to analyze work practices in the detail necessary for LCD, we need a range of methods, each addressing a portion of our work analysis requirements. This is no surprise; if we are trying to fully understand a complex work practice, then the necessary analysis should be expected to be complex.

The question for HCI researchers, then, is how can we assemble a variety of these methods into a viable, single work analysis model that gives the learner-centered design team all of the explicit information needed to fully understand the target work practice? Also, can we devise such a wide-ranging model that can still be used in a timely manner within the learner-centered design process? While in reality, we may incorporate bits and pieces from different analysis methods to analyze work, we need to explore a single overriding work analysis model. We need to articulate a common model and a common vocabulary for analyzing a work practice with an eye toward the goals and requirements of learner-centered design.

As a final question, we should also consider the situations in which work analysis may not be as fruitful as we might think for the software design. In our experience, our analysis of working scientists has been important for us in designing science tools for learners (Quintana et al. 1999). However, some work practices may be more abstract and less observable than others and it is not as easy to analyze and gather information. While some sort of task or work analysis seems intuitively necessary, it is still a question as to whether analyzing any work practice will always yield useful results for a LCD team.

27.3.2 Issues in Learner-Centered Requirements Specification

In traditional UCD, software requirements define what functions the software needs to have in order to help the user complete their work efficiently. For LCD, we need to consider another type of software requirement. Specifically, we consider a "learner-centered requirement" to be an identified area where a learner needs support to engage in certain work activity. In terms of determining learner-centered system requirements, LCD teams still need guides and methods to aid them with determining the following.

- Can the learner engage in the activity? The educational experts on the LCD team need to gauge the extent to which the learner can or cannot engage in the activity.

- Why does a learner need support to engage in the activity? The educational experts should articulate the stumbling blocks for the learner and the kind of knowledge needed for the learner to engage in the activity (in other words, what kind of knowledge does the learner lack?).

- What kind of possible support could be useful for the learner to engage in the activity? The educational experts need to outline some general, high-level ways that the learner could be supported to engage in the activity.

This rather informal description of what kind of information goes into a learner-centered requirement highlights the problem with requirements specification for LCD—namely, what exactly is the information needed to fully define a learner support need? There is still a lack of formal requirement definitions for LCD and methods for determining them. More work is needed to define learner-centered requirements in a more methodical fashion.

27.3.3 Issues in Learner-Centered Software Design

Preece et al. (1994) describe two major phases for software design. First, there is the conceptual design phase where the designers determine the conceptual overview and strategies for addressing the software requirements. Second, there is the physical design phases where the designers determine the physical instantiations of the conceptual strategies in software.

For LCD, these design phases involve the following work. Conceptual design involves determining the *conceptual scaffolding strategies* that will be used to address individual learner-centered support requirements. Physical design involves implementing the conceptual scaffolding strategies in software in a way that learners can understand and perform the supported activity.

Conceptual and physical design are still intuitive activities informed by the prior experience of designers. This is true with UCD and LCD. However, while there are good examples of user-centered software, the corpus of good, rationalized, and evaluated design examples for LCD is still sparse (although growing). Learner-centered designers need design guides and guidelines for developing effective scaffolding strategies that address the following issues.

What kind of scaffolding can address the diversity of learners? Different aspects of the diverse learner audience need to be addressed in learner-centered tools. For example, learners' different learning styles need to be addressed. There is work focusing on identifying different learning styles and "intelligences" (for example, linguistic, spatial, logical-mathematical intelligences [Gardner 1993]. However, we need further research to determine how to design scaffolding strategies that address learners exhibiting different learning styles. Similarly, we need more work that considers the differences in age groups to design effective software for "big" learners (grown-ups) and "small" learners (kids). Just as we would like scaffolding that addresses the diversity of learning styles, we also need research into the kinds of scaffolding needed to support learners in a variety of age groups.

What kind of scaffolding can address motivation? Along with addressing learner diversity, we need much more research into "motivational scaffolding." That is, scaffolding strategies that can keep the learner focused on their task and motivated in their work. There are promising areas of research along these lines. Reeves and Nass (1996) study how people personally interact with computers to better understand how computers can offer people advice in nonthreatening ways. Picard (1997) studies how computers can address the fear and frustration that many computer users can exhibit when using technology.

These researchers explore motivation in a computing context, but there is research in other fields outside computing, such as psychology, that can be useful for LCD. For example, Csikszentmihalyi (1990) studies the creative process and the "flow consciousness"—the state of concentration and enjoyment that leads to "optimal experience." Research in psychology, education, creativity, and even game design can provide other fruitful avenues to explore supporting motivation. Usage and expansion of all areas of motivation research can be useful for LCD to determine strategies that support the creative process and address the anxiety and lack of motivation learners exhibit when attempting to engage in new, complex work.

What is the best way to remove scaffolding? In LCD, there arises an issue that does not necessarily need to be addressed in traditional UCD. Namely, how is the scaffolding removed or faded when it is no longer needed by the learner? There is work that explores issues involved with fading scaffolding (Jackson et al. 1998) and work on re-introducing complex functionality that was removed earlier (Carroll and Carrithers 1984). However, there are still many open questions pertaining to the fading of scaffolding. Who should fade the scaffold: the learner, the teacher or work expert, the system, or a combination of the three? What is the mechanism for fading scaffolds: learner preferences or automatic system control? How much of the scaffold should fade: Should a scaffold fade completely or progressively in different levels?

How can designers determine what scaffolding to include, and not include, *in the tool?* Learner-centered software is part of an overall context where learning takes place. Therefore, some of the support that is needed by the learner might be better provided by the teacher or work expert who might be available in the work context. Determining what *not* to scaffold in software is a difficult question in itself being addressed by some LCD researchers (for example, Smith and Reiser's [1998] view of classroom-centered design).

How can scaffolding frameworks and libraries be developed? Designers need access to good design information and scaffolding examples. To aid in the design of LCD software and to avoid wasting effort reproducing prior work, we anticipate the creation of frameworks and libraries of learner-centered scaffolding components. Many groups are researching the development of such learner-centered software components including the *Educational Object Economy* project and the *Educational Software Components of Tomorrow* project (see References for Web sites). Such projects need to continue to help designers make their ideas for LCD "widgets" and techniques more widely available to the design community.

What are the differences between user-centered and learner-centered strategies? Learner-centered tools need to be usable, so a LCD team certainly needs to keep good usability principles in mind when designing learner-centered software. After all, an unusable tool will not be of any benefit to a learner. However, there is a question as to when a learner-centered tool may be too user-centered.

LCD constructivist principles state that in order for learners to begin developing work practice expertise, they must actively and mindfully complete work tasks. UCD focuses on efficiency, helping users complete work tasks easily. However, if a learner-centered tool is too user-centered, the tool may make it too easy for the learner to complete his or her tasks. In this case, the learner may not be forced to apply the cognitive effort needed to mindfully complete the work tasks and, in turn, learn the work practice. It would be helpful to LCD designers to identify design strategies that are good user-centered techniques but not good learner-centered techniques. For example, consider software "wizards." Wizards are good user-centered techniques because they help users get a task done easily. But wizards are not good learner-centered techniques because they do too much work for the learner without requiring significant thought on the task (the wizard is essentially completing the task) (Cooper 1995). So a wizard would probably not support the learner in learning the task.

Thus, one area of future work needs to involve helping designers straddle this fine line between "user-centeredness" and "learner-centeredness." There is some work exploring the tightrope between tool efficiency and mindful work (Rappin et al. 1997; Sedighian et al. 2001). Designers need to better understand how to design usable tools that still allow learners to actively engage in the work practice without the system being so usable that the system is doing too much of the work task for the learner.

27.3.4 Issues in Learner-Centered Software Evaluation

In traditional UCD, designers focus on evaluating tool use and consider evaluation criteria such as error rates with the tool, efficiency measures, and so on. However, software evaluation for LCD needs to consider different approaches. LCD teams need to evaluate individual scaffolds and scaffolding strategies plus the overall effectiveness of the software to see how well a learner understands the work practice after using the software. Thus, LCD needs evaluation methods and criteria that evaluate the different cognitive effects resulting from technology use (Salomon et al. 1991).

- "Effects of" technology: the changes in the learner's understanding of the work practice (or the "cognitive residue") after learners have used the software. By evaluating these "global effects" of technology, we analyze the effectiveness of the learner-centered software as a whole.
- "Effects with" technology: the changes in performance on the work activity that learners display as they use the software. By evaluating these "local effects" of technology, we analyze how learners use the different scaffolds in the software.

Aside from exploring the specific evaluation targets and criteria for a learner-centered tool, another challenge that arises is determining what approach to take in evaluating the software: Do we perform quantitative assessment, qualitative assessment, or a combination of the two? Many LCD researchers have encountered obstacles in carrying out more traditional, controlled studies of a learner-centered tool given the long-term use of the software within a more "real-world" setting (such as a classroom). While a more controlled, laboratory study might be possible, questions arise whether the results generalize when the software use moves from the lab to the actual context of use (Chi 1997). Such problems are faced not just by the LCD community but by the greater HCI community studying software in the context of use. Evaluation methods and metrics that can make objective evaluations of observational data are needed and can be beneficial for many software designers, learner-centered and otherwise.

27.4 Conclusion

Learner-centered design is a complex enterprise that entails a range of different challenges, many of which we have summarized in this chapter. LCD teams need to study wide-ranging work practices. LCD tools need to be designed for a diverse audience that will change and grow—necessitating that the tools also change along the way. LCD teams need to incorporate the viewpoints and expertise of work experts, HCI experts, teachers, and educators. And LCD tools need to be evaluated not just in terms of work efficiency and ease-of-use but in terms of the changes in work understanding that have been mediated in the user of the tool.

There are many other issues to consider for learner-centered design that are beyond the scope of this chapter. Here, we have primarily focused on a technology-centric presentation of learner-centered design. However, there are other important issues to consider concerning the learning context and the learning environment in which a learner-centered tool will be used. For example, in a classroom setting, the design of the curriculum and other supporting materials will not only impact the use of the software but also the design of the software. Similarly, as we alluded earlier, the role of the teacher (if present) in the learning environment will also impact the software design. These are issues that are external to the actual software but that must also be considered because of their impact on the software design. Thus, LCD must also take into consideration the makeup of the learning environment, the role of teacher or other work experts in the environment, and the role of external materials that are used with the technology.

Many of the research directions that we have outlined here are not unique to learner-centered design. We are all aware of the ongoing shifts in HCI research: from tasks to context and practice; from desktop computers to ubiquitous computing in homes, schools, and the workplace; from tools for highly specified user audiences to tools for diverse, wide-ranging user audiences. All of these areas of HCI research impact learner-centered design. By better specifying LCD and identifying the challenges involved therein, we hope to continue to push the HCI agenda and set a wide-ranging research agenda to fully realize the potential of computing technology to educate learners in all walks of life into the twenty-first century.

Acknowledgments

This material is based on work supported by the National Science Foundation under NSF REC 9980055. Any opinions, findings, and conclusions or recommendations expressed in this material are those of the author(s) and do not necessarily reflect the views of the National Science Foundation.

References

Belamy, R.K.E. (1996). Designing educational technology: Computer-mediated change. In B.A. Nardi (Ed.), *Context and Consciousness: Activity Theory and Human-Computer Interaction.* Cambridge, MA: MIT Press.

Beyer, H., and Holtzblatt, K. (1999). Contextual design. *Interactions,* 6, 1.

Boehm, B.W. (1988). A spiral model of software development and enhancement. *IEEE Computer,* 21, 2, 61–72.

Brown, J.S., Collins, A., and Duguid, P. (1989). Situated cognition and the culture of learning. *Educational Researcher,* 18, 32–42.

Carroll, J.M. (1995). Introduction: The scenario perspective on system development. In J.M. Carroll (Ed.), *Scenario-Based Design: Envisioning Work and Technology in System Development.* New York: John Wiley & Sons, Inc.

Carroll, J.M., and Carrithers, C. (1984). Training wheels in a user interface. *Communications of the ACM,* 27, 8, 800–806.

Chi, M.T.H. (1997). Quantifying qualitative analyses of verbal data: A practical guide, *The Journal of the Learning Sciences,* 6, 3, 271–315.

Communications of the ACM. (1996). 39, 4, 24–49.

Communications of the ACM. (1996). 39, 8, 83–109.

Cooper, A. (1995). *About face: The essentials of user interface design.* Foster City, CA: IDG Books Worldwide.

Csikszentmihalyi, M. (1990). *Flow: The psychology of optimal experience.* New York: Harper Perennial Press.

Educational Object Economy (EOE) Web site: http://www.eoe.org.

Educational Software Components of Tomorrow (ESCOT) Web site: http://www.escot.org.

Fitzpatrick, G., and Welsh, J. (1995). Process support: Inflexible imposition or chaotic composition. *Interacting with Computers,* 7, 2.

Gardner, H. (1993). *Multiple intelligences: The theory in practice.* New York: Basic Books.

Hartson, H.R., and Hix, D. (1989). Human-computer interface development: Concepts and systems for its management. *ACM Computing Surveys,* 21, 1, 5–92.

Hogan, K., Nastasi, B.K., and Pressley, M. (2000). Discourse patterns and collaborative scientific reasoning in peer and teacher-guided discussions. *Cognition and Instruction,* 17, 4, 379–432.

Jackson, S.L., Krajcik, J., and Soloway, E. (1998). The design of guided learner-adaptable scaffolding in interactive learning environments. *Human Factors in Computing Systems: CHI'98 Conference Proceedings.* Reading, MA: Addison-Wesley.

John, B.E., and Kieras, D.E. (1994). The GOMS family of analysis techniques: Tools for design and evaluation. *ACM Transactions on Computer-Human Interaction,* 3, 4 (Dec. 1996), 287–319.

Lave, J., and Wenger, E. (1991). *Situated learning: Legitimate peripheral participation.* Cambridge, UK: Cambridge University Press.

Lawson, B. (1990). *How designers think.* London; Boston: Butterworth Architecture.

Leont'ev, A. (1974). The problem of activity in psychology. *Soviet Psychology,* 13, 2, 4–33.

Lesgold, A. (1986). *Guide to cognitive task analysis.* University of Pittsburgh Learning Research and Development Center.

Mayhew, D.J. (1999). *The usability engineering lifecycle.* San Francisco, CA: Morgan Kaufman Press.

Medina-Mora, R., Winograd, T., Flores, R., and Flores, F. (1992). The action workflow approach to workflow management technology. *Proceedings of CSCW '92,* 281–288. New York: ACM Press.

Nardi, B.A. (1992). Studying context: A comparison of activity theory, situated action models, and distributed cognition. *Proceedings of the East-West Conference on Human-Computer Interaction,* 352–359.

Norman, D.A. (1986). Cognitive engineering. In D.A. Norman and S.W. Draper (Eds.), *User Centered System Design.* Hillsdale, NJ: Lawrence Erlbaum Associates.

Norman, D.A., and Draper, S.W. (Eds.). (1986). *User Centered System Design.* Hillsdale, NJ: Lawrence Erlbaum Associates.

Papert, S. (1993). *The children's machine: Rethinking school in the age of the computer.* New York: Basic Books.

Piaget, J. (1954). *The construction of reality in the child.* New York: Basic Books.

Picard, R.W. (1997). *Affective computing.* Cambridge, MA: MIT Press.

Preece, J., Rogers, Y., Sharp, H., and Benyon, D. (1994). *Human-computer interaction.* Reading, MA: Addison-Wesley.

Quintana, C., Eng., J., Carra, A., Wu, H., and Soloway, E. (1999). Symphony: A case study in extending learner-centered design through process space analysis. *Human Factors in Computing Systems: CHI'99 Conference Proceedings.* New York: ACM Press.

Rappin, N., Guzdial, M., Realff, M., and Ludovice, P. (1997). Balancing usability and learning in an interface. *Human Factors in Computing Systems: CHI'97 Proceedings.* Reading, MA: Addison-Wesley.

Reeves, B., and Nass, C. (1996). *The media equation: How people treat computers, television, and new media like real people and places.* Cambridge, UK: Cambridge University Press.

Salomon, G., Perkins, D.N., and Globerson, T. (1991). Partners in cognition: Extending human intelligence with intelligent technologies. *Educational Researcher,* April, 2–9.

Schoenfeld, A.H. (1987). What's all the fuss about metacognition? In A.H. Schoenfeld (Ed.), *Cognitive Science and Mathematics Education.* Hillsdale, NJ: Lawrence Erlbaum Associates.

Sedighian, K., Klawe, M., and Westrom, M. (2001). Role of interface manipulation style and scaffolding in cognition and concept learning in learnware. *ACM Transactions on Computer-Human Interaction,* 8, 1 (March 2001), 34–59.

Smith, B.K., and Reiser, B.J. (1998). National Geographic unplugged: Classroom-centered design of interactive nature films. *Human Factors in Computing Systems: CHI'98 Conference Proceedings,* 424–431. Reading, MA: Addison-Wesley.

Soloway, E., Guzdial, M., and Hay, K.H. (1994). Learner-centered design: The challenge for HCI in the 21st century. *Interactions,* 1, 2.

Soloway, E., Jackson, S.L., Klein, J., Quintana, C., Reed, J., Spitulnik, J., Stratford, S.J., Studer, S., Eng, J., and Scala, N. (1996). Learning theory in practice: Case studies in learner-centered design. *Human Factors in Computing Systems: CHI'96 Conference Proceedings.* Reading, MA: Addison-Wesley.

Soloway, E., and Pryor, A. (1996). The next generation in human-computer interaction. *Communications of the ACM,* 39, 4.

Squires, D., and Preece, J. (1999). Predicting quality in educational software: Evaluating for learning, usability and the synergy between them. *Interacting with Computers,* 11, 467–483.

28

HCI Meets the "Real World": Designing Technologies for Civic Sector Use

Douglas Schuler

> *Sitting at your PC, you can do your taxes, surf the web,*
> *write letters, e-mail friends, play games, plan a business, buy a car,*
> *do your homework . . . in fact, do whatever you want.*
> —BILL GATES (*NEWSWEEK,* MAY 31, 1999)

> *Men make their own history but not under conditions of their own choosing.*
> —KARL MARX (PARAPHRASED)

> *Active, informed, citizen participation is the key to*
> *shaping the network society. A new "Public Sphere" is required.*
> FROM THE "SEATTLE STATEMENT" (MAY 23, 2000)

An eve-of-the-millennium cover story from *Newsweek* (May 31, 1999) showcases a variety of gee-whiz technologies under the authoritative heading of "Technology: What You Will Want Next." Although the technology that we apparently will all "want next" introduces a staggering number of social implications, there is not the vaguest whisper of human agency, human aspiration, or human struggle in the creation and use of this new technology. People exist, or so it would seem, only to consort with technological gadgetry. The world implicitly portrayed in the article is inert, an eternal suburb populated by white collared professionals nattering around in a technologically mediated cocoon.

627

28.1   Introduction: A "Network Society"

Manuel Castells (1996) has presented ample evidence that a globalized "Network Society" has arrived; all or nearly all of the readers of this book are part of it. The Internet is still growing at a geometric rate, doubling its user population at least once per year. The growth, moreover, is global; the largest increases are taking place outside of the United States. This burgeoning growth offers significant opportunities for public involvement. The Internet is two-way (at least for now), and "ordinary people" are becoming connected to the Internet in record numbers. These large numbers of people who are less likely to be guided along specific professional or organizational trajectories than their predecessors are increasingly likely to be engaged in new computer-mediated social interactions (Smith and Kollock 1999). These demographic, social, and technological changes bring up important challenges for HCI.

Although the demographics of Internet use have changed and continue to change, it would be a big mistake to assume that some inexorable "democratization" process is underway.

The rapid growth of the Internet suggests (at a crude level of analysis) that soon all inhabitants—rich and poor, young and old, male and female—will have access to this vast communication network. Statistics, however, deflate this utopian dream. Although Castells believes that the network society represents a profound global reorientation, he points out that this new structure is no more equitable than before. As a matter of fact, because it separates the poor from the forces that are keeping them that way, it generally makes inequity more intractable. Massive divisions between rich and poor still exist, a social fact that is reflected in access to communication technology. As of 1997, 65 percent of the world's 1.4 billion households had no telephone (Hamelink 1999). In the United States there exists a "digital divide" between Internet users, who are largely drawn from the middle and upper classes, and non-Internet users, who are often poor and from ethnic minorities (U.S. Department of Commerce 1999; Novak and Hoffman 1998). If, as many suggest, the Internet is a powerful tool that benefits its users, it follows logically that users will derive greater benefit than non-users. The "computer revolution," in other words, is exacerbating these gaps.

28.2   Support for the Community

Girded by basic democratic theory (Dahl 1989, for example) and recent work by Habermas (Sparks 1998) and others, many researchers, policymakers, and activists believe that strengthening the civic sector, the sector of society which is neither governmental nor commercial (though intimately connected to both), could ultimately help to address these problems. The civic sector contains educational institutions and a staggering array of voluntary associations worldwide. Democracy, ideally, is a form of organized collective intelligence that could help society address major problems associated with social injustice and environmental degradation. The major movements of the twentieth century for human rights, civil liberties, sexual freedom, environmentalism, and women's liberation were, in fact, sparked by the civic sector (Keck and Sikkink 1998). HCI research, like other applied computer science, has traditionally not directly supported civic society. People not affiliated with government or business have not traditionally had any access to computers, let alone cutting edge research projects. This bias is exemplified by the paper by Arias et al. (Chapter 16). Big media interests are interested in applications that allow people to more easily consume commercial media and commercial goods—not to produce alternatives to commercialism. If HCI and other computer professionals decide to direct more attention to the civic sector, they will find, however, that it is not just a matter of changing audiences or clients; this shift in focus is philosophical as well, and changes are likely to resonate through the entire enterprise.

In my book *Community Networks* (1996) I postulated that a community (inherently a civic sector body) has *systems* or *core values* that maintain its "web of unity" (MacIver 1970). These six core values—conviviality and culture; education; strong democracy; health and well-being; economic equity; opportunity; and sustainability; and information and communication (Figure 28.1)— are all strongly interrelated. Each system influences each of the others, and any deficiency in one promotes a deficiency

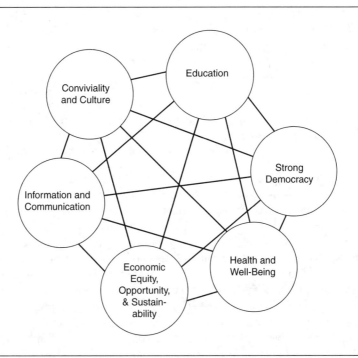

FIGURE 28.1   Community core values

of the whole (Schuler 1996). It has long been known, to illustrate the interconnectedness of the core values with just one example, that the higher an individual's education and economic levels, the higher the amount of his or her political participation (Greider 1993; Goel 1980). Strengthening these community core values, therefore, is likely to result in stronger, more coherent communities.

The civic sector certainly has not allowed the implications of the Network Society and new communication technology (like the Internet) to escape them. A complete catalog of civic sector efforts, grounded and motivated by "community core values" and the promise of richer communication, is too large to be considered exhaustively here. For that reason we focus on one effort, the Seattle Community Network, and make references to other relevant projects and opportunities.

28.3   Community Networks

The associations in community are interdependent. To weaken one is to weaken all. If the local newspaper closes, the garden club and the township meeting will each diminish as they lose a voice. If the American Legion disbands, several community fundraising events and the maintenance of the ballpark will stop. If the Baptist Church closes, several self-help groups that meet in the basement will be without a home and folks in the old peoples' home will lose their weekly visitors. The interdependence of associations and the dependence of community upon their work is the vital center of an effective society.

—John McKnight (1987)

Networks of civic engagement embody past success at collaboration which can serve as a cultural template for future collaboration.

—Robert Putnam (1993)

Before computers and digital networks became prominent, the term "community network" was a sociological concept that described the pattern of communications and relationships in a community (Wellman 1999). This was the web of community, described by McKnight and Putnam in the quotations above, that helped us better understand how news traveled and how social problems were addressed in the community. New computer-based "community networks" are a recent innovation that are intended to help revitalize, strengthen, and expand existing *people-based* community networks much in the same way that previous civic innovations (such as the print-media inspired public library) have helped communities historically.

For over a decade, community members and activists all over the world, often in conjunction with other local institutions including colleges and universities, K–12 schools, local governmental agencies, libraries, or nonprofit organizations, have been developing community networks. In fact, by the mid-1990s, there were nearly 300 operational systems, with nearly 200 more in development (Doctor and Ankem 1995), and the number of registered users exceeded 500,000 people worldwide. (Unfortunately user demographics for the aggregate are nearly impossible to obtain. At the same time, there has been an explosion of efforts and no inclusive shared concept of what a "community network" is!) Innovative examples can be found in Amsterdam (www.dds.nl), Milan (wrcm.dsi.unimi.it), Barcelona (www.ravalnet.org), Japan (www.can.or.jp/index-e.html), and, more recently, in Russia (www.friendspartners.org/civnet/index.html), where the development of civil society is an urgent matter after the sudden breakup of the Soviet Union. These community networks (sometimes called civic networks, digital cities, Free-Nets, community computing-centers, or public access networks), some with user populations in the tens of thousands, are intended to advance social goals, such as building community awareness, encouraging involvement in local decision making, or developing economic opportunities in disadvantaged communities. In other words, the community network's services are intended to support the core values of the community (Figure 28.2).

A community network addresses these goals by supporting smaller communities within the larger community and by facilitating the exchange of information between individuals and these smaller communities. Another community-network objective is to aggregate digital community information and communication, thus focusing attention on civic matters. This is done in a variety of ways: through discussion forums, question and answer forums, electronic access for government employees, information and access to social services, electronic mail, and, in most cases, Internet services, including access to the World Wide Web and Usenet news groups. Some organizations highlight related work—such as low-power community radio in the United States (recently scuttled by Congress)—and policy issues specifically related to communication systems. The most important aspect of community networks, however, is probably their potential for increasing participation in community affairs. The Internet's original design makes little distinction between information consumers and producers and has helped spur idealism among community network developers that is not shared among reformers of traditional media such as newspapers, radio, or television.

Community members interact with community networks in various ways. Community-network terminals can be set up at public places like libraries, bus stations, schools, laundromats, community and senior centers, social service agencies, public markets, and shopping malls. Community networks are also accessible from home via dial-up computers and from the Internet. In recent years, activists have also been establishing community computing centers or telecenters where people, often those in low-income neighborhoods, can become comfortable and adept with computer applications and network services (see, for example, http://www.ctcnet.org).

Community networks are currently local and independent. Many were affiliated with the National Public Telecomputing Network (NPTN), a now-defunct organization that helped establish a large number of community networks—or *Free-Nets* in NPTN's terminology. New organizations, such as the Association for Community Networks (AFCN) in the United States, the European Association of Community Networks (EACN), and the CAN (Community Area Networks) Forum in Japan have recently

Conviviality and Culture

- Forums for ethnic, religious, neighborhood interest groups
- Recreation and parks information
- Arts, crafts, and music classes, events, and festivals
- Community calendar

Education

- Online homework help
- Forums for educators, students
- Q&A on major topics
- Distributed experiments
- Penpals

Strong Democracy

- Contact information for elected officials—"Ask the Mayor"
- E-mail to elected officials
- E-mail to government agencies
- Forums on major issues
- Online versions of legislation, judicial decisions, regulations, and other government information

Health and Well-Being

- Q&A on medical and dental information
- Alternative and traditional health care information
- Community clinics information
- Self-help forums
- Public safety bulletins
- Where to find help for substance abuse and related issues
- Resources for the homeless; shelter information and forums

Economic Equity, Opportunity, and Sustainability

- Want ads and job listings
- Labor news
- Ethical investing information
- Job training and community-development projects
- Unemployed, laid-off, and striking worker discussion forums

Information and Communication

- Access to alternative news and opinion
- E-mail to all Internet addresses
- Cooperation with community radio
- Access to library information and services
- Access to online databases
- Online "Quick Information"
- Access to online periodicals, wire services

FIGURE 28.2 Example services for a community network

been launched, but, in general, community network developers have not explored deeply, in theory or in practice, the idea of stronger and closer relationships between them, thus diminishing the chances that a community networking "movement" will develop. This shows some signs of changing lately. The "Global 2000 Virtual Community Coalition" (Serra 1999) is helping to coordinate over a dozen conferences, both face-to-face and online, on community-oriented "network society" topics.

Community network systems have almost always had a difficult time financially. Increased public interest and some limited financial infusions from the government, businesses, and foundations have helped to alleviate some of the problems with some of the systems. For example, in Texas, a new initiative, the largest ever in the United States, is devoting some 30 million dollars for community networking. This effort, however, is a major exception. Very few community networks—in Texas or elsewhere—have been adequately staffed or have had adequate office space, hardware, software, or telecommunications. Whether or not community networks in one form or another succeed hinges on the question of whether community and/or other institutions can coalesce around the idea of democratic community communication as a permanent institution worthy of financial and other support.

28.4 The Seattle Community Network— A Whirlwind Tour

Community networks take different forms in different communities, depending on who develops them and how people use them. Historical and demographic factors in the community, what types of services and institutions—computer based or not— already exist in the community, and what resources are available, are also important factors. Changes in computer technology (new databases, graphical interfaces, plug ins, and distributed applications) also influence the design of future systems. The earlier text-based systems have been largely replaced with Web-based systems. Although the Seattle Community Network (SCN) was launched with the text-based Free-Net software pioneered in Cleveland, the system is now mostly Web-based. Over 13,000 registered users of SCN log in 75,000 times a month, and the Web site gets hundreds of thousands of visits every year.

When a user encounters the Seattle Community Network (Figure 28.3; http://www.scn.org), the first thing he or she sees is the SCN logo, replete with communication metaphors and Seattle imagery: Hermes, the Greek messenger of the gods, reclining on snowcapped Mount Rainier, beckons to future users; the Seattle Space Needle, an icon from the 1963 World's Fair, now retooled as a communications beacon, is held tightly in his hand. (The uncropped version of the logo is framed with the perforated border found on postage stamps, referring to another communication approach—the traditional letter.) Clicking the "About SCN" link reveals information about SCN's policy (http://www.scn.org/policy.html) and principles (http://www.scn.org/ip/commnet/principles.html). Their policy stresses freedom of speech, privacy, and due process for users, while the principles include commitments to *access, service, democracy, the world community,* and to *the future*

In addition to providing free Web space and e-mail, SCN also provides free support for electronic distribution lists via the *Major Cool* program. Basic information about contacting SCN, getting an account, and publishing information on the SCN Web site

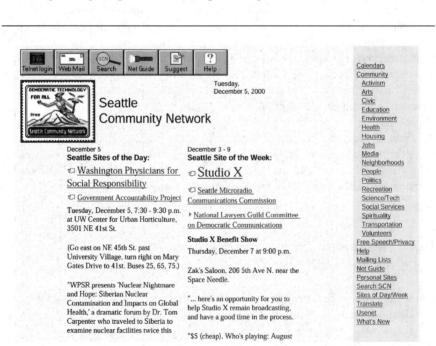

FIGURE 28.3

are found on the left side of the page, below the logo and the welcome message. Under that, the "Seattle Site of the Week" is featured. (The last time I looked, it linked to various events linked to the anniversary of the WTO meeting held the previous year in Seattle.)

The SCN developers decided in an early design phase not to employ the building metaphor that was often used to organize information in Free-Net Systems ("Post Office," "Public Square," "Arts Building," "School House," "Sciences and Technology Center," "Library," etc.). Instead they devised less concrete descriptors such as "Activism" and "Arts." These main SCN categories ("Activism," "Arts," "Civil," "Earth," "Education," "Health," "Marketplace," "Neighborhoods," "News," "People," "Recreation," "Sci-Tech," and "Spiritual") are lined up along the right edge of the page. Since the categories are arranged alphabetically, the "activism" category heads the list. While the placement is accidental, its prominent location does help ensure prominence of activism to SCN Web site users and of the idea in general, a major part of the SCN project philosophy. Commercial search engines and other major portals on the Web are, of course, unlikely to highlight this category at all: Selling things is the primary objective of those systems, and social activism is generally neutral or even hostile to the concerns and objectives of corporations.

Clicking on the "Activism" link on SCN brings up a wide range of information, including links to "Environmental," "Human Rights," "Hunger and Homelessness,"

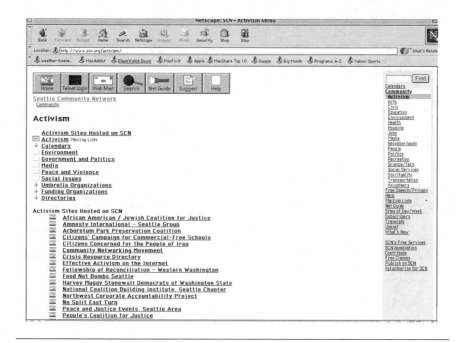

FIGURE 28.4

and "Women" (Figure 28.4; http://www.scn.org/activism). All of this information relates to activism generally in the Seattle area and generally on SCN but not exclusively. The "Activism" page, like all the other category pages on SCN, is coordinated and managed by a "Section Area Editor," one of the many volunteer roles at SCN. SCN, as of this writing, is run entirely by volunteers with few top-down directives. Subject Area Editors, then, are basically free to organize their Web page in the manner they prefer as long as they include the basic SCN header (which contains links to the other SCN subject pages) and are responsive to the information providers (IPs) who are adding information in that subject area.

The "Civic" section (Figure 28.5; http://www.scn.org/civic) has links to "Social Services," "Politics," "Legal," "Non-Profit," "Philanthropy," "Public Agencies," and "International." The *Sustainable Seattle* project deserves particular attention because of its potent model that integrates community research, activism, and civic engagement. Sustainable Seattle has been developing a set of sustainability "indicators" that—taken as a whole—provide a meaningful snapshot of the Seattle region's ability to provide long-range social and environmental health for all of its inhabitants, human and otherwise. Given Seattle's natural surroundings and environmental ethos, it's not surprising that the "Earth" section (Figure 28.6; http://www.scn.org/earth) is

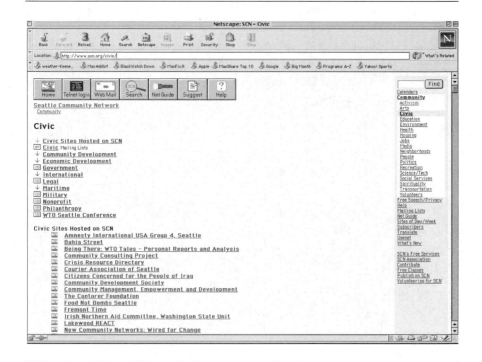

FIGURE 28.5

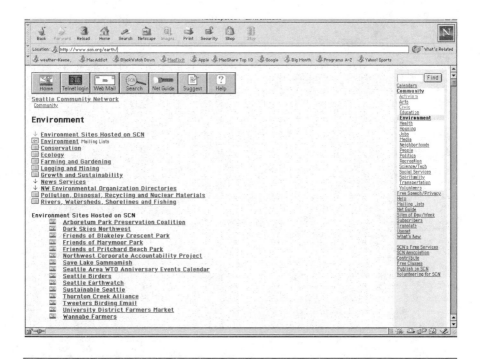

FIGURE 28.6

fairly rich. Links here point to "University District Farmer's Market," "Wannabe Farmers," "Save Lake Sammamish," and many others.

The fact that the SCN "Neighborhood" (Figure 28.7; http://www.scn.org/neighbors) section has been growing steadily over the years is important to the SCN organizers because supporting geographical communities of various sizes has been a primary motivation from the project's onset. Although, ideally, a community network would exist for every community on the planet, it's clear that this is unlikely to happen in the near future. Although SCN places its main focus on the Seattle area, it is not intended to be its *exclusive* focus. Therefore, neighborhoods such as Kenmore, Lakewood, and Bellingham use the SCN site (as do such global neighbors as the "Uganda Community Management Program" and the "USTAWI: Promoting Self-Sufficiency in Africa") sites, which can be found on the "Civic" section area. Neighborhood coalition groups such as the "Seattle Neighborhood Coalition" and the "Washington State Neighborhood Networks Consortium" also have links on SCN.

The "Science and Technology" (Figure 28.8; http://www.scn.org/tech) section points to a large selection of important resources both on SCN and other locations. This page also lets users post a URL to science and technology resources or information about upcoming meetings. There are links to several innovative projects such as the

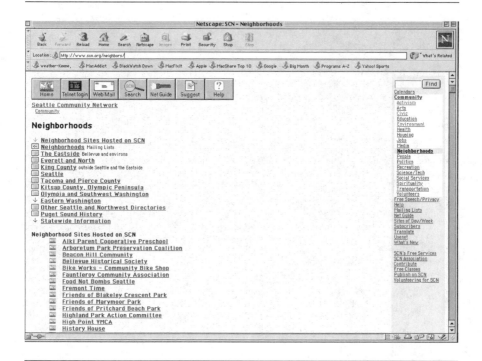

FIGURE 28.7

Community Technology Institute (which offers free voice mail to homeless and phoneless people around the country); *The Network,* a cooperative effort of community network activists and researchers worldwide; and the volunteer-run Vintage Telephone Equipment Museum in Seattle. The "Ask Mr. Science" service, currently not being conducted, allowed people to submit science questions to "Mr. Science," who would then post the answers online. This feature, based on Cleveland Free-Net examples, was one of SCN's oldest features and has been used by many Seattle area classrooms.

SCN, as of this writing, is a thriving computer system that has served as a model for many others throughout the world. On the other hand, its future is far from secure. After many years, it still relies on volunteer labor and on financial donations, a reliance that mitigates against keeping the technological infrastructure up to date. The search for sustainability is not an issue for Seattle alone. Most, if not all, community networks are finding it difficult to find the necessary support. For that reason many people suspect that community networks will need to rely on the government in the future for support. There is also a strong fear that as billions of dollars are invested in commercial Internet ventures, community networks and other new civic institutions that employ digital technology may simply become more and more marginalized as time goes on. While relying on volunteers may be seen as virtuous by some, the drawbacks are numerous: Volunteer labor can be unreliable and the available skills inadequate for the tasks.

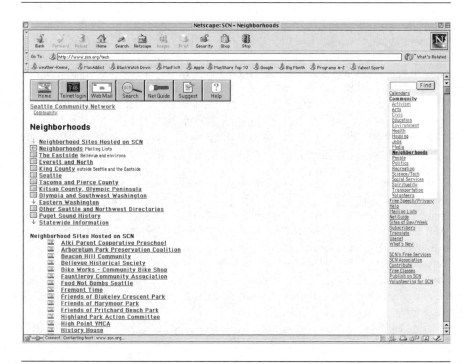

FIGURE 28.8

"Democratic self-management" may also be considered an asset, but in the absence of established chains of command, paralysis can set in.

Because there is no paid staff or office space to rent, its operating costs are very low—basically telephone lines and new equipment. Although its budget is low while its potential and objectives are great, SCN (and similar projects) offer intriguing platforms for collaboration with HCI and other professionals. Some of these include usability studies, alternative user interfaces (including voice), new collaborative work environments (Arias et al., Chapter 16), and communication spaces (Sack 2000), and new design processes.

28.5   Opportunities and Ideas

There are scores of possible civic applications awaiting exploration by HCI professionals. Search engines, for example, are rapidly turning into *TV Guides* for the Internet. What types of new search engines could support public, nonprofit, and educational uses? How would a public classification system, analogous to the Dewey

Decimal system but geared toward network resources and without its strong bias toward English language and Western culture, help support a vast digital library to which everybody could contribute? What new online meeting tools for deliberation and decision making are needed? A revised *Robert's Rules of Order,* for example, could extend into the electronic digital room the same respect for process that Henry Robert devised in the 1800s for face-to-face meetings (Adams and Powell 2000). New tools are becoming available that help us understand large public conversations (Sack 2000). Web publishing kits (including those that use low-bandwidth connections and older technology) could help grassroots organizations publish high-quality information electronically. What new user interfaces to these devices can be devised?

Many civic organizations are designing new systems for use by nonprofessionals. The RTKnet (for "Right To Know" network) Web site allows people to see what chemicals are being used in their communities. In Chicago, the Center for Neighborhood Technology established the Neighborhood Early Warning System (NEWS) that aggregates data from a variety of government agencies. Both systems are providing a consistent metaphor to describe and present information from disparate sources. Complex situations demand data from various sources, but finding and assimilating the necessary constellation of interrelated information is one of the prime obstacles to effective data utilization (Durrance 1994).

Using computers and communications in developing countries provides additional challenges. Although these countries contain 75 percent of the world's population, they are home to only 3 percent of the Web sites. How can these countries effectively reap the benefits that the Internet offers? What tools can be devised that will help people in the developing countries preserve their own languages and cultures? Since money is in short supply in the developing world, low-cost approaches are particularly apt. For that reason, many developers in these countries are focusing on free software alternatives like Linux and older hardware. Developing tools that could be used on those systems could also help leverage their development efforts. At a more fundamental level, the development of protocols for exchanging "community work" information (such as task descriptions, schedules, etc.) could help spur work in inexpensive community "groupware" systems. (This approach was suggested to me by Jakob Kaivo.)

HCI professionals can also increase their involvement in the development and refinement of design processes that are well suited to civic applications. Civic applications are intended to be used by a wide variety of users, and hence the design processes that are to be used are often more participatory. In some cases "maximum participation" on the part of the citizenry is stipulated by law. There are various group processes that can be facilitated by computer technology (see Turner and Pinkett 2000). GIS systems, for example (Krygier 1998; Lentz 2000), can also be key components in the participatory design of neighborhoods and public transportation.

28.6   How Can HCI Research Get Transferred to the Community?

As media converges (at least by virtue of being digital), the computer, as a programmable and powerful portal that connects people to the rest of the world, becomes a critical component in the vast network of increasingly global communication. Hence, HCI is thrust into a position of intensified responsibility: What HCI professionals do is likely to have major implications for the future of the planet.

"Ordinary" people, outside of business and governmental settings, are increasingly becoming computer users. What new objectives, perspectives, and methodologies emerge if the "community" or the "civic sector" becomes the client or ultimate user of HCI research? If nothing new emerges from this new point of view then the HCI community can feel confident that their current course is sufficient and no adjustment is needed.

One approach to answering this question is to think of "ordinary citizens" as "customers" for the systems being designed by HCI professionals. Although the money coming from these "customers" arrives via a circuitous and indirect route (as was the case of U.S. taxpayers who dutifully yet ignorantly funded the development of the Internet), they nevertheless do assist in the funding of research. If we assume that the "product" produced by researchers is something that these customers actually want, then the speed by which the products arrive ready for use would surely be a point of contention for those "customers" who are the last to receive the product. Arguably, in fact, any product that relied on state-of-the-art processors and very fast networks might be considered a poor investment by those people. If, for example, a large number of these not-entirely-hypothetical customers do not currently have access to the Internet and do not expect to gain this access soon, they are unlikely to be interested in expensive, bandwidth-greedy applications. For these reasons, research that relies on low-cost technology is more likely to be transferred to low-income communities at a swifter rate than high-cost technology, all other things being equal.

Whether or not the research is ultimately appropriate to the bulk of the citizenry, the fact remains that the "feedback loop" between the research community and the citizenry, especially the low-income community, is so indistinct as to be nonexistent. Therefore, another strategy for making HCI work directly relevant to the citizenry is to enrich this feedback loop by working directly with community and social activist organizations with low income and other marginalized populations. This can take several forms, of course, but the design charette model that architects employ and participatory design methods generally (Schuler and Namioka 1993; Greenbaum and Kyng 1991) are particularly relevant.

28.7 Challenges for HCI

New historical circumstances present formidable challenges for HCI professionals and the discipline as a whole. There are two major tasks ahead for HCI professionals. The first is placing HCI in "the context of social systems," in the words of Erickson and Kellogg. This work involves an investigation into the web of actual and *possible* relationships that HCI is or *could be* embedded within. The second task is developing research techniques, experiments, applications, and services that advance HCI, while systematically exercising and exploring the web of relationships (both actual and potential) identified by the first task.

Other facts confound the difficulty of these new tasks. The first is that these tasks require languages and perspectives that HCI professionals may not possess. One approach to this problem is to develop interdisciplinary teams that combine various expertises into broad-spectrum, grounded research programs. An interdisciplinary project team might include social scientists, community activists, decision makers, policy makers, educators, HCI specialists, and artists. This approach, of course, suggests another substantial problem: the institutionalized bias against interdisciplinary work by both funding agencies, departmental units within the university and commercial concerns.

There are, however, some hopeful signs. The first is a growing interest among researchers in working with communities outside their traditional purview (white-collar work situations). In early 2000, over 100 researchers responded within two months to a call for abstracts to the "Shaping the Network Society: The Future of the Public Space" Symposium. Attendees from the symposium drafted the "Seattle Statement" (Appendix A), which directly links the needs of civil society to communication technology policy, research, and development agenda. Another hopeful sign is the fact that the National Science Foundation and a number of nonprofit foundations are beginning to invest more substantially in "digital divide" (U.S. 1999) issues and other social implications of network technology.

28.8 Discussion

HCI authors realize the importance of their work. Jonathan Grudin points out that computer-mediated interaction is an increasingly important focus of human-computer interaction, while other researchers believe that computers will increasingly mediate the interaction between people. Many researchers believe, furthermore, that computer programs will increasingly offer advice and develop and execute plans that are deemed appropriate according to various criteria and objectives supplied by human users.

Thus, among HCI professionals there is an acknowledgment, often casually articulated, of the potentially vast implications that their work is unleashing for social relationships in the future. At the same time, there doesn't seem to be a corresponding analysis or interest in the ultimate effects of the system, who benefits and who is left behind. Most of the rhetoric stresses the *beneficial* aspects of their work, as if the work has an inherent momentum toward goodness. Although, as Erickson and Kellogg point out, "Technology is always deployed in the context of social systems," HCI work often seems to ignore this context. As just suggested, this limitation shows up most clearly in (1) the lack of grounding in actual social (including economic, political, and cultural) contexts, assuming instead a somewhat disembodied focus on rationalized white collar work, and (2) the absence of feedback and involvement in HCI research and development among communities outside traditional HCI constituencies. As previously discussed, new circumstances—both social and technical— suggest a number of fruitful directions for HCI.

28.9 Conclusion

According to several authors in this book, computer technology is likely to usher in radical changes in social relationships. At the same time, a new "network society" with a vast chasm between rich (usually wired) people and poor (usually unwired) people is emerging. Yet computer scientists in the trenches usually stay in their trenches when it comes to relating their work to these broader issues. They are surprisingly silent about the implications—both positive and negative—that their activities could possibly engender. Their historical connection to "pure" research and business interests has perhaps helped sustain an inertia that isn't keeping pace with changing social, economic, and political changes. Perhaps they believe that exploring this line of critical thinking would be unwise for their careers and there is definite risk there. The reasons, however, are likely to be more mundane. Computer scientists and developers are generally focused on technical challenges. They basically just don't have the time or inclination to concern themselves with complex, technically nontractable problems of human society. *But who will?*

HCI and other computer professionals can assume a leadership role in the development of new technology that supports human values. HCI doesn't stop at the computer screen. What happens at the interface between the computer screen and a person in front of it is important, but it's just one link in a vast network of relationships between people and information and between people and people. Each link is a node in a rapidly expanding system of collective intelligence. We make a major mistake if we assume that "magic" exists in technology or that technology exists independently of a social context. New technology offers new potential to civil society, but it takes human intelligence and struggle to make it suit civic purposes.

The future of communication technology—a key part of our collective intelligence—is being created now. What will our role as computer professionals be? Which possible histories of the future will we invent? Working in the community on community networks and other civic sector applications can provide challenging and satisfying work for HCI and other computer professionals.

Appendix A

Seattle Statement

http://www.scn.org/cpsr/diac-00/seattle-statement.html

Citizens Shaping the Network Society
May 23, 2000

Developed by a committee of participants in the final session of the Shaping the Network Society: The Future of the Public Sphere in Cyberspace symposium sponsored by Computer Professionals for Social Responsibility.

Show your support for the Seattle Statement!

1. Send e-mail to douglas@scn.org with your name and affiliation (optional) if you'd like to "sign!" — or —

2. Fill out form at http://www.scn.org/cpsr/diac-00/sign-it.html.

- The world is becoming globalized, and communications technology is an important part of that process.

- The human race is faced with a multitude of major problems that are receiving inadequate attention.

- Civic society throughout the world has enormous—insufficiently tapped—resources including creativity, compassion, intelligence, dedication, which can help address these problems.

- At the same time, civic society is undervalued and threatened.

- Information and communication technology offers enormous potential for civic society for education, health, arts and culture, social services, social activism, deliberation, agenda setting, discussion, and democratic governance.

- Active, informed citizen participation is the key to shaping the network society. A new "Public Sphere" is required.

References

Adams, J., and Powell, M. (2000). Deliberations in the digital age (workshop). *Proceedings of DIAC-2000, Shaping the Network Society: The Future of the Public Sphere in Cyberspace.* Palo Alto, CA: Computer Professionals for Social Responsibility.

Castells, M. (1996). *The information age: Economy, society, and culture.* Oxford: Blackwell.

Dahl, R.(1989). *Democracy and its critics.* New Haven, CT: Yale University Press.

Doctor, R., and Ankem, K. (1995). *A directory of computerized community information systems.* Unpublished report. Tuscaloosa, AL: School of Library and Information Studies, University of Alabama.

Durrance, J. (1994). *Armed for action: Library response to citizen information needs.* New York: Neal-Schuman Publishers.

Goel, M. (1980). Conventional political participation. In D. Smith and J. Macaulay (Eds.), *Participation in Social and Political Activities.* San Francisco, CA: Jossey-Bass.

Greider, W. (1993). *Who will tell the people?* New York: Simon and Schuster.

Greenbaum, J., and Kyng, M. (1991). *Design at work: Cooperative design of computer systems.* Hillsdale, NJ: Lawrence Erlbaum Associates.

Hamelink, C. (1999). The elusive concept of globalization. *Global Discourse,* 1, 1.

Keck, M., and Sikkink, K. (1998). *Activists beyond borders: Advocacy networks in international politics.* Ithaca, NY: Cornell University Press.

Krygier, J. (1998). Public participation visualization: Conceptual and applied research issues. http://www.owu.edu/~jbkrygie/krygier_html/lws/ppviz.html.

Lentz, B. (2000). Place matters, even in cyberspace: Exploring online maps as forms of alternative community media. *Proceedings of DIAC-2000, Shaping the Network Society: The Future of the Public Sphere in Cyberspace.* Palo Alto, CA: Computer Professionals for Social Responsibility.

MacIver, R. (1970). *On community, society and power.* Chicago, IL: University of Chicago Press.

Novak, T., and Hoffman, D. (1998). Bridging the digitial divide: The impact of race on computer access and internet use. http://www.2000.ogsm.vanderbilt.edu/papers/race/science.html.

Sack, W. (2000). Navigating very large-scale conversations. *Proceedings of DIAC-2000, Shaping the Network Society: The Future of the Public Sphere in Cyberspace.* Palo Alto, CA: Computer Professionals for Social Responsibility.

Schuler, D. (1996). *New community networks: Wired for change.* Reading, MA: Addison-Wesley.

Schuler, D. ,and Namioka, A. (1993). *Participatory design: Principles and practices.* Hillsdale, NJ: Lawrence Erlbaum Associates.

Seattle Statement. http://www.scn.org/cpsr/diac-00/seattle-statement.html.

Serra, A. (1999). E-mail communication.

Smith, M. and Kollock, P. (Eds.). (1999). *Communities in cyberspace.* Routledge.

Sparks, C. (1998). Is there a global public sphere? In Thussu, D. (Ed.), *Electronic Empires: Global Media and Local Resistance.* London: Arnold.

Turner, N., and Pinkett, R. (2000). An asset-based approach to community building and community technology. *Proceedings of DIAC-2000, Shaping the Network Society: The Future of the Public Sphere in Cyberspace.* Palo Alto, CA: Computer Professionals for Social Responsibility.

U.S. Department of Commerce. (1999). Falling through the net: Defining the digital divide. http://www.ntia.doc.gov/ntiahome/fttn99/contents.html.

Wellman, B. (1999). The network community, an introduction. B. Wellman, (Ed.), Boulder, CO: Westview.

29

Beyond Bowling Together: SocioTechnical Capital

Paul Resnick

29.1 Introduction

The notion of capital suggests a resource that can be accumulated and whose availability allows people to create value for themselves or others. People can do more when they have access to physical resources like buildings and tools, which are usually referred to as physical capital. Money, or financial capital, allows people to acquire many other kinds of resources. In the latter half of the twentieth century, economists began to think about education as human capital. People who have more knowledge and skills can produce more, so it makes sense to think about spending on education as a form of investment rather than consumption (Schultz 1961).

Productive resources can reside not just in things and in people but also in social relations among people (Coleman 1988; Putnam 1993). A network of people who have developed communication patterns and trust can accomplish much more than a bunch of strangers, even if the two sets of people have similar human, physical, and financial capital available. The productive capacity can be used to benefit individuals, the network as a whole, or society at large. Typically, productive social structures and dynamics emerge as a by-product of interactions that occur naturally in the course of work or recreation. Conceptualizing such resources as "social capital" suggests, however, that it is also possible to make conscious investments to develop resources that inhere in social relations.

A growing body of literature has confirmed that social capital is correlated with positive individual and collective outcomes in areas such as better health (Lochner et al. 1999; Parker 2000), lower crime (Sampson 1997), better educational outcomes (Putnam 2000), economic development (Putnam 1993; Knack and Keefer 1997; Putnam 2000), and good government (Putnam 1993). These studies either measure social capital directly, usually through survey questions about attitudes and expectations of others' behavior, or indirectly by measuring the amounts of certain activities that are thought to produce social capital, such as attendance at meetings. The measures of social capital are then correlated with the outcome variables. For example, in his study of regional differences in Italy, Putnam found that participation in choral societies and soccer clubs, activities that might be expected to generate social capital, was the best predictor of regional variation in economic development and political corruption (Putnam 1993).

Social capital is a residual or side effect of social interactions and an enabler of future interactions, as shown in Figure 29.1. For example, a neighborhood trash pickup has the direct effect of leaving a cleaner neighborhood. If many people participate in the pickup, there may also be side effects on their stock of social capital. They may meet each other and develop ties that make it easier to organize a block party or arrange shared babysitting in the future. They may begin to share information about crime incidents and feel a sense of emotional support. They may become more able to mobilize in response to perceived external threats such as noise from airplanes. This example illustrates that social capital, like many other aspects of social life, is not only produced but also reproduced. Use doesn't use it up; when a group draws on its social capital to act collectively, it will often generate even more social capital. Conversely, if a group tries to mobilize but fails to act collectively, some of its social capital may dissipate as members lose faith in each other.

Information and communication technologies (ICTs) should also increase people's ability to act together, which has prompted large investments in such technologies. Surprisingly, economists' initial studies failed to find productivity increases resulting from those investments (Brynjolfsson 1993), which spurred a call for more efforts in the field of human-computer interaction (Landauer 1995). More recent studies have demonstrated productivity gains (Brynjolfsson and Hitt 1998). The challenge remains, however, for human-computer interaction research and development to maximize the productive value of investments in information and communications technology.

It is especially interesting to think about interaction effects between social relations and ICTs. Some communication services may be useful only to groups of

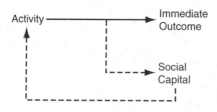

FIGURE 29.1 Social capital as a side effect of previous activities and enabler of future activities.

people who have already developed strong social ties and who develop certain norms for how to use it. Other groups of people might find the same communication service a nuisance rather than a helpful tool. Conversely, some social practices might be productive only in the presence of particular communication and computational tools. For example, a convention of broadcasting event announcements to large groups of people, only a few of whom will be interested, may be productive if most of the people have sophisticated tools for filtering their messages but unproductive otherwise. I will use the term "sociotechnical capital" to refer to productive combinations of social relations and information and communication technology.[1] It is thus a special case, a subset of social capital, but an important one because technological advances have opened many new opportunities that have not been examined from the social capital perspective.

The field of human-computer interaction deals frequently with systems that combine technology and social practices. Previous work on "sociotechnical systems" has emphasized dynamic coevolution between technical and social subsystems (Bikson and Eveland 1996). The emphasis here is not so much on how the social and technical affect each other, but how they jointly influence the ability of people to act together.

The novel conceptual lens here is that of capital, a resource that can be accumulated over time through deliberate investment. As with purely social capital, resources are accumulated as a side effect of previous interactions. The resources may consist of artifacts created during the earlier interactions or social ties and practices that developed. They constitute capital if they help a group of people to accomplish more together, improving the routing of information, the exchange of resources, the provision of emotional support, or the ability to coordinate and to mobilize for collective action. The resources are sociotechnical in nature if their production or use requires a combination of social relations and information and communications technologies.

For HCI designers, the lens of sociotechnical capital suggests a new place to look for the success factors behind information systems deployments. It may be that a system can be used effectively only after its users have developed trust in each other, a shared identity, or some other form of social capital.[2]

Perhaps more importantly, the lens also suggests a new definition of success for system deployments, one that accounts for sociotechnical capital side effects as well as direct impacts on immediate tasks. If, for example, a system allows a worker to find information on her own without consulting colleagues, there is a positive time efficiency gain. There is also a negative effect from losing opportunities to build and maintain ties with her colleagues, which might be useful for other reasons beyond the immediate task. In some cases, the tradeoffs may be worth it, in other cases not. Moreover, an alternative design of the system might improve immediate productivity and the formation of sociotechnical capital as well, once we set that as a goal.

---

[1] I thank Tora Bikson for an analogy to interaction terms in regression models, which led to this formulation.
[2] Olson and Olson (Chapter 18) suggest that "readiness to collaborate" is an important precondition for effective use of group communication. I would argue that social capital is the key determinant of such readiness.

29.1.1 The Civic Challenge

The conceptual lens of sociotechnical capital can inform design and evaluation of systems that support work and education, which have been the traditional domains of HCI. Recent research on social capital, however, suggests that supporting civic activity is of special importance and that new forms of social capital are needed to replace older forms that are declining. This is a special challenge that human-computer interaction as a field should rise to meet.

At least in the United States, many of the formal and informal activities that produce social capital have been declining in the last few decades, as documented in Putnam's (2000) recent book, *Bowling Alone*. Participation in clubs and civic organizations has dropped by more than half over the last 25 years. Church attendance is down by roughly one-third since the 1960s. Participation in bowling leagues is down. Even family dinners and vacations are way down.[3] As expected, this decline in the generators of social capital is matched by declines in attitudinal and behavioral indicators of social capital. Americans vote less, are less trusting of institutions and each other, and are less civil to each other (witness road rage).

There are many possible explanations for these declines, including differential generational coming-of-age experiences (Strauss and Howe 1992), changing residential and work patterns, and changing media consumption. If individual technology use were to be seriously implicated as a culprit, it would have to be TV (and perhaps radio and telephones) rather than the Internet, since the Internet is too recent a phenomenon. Still, there is cause for concern that the Internet may make things worse. Though not definitive, the best study to date suggests that among new users of the Internet, heavier users experienced more negative changes in their level of social isolation than light users, as measured by loneliness and depression survey questions (Kraut et al. 1998).[4]

Rather than assessing blame, this essay explores how technology, when paired with certain social practices, might help to reverse declining social capital in the civic sector. One approach is to try to reinvigorate the organizations and activities that have been sources of social capital in the past by reducing the costs of coordinating and publicizing activities or making the activities themselves more lively and exciting. Perhaps participation in the Boy Scouts, religious services, and even bowling leagues could be increased. For example, scheduling tools or even just e-mail might reduce the costs of arranging meetings. Desktop publishing and Web sites might provide new avenues for publicizing organizations and their activities and thus recruiting new members. Video screens and automatic scoring might even make bowling more fun. While this approach is certainly worth pursuing, it's unlikely that what we

---

[3]Some skeptics might argue that this is a spurious result of mismeasurement (for example, surveys might not ask about new informal activities, and people may answer survey questions differently than they did 30 years ago). The preponderance of data, however, from many different sources, all yielding trends in the same direction, have convinced the author of this essay that the overall declines are real.

[4]Preliminary data from a follow-on study suggest that heavy use of the Internet acts more as a magnifier of underlying personality traits: The lonely get lonelier but the connected get even more connected (Bob Kraut, personal communication, July 8, 2000).

now consider traditional social capital-building activities will regain the popularity they had in 1960.

A second approach is to try to invent new forms of togetherness that may be more suited to current lifestyles. Perhaps, with the aid of technology, it is possible to go beyond bowling together[5] to form even more productive social relations even more conveniently. For example, a dormant e-mail list may provide a just-in-case communication channel, allowing quick mobilization of a group when necessary, without creating any burdens during off-times. Feedback and reputation systems may enable trust to develop quickly in large groups. Technologies that enable lurking and catching up (like FAQs or well-indexed meeting notes) may enable peripheral participation without disrupting central activities. Introducer systems may enable just-in-time expansion of social networks.

Around the turn of the last century, social innovators created many new organizations, including Kiwanis, the Boy Scouts, and labor unions, in response to changing social conditions (factory work, immigration, urbanization). For a twenty-first century information society, an analogous spree of sociotechnical innovation will be needed.

In our own day, there are already some promising developments. Community networks are helping to publicize local organizations and activities and are creating new spaces for public deliberation about civic matters (Schuler, Chapter 28). Sites like myfamily.com help people to rebuild extended kinship networks frayed by geographic dispersion. Sites like evite.com make it easier to invite people to social events and keep track of their responses. Additionally, by putting entertaining online, it helps to lend an aura of modernity to something that many people had viewed as passé. Webgrrls and other New Economy networking sites are jumping off the screen into face-to-face local chapter meetings.

This essay provides a conceptual framework, some examples, and a research agenda for understanding and generating sociotechnical capital in the civic sector, but also in education and the workplace. The next two sections dissect the idea of social capital in more detail, first examining the kinds of productive activity it enables and then the kinds of social relations in which it inheres. Sections 29.4 and 29.5 explore the space of sociotechnical opportunities, including new kinds of interactions and new ways of capturing and managing the residuals of interactions. Section 29.6 provides a research agenda on understanding what features of sociotechnical relations are productive and measuring those features.

29.2 How Social Capital Works

It is clear that social capital makes a difference at a macro scale, but at a micro scale, how does it work? What can people who have social capital do together that otherwise would be difficult for them to do (see Figure 29.2)?

---

[5]This phrasing is inspired by an influential paper titled "Beyond Being There," which suggested that computer-mediated communication could aspire to improve on face-to-face, not merely approximate it (Hollan and Stornetta 1992).

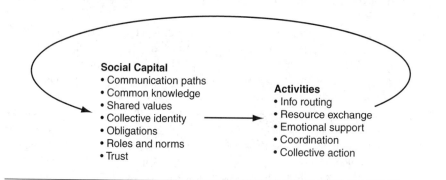

FIGURE 29.2   The forms of social capital and the kinds of interactions they enable.

First, social capital can facilitate information routing. In an era of information overload, this cannot be accomplished simply by increasing flows of information. It requires selective highlighting of what is important, so that the people who can benefit from it will attend to it. Social capital can help in this regard. People who have interacted previously learn something about each other's interests and can bring useful information to each other's attention. Prior interactions can also help decide which sources of information are worth attending to. For example, someone searching for a job will get better leads from people more familiar with the candidate and will be more likely to follow leads from people whose prior leads were valuable.

Second, social capital can help people to exchange other resources besides information. In a frictionless market, whenever one person valued a good more than another person did, an exchange would occur, creating a net increase in value for them. But many transaction costs can intervene to hinder such exchanges. First, the two parties must be aware of the exchange opportunity. Second, it may be difficult to quantify the value of the resources exchanged (consider, for example, small favors that neighbors or coworkers do for each other). The costs of accounting could easily consume the entire surplus from trade. Third, there may be difficult negotiations over division of the surplus from trade, with posturing during negotiation causing some valuable trades to be missed.[6] Finally, there may be risks in the consummation of trade. For example, a seller may take the buyer's money but not provide the expected good or service.

People who have social capital can reduce some of these transaction costs and thus accomplish more beneficial resource exchanges. For example, people who know each other well may provide gifts or favors without payments or maintenance of

---

[6]Economists have demonstrated that there is no mechanism for two-party price negotiation that will induce rational negotiators to trade whenever such a trade would be beneficial. Rational efforts to capture the surplus will, of necessity, sometimes lead to dissipation of that surplus (Myerson and Satterthwaite 1983).

explicit accounts. They also may be more willing to accept risks in trading with each other.[7]

Third, social capital makes it easier for people to provide emotional support to each other. People who know and trust each other are more likely to share personal information. If they have a background of shared experience, they can more easily convey that information, and responses are more likely to be interpreted as supportive.

Fourth, social capital enables coordination of interdependent actions. To complete a large project, some tasks may need to be completed before others or undertaken simultaneously. (For a comprehensive taxonomy of dependencies that require coordination, see Malone et al. 1999.) Groups of people who have social capital are better able to schedule their activities and use of shared resources in a way that respects these interdependencies.

Finally, social capital can help people overcome dilemmas of collective action. One collective action problem is procurement of public goods, where people might free ride, hoping that others will supply them.[8] A related problem is the overuse of common pool resources, where individuals might consume more than their fair share, creating a "tragedy of the commons" such as overgrazing a shared pasture (Hardin 1968). Another related dilemma of collective action is social mobilization, where everyone may realize that all will benefit if they all act, but individuals who act without others will fare badly and no one acts out of fear that others will not join. Starting a labor strike (Kollock and O'Brien 1992) or starting the dancing at a party are examples of this problem.

One solution to these dilemmas of collection action is to rely on some outside agent, a Leviathan, to force individuals to act collectively (Olson 1965). For example, governments force people to pay taxes to build and maintain roads. A second solution is to privatize the problem—for example, by fencing in common grazing lands as a set of private grazing areas. The last solution is to rely on social capital through social norms and sanctioning mechanisms that a group can enforce itself without the aid of an outside Leviathan (Ostrom 1990).

29.3   The Anatomy of Social Capital

Thus far, social capital has served as a metaphor, defined as productive resources that inhere in social relations, as a residual of previous interactions. What exactly are these resources that develop in a social network over time, and why are they productive?

---

[7]It is interesting to note that taking risks and exchanging without keeping accounts also have feedback effects on the stock of social capital. If these interactions turn out well for all parties, they are more likely to do them again in the future. Conversely, Amy Tan's novel *The Joy Luck Club* includes a cautionary tale of the detrimental effects of strict accounting on a couple's social capital. Because they divide household costs based on actual use of resources, right down to the last spoonful of ice cream, they do not develop the trust and habits of sharing necessary to navigate more difficult problems.

[8]Economists define a public good as one that is *non-rival,* meaning that everyone can enjoy it without reducing the benefit it provides to others, and *non-excludable,* meaning that if procured, it is available to everyone, regardless of their contribution to its procurement. Examples include roads, public safety, and radio and TV broadcasts.

The first productive resource is communication paths. Prior (useful) communication from one person to another often establishes a path for future information flow as well: Not only may it be easier for the sender to send, but the receiver will be more likely to attend to the information sent. These communication paths can be represented as a graph, with people as nodes and communications paths between people as links. Coleman (1988) has argued that graphs with closure provide a better base for collective action. Here, closure means roughly that the people that person A interacts with interact with each other. Sometimes the closure need not be so direct, as when an adult's children's friends are also the adult's friends' children. Behavior monitoring, social support, and reciprocal aid are more likely to occur in such networks. Sometimes these within-group ties are referred to as *bonding* social capital. Granovetter (1973) and others have noted that information flows better when there are bridging, or weak, ties. In contrast, if a clique is very tight, then members of the clique are less likely to have access to information or resources from outside the clique. These two arguments about desirable social network structure are somewhat at odds with each other, suggesting that different structures may be productive in different ways. Recent research has suggested that graphs that have significant closure (that is, mostly cliques) with just a few bridging links can still exhibit a small-world phenomenon where everyone is only a few links away from everyone else (Watts 1999). So perhaps these two desirable features, closure and bridging ties, can both be achieved.

The second productive resource is shared knowledge. This can include not only knowledge of facts, events, or stories but also a shared vocabulary and repertoire of ways of interacting (Wenger 1998). These make it easier to communicate and negotiate shared meaning in new situations. Shared knowledge can also contribute to a sense of emotional support, if people sense that others "understand" them.

The third productive resource is shared values. People with shared values find it easier to unite for a common purpose and thus overcome problems of collective action. It is especially helpful if the shared values have been articulated explicitly, as this then permits explicit appeals to those shared values when exhorting people to act together.

The fourth productive resource is a shared sense of collective identity (Wenger 1998). Identity results from the interplay of three related factors: whether one considers oneself part of a group, whether other group members treat one as a member, and whether people outside the group do (Minow 1997). An individual who feels herself to be a member of a group may internalize the group's utility as part of her own preferences, which will help overcome problems of collective action and barriers to resource exchange. For example, parents who make personal sacrifices for the good of their children may not experience the actions as a sacrifice. An individual who is treated by other members as part of a group may be included in information and resource exchanges or be offered emotional support. Finally, if outsiders treat an individual as a member of a group, the welfare of that group becomes important to the individual, even if the individual does not otherwise personally identify with the group. Again, this can internalize group welfare into individual preferences, alleviating problems of collective action.

The fifth productive resource is obligations, debts that have been incurred during prior interactions. The obligations may be explicitly acknowledged, or implicit. In either case, the fulfillment of these obligations will create value for the group in the future.[9]

The sixth productive resource is roles and norms of behavior for people playing those roles. For example, someone playing the lecturer role does most of the talking, while people playing the audience member role are expected to signal a desire to speak and wait until the lecturer recognizes them. Well-defined roles create clear expectations of what people will do, enabling them to route information and exchange resources more efficiently. These roles and expectations can be codified into routines, patterns of behavior that become so automatic that people do not have to consciously decide to follow them (Nelson and Winter 1982). For example, a basketball team can execute a fast break if players know the roles involved. The person dribbling the ball knows where the other players will go, not because of who they are but because of their relative position on the court, which defines the role they will play this time down the court.

Certain norms can be especially productive. For example, a norm of joining in when someone takes a risky action can enable a group to overcome the collective action problem of mobilizing. The norm of reciprocity creates an expectation that an individual who receives a favor will feel obliged to pass it on, either back to the original source (direct reciprocity) or to someone else (indirect or generalized reciprocity). A norm of reciprocity is especially useful for resource exchange when the transaction costs of explicit accounting would be high. Exchanges based on a norm of reciprocity also have the side benefit of creating a feeling of emotional support, since it is validating to one's self-worth to receive something without an expectation of immediate, direct payback.

The seventh and final productive resource is trust. Trust is an expectation that others will act in a way favorable to one's interests, even if they have an opportunity to do otherwise. If, in fact, the people in one's environment are trustworthy, trust is productive because it enables risk-taking in resource exchange and in overcoming dilemmas of collective action.[10] Trust also colors how an individual interprets the actions of others, so that information from trusted sources is more likely to be heeded, and aid from trusted people is more likely to create a sense of emotional support.

An expectation of continued interaction in the future is helpful in maintaining trust. A person might reason as follows. If I make myself vulnerable, my interaction partner might take advantage of me. That will help him in the short run, but it will harm his reputation, so he might be treated badly in the future. This "shadow of the future" (Axelrod 1984) will prevent him from taking advantage of me, and thus it is safe to trust him. Future consequences of current actions are essential to this reasoning. Thus, spread of reputational information can enable trust, because other members of the

---

[9]This suggests a curious inversion of the adage "Neither a borrower nor a lender be." When I move into a new neighborhood or a new work environment, I take every opportunity to borrow and lend.

[10]Of course, if others are not trustworthy, then trust is actually counterproductive, and not sustainable.

group can carry out retaliation against someone who is opportunistic. For a similar reason, multivalent or multiplex relations, where the same people interact in multiple roles or contexts, also enable trust. If my plumber also plays tennis with me, he is less likely to overcharge for plumbing work, since I might not only stop calling on his professional services but also stop calling him for tennis.

In summary, social capital is both a residual of previous interactions and an enabler of future interactions. The residuals can include activatable communication paths; shared knowledge and values; identities, obligations, and norms that people take on; and expectations that people form about others' behaviors. These residuals are a resource that help people route information, exchange resources, provide emotional support, coordinate activity, and overcome dilemmas of collective action.

No comprehensive theory of how social capital grows or erodes has come to my attention, and I have not yet been able to develop an adequate one. It is clear, however, that the shadow of the future created by repeated interaction is a necessary condition. It is also clear that the generation and use of social capital act in a virtuous or vicious cycle. Successful collective action typically generates social capital, while inaction or failed attempts to act together make it even harder to do so in the future.

29.4 SocioTechnical Capital Opportunities

Given this background on how social capital works, it is now possible to explore the new opportunities and pitfalls that ICTs present. In the absence of a comprehensive theory of how social capital builds and erodes, the exploration is organized around categories of technological affordances rather than social capital needs.

29.4.1 Removing Barriers to Interaction

The first and most obvious affordance of ICTs is that they enable interactions that would otherwise be cumbersome or impossible, as summarized in Table 29.1. Researchers in computer-supported cooperative work long ago noted that computer-mediated communication enables communication at a distance and communication across time. In addition, technology can present information in unobtrusive ways, so that interaction can take place without unduly disturbing other activities.

Interaction of some kind is a necessary condition for building social capital, so using ICTs to overcome these barriers to interaction is a potential opportunity. But interaction is not a sufficient condition. A long line of research has investigated various limitations of computer mediated interactions (Turoff, Chapter 13), and there are good arguments that there may be inherent limitations to interaction at a distance that technology will never overcome (Olson and Olson, Chapter 18). Moreover, there are opportunity costs: If mediated interactions use time that would otherwise be used in

TABLE 29.1 How Technology Can Remove Barriers to Interaction

Affordance	Description	Examples
Distant Communication	The sender and receiver need not be collocated.	Videoconferencing, e-mail, instant messaging, Webcam
Asynchronous Communication	The recipient of communication accesses it at a later time.	Voice mail, e-mail
Peripheral Presentation	An interaction need not take the user's full attention and may not come to the attention of other people who are copresent.	Vibrating beeper, headphones, heads-up display in automobile

face-to-face interactions, the net effect could be to reduce social capital. On the other hand, if the displaced activities are driving and television watching, or if the mediated interactions are in some way better than face-to-face at building social capital, the effect could be positive.

29.4.2 Expanding Interaction Networks

ICTs make it possible to interact with much larger social networks (Table 29.2). Messages can routinely reach hundreds or thousands of people on mailing lists and computers can help people monitor and aggregate information from many sources. Again, the social capital impacts are ambiguous: If weak ties with a larger social network displace stronger ties with a few people, there are both gains and losses to social capital.

29.4.3 Restricting Information Flows

A third opportunity is to use ICTs to restrict information flows (Table 29.3). Interactions where people are not informed about each other's identity can sometimes allow people to transcend their stereotypes or take productive risks (Turoff, Chapter 13).

TABLE 29.2 How Technology Can Expand Interaction Networks

Affordance	Description	Examples
Large Fan-Out	One sender can send information to a large number of recipients.	E-mail lists, news groups, Web sites
Large Fan-In	One recipient can receive information from many sources and have them automatically aggregated.	Voting, information filtering and summarization, shopbots

TABLE 29.3   How Technology Can Restrict Information Flows

Affordance	Description	Examples
Anonymity	Information about the identity of interaction partners may be partially or completely hidden.	Anonymous remailers, pseudonyms
Restricted Modality	Communication may not have the full richness and nuance of face-to-face communication.	Text-only for e-mail messages, voice-only for voice mail, no smell in videoconferencing
Access Controls	Some people may be prevented from reading or writing information or interacting with certain people or services.	Password-restricted areas on Web sites, firewalls, moderated e-mail lists

Similarly, the suppression of certain sensory information (smell, tone of voice, facial expressions) can, in some circumstances, allow people to transcend emotional reactions that would interfere with working together.

Access controls (for example, an e-mail list where moderators approve new members and new messages) are another example of restricting information flows. This can help build social capital in two ways. First, it can create a sense of boundaries, reducing the risks of participation and fostering a group identity among those who do have access. Second, according people different access privileges can reify roles. For example, when someone has moderator privileges, other people may interact with them in certain ways, triggering them to enact the role of moderator in whatever way is customary for the group.

29.4.4 Managing Dependencies

Technology support can be incorporated into routines for managing dependencies (Table 29.4). Calendar programs remind people of appointments and notification services alert them when messages arrive or other events occur. Concurrency controls help people work in parallel, preventing them from interfering with each other's work or alerting them when potential conflicts have occurred.

29.4.5 Maintaining History

Technology is also useful in maintaining history, making the residuals of previous interactions visible in some way (Table 29.5). History can be useful in several ways, contributing to common knowledge (people can consult an archive or FAQ), to the development of roles and a sense of collective identity (people can reflect on past patterns of interactions), and to trust (the visibility of interaction logs and explicit feedback can create accountability).

TABLE 29.4   How Technology Can Help Manage Dependencies

Affordance	Description	Examples
Notification	When an event occurs, the user is notified, so that user need not keep checking to see whether the event has occurred yet.	Beeper, smoke alarm
Concurrency Controls	When people work together, technology can prevent them from overwriting each other's work, either by preventing simultaneous access or by merging changes that result from simultaneous access.	Transaction processing; check-out, check-in, and merge features in RCS and CVS for software source code

TABLE 29.5   How Technology Can Maintain History

Affordance	Description	Examples
Document Versioning	Track the history of all previous versions of a document and note forks in the version tree where versions diverged from a common ancestor.	CVS for code versioning, "Track changes" feature in MS Word
Interaction Logs	If interactions are mediated, the mediating computer logs user behaviors.	Web log files, e-mail logs, purchasing history
Explicit Feedback	People comment on the quality of information or interactions.	Buyer and seller feedback about each other on eBay, epinions.com
Network Maps	Group members can reflect on their own interaction patterns by looking at a visual representation of the graph of connections between members.	IKNOW (Contractor et al. 1998), Krackplot (Krackhardt et al. 1995)

29.4.6 Naming

Finally, ICTs can contribute to social capital through indirection in naming (Table 29.6). Names can reify roles. For example, when a person sends e-mail to editor@ journal.org, and it automatically forwards to the current editor, the sender is likely to interact with the recipient as editor, even if the two might interact in different ways in other contexts. Similarly, a named e-mail lists can help establish a group identity. The group's membership can change over time, and individuals need not even be aware of

TABLE 29.6   How Technology Contributes to Establishing Names for Roles and Groups

Affordance	Description	Examples
Local Names with Late Binding	People refer to information and other people by names that are resolved at the last possible moment. Thus, the referent can change dynamically, and the user need not even be aware of its exact binding.	URLs for Web pages; e-mail groups such as listservs, which are addressable by name but whose membership can change over time

the current membership when they send messages, but the name persists and acts as a marker of a single, collective identity.

29.4.7 Summary

Of course, none of these technology-mediated interactions or residuals will improve the social capital of all groups in all situations. For example, a Webcam may enable peripheral participation, but it may also engender distrust if people feel that they are being spied on. The purpose of the inventory of affordances is merely to spark the imagination.

29.5   Examples of New SocioTechnical Relations

Given these building blocks, what new kinds of social relations seem like promising forms of sociotechnical capital? There are a few categories of opportunities, including enhanced group self-awareness, reliance on brief and intermittent interactions, low-maintenance (in terms of time) social ties, support for collective action in large groups, and just-in-time introductions.

29.5.1 Enhanced Group Self-Awareness

Groups can use captured traces as a basis for reflection on their own activities. For example, visualizations of who knows or interacts with whom (Contractor 1998) or of overlaps in mailing-list subscriptions (Donath 1995) can highlight connections among people. Greater awareness may lead to greater investment in activities that build these networks, creating a positive feedback loop. Both visual representations of activity and assigning a name to a group may also aid in formation of a sense of group identity.

29.5.2 Brief interactions

Lee Sproull and John Patterson (2000) have noted a serious limitation of traditional civic activities: They almost all require synchronous, colocated participation in two- to three-hour chunks of time. Perhaps there is another way. People can engage in short interactions if the setup for each interaction is easy enough. Setup can involve costs of coordinating schedules and locations and cognitive costs of recalling the context of previous interactions. Technology-mediated communication can eliminate the need for colocation, reducing transportation costs. Monitoring and notification technologies can make it easy to coordinate schedules, and use of asynchronous communication can eliminate the need to coordinate schedules entirely. Technology-mediated histories can help people recall the context of previous interactions.

For example, some people are using buddy lists and instant messaging to maintain frequent, brief contacts with their friends or coworkers throughout the day (Nardi et al. 2000). Similarly, people are using pagers and text messaging features in cell phones to exchange very brief messages. On a larger time scale, some college students today are exchanging short e-mail messages with their parents, siblings, and high school friends, enabling them to maintain relations that likely would have atrophied when their counterparts went to college two decades ago.

29.5.3 Maintaining Ties While Spending Less Time

People can maintain ties while effectively using less time, either by actually spending less time interacting or by doing other things while interacting. This can either free up time for other activities or allow people to maintain more interaction overall.

Technology can reduce the time-burden that initiating newcomers places on other group members. The FAQ document[11] is becoming an accepted norm for online discussion spaces (news groups, e-mail lists, and Web sites). A social norm is emerging that newcomers to any group should read the FAQ (and other documentation) before posting a request for help. The availability of an FAQ, together with the social convention of checking it, allows a group to welcome newcomers without having them hold back the conversation or other activity of veteran participants.

Some people are always more active than others in any group. Previous theories have emphasized peripheral participation as an important steppingstone toward full membership in a community of practice (Lave and Wenger 1991). But technology may also enable people to remain productively at the periphery. For example, if records of meetings are captured and easily accessed, a person who only rarely attends meetings may still be able to participate fully in those meetings she attends. If

---

[11]FAQ stands for Frequently Asked Questions. The questions act as an index to the answers, which provide important information for newcomers. Sometimes the questions truly have been asked frequently, but even new groups will provide an FAQ document, reflecting questions that the authors think newcomers might ask if the FAQ weren't available.

speech recognition improves, computers might scan records of conversations and highlight the parts that were relevant to particular people. It might even be possible to monitor conversations in real time and notify participants when they should tune in. For example, in large software development projects, there are often people present at meetings just in case something comes up that will affect their organization or functional area. They could perhaps participate more peripherally and just as effectively.

Rather than occasional activity from some members, the group as a whole may be dormant for a long period of time but activatable just in case it's needed. Dormant groups can be difficult to reactivate, but technology may make this easier to do. For example, a year ago I created an e-mail list for the people who live on my block. It's almost never used (about one message a month), and only a few people have posted messages, so by conventional HCI evaluation methods it would be considered a failure. However, it turned out to be extremely useful on a few occasions: for arranging a block party, announcing funeral arrangements for a neighbor, and alerting people to a car break-in. People don't often have messages they want to broadcast to the block, but the list is there just in case.

Multitasking is another way to stretch the available time. Lawyers have long had more than 24 (billable) hours in a day, and everyone else seems to be catching on to the practice of doing more than one thing at a time. Cell phones have made it possible to talk while walking or, unfortunately, driving. Teenagers are apt to talk on the phone while watching TV.[12] At my health club, people watch TV, listen to music, or read a book while exercising. People often take advantage of multitasking to negotiate possible interactions (Nardi et al. 2000)—for example, sending a text message to someone who may be in a meeting. Instant messaging and vibrating pagers or handhelds make this possible without interrupting the meeting.

29.5.4 Support for Large Groups

New forms of sociotechnical relations may be especially useful for large groups of people, groups so large that it's impossible for everyone to know everyone else. In larger groups, there are more opportunities for information and resource sharing, but it's difficult to coordinate these, and it is also difficult to overcome problems of collection action. SocioTechnical Capital may enable productive activity in these larger groups.

Word of mouth normally travels from person to person in a social network. Recommender systems (Resnick and Varian 1997) can supercharge this process, allowing recommendation sharing among people who may not know each other or be explicitly aware of each other's interests. Computers provide support for gathering feedback about information, products, or even people, either in the form of explicit ratings or

---

[12]Jorge Schement (personal communication) relays an amusing story about his observation of a teenage relative who had on the TV and an active chat window on the computer while she chatted on the phone. Jorge asked, "What are you doing?" She replied, of course, "Watching TV with my friend."

traces of behavior such as clickstream or purchasing history. For example, Amazon. com gathers explicit book reviews from readers and also mines purchasing behavior to generate bestseller lists and links from individual books to other related books. Recommender systems can aggregate feedback from multiple people in a personalized way, identifying people who have similar interests and then weighting their feedback more heavily. One potential downside to recommender systems is social fragmentation if people share information only with others who are like-minded (Sunstein 2001). Mathematical models suggest this could occur even if each individual has only a slight preference for homogeneity (Van Alstyne and Brynjolfsson 1996). That is, communication paths might form cliques rather than bridging ties, thus destroying the social capital benefits that come from the small-world phenomenon. Terveen and Hill (Chapter 22) explore the future of recommender systems in more detail.

In large groups, it is hard for individuals to determine who to trust, and it is hard for the groups as a whole to encourage trustworthy behavior. This acts as an inhibitor to transactions that require risk-taking and to collective mobilization whenever there is an opportunity for free-riding. A reputation system gathers information about people's past behavior and makes it available to others. For example, at eBay and other auction sites, a buyer and seller can leave comments about each other after completing a transaction, and these comments are visible to future buyers and sellers.

If people regularly provide honest feedback, and those with more positive feedback are treated better in the future, this can enable the maintenance of trust in a large online interaction environment (Resnick et al. 2000). Game-theoretic analysis suggests that this can be fairly effective, though not optimal, even if people remain anonymous and thus have the option of shedding bad reputations and starting over (Friedman and Resnick, in press). Empirical analysis of eBay auctions suggests that social practices have indeed evolved at eBay that help buyers and problem sellers and reward sellers who have better reputations with higher profits for their goods (Bajari and Hortascu 2000; Lucking-Reiley et al. 2000; Resnick and Zeckhauser 2001).

One of the most exciting trends in software development is the success of open-source projects (Raymond 1999). Much has been made of the surprising economic viability of these projects, given that users of the software don't pay for it. The interesting feature from the sociotechnical capital perspective is the ability of a large group of people, most of whom will never meet each other, to together create really good software. Each project has a central coordinating body that maintains the recognized "source tree," including a version history and, in some cases, alternate versions (updates to the official release version may not be reflected in the code people are working on for the next release). Anyone can check out a copy of code files and contribute updated files or new files as candidates for inclusion in the official source tree. Concurrency control features make it easy to merge changes from several people who have worked in parallel and to identify any conflicting changes they have proposed. Over time, contributors can develop reputations for writing good code, and their suggested code is more likely to be included in the official versions.

Software is not the only mass-collaboration authoring happening on the Internet. For example, the online documentation for the programming language PHP allows anyone to add a question or comment to the bottom of any page in the manual (see php.net). The reader contributions tend to be quite helpful, clearing up infelicities and omissions in the original and providing useful code samples that official documentation writers might otherwise be expected to provide. The site BetterTogether. org applies this widely distributed authoring idea recursively to the topic of building social capital. It invites readers to contribute stories about new ways of building social capital, or to add comments about others' stories.

New technology and social practices can also support conversation in very large groups. The division of netnews into a hierarchy of topics, with response threads within each topic, was an early way of structuring large conversations. Some of the early work on recommendation sharing was motivated by the need to find personally relevant messages in netnews (Resnick et al. 1994). Recent work explores visual representations of social networks and topic relations as a way to keep conversations manageable as the number of participants grows (Sack 2000).

29.5.5 Introducer Systems: Just-in-Time Social Ties

In everyday life, people introduce friends and colleagues to each other. In larger, more diffuse groups, computer technology can assist in this social process. Some of the early writings on recommender systems suggested that people who shared tastes in movies or music should be introduced to each other (Hill et al. 1995). The site sixdegrees.com explicitly represents social networks and then automatically passes on messages to "friends-of-friends," a form of automatic introduction. ReferralWeb automatically finds paths in social networks, suggesting a sequence of intermediaries could serve as personal introducers in order to make a connection with someone else (Kautz et al. 1997). Modern personal ads, which seem to be quite popular based on their volume in local papers, introduce people to each other and mediate the exchange of messages (often through voice mail) while people decide whether they want to strike up a relationship. The Yenta system takes this cloaking of identities to the next level, making matches based on common interests (personal or professional) while providing cryptographic guarantees of anonymity until participants decide to reveal their identities or other personal information (Foner 1999).

Documents can act as interesting focal points for introducing people. Common interest in a document suggests that an introduction might be worthwhile, and the document itself can act as a natural first topic for conversation. For example, in the BetterTogether.org story collector mentioned previously, each story has the potential to act as a focal point for introducing readers to each other.

Finally, directories can help to break the ice among people who are members of new or loosely knit groups. The directories can include photos, contact information, offers or requests for resources, and something fun or personal that acts as a conversation starter when people meet. Neighborhoods, church groups, sports teams, civic organizations, and even entering classes of graduate schools are all good candidates (see, for example, www.whothat.org).

29.6   Research Agenda

The preceding examples suggest that there are rich opportunities for new sociotechnical relations. Research is needed in several areas to better understand which kinds of sociotechnical relations can properly be called sociotechnical capital.

29.6.1 Measurement of SocioTechnical Capital

First, research is needed on ways of measuring sociotechnical capital. Social capital is an intermediate outcome, both a residual of some activities and an enabler of others. Thus, social capital metrics need to function in some studies as independent variables. For example, in Putnam's study of Italy, regions with greater social capital in the late nineteenth century had better political and economic outcomes in the late twentieth century, even controlling for political and economic conditions in the earlier period (Putnam 1993). For designers and evaluators of information systems, however, social capital metrics will more often serve as a dependent variable. If the social capital metrics increase as a result of a group of people adopting certain technology and social practices, it is a marker of success of that combination.

Some traditional social capital metrics will be appropriate for sociotechnical capital as well. But some are based on implicit assumptions about what social relations are productive and what activities generate them, assumptions that may not hold when information and communication technologies are available. The inventory below pays special attention to potential limitations and suggests avenues for development of new metrics. Previous social capital metrics measure activities, attitudes, and networks. Consider each of these in turn.

Activity-based social capital measures include membership in organizations, participation in elections, and attendance at meetings and other face-to-face events. For example, Putnam (2000) reports survey data about how often Americans attend club meetings, participate in neighborhood activities, play cards, go on picnics, and eat dinner with friends.[13] These measures, however, would miss trends in interactions that are not face to face. It may be that these other forms of interactions are not as good at building social capital, but that needs to be determined independently, using some metric of social capital that does not privilege face-to-face interaction.

Attitude-based social capital measures focus on people's dispositions and their expectations about how others will act. These are typically measured through surveys and include measures of collective efficacy (members' belief in the ability of the collective to act effectively), psychological sense of community, and neighborhood cohesion (Lochner et al. 1999). There have also been attempts to develop behavioral measures of these attitudes. For example, experimental economists ask subjects how much they would be willing to pay the experimenter to have the experimenter drop

---

[13]Some of the data sets are available for download at bowlingalone.com.

on their street an unsealed envelope with $10 in it and with the subject's name written on it (Gleaser et al. 1999). This measures the subject's level of trust in the people on that street to return the money to her.

Some attitude-based measures are situational, reflecting who a person is expecting to interact with and in what context. Others measure more universal dispositions, such as the general social survey question, "Most people can be trusted—or you can't be too careful dealing with people." The measures of universal dispositions are generally more useful when social capital is an independent variable because one would not expect them to change quickly in response to adoption of new information systems or social practices. Contextualized measures will be quite useful in studying sociotechnical capital but need to be adapted to reflect situations where people expect information systems to be available and used in particular ways. Thus, for example, in measuring the sociotechnical capital resulting from eBay's feedback system, it is not enough to inquire about participants' beliefs in how trustworthy sellers are in general. What matters is how trustworthy they are, given their reputations, given the ability of the buyer to provide feedback at the end of transaction, and given the expectation that others will look at that feedback in the future.

Finally, network measures of social capital reflect which people know each other and tend to interact with each other. Networks are usually represented as graphs, with people as nodes and links between nodes if the people know each other or tend to interact with each other. Many metrics can be computed over these graphs. For example, the diameter of the graph is an indicator of how quickly information might spread through the network (Watts 1999). The presence of cliques or near-cliques may indicate a group with strong ties, and the absence of links connecting subgraphs is an indicator of boundaries where information or trust might stop (Burt 1995).

When using network measures of sociotechnical capital, extreme care must be taken. As suggested in the previous section, one of the new and productive forms of sociotechnical relations may be dormant but activatable social ties. Other ties may be latent, with introducer systems making it possible to connect people when the need arises. Metrics on graphs may still be useful but only after creative definition of links between nodes that takes into account the potential for future interaction and not simply the history of past interaction.

Creating and validating metrics of sociotechnical capital is an important research problem. When appropriate, it is advantageous to use existing measures of social capital because many of these measures have already been validated through correlation with positive final outcomes such as health, education, and crime reduction. In some cases, however, new measures may be needed. There may also be opportunities for new kinds of metrics. For example, it may be possible to mine transactional or clickstream data (like bidding behavior at eBay) to determine behavioral measures of trust. It may also be possible to have a group conduct a stylized activity online (for example, play a social dilemma or negotiation game; Rocco 1998) to determine how effectively the group can act together. Any new metrics, however, will have to be validated, either by showing a correlation with existing metrics or by showing a correlation with the ability of a group to achieve desirable individual or collective outcomes.

29.6.2 Case Studies of New SocioTechnical Relations

A second line of research is further exploration of new forms of sociotechnical relations. The previous examples of new ways that people might interact and the new kinds of residuals they might rely on only scratch the surface of what is possible. Concerted efforts are required to imagine new technologies and social practices that plausibly could enhance the capability of a collective to serve individual and collective needs. Similar effort is required to evaluate social capital impacts, both controlled experiments testing interventions and natural experiments where new social relations are emerging without the experimenter's intervention. This process will yield a set of case studies that are fodder for more systematic theorizing.

One case study that I have been working on measures the impact of a photo directory on the way that neighbors interact with each other. The intervention is for a block captain to interview his or her neighbors and distribute paper directories with names, contact information, hobbies or interests, and photos to everyone who wants to participate. Before and after the intervention, everyone on the block is asked to complete a survey with a number of social capital questions. Details can be found at www.whothat.org.

29.6.3 Codification of the Opportunity Space and Determining Which Features Are Productive

More systematic theorizing needs to begin with a codification of the space of opportunities for new sociotechnical relations. Ideally, this codification would identify basic building blocks, independent features of sociotechnical relations whose utility could be evaluated semi-independently of other features. This is a common goal in characterizing the design space for technical systems. One strategy is to collect examples of different designs and ask what they have in common and how they differ. The ways that they differ often fall naturally onto one or more independent dimensions. For this strategy, a large collection of case studies is especially useful.

One approach would be to consider features of technology and features of social practices separately. This is unlikely to be fruitful, however, if the evenutal goal is to make claims about the utility of different configurations. As suggested in the introduction, the most interesting forms of sociotechnical capital are likely to be those where there is an interaction effect between the technology and the social practices. For example, the practice of allowing a group to go dormant when there is nothing it needs to do may only be effective if technology mechanisms are available that make it easy to reassemble the group when it is needed. Thus, the research challenge is to break down the space of opportunities along dimensions that capture both technical and social aspects and that have identifiable impacts on the ability of a collective to act effectively.

It would also be helpful to develop a grand theory of how social capital builds and is destroyed. As mentioned previously, repetition and reputation are important preconditions, and successful use of existing social capital is often a way to build more. A more comprehensive theory, however, would account for the permeability of boundaries, the effects of homogeneity and heterogeneity in group composition, and many other factors.

With a characterization of both the opportunity space and the sources of social capital, it may then be possible to make claims about the social capital effects of various sociotechnical features. For example, a long line of research has investigated the effects of restricted communication modalities (such as text only, voice + text, video) on the ability of a pair or group to carry out specific tasks, such as design, negotiation, or cooperation in a social dilemma (Rocco 1998; Olson and Olson, Chapter 18). Similarly, if periodically dormant communication channels were one of the dimensions of the space of opportunities, a research goal would be to make claims about the extent to which that kind of sociotechnical relation supports various kinds of collective activity (information routing, resource exchange, emotional support, coordination, public goods production).

Even if researchers are successful in identifying types of sociotechnical relations that are resources people can use to act together, it will not follow automatically that these sociotechnical relations will emerge naturally. Further research will be necessary to identify ways to introduce technology and seed practices so that the desired sociotechnical capital will grow.

29.7   Conclusion

This essay has suggested a reorientation of researchers' attention away from the immediate ability of people to complete tasks toward the longer-term effects on their ability to act collectively. But long-term effects are distant and highly contingent. The concept of social capital provides a way of thinking about intermediate states, immediate effects of people's interactions that have long-term consequences. This makes social capital a good focal point for research, especially for HCI designers and evaluators.

First, social capital effects may appear sooner and be easier to measure than some of the long-term outcomes that we might care about, such as organizational productivity or improved health. Thus, social capital measures can be useful outcome variables in evaluations of information system interventions. Do networks become denser? Do ties form between groups? Do people interact more frequently and share more information when they do? Do they provide more favors for others without keeping strict accounts, thus indicating a norm of reciprocity? Do they trust one another more or feel a greater sense of belonging?

Second, information systems designers may have a special role to play in helping to resolve social science controversies about whether observed correlations between social capital measures and positive outcomes are actually causal. Few previous studies have made causal claims. It is possible in some cases to argue causality from the temporal sequence of observed changes in social capital variables and end outcomes (for example, Putnam's [1993] study of Italy). But it is rare to find such natural experiments and still rarer to find sufficient data about them to yield strong conclusions. If information systems interventions can be found that reliably cause changes in certain measures of social capital, these interventions can be used to manipulate social capital as an independent variable in experimental or quasi-experimental studies and hence study their causal impact on end outcomes.

Technology is not just a creator (and destroyer) of old forms of social capital. New forms of social relations can emerge that would be infeasible without computers mediating interactions and managing the interaction traces and artifacts that are created during interactions. The challenge for activist researchers is to identify and promote those new social relations that truly are productive. There seem to be some promising opportunities, including maintaining ties with occasional, short, or peripheral interactions, and loosely coupled collective activity in large groups. Some variants of these social relations seem to be beneficial while seemingly similar variants leave people feeling disconnected and unable to act collectively.

Exploring and codifying the space of opportunities, and evaluating the effects of various options on sociotechnical capital, is extremely important work. It is clear that society is changing and that older forms of togetherness that generated social capital no longer draw people in the way they once did. The pure entertainment value of computer-based interactions is another lure away from face-to-face interactions. If we do not succeed in generating new forms of sociotechnical capital from these online interactions, our society will decline in its ability to provide emotional support to its members, to overcome transaction costs that hinder resource exchange, and to overcome dilemmas of collective action. In the long run, our economy, our health, and our safety may all be at stake. The future needs us to succeed in identifying and promoting new forms of sociotechnical capital, in the workplace, in learning environments, and especially in civic life. Are we up to the challenge?

Acknowledgments

For useful comments and conversations, I would like to thank Tora Bikson, Michael Cohen, George Furnas, Rob Kling, Bob Putnam, Lee Sproull, an anonymous reviewer, and all the participants at a workshop on SocioTechnical Capital held in Ann Arbor in March 2000.

References

Axelrod, R. (1984). *The evolution of cooperation.* New York: Basic Books.

Bajari, P., and Hortascu, A. (2000). Winner's curse, reserve prices and endogenous entry: Empirical insights from eBay auctions. Stanford. http://www.stanford.edu/~bajari/wp/auction/ebay.pdf.

Bikson, T., and Eveland, J.D. (1996). Groupware implementation: Reinvention in the sociotechnical frame *(CSCW 96)*. *Conference on Computer Supported Cooperative Work,* 428–437. New York: ACM Press.

Brynjolfsson, E. (1993). The productivity paradox of information technology. *Communications of the ACM,* 36, 12, 66–77.

Brynjolfsson, E., and Hitt, L. (1998). Beyond the productivity paradox. *Communications of the ACM,* 41, 8, 49–55.

Burt, R.S. (1992). *Structural holes: The social structure of competition.* Cambridge, MA: Harvard University Press.

Coleman, J.S. (1988). Social capital in the creation of human capital. *American Journal of Sociology,* 94 (Supplement), S95–S120.

Contractor, N., Zink, D., et al. (1998). IKNOW: A tool to assist and study the creation, maintenance, and dissolution of knowledge networks. In T. Ishida (Ed.), *Community Computing and Support Systems,* 201–217. Berlin: Springer-Verlag.

Donath, J.S. (1995). *Visual who: Animating the affinities and activities of an electronic community.* San Francisco, CA: ACM Multimedia.

Foner, L.N. (1999). Political artifacts and personal privacy: The Yenta multi-agent distributed matchmaking system. MIT: Thesis. http://foner.www.media.mit.edu/people/foner/PhD-Thesis/Dissertation/.

Friedman, E., and Resnick, P. (In press). The social cost of cheap pseudonyms. *Journal of Economics and Management Strategy.*

Glaeser, E.L., Laibson, D., Scheinkman, J., and Sutter, C. 2000. Measuring trust. *Quarterly Journal of Economics* 115, 3, August, 811–846.

Granovetter, M.S. (1973). The strength of weak ties. *American Journal of Sociology,* 76, 6, 1360–1380.

Hardin, G. (1968). The tragedy of the commons. *Science,* 162, 1243–1248.

Hill, W., Stead, L., Rosenstein, M. (1995). Recommending and evaluating choices in a virtual community of use. *CHI'95 Conference on Human Factors in Computing Systems,* 194–201. Denver: ACM Press.

Hollan, J., and Stornetta, S. (1992). Beyond being there. *CHI'92 Conference on Human Factors in Computing Systems,* 119–125. New York: ACM Press.

Kautz, H., Selman, B., Shah, M. (1997). The hidden web. *The AI Magazine,* 18, 2, 27–36.

Knack, S., and Keefer, P. (1997). Does social capital have an economic payoff? A cross-country investigation. *The Quarterly Journal of Economics,* 112, 4, 1251–1288.

Kollock, P., and O'Brien, J. (1992). The social construction of exchange. *Advances in Group Processes,* 9, 89–112.

Krackhardt, D., Blythe, J., McGrath, C. (1995). *Krackplot 3.0: User's manual.* Carnegie Mellon University. http://www.contrib.andrew.cmu.edu/~krack/.

Kraut, R., Patterson, M., Lundmanc, V., Kiesler, S., Mukophadyay, T., Scherlis, W. (1998). Internet paradox: A social technology that reduces social involvement and psychological well-being? *American Psychologist,* 53, 9, 1017–1031.

Landauer, T.K. (1995). *The trouble with computers: Usefulness, usability, and productivity.* Cambridge, MA: MIT Press.

Lave, J., and Wenger, E. (1991). *Situated learning: Legitimate peripheral participation.* Cambridge, UK: Cambridge University Press.

Lochner, K., Kawachi, I., Kennedy, B-P. (1999). Social capital: A guide to its measurement. *Health & Place,* 5, 259–270.

Lucking-Reiley, D., Bryan, D., Prasad, N., Reeves, D. (2000). Pennies from eBay: The determinants of price in online auctions. Vanderbilt: Working paper. http://www.vanderbilt.edu/econ/reiley/papers/PenniesFromEBay.pdf.

Malone, T.W., Crowston, K., Lee, J., Pentland, B., Dellarocas, C., Wyrer, G., Quimby, J., Osborn, C., Herman, G., Klein, M., O'Donnell, E. (1999). Tools for inventing organizations: Toward a handbook of organizational processes. *Management Science,* 45, 3, 425–443.

Minow, M. (1997). *Not only for myself: Identity politics and the law.* New York: The New Press.

Myerson, R., and Satterthwaite, M. (1983). Efficient mechanisms for bilateral trade. *Journal of Economic Theory,* 28, 265–281.

Nardi, B., Whittaker, S., et al. (2000). Interaction and outeraction: Instant messaging in action. *Conference on Computer-Supported Cooperative Work.* (CSCW'00). New York: ACM Press.

Nelson, R.R., and Winter, S.G. (1982). *An evolutionary theory of economic change.* Cambridge, MA: Harvard University Press.

Olson, M. (1965). *The logic of collective action.* Cambridge, MA: Harvard University Press.

Ostrom, E. (1990). *Governing the commons: The evolution of institutions for collective action.* Cambridge, UK: Cambridge University Press.

Parker, E.A., Lichtenstein, R.L., et al. (2000). Disentangling measures of community social dynamics: Results of a community survey. University of Michigan School of Public Health: Draft.

Putnam, R. (2000). *Bowling alone: The crumbling and revival of American community.* New York: Simon & Schuster.

Putnam, R.D. (1993). *Making democracy work: Civic traditions in modern Italy.* Princeton, NJ: Princeton University Press.

Raymond, E. (1999). *The cathedral & the bazaar: Musings on Linux and Open Source by an accidental revolutionary.* Cambridge, MA: O'Reilly.

Resnick, P., Iacovou, N., et al. (1994). GroupLens: An open architecture for collaborative filtering of netnews. *Conference on Computer Supported Cooperative Work (CSCW'94),* 175–186. New York: ACM Press.

Resnick, P., and Varian, H. (1997). Recommender systems (introduction to special section). *Communications of the ACM, 40*, 3, 56–58.

Resnick, P. and Zeckhauser, R. (2001) Trust among strangers in Internet transactions: Empirical analysis of eBay's reputation system. Working paper. http://www.si.umich.edu/~presnick/papers/ebay NBER/.

Resnick, P., Zeckhauser, R., et al. (2000). Reputation systems: Facilitating trust in Internet interactions. *Communications of the ACM, 43*, 12.

Rocco, E. (1998). Trust breaks down in electronic contexts but can be repaired by some initial face-to-face contact. *ACM CHI'98 Conference on Human Factors in Computing Systems,* 496–502. New York: ACM Press.

Sack, W. (2001) Conversation map: An interface for very large-scale conversations. *Journal of Management Information Systems, 17*, 3, 73–92.

Sampson, R.J., Raudenbush, S.W., et al. (1997). Neighborhoods and violent crime: A multilevel study of collective efficacy. *Science, 277*, 918–924.

Schultz, T.W. (1961). Investment in human capital. *The American Economic Review, 51*, 1, 1–17.

Sproull, L., and Patterson, J. (2000). Computer support for local communities. NYU Stern School of Business: Working paper. April 2000.

Strauss, W., and Howe, N. (1992). *Generations: The history of America's future, 1584 to 2069.* New York: William Morrow & Co.

Sunstein, C. (2001) *Republic.com.* Princeton, NJ: Princeton University Press.

Van Alstyne, M., and Brynjolfsson, E. (1996). Widening access and narrowing focus: Could the Internet balkanize science? *Science, 274*, 5292, 1479–1480.

Watts, D. (1999). *Small worlds: The dynamics of networks between order and randomness.* Princeton, NJ: Princeton University Press.

Wenger, E. (1998). *Communities of practice: Learning, meaning, and identity.* Cambridge, UK: Cambridge University Press.

Contributors

Gregory D. Abowd is an associate professor in the College of Computing and a member of the GVU Center and Broadband Institute at Georgia Tech. His research focuses on HCI and software engineering aspects of ubiquitous computing. He founded the Future Computing Environments Group within the College of Computing and is responsible for building living laboratories for ubiquitous computing experimentation in the classroom and the home. He is co-author of *Human-Computer Interaction* (Prentice-Hall, 1998).

Mark S. Ackerman is associate professor of Information and Computer Science at the University of California, Irvine. He has published on computer-supported cooperative work, collaborative information access, virtual communities, organizational memory, hypermedia, and other human-computer interaction topics.

Ernesto G. Arias is professor of Urban and Regional Planning in the College of Architecture and Planning, courtesy professor of Computer Science, faculty fellow of the Institute of Cognitive Science, and associate director of the Center for Life-Long Learning & Design at the University of Colorado. His research interests include the roles of information technology in face-to-face and distributed interactions in the human processes of planning, design, and learning. His HCI work focuses on developing systems that support design as the resolution of "ill-structured and ill-behaved" problems, whose nature is defined by change and the involvement of multiple stakeholders. He has published in various disciplines ranging from design, planning, and policy to computer science, environmental psychology, and operations research.

Philip Barnard is a cognitive psychologist with an interest in theories of mental architecture and their application to the kinds of complex tasks characteristic of HCI. He also applies the same work on mental architecture in research on human emotion and psychopathologies, such as depression and schizophrenia. He is on the scientific staff of the Medical Research Council's Cognition and Brain Sciences Unit in Cambridge, UK.

Gordon D. Baxter is currently working as a researcher in the Department of Psychology at the University of York in the UK, having previously spent several years in systems development in industry. He is part of the Interdisciplinary Research Collaboration, which is investigating the dependability of computer-based systems (www. DIRC.org.uk). In particular, he is interested in the ways that aspects of timeliness affect human-machine interaction in such systems. He is a chartered engineer and a member of the British Computer Society.

Josh Bers is a software developer in the Speech and Language Processing Department of BBN Technologies. He has designed and developed many speech and multi-modal interfaces. Prior to joining BBN he received a masters degree from the Media Lab at MIT. His interests include conversational interfaces, distributed software design, and methods for text understanding.

Suresh K. Bhavnani specializes in computational design and human-computer interaction with a research focus on the identification, acquisition, and performance of efficient strategies to use in complex computer systems. He is assistant professor at the School of Information, University of Michigan.

Michael Bieber is associate professor of Information Systems at the New Jersey Institute of Technology, where he co-directs the Collaborative Hypermedia Research Lab and teaches in the distance learning program. He is active in hypermedia, relationship management, WWW, virtual community, and asynchronous learning networks research.

Andrew Carra is a consultant and software engineer for Parlano, Inc., in Chicago. He studied at the Center for Highly Interactive Computing in Education at the University of Michigan from 1997 to 2000. His current interests include pen-based computing, wireless networking, immersive interfaces, and computer security.

John M. Carroll is professor of Computer Science, Education, and Psychology, and director of the Center for Human-Computer Interaction at Virginia Tech. His research interests include methods and theory in human-computer interaction, particularly as applied to networking tools for collaborative learning and problem-solving. His most recent books are *Minimalism beyond "The Nurnberg Funnel"* (MIT Press, 1998) and *Making Use: Scenario-Based Design of Human-Computer Interactions* (MIT Press, 2000).

George Chin is a senior research scientist at Battelle Pacific Northwest Laboratory. Prior to joining Battelle, he studied at the Center for Human-Computer Interaction at Virginia Tech. His research has focused on the areas of participatory design, ethnographic methods, computer-supported collaborative work, computer-supported collaborative learning, problem-solving environments, and human-computer interaction.

Phil Cohen received his B.A. in mathematics from Cornell University and his M.Sc. and Ph.D. in computer science from the University of Toronto. Dr. Cohen is currently a professor and co-director of the Center for Human-Computer Communication in the Department of Computer Science at the Oregon Graduate Institute of Science and Technology. His research interests include multimodal interaction, multiagent systems, dialogue, natural language processing, and theories of collaboration and communication. Cohen was president of the Association for Computational Linguistics in 1999 and is a fellow of the American Association for Artificial Intelligence.

Andrew Dillon is associate professor of Information Science and of Informatics at Indiana University, where he directs the IU Program in HCI. He conducts research on human response to information technology, the emotional and affective dimensions of acceptance, and the design of information architectures that support learning. He has published more than 80 papers on his work and serves on several editorial boards, including *International Journal of Human-Computer Studies, Interacting with Computers, and the Journal of Digital Information.*

David Duce is a professor of Computing at Oxford Brookes University, where he leads the Distributed Systems Research Group. His research interests include Web graphics, distributed cooperative visualization, and applications of formal techniques in human computer interaction.

David Duke is a lecturer in Computer Science at the University of Bath, UK. Over the last ten years his work has spanned formal methods, standards for distributed multimedia, information visualization, and human-computer interaction. He currently holds an Advanced Research Fellowship funded by the UK Engineering and Physical Sciences Research Council.

Lisbeth Duncan is an associate technical fellow in the Mathematics and Computing Technology Division of The Boeing Company in Seattle, Washington. She has worked in research and development there for the past 15 years, focusing on natural language processing and human-computer interface design. She has authored and co-authored several papers and technical reports on Boeing's work in these areas.

Hal Eden is a research associate in the Department of Computer Science, a member of the Institute of Cognitive Science, and associate director of the Center for Life-Long Learning & Design at the University of Colorado at Boulder. His current research interests center on the creation of co-present group interfaces supporting collaboration, learning, and social creativity. He has worked and directed several projects focused on combining social and technical elements that enable and encourage learning and the creation of community.

Thomas Erickson is a research staff member at the IBM T.J. Watson Research Center in New York, where he works on designing systems that support network-mediated group interaction. An interaction designer and researcher, his approach to systems design is shaped by work in sociology, rhetoric, architecture, and urban design. He has contributed to the design of many products and authored numerous publications on topics ranging from personal electronic notebooks and information retrieval systems to pattern languages and virtual community.

David Ferro is senior manager of e-Business Operations at Iomega Corporation in Roy, Utah. Prior to Iomega he worked in natural language understanding at Unisys

Corporation. His interests include participatory HCI and the engineering culture. He received his Ph.D. in the Social Study of Science and Technology from Virginia Tech.

Gerhard Fischer is professor of Computer Science, fellow of the Institute of Cognitive Science, and director of the Center for Lifelong Learning & Design at the University of Colorado at Boulder. His research includes new conceptual frameworks and new media for learning, working, and collaboration; human-computer interaction; cognitive science; artificial intelligence; software design; and domain-oriented design environments. Over the last 20 years, he has directed research projects and published extensively in these areas.

Jerry Fjermestad is an associate professor in the School of Management at NJIT. He received his B.A. in Chemistry from Pacific Lutheran University, an M.S. in Operations Research from Polytechnic University, an M.B.A in Operations Management from Iona College, and an M.B.A. and Ph.D. from Rutgers University in Management Information Systems. His current research interests are in collaborative technology, decision support systems, data warehousing, electronic commerce, and enterprise information systems.

George W. Furnas is a professor at the School of Information and in the College of Engineering at the University of Michigan. He was formerly director of Computer Graphics and Interactive Media research at Bell Communications Research. A principal focus of his research has been in human computer interaction, specializing in areas related to information access and visualization, but he has also published work in multivariate statistics and graphical reasoning.

Andrew Gorman is a senior research assistant in the Department of Computer Science, a member of the Institute of Cognitive Science, and member of the Center for Lifelong Learning & Design at the University of Colorado at Boulder. His research interests include computer-supported cooperation, human-computer interaction, cognitive science, and user modeling. He has more than ten years' experience developing large-scale information systems for industry and is now applying his system design expertise to the area of collaborative knowledge management systems.

Will Hill is a technology consultant at AT&T Shannon Labs, where his research interests include data-mining of public preferences, information visualization, and novel input devices. Prior to joining AT&T, he conducted human interface research at Bellcore, MCC, and Northwestern University.

Starr Roxanne Hiltz is distinguished professor of Computer and Information Science at New Jersey Institute of Technology, where she also directs the Ph.D. program in Information Systems. She does research on applications and the social impact of computer technology, publishing widely in journals such as *JMIS, MISQ, Communications of the ACM,* and *Management Science.* Her research interests currently include group support systems, asynchronous learning networks, and pervasive computing.

James Hollan is professor of Cognitive Science at the University of California, San Diego. He has served as director of the Human Interface Laboratory at MCC, director of the Computer Graphics and Interactive Media Research Group at Bellcore, and chair of the Computer Science Department at the University of New Mexico. His research focuses on human-computer interaction and information visualization. In collaboration with Edwin Hutchins and David Kirsh, he established the Distributed Cognition and Human Computer Interaction Laboratory at UCSD.

Thomas Holzman is senior human factors engineering consultant at NCR Corporation and adjunct professor of Instructional Technology at Georgia State University. He has also served in NCR's Corporate Technology organization as director of Cognitive Engineering. His research and development activities have focused on the way that media and human-computer interaction parameters influence the effectiveness and attractiveness of user interfaces, computer-based instruction, and electronic performance support systems.

Scott E. Hudson is associate professor of Human Computer Interaction in the HCI Institute at Carnegie Mellon, where he serves as the director of the HCII Ph.D. program. He has been the general and program chair for the ACM UIST conference, currently serves as an associate editor for *ACM Transactions on CHI,* and has published more than 70 papers. His research interests cover a wide range of topics in user interface software and technology.

Edwin Hutchins is professor of Cognitive Science at the University of California, San Diego. He studies cognition in naturally occurring, culturally constituted settings using an approach called distributed cognition. Trained as a cognitive anthropologist, he has studied litigation in Melanesia, traditional Micronesian navigation, modern navigation, and automation in airliners. His book *Cognition in the Wild* (MIT Press, 1996) is a classic in cognitive science.

Hiroshi Ishii is an associate professor at the MIT Media Lab, where he founded and directs the Tangible Media Group. Prior to MIT, he led a CSCW research group at the NTT Human Interface Laboratories and was a visiting assistant professor at the University of Toronto. He is active in the research fields of human-computer interaction and computer-supported cooperative work, and he has been an associate editor of *ACM TOCHI* and *TOIS.*

Bonnie E. John is an associate professor in the Human-Computer Interaction Institute and Department of Psychology at Carnegie Mellon University. She was a founding member of the HCI Institute and serves as the director of its professional Masters Program in HCI. She was a founding associate editor for the *ACM Transaction on CHI* and is a member of the National Research Council's Committee on Human Factors. Her research involves engineering models of human behavior, usability evaluation methods, and the relationship between usability and software architecture.

Gary Jones is a lecturer in cognitive psychology at the University of Derby (UK). His research interests focus on the computational modeling of different aspects of development, primarily what develops in children's thinking and how children acquire language. Jones is also on the board of the Society for the Study of Artificial Intelligence and Behaviour (AISB).

Wendy A. Kellogg is manager of Social Computing at IBM's T.J. Watson Research Center. Her current work involves designing and studying systems for supporting computer-mediated communication in groups and organizations that mesh with social processes. She is author of numerous papers in the field of human-computer interaction and was co-editor in 2000 of a special issue of *Human-Computer Interaction* entitled "New Agendas for Human-Computer Interaction." She recently served as technical program co-chair for ACM's DIS 2000 (Designing Interactive Systems) conference and as general co-chair for ACM's CSCW 2000 (Computer-Supported Cooperative Work) conference.

David Kirsh is associate professor of Cognitive Science at the University of California, San Diego. He was originally trained in the philosophy of mind and logic at Oxford and spent several years in the AI Lab at MIT before coming to UCSD, where he has been working on theories of embodied activity, cognitive engineering, and how to better design highly interactive environments. He has published in journals in artificial intelligence, philosophy, cognitive science, and architecture.

Shin'ichi Konomi is a research fellow at the Center for LifeLong Learning and Design at the University of Colorado, Boulder. Previously he was a research scientist at the German National Research Center for Information Technology (GMD-IPSI) in Darmstadt, working in the AMBIENTE division. His research has been in the areas of ubiquitous and mobile computing, augmented reality, computer-supported cooperative work (CSCW), and cooperative information bases.

Joseph Krajcik is professor of Science Education at the University of Michigan and a co-director of the Center for Highly Interactive Computing in Education. He works with science teachers to re-engineer classrooms so that students engage in solving authentic, meaningful problems through inquiry and the use of learning technologies. A major aspect of his work involves the design of curriculum materials and computing tools that support inquiry.

James Landay is assistant professor of Computer Science at the University of California, Berkeley. His Ph.D. dissertation was the first to demonstrate the use of sketching in user interface design tools. He has published extensively in the area of user interfaces, including articles on user interface design and evaluation tools, gesture recognition, pen-based user interfaces, mobile computing, and visual languages.

Jim Larson is the author of several books and articles, including *Interactive Software-Tools for Building Interactive User Interfaces* (Yourdon Press, 1992). Larson is manager of Advanced Human Input/Output at the Intel Architecture Labs and is chairman of the W3C Voice Browser Working Group, which is standardizing VoiceXML and related voice application languages. He is an adjunct professor at Oregon Graduate Institute and Portland State University.

Henry Lieberman is a research scientist at the Media Laboratory of MIT in the Software Agents group. Prior to that, he held the same position at the MIT Artificial Intelligence Lab. His interests are in the intersection of artificial intelligence and the human interface. He holds a doctoral-equivalent degree from the University of Paris VI and was a visiting professor there. He recently edited a book, *Your Wish Is My Command: Programming by Example* (Morgan Kaufmann, 2001), showing how computers can learn new behavior by watching the user demonstrate procedures on concrete examples and constructing generalized programs.

Jon May is a cognitive psychologist who has been researching the role that psychological theory can play in interface design since the late 1980s. His other research interests include cognition and emotion, reasoning, and complex task performance. He is a lecturer in Psychology at the University of Sheffield, UK.

Ken Maxwell is a cofounder of Stick Networks Inc. (www.sticknetworks.com), where he solves human factors problems involving wireless connected services. He has worked in a variety of human factors areas for more than 15 years. Prior to Stick Networks he designed and tested human-computer interfaces for Tandem Computers and Compaq Computers. He was an associate faculty member of the Human Performance Institute at the University of Texas at Arlington. He worked on cockpit automation and information display technologies while working for General Dynamics.

Kevin L. Mills is a senior research scientist at the National Institute of Standards and Technology, where his research interests include evaluating and improving the performance and robustness of distributed software systems. Dr. Mills also serves as Adjunct Professor of Software Engineering at George Mason University, where he teaches graduate courses in software design, distributed systems, and data communications.

Christian Müller-Tomfelde is a research scientist at GMD-IPSI's division "AMBIENTE-Workspaces of the Future" in Darmstadt, Germany. Before joining GMD in 1997, he worked at the Center for Art and Media Technology (ZKM) in Karlsruhe in the area of interactive and virtual room acoustics. At GMD-IPSI, he worked especially on the design and realization of the roomware components of the first and the second generation. He is active in the fields of human-computer interaction, auditory display, computer-supported cooperative work (CSCW), and the disappearing computer.

Brad Myers is a senior research scientist in the Human-Computer Interaction Institute in the School of Computer Science at Carnegie Mellon University. He is the author or editor of over 200 publications, and he is on the editorial board of five journals. He has been a consultant on user interface design and implementation to about 40 companies.

Elizabeth D. Mynatt is an assistant professor in the College of Computing and the associate director of the GVU Center at the Georgia Institute of Technology. There she directs the Everyday Computing Laboratory, examining the HCI implications of the continuous presence of computation in everyday life. Previously she was on the research staff at Xerox PARC. Dr. Mynatt received her Ph.D. in Computer Science from Georgia Tech in 1995.

Bonnie A. Nardi is a research scientist in the Bioscience Information Solutions Department at Agilent Laboratories in Palo Alto, California. She is conducting ethnographic studies of molecular biologists to understand their information needs. She is the author of *A Small Matter of Programming: Perspectives on End User Computing* (MIT Press, 1993), *Context and Consciousness: Activity Theory and Human Computer Interaction* (MIT Press, 1996), and coauthor of *Information Ecologies: Using Technology with Heart* (MIT Press, 1999).

Dennis C. Neale is a human factors engineer who recently worked as an evaluation specialist for the Center for Human-Computer Interaction at Virginia Tech. He is currently pursuing a doctorate degree in Industrial and Systems Engineering at Virginia Tech. His current research interests include usability engineering, collaborative systems, and video-mediated communication.

Gary M. Olson is Paul M. Fitts professor of Human-Computer Interaction in the School of Information at the University of Michigan. He is also a professor in the Department of Psychology. His principal research interest for the past decade has been what kinds of tools and processes can enable people to work together who are not geographically collocated.

Judith S. Olson is Richard W. Pew professor of Human-Computer Interaction in the School of Information at the University of Michigan. She is also a professor in the Michigan Business School and the Department of Psychology. Her principal research interest is in the nature of group work and the design of technology to support it, especially for groups with distributed members.

Sharon Oviatt is professor of Computer Science and co-director of the Center for Human-Computer Communication at the Oregon Graduate Institute of Science & Technology. Her current research focuses on human-computer interaction, spoken language and multimodal interfaces, and mobile and highly interactive systems. She is an active member of the international HCI and speech communities, has published more than 70 scientific articles, and has served on numerous government advisory panels, editorial boards, and program committees. Her work is featured in recent special issues of *Communications for the ACM, Human-Computer Interaction,* and *IEEE Multimedia.*

Randy Pausch is professor of Computer Science, Human-Computer Interaction, and Design at Carnegie Mellon, where he is the co-director of the Entertainment Technology Center (ETC). He was a National Science Foundation Presidential Young Investigator and a Lilly Foundation Teaching fellow. In 1995, he spent a sabbatical with the Walt Disney Imagineering Virtual Reality Studio, and he currently consults with Imagineering on interactive theme park attractions, particularly for the "DisneyQuest" virtual-reality-based theme park.

Chris Quintana is an assistant research scientist in the School of Education and College of Engineering at the University of Michigan. Dr. Quintana works at the Center for Highly Interactive Computing in Education. His research interests include the application of human-computer interaction, software engineering, and information visualization principles to the design of educational technology.

Paul Resnick is an associate professor at the University of Michigan School of Information, where he coordinates the Community Information Corps. His research focuses on recommender systems, reputation systems, and other ways that information systems can contribute to social capital.

Frank E. Ritter joined Penn State in 1999 to help found a new interdisciplinary School of Information Sciences and Technology. He is also an associate professor of Psychology. He is interested in the interaction of cognitive models and HCI and is on the board of the UK's Society for the Study of AI and Simulation of Behaviour (AISB) and a member of the editorial board of Human Factors.

Mary Beth Rosson is associate professor of Computer Science and fellow of the Center for Human-Computer Interaction at Virginia Tech, where she is working in the areas of human-computer interaction, computer-supported cooperative work, and usability engineering. She recently co-authored a book with John Carroll, *Usability Engineering: Scenario-Based Development of Human-Computer Interaction* (Morgan Kaufmann, forthcoming).

Eric Scharff is a Ph.D. student studying computer science at the University of Colorado at Boulder. His research interests include collaborative technologies, open source software, open systems, human-computer interaction, and multimedia systems. He has created numerous software systems that enhance the way we collaborate using computers.

Jean Scholtz is a computer science researcher at the National Institute of Standards and Technology, where her research interests are in evaluation of interactive systems. She is currently on detail to the Defense Advanced Research Projects Agency (DARPA), where she manages the Information Management Program and ubiquitous computing efforts.

Douglas Schuler has been working at the intersection of technology and society for nearly 20 years. Doug believes that positive social change is *possible* and that technology *could* play a role in promoting it. He is a cofounder of the Seattle Community Network and is currently a member of the faculty at the Evergreen State College in Olympia, Washington, and program director for the Public Sphere Project for Computer Professionals for Social Responsibility.

Ben Shneiderman is a professor in the Department of Computer Science at the University of Maryland at College Park, founding director (1983–2000) of the Human-Computer Interaction Laboratory, and member of the Institutes for Advanced

Computer Studies & for Systems Research. Dr. Shneiderman is the author of *Software Psychology: Human Factors in Computer and Information Systems* (Little, Brown, 1980) and *Designing the User Interface: Strategies for Effective Human-Computer Interaction,* now in its third edition (Addison-Wesley, 1998).

Elliot Soloway is a professor in the College of Engineering, the School of Information, and the School of Education at the University of Michigan, and is cofounder of the Center for Highly-Interactive Computing in Education, a multidisciplinary project aimed at developing standards-based, inquiry-driven, technology-pervasive curriculum for K–12.

Norbert A. Streitz is the manager of the research division of AMBIENTE-Workspaces of the Future, which he founded in 1997 at the Integrated Publication and Information Systems Institute of the German National Research Center for Information Technology in Darmstadt, after serving as deputy director of GMD-IPSI for six years. He also teaches in the Computer Science Department of the Technical University Darmstadt. Before joining GMD in 1987, he was an assistant professor at the Technical University in Aachen in the area of human factors and cognitive psychology. His research has focused on human-computer interaction, hypermedia, CSCW, ubiquitous computing, augmented reality, cooperative buildings, and roomware. He is also chair of the Steering Group of the European proactive initiative "The Disappearing Computer" (www. disappearing-computer.net).

Bernhard Suhm is a senior scientist in the Speech and Language Processing Group at BBN Technologies, a Verizon company, where he develops methods for evaluating telephone user interfaces, and he consults call-centers on redesigning and speech-enabling IVRs. He also leads research and development of advanced audio mining and natural language-processing technologies. Prior to joining BBN Technologies, he worked for five years at Carnegie Mellon University, conducting research on speech-to-speech translation and multimodal error correction. He has published in the areas of speech recognition and multimodal interfaces, including *Multimodal Error Correction for Speech User Interfaces* (Shaker, Germany, 1999). Dr. Suhm holds a Ph.D. in Computer Science from Karlsruhe University, Germany.

Alistair Sutcliffe is professor of Systems Engineering at the Department of Computation, University of Manchester Institute of Science and Technology, and director of the Centre for Human Computer Interface Design. His research interests in HCI cover usability engineering methods and tools for multimedia and virtual reality, design of information searching and safety critical user interfaces, evaluation methods, theories of interaction, and knowledge representation. His software engineering research includes work on component engineering, requirements engineering, and the design of complex socio-technical systems.

Peter Tandler is a research scientist responsible for software development in the AMBIENTE division of the Integrated Publication and Information Systems Institute of the German National Research Center for Information Technology. His research interests are computer-supported cooperative work (CSCW), human-computer interaction, and integrated work environments, with a focus on software architectures for interactive roomware environments.

Loren Terveen received a Ph.D. in Computer Science from the University of Texas at Austin in 1991 and has been a research scientist at AT&T Laboratories since then. His general research area is human-computer interaction, with specific interests in recommender systems and online communities.

Murray Turoff is distinguished professor of Computer and Information Science at the New Jersey Institute of Technology. He has recently assumed the acting chair for the new Department of Information Systems in the new college of Computing Sciences at NJIT. Dr. Turoff is noted for his work on the design of applications of computer-mediated communications systems, having developed the first such group communication system in 1969. Currently he is working on collaborative knowledge bases for use by professional and learning communities.

Brygg Ullmer is a final-year Ph.D. student and IBM Media Lab Fellow at the MIT Media Lab, where he studies with Professor Hiroshi Ishii in the Tangible Media Group. He has held summer research positions at Interval Research and Sony CSL. His research interests include user interfaces for information infrastructure and biological systems, as well as rapid physical and functional prototyping.

John Vergo is the manager of the User Experience Research group at the IBM T.J. Watson Research Center in Hawthorne, New York. His research interests include human-computer interaction, user-centered design methods, multimodal user interfaces, e-commerce user experiences, speech recognition, natural language understanding, scientific visualization, 3D graphics, and software development methods. He has a B.S. in mathematics and psychology from the University at Albany and an M.S. in computer science from Polytechnic University.

Kim J. Vicente is professor of Mechanical & Industrial Engineering, Biomaterials & Biomedical Engineering, Computer Science, and Electrical & Computer Engineering at the University of Toronto, where he is also founding director of the Cognitive Engineering Laboratory. He has authored more than 135 refereed publications, as well as *Cognitive Work Analysis: Toward Safe, Productive, and Healthy Computer-Based Work* (Lawrence Erlbaum Associates, 1999).

Steve Whittaker is a senior research scientist at AT&T Labs, Florham Park, New Jersey, where he works in the Human Computer Interface Department. He has researched various aspects of computer-supported cooperative work, with a particular focus on how theories of human interaction can be used to inform the design of computer-mediated communication systems. He is the author of more than 60 refereed publications.

Brian Whitworth is an assistant professor in the Department of Computer and Information Science at New Jersey Institute of Technology. After completing two degrees, one in mathematics and one in psychology, he did a masters thesis in neuro-psychology on the implications of split-brain research for the concept of self. He was senior Army psychologist in the New Zealand Army, where he moved into computing, developing operational software and simulations, and working in liaison with the Australian, Singapore, and Malaysian Army War Game Centers. For the last ten years he has studied distributed electronic groups, completing an IS doctorate on Generating Agreement in Computer-Mediated Groups. His interests are cognition and computer-human interaction, and designing systems to enable group interaction and virtual communities.

Terry Winograd is professor of Computer Science at Stanford University, where he directs the program in Human-Computer Interaction. His current research is on the design of interactive information spaces. He has written and edited books on natural language understanding and interaction design, including *Understanding Computers and Cognition: A New Foundation for Design* (Addison-Wesley, 1987) and *Bringing Design to Software* (Addison-Wesley, 1996).

Lizhong Wu is a senior staff scientist at HNC Software Inc. He has 20 years of research and development experience in multimedia signal processing, machine learning, and natural language processing. Dr. Wu has authored and coauthored more than 50 technical articles and book chapters, and he is a regular reviewer of several international conferences and journals, an active technical member of the IEEE Neural Network Signal Processing Committee, and a member of IEEE and ACM associations. He was a Program and Organizing Committee member of International Symposium on Intelligent Data Engineering and Learning. Prior to joining HNC, Dr. Wu held positions at Oregon Graduate Institute, Nonlinear Prediction Systems, and Cambridge University. He obtained his Ph.D. in Information Engineering from Cambridge University in 1992 and his M.S. and B.S. in Electrical Engineering from South China University of Science and Technology in 1986 and 1983.

Richard M. Young is professor of Cognitive Science at the University of Hertfordshire, UK, where he has been since 1997 after spending many years at the Medical Research Council's Applied Psychology Unit in Cambridge, UK. His research interests are in cognitive modeling and its applications to human-computer interaction and in the use of cognitive architectures in understanding human cognition. He is on the editorial boards of *Human-Computer Interaction* and *Cognitive Science Quarterly* and is a past chair of the Society for the Study of Artificial Intelligence and Simulation of Behaviour (AISB).

Index

A

About.com, 495
Abowd, Gregory D., 513–535
Access, to live experiences, 522–524
ACE (Application Construction Environment), 203
Ackerman, Mark S., 303–324, 333, 498
ACM (Association for Computing Machinery), xxx, xxxi, xxxiii, xxxv, 194, 461
ACT-R, 5, 35, 135–136
ACT-R/PM (process motor extension), 5–6, 140, 142
Action
    CSCW and, 307–319
    EDC and, 362–364
    integration of, with reflection, 362–364
    perception and, 268–272
    social-technical gap in, 307–313
Active Badge, 518
ActiveX controls (Microsoft), 217
Activity, visibility of, 333–334
Adaptation
    demand for, 152–157
    learning and, relationship between, 155–157
Adaptive strategy choice model (ASCM). See ASCM (adaptive strategy choice model)
Adobe PhotoDeluxe, 250
Advanced Research Projects Agency (ARPA). See ARPA (Advanced Research Projects Agency)
Advice-based interfaces
    agents and, 476–477

AI (Artificial Intelligence) and, 481
    anytime algorithms and, 482
    context-sensitivity and, 483
    designing, 475–484
    examples of, 481–483
    future of, 483–485
    Internet applications and, 483
    introduction to, 475–477
    Letizia browser and, 477–479, 483–485
    Mondrian graphical editor and, 479–480, 483–485
    physically-based interfaces and, 484
    programming by example and, 482
    as a tool for helping people learn, 483
    visual communication and, 484
AFCN (Association for Community Networks), 631
Agent(s)
    advice-based interfaces and, 476–477
    use of the term, 431
Aggregate-ModifyAll-Modify Exception strategy, 101–102, 110
Aggregate-Modify strategy, 100, 106, 107–108, 116
Aggregation strategies, 103–110
AI (Artificial Intelligence), xxxv, 265–266, 315
    advice-based interfaces in, 481–483
    flexible planning and, 481
    reasoning and, 481
    reference tasks and, 175
Airas, Ernesto G., 347–372
Air Force (United States), 202
Airline cockpit automation, 83

Also Available from Addison-Wesley

The Humane Interface

New Directions for Designing Interactive Systems

ACM Press

Jef Raskin

This unique guide to interactive system design reflects the experience and vision of Jef Raskin, the creator of the Apple Macintosh. Other books may show how to use today's widgets and interface ideas effectively. Raskin, however, demonstrates that many current interface paradigms are dead ends, and that to make computers significantly easier to use requires new approaches. He explains how to effect desperately needed changes, offering a wealth of innovative and specific interface ideas for software designers, developers, and product managers. *The Humane Interface* delivers a way for computers, information appliances, and other technology-driven products to continue to advance in power and expand their range of applicability, while becoming free of the hassles and obscurities that plague present products.

0-201-37937-6 • Paperback • 256 pages • © 2000

Designing the User Interface

Strategies for Effective Human-Computer Interaction, Third Edition

Ben Shneiderman

With the third edition of this popular text and reference, Ben Shneiderman provides a complete and authoritative introduction to user-interface design, discussing the principles and practices needed to design effective interaction. Based on 20 years' experience, Shneiderman offers readers practical techniques and guidelines for interface design; as a scientist, he also takes great care to discuss underlying issues and to support conclusions with empirical results. Coverage includes the human factors of interactive software (with added discussion of diverse user communities); tested methods to develop and assess interfaces; interaction styles (like direct manipulation for graphical user interfaces); and design considerations (effective messages, consistent screen design, appropriate color). The book also features chapters on the World Wide Web, information visualization, and computer-supported cooperative work.

0-201-69497-2 • Hardcover • 640 pages • © 1998

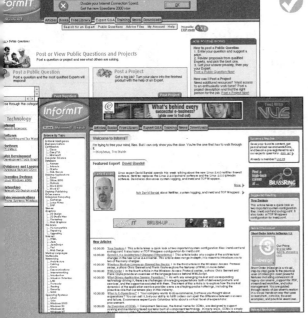

Register
Your Book
at www.aw.com/cseng/register

You may be eligible to receive:
- Advance notice of forthcoming editions of the book
- Related book recommendations
- Chapter excerpts and supplements of forthcoming titles
- Information about special contests and promotions throughout the year
- Notices and reminders about author appearances, tradeshows, and online chats with special guests

Contact us

If you are interested in writing a book or reviewing manuscripts prior to publication, please write to us at:

Editorial Department
Addison-Wesley Professional
75 Arlington Street, Suite 300
Boston, MA 02116 USA
Email: AWPro@aw.com

Addison-Wesley

Visit us on the Web: http://www.aw.com/cseng